Family Law

PRINCIPLES, POLICY
AND PRACTICE

Family Law
PRINCIPLES, POLICY
AND PRACTICE

Mary Hayes BA (Law), JP
Reader in Law, University of Sheffield
of Lincoln's Inn, Barrister

Catherine Williams LLB
Lecturer in Law, University of Sheffield

Butterworths
London, Dublin, Edinburgh
1995

United Kingdom	Butterworths a Division of Reed Elsevier (UK) Ltd, Halsbury House, 35 Chancery Lane, LONDON WC2A 1EL and 4 Hill Street, EDINBURGH EH2 3JZ
Australia	Butterworths, SYDNEY, MELBOURNE, BRISBANE, ADELAIDE, PERTH, CANBERRA and HOBART
Canada	Butterworths Canada Ltd, TORONTO and VANCOUVER
Ireland	Butterworth (Ireland) Ltd, DUBLIN
Malaysia	Malayan Law Journal Sdn Bhd, KUALA LUMPUR
New Zealand	Butterworths of New Zealand Ltd, WELLINGTON and AUCKLAND
Puerto Rico	Butterworth of Puerto Rico, Inc, SAN JUAN
Singapore	Butterworths Asia, SINGAPORE
South Africa	Butterworths Publishers (Pty) Ltd, DURBAN
USA	Butterworth Legal Publishers, CARLSBAD, California and SALEM, New Hampshire

A CIP Catalogue record for this book is available from the British Library.

ISBN 0 406 06329 X

Printed by Mackays of Chatham PLC, Chatham, Kent

Preface

The aims and objectives of this book

The aims and objectives of this book are to assist readers to understand, and to enjoy, the study of Family Law. When selecting material, we decided to concentrate on those areas of Family Law with which students, practitioners and policy-makers need to be familiar in order to build their knowledge and skills on secure foundations. Thus our chapters focus on those matters which are likely to occur frequently in practice; those which have a tendency to give rise to difficult and controversial litigation; those which are a matter of general public interest; and those where proposed reforms are likely to be implemented.

Our book aims to encourage readers critically to weigh and to evaluate statutory and common law developments. With this in mind, we provide a descriptive account of the legal framework; we explain and discuss considerations of policy where these have been influential on the law's development; we impress on the reader the discretionary nature of much of Family Law; we draw to the reader's attention those primary sources and articles which will give them closer insight into the area of law currently being examined; and we insert our own comments within the body of the text.

How this book will assist students

Because we were asked by our publishers, Butterworths, to give particular consideration to the needs of students, we took as our starting point that we should set out to explain the law in a manner which is 'user friendly'. The study of law undoubtedly requires a meticulous attention to accuracy, and to detail, but there is a danger that an excessively legalistic approach can obfuscate the underlying principles and policy considerations which inform the main body of the law. Our purpose has been to make these central considerations clear. We have also introduced some critiques into the text, and made suggestions about how the law might develop and be improved. We like to think that this approach will encourage students to engage in animated discussion and debate. Law is, of course, a living, moving subject, and there are arguments to be made about whether it is moving in the right direction. In our more optimistic moments, we hope that some of our suggestions will excite the students' curiosity, stimulate their imagination and create in them a desire to know more about this fascinating area of law.

Used as a student text, we believe that our book is particularly well-suited to a modular structure because it naturally divides into two halves. The first four chapters are devoted to developments in private and public child law since the implementation of the Children Act 1989. The other half of the book concentrates on the law relating to domestic violence, ending a marriage by decree, and the financial and property implications of marriage and relationship breakdown. Thus it could be used either as a main text for a full family law module, or for a course devoted solely to child law, or for one concerned with the rights and obligations of spouses and unmarried partners.

How this book will assist practitioners and other professionals

Because of the essentially discretionary nature of much of Family Law, the courts are often feeling their way towards the best outcome. Where this is the case, it gives the practitioner an unrivalled opportunity to use his or her advocacy skills to persuade the court towards a particular solution. An examination of case law reveals that articulated, and unarticulated, theories of rights, or appeals to notions of justice and fairness, or special policy considerations, are often influencing the courts' decisions. The family law practitioner needs to have access to this key information, alongside an up-to-date account of the substantive law. We would like to think that this book will be of real assistance to advocates and to solicitors. We believe that it will provide them with a sound knowledge of precedent; that it explains the ideas upon which the present law is based; and that it contains useful suggestions as to how the law might be developed. Thus it should assist them both when negotiating a settlement, and when formulating arguments in order to present a client's case in court.

Much of the text is devoted to the law relating to children. Social workers, and others working with children, are often daunted by the weight of legal knowledge they are expected to have, and find the study of law an alien discipline. We have tried to explain the intricacies of child law in a

comprehensible manner and to get across the 'feel' of the subject. We
therefore believe that professionals working with children will find this a
useful book in helping them better to understand the legal framework
within which they carry out some of their work.

Acknowledgments

Between us we have two husbands and nine children. We owe a great debt
of gratitude to our families for their forbearance whilst this book has been
in preparation. The welfare of our children has definitely not been treated
as paramount, particularly in the weeks running up to Christmas 1994,
when the text had to be completed. The children have nonetheless put up
with a poor quality of maternal care with good humour and patience. Our
husbands have been enormously supportive, and have encouraged us
throughout. We also thank all those persons who have read parts of the
manuscript in draft. Their helpful comments and suggestions provided us
with invaluable practical and moral support. Finally we would like to thank
Butterworths for their generosity in offering a prize for a new text in a
main-stream area of law. This has assisted our motivation when the task
seemed arduous, and the finished version a long way off. The chance of
winning the prize has added an element of excitement to what to us has,
in any event, been an enjoyable venture.
    The law is as at Christmas 1994.

Mary Hayes **and** *Catherine Williams*

Contents

CHAPTER 4

Approaches to welfare in children cases   **185**

CHAPTER 7

Money and property on marriage breakdown 445

CHAPTER 8

Child support, and homes for unmarried partners and children   **541**

Table of statutes

References in this Table of Statutes are to Halsbury's Statutes of England (Fourth Edition) showing the volume and page at which the annotated text of the Act may be found.

Table of cases

B

C

PAGE

H

PAGE

L

M

PAGE

N

O

P

PAGE

Q

R

PAGE

PAGE

T

PAGE

X

Chapter 1

Responsibility for bringing up children

Chapter 1

Responsibility for bringing up children

The responsibility to decide about a child's upbringing

When there is disagreement over a child's upbringing, various persons may have an interest in, or views about, what should happen to the child. These persons may include the child, the parents, a step-parent, grandparents and other relatives, a local authority, a foster parent, an 'expert' such as a paediatrician, psychologist or psychiatrist, and other concerned individuals. Normally, such disagreement is best resolved through discussions and compromise. Indeed, agencies and systems exist to encourage conciliatory methods of resolving children cases.[1] However, it is inevitable that circumstances will occur in which an amicable resolution of conflict cannot be achieved. Identifying who has the responsibility to make decisions about a child's upbringing may then be of crucial importance. It will be seen in the pages which follow that much of child law centres around this issue.

Parental responsibility

'Parental responsibility' is a key principle and a key concept in child law.[2] It permeates the Children Act 1989. This Act provides the statutory framework around which most of child law is based, and is the bedrock in which burgeoning ideas and principles relating to the upbringing of children are firmly rooted.[3] Parental responsibility is defined in section 3(1) to mean—

1 See ch 4.
2 See J Eekelaar *Parental Responsibility: State of Nature or Nature of the State?* [1991] JSWFL 37.
3 Any statutory references in this chapter are to the Children Act 1989 unless otherwise stated.

'All the rights, duties, powers, responsibility and authority which by law a parent of a child has in relation to the child and his property.'

This definition reveals that parental responsibility is a compilation of attributes of parenthood. It is a concept which can be encapsulated in the notion that it is those with parental responsibility who have the power and responsibility to determine how a child is brought up. Babies and young children cannot make decisions about their own upbringing because they lack the capacity to do so. In the case of older children, they may have the intellectual capacity to make decisions, but they are nonetheless likely to be dependent on adults to provide them with their basic needs. Also, whilst older children may have the ability to understand and make choices, they may lack the maturity and foresight to make decisions which are wise and in their own interests.[4] The law therefore throws a ring of care around children by imposing parental responsibility for their upbringing on specified persons until the children reach adulthood.[5] However, recognising that those with parental responsibility have the right to control most aspects of a child's upbringing does not imply that the means used will always be acceptable. 'The principle of law... is that parental rights are derived from parental duty and exist only so long as they are needed for the protection of the person and property of the child.'[6] Thus parental responsibility can be challenged, and even overridden, when parents and others with parental responsibility act in violation of this principle.[7]

There is no definitive list of the 'rights, duties, powers, responsibility and authority' which belong to those with parental responsibility; essentially they comprise those attributes of parenthood which are needed to enable parents to perform their duty properly to bring up their children until the children are capable of looking after themselves. Because there are no written rules about the nature and scope of parental responsibility this creates some degree of uncertainty. This tension between flexibility and certainty is endemic in child law. On the one hand it will be seen that Parliament and the courts have resisted formulating rules which would create certainty about the responsibilities of parents, in order to enable the law to respond flexibly to changing social circumstances, and to be sensitive to alterations in customs and values relating to the upbringing of children. On the other hand it is desirable that others who have dealings

4   See below in relation to 'Gillick competent' children.
5   Not only do persons with parental responsibility have all the responsibilities of parenthood, they also are not allowed to surrender or transfer any part of that responsibility to another: s.2(9). Only a court can deprive a person of parental responsibility.
6   *Gillick v West Norfolk and Wisbech Area Health Authority* [1985] 3 All ER 402 per Lord Scarman at p 420.
7   See ch 3.

with a child know what is, or is not, permissible without parental agreement, and it will be seen that the courts have been responsive to this pressure too.[8]

Parents and parental responsibility

A mother always has parental responsibility. The position of fathers is more complicated. Section 2(1) of the Children Act 1989 provides—

> 'Where a child's father and mother were married to each other at the time of his birth, they shall each have parental responsibility for the child.'

Clearly this means that a father who was married to the child's mother at the time when the child was born has automatic parental responsibility. However, on its face, this provision is slightly misleading because the meaning of 'being married to each other at the time of the child's birth' is extended by section 1 of the Family Law Reform Act 1987 to include relationships in which the parties clearly were not married to each other at the time of the child's birth. Thus parents who are parties to a void marriage fall within section 2(1) provided that at the time of the child's conception, or the time of the marriage if later, either or both of them reasonably believed that the marriage was valid.[9] This means, for example, that both parents enjoy parental responsibility if one of the parents was aged under 16 at the date of the marriage, if either or both of them did not realise this. It means that a man who is already married to someone else, and who knowingly enters into a bigamous marriage, has parental responsibility for any child of the new marriage if his 'wife' reasonably believed that their marriage was valid at one of the relevant times.

Furthermore, it is relatively common for parents who were not married to each other at the time of the child's birth subsequently to marry. Such parents are treated as if they were married to each other at the time of the child's birth.[10] The father's status alters from being a parent without parental responsibility to being a parent with parental responsibility through the act of marrying. Parents of adopted children are included within the definition of parents married to each other at the time of the child's birth.[11] This reinforces the principle that, where the adopters are a married couple, an adopted child shall be treated in law as if he had been

8   For example, the law relating to the medical treatment of children, see below. For a general analysis, see *Report on Family Law*, Scot Law Com No 135, paras 2.1–2.13.
9   Legitimacy Act 1976, s.1. Void marriages are explained in ch 6.
10 Ibid, s.2.
11 Family Law Reform Act 1987, s.1(3)(c).

born as a child of the marriage.[12] Finally, parents of any person who is otherwise treated in law as legitimate also fall within section 2(1).[13] This provision draws in those cases, usually where there is a foreign element, where a child is treated by law as a child of parents who are married at the time of his birth even though this is not factually the case.

Unmarried fathers and parental responsibility

All other parents are treated as parents who were not married to each other at the time of the child's birth. In relation to unmarried parents, section 2(2) provides—

'Where a child's mother and father were not married to each other at the time of his birth—
  (a) the mother shall have parental responsibility for the child;
  (b) the father shall not have parental responsibility for the child, unless he acquires it in accordance with the provisions of this Act.'

However, although unmarried mothers enjoy all the rights, duties, powers, responsibility and authority of parenthood to the exclusion of the father, the fact that the father does not have parental responsibility for a child does not affect any obligations he may have, in particular the statutory duty to maintain the child. Nor does it affect any rights he may have in the event of the child's death in relation to the child's property.[14]

It has been seen that a child's father automatically has parental responsibility if he was married to the mother at the time of the child's birth. Why is an unmarried father treated differently? In 1979 the Law Commission suggested in a working paper on the reform of the law relating to illegitimacy that unmarried fathers should have the same rights in relation to their children as married fathers.[15] However, the process of consultation which followed publication of the working paper revealed that there was widespread opposition to this proposal, and by the time the Law Commission published its final report it had moved away from its original suggestion.[16] The Law Commission pointed out that in most other countries an unmarried father did not automatically have the full range of rights, powers and authority enjoyed by a married father, and it gave reasons why a similar approach should be taken in England.

These reasons took account of the response that the Law Commission had received from organisations representing single parents which stated

12 Adoption Act 1976, s.39.
13 Family Law Reform Act 1987, s.1(3)(d).
14 Children Act 1989, s.3(4).
15 Law Com W P No 74.
16 *Illegitimacy*, Law Com No 118.

that each year they received numerous enquiries from unmarried mothers seeking reassurance about their rights over their children, and whether these could be challenged, particularly by the father. The Law Commission reported that some respondents had indicated that there was reason to fear that mothers would be tempted to conceal the identity of the child's father in order to ensure that he did not have any rights in relation to the child's upbringing. Other respondents had pointed out that the welfare of children could be imperilled by conferring rights on all fathers.[17] After balancing the advantages and disadvantages of alternative proposals, the Law Commission recommended that unmarried fathers should not have rights automatically, but that they should be entitled to apply to a court for such rights. This recommendation led to the enactment of section 4 of the Family Law Reform Act 1987 which enabled an unmarried father to apply to a court for a parental rights and duties order. Such an order gave him the same status as a married father.

This provision has been repeated in very similar terms in section 4 of the Children Act 1989.[18] A further innovation is that an unmarried father may obtain parental responsibility by agreement with the child's mother, provided certain provisions in the Act are complied with. Section 4 provides—

'(1) Where a child's father and mother were not married to each other at the time of his birth—

(a) the court may, on the application of the father, order that he shall have parental responsibility for the child; or

(b) the father and mother may by agreement ('a parental responsibility agreement') provide for the father to have parental responsibility for the child.'

Should unmarried fathers be afforded equal treatment?

There is a strong body of opinion which would afford equal treatment to unmarried fathers which is matched by an equally strong body of opinion which is resistant to any alteration in the present law.[19] It has been suggested that English law may be out of line with Articles 8 and 14 of the European Convention on Human Rights and Fundamental Freedoms.[20] Article 8(1) provides that—

---

17 M Hayes *Law Commission Working Paper No 74: Illegitimacy* (1980) 43 MLR 299.

18 Parental responsibility orders are discussed in detail below.

19 See A Bainham *Children the Modern Law* (Family Law, 1993) pp 162-179 for a helpful account of the literature on this debate.

20 A Bainham '*When is a Parent not a Parent?' Reflections on the Unmarried Father and his Child in English Law* (1989) IJFL 208; for a contrary view, see R Deech *The Unmarried Father and Human Rights* (1992) 4 JCL 3.

'Everyone has the right to respect for his private and family life, his home and his correspondence'.

Article 14 provides that—

'The enjoyment of the rights and freedoms set forth in this Convention shall be secured without discrimination on any ground such as sex, race, colour, language, religion, political or other opinion, national or social origin, association with a national minority, property, birth or other status.'

This latter article has no independent existence, rather it complements the other articles. There has been no direct consideration of the question whether the Convention demands that an unmarried father should be as equally entitled to exercise his parental role as a parent with parental responsibility. It is clear from the ruling of the European Court of Human Rights in *Marckx v Belgium*[1] that the Convention draws no distinction between the married and the unmarried family life when interpreting 'respect for ... family life'. However, the Law Commission took the view that the *Marckx* case only required English law to prevent discrimination against the *child* of unmarried parents, rather than against the father, in order to bring it into line with its treaty obligations.

More recently, Article 18 of the United Nations Convention on the Rights of the Child provides under the heading *'parental support'* that—

'States Parties shall use their best efforts to ensure recognition of the principle that both parties have common responsibilities for the upbringing and development of the child. Parents, or as the case may be, legal guardians, have the primary responsibility for the upbringing and development of the child. The best interest of the child will be their basic concern.'

This is one factor which has influenced the Scottish Law Commission to recommend that 'in the absence of any court order regulating the position, both parents of the child should have parental responsibilities and rights whether or not they are or have been married to each other.'[2]

Clearly there is a divide between the English and Scottish Law Commissions, and in the populace generally, between those who support and those who oppose the automatic conferment of parental responsibility on all fathers. Each group advances the notion that the welfare of children is best served by adopting their point of view. Those in favour of removing all

1 EUR Court HR Series A No 31; and see S Maidmant *The Marckx Case* (1979) 9 Fam Law 228.
2 Scot Law Com No 135 recommendation 5. For their more general reasoning, see paras 2.36–2.49.

discrimination assert that it is wrong to deprive a child of a parent who has the normal parental responsibilities and rights in relation to the child, merely because that parent, perhaps through no fault of his own, was not married to the mother. Furthermore, they assert that, by discriminating against unmarried fathers, the law may be fostering irresponsible parental attitudes which it ought to be doing everything possible to discourage.[3]

Those who take the contrary view point to how conferring parental responsibility on all fathers may damage the rights and interests of children. When parents are married the identity of the father of a child conceived, or born, in wedlock is either known to be, or is presumed by law to be, the husband of the mother.[4] There can be no such presumption in the case of unmarried fathers, and in some cases, for example when a child has been conceived as a result of a casual relationship, or when one of several men could be the father of the child, it may be difficult to identify who the father is. Often this will not matter. But sometimes it will. Once rights have been given to a father they must be accorded respect by law. An inevitable consequence of conferring parental responsibility on all fathers is to add to the persons who have the right to be consulted in relation to the child's upbringing.[5] This is liable to cause delays in decision-making about the child whilst steps are taken to trace, and in some cases to identify, the father.[6] Yet there is a general principle that any delay in determining a question in relation to a child's upbringing is likely to prejudice the welfare of a child, as section 1(2) of the Children Act 1989 recognises and stresses.

Other reasons advanced for opposing any change in the existing law include the offence this could cause to unmarried mothers struggling to bring up their children without support from the children's fathers, and the fears of some mothers that they might be at risk of interference and harassment. The Scottish Law Commission was fairly dismissive of the former objection, pointing out that it is not the feelings of one parent which should determine the content of the law but rather the interests of children and responsible parents. It said that the answer to the latter problem is for the law to remove or regulate parental rights. But it could be maintained that this response ignores the issue of the delay which will occur while legal proceedings are taken, and fails to give weight to the potential for disruption of the child's upbringing. It is also open to the more profound objection that it makes too many assumptions about the efficacy of legal proceedings in dealing with family conflict, and the ability of the principle that the child's welfare must be the court's paramount consideration when

3   Ibid, paras 2.45 and 2.43.
4   See below.
5   For example, in adoption proceedings if unmarried fathers had the same rights as married fathers it would be essential to obtain the father's agreement to his child's adoption, or to find grounds for dispensing with that agreement: see further ch 4.
6   Cf *Re P (Adoption) (Natural Father's Rights)* [1994] 1 FLR 771.

an issue arises with respect to his upbringing adequately to embrace strife of this nature.[7]

Parental responsibility agreements

English law effects what the Scottish Law Commission have described as a 'second best solution',[8] namely section 4(1)(b) of the Children Act 1989 enables the unmarried father to acquire parental responsibility by making an agreement with the mother. This is a formal agreement which must be made on a set form, be signed and witnessed, and be registered in the Principal Registry of the Family Division in London.[9] The Children Act Advisory Committee, which was established to monitor the working of the Act, has detected that there have been some attempts to forge a mother's signature to an agreement, and it has proposed that agreements should in future be witnessed by a lay justice or an officer of the court.[10] Both parties are advised to seek legal advice before signing the agreement. Any person giving legal advice to the mother would need to explain to her that once a parental responsibility agreement has been made it cannot be revoked by either party.[11] Only a court may bring a parental responsibility agreement to an end, and it may only do this if an application is made either by any person who has parental responsibility for the child, or by the child himself who has been given leave of the court to apply.[12] A court cannot either make or end a parental responsibility agreement using its own motion powers.

Parental responsibility orders: analysis of the case law

When an agreement with the mother cannot be effected for whatever reason an unmarried father is entitled to apply for a parental responsibility order.[13] There is no specific guidance in section 4 on how a court should determine

7 See M Hayes *Law Commission Working Paper No 74: Illegitimacy* (1980) 43 MLR 299. On the application of the welfare principle to disputes between parents over the upbringing of their children, see ch 4.

8 Scot Law Com No 135 para 2.51.

9 Parental Responsibility Agreement Regulations 1991 (SI 1991 No 1478). 5,141 agreements had been registered by June 1993. These forms do not appear to be readily available, for example in post offices. If the intention is to increase the number of fathers who have full parental responsibility, then it seems that a programme of publicity and information on the scheme needs to be introduced.

10 Children Act Advisory Committee annual report 1992-3 p 13.

11 This can be contrasted with the appointment of a guardian for a child by deed or will or other formal document, which can be revoked at any time before the guardianship takes effect. On guardianship generally, see below.

12 S.4(3).

13 S.4(1)(a).

whether to confer parental responsibility, and the court is not required to apply the checklist in section 1(3) which identifies those matters to which a court must have regard when deciding what course of action will best promote a child's welfare.[14] However, who should have parental responsibility is undoubtedly a question with respect to the upbringing of a child, and the child's welfare is therefore the court's paramount consideration in determining the issue.[15] But parental responsibility is also a matter of status, and the issue for the court to resolve is whether the father should be treated in the same way by law as a married father. Those who have parental responsibility have an advantage when decisions must be made about a child's future because they are entitled to be consulted. By contrast, the status of being a parent without parental responsibility does not always afford a father the same protection of his interest to be involved in decisions about his child's upbringing. This can be of crucial importance where a local authority are treating a child as a child in need of accommodation,[16] or if there are adoption proceedings about the child.[17]

Guidance from case law on when it is appropriate for a court to make a parental responsibility order stems both from cases decided under section 4 of the Family Law Reform Act 1987, and from cases decided under section 4 of the Children Act 1989 which replaced it. In *Re CB (A Minor) (Parental Responsibility Order)*[18] Waite J said that, in his view, Parliament intended to carry forward the case law decided under the 1987 Act, and it will be seen that this case law has been influential on how cases brought under section 4 of the Children Act 1989 have been approached. The courts have taken the view that an application for a parental responsibility order is a discrete application which must be determined separately from other matters which may have arisen in the proceedings.

Under the law which preceded the Children Act 1989 an unmarried father did not have the right to apply for contact with his child who was in local authority care, and there was no other way open to him to challenge the decision of the local authority to deny him contact. Clearly this placed him at an enormous disadvantage by contrast with mothers and married fathers who were entitled to challenge a refusal to allow contact. In *D v Hereford and Worcester County Council*[19] an unmarried father wished to apply for contact with his child in care. He therefore applied for a joint parental rights and duties order under section 4 of the Family Law Reform Act 1987 in order to obtain the locus standi to make a further application challenging the decision to refuse him contact. Ward J ruled that the essence

14 See ch 4, where the provisions in the checklist are explained.
15 S.1(1), and see *Re G (A Minor) (Parental Responsibility Order)* [1994] 1 FLR 504.
16 S.20; and see ch 3.
17 See ch 4.
18 [1993] 1 FLR 920.
19 [1991] 1 FLR 205.

of the question to be determined by the court when making a parental responsibility order was: 'can [the natural father] show that he is a father to the child, not in a biological sense, but in the sense that he has established or is likely to establish such a real family tie with the child that he should now be afforded the corresponding legal tie.'[20] He said that another way of framing the question is to ask: 'Has he behaved or will he behave with parental responsibility towards the child?'[1] He added that the burden of proof was on the father, and there may be obvious reasons for rejecting his application such as when the mother is implacably hostile to the intervention of the father into her life, perhaps after the most casual of relationships. He said that if the father had nothing to offer the child it would be right to refuse his application.

An unmarried father without parental responsibility was, and still is, at a disadvantage in adoption proceedings in comparison with a married father. Neither his agreement to an order which would free his child for adoption, nor his consent to an adoption order is required.[2] In *Re H (Illegitimate Children: Father: Parental Rights) (No 2)*[3] an unmarried father was seeking a parental rights and duties order under the 1987 Act in the course of proceedings to free his children for adoption. Such an order would give him the locus standi to oppose the freeing order. It would also give him residual rights under the Adoption Act 1976 to receive progress reports on the children, and to apply for the freeing order to be revoked if the children were not placed for adoption within 12 months.[4] Balcombe LJ said that in determining whether to make an order the court should take account of the degree of commitment the father had shown towards the child, the degree of attachment that existed between father and child, and the reasons why the father was applying for the order.[5] The court found that there had been contact between the father and his children and that there was evidence of some attachment between them. It therefore determined that a parental rights and duties order should be made. However, it went on to rule that grounds for dispensing with the father's agreement to the freeing order had been established.

Re H (Illegitimate Children: Father: Parental Rights) (No 2) illustrates the principle that a court may think it right to confer parental responsibility

20 Ibid, at p 212.
1   Ibid.
2   A parent for the purposes of the Adoption Act 1976, ss.18 and 16 means a parent with parental responsibility: see the Adoption Act 1976, s.72. An unmarried father is, however, afforded lesser measures of protection: see ch 4.
3   [1991] 1 FLR 214.
4   Adoption Act 1976, ss.19 and 20.
5   In *Re G (A Minor) (Parental Responsibility Order)* [1994] 1 FLR 504 Balcombe LJ, when told that this list 'had become used almost as if it were a statutory definition', said that it was certainly not so intended, and that the factors were not intended to be exclusive, see p 507.

on a father even if during the course of the same legal proceedings that responsibility is then removed. Whether a father should be given all the responsibilities of a married father is determined by one set of principles; whether he should then be deprived of these responsibilities is a completely separate question which is determined by a different set of principles. These latter principles relate to the nature of the proceedings which have been brought about the child. In relation to the application for parental responsibility, the concern of the court is whether the unmarried father should be afforded the same status, and therefore the same rights, as a married father. In relation to dispensing with agreement to adoption, the concern of the court is to determine whether a parent who enjoys the privileges of parental responsibility is unreasonably withholding his agreement to an adoption order being made.[6]

The principle that an application for parental responsibility is a discrete application was illustrated in a different way in *Re C (Minors) (Parental Rights)*,[7] which was also decided under the 1987 Act. Here the issue to be resolved was whether a court should make a parental rights and duties order even though some, or all, of the rights given to the father would be incapable of being enforced. Unmarried parents of two children had parted and there was medical evidence to the effect that the mother's mental stability would be at risk if the father was allowed contact with the children. The court therefore determined that contact should be denied for the time being. However, in relation to the parental rights and duties order Waite J said that the question to ask was: 'was the association between the parties sufficiently enduring, and has the father by his conduct during and since the application shown sufficient commitment to the children, to justify giving the father a legal status equivalent to that which he would have enjoyed if the parties had been married.'[8] Waite J said that the order 'will have real and tangible value, not only as something [the father] can cherish for the sake of his own peace of mind, but also as a status carrying with it rights in waiting, which it may be possible to call into play when circumstances change with the passage of time.'[9] The court concluded that it could never be right to refuse a parental rights and duties order on the automatic ground that it would be vitiated by an inability to enforce it.

A similar approach has been adopted in cases decided under section 4 of the Children Act 1989. In *Re CB (A Minor) (Parental Responsibility Order)*[10] the court ruled that magistrates hearing an application brought in care proceedings should have given independent assessment to whether the father should have a parental responsibility order. In determining this

6   See ch 4.
7   [1992] 1 FLR 1
8   Ibid, at p 8.
9   Ibid, at p 4.
10 [1993] 1 FLR 920.

matter the court should have regard to the father's commitment and attachment to the child and to his motives. In *Re H (A Minor) (Parental Responsibility)*,[11] in which a father was seeking parental responsibility and contact orders, the Court of Appeal found that the trial judge could not be faulted in the reasoning which led him to deny contact by the father with his child, but held that he had been plainly wrong to apply the same kind of reasoning to whether the father should be given a parental responsibility order. In *Re H (A Minor)*, measuring the order against the child's best interests, the judge had found that it would have no benefits and some disadvantages. He took the view that a parental responsibility order might raise false hopes in the father, and would tend to disrupt relationships in the mother's household with her new husband to the child's disadvantage in the same way as allowing contact would. The Court of Appeal held that this approach had been wrong. The evidence showed that the father had shown commitment and attachment to the child, and that in the light of the authorities a parental responsibility order should therefore have been made.[12]

A mother who is alienated from the father is likely to fear that a parental responsibility order will lead to the father interfering in the day-to-day upbringing of her child. However, in *Re P (A Minor) (Parental Responsibility Order)*,[13] Wilson J held that this was to misunderstand the effect of the order. He emphasised that a parental responsibility order does not permit the father to interfere in the day-to-day management of the child's life; it is the mother who has the right to determine such matters. Nor does it give him the power to override the mother's decisions. Furthermore, he pointed out that if a father were to misuse the rights given to him under section 4, they could be controlled by orders made under section 8 of the Act.[14] As a last resort, the parental responsibility order itself could be discharged. In relation to the case before him, Wilson J held that the fact that there was acrimony between the parties was not a reason for denying the father parental responsibility. He found that the father had shown great love and concern for the child, and it was therefore in her interests that both parents should have parental responsibility for her.[15]

However, a judge may be entitled to refuse an application for a parental responsibility order where the motivation for the application is to frustrate

---

11 [1993] 1 FLR 484.
12 Subsequently, in *Re G (A Minor) (Parental Responsibility Order)* [1994] 1 FLR 504 the Court of Appeal accepted for the purposes of the case that the welfare principle applies to parental responsibility orders; see too the observations of Butler-Sloss LJ in *Re T (A Minor) (Parental Responsibility: Contact)* [1993] 2 FLR 450.
13 [1994] 1 FLR 578.
14 These allow a court to control with whom the child will live and with whom he may have contact, to prohibit the manner in which a parent is otherwise entitled to exercise his parental responsibility, and to deal with any specific issue which has arisen. Such orders may contain directions and impose conditions. For a full account, see ch 2.
15 See too, *Re E (A Minor) (Parental Responsibility)* [1994] 2 FCR 709.

plans for a child's upbringing. This was the position in *W v Ealing London Borough Council.*[16] The children were in the care of the local authority, and leave had been given to the authority to terminate contact between the children and their parents prior to placing the children with long-term foster parents with a view to their adoption. The children had been prepared for separation from their parents, and two possible adoptive families had been found, neither of whom wanted contact between the children and their mother and father to continue. The father applied for contact and for a parental responsibility order.[17] The court found that an order for contact would inevitably be disruptive of plans for the children's future, and that the father's only reason for applying for a parental responsibility order was the hope that he might thereby thwart the making of an adoption order. The father had relied on the authorities and submitted that he should have a parental responsibility order in the light of the principles enunciated in them. To this Sir Stephen Brown P responded: 'the principle that an order is not precluded merely because parental rights may not in practice be exercisable is no authority for the converse proposition that an order must be made in such circumstances.'[18]

Who, in law, *are* a child's parents?

Almost all children know with certainty who their mother is, and the great majority of children know who their father is; however, in some cases the identity of a child's parents may be in doubt. This situation may arise for a variety of reasons. Sometimes a woman deceives a man into thinking that he is the father of her child, and sometimes the woman herself may not know which of two (or more) men is the child's father. The position is further complicated because modern methods of assisted conception mean that a woman may conceive a child other than through having sexual intercourse with a man. She may become pregnant by means of artificial insemination. The semen used to fertilise her egg may have been donated by a man who is not her husband or, in the case of unmarried couples, not the man with whom she is living. Instead, the donor of the semen is likely to be anonymous. Eggs, as well as semen, can be donated, and this can result in a woman giving birth to a child which has grown from another woman's egg. In all these situations, and others, the law must find an answer to the question 'who, in law, are the child's parents?'[19]

---

16 [1993] 2 FLR 788.
17 Because the children were in care, the contact application was made under s.34 of the Children Act 1989: see ch 3.
18 [1993] 2 FLR 788, at p 796.
19 For a detailed account of the law relating to artificial reproduction, see G Douglas *Law, Fertility and Reproduction* (Sweet and Maxwell, 1991).

Who is the child's mother?

The only situation in which the question 'who is a child's mother?' arises is when a woman has sperm and eggs, or an embryo, implanted in her which uses eggs obtained from another woman. This means that the child contains none of the woman's genetic material. Is the woman who gives birth the mother of the child, or is the woman who donated her egg the mother? The law answers this question without equivocation. Section 27(1) of the Human Fertilisation and Embryology Act 1990 provides:

> 'The woman who is carrying or who has carried a child as a result of the placing in her of an embryo or of sperm and eggs, and no other woman, is to be treated as the mother of the child.'

Section 29(1) further provides that a woman treated as the child's mother under section 27 is to be treated in law as the mother of the child for all purposes. Thus here there is certainty. The woman who gives birth to a child is the child's mother whether or not the child is genetically related to her.[20]

Occasionally a woman may be willing to act as a surrogate mother for a married woman who is unable to carry a child to term herself, with the intention of handing the child over to her and her husband after birth. In a situation of this kind there is no doubt that the woman who gives birth is the child's mother. But, in some instances, section 30(1) of the Human Fertilisation and Embryology Act 1990 provides that a court may make an order in favour of the commissioning couple 'providing for a child to be treated in law as the child of the parties to a marriage.'[1] Before such an order can be made a court must be satisfied that the child has been carried by a woman other than the wife as the result of placing in her of an embryo, or sperm and eggs, or her artificial insemination, and that the gametes of the husband or the wife, or both, were used to bring about the creation of the embryo. In addition it must be satisfied that various conditions specified in subsections (2) to (7) of section 30 have been complied with. These conditions include that the application for the order has been made within six months of the child's birth; that both the woman who carried the child, and the father[2] of the child agree unconditionally to the making of the

---

20 The Warnock Committee *Report of the Committee of Inquiry into Human Fertilisation and Embryology* (1984) Cmnd 9314, took the view that the law should always regard the carrying mother as the child's real mother. There is one exception to this rule: s.29(4) provides that it does not apply to 'the succession to any dignity or title of honour.'

1 Thus avoiding the situation which occurred in *Re W (Minors) (Surrogacy)* [1991] 1 FLR 385, which arose before s.30 came into force.

2 For these purposes the 'father' includes the man who is recognised by law as being the child's father under s.28 (see below) where he is not the commissioning father: s.30(5).

order; and that no money or other benefit has been given or received by the commissioning couple for the purposes of the surrogacy arrangements and the making of the order.

Once an order is made under section 30 the child becomes the child of the commissioning parents, and the woman who gave birth to him is no longer recognised by law as his mother. However, it should be noted that proceedings under section 30 are family proceedings for the purposes of the Children Act 1989,[3] so a court could make an order under section 8 of that Act[4] in addition to the section 30 order, or instead of a section 30 order. This is an important safeguard, which would allow a court to base any order it made on the principle that the child's welfare is the court's paramount consideration. However, it seems most unlikely that an order under section 8 would be made unless either an issue arose over contact with the child, or one or other of the child's legal parents changed his or her mind about agreeing to the section 30 order during the course of the proceedings.

Who is the child's father?

Identifying a child's father can be complicated,[5] though it is less complicated than hitherto. Modern forensic methods can determine with certainty whether a man is a child's father where genetic samples are available for analysis. The question 'who is the child's father?' may arise in various contexts, the most commonplace being when a married woman gives birth to a child and there is doubt about whether her husband is the child's father; when an unmarried woman gives birth to a child and the man whom she alleges is the father denies paternity; and when a child is conceived either as the result of the artificial insemination of the mother, or by some other method of fertilisation not involving sexual intercourse.

The presumption of legitimacy

When a married woman gives birth to a child, the law dictates that the child should be presumed to be the offspring of her husband unless or until it is proven to be otherwise. This presumption of legitimacy applies to children conceived during a marriage; to children conceived before marriage but born during the marriage; and to children born within the

3   S.30(8).
4   See ch 2.
5   As Shakespeare (who understood more than most about the vagaries of family life) realised when he commented through the mouthpiece of Young Gobbo in *The Merchant of Venice* 'it is a wise father that knows his own child.'

normal gestation period after a marriage has ended by death or divorce. The presumption, which is a presumption of law, may be rebutted by evidence which shows that it is more probable than not that the husband is not the father.[6] Before issues relating to paternity could be resolved through blood tests and, more recently, DNA profiling, a body of case law had developed around this presumption and how it could be rebutted. This case law is now mainly of historic interest. However, if the husband has died, or cannot be traced, and if doubt is thrown on his paternity, it may be necessary to have recourse to this body of law because forensic testing will not be available.[7] There is no corresponding presumption relating to the paternity of a child who is born of parents who are unmarried.

Forensic testing

Nowadays, when doubt is cast on a husband's paternity, or when a man denies that he is the father of a child, a court has a discretion to order either blood or DNA testing under the Family Law Reform Act 1969, section 20. The court may exercise this power either of its own motion, or on an application by any party to the proceedings. However, jurisdiction to make an order for blood tests only arises where there are civil proceedings before the court in which the paternity of a child is in issue.[8] A court cannot make an order for blood tests on a free-standing application. This type of forensic evidence is far preferable to evidence relating to whether the husband and wife had sexual intercourse around the time when the child is believed to have been conceived, and to evidence relating to whether the wife had sexual intercourse with another man or men during the relevant period. Similarly, when the issue of paternity relates to an unmarried woman, unless forensic evidence is available, the evidence is likely to consist of statements made by the mother, and by the man she alleges to be the father, and of statements made by other witnesses. These statements will mainly relate to whether the alleged father had the opportunity and the inclination to have sexual intercourse with the mother. As people normally have sexual intercourse in private, such witness statements are usually of limited assistance. The disadvantage of placing reliance on this type of evidence is manifest. Apart from the fact that such evidence is often somewhat distasteful, embarrassing to all concerned, and may sometimes cause distress to the parties because of the type of detail about the parties' sexual activities which is required in a contested case, it is also not the best evidence available. Forensic evidence is the best evidence and, of the

6   Family Law Reform Act 1969, s.26.
7   For an account of the case law see Bromley and Lowe *Bromley's Family Law* (Butterworths, 7th edn) pp 240-244.
8   *Re E (A Minor) (Parental Responsibility)* [1994] 2 FCR 709.

choices available, DNA testing is preferable to blood-matching testing because it can establish paternity with certainty. By contrast, a blood-matching test can establish that a man is not the child's father, but can only give a statistical likelihood of whether he is the father.

Guidance on the discretion to order blood testing was given by the House of Lords in *S v S; W v Official Solicitor*.[9] The point of law to be resolved was whether a test could be ordered despite the fact that the child might not benefit from the outcome of the test. The House of Lords ruled that where there is, or may be, a conflict between the interests of the child and the general requirements of justice, justice requires that available evidence should not be suppressed. It held that a court's duty to protect children will not ordinarily provide a ground for refusing to order forensic testing merely because it might, in revealing the truth, prove that the child is not the husband's child, and thus not born in lawful wedlock.[10] In relation to the child's interests, Lord Reid said: 'On the one hand, it is said that with rare exceptions it is always in the child's interests to have a decision that it is legitimate. On the other hand, it is said that the value to the child of a finding of legitimacy is now much less than it used to be, and that it is generally better for the child that the truth should out than that the child should go through life with a lurking doubt as to the validity of a decision when evidence, which would very likely have disclosed the truth, has been suppressed'.[11]

Despite the recognition by the House of Lords in *S v S; W v Official Solicitor* that to allow the truth to emerge normally serves both the interests of justice and the welfare of the child, the child's best interests may occasionally demand that forensic testing does not take place. In *Re F (A Minor) (Blood Tests: Parental Rights)*[12] the mother was having a sexual relationship with both her husband and another man during the period when the child was conceived. The child had been brought up by her mother and the mother's husband since her birth, and had had no contact with the other man. This man, believing that he was the child's father, applied for a parental responsibility order, an order allowing him to have contact with the child, and for blood tests to determine her paternity. Clearly, unless the man was the child's father, the applications for parental responsibility and contact would be without basis. The trial judge dismissed the man's application for forensic tests to be carried out, and the man's appeal was dismissed. The Court of Appeal held that the judge had properly exercised his discretion to refuse the application for blood tests. It held that the probable outcome of his application for a parental responsibility and contact

9   [1970] 3 All ER 107.
10 Although the law does not distinguish between children born inside and outside marriage, in some circles there is still a stigma attached to illegitimacy.
11 [1970] 3 All ER 107 at p 111.
12 [1993] 3 All ER 596.

order was that both orders would be refused because they could not possibly benefit the child. It said that the decisive factor was the child's welfare, and that the stability of the family unit on which the child's security depended might be disturbed if blood testing was ordered. It further held that a court will not order a blood test to be carried out on a child against the will of a parent who has had sole parental responsibility for the child since the child's birth.[13]

The fact that a parent is adamant in refusing to be tested, or to allow her child to be tested, may in itself influence the court in its decision whether to order tests. In *Re CB (A Minor) (Blood Tests)*,[14] when refusing the applicant's request that orders for blood tests be made in respect of the mother, a married woman, and her youngest child, Wall J held that if blood tests were to establish that the applicant was the child's father, but if as a consequence the adults became involved in a bitter dispute over the child's upbringing, this would be contrary to the child's interests.

Refusing forensic testing

It seems likely that cases in which paternity is in issue will increase in the future because of the implications of the Child Support Act 1991. This Act imposes an obligation on all absent parents to support their children financially, and provides for tracing and enforcement methods which have the potential to draw far more unmarried fathers into the net of child support than hitherto.[15] It also gives fathers a stronger motive than hitherto to deny paternity because the amount they are likely to be ordered to pay may be substantial, in which case the matter can be referred to a court. What inferences may a court properly draw from the refusal of a person to be tested or to agree to the child being tested?

Section 21(1) of the Family Law Reform Act 1969 makes it clear that a court cannot force an adult to undergo forensic testing.[16] In relation to children, a child of 16 can give consent to the taking of a bodily sample.[17] Where the child is under 16 a sample can be taken if the person who has care and control of him consents.[18] In relation to the position where a person refuses to agree to forensic testing, or refuses to allow the child to be tested, section 23(1) of the Family Law Reform Act 1969 provides that—

---

13 For a critique, see J Fortin *Re F: 'The Gooseberry Bush Approach'* (1994) 57 MLR 296.
14 [1994] 2 FCR 925.
15 See ch 8.
16 And see *Re CB (A Minor) (Blood Tests)* [1994] 2 FCR 925.
17 S.21(2).
18 S.21(3); it may also be the case that a 'Gillick competent' child can consent to giving a bodily sample: see below.

'Where a court gives a direction under section 20 of this Act and any person fails to take any step required of him for the purpose of giving effect to the direction, the court may draw such inferences, if any, from that fact as appear proper in the circumstances.'

Section 23(2) provides that—

'Where in any proceedings in which the parentage of any person falls to be determined by the court hearing the proceedings there is a presumption of law that that person is legitimate, then if—
(a) a direction is given under section 20 of this Act in those proceedings, and
(b) any party who is claiming relief in the proceedings and who for the purposes of obtaining that relief is entitled to rely on the presumption fails to take any step required of him for the purpose of giving effect to the direction,
the court may adjourn the hearing for such period as it thinks fit to enable that party to take that step, and if at the end of that period he has failed without reasonable cause to take it the court may, without prejudice to subsection (1) of this section, dismiss his claim for relief notwithstanding the absence of evidence to rebut the presumption.'

Section 23(3) provides that—

'where any person named in a direction under section 20 of this Act fails to consent to the taking of a bodily sample from himself or from any person named in the section over whom he has care and control he shall be deemed for the purposes of this section to have failed to take a step required of him for the purpose of giving effect to the direction.'

In *Re A (A Minor) (Paternity)*[19] the Court of Appeal held that the court's powers to draw inferences under section 23(1) are wholly at large and unconfined, including about the fact in issue, namely the child's paternity. It concluded that where an alleged father chooses to exercise his right not to be tested, the inference that he is the father of the child would be virtually inescapable. It pointed out that, in the light of recent scientific advance, a man cannot be forced against his will to accept paternity of a child whom he does not believe is his. But, as Waite LJ said, 'any man who is unsure of his own paternity and harbours the least doubt as to whether the child he is alleged to have fathered may be that of another man now has it within

19 [1994] 2 FLR 463.

his power to set all doubt at rest by submitting to a test.'[20] Equally it seems that a court could properly draw the inference that a particular man is the child's father in a case where the mother denies this, but refuses to be tested, or to allow her child to be tested.

In the light of *Re A (A Minor) (Paternity)* it seems likely that courts will adopt a robust approach where one of the parties refuses to be tested, or to allow the child to be tested, and will take full advantage of their entitlement to draw such inferences as appear proper.[1] However, in a case when a child is born to a married woman the position is made more complicated by the presumption of legitimacy. It can be seen that section 23(2) separates the presumption of legitimacy from claiming relief in reliance on the presumption. In a case in which a party who is relying on the presumption refuses to be tested, or to allow the child to be tested, the court may dismiss the claim for relief even though there may be an absence of evidence to rebut the presumption. An example might be where a married woman alleges that a man other than her husband is the father of her child for child support purposes. Where the man denies paternity, but refuses to be tested, it seems that it would be possible for a court to order that the man should be liable to make child support payments, even though there is an absence of evidence to rebut the presumption of legitimacy.[2]

Assisted conception and paternity

It has been seen that methods of assisting an infertile couple to conceive a child may include impregnating the woman with sperm from a man who is not the woman's husband, or partner. However, despite the lack of genetic relationship between the husband, or partner, and the child, these men will usually be accorded the status of father of the child as a matter of law. Consider first the case of married couples. When a child is born to a married woman, section 28 of the Human Fertilisation and Embryology Act 1990 provides that her husband shall be treated as the child's father for all purposes, unless he has not consented to the artificial form of treatment she received to bring about conception. Where he has not consented, the common law presumption of legitimacy will nonetheless apply unless rebutted by evidence to the contrary.[3] In the case of unmarried couples, a

20 Ibid, at pp 472-3.
1 There is, however, a risk that a man may sometimes be dissuaded from asking for DNA testing, even though he has reasonable cause for believing that he is not the father, because the court could order him to pay the costs, which are substantial (currently about £500).
2 This could only occur in a case where the husband is unavailable for testing but where there is evidence that he could be the father, for otherwise whether or not the husband is the child's father could be established with certainty by taking samples from him and the child.
3 Human Fertilisation and Embryology Act 1990, s.28(5)(a).

man who is not the child's genetic father is treated by law as the father, provided that the methods used to assist conception were carried out 'in the course of treatment services provided for her and a man together by a person to whom a licence applies.'[4] Thus the child's status is dependent on whether an unmarried couple have been able to secure the donation of sperm with the assistance of a licensed clinic. The donor of the sperm is not treated as the child's father for any purposes.[5]

On the other hand, and by contrast, where a woman conceives through donor insemination using self-help methods, then it is the donor, not her partner, who is the child's father.[6] This outcome is inevitable, for there is no regulated framework within which the conception occurs. However, where such self-help methods have been used, and where the woman's partner holds himself out as the child's father with the agreement of the mother, he will of course be recognised and treated by others as the father because no one will have cause to think otherwise. Where couples disguise the truth about the child's paternity in cases of this kind, the true position is unlikely to emerge provided that the family relationships remain stable. However, serious questions may arise about whether forensic testing should be ordered in a case where the relationship between the man and the woman subsequently breaks down, and where the 'father' denies paternity. Is it in the best interests of a child for tests to take place where the child has had a relationship of many years with the man, and where he believes that the man is his father? Should a man who has agreed to the donor insemination of his partner be entitled to avoid having any further responsibility for the upbringing of the child?[7] And if the mother refuses to undergo forensic testing, or to allow the child to be tested, what inferences, if any, would it be proper for the court to draw under section 23(1) of the Family Law Reform Act 1969?

Parental responsibility and third parties

The concept of parental responsibility underpins decision-making about children. It is the fact that a decision-maker enjoys this responsibility which gives him or her the power and the authority to make choices about a child's upbringing. Consequently it may be essential for persons other than

4   S.28(3); that is a licence issued by the Human Fertilisation and Embryology Authority which regulates treatment and research in the area of fertility treatment and maintains a Code of Practice.

5   S.28(4); see too s.28(6)(a).

6   Self-help may involve the woman having sexual intercourse with a man on the understanding that any child conceived will not be treated as his child; or by the man producing his sperm and the woman inserting it into her body by a syringe.

7   This question is particularly likely to arise where an unmarried mother is claiming child support from the 'father'. Unless the man is indeed the child's father, he has no duty to support the child: see further ch 8.

parents to have parental responsibility so that they are empowered to act on the child's behalf. Unless a decision is made by a person with parental responsibility it is not normally a decision which can safely be acted upon. Parental responsibility can be acquired by persons who are not parents of the child in the following circumstances: when a person is appointed as guardian of the child; when a court makes a residence order to a third person; when a local authority obtains a care order, including an interim care order; or when an emergency protection order is made. In each of these circumstances there are reasons why the fact that the child's mother, and sometimes his father, have parental responsibility provides insufficient safeguards for the child.[8] In the case of guardianship, a parent with parental responsibility will be dead.[9] In the case of a residence order to a third party, a court will have made an order that the third party is the person with whom the child is to live because the child's welfare requires this.[10] In the case of a care order, or an emergency protection order, it will have been established that the child is suffering, or is likely to suffer, significant harm attributable to a lack of reasonable parental care, or because the child is beyond parental control, and that it is for the welfare of the child that parental responsibility is given to the local authority.[11] With the exception of guardianship, parental responsibility can only be conferred on a person other than a parent by means of a court order.

Sharing parental responsibility

A person who already has parental responsibility for a child does not cease to have that responsibility solely because some other person subsequently acquires it.[12] The Children Act 1989 makes it explicit that more than one person may have parental responsibility for the same child at the same time.[13] This is a vital principle which underpins much of the thinking in the Children Act 1989.[14] It means that parental responsibility is not only shared between parents, but also that it may sometimes be shared between parents and a third party. But if each person with parental responsibility has 'all the rights, duties, powers, responsibilities and authority which by law a parent of a child has in relation to the child and his property',[15] how

8   It has been explained above how an unmarried father can acquire parental responsibility either by making a formal agreement with the mother, or by a court order.
9   Guardianship is considered below.
10 See ch 2.
11 Care orders and emergency protection orders are considered in detail in ch 3.
12 S.2(6).
13 S.2(5).
14 In particular, it underpins the notion that local authorities who are looking after a child in their care, and for whom they therefore have parental responsibility, should work in partnership with parents: see ch 3.
15 The meaning of parental responsibility given in s.3(1).

can such persons exercise parental responsibility independently of the other where their parental responsibility is shared? This question is answered in various provisions in the Act, and in the accompanying regulations and guidance.

Section 2(7) provides that—

'Where more than one person has parental responsibility for a child, each of them may act alone and without the other (or others) in meeting that responsibility; but nothing in this Part shall be taken to affect the operation of any enactment which requires the consent of more than one person in a matter affecting the child.'

This clearly allows unilateral decisions to be made about a child's upbringing by a person with parental responsibility. This is essential for practical reasons. If every time a decision was made about a child which required authorisation from someone with the requisite authority, it would often be impossible to proceed if agreement was first required from all persons with parental responsibility. There may also be psychological benefits in the notion that each person with parental responsibility may act alone in meeting that responsibility. When parents are estranged, they often disagree over matters relating to the upbringing of their children. There are advantages in the notion that one parent is not entitled to dictate to the other parent how he or she looks after the child when that child is in the other's care.[16] If a residence order is made to a third party, which means that the child will have his home with that third party, he or she is likely to need to have the authority to make decisions about the child without prior consultation with the parents.

On the other hand there are disadvantages in allowing unilateral decision-making by persons with parental responsibility. Some decisions about the upbringing of a child are so important that it may be thought right that all persons with parental responsibility should have the opportunity to express an opinion before action on the decision is taken. Thus in *Re G (Parental Responsibility: Education)*[17] Glidewell LJ had no doubt that the mother ought to have been consulted by the father before he made the important decision to remove the child from his day school and to send him to a boarding school.[18] However, section 2(7) affords protection to the parent who acts unilaterally in a case of this kind, and no sanction can be imposed on a parent who fails to consult the other. Indeed, the court may feel that it is inappropriate to intervene once a decision

16 For example after divorce the child will normally live with one parent and have contact with the other. When the non-residential parent looks after the child on a contact visit he or she is entitled to care for the child in whatever manner he or she chooses.
17 [1994] 2 FLR 964.
18 A different example might be where the child requires medical treatment, and where there are different views about whether such treatment is in the child's best interests.

about the child's upbringing has been made by one parent.[19] Furthermore, where the issue is discussed, but where agreement cannot be reached, a person with parental responsibility who objects to the exercise by the other of his or her parental responsibility has the burden of pursuing the matter before a court. An exception to this general principle applies where the law dictates that the consent of all persons with parental responsibility is required. The law requires the consent of both parents with parental responsibility to their child's adoption;[20] or to his permanent removal from England.[1] In other cases the law normally requires the consent of both parents to the child's marriage while he is a minor;[2] to his temporary removal from England;[3] or to his reception into local authority accommodation.[4] But it will be seen that these matters are affected by whether one parent has the benefit of a residence order.[5]

The other way in which the sharing of parental responsibility is made workable is through the 'incompatibility' principle which is embodied in section 2(8). This provides that—

> 'The fact that a person has parental responsibility for a child shall not entitle him to act in any way which would be incompatible with any order made with respect to the child under this Act.'

Thus when a court has made a decision about a child which has been embodied in a court order, that decision takes priority over the parental responsibility of the parents and others. For example, the parents might not wish the child to have contact with his grandparents. Normally parents have the power to decide whether such contact should take place. But where that decision is challenged in a court, and the court rules that contact should be permitted, the court's order must be obeyed. Similarly, a local authority which is looking after a child in care is normally entitled to decide whether a child has contact with his grandparents. However, if the grandparents successfully challenge this decision in a court, the local authority must allow such contact to take place in accordance with the court's ruling. Any other outcome would be incompatible with the court's order. Or one parent might be empowered by a court order to make all decisions about a child's medical treatment in a case where the other parent holds strong views against traditional forms of medical intervention. Thus

19 Thus in *Re G (Parental Responsibility: Education)* [1994] 2 FLR 964, the court refused to make an ex parte prohibited steps order to prevent the child attending the boarding school, despite finding that the mother should first have been consulted.
20 Adoption Act 1976, s.16.
1 Child Abduction Act 1984, s.1; Children Act 1989, s.13.
2 Marriage Act 1949, s.3(1A).
3 Children Act 1989, s.13.
4 Ibid, s.20(7)(8).
5 See ch 2.

the incompatibility principle diminishes the decision-making powers of those with parental responsibility, and in some cases determines how decision-making will be shared.

Where a child is in care under a care order, which means that the local authority have parental responsibility for him, the general principles in section 2 apply. The local authority must share their parental responsibility with the parents. However, the provisions in section 2 are qualified by section 33(3)(b). This provides that the local authority have the power to determine the extent to which the parents may meet their parental responsibility for a child where a care order has been made. However, provisions in Part III of the Act, and regulations and guidance issued under the Act, require local authorities to work in partnership with parents, and to involve them in decision-making about their child's upbringing.[6] Periodic reviews must be held about the child, and the views of the parents must be sought.[7] Procedures must be established which enable a parent to make representations, including any complaint, to the local authority about their child's upbringing, and at least one person who is not a member or officer of the local authority must be a member of such a reviewing body.[8] Thus mechanisms have been put in place which are designed to ensure that responsibility between parents and the local authority is shared, despite the fact that it is the local authority which has the primary responsibility to make decisions about the child.

Delegating parental responsibility

It is often necessary for persons who have dealings with the day-to-day care of a child to be empowered to make decisions on the child's behalf despite the fact that they do not have parental responsibility. Relatives, school teachers, child minders and nannies are obvious examples of such persons. Section 2(9) specifically stipulates that a person who has parental responsibility for a child may not surrender or transfer any part of that responsibility to another, but the subsection does allow a person with parental responsibility to arrange for some or all of it to be met by one or more persons acting on his behalf. For example, it is common practice for schools to receive written authority from parents delegating their power to give consent to medical treatment for children to the teachers. When the main body of care for a child is provided in an institution, such as when a child is accommodated in a boarding school, or in a local authority childrens' home, a wide variety of decisions about the child's upbringing will be formally delegated to the persons running these institutions.

6 See ch 3.
7 S.26(2).
8 S.26(3)(4).

In the usual course of daily living, parents do not normally make formal provision for the day-to-day arrangements they make with others about the care of their children. However, this can sometimes cause problems. The Act places considerable emphasis on the concept of parental responsibility as providing the basis for decision-making, and this is gradually permeating into public awareness.[9] In the context of medical treatment there is evidence that some hospital personnel refuse to provide medical treatment for a child until they receive parental authority to do so (unless the situation is one of an emergency).[10] It would be most unfortunate if medical decisions about a child were to be delayed whilst parents are contacted if such delay would cause a child avoidable pain and suffering. It is suggested that such an approach to the formal provision of consent from a parent stems from a misunderstanding of the formality which is required by law for the delegation of parental responsibility. For the law to be workable, it would appear essential for the delegation of parental responsibility to be capable of being implied. It is suggested that if a relative, nanny, child-minder or other person is caring for a child, and has been told informally to seek medical assistance if the child needs it, that this should be sufficient to amount to delegated authorisation from the parent to consent to whatever type of medical treatment is suggested until the parent can be contacted.

The position of persons without parental responsibility

Many people have the day-to-day care of children without having parental responsibility for them. Yet it has been seen that only those with parental responsibility have all the responsibilities of parenthood, and the position of others who have the care of children therefore requires some clarification. Can they make important decisions about the child? If such a person were to smack the child, would this be an assault on the child?[11] If not, where does the power to smack or otherwise punish the child come from? Section 3(5) contains only a partial answer to these and other questions. It provides—

---

9   For example, in *B v B (A Minor) (Residence Order)* [1992] 2 FLR 327 a local education authority were refusing to accept the consent of a grandmother to her grandchild going on school trips, and were demanding the written consent of the mother: see ch 2.

10 The evidence is anecdotal, rather than derived from a properly conducted research study. However, it seems highly unlikely that a doctor would ask a father whether he is married to the child's mother and, if not, whether he has a parental responsibility order, before obtaining his consent to treat the child! In this way, strict law and day-to-day practice completely part company for obvious and practical reasons.

11 Cf the position of child-minders under Part X of the Act, see *Sutton London Borough Council v Davis* [1994] 1 FLR 737.

'A person who—
(a) does not have parental responsibility for a particular child; but
(b) has care of the child,
may (subject to the provisions of this Act) do what is reasonable in all the circumstances of the case for the purpose of safeguarding or promoting the child's welfare.'

This is a broadly based provision the scope of which has yet to be ascertained. It is suggested that reliance could be placed by medical personnel on section 3(5) where persons with parental responsibility cannot be contacted, but where others who have care of the child consent to medical treatment. It is suggested that section 3(5) could be wide enough to encompass giving consent to most orthodox forms of medical treatment. Furthermore, it might be a sustainable argument that the doctor himself 'has care of the child' and can do what is reasonable to safeguard or promote the child's health, which is an aspect of his welfare, until the parents can be found. Such an approach gives respect to the notion that parental responsibility is conferred in order to enable a parent to fulfil his parental duties. When a parent is not available to do this, then there is merit in allowing other persons, who are motivated by the purpose of safeguarding the child's welfare, to step in. The alternative approach, namely that persons cannot normally act until a parent agrees, may give too much weight to the notion that parents have *rights* in respect of their children rather than *responsibilities*, and give insufficient weight to the right of the child to be treated as an autonomous individual, who is entitled to receive the aid and assistance of others who are acting in the course of their professional duties.

Whether section 3(5) permits a person with care of the child to take steps for the purposes of safeguarding or promoting the child's welfare contrary to the express wishes of a person with parental responsibility is more controversial. The context in which this question is most likely to arise is where the person with care forms the view that it would be against the interests of the child to return him to the care of a parent. For example, if parents returned home drunk, and a baby sitter formed the opinion that it would be unsafe to leave the child in the house with them, could she lawfully remove the child from the premises and take the child to her own home? It would seem desirable that the law should authorise such a properly motivated action, and section 3(5) would almost certainly cover this situation. More difficult is the position when a child is being accommodated by a local authority under section 20, and a parent wishes immediately to remove his child from that accommodation. A local authority does not have parental responsibility for an accommodated child, and section 20(8) specifically states that any person who has parental responsibility may at any time remove the child from accommodation provided by the local authority under that section.[12] Whether section 3(5) would allow a foster parent, or a person in charge of a children's home, to refuse to hand the child over in express disregard of section 20(8) has yet to be determined. It would seem desirable that section 3(5) should provide such persons with protection for a short period, provided that during that period steps were being taken to obtain a court order authorising the retention of the child.

Guardians and parental responsibility

Many parents are anxious to make provision for a person to have parental responsibility for their children in the event of their death. They can achieve this by appointing a person to be the child's guardian. The law relating to the appointment of guardians is contained in section 5 of the Act. In the case of married parents, each parent is entitled to appoint an individual to be the child's guardian in the event of his or her death. In the case of unmarried parents, the father may not appoint a guardian unless he has parental responsibility. Guardians can be appointed in a relatively informal manner. The appointment can be made by deed or will, but it is also sufficient if it is 'made in writing, is dated and is signed by the person making the appointment.'[13]

When does the appointment of a guardian take effect?

Although the purpose of appointing a guardian is to arrange for someone to act in the deceased's place, section 5 provides that the actual appointment does not take effect unless both parents with parental responsibility have died.[14] When parents are living together in harmony this rule creates no difficulties, though it may be that the surviving parent would sometimes have welcomed sharing parental responsibility with the guardian appointed by his deceased spouse. The benefits and burdens of bringing up children are often easier to manage when the task is shared. It is suggested that the Law Commission, when they recommended that the law be changed from the common law position under which the testamentary guardianship took effect from death, may have been unduly influenced by the notion that the deceased spouse was seeking to rule the other from the grave.[15]

12 See further ch 3.
13 S.5(5).
14 S.5(7)(8); a person can disclaim his appointment 'within a reasonable time of his knowing that the appointment has taken effect': s.6(5).
15 Law Com No 172, para 2.27.

In the event of estrangement or divorce, neither party may be content with the notion that the surviving spouse will have sole responsibility for their child's upbringing, and they may wish to appoint a guardian to have parental responsibility in conjunction with the survivor. This is particularly likely where a parent anticipates his or her premature death, and where he or she wants a relative to have care of his or her children; or where a parent has remarried, and wants the new spouse to be the children's guardian. However, it has been seen that normally guardianship does not take effect where there is a surviving parent with parental responsibility.[16] The only way in which the appointment of a guardian can take immediate effect is when the deceased parent had a residence order. Section 5(7)(b) provides that where—

> 'immediately before the death of any person making such an appointment, a residence order in his favour was in force with respect to the child, the appointment shall take effect on the death of that person.'

When such an appointment takes place, parental responsibility is shared by the guardian with the surviving spouse. Where they cannot agree over the child's upbringing, for example whether the child should have his home with the parent, or with the guardian, the matter in dispute will have to be resolved by an application for an order under section 8.[17]

Where a child has no parent with parental responsibility for him, or where a parent with a residence order has died, an application may be made by any individual to a court, and the court may appoint that individual to be the child's guardian.[18] A court may also exercise this power in any family proceedings where it considers that a guardianship order should be made, even though no application has been made for the order.[19] Such an appointment may have an advantage over a residence order in a case where a child has been orphaned, because a guardian obtains greater powers. He can himself appoint a guardian for the child,[20] and his agreement to the child's adoption is required.[1]

---

16 S.5(7)(8).
17 The guardian is entitled to apply for a section 8 order, and need not first obtain the leave of the court. The implications of having entitlement, as distinct from requiring the court's leave, are explained in ch 2.
18 S.5(1).
19 S.5(2).
20 S.5(4). See ch 2 in relation to local authority foster parents and guardianship.
1 Adoption Act 1976, ss.16 and 18.

Guardianship, and children who are being looked after by a local authority

Only an 'individual' as distinct from a 'person' may be appointed a child's guardian. This means that a local authority may not apply for guardianship in respect of an orphaned child. Furthermore, it was held by Thorpe J in *Birmingham City Council v D and M*[2] that the fact of being an orphan does not mean that a child is suffering, or is likely to suffer, significant harm for the purposes of section 31 of the Act, and that therefore a care order cannot be made in respect of such a child thereby conferring parental responsibility on the local authority. It is suggested that there is a gap here in the law which creates difficulties for local authorities seeking to make the most appropriate provision for orphaned children.[3]

Competent children, parental responsibility and decision-making

So far in this chapter the assumption has been made that it is parents, and others with parental responsibility, who are the persons who are entitled to make decisions about a child's upbringing. But of course children themselves hold strong opinions about their own upbringing, and these opinions may not coincide with the opinions of the persons who have parental responsibility for them. It seems likely that the large majority of parents will normally discuss important matters about their children's upbringing with their children. The extent to which, in any particular household, decisions are made in an authoritarian manner by parents, in a more relaxed and consultative manner by parents and children together, or by the children themselves, will depend on how the parents see their role as parents. It will also depend on whether the children are old enough to understand and to express a point of view, and how forceful they are in asserting their own wishes and feelings. Where others have parental responsibility for a child under a residence order, or through guardianship, it seems likely that the dynamics of decision-making about the child's upbringing will operate in a similar manner. In most families some degree of conflict occurs between parents and children over the exercise of parental responsibility and authority, and each family handles this conflict in its own way. It is only where areas of disagreement between children and those who have parental responsibility for them cannot be resolved within the family, by whatever means, that the law may have a part to play.

---

2   [1994] 2 FLR 502: see further ch 3.
3   See *Re S (Minors) (Care: Orders in Respect of Orphans)* [1994] Fam Law 356 in which a
     circuit judge had taken a contrary view; and for commentary on this issue see (1994) 24
     Fam Law 152.

Where a child is being looked after by a local authority, conflict is just as likely to occur between the child's carers and the child himself in this situation as it does in families. Whether the child is being looked after by foster parents, or is living in residential accommodation, day-to-day decisions about the child's upbringing must be made by the persons who are looking after him. Furthermore, it should be borne in mind that children being looked after by local authorities have often suffered at the hands of those who have hitherto had charge of them, and this may make such children less amenable to the assertion of adult authority than those children who come from more stable home backgrounds. The responsibility of a local authority when making decisions about children is somewhat different from the responsibility of parents, because the manner in which this responsibility is exercised is governed in part by the Children Act 1989, and its associated regulations. A local authority have a duty to consult with children. They must, so far as is reasonably practicable, ascertain the child's wishes and feelings before making any decision with respect to a child whom they are looking after, or are proposing to look after.[4] They are obliged by law periodically to review the position of a child whom they are looking after and, when holding such a review, must take steps to ascertain the child's views.[5]

In the case of a young child it is inevitable that adults will make decisions on the child's behalf because the child does not have the requisite competence to decide himself. However, as children grow older they become increasingly capable of making their own choices about their own upbringing. When adults are in serious conflict with the child over a matter relating to a child's upbringing, difficult issues arise about who has the right to determine what should happen to the child.

The 'Gillick' case

The starting point of any discussion about decision-making by children is the House of Lords' decision in *Gillick v West Norfolk and Wisbech Area Health Authority*.[6] The case itself was concerned with whether a doctor could lawfully give contraceptive advice and treatment to a girl aged under 16 without the knowledge and consent of her parents.[7] Mrs Gillick sought

4 S.22(4).
5 S.26(2).
6 [1985] 3 All ER 402; it is impossible here to do justice to the complexity of the ruling in *Gillick* which has been the subject of extensive analysis. See, for example, J Eekelaar *The Eclipse of Parental Rights* (1986) 102 LQR 4; J Eekelaar *The Emergence of Children's Rights* (1986) 6 Ox JLS 161; A Bainham *The Balance of Power in Family Decisions* (1986) CLJ 262.
7 The reason why the age of 16, rather than 18, was the age in issue is because the Family Law Reform Act 1969, s.8 specifically provides that the consent to medical treatment of a minor aged 16 is a valid consent.

a declaration stating that such action would be unlawful. Various arguments were advanced on her behalf. These included the assertion that it would be unlawful to provide such advice and treatment, because a child below the age of 16 lacks the capacity to give valid consent to medical treatment; and the assertion that to give advice and treatment without parental consent would be inconsistent with Mrs Gillick's rights as a mother. The House of Lords ruled by a majority that, in relation to when a child acquires capacity to make decisions, 'a minor's capacity to make his or her own decision depends on the minor having sufficient understanding and intelligence to make the decision and is not to be determined by reference to any judicially fixed age limit.'[8] In relation to the notion that parents have rights in relation to the upbringing of their children which cannot be displaced by others, the House of Lords acknowledged that parental rights clearly do exist, and that they do not wholly disappear until the age of majority. However, it then affirmed the centrality of the principle that 'the common law has never treated such rights as sovereign or beyond review or control. Nor has our law ever treated a child as other than a person with capacities and rights recognised by law. The principle of law ... is that parental rights are derived from parental duty and exist only so long as they are needed for the protection of the person and property of the child.'[9] Accordingly, the House of Lords refused to grant the plaintiff the declaration which she sought.

Gillick v West Norfolk and Wisbech Area Health Authority was undoubtedly an enormously important decision even when restricted to its material facts. As a consequence, a child is entitled to have a confidential relationship with her doctor and to obtain contraceptive advice and treatment without parental consent. Guidance on when it would be justifiable for a doctor to proceed in this manner was given by Lord Fraser; this guidance includes the prerequisites that the girl 'is very likely to begin or to continue having sexual intercourse with or without contraceptive treatment', 'that unless she receives contraceptive advice or treatment her physical or mental health or both are likely to suffer' and that 'her best interests require him to give her contraceptive advice, treatment or both without parental consent.'[10] Clearly this guidance encompasses additional factors to those which a doctor would have in mind when deciding whether to prescribe contraception for an adult. A doctor who sought to ascertain from an adult patient whether she was 'very likely to begin or to continue having sexual intercourse' before he would agree to prescribe for

8 [1985] 3 All ER 402, per Lord Scarman at p 423.

9 Ibid, per Lord Scarman, at p 420.

10 At p 413. This guidance has been incorporated in DOH guidelines. More general guidance on the level of capacity required in the child was given by Lord Scarman at pp 423-4. This was put at a very high level of comprehension, and appreciation, of the issues involved.

her might risk receiving a fairly hostile response! It might therefore be argued that all the House of Lords did in *Gillick* was to substitute professional decision-making by a doctor for parental decision-making, and that it did not give a child a positive right to make her own choices irrespective of the view taken by adults of their desirability. However, whilst such an argument has some merit in respect of the confines of the actual decision in *Gillick* itself, it ignores the wide impact which the ruling has had on the development of child law in recent years.

Essentially what *Gillick* achieved was to create a climate of expectation that a child will be consulted, and his or her wishes and feelings will be taken into account, when any important decision is made in respect of his or her upbringing. What *Gillick* did *not* achieve was to create a rule that the wishes and feelings of a child will always prevail over the wishes and feelings of the persons with parental responsibility, even though the child has sufficient competence to understand the full implications of the decision to be made. The opportunity to suggest the incorporation of such a rule in legislation was afforded during the massive review of child law which took place before the Children Act 1989 was enacted, but no suggestion for such a rule was made. Rather, the definition of parental responsibility was made in terms that it means 'all the rights, duties, powers, responsibility and authority which by law a parent has in relation to the child and his property.'[11] The use of the phrase 'which by law a parent has in relation to the child' allows for development and change in the law, and gives scope for further judicial interpretation of what the phrase encompasses.

Competent children and medical decisions

The question of who has the responsibility to decide when there is disagreement between a competent child and the persons with parental responsibility for him has arisen mainly in the context of medical decisions. It should be recalled that *Gillick v West Norfolk and Wisbech Area Health Authority*[12] was concerned with whether a competent child could *consent* to medical treatment, and whether such consent could be countermanded by a person with parental responsibility. Subsequently two serious cases involving very sick children came before the courts in which the children concerned were *refusing* medical treatment, and where there was doubt about whether there was authority to treat the children without their consent.[13] In *Re R (A Minor) (Wardship: Medical Treatment)*[14] the girl

---

11 S.3(1).
12 [1985] 3 All ER 402.
13 See too *Re E (A Minor) (Wardship: Medical Treatment)* [1993] 1 FLR 386; *Re S (A Minor) (Consent to Medical Treatment)* [1994] 2 FLR 1065.
14 [1991] 4 All ER 177.

concerned was aged 15 and in *Re W (A Minor) (Wardship: Medical Treatment)*[15] she was 16.

In *Re R (A Minor) (Wardship: Medical Treatment)* the child had a history of serious mental illness such that, in the past, she had been ill enough to be admitted to hospital under sections 2 and 3 of the Mental Health Act 1983. Subsequently she was placed in an adolescent psychiatric unit. Concern grew about her mental state such that the senior consultant in the unit stated that he believed R to be in a psychotic state, and he wanted the permission of the local authority, who had parental responsibility for R under a care order, to administer anti-psychotic medication to her. This consent was given, but R refused to take the drugs. A social worker, who had experience with cases involving persons who are mentally ill, then had a three-hour telephone conversation with R after which he decided that R sounded lucid and rational and he did not regard her as 'sectionable'.[16] The local authority therefore took the view that they could not give permission for R to have drugs administered against her will. As a consequence of this refusal of permission, the adolescent unit took the view that they could not continue to care for R unless they were given a free hand in relation to the administration of medication. The psychiatrist was of the opinion that, without medication, R was likely to lapse into a fully psychotic state under which she would be a serious suicidal risk, and potentially very violent and unpredictable in her behaviour. He was also of the opinion that R was currently mature enough to understand the nature and the implications of the treatment proposed, and of sufficient understanding to make a decision in her own right. The local authority therefore made the child a ward of court, and asked the court to determine whether R could be treated without her consent in the light of the House of Lords ruling in *Gillick v West Norfolk and Wisbech Area Health Authority*.

In *Re R (A Minor)* there were three issues to be resolved: did R have the capacity to refuse consent to medical treatment; if she did, could she nonetheless be treated if a person with parental responsibility gave consent; and did the court have the power to override the decision of a child irrespective of whether the child was competent to give consent?

In relation to capacity, the Court of Appeal ruled that R did not have the capacity to make decisions about her own medical treatment. It was by no means satisfied that R understood the implications of the treatment being withheld, as distinct from understanding what was proposed to be done by way of treatment. The evidence had established that R's mental state fluctuated, so that even if, on a good day, she was capable of reaching the standard of competence required to meet the *Gillick* criteria, on other days she was not only *Gillick* incompetent, she was actually sectionable. Lord

15 [1992] 4 All ER 627.
16 That is, liable to be made the subject of an application under ss.2 and 3 of the Mental Health Act 1983.

Donaldson MR ruled that 'no child in that situation can be regarded as "*Gillick* competent"... "*Gillick* competence" is developmental concept and will not be lost or acquired on a day-to-day or week-to-week basis. In the case of mental disability, that disability must also be taken into account, particularly where it is fluctuating in effect.'[17]

In relation to whether a person with parental responsibility had the power to override the refusal to consent to medical treatment by a competent child, only Lord Donaldson expressed a view. He was clearly of the opinion that in a case where a '*Gillick* competent' child refuses treatment, but someone with parental responsibility consents, that treatment can lawfully be given to the child. He acknowledged that the child's refusal of consent will be a very important factor in the doctor's decision whether or not to treat, but held that it does not stop treatment going ahead if consent is obtained from another person with parental responsibility. In relation to the court's position, all of the judges had no hesitation in finding that a court has the power to override the refusal of consent by a competent child.[18]

In *Re W (A Minor) (Wardship: Medical Treatment)*[19] the girl was suffering from anorexia nervosa. By the time the case came to court her weight had dropped to such a low level that, should she continue to lose weight for more than a few days, her capacity to have children in later life would be put seriously at risk, and a little later her life itself might be in danger. The court granted the local authority leave to make an application for the exercise by the court of the inherent jurisdiction of the High Court.[20] The local authority applied for leave to move the girl from the clinic in which she was currently being treated to a specialist unit for the treatment of eating disorders, and for leave to treat the girl without her consent. The girl wished to remain where she was. This case differed from the case of *Re R (A Minor)* in two significant respects: the girl concerned was aged 16; and the trial judge, Thorpe J, had found that she was of sufficient understanding to make an informed choice, a finding that was accepted by the Court of Appeal.[1] By contrast with *Re R (A Minor)*, the determination

---

17 [1991] 4 All ER 177 at pp 187-8. Because the court found that R did not have the capacity to make an informed decision then, strictly speaking, what it had to say about the power to override the consent of a competent child was obiter. Nonetheless, it was highly influential on subsequent decisions.

18 The ruling in *Re R (A Minor) (Wardship: Medical Treatment)* was subject to considerable criticism. See, for example, C Dyer (ed) *Doctors, Patients and the Law* (Blackwell, 1992) pp 60-61 and 156-7; R Thornton *Multiple Keyholders – Wardship and Consent to Medical Treatment* (1992) 51 CLJ 34.

19 [1992] 4 All ER 627.

20 For the use of the High Court's inherent jurisdiction, see ch 2.

1 Though Lord Donaldson MR expressed doubt whether Thorpe J had taken sufficient account of the fact that it is a feature of anorexia nervosa that it is capable of destroying the ability to make an informed choice.

in *Re W (A Minor)* was made against the background that section 8 of the Family Law Reform Act 1969 enables a person who has attained the age of 16 to give a valid consent to medical treatment.

The two main questions for the court to resolve were: could persons with parental responsibility for a competent minor aged 16 authorise medical treatment in the face of the minor's refusal; and did the court's power to override the wishes of a competent minor who *refuses* treatment extend to a minor aged over 16? The court also considered whether a court could override a competent minor's *consent* to medical treatment. Lord Donaldson MR and Balcombe LJ were of the view that the consent of a person with parental responsibility suffices to authorise the medical treatment of a minor of whatever age, and that no minor by refusing consent to medical treatment has the power to override such consent. Nolan LJ appeared to have some reservations about this point.[2] The court was united in its view that a court has the power to override a minor's consent to medical treatment. In relation to whether a court can override the consent of a competent child, Lord Donaldson asserted that this was accepted by all parties in *Gillick v West Norfolk and Wisbech Area Health Authority.*

When the rulings in *Re R (A Minor) (Wardship: Medical Treatment)* and *Re W (A Minor) (Wardship: Medical Treatment)* are separated from their factual context they raise all sorts of alarming possibilities of invasive forms of medical treatment being forced on unwilling teenagers who have the competence to make their own choices. The possibility that sedative medication will be forced on resisting adolescents with behavioural difficulties, who are being looked after in residential homes and treatment units run by local authorities or health trusts is particularly disturbing. An example arose in *Re K, W and H (Minors) (Medical Treatment)*[3] in which Thorpe J said that applications for orders authorising medical treatment, made by a hospital in respect of three highly disturbed 15-year-old girls who might not wish to consent in the future to the emergency use of medication, had been misconceived and unnecessary. He ruled that the girls were not '*Gillick* competent' to make decisions about their own medical treatment but that, even if they were, it was clear that the law allowed treatment to be given provided that someone with parental responsibility had given consent. An alarming feature of this case was that the judge took the view that the law was 'perfectly clear in this field', and that 'where more than one person has the power to consent, only a refusal by all having that power will create a veto.' He rejected the hospital's appraisal of the situation as being highly complex and confusing.

2   See below.
3   [1993] 1 FLR 854, which occurred after *Re R (A Minor)* but before *Re W (A Minor)*.

The weight to be given to the competent child's wishes in medical cases

It is suggested that Thorpe J's certain approach in *Re K, W and H (Minors)*,[4] coupled in that case with a finding that the girls did not have sufficient competence to instruct their own lawyers, despite the beliefs of their lawyers to the contrary,[5] bodes ill for competent and incompetent children who are in conflict with persons with parental responsibility in relation to medical decisions.[6] It illustrates the dangers of translating reasoned judgments, in which various reservations are expressed, into a simplified rule of law. It is important, therefore, that some of the thinking of the judges in *Re W (A Minor) (Wardship: Medical Treatment)* about the weight to be given to the competent child's wishes in medical cases is not lost.

The Court of Appeal clearly expected great weight to be given by medical practitioners to the wishes of the competent child. However, the court's pronouncements in this regard were made in the context of what Lord Donaldson MR described as the 'hair-raising' possibility, which had been canvassed before him, of abortions being carried out by doctors with the consent of parents on unwilling 16- and 17-year-olds. Lord Donaldson MR had no doubt that the wishes of a competent child were of the greatest clinical importance, and was content to place reliance on medical ethics to act as a restraining influence in cases of this kind. Balcombe LJ was also of the opinion that a doctor would not terminate the pregnancy of a mentally competent 16-year-old merely upon the consent of the child's parents. He added that it would seem inevitable that the matter would have to come before the court in such highly unlikely circumstances. Nolan LJ offered the child the strongest safeguard when he said—

'We are not directly concerned with cases in which the jurisdiction of the court has not been invoked, and in which accordingly the decision on treatment may depend upon the consent of the child or of the parent. I for my part would think it axiomatic, however, in order to avoid the risk of grave breaches of the law that in any case where time permitted, where major surgical or other procedures (such as an abortion) were proposed, and whereby the parents or those in loco parentis were prepared to give consent but the child (having sufficient understanding to make an informed decision) was not, the jurisdiction of the court should always be invoked.'[7]

4   Even though at the time of his judgment the only ruling on parental consent and *Gillick* competence had been in *Re R (A Minor) (Wardship: Medical Treatment)*, on which only Lord Donaldson MR had expressed a concluded view.

5   See further ch 2.

6   See too *South Glamorgan County Council v W and B* [1993] 1 FLR 574 which is discussed in ch 2.

7   [1992] 4 All ER 627 at pp 648-9.

Furthermore, Balcombe LJ was clearly unhappy with the approach which had been taken by Thorpe J when trying *Re W (A Minor)* at first instance. Thorpe J had treated the case 'as one for the unfettered exercise of his discretion, in which W's views were merely a relatively unimportant factor.' Balcombe LJ, by contrast, stressed that 'the judge should approach the exercise of the discretion with a predeliction to give effect to the child's wishes on the basis that prima facie that will be in his or her best interests.'[8] He added that W's wishes should have been respected 'unless there were very strong reasons for rejecting them.' Nolan LJ was certain that a court had not only the power, but also the inescapable responsibility, of deciding what should be done in W's case, guided by the welfare principle in section 1(1) of the Children Act 1989, and the checklist of matters in section 1(3) to which a court is required to have regard.[9] However, he commented:

'I am very far from asserting any general rule that the court should prefer its own view of what is in the best interests of the child to those of the child itself. In considering the welfare of the child, the court must not only recognise but if necessary defend the right of the child, having sufficient understanding to make an informed decision, to make his or her own choice.'[10]

This thinking gives great weight to the wishes and feelings of the competent child, and affords the child's interest in the decision-making process some considerable protection when a case comes before a court. However, what it also exposes is that a child may not obtain the benefit of such protection where a person with parental responsibility authorises medical treatment. Whilst persons with parental responsibility may generally be presumed to make decisions in a child's best interests, this is not inevitably the case. Such a person's perception of a child's best interests may be misguided. It may give insufficient weight to the wishes and feelings of the child. Or it may be over-influenced by the consenting person's own wishes and feelings. What might a '*Gillick* competent' child do when medical treatment is authorised without his or her consent? It is suggested that he or she would be best advised either to seek leave to apply for a specific issue order, or for a prohibited steps order, under section 8 of the Children Act 1989, or that he or she should seek leave to make an application for the exercise by the High Court of its inherent jurisdiction. Each of these options is discussed in the next chapter.

8   Ibid, at p 644.
9   See further ch 4.
10 [1992] 4 All ER 627 at p 648.

Chapter 2

Section 8 orders, and orders under the High Court's inherent jurisdiction

The nature of the proposed application, and the applicant's connection
with the child
Any risk of harm or disruption
The local authority's plans for the child
The wishes and feelings of the child's parents
Ex parte or inter partes applications for leave
The child concerned and leave
Leave and the welfare of the child where the child is the applicant
Who should represent the child?
Local authority foster parents and section 8 orders
Foster parents and leave to apply for a section 8 order
Local authority foster parents and guardianship
Local authorities and section 8 orders
A court may only make a residence order with respect to a child in care
A local authority may not apply for a residence or contact order
A local authority may apply for a specific issue, or prohibited steps, order
The inherent jurisdiction of the High Court
Situations not covered by the Children Act 1989
The inherent jurisdiction and local authorities
Who decides in children cases?
How the Children Act 1989 has affected the ruling in *W v Hertfordshire
County Council*

Chapter 2

Section 8 orders, and orders under the High Court's inherent jurisdiction

Court orders about children

Where opposing points of view about a child's upbringing are being expressed by persons who have equal parental responsibility for a child, and when neither will give way, then legal proceedings to resolve the matter in dispute may become inescapable. Persons without parental responsibility may also feel compelled to go to court when they disagree with those who have the right to decide about some matter concerning the child's upbringing. Local authorities have specific statutory duties to take steps to protect children, and in some cases these may warrant the institution of legal proceedings. The Children Act 1989 contains a range of orders which can be made about children. Between them, they cover almost all aspects of a child's upbringing, and the areas of disagreement which are likely to arise.[1] In this chapter the making of orders under section 8 of the Act is discussed. This is followed by an analysis of when the inherent jurisdiction of the High Court can be invoked.

No order unless better for the child

It will be seen that court's have wide powers to make orders and that, in some cases, there are few restraints on how these powers should be exercised. But there is a risk, therefore, that a court might be tempted to be too interventionist, and to make orders about matters which should normally be decided by those with parental responsibility. For example, it has not been unknown for a court to think that it properly falls within its powers to order at what time a child should be put to bed![2] A restraining

1   Adoption law is the main exception; this is covered by the Adoption Act 1976: see ch 4. Parental responsibility and guardianship orders have been considered in ch 1; public law orders under Parts IV and V are considered in ch 3.
2   *B v B (Custody: Conditions)* (1979) 1 FLR 385.

feature on the use and misuse of orders is embodied in section 1(5) which provides that—

> 'Where a court is considering whether or not to make one or more orders under this Act with respect to a child, it shall not make the order or any of the orders unless it considers that doing so would be better for the child than making no order at all.'

These words encapsulate an important principle, namely that a court should not make an order which will influence the upbringing of a child unless it is satisfied that the order will improve matters for the child. Another way of expressing this might be to say that court orders are designed to achieve a purpose and should not be granted automatically and without thought as to their consequences.

Before the enactment of the Children Act 1989 court orders were used in almost all divorce cases involving children.[3] The relationship between parents and children was formalised and characterised in legal language without much thought as to whether this was either desirable in the interests of children, or wanted by their parents. In court the following dialogue would be typical—'The children are living with you Mrs Smith?' 'Yes.' 'They see their father regularly?' 'Yes.' 'You have no objection to Mr Smith having reasonable access to them?' 'No.' 'The court orders custody, care and control to Mrs Smith and reasonable access to Mr Smith.' This approach had the major disadvantage of putting labels on the forthcoming relationship between parents and children. Whilst, legally speaking, each parent would still be entitled to be involved in major decisions about the child's upbringing,[4] this was not generally realised and the language of 'custody' and 'access' made the situation appear to be otherwise. The very fact that a court order was made appeared to reduce the parental responsibility of the non-custodial parent to one of having a right of access only, and to diminish his or her future role in the child's life. Consequently the non-custodial parent may have been both physically and emotionally distanced from his child, sometimes with damaging consequences for the child if this led to a loss of contact. Furthermore some parents experienced the role of courts as being unnecessarily, and sometimes offensively, intrusive in cases in which they could agree over arrangements for their children; such parents were sometimes forced to accede to court orders which they did not necessarily want.

The Children Act 1989 turns its face away from this approach. It recognises that a court order may be neither necessary nor helpful where

---

3   See further J Priest and J Whybrow *Custody Law in Practice in the Divorce and Domestic Courts* supplement to Law Com WP No 96.
4   *Dipper v Dipper* [1980] 2 All ER 722.

there is agreement between the parties about the upbringing of a child. In many cases parents are able to make arrangements about their children without assistance from either conciliators or lawyers. Indeed, intervention from an outsider may sometimes cause annoyance and distress to the divorcing parents. Conciliators or lawyers may be useful in those cases where the parents cannot agree; and where acceptable arrangements prove difficult to negotiate it may be advisable for the lawyers to incorporate the arrangements in a written agreement, so that they are on record, and no one has any doubt about their exact nature. But again no court order may be necessary. Indeed an order could in some circumstances be counter-productive, because it might create, or exacerbate, hostility between the adults.

The concern of the law is to identify those cases where the proposed order will be better for the child than making no order. Just as there are likely to be many cases where an order is unhelpful or unnecessary, so too it is probable that there will be many cases when an order will prove beneficial. For example, a parent may be determined to fight a case, or just be utterly unreasonable in the arrangements he or she proposes. Even where the parties can be persuaded to agree, it may be sensible for their understanding of the agreed arrangements to be embodied in a court order, for the avoidance of doubt, and so that it puts an imprint of authority on the agreement. Sometimes a court order might be needed to satisfy a bureaucratic requirement for 'evidence' that a certain state of affairs exists. An example might be a case where a court order would assist a parent to obtain local authority housing, or to be granted other types of public, or charitable, assistance which will benefit the child. Here the order will be better for the child not because it resolves an argument, but because it increases the child's chances of being properly housed, or otherwise well looked after.

The principle in section 1(5) applies to all orders made under the Children Act 1989, be they orders made between private individuals or orders made when a local authority is involved. This means that in all cases the applicant has the burden of proving why making the order sought will improve matters for the child. The 'no order' approach means that persons seeking an order must normally explain to the court why an order is needed, and what they will do with the order if it is granted. In the case of applications for orders made by a local authority this may have the desirable effect of promoting considered forward planning for children, and introducing a measure of accountability in an area of decision-making which normally is not subject to judicial scrutiny. It will be seen below that courts may not make certain orders once a child has been placed in the care of a local authority. Hence there may be all the more reason for a court to be satisfied, at the outset, that an order which vests major decision-making powers in a local authority will be better for the child than making no order at all.

Section 8 orders

The four orders which can be made under section 8 are designed to deal with practical issues concerning a child's upbringing in a flexible fashion. The Act explains what each order means in the following manner:

'**A residence order**' means an order settling the arrangements to be made as to the person with whom a child is to live.

'**A contact order**' means an order requiring the person with whom a child lives, or is to live, to allow the child to visit or stay with the person named in the order, or for that person and the child otherwise to have contact with each other.

'**A prohibited steps order**' means an order that no step which could be taken by a parent in meeting his parental responsibility for a child, and which is of a kind specified in the order, shall be taken by any person without the consent of the court.

'**A specific issue order**' means an order giving directions for the purpose of determining a specific question which has arisen, or which may arise, in connection with any aspect of parental responsibility for a child.

On its face, a specific issue order could be made in most of the situations which are covered by the meanings given to the other three section 8 orders. Identifying the person with whom the child is to live, or the persons with whom he is to have contact, are each specific questions which may arise in connection with the exercise of parental responsibility. However, section 9(5) provides that—

'No court shall exercise its powers to make a specific issue or prohibited steps order—
(a) with a view to achieving a result which could be achieved by making a residence or contact order.'

It is clear, therefore, that the orders are not interchangeable.[5] Consequently it is important to know exactly what each order covers, and the legal consequences of each order.

---

5   The reason for this is explained below; essentially it is to prevent local authorities from by-passing the care framework when intervening in a child's family life. See too *Re B (Minors) (Residence Order)* [1992] 3 All ER 867.

A residence order

A residence order is easily explained. As the Act states, a residence order means—

'an order settling the arrangements to be made as to the person with whom a child is to live.'

An increasing number of children born both in and outside marriage are experiencing the breakdown of their parents' relationship. Discord over where the children are to have their main home may be one of the more distressing and difficult issues to be resolved through court proceedings. Other persons such as relatives or foster parents may also be caught up in this type of strife. In some cases it may be appropriate for more than one person to have a residence order, for example where two relatives such as grandparents are looking after their grandchild.

Normally when more than one person has a residence order the persons concerned will live together in the same household, but this is not essential. Section 11(4) provides that—

'Where a residence order is made in favour of two or more persons who do not themselves all live together, the order may specify the periods during which the child is to live in the different households concerned.'

This provision may have particular significance for parents who each wish to provide a home for the child. It is easy to understand why it may occasionally be important to a child, and to the parent who spends less time with the child than the other parent, that their time spent together is dignified by the word 'residence' rather than 'contact'. Residence is a concept which brings with it connotations of shared care, similarity of status and the equal exercise of parental responsibility. The emotional impact of a court order on the parties to the proceedings is one of the many considerations a court may have in mind when assessing whether the order proposed will advance a child's best interests. The Court of Appeal has confirmed that there is no reason in principle why a parent who has his child to stay for regular periods of time, on an agreed or defined basis, should not have the arrangement incorporated in a residence order rather than a contact order. However the court also said that an order in which residence was shared between the parents would be unusual, and there would have to be positive benefit to the child in making such an order.[6]

6   *A v A (Minors) (Shared Residence Order)* [1994] 1 FLR 669. See also *Re H (A Minor) (Shared Residence)* [1994] 1 FLR 717 where Cazalet J expressed his views in much the same terms, but where Purchas LJ thought a shared residence order should only be made in 'exceptional circumstances'. See further, ch 4.

A residence order has specific legal consequences in addition to settling the person(s) with whom the child is to live. These are broadly (i) that it confers parental responsibility on persons who would not otherwise have it; (ii) it diminishes the existing parental responsibility of the non-residential parent; and (iii) it discharges a care order.

A residence order confers parental responsibility

It has been explained already that an unmarried father is a parent without parental responsibility, but that he can acquire parental responsibility for his child either by making a formal agreement to this effect with the mother, or by obtaining a parental responsibility order.[7] Where a court makes a residence order in favour of an unmarried father it must also make an order giving him parental responsibility under section 4.[8] This has the advantage for the father that not only does he have parental respons-ibility for his child while ever the residence order is in force, he also retains his parental responsibility where the residence order is subsequently brought to an end. The law in this way recognises that once a court has decided that an unmarried father is suitable to act as a residential parent, it is only logical that he should henceforth be treated in the same way as a father who was married to the child's mother. It also means that he is in the position to appoint a guardian for his child in the event of his death.[9]

When a person who is not the child's parent or guardian obtains a residence order, section 12(2) provides that he or she shall have parental responsibility for the child, but only while the residence order remains in force. The reason why a residence order confers parental responsibility on such a person is because the person who provides the child with a home will normally make most, or all, of the day-to-day decisions about the child's upbringing, and he or she is therefore likely to need parental responsibility. The value of this provision is illustrated by *B v B (A Minor) (Residence Order)*.[10] Here a grandmother had applied for a residence order in the family proceedings court. The magistrates, applying the 'no order unless better for the child' principle in section 1(5),[11] had refused to make the order on the grounds that it was not necessary since the child was already living with the grandmother, and the matter was not in dispute. On appeal it was held that the court had been wrong to refuse to make a residence order. The grandmother had found that her lack of parental responsibility was giving rise to practical difficulties, in particular the local education

7   S.4, and see ch 1.
8   S.12(1).
9   See ch 1.
10 [1992] 2 FLR 327.
11 See above.

authority were unwilling to accept her consent to the child going on school trips, and were demanding the written consent of the mother. It was also pointed out that she might need the power to consent to the child receiving both routine and emergency medical treatment. The grandmother needed parental responsibility for the child while she had charge of the child's upbringing, and this could only be conferred by means of a residence order.

The status of having had parental responsibility for a child is relevant if the child subsequently goes into local authority care. Although section 12(2) provides that a non-parent has parental responsibility only while the residence order remains in force, and although the making of a care order discharges any order made under section 8,[12] the preceding parental responsibility of a non-parent continues to be recognised. Section 34 provides that a local authority shall allow the child reasonable contact with 'a person in whose favour a residence order was in force immediately before the care order was made'. It also entitles such a person to apply for a contact order when there is a dispute with the local authority about what arrangements are reasonable.[13] More generally, when a child is being looked after by a local authority they must involve any person with parental responsibility in decision-making about the child.[14]

A residence order diminishes the parental responsibility of the non-residential parent

Part of the rhetoric surrounding the period preceding the implementation of the Children Act 1989 was that residence orders would 'lower the stakes', and avoid the impression that the 'loser takes all' when parents part.[15] It is certainly the case that each parent still retains parental responsibility whether or not a residence order is made in his or her favour. However a residence order, like any other order, is covered by the incompatibility principle in section 2(8). This provides that—

> 'The fact that a person has parental responsibility for a child shall not entitle him to act in any way which would be incompatible with any order made with respect to the child under this Act.'

The incompatibility principle inevitably affects the exercise of parental responsibility of the non-residential parent because the person with whom the child lives will make the day-to-day decisions about the child's

12 S.91(2).
13 S.34(3)(a).
14 S.22(4)(c).
15 See R White, P Carr and N Lowe *A Guide to the Children Act 1989* (Butterworths, 1990) para 3.3.

upbringing. Nonetheless it is clear that the non-residential parent has the right to act independently in meeting his or her parental responsibility[16] and, when there is disagreement between parents on any major aspect of the child's upbringing, neither has the absolute right to decide. However it is suggested that it is somewhat misleading to state that a residence order does not award a 'bundle of proprietorial rights in the child' to the residential parent.[17] A residence order undoubtedly does give additional rights to the residential parent, and does diminish the parental responsibility of the non-residential natural parent in various ways.

It is normally the case that a person who takes, or sends, a child out of the United Kingdom without the consent of a parent with parental responsibility commits an offence.[18] However, such a person does not commit an offence where he has a residence order, and where he takes or sends the child from the United Kingdom for less than one month.[19] The aim of the one-month provision is to allow holidays abroad to be taken without prior consent or the court's approval. But a law which permits the removal of some children from the United Kingdom by a residential parent, or other person with a residence order, runs the risk that occasionally a child will not be returned. Because no consent is needed, the non-residential parent does not need to be notified about the residential parent's intentions, and he or she may therefore be in no position to take action to prevent the removal by applying for a prohibited steps order.

A residence order affects the appointment of a guardian. Each parent with parental responsibility is entitled to appoint a person to act as guardian of the child in the event of his or her death. However, such an appointment does not take effect when there is a surviving parent with parental responsibility *unless* the deceased parent had a residence order.[20] It is only in the latter situation that the guardian shares parental responsibility with the surviving parent. This could expose the non-residential parent to forms of interference in the child's upbringing which he would not experience where no residence order had been made, and to that extent it may diminish his or her parental responsibility. A parent may also take the view that his responsibility has been diminished when he discovers that the normal rule that the consent of each parent with parental responsibility to the marriage of their child aged under 18 is abrogated when a residence order is in force. It is only the consent of the person who has a residence order which is needed.[1] A residence order also

---

16 S.2(7).
17 Hoggett *Parents and Children* (Sweet and Maxwell, 4th edn) p 67.
18 Child Abduction Act 1984, s.1.
19 Ibid, s.1(4); Children Act 1989, s.13(2).
20 Children Act 1989, s.5(7)(8).
1   Marriage Act 1949, s.3.

affects who may confer entitlement to apply for a residence or contact order on a third party.[2]

The parental responsibility of the non-residential parent can be seriously affected in a case where a person with a residence order wishes to make use of accommodation provided for children in need by a local authority. The law makes it clear that a local authority may not provide accommodation for a child if any person with parental responsibility is willing and able to provide, or to arrange for accommodation to be provided, for the child.[3] Furthermore, any person with parental responsibility may remove the child at any time from local authority accommodation.[4] The thinking behind these provisions is that the state should not be able to keep a child away from a parent with parental responsibility who is offering to care for the child unless there are grounds for a care order. However, this rule does not apply when a residence order is in force.[5] Thus, for example, if parents divorce and no residence order is made, the parent who does not have the day-to-day care of the child can prevent the child going into local authority accommodation, and can remove the child who is being accommodated at any time. But where there is a residence order and the residential parent wants the child to be accommodated, the local authority have a discretion as to whether to accommodate the child against the wishes of the non-residential parent. The extent to which these accommodation provisions diminish parental responsibility is therefore dependent on the approach adopted by the local authority. When the authority is insistent on accommodating the child, the remedy for the aggrieved parent is to apply for a residence order.[6]

A residence order and the child's surname

It has long been customary for a woman to take her husband's surname on marriage. In recent years this custom has been observed to a lesser extent, but in those cases where a married woman retains her maiden, or professional, name it is still normally customary for the child to be registered in his father's surname. One anxiety of an ex-husband may be that his ex-wife will change his child's surname, thus severing all public acknowledgment of the father's parental link. He is particularly likely to find this objectionable where the child's surname is changed to that of his step-father. Section 13(1) protects the sensibilities of such fathers by providing that—

2 This is explained below.
3 Children Act 1989, s.20(7).
4 S.20(8).
5 S.20(9).
6 See ch 3 for a fuller examination of the accommodation provisions in s.20.

'Where a residence order is in force with respect to a child, no person may—
(a) cause the child to be known by a new surname;
...without either the written consent of every person who has parental responsibility or the court's leave.'

This provision also protects the rights of both parents when a residence order is made in favour of a third party. However, it can be seen that the prohibition only applies where there is a residence order in force, and residence orders are not commonplace when parents part. Where they disagree over a child's upbringing, it is usually about matters relating to contact, and where a court order is obtained, it is usually a contact order only. Thus where an ex-husband discovers that the mother has changed the child's surname, where there is no residence order, and where he wishes to obtain an order requiring the child to be known by his surname, he will need to apply for a specific issue order. In *W v A (Child Surname)*[7] the Court of Appeal took the view that the change of a child's surname was an important matter, not to be undertaken lightly. This approach was followed in *Re F (Children: Surname)*,[8] and change of surname was refused because the mother had failed to establish that the child was going to be embarrassed, or that there was anything particularly unusual in her being registered at school in a name different from the current surname of her mother.

A residence order discharges a care order

When a child is the subject of a care order only a very limited class of persons are entitled to apply for the order to be discharged.[9] Fathers without parental responsibility, relatives and other interested persons fall outside this class. However, section 91(1) provides that a residence order discharges a care order. It will be seen below that a fairly wide group of persons are entitled to apply for a residence order, and that any other person may seek the court's leave to apply for a residence order.[10] Thus it may be possible for a relative, or other interested person, to take steps to bring a care order to an end by obtaining a residence order. This is a vitally important provision where a relative wishes to look after a child, but where a local authority refuse to place the child in the care of that relative.[11]

7   [1981] 1 All ER 100.
8   [1994] 1 FCR 110.
9   S.39(1).
10 An exception to this rule is made in relation to local authority foster parents to whom special provisions apply: see below.
11 The importance of the provision is further discussed below.

A contact order

A contact order means —

> 'an order requiring the person with whom a child lives, or is to live, to allow the child to visit or stay with the person named in the order, or for that person and the child otherwise to have contact with each other.'

Contact can be maintained with a child in a variety of ways. Normally it will involve visits by the child and staying contact, but in some situations it may not be possible, or it may not be appropriate, for physical contact to take place. In these circumstances a court may order indirect contact by means of letters, cards, presents for birthdays and Christmas, and telephone calls.[12] Occasionally it may be thought that contact should be informally supervised. Many court welfare services provide contact centres which are aimed at facilitating contact. These centres provide a particularly useful service where contact poses some risk to the child, or where there is so much distrust and animosity between the parents that contact will only be possible if it takes place in a neutral setting.

Directions and conditions in a contact order

Section 11(7) permits a court to supplement any section 8 order by giving directions about how it is to be carried into effect, and by imposing conditions on specified persons. The order can be made to have effect for a specified period, and contain provisions which are to have effect for a specified period. In addition the court is given the power to 'make such incidental, supplemental or consequential provision as the court thinks fit.' However this power does not entitle a court to give directions and impose conditions which fall outside the scope of the order. Whilst the desirability of giving directions and imposing conditions may arise in relation to any of the section 8 orders, it is particularly likely to occur in cases where there is conflict about contact arrangements. When parties cannot agree, the burden will fall on the court to determine how and when contact is to take place.

The onus to facilitate contact is placed on the person with whom the child is living. It requires that person to allow the child to have contact with the person in whose favour the contact order has been made. In *Re M*

---

12 See, for example, *Re J (A Minor) (Contact)* [1994] 1 FLR 729, where the court allowed the father to send letters and presents. Itemisation of telephone calls should make orders of this type easier to make because the recipient of calls from a child could agree to pay for their cost.

(A Minor) (Contact: Conditions)[13] magistrates directed the mother to write a letter every three months to the child's father, who was in prison, telling him about the progress of his child. Wall J held that they had acted beyond their jurisdiction. He said that the effect of their order would have been to require the parents to have contact with each other, and that the court had no power to make such an order.[14] He held that an obligation could be imposed on the mother to keep the father informed of the child's whereabouts, but this obligation should be distinguished from requiring her to communicate with him generally about the child's welfare. *Re M (A Minor)* also raised a more difficult question, namely whether courts have the power to compel a parent to undertake an act which facilitates contact. The magistrates had ordered the mother to read letters from the father to their three-year-old child. Wall J said that he was 'profoundly unhappy' about orders which require a parent to be pro-active in facilitating contact. He said that although the court may have had jurisdiction to give such a direction, that nonetheless it should not have made such a direction unless the other parent consented, and was willing to undertake the task. He ruled that the direction was wrong in principle, and unwise on the facts, and therefore that it could not stand.

Re M (A Minor) (Contact: Conditions) highlights the inevitable fact that, when a young child is involved, it will often be impossible for a contact order to take effect without the co-operation of the caring parent. But when parents are badly estranged such co-operation may not be forthcoming. During the course of his judgment Wall J commented that the magistrates had rejected any suggestion that the child should be taken to see his father in prison. But what would the position have been if the court had taken the view that such an arrangement would have been in the interests of the child? This case leaves open the question whether, and in what circumstances, a parent or other person can be ordered to take active steps to facilitate contact. The wording in section 8, which explains what a contact order means, requires the person with whom the child lives 'to allow the child to visit or stay with the person named in the order, or for that person and the child otherwise to have contact with each other.' In *Re M (A Minor)* the court held that there is power under section 11(7) to direct the residential parent to keep the other parent informed of the child's whereabouts as a necessary condition of contact taking place. It would seem that the court's powers are probably broad enough to require the person with whom the child is living to send a copy of the child's school report to the non-residential parent, and to notify him or her of any special activities in which the child is taking part, such as a sporting event, play or concert. But this is a long way away from requiring the residential parent to take

---

13 [1994] 1 FLR 272.
14 Similarly a court cannot order that parents do not have contact with one another: *Croydon London Borough Council v A (No 1)* [1992] 2 FLR 341.

the child to visit the non-residential parent. Perhaps the solution lies in making such an order a condition of the residence order. However, the problem of enforcing the order if the residential parent refuses to co-operate remains. Threatening to remove the child is usually an empty threat since to do so would normally be against the child's best interests.

Ordering no contact

When a court wishes to order that no contact should take place it is a moot point whether it should order no contact, or whether it should make a prohibited steps order. This is a real issue because section 9(5)(a) provides that a prohibited steps order cannot be made with a view to achieving a result which could be achieved by making a residence or contact order. In *Re H (A Minor)*[15] the question of which order should be made was not raised, but Scott Baker J took the view that the appropriate order to prevent contact between parent and child was a prohibited steps order. In the particular case with which he was dealing he stated that the order should be drafted in the nature of an injunction, with a penal notice attached, stating that the natural parents should not assume physical possession of, or contact with, their child in any way without the court's further order. However, in the later case of *Nottinghamshire County Council v P*[16] it was held that the sensible and appropriate construction of the term 'contact order' includes a situation where a court is required to consider whether any contact at all should be allowed. It was further held that an order for no contact falls within the general concept of contact, and that, applying section 9(5)(a), a prohibited steps order cannot be made where it would be a disguised form of contact order. In *Re J (A Minor) (Contact)*[17] the judge ruled that there should be no order on the father's application for contact, and the Court of Appeal made no comment on the choice of means to deny contact.

Which approach is preferable? Contact orders are drafted in a positive manner in section 8 and, prima facie, to order that a child should not have contact with his parent appears to be a clumsy way of expressing this positive drafting in negative terms. Applying the no order principle under section 1(5) and making no order for contact seems to be the better solution.[18] But a prohibited steps order may be more appropriate where it

---

15 [1993] Fam Law 205; see too *Croydon London Borough Council v A (No 1)* above, where contact was prevented by a prohibited steps order.

16 [1993] 2 FLR 134.

17 [1994] 1 FLR 729; the Court of Appeal held that such a ruling gave the father an automatic right of appeal, RSC Ord 59, r.1B(1)(f)(ii),(iii).

18 See *Re J (A Minor) (Contact)*, above; and *Re W (A Minor) (Contact)* [1994] 1 FLR 843 where such an approach by magistrates was accepted without comment by the Court of Appeal. (The case was remitted for other reasons).

is thought desirable to add a penal notice, as in *Re H (A Minor)*. It seems doubtful whether a penal notice could be issued when a court refuses to make an order, though it might be possible to attach this to the statement of reasons which must be given whenever a court makes, or refuses to make, an order.[19] However, the position is complicated by the existence of the special rule in section 9(2) which prevents a local authority from applying for a contact order and prevents such an order being made in their favour. The reason for this rule is to prevent a local authority from using a private law order to supervise a child (for contact could be used in a supervisory way). When a local authority believe that a child is in need of supervision they must apply for a supervision order under Part IV. On the other hand, a local authority may apply for a prohibited steps order provided that they first obtain the court's leave. In *Nottinghamshire County Council v P*[20] the Court of Appeal took the view that the local authority were attempting to by-pass the rule in section 9(2) by applying for a prohibited steps order to prevent a father from having contact with his daughters. The court ruled that to make an order which prohibited contact was in essence to make a contact order. The importance of determining whether a prohibited steps order, or a contact order, should more appropriately be used to deny contact is probably limited to those situations in which a local authority are involved. In that regard the issue has been resolved by the ruling in *Nottinghamshire County Council v P*.

A prohibited steps order

A prohibited steps order means—

> 'an order that no step which could be taken by a parent in meeting his parental responsibility for a child, and which is of the kind specified in the order, shall be taken by any person without the consent of the court.'

It can be seen that this is an order which can impose limits on the exercise of parental responsibility by a parent, but that it can also be used to control the behaviour of 'any person' towards a child, which therefore includes a person who does not have parental responsibility. The purpose of a prohibited steps order is to enable a court to play a continuing parental role in relation to the child by empowering it to identify those matters of parental responsibility which must be referred back to the court.[1]

---

19 Family Proceedings Rules 1991, r.4.21(4).
20 [1993] 2 FLR 134.
1 See the Law Commission review of child law, guardianship and custody, Law Com No 172, para 4.20.

The scope of the order

It is important to realise that a prohibited steps order cannot be used to forbid any action which the applicant or court wish to prevent, for the order is confined to controlling those steps which could be taken by a parent in meeting his parental responsibility for a child.[2] In *Croydon London Borough Council v A (No 1)*[3] it was held that while the trial court had been correct to make an order prohibiting a father from having any contact with his children, and prohibiting the mother from allowing him to have contact with the children, it had been plainly wrong to make an order that the parents could not have contact with each other, as contact between parents has nothing to do with the exercise of parental responsibility. It is for this reason, too, that a prohibited steps order cannot be used as a means to oust a parent from the home.[4] However, it may be that the order can be used to require a parent to prevent a person who has no legal entitlement to go on the premises from entering her home. In *W v Hertfordshire County Council*[5] justices made an order prohibiting a mother from allowing her partner, who had allegedly caused her child's injury, into her house. This was referred to without comment when the case was appealed on other grounds. It is suggested that an order of this type could be valuable because it places a burden of responsibility on the parent, but that such an order should also be made against the partner so that it is clearly he who is in breach of the court's order, as well as the mother.

Removal of children from the United Kingdom without the appropriate consents is a criminal offence,[6] but parents and others may either not be aware of this, or they may be prepared to break the criminal law. In addition, section 13 provides that a person with a residence order can take or send the child out of the United Kingdom for less than one month without either the consent of all those with parental responsibility or the court's leave. But in some cases any removal could expose the child to the risk of being taken permanently abroad and a prohibited steps order might be necessary to obviate this risk. Certainly it is advisable that such an order is sought when there is a perceived risk of the child being taken overseas without consent, for once a child has been taken from the country it may be extremely difficult to secure his return. In these circumstances, a person without parental responsibility, such as an unmarried father or other close relative, might also wish to apply for such an order, for such persons have no right to prevent a child being taken abroad. Where they enjoy a close

2   For example, it could not be used to prohibit publicity about a child; an injunction under the court's inherent jurisdiction would be the proper remedy.
3   [1992] 2 FLR 341.
4   *Nottinghamshire County Council v P* [1993] 2 FLR 134.
5   [1993] 1 FLR 118.
6   See the Child Abduction Act 1984, s.1.

relationship with the child, a court might be persuaded to prohibit the child's removal unless those with parental responsibility first gained the permission of the court.

The relationship between prohibited steps orders and public law orders

The full scope of prohibited steps orders has yet to be explored by the courts, in particular their relationship with the public law orders under Parts IV and V. Local authorities are encouraged to work in partnership with parents, and to take the least intrusive steps into the family life of a child which are consistent with protecting him from harm.[7] It is not clear whether prohibited steps orders may ever be used as a substitute for the initiation of care proceedings. This approach was certainly disapproved in *Nottinghamshire County Council v P*,[8] but it is uncertain how far the ruling in that case extends. There may be occasions when a more limited form of intervention than an application brought in care proceedings might be sufficient to protect a child. For example, if the feared risk of significant harm to a child was from too severe forms of punishment, and if a local authority were to apply for an order that a parent did not use any form of corporal punishment on a child, it remains to be seen whether a court would be willing to make such an order.

Controversy over whether a prohibited steps order may be used to restrain a local authority in the manner in which they are exercising their statutory powers and duties in relation to a child arose in *D v D (County Court Jurisdiction: Injunctions)*.[9] The Court of Appeal ruled that the trial judge did not have jurisdiction to issue a direction which had the effect of inhibiting a local authority from carrying out their investigative function in response to a suspicion of child abuse[10] in proceedings brought by parents for residence orders. This investigation had been set in motion when the father made an allegation of child abuse against the mother.[11] However, the court also ruled that if a parent is exercising her parental responsibility in a way which is detrimental to the welfare of the child, she can be restrained by an order under section 8 from doing so; and, importantly, there is obiter dicta in *D v D* to the effect that a court may make a prohibited steps order against a person with parental responsibility where she is permitting her child to be exposed to unnecessary interviews and examinations. The court added that neither the local authority, nor the police

7   See the several volumes of *The Children Act 1989 Guidance and Regulations* issued by the Department of Health (HMSO, 1991).
8   [1993] 2 FLR 134.
9   [1993] 2 FLR 802.
10   Whether a High Court judge has such power was doubted, but left open: ibid, at p 811.
11   The trial judge clearly suspected the father's motives, and described the intervention by the police and social services department as 'ham-fisted'.

(except in the exercise of their emergency powers under section 46[12]), may take any step which is invasive of the life of the child, once such a prohibited steps order has been made, without first applying to the court.

The ruling in *D v D (County Court Jurisdiction: Injunctions)* may have significant implications for a local authority where they have reasonable cause to suspect that a child is suffering, or is likely to suffer, significant harm and where they are carrying out an investigation.[13] Where such an investigation requires the co-operation of a parent with parental responsibility, and where the parent has been prohibited by the court from permitting the child to be medically examined, or otherwise investigated, without the leave of the court, the local authority will either be forced to abandon the investigation, or it will require authority from the court to proceed.[14]

A specific issue order

A specific issue order means—

> 'an order giving directions for the purpose of determining a specific question which has arisen, or which may arise, in connection with any aspect of parental responsibility for a child.'

A specific issue order may be of particular value to a parent in a situation when the child has his home elsewhere. Clearly, the parent in charge of the day-to-day care of the child will make most decisions about the child's upbringing, but the other parent still retains an interest in these decisions and, where they are in dispute, the issue can be placed before a court and the court asked to decide. Examples of when a specific issue order might be useful are where parents disagree over where their child is to be educated,[15] or over the religion in which he is to receive instruction. It was stated in *Re C (A Minor) (Leave to Seek Section 8 Orders)*[16] that specific issue orders should be reserved for the resolution of matters of importance. The court therefore refused to give leave to a child to apply for an order determining whether she could go on holiday to Bulgaria with the family with whom she was living, against the wishes of her parents.

A specific issue order may also be of value to a third party who wishes to challenge a decision of a person with parental responsibility. In *Re F (A Minor) (Criminal Proceedings)*[17] a father was accused of assaulting the mother of two children, and had been committed for trial. His solicitor

---

12 This is further discussed in ch 3.
13 Under s.47: see ch 3.
14 The implications of *D v D (County Court Jurisdiction: Injunctions)* [1993] 2 FLR 802 are further discussed in ch 3.
15 See, for example, *Re G (Parental Responsibility: Education)* [1994] 2 FLR 964.
16 [1994] 1 FLR 26. See below.
17 (1994) Times, 12 December.

wished to interview the children, who may have witnessed the alleged assault. The mother, who had sole parental responsibility for the children, refused to consent to the interview taking place. Dismissing the mother's appeal against the granting of a specific issue order permitting the solicitor to interview the children, the Court of Appeal held that 'children ... are citizens owing duties to society as a whole ... which are appropriate to their years and understanding.'[18] Waite LJ said that the interview would be an ordeal the boys would want to be spared if possible, but that consideration had to be weighed against the advantages of securing a fair trial.[19]

Specific issue orders and medical treatment

Decisions relating to medical treatment can pose particular difficulties when persons with parental responsibility disagree. In this situation it should be recalled that each person with parental responsibility may act alone in meeting that responsibility, which means that a medical practitioner is authorised to provide treatment with the consent of one parent alone.[20] However, unless asked to do so in an emergency, it is most unlikely that a medical practitioner would be willing to give medical treatment in a situation where the persons with parental responsibility are in conflict, because the ethics of so doing may not be clear. Consequently, the person who wishes the treatment to take place might feel impelled to ask a court to rule that the treatment is in the best interests of the child, and that the consent of one parent alone is all that is required in the circumstances.

Parents may also seek a form of medical treatment for their child which raises profound moral and ethical dilemmas. In *Re HG (Specific Issue Order: Sterilisation)*[1] a girl aged nearly 18 had severe epilepsy and a form of chromosomal deficiency which meant that she was an infant in terms of abilities. She lived in a school which meant she was likely at some time to be at risk of sexual relationships leading to pregnancy. The contraceptive pill was not suitable because of her epilepsy. It was accepted by all that it would be disastrous for the girl if she were to become pregnant because she would not be capable of understanding what was happening to her. Her parents wished to raise the question whether their daughter could be sterilised by making an application as the child's next friend for a specific

18 See *Re R (A Minor) (Wardship: Criminal Proceedings)* [1991] Fam 56, per Lord Donaldson MR, at p 65.
19 In relation to balancing the welfare of children against other profoundly important principles, see further ch 4.
20 S.2(7); *Re R (A Minor) (Wardship: Medical Treatment)* [1991] 4 All ER 177; *Re W (A Minor) (Medical Treatment: Court's Jurisdiction)* [1993] Fam 64.
1   [1993] 1 FLR 587.

issue order. Their application raised two matters of principle: namely whether sterilisation is a matter which falls within the scope of a specific issue order because, the argument ran, parental responsibility does not extend to authorising a sterilisation operation to take place; and whether a specific issue order can be made when there is no issue between the persons having parental responsibility. The court ruled that the fact that a High Court judge must rule on sterilisation does not take from the parents their responsibility to form their own conclusion and to take the necessary steps to implement that conclusion. Indeed, the court suggested that it may be one of the responsibilities of parenthood to bring the issue of sterilisation before a judge. On the second matter the court ruled that a specific question had arisen, and that is what had given rise to the issue, not that there were protagonists on either side of the debate. The parents could, and should, therefore, bring the issue before the court.

Re HG (Specific Issue Order: Sterilisation) is illustrative of how an application for a specific issue order can be made by a child who does not have the capacity herself to initiate proceedings. Section 10(7) entitles any person who falls within a category of persons prescribed by rules of court to apply for a section 8 order, and rules of court provide that a person under a disability may begin and prosecute proceedings by her next friend, in this case the parents.[2] The parents could, of course, have made their own application for a specific issue order; however they were not entitled to legal aid to make an application themselves, and legal proceedings in the High Court are very expensive. On the other hand they could obtain legal aid to bring proceedings on behalf of their child. The court found this approach to be acceptable.

As with a prohibited steps order, the court's order must relate to an aspect of parental responsibility, and a specific issue order cannot be used to achieve a result which could be obtained by making a residence or contact order.[3] The courts have been on their guard to prevent these orders from being used for ulterior purposes because in theory any issue about a child can be characterised as a specific issue. Thus in *Pearson v Franklin*[4] the court refused to accept the argument that a specific issue order could be used to oust a father from the home because such an order would be in the best interests of the child. Ouster orders are governed by different statutes, and the Court of Appeal ruled that they cannot be made under the guise of a specific issue order.[5]

---

2 Family Proceedings Rules 1991 (SI 1991/1247), r.9.2 (as amended).
3 S.9(5).
4 [1994] 1 FLR 246.
5 See further ch 5.

Specific issue orders, medical treatment and local authorities

Cases in which all persons with parental responsibility are refusing to agree to a child receiving medical treatment may be of the utmost gravity. Any decision of the court to order medical treatment may run counter to the most profound and sincerely held beliefs of the parents. In *Re O (A Minor) (Medical Treatment)*[6] and *Re R (A minor) (Blood Transfusion)*[7] it was held that such cases should be determined, wherever possible, by a High Court judge, and that strenuous efforts should be made to ensure an inter partes hearing. Usually it will be the local authority who will initiate legal proceedings on behalf of the child because they are under a statutory duty to intervene when a child is at risk of significant harm. This raises questions about which proceedings are the most appropriate when a local authority are the applicant; should they apply under the public law provisions in the Act; under the inherent jurisdiction of the High Court; or for a specific issue order?

In *Re O (A Minor) (Medical Treatment)* parents who were Jehovah's Witnesses were refusing to authorise blood transfusions for their gravely ill child. A family proceedings court made an emergency protection order[8] in ex parte proceedings followed by an interim care order, and the case was then transferred for hearing to the High Court. Johnson J was asked to express a view about the most appropriate legal framework in which such decisions should be made. He agreed with counsel, who had been unanimous in rejecting all proceedings governed by the Children Act 1989, and ruled that the inherent jurisdiction of the High Court was the only one appropriate. However, when subsequently *Re R (A Minor) (Blood Transfusion)*, a case with similar facts, came before Booth J, she distinguished *Re O (A Minor)* on the grounds that it was a case in which the local authority were seeking parental responsibility for the child, and held that the case before her could be determined on an application for a specific issue order. She ruled that it is unnecessary, and inappropriate, for the court to exercise its inherent jurisdiction where there is no need for the court to intervene otherwise to safeguard the child.

Which approach is the most appropriate? Orders under section 44 for an emergency protection order, and under section 31 for a care order, confer parental responsibility on the local authority, which means that the local authority become entitled to authorise a blood transfusion. However, in *Re R (A Minor)* and *Re O (A Minor)* the courts have taken the view that such a decision should be made by a High Court judge where it is to be made against the strongly held beliefs of the child's parents. The difficulty

6   [1993] 2 FLR 149.
7   [1993] 2 FLR 757.
8   It was pointed out in the appeal that it was difficult to bring the case within any of the three situations envisaged by s.44(1): see ch 3.

which arises once the child is in the care of a local authority is that a court is prevented by section 9(1) from making any section 8 order other than a residence order.[9] Thus a High Court judge cannot make a specific issue order about a child in care. Consequently, once a child is in care, the only possible way of transferring decision-making powers from a local authority to a High Court judge is for the local authority to make an application for leave to apply under section 100 for the exercise of the court's inherent jurisdiction. Section 100(3), (4) provide that leave to make such an application may be granted only if the court is satisfied that the result which the local authority wish to achieve could not be achieved through the making of any other order for which they are entitled to apply.

It is suggested that the choice of which proceedings are appropriate depends on whether the local authority's only anxiety about the child's well-being relates to medical treatment, or whether they have other concerns about significant harm to the child, and are seeking parental responsibility for the child. In the former situation they are better advised to apply for leave to apply for a specific issue order, and for the leave court to direct that the matter should come before a High Court judge as a matter of urgency. In the latter situation their initial difficulty is that care proceedings must commence in a magistrates court; however that court can, and in a case of this kind clearly should, ensure that the case is transferred to the High Court.[10]

A family assistance order

A family assistance order complements section 8 orders. It may be made with respect to any child where, in family proceedings, the court has power to make an order under Part II of the Act, irrespective of whether or not it makes such an order. The purpose of the order is to provide assistance for the family, for a relatively brief period.

Features of a family assistance order

Section 16(1) provides that a court may make an order requiring—

'(a) a probation officer to be made available; or
(b) a local authority to make an officer of the authority available,
to advise, assist and (where appropriate) befriend any person named in the order.'

9   This provision is to prevent a court from exercising decision-making powers which properly belong to a local authority.
10 The Children Act (Allocation of Proceedings) Order 1991 (SI 1991 No 1677).

The persons who may be named in the order are any parent or guardian; any person with whom the child is living, or in whose favour a contact order is in force; and the child himself. The court may not make an order unless satisfied that the circumstances of the case are exceptional. The meaning of this provision has yet to be clarified; however it recognises that welfare resources are scarce, and that were probation officers and social workers frequently to be called upon to provide assistance under these orders, it would put an intolerable strain on these resources. An order cannot be made without the prior consent of every person named in the order, with the exception of the child. Thus it can be seen that the purpose of the order is to provide voluntary assistance, for a maximum period of six months. It seems most likely to be made where parties have separated or divorced, and where they need help with coping with the changes in their personal relationships. Where both a family assistance order and an order under section 8 are in force in respect of the same child, the supervising officer may refer to the court the question whether the section 8 order should be varied or discharged. Thus where, for example, a defined contact order has been made, and where this order is not working and is causing distress to the child, the supervising officer could refer the matter back to court. Similarly, he could refer back an order where one of the parties was refusing to obey it. It would then be a matter for the court to determine whether the order should be varied or discharged.[11]

Applying for a section 8 order

A section 8 order can be made when someone makes a free-standing application for an order under section 10(2), on an application made in family proceedings under section 10(1)(a), and when the court makes an order of its own motion under section 10(1)(b). It is often the case that an issue about a child arises in the context of other proceedings, yet it is wasteful of time and resources if different proceedings are commenced to resolve inter-related family matters; also a proliferation of court hearings can cause extra anxiety and stress for the parties concerned. The Children Act 1989 recognises this, designates certain proceedings as 'family proceedings', and empowers a court to make a section 8 order 'in any family proceedings in which a question arises with respect to the welfare of any child.'[12] 'Family proceedings' means any proceedings 'under the inherent jurisdiction of the High Court in relation to children'[13] or under any of the enactments listed under section 8(4). These enactments are—

11 Guidance on how court welfare officers should approach family assistance orders is provided in *National Standards for Probation Service Family Court Welfare Work* HMSO (1994).
12 S.10(1)(a).
13 S.8(3).

- Parts I, II and IV of the Children Act 1989;
- the Matrimonial Causes Act 1973;
- the Domestic Violence and Matrimonial Proceedings Act 1976;
- the Adoption Act 1976;
- the Domestic Proceedings and Magistrates' Courts Act 1978;
- sections 1 and 9 of the Matrimonial Homes Act 1983; and
- Part III of the Matrimonial and Family Proceedings Act 1984.

The availability of section 8 orders in family proceedings allows a court to choose how best to respond to an application for a different order. It is not limited to making, or refusing to make, the order which has been requested. For example, a court might decide that there is sufficient evidence to enable it to make a care order under section 31, but that the child's interests would better be served by making a residence order in favour of a concerned relative. Similarly it might be satisfied that an adoption order could properly be made under the Adoption Act 1976, but that a residence order to the applicants to adopt, coupled with a contact order to the natural mother, would be a better alternative for the child.

A court in free-standing or family proceedings has power to make a section 8 order of its 'own motion'. If the court takes the view that a section 8 order would be in the child's best interests then it can make such an order even though no application for an order has been made.[14] It has been held in the context of contact orders with children in care, when a court may also make an order of its own motion, that normally a court should give a party to the proceedings the opportunity to oppose an order before it exercises its own motion powers, but that where an adjournment would be contrary to the child's welfare, the court can make the order despite the fact that no advance warning has been given.[15]

Applying for a section 8 order—entitlement and leave

When there is disagreement over a child's upbringing the person, or persons, with parental responsibility are entitled to decide what should happen. Where those with parental responsibility are resolute about their decision then, unless their decision can be reviewed and, where appropriate, be overturned by a court, those without parental responsibility have no choice but to abide by the will of those with the power to decide. It has been seen that section 8 orders are designed to provide solutions to areas of disagreement which cover all practical aspects of a child's upbringing. On its face it may seem an attractive proposition that the law should be so

---

14   S.10(1)(b).
15   *Re SW (A Minor) (Care Proceedings)* [1993] 2 FLR 609; see further ch 3.

structured that the door to the court is open to everyone who has an interest in the child. However, there are various objections to such an approach.

There is the pragmatic objection that it could lead to a flood of applications, some of which might be wholly without merit, which would use up valuable court time and divert attention and resources from those genuine cases in need of resolution. A more powerful objection is that an open door policy would be against the best interests of children. Section 8 orders are powerful orders, with the potential to have a major impact on the life of a child, and on those with parental responsibility for him. Consequently, even the suggestion that an application for an order will be made could cause distress to a child and undue anxiety to his parents or others with parental responsibility. Opening the door of the court to all might also be disruptive, and prevent arrangements for a child's upbringing from being implemented until the litigation had been completed. But, as section 1(2) of the Act recognises, any delay in determining a question about a child's upbringing is likely to prejudice the welfare of the child.

On the other hand to deny access to the courts to anyone other than a limited and named class of persons also has disadvantages. This approach could prevent excluded persons with a genuine interest in a child's upbringing from pursuing the matter, and challenging the decisions of parents, and others with parental responsibility, in the courts. This approach could operate to the disadvantage of the child and could put his welfare at risk. The law therefore seeks to strike a delicate balance between making courts readily accessible to all with a genuine interest in the child, and exposing the child, and others, to unnecessary and possibly damaging litigation. This balance is achieved by designating certain persons as entitled to apply for section 8 orders, and by allowing all other persons to apply only if the court is first prepared to give them leave. In addition, there are special rules which apply to children, local authorities and local authority foster parents.

Persons entitled to apply for any section 8 order

Section 10(4) provides:

> 'The following persons are entitled to apply to the court for any section 8 order with respect to a child—
> (a) any parent or guardian of the child;
> (b) any person in whose favour a residence order is in force with respect to the child.'

The entitlement of all parents to apply for any section 8 order recognises their prime position. It is also a provision which comes to the assistance of the unmarried father. He is entitled to apply whether or not he has parental responsibility.[16] However, once parents cease to be their child's parents because their child has been adopted, or has been freed for adoption, they cease to fall within section 10(4) and are therefore not entitled to apply for a residence order.[17] The other entitled persons, namely a guardian or a person with a residence order, already have parental responsibility for the child which is why they too are especially favoured. In the case of a guardian, difficulties are most likely to arise when his or her appointment takes place despite the fact that there is a surviving parent, a position which arises when the deceased parent had a residence order.[18] In this situation, parental responsibility is shared between the guardian and the surviving parent, and where they cannot agree about any aspect relating to the child's upbringing a court ruling may be the only way of resolving the matter.

It has already been explained that parental responsibility is acquired incrementally, and that acquisition of parental responsibility by a third party does not diminish the parental responsibility of parents.[19] Rather, parental responsibility is shared, and its exercise inhibited only by the incompatibility principle enshrined in section 2(8). Plainly, there will be occasions when the person with a residence order finds himself in disagreement with parents. When this occurs it may then be essential for either party to have access to a court to resolve the matter by means of a section 8 order. Hence a person with a residence order is also entitled to apply for any section 8 order.

Persons entitled to apply for a residence or contact order

Section 10(5) identifies a privileged group of persons who are entitled to apply for a residence or contact order. It provides:

'The following persons are entitled to apply for a residence or contact order with respect to a child—
(a) any party to a marriage (whether or not subsisting) in relation to whom a child is a child of the family;
(b) any person with whom the child has lived for a period of at least three years;
(c) any person who—
  (i) in any case where a residence order is in force with respect to the child, has the consent of each of the persons in whose favour the order is made;

---

16 *M v C and Calderdale Metropolitan Borough Council* [1993] 1 FLR 505.
17 Ibid; *Re C (A Minor) (Adopted Child: Contact)* [1993] 2 FLR 431.
18 See ch 1.
19 See ch 1.

(ii) in any case where the child is in the care of a local authority, has the consent of that authority; or

(iii) in any other case, has the consent of each of those (if any) who have parental responsibility for the child.'

Why are these persons accorded special treatment? What is their uniting characteristic? According to the Law Commission they were selected because to require such persons to seek the court's leave to apply would amount to a meaningless formality because it would almost invariably be granted.[20] However, the applicant who falls within section 10(5) is only entitled to apply for those orders which are concerned with where the child lives and whom he sees. This is presumably because such matters are determined by the quality of the applicant's personal relationship with the child, and the perceived value of that relationship to the child. However, in this regard it is curious that such persons are not also entitled to apply for a specific issue or prohibited steps order, for it would seem that the same reasoning applies to these orders too.

Any party to a marriage in relation to whom a child is a child of the family

A step-parent who is, or has been, married to a parent is entitled to apply for a residence or contact order provided that he or she has treated the child as a child of their family.[1] Sometimes a husband may falsely believe that he is the father of his wife's child and not discover the true facts until after the marriage has broken down. In a case of this kind the child will nonetheless be a child of the family because he will have been treated as such, albeit on a mistaken basis.[2]

In the past, if a custodial parent remarried and she and her second husband applied to adopt her child a court would sometimes make a joint custody order as an alternative to adoption. Indeed, legislation specifically required an adoption court to consider that option.[3] Under the present law the only way in which a step-parent can obtain parental responsibility for a step-child (other than through adoption, or appointment as the child's guardian), is by applying for a residence order. Section 10(5)(a) entitles the step-parent to make such an application. It has yet to be determined whether a court will make a residence order to a step-parent, not in truth to settle the arrangements to be made as to the person with whom the

20 Law Com No 172, para 4.45.
1 A child of the family is defined in s.105(1).
2 *W (RJ) v W (SJ)* [1971] 3 All ER 303. Cf *Re H (A Minor) (Contact)* [1994] 2 FLR 776, where a husband who knew he was not the father of the child was given a contact order with the child.
3 Adoption Act 1976, s.14(3).

child is to live, for this will not be in dispute, but in order to confer parental responsibility on the step-parent. It could be argued that as the child is living with the step-parent he or she needs parental responsibility in order properly to care for the child. In a case of this kind it would be important that the natural parent made a joint application with the step-parent for a residence order, otherwise, if the step-parent's application was successful, he or she would have more rights in relation to the child than the natural parent, because that parent's parental responsibility could otherwise be diminished.

Any person with whom the child has lived for a period of at least three years

Any person with whom the child has lived for a period of at least three years is entitled to apply for a residence or contact order.[4] Section 10(10) provides that the period of three years need not be continuous but must not have begun more than five years before, or ended more than three months before, the making of the application. This three-year provision recognises that it is in the interests of children that persons who have provided a child with a home over a considerable period of time are able to apply for an order, either to secure that position, or to ensure that contact with the child is maintained. Furthermore, no one is able to pre-empt an application simply by removing the child, as there is the three-month period of grace within which proceedings can be commenced. Three years is an arbitrary period which may bear no relationship either to a child's sense of time, or to the strength of his personal attachments. These will vary considerably according to the child's particular circumstances, and will be influenced by the child's age, personality and stage of development. However, the chosen period seeks to strike a balance between recognising the importance of a child's attachments to persons other than parents, and not exposing parents to the threat of legal proceedings, and the fear of losing their children to substitute carers, without the preliminary safeguard of an application for leave.[5]

Any person who has the necessary consents

The third category of persons entitled to apply for a residence or contact order are those who have obtained the necessary consents. By providing that it is only the consent of each of the persons in whose favour the

4   S.10(5)(b).
5   The conferment of the right to apply for an order which will secure the child's position after the lapse of three years is not new; it was first introduced by the Children Act 1975.

residence order was made which must be given in order to confer entitlement on an applicant, section 10(5)(c)(i) is another example of how a residence order gives increased authority to a parent or third person who has the benefit of such an order.[6] Others who share parental responsibility for the child have no power to give or withhold consent. This can be illustrated by the following example: after divorce a mother obtains a residence order; later she falls ill and is unable to look after her child. A friend of the mother offers to care for the child, but the child's father disagrees because he wishes to care for the child himself. Provided that the friend has the mother's consent, she is entitled to apply to a court for a residence order. By contrast, if the facts were the same, but no residence order had been made, the consent of *both* parents would be required under section 10(5)(c)(iii) to confer entitlement to apply; without these consents the friend would first need to obtain the leave of the court to make an application.

In a case where the child is in the care of a local authority it is the consent of the authority which confers entitlement to apply. Section 9(1) prohibits a court from making any section 8 order other than a residence order with respect to a child in care, so in fact an application for a residence order is the only one which can be made in relation to a child in care. The reason for this exception is because a residence order goes to the source of the local authority's power and not to the manner in which it is exercised; the effect of a residence order is to discharge the care order.[7] Contact with a child in care is governed by section 34 (which has its own provisions about entitlement and leave to apply). In a case where the child is merely being accommodated by a local authority it is, of course, the consent of those with parental responsibility which is needed under sub-paragraphs (i) and (iii).[8]

In any other case, that is to say when there is no residence order in force and the child is not in local authority care, a person is entitled to apply who has the consent of each of those (if any) who have parental responsibility for the child. Where there is no one with parental responsibility there is no one with the capacity to give consent, which means that anyone is entitled to apply for a residence or contact order. When parents are unmarried, normally the mother alone has parental responsibility, so it is her consent which is needed. If she has died, no one has parental responsibility for the child despite the fact that the unmarried father survives. The effect of this, in practice, can be illustrated by the following example: an unmarried mother dies and her parents wish to apply for a residence order in respect of their granddaughter. If the child's father has

6 See above.
7 S.91(1).
8 In relation to how this might affect the entitlement to apply of a local authority foster parent, see below.

parental responsibility they will need his consent to entitle them to apply for the order. Without that consent they must obtain the leave of the court to make their application. But if the father does not have parental responsibility, then the grandparents are entitled to apply for a residence or contact order.

Leave to apply for a section 8 order

It has been seen already that the class of persons who are entitled to apply for section 8 orders is limited; however the door of the court is not necessarily closed to non-entitled persons. Such persons may seek the leave of the court to apply for an order either in family proceedings or on a free-standing application.[9] An alternative route to a hearing for a non-entitled person is to apply to be joined as a party to existing family proceedings. As a party, a non-entitled person has the opportunity to adduce evidence and to make submissions with a view to persuading a court to exercise its own motion powers to make a section 8 order in his or her favour. Rules of court[10] which permit an application to be made to be joined as a party provide no guidelines as to the test to be applied in determining the application. However in *G v Kirklees Metropolitan Borough Council*[11] Booth J stated that the criteria which apply to an application for leave are equally applicable to an application to be joined as a party.

The criteria for an application for leave

Section 10(9) provides—

> 'Where the person applying for leave to make an application for a section 8 order is not the child concerned, the court shall, in deciding whether or not to grant leave, have particular regard to—
> (a) the nature of the proposed application for the section 8 order;
> (b) the applicant's connection with the child;
> (c) any risk there might be of that proposed application disrupting the child's life to such an extent that he would be harmed by it; and
> (d) where the child is being looked after by a local authority—
>   (i) the authority's plans for the child's future; and
>   (ii) the wishes and feelings of the child's parents.'

9   S.10(1)(a)(ii); s.10(2)(b).
10 Family Proceedings Court (Children Act 1989) Rules 1991, r.7; Family Proceedings Rules 1991, r.4.7.
11 [1993] 1 FLR 805; see too *North Yorkshire County Council v G* [1993] 2 FLR 732.

In *Re A (Minors) (Residence Order)*[12] the trial judge held that a court must give paramount consideration to the welfare of the child on an application for leave. The Court of Appeal held that in this regard the judge had been plainly wrong. It ruled that the court must be guided by the specific criteria contained in section 10(9) when deciding whether to grant leave and held that the paramountcy principle does not apply. It held that in granting, or refusing, leave a court is not determining a question with respect to the upbringing of the child concerned, and therefore section 1(1) is not applicable.[13] The court reinforced its argument by pointing out that some of the criteria in section 10(9) would be otiose if the whole matter were subject to the overriding provisions of section 1(1).

Whether leave is granted to a non-entitled person is usually of crucial importance to that person. Often an applicant for leave has already been excluded from the child's life by the persons who have parental responsibility, or plans for the child's future include his or her exclusion from having any say in the child's upbringing. Unless the applicant for leave can get through the door of the court to obtain a hearing there is no other way in which the merits of decisions of this nature can be challenged and subjected to scrutiny.

The nature of the proposed application, and the applicant's connection with the child

Whilst the nature of the proposed application, and the applicant's connection with the child, are distinct criteria they are usually closely inter-related. These criteria appear to indicate that any person who can demonstrate a genuine relationship with, and a legitimate concern about, some matter relating to the child's upbringing will normally be granted leave. However, the fact that the applicant is a relative may not outweigh different considerations in the other paragraphs. Thus in *Re A (A Minor) (Residence Order: Leave to Apply)*[14] a request was made by an aunt for leave to apply for a residence order in the course of care proceedings which were already under way. The trial court took the view that sufficient persons were already involved in the case, and that to join another would not be in the interests of the child because it would lead to delays and be disruptive. This approach was confirmed on appeal.

When a child has been adopted then, as a matter of law, his natural parents are no longer his parents.[15] Consequently if a natural parent wishes

---

12 [1992] 3 All ER 872.
13 The court cited *F v S (Adoption: Ward)* [1973] 1 All ER 722 in support of this ruling.
14 [1993] 1 FLR 425.
15 Adoption Act 1976, s.39(2).

to apply for a section 8 order he or she must first obtain the court's leave.[16] It is easy to understand why it could be manifestly undesirable if an application for, say, contact could be made by a natural parent without the prior screening of leave. This could cause emotional turmoil and feelings of insecurity both for the child and for the adoptive parents. Difficulty then arises as to who should be notified about the leave application, because these feelings could be generated merely by the knowledge that a leave application was being made. In *Re C (A Minor) (Adopted Child: Contact)*[17] the court was of the opinion that the vast majority of leave applications by natural parents would fail. It was concerned to shield the adoptive parents from unnecessary anxiety, and it took the view that an application for leave could safely be refused without the adoptive parents' involvement. It therefore ruled that the Official Solicitor should be brought in as respondent in a case of this kind, his function being to represent the child's interests. In addition the local authority, which had been a party to the adoption proceedings, should be invited to take part where they had a relevant contribution to make. Only if, having heard from the applicant, and from the Official Solicitor and/or the local authority, the court was satisfied that the natural parent had made out a prima facie case for leave should notice be given to the adoptive parents. In this way the court would ensure that no application for leave was granted without the adoptive parents having first been given an opportunity to oppose it. In *Re C (A Minor)* itself, the court refused the natural parent leave to apply for either a specific issue order, which would result in her learning the identity of the adoptive parents, or a contact order. It held that adoption orders are intended to be permanent and final, and that a fundamental question such as contact should not be subsequently reopened unless there is some fundamental change in circumstances.

It should be recalled that section 10(5), which draws persons other than parents and those with parental responsibility into the net of those who are entitled to apply, confers such entitlement only in respect of residence and contact orders, and not in respect of specific issue and prohibited steps orders. Somewhat surprisingly, even those who are able to obtain the consent of persons with parental responsibility are not entitled to apply for a specific issue or prohibited steps order; they must first obtain leave. Whilst in the majority of cases it seems extremely unlikely that most persons falling within section 10(5) would be refused leave, occasionally there may be a good reason for refusing such a person leave. An application for a prohibited steps or specific issue order, if successful, could result in a court making an order which controls the way in which a person behaves towards a child; prevents a parent, or other person, from exercising full

---

16 *Re C (A Minor) (Adopted Child: Contact)* [1993] 2 FLR 431; *M v C and Calderdale Metropolitan Borough Council* [1993] 1 FLR 505.

17 Above.

parental responsibility; or temporarily transfers decision-making powers to the court. In some situations an order of this nature could amount to an unwarranted attempt to interfere in a child's family life, and there may therefore be sound arguments as to why even an attempt to make an application for an order should be curtailed at an early stage.

In *G v Kirklees Metropolitan Borough Council*,[18] Booth J ruled that the court is entitled to consider the overall merits of the applicant's case for a section 8 order before granting leave. The court held that it is not enough simply to establish that the applicant has an arguable case; he or she must establish a case that is reasonably likely to succeed.[19] The nature of the proposed application and the applicant's connection with the child may often be relevant to this assessment. In *G v Kirklees Metropolitan Borough Council* an aunt had acted for a short period as an approved foster parent for her nephew, but then had ceased to have contact with him. Subsequently the local authority had instituted care proceedings, and the aunt was seeking to be joined as a party to these proceedings with a view to obtaining a residence order. The court's findings that the child's mother was strongly opposed to any family placement, coupled with opposition from the local authority to the aunt having further involvement with her nephew, were fatal to her application.

The use of leave as a sifting process to prevent undesirable applications coming before a court applies not only when an individual is the applicant, but also when an application for leave is made by a local authority. Local authorities are limited by section 9 in respect of the applications they may make,[20] however they may apply for leave to apply for specific issue and prohibited steps orders. There is a risk in allowing local authorities to do this, namely that an authority might apply for leave to apply for one of these orders in inappropriate circumstances, and refrain from exercising their statutory powers and duties to apply for appropriate orders under Part IV of the Act. This risk materialised in *Nottinghamshire County Council v P.*[1] In that case the Court of Appeal ruled that the local authority's application for a prohibited steps order, rather than a care order, had been inappropriate and misconceived. The court took the view that it was likely that the application would have been refused if the matter had been referred to the county court. It therefore gave a direction that, in future, a local authority should not apply ex parte before a single justice of the family proceedings court for leave to apply for a section 8 order; instead such proceedings should be transferred to the county court and should be dealt with inter partes.

18 [1993] 1 FLR 805.
19 In support of her ruling, Booth J commented that the Court of Appeal had examined the merits of the substantive application in *Re A (Minors) (Residence Order)* [1992] 3 All ER 872; see too *F v S (Adoption: Ward)* [1973] 1 All ER 722.
20 See below.
1 [1993] 2 FLR 134.

Any risk of harm or disruption

It has been explained already that one reason why the door of the court is not open to all is because this could have the potential to cause disturbance to the child's life. When determining whether to grant leave, the court is required to have particular regard to 'any risk there might be of the proposed application disrupting the child's life to such an extent that he would be harmed by it.' 'Harm' for these purposes means harm as defined by section 31(9).[2] It will sometimes be the case that a court cannot properly determine whether disruption and harm will be caused unless it considers the child's wishes and feelings, and some or all of the other factors specified in the checklist in section 1(3). The question then arises as to what extent a court, at the leave stage, may hear evidence which relates to the merits of the substantive application.

In *Re A (A Minor) (Residence Order: Leave to Apply)*[3] it was recognised that a court may inevitably be drawn into considering matters of substance when considering the disruption issue in the leave criteria. In *Re A (A Minor)* the aunt of a child aged seven was requesting leave to apply for a residence order. On an appeal against a refusal by magistrates to grant the aunt's request, Hollings J held that it had been correct for a court to consider the child's wishes and feelings when determining whether the proposed application would be disruptive and harmful to him. He also held that a court is entitled to consider matters which relate to the substantive application when considering whether the application might prove to be disruptive, and that the amount of cross-examination allowed is essentially a matter for the court. Similarly, in *North Yorkshire County Council v G*[4] the court ruled that the tests the court should apply are the criteria in section 10(9) coupled with those in section 1(3). In *Re A (Minors) (Residence Order)*[5] a foster mother of several children in local authority care was applying for leave to apply for a residence order. The Court of Appeal admitted information from the Official Solicitor relating to the wishes and feelings of the children; it took account of the inevitable delay a successful leave application would cause in making long-term arrangements for the children; and it took account of the disruption and harm which would occur if all the children had to be examined by a psychiatrist and were caught up in proceedings which were bound to be bitter. In the light of these findings the court refused leave.

---

2   *Re A (Minors) (Residence Order)* [1992] 3 All ER 872. S.31(9) provides: '"harm" means ill-treatment or the impairment of health or development.'
3   [1993] 1 FLR 425.
4   [1993] 2 FLR 732.
5   [1992] 3 All ER 872.

The local authority's plans for the child

In a case where a child is being looked after by a local authority a court is required to have particular regard to the authority's plans for the child's future. In *Re A (Minors) (Residence Order)*[6] counsel for the local authority, relying on pre-Children Act authority,[7] submitted that, save in the most exceptional circumstances, a court should not allow an application for leave where a child is in the care of a local authority when this would interfere with the authority's care of the child. The Court of Appeal rejected this submission, pointing out that while that principle is maintained in relation to most matters concerning a child in care, an application for a residence order is expressly excepted under section 9(1). However, the court added that this does not mean that the court should give no weight to the authority's plans. On the contrary, section 10(9)(d)(i) requires a court to have particular regard to the authority's plans. The court went on to explain how a court should approach a case where a local authority have plans for the child's future which are inconsistent with the application for leave. It reasoned as follows: a local authority have a duty under section 22(3) to safeguard and promote the welfare of any child in their care:

> 'Accordingly, the court should approach the application for leave on the basis that the authority's plans for the child's future are designed to safeguard and promote the child's welfare and that any departure from those plans might well "disrupt the child's life to such an extent that he would be harmed by it"'.[8]

This ruling highlights the dilemma faced by courts when a challenge is made to the way in which a local authority are choosing to exercise their statutory powers, namely when is it proper for a court to substitute its own judgment for the judgment of the authority about what decision will best promote the welfare of the child? An analysis of the ruling in *Re A (Minors) (Residence Order)* reveals that it is clear that the decision whether or not to grant leave is one for a court to make, and the fact that a child is in care does not detract from the court's decision-making function. However, the Court of Appeal ruled that a court must take as its starting point the notion that a local authority is under a statutory duty to promote the child's welfare, and a fortiori the authority's plans are therefore designed to advance the welfare of the child. Thus the court created what appears to amount to a presumption in favour of not disrupting the authority's plans for the child, and put the burden of rebutting that presumption squarely on the applicant. It seems that this will be an extremely difficult burden

6   [1992] 3 All ER 872.
7   *A v Liverpool City Council* [1981] 2 All ER 385.
8   [1992] 3 All ER 872 at p 879.

to discharge, since it should be borne in mind that there are often conflicting views about how the child's interests will best be served, and a court may be no better equipped to identify the welfare of the child than a local authority. It should also be borne in mind that the applicant must demonstrate that he or she has more than an arguable case; rather it must be established that it has a reasonable prospect of success.[9]

It is not clear how much evidence a court ought to be prepared to accept on a leave application, which is, of course, a preliminary application only. It is, nonetheless, an application of enormous importance to the parties, and it seems likely that where an applicant is in conflict with a local authority he or she will need to take advantage of the rulings in *Re A (A Minor) (Residence Order: Leave to Apply)*[10] and *North Yorkshire County Council v G*[11] that information relating to the welfare checklist, as well as that relating to section 10(9), can be put before the court. It also seems likely that the applicant will need to seek the indulgence of the court to allow the cross-examination of witnesses.[12]

It is suggested that where there is evidence which might open a local authority to challenge in judicial review, that this could provide a sound base on which to question the judgment of the local authority. In *R v Hereford and Worcester County Council, ex p D*[13] it was held in judicial review proceedings to have been wrong to remove a child without warning from her aunt who was acting as her foster parent. The removal occurred during the course of care proceedings. Initially the understanding with the aunt had been that the child would be placed on a long-term basis with her, but there was a change of care plan, and the child was taken from her without consultation. In that case the court ruled that any decision about the child's future should be made on the fullest information, and that the local authority had been wrong not to listen to the aunt and to give her views due weight. The Children Act 1989 was not in force when *R v Hereford and Worcester County Council, ex p D* was decided, so the only remedy for the aunt was in judicial review. Now she would be able to apply for leave to apply for a residence order.

The phrase 'being looked after' by a local authority embraces both a child being provided with accommodation by the authority and one in their care under a care order.[14] In relation to an accommodated child the authority do not have parental responsibility, and it could be somewhat anomalous to give significant weight to the local authority's plans for a child's future in circumstances when they do not have the power to implement these

9   See above.
10 [1993] 1 FLR 425.
11 [1993] 2 FLR 732.
12 *Re A (A Minor) (Residence Order: Leave to Apply)* [1992] 3 All ER 872.
13 [1992] 1 FLR 448.
14 S.22(1).

plans. It might therefore be maintained that less weight ought to be given to the authority's plans for an accommodated child than when the child is in care.

The wishes and feelings of the child's parents

Curiously, section 10(9) requires the wishes and feelings of the child's parents to be taken into account only when the child is being looked after by the local authority. Yet parents (and persons with parental responsibility) will normally have the greatest interest in whether or not an application is allowed to proceed. However, it seems that this somewhat anomalous provision[15] will be relied upon to ensure that the views of the parents are taken into account when the child is being looked after by a local authority, but that it will not be used to exclude the wishes and feelings of the parents in other cases. In *Re A (Minors) (Residence Order)*[16] a foster mother had applied for a residence order in respect of four children who were in the care of a local authority. No notification of her application had been given to the children's mother. The Court of Appeal stated that the children's mother should have been notified of the leave application although there was no notification requirement under the rules, and that by failing to give the mother notice the judge had deprived himself of information which was necessary for the proper exercise of his discretion.

Ex parte or inter partes applications for leave

A request for leave to apply for a section 8 order can either be made ex parte before a single magistrate or judge, or at an inter partes hearing. It seems probable that a request for leave which is made ex parte is more likely to succeed than an application made at an inter partes hearing, bearing in mind that the applicant will not draw to the attention of the court any risk that the application might prove disruptive and harmful to the child. The ex parte nature of the leave process has caused anxiety to judges hearing contentious and difficult cases. In *Re S (Adopted Child: Contact)*[17] Thorpe J stated that where a natural mother of an adopted child is seeking leave to apply for a contact order, the request should always be heard in the Family Division and not be granted on an ex parte application. In *Nottinghamshire County Council v P*[18] the Court of Appeal

15 Particularly bearing in mind that in the case of an accommodated child, it is the parents who have parental responsibility, not the local authority.
16 [1992] 3 All ER 872.
17 [1993] 2 FCR 234.
18 [1993] 2 FLR 134.

stated that it was wholly inappropriate for a local authority to apply ex parte before a single justice for leave to issue an application for a prohibited steps order. The court added that, in future, any such application should be transferred to the county court and that it should not be dealt with ex parte. In *Re SC (A Minor) (Leave to Seek Residence Order)*[19] the court held that where the applicant for leave is a child, it was desirable that everyone with parental responsibility should be given notice of the application even though an application for leave can be made ex parte. In *Re M (Prohibited Steps Order: Application for Leave)*[20] Johnson J emphasised the importance of the leave decision. He stated that while there may well be cases of urgency, or other circumstances, which make it right to grant leave on an ex parte application, in the ordinary case the interests of justice require that notice of the application should be given to other parties who are likely to be affected if leave is granted. He added that such persons should be given the opportunity to adduce evidence and to make submissions.

A court at the leave stage, whether the hearing is ex parte or inter partes, may find itself confronted with a difficult choice between either granting, or refusing, an application for leave after allowing only brief evidence, or holding a 'trial within a trial' in which issues relating to the substantive application are put before the court at this preliminary stage. A court may have difficulty in determining whether a person ought to be granted leave on minimal information provided by the applicant. However, obtaining adequate information upon which to base a ruling is liable to be time-consuming, which in itself could be disruptive and harmful to the child. Exercising judicial restraint, and refusing leave because the alternative is to embark on a detailed enquiry, may sometimes be as proper a way of advancing a child's best interests as allowing the leave application to be conducted at an inter partes hearing.

The child concerned and leave

No one has a greater interest in decisions about a child's future than the child himself. The Children Act 1989 recognises that in some instances the child should be given the opportunity to communicate his own views by initiating proceedings on his own behalf. Children do not fall within the categories of persons who are entitled to apply for a section 8 order, but a child is entitled to make a leave application, subject to the proviso in section 10(8) that—

'where the person applying for leave to make a section 8 application is the child concerned, the court may only grant leave if it is satisfied

19 [1994] 1 FLR 96.
20 [1993] 1 FLR 275.

that he has sufficient understanding to make the proposed application for the section 8 order.'

The constraint in section 10(8) is the only statutory restriction imposed and the criteria for leave in section 10(9) do not apply. This may be of advantage to the child in a case where, as in *Re SC (A Minor) (Leave to Seek Residence Order)*[1] she wishes to live with a person who, because of section 10(9), would be unlikely to succeed on her own application. In that case it was made clear that whilst a residence order could not be made in favour of the child herself, the child could nonetheless seek leave to apply for a residence order in favour of someone else.

In relation to a child's understanding, in *Re S (A Minor) (Independent Representation)*[2] the Court of Appeal stated that a balance must be struck between two considerations. First is the principle that the child's views, wishes and feelings should command serious attention, and are not to be discounted simply because he is a child. Second is the fact that a child is liable to be vulnerable and impressionable which is why the law is particularly solicitous in protecting his interests. A child may lack the maturity and experience to weigh the longer term against the short term, or the insight to know how he may react to certain outcomes, or how others will react in certain situations. Different children have differing levels of understanding at the same age, and understanding must be assessed relatively to the issues in the proceedings. The court concluded that where any sound judgment on the issues calls for insight and imagination which only maturity and experience can bring, both a court and a solicitor should be slow to conclude that the child's understanding is sufficient to enable him to take an independent part in the proceedings.[3]

Thus the degree of understanding required under section 10(8) appears to be relatively high. Yet if a court is too ready to assume that a child lacks the capacity to institute proceedings on his own behalf this could amount to a denial of the child's right to be treated as an autonomous individual.[4] It is suggested that, in many cases, the only understanding he ought to be required to demonstrate is an understanding that he wants a court to intervene in his life, and for the court to substitute its own view of his best interests for the view of the person(s) who have parental responsibility for him.

1   [1994] 1 FLR 96.
2   [1993] 2 FLR 437.
3   See too *Re H (A Minor)* [1992] Fam Law 368, where, in the context of care proceedings, the court held that if there was any real question as to whether the child's emotional disturbance was so intense that he could not give instructions, it should be the subject of expert opinion.
4   As established in *Gillick v West Norfolk and Wisbech Area Health Authority* [1986] AC 112, and see ch 1.

Leave and the welfare of the child where the child is the applicant

The limit on children applying for a section 8 order, on its face, is concerned simply with whether the child has sufficient understanding to make an application. However, in *Re SC (A Minor) (Leave to Seek Residence Order)*[5] Booth J pointed out that a court has a discretion whether to grant leave even if it has been established under section 10(8) that the child has sufficient understanding to make the application. But she added that as the initial application for leave did not raise any question about the child's upbringing, the child's welfare was not the court's paramount consideration when exercising its discretion in deciding whether or not to grant leave.[6] In that regard, she said, no distinction could be drawn between an application by a child for leave, and an application made by any other person. On the other hand she held that it is right for the court to have regard to the likelihood of success of the proposed application, and to be satisfied that the child is not embarking on proceedings which are doomed to failure.

By contrast, in *Re C (A Minor) (Leave to Seek Section 8 Orders)*[7] Johnson J extended the application of the welfare principle to the whole question of leave on an application made by a child. A 15-year-old girl was seeking leave to apply for a residence order to live at the home of a friend and her family, and for a specific issue order to go on holiday with them to Bulgaria. Johnson J ruled that as the considerations laid down in section 10(9) do not apply where the applicant is the child concerned, he must be guided in respect of both leave applications by the welfare principle.[8] In relation to the residence order he took the view that there was no identifiable advantage in making a residence order at the present time. He therefore adjourned the child's application for leave. In relation to the application for leave to apply for a specific issue order, he recognised that the question whether the child should be allowed to go on holiday to Bulgaria had important significance both for her and for her parents. However he took the view that this was not the kind of issue which Parliament had envisaged as being litigated in a court when it allowed children to make applications for leave. He therefore refused the child's leave application.

It is suggested that normally it should only be at the trial of the substantive issue that a court should be influenced by whether a child's wishes coincide with his best interests, and not at the stage of leave. Any

---

5   [1994] 1 FLR 96.

6   Following *Re A (Minors) (Residence Order)* [1992] 3 All ER 872.

7   [1994] 1 FLR 26.

8   *Re A (Minors) (Residence Order)* [1992] 3 All ER 872, in which the Court of Appeal ruled that the welfare principle does not apply to leave applications made under s.10(1)(2), does not appear to have been brought to the court's attention.

other approach brings with it the danger that the child will be denied the right to litigate about his upbringing, which is a right enjoyed by adults. It is suggested that treating a child differently from an adult in the area of rights, particularly when these have apparently been given to the child by Parliament, requires stronger justification than that advanced in *Re C (A Minor) (Leave to Seek Section 8 Orders)*,[9] and that the approach taken by Booth J in *Re SC (A Minor) (Leave to Seek Residence Order)*[10] is preferable.

Where the child is the applicant for leave this may create a difficult practical problem namely, where is the child to live in the period between the application for leave and the hearing? Apart from the normal notice requirements (which can in certain circumstances be abridged), a case of this nature is likely to be difficult and may take several days to prepare. Also, such cases must be heard by a High Court judge which may add to the delay. In the meanwhile the child may be living with a parent or other person, such as a step-parent, in circumstances of considerable animosity. An interim order, temporarily to settle the arrangements as to the person with whom the child is to live, would seem essential. An interim order may be made at any stage during the course of the proceedings in question,[11] but it is doubtful whether one can be made at the leave to apply stage. Furthermore, the difficulty presented in taking this step is that it interferes in a parent's parental responsibility on the basis of incomplete information, and makes an order which could be influential against the parent when the case comes for trial. Therefore, where the child should live pending the hearing for leave raises some awkward questions of principle as well as the practical question of what should be done.

Who should represent the child?

Shortly after the Act came into force a number of cases occurred in which the child was the applicant for leave either to be joined as a party to existing family proceedings, or to make a free-standing application. Some senior judges expressed the view that such applications raised issues which were more appropriate for determination in the High Court and subsequently a *Practice Direction* was issued requiring such cases to be transferred there.[12] This Direction has significant procedural implications. Under the High Court and County Court Rules, a child must seek leave to institute or participate in existing proceedings through a next friend or guardian ad

9 [1994] 1 FLR 26.
10 [1994] 1 FLR 96.
11 S.11(3).
12 *Practice Direction (Family Proceedings Orders: Applications by Children)* [1993] 1 All ER 820.

litem,[13] who is normally the Official Solicitor.[14] A child, for the purposes of the Rules, is treated as a person under a disability. However, the Rules also provide that when the child has sufficient understanding, or is represented by a lawyer, he may be a party to the proceedings without this assistance;[15] indeed, he cannot be represented by both.

It is important to keep distinct the question whether leave should be granted from who, if anyone, should represent the child. There are significant differences between not allowing a child to take part in existing family proceedings; not allowing him to do so unless represented; not allowing him to conduct the remaining stages of existing proceedings without a guardian ad litem; and not allowing him to commence proceedings at all. In family proceedings, issues about the child are already before a court and, where these are contested, the court is bound to have regard to the child's wishes and feelings before formulating its judgment.[16] Usually it will have a report which gives an account of the child's views from a court welfare officer; alternatively, the child will be represented. This means that the voice of the child will be heard in some way, even if not always in the manner in which the child would most prefer it to be expressed. But where a child is applying for leave to make a free-standing application for a section 8 order, the matter relating to his upbringing which he wishes to have investigated will never come under the scrutiny of a court if leave is refused.

Where a child applies for leave to participate in proceedings without a next friend or guardian ad litem, it is the judge, not the solicitor, who is required to assess the individual child's understanding in the context of the proceedings in which he has applied to take part.[17] However, in *Re CT (A Minor) (Wardship: Representation)*[18] Waite LJ said that he would hope, and expect, that instances where a challenge is directed to a solicitor's view of his minor client's ability to instruct him would be rare, and that cases where the court felt bound to question such ability of its own motion would be rarer still.[19] In *Re S (A Minor) (Independent Representation)*[20] the Court of Appeal held that a court would be unlikely to grant leave to a child to take part in proceedings without a next friend or guardian ad litem unless the child had already instructed a solicitor. When, as in *Re S*

13 Family Proceedings Rules 1991, r.9.2.
14 R. 9.2(3)(7); this replicates the long-standing practice of the wardship jurisdiction which allows the ward's best interests to be examined independently of the competing claims or arguments of the main parties.
15 R. 9.2A.
16 S.1(3)(a), and s.1(4).
17 See *Re S (A Minor) (Independent Representation)* [1993] 2 FLR 437; *Re CT (A Minor) (Wardship: Representation)* [1993] 2 FLR 278.
18 Above.
19 But cf *Re K, W and H (Minors) (Medical Treatment)* [1993] 1 FLR 854.
20 [1993] 2 FLR 437.

(A Minor), a next friend or guardian ad litem had been appointed, and the child wished to continue the proceedings without that person's participation, this too required the court's leave; whether leave was granted was also dependent on the child's capacity to understand. Consequently, at the leave stage a court has two issues to resolve: does the child have sufficient understanding to make the proposed application; and what form of representation, if any, should the child have.

There may be a vital difference for the child in being represented by a guardian ad litem or next friend, and having a solicitor to conduct his case. The role of a guardian ad litem is to listen to the child, understand his point of view and explain it to the court, but the guardian's overriding duty is to safeguard and represent the child's best interests. Where the guardian ad litem forms the opinion that the child's welfare will not be served by taking steps which accord with the child's wishes and feelings, the guardian has a duty to protect the child against himself.[1] However, the role of the solicitor is to take the child's instructions and to pursue the case simply on the basis of those instructions.

A disturbing example of a court refusing to allow children to be separately legally represented in existing legal proceedings, and instead requiring them to be represented by a guardian ad litem, arose in *Re K, W and H (Minors) (Medical Treatment)*.[2] Three 15-year-old girls were being looked after in a specialist unit for disturbed adolescents. A question arose over whether they were consenting to emergency medication and whether they might not wish to consent to such treatment in the future. The hospital therefore applied for orders under section 8 to confirm that they could treat the girls in reliance on the consent of a person with parental responsibility. Thorpe J ruled that he was confident that none of the girls was '*Gillick* competent'[3] for the purposes of giving consent to medical treatment. But he also said that, even if they were, the application was misconceived because the doctors had the necessary consents from the persons with parental responsibility. When the case had first come before the court each of the girls had applied to be independently represented by her own lawyer. Although the lawyers were of the opinion that all the girls had sufficient understanding to instruct their own legal representatives, Thorpe J preferred the view of the childrens' previous guardians ad litem, who had expressed the opinion that the children did not have sufficient understanding to participate in the proceedings without a next friend or guardian ad litem. The girls' applications for independent representation were therefore refused, and they were represented by the Official Solicitor for the remainder of the proceedings.

1   See *Re CT (A Minor) (Wardship: Representation)* [1993] 2 FLR 278.
2   [1993] 1 FLR 854.
3   For the meaning of this phrase, see ch 1.

It is suggested that by preventing the girls from being independently represented in a case where the question of compulsory medication of an unwilling and possibly '*Gillick* competent' child was in issue, and where the consent being relied upon was that of the parent rather than the court, the court was depriving the children of the separate representation of their voice in exactly the type of case where this safeguard is needed.

Local authority foster parents and section 8 orders

Where a local authority foster parent has had the care of a child for a considerable period of time she may wish to apply for a residence order so that the child will continue to have his home with her. There are special, and somewhat complicated provisions which apply to local authority foster parents. The first question to be resolved is: 'is the foster parent entitled to apply for a residence order?' The answer to this question is discovered in section 10(5). If she falls within the scope of the provisions in that subsection, then she is entitled to apply for a residence order.[4] Thus where the child has lived with the foster parent for a period of at least three years, not ending more than three months before the date of the application, she is entitled to apply for an order under section 10(5)(b).[5] Where she has looked after the child for less than three years, and where the child is being looked after by the local authority under a care order, she would need the consent of the local authority under section 10(5)(c)(ii) in order to be entitled to make an application for a residence order.[6] But where the child is an accommodated child, then before the foster parent can be entitled to apply, she would either have to obtain the consent of each person with a residence order under section 10(5)(c)(i); or in any other case, the consent of each of those (if any) who have parental responsibility for the child under section 10(5)(c)(iii).

Where an accommodated child has lived with the foster parents for some considerable period (but less than the three years which would entitle them to apply), and where the relationship between the foster parents and the natural parent(s) is good, the provisions relating to the consent of persons with parental responsibility could be important. Local authorities sometimes operate fostering policies which do not necessarily command

---

4   She is also entitled to apply for a contact order unless the child is in the care of the local authority. In practice this will almost certainly be the situation. Contact applications in relation to children in care are governed by s.34. A foster parent would need the leave of the court to apply for a contact order under that section.

5   As qualified by s.10(10).

6   S.10(5)(c)(ii) requires the consent of the local authority only where the child is in the care of the local authority; this provision should be contrasted with the consent provision in s.9(3)(a), which also applies where the child is accommodated, and which is discussed below.

the full support of the parents of the children whom they are looking after: always treating children of mixed race parentage as being black being one such policy which does not necessarily enjoy widespread acceptance. On the one hand a local authority might wish to alter the child's placement in pursuance of such a fostering policy.[7] On the other hand, the natural parent(s) might prefer the child to stay with the foster parents to whom he has become attached. In a case of this kind the parents might be willing to consent to the foster parents making an application for a residence order despite objections from the local authority.[8]

While this is likely to be a rare occurrence, it reinforces an important principle: local authorities only have power to determine the course of the lives of other people's children either because this power has been conferred on them by Parliament, or by a court, or because those with parental responsibility agree. In the case of accommodated children, foster parents are in a somewhat curious position. Their relationship with a local authority is controlled by regulations and they must abide by the authority's instructions.[9] However, where foster parents are in disagreement with a local authority over residence and contact, the ultimate decision-making power about conferring entitlement on the foster parents to apply for a residence, or contact order, rests with the person(s) who have parental responsibility, which in the case of accommodated children is not the local authority.

Foster parents and leave to apply for a section 8 order

A foster parent who is not entitled to apply for an order must, like any other non-entitled applicant, apply to the court for leave to apply for the order. However, special rules apply to foster parents. Section 9(3) provides that—

'A person who is, or was at any time within the last six months, a local authority foster parent of a child may not apply for leave to apply for a section 8 order with respect to the child unless—

---

7   It is not fanciful to suggest that local authorities sometimes vigorously pursue such policies despite there being apparently compelling reasons to allow the child to remain where he is: see *Re A (A Minor) (Cultural Background)* [1987] 2 FLR 429; *Re N (A Minor) (Adoption)* [1990] 1 FLR 58; *Re P (A Minor) (Adoption)* [1990] 1 FLR 96; *Re JK (Adoption: Transracial Placement)* [1991] 2 FLR 340. These cases are discussed in ch 4.

8   In such a situation there would need to be a strong degree of trust between the parents and foster parents. The latter would acquire parental responsibility if a residence order was made, and the parents would be likely to experience difficulty in persuading a court to substitute an order restoring the child's residence to them at a later date, unless the foster parents were in agreement.

9   Foster Placement (Children) Regulations 1991 (SI 1991/910).

(a) he has the consent of the authority;
(b) he is a relative of the child; or
(c) the child has lived with him for at least three years preceding the application.'

Why are local authority foster parents who require the court's leave singled out for special treatment? One of the many aims of the Children Act 1989 is to instil confidence in parents in state provision of social services for children in need and in care. Parents are encouraged to work in partnership with local authorities for the benefit of their children. Foster parents may often have more material possessions than a natural parent, and the opportunities afforded in the foster home to develop and enhance a child's physical, emotional and educational progress may be superior to those that a natural parent is able to provide. These are all matters which are relevant to the application of the welfare principle which governs the determination of applications for section 8 orders.[10] If a foster parent could apply like any other person for leave to apply for a residence order a natural parent might be fearful of making temporary arrangements for his or her child with a local authority. This could rebound to the general disadvantage of children in need and in care, because parents might be tempted to make private arrangements for their children which are less appropriate to their child's needs, or they might become hostile to a foster placement simply because it appeared to be particularly well-suited to their child's circumstances.

Unless a foster parent is a relative, or has looked after the child for at least three years, he or she must obtain the consent of the local authority to apply to the court for leave to apply for a section 8 order. Unless that consent is forthcoming, the foster parent is precluded from seeking a section 8 order. The requirement of local authority consent is included to reassure parents that it is safe to allow their children to go into foster care. It operates, too, as a reminder to foster parents that normally their role is to work alongside parents, so far as is reasonable and possible, in all aspects of the child's upbringing. If foster parents could seek a court's leave to apply for an order that the child should live with them, without further restraint, some might be tempted to exclude the natural parents, rather than to work co-operatively with them. The consent provision is also there to reassure local authorities that they can develop their fostering services without losing control over the children.[11]

---

10 See ch 4.
11 Where a child has been orphaned, or when a parent with a residence order has died, many of these arguments do not apply; in these circumstances there is nothing in s.5 of the Children Act 1989 to prevent a foster parent from applying for a guardianship order, see below.

In *Re P (A Minor) (Leave to Apply: Foster Parents)*[12] the question arose whether the local authority had the entitlement to give consent under section 9(3)(a) where the child was an accommodated child, and where the local authority therefore did not have parental responsibility for the child. It was argued that if a local authority were able to give leave under section 9(3), this would, in effect, allow the authority to circumvent the clear prohibition in section 9(2) that no application may be made by a local authority for a residence order or a contact order.[13] Hale J dismissed this argument. She said that it was absolutely plain from the wording that the consent of the local authority accommodating the child was the consent which was needed. Whilst this ruling was unremarkable on the point of law which it settled, the argument raised by counsel that this was a back-door way of allowing a local authority to apply for a residence order was uncomfortably close to the mark. Of course it was not the local authority who were applying for the residence order, it was the foster parents. Furthermore, it would be the court which would decide whether leave should be given for the foster parents to make the substantive application; and it would be for the court to decide whether to make a residence order in their favour. However, it does expose an uncomfortable tension between the various policies which underpin different provisions in the Act. The ruling makes it clear that a local authority, where they take the view that the welfare of the child requires that he should remain in the care of his foster parents, but where they also take the view that they do not have sufficient grounds to satisfy the test for making a care order,[14] can encourage the foster parents to make their own application for a residence order, and give them the leave to do so.[15] Were this to happen with any frequency, it could undermine confidence in the accommodation provisions in the Act which section 9(2) and (3), amongst other provisions in the Act, are designed to promote.[16]

A relative[17] who acts as local authority foster parent may apply to a court for leave to apply for a section 8 order without first obtaining the local authority's consent. This provision could come to the assistance of a relative in circumstances similar to those that occurred in *R v Hereford and Worcester County Council, ex p D*.[18] In that case a local authority had initially decided to place a child (about whom care proceedings had been

---

12 [1994] 2 FCR 1093.
13 See below.
14 S.31(2), and see ch 3.
15 Which indeed was close to what happened in *Re P (A Minor) (Leave to Apply: Foster Parents)*. The local authority were also acting as an adoption agency in respect of the child. The parents, who were Orthodox Jews, objected to the foster parents as adoptive parents because they were Roman Catholics. The court granted the foster parents leave to apply for a residence order.
16 Particularly s.20(8): see ch 3.
17 For the definition of 'a relative', see s.105.
18 [1992] 1 FLR 448.

commenced and who was in their care under an interim care order) with her aunt as foster parent. However, the child's guardian ad litem formed the opinion that the aunt would not be able to protect the child from her mother. This led the local authority to change their mind about the suitability of the placement, and to the removal of the child from her aunt's care. Prior to the Children Act 1989 the only possible redress open to the aunt was in judicial review. Nowadays a relative in a similar position would be able to apply to a court for leave to apply for a residence order. However, a relative might still find that access to a full court hearing would be prevented by the refusal of leave under the criteria in section 10(9).[19]

What is the difference between the provision in section 10(5)(b) which entitles anyone to apply for a residence or contact order after the child has lived with the applicant for at least three years, and the provision in section 9(3)(c) which allows a local authority foster parent with whom the child has lived for at least three years to apply for leave to apply for a section 8 order without the consent of the local authority? The answer is found in a close examination of sections 10(10) and 9(4). Under both provisions the three-year period must have begun not more than five years before the making of the application, but *entitlement* to apply for an order arises only when the three-year period has ended not more than three months before the application. Thus if the child has been removed from the foster parents, and more than three months elapses before they make their application, they must overcome the hurdle of leave before they can get through the door of the court.

It should be noticed that the requirements in section 9(3) apply only to a person who is, or was at any time within the last six months, a local authority foster parent of the child in question. Once six months have elapsed since the foster parent last looked after the child, the foster parent is free to apply to the court for leave to apply for a section 8 order without first obtaining the consent of the local authority. Thus, for example, a local authority foster parent who had looked after a child for two years, and who is not a relative of the child, could not apply for leave to apply for a section 8 order. But if the child were to be taken from her, and six months were to elapse, she could then apply directly to a court for leave to apply for a residence order. Of course her difficulty in overcoming the hurdle of the criteria in section 10(9) would almost certainly be accentuated by the lapse of time. However, a foster parent who was determined to apply for leave once the six months elapsed might persuade the local authority to consent to her making a leave application at once. This would resolve the matter at an early stage and allow the child's future to be planned without the threat of future litigation.[20]

---

19 See above.
20 In *Re A (Minors) (Residence Order)* [1992] 3 All ER 872 the local authority gave their consent to the foster mother applying for leave to apply for a residence order, but opposed her application to the court for leave.

Local authority foster parents and guardianship

There is no control, or filtering mechanism, over who is entitled to make an application for guardianship. Any individual may apply to a court for such an appointment if the child has no parent with parental responsibility for him; or where a residence order has been made in favour of a parent or guardian of the child, and that person has died while the order was in force.[1] Thus it seems that, in these circumstances, an application may be made in respect of a child who is being looked after by a local authority,[2] and that the application must come before the court despite any objections from the local authority, or from anyone else.

Where a guardianship order is made it confers parental responsibility on the applicant. However, a guardianship order has no other effect on any existing orders; in particular it has no effect on an existing care order. However, guardianship proceedings are family proceedings, consequently the court can make any section 8 order of its own motion during their course (including a residence order which would have the effect of discharging the care order).[3] The advantage of a court hearing is that a new decision-maker is able to consider the merits of the case: decision-making is vested in the court and not in the local authority. If the court were to contemplate using its own motion powers to make a residence order in addition to a guardianship order, and where the effect of the order would be to discharge a care order, a guardian ad litem would have to be appointed to protect the child's interests.[4] This would mean that the local authority's plans for the child would be subjected to an independent professional assessment, and occasionally the alternative plans offered by the foster parent might be thought by the guardian ad litem to be more in the interests of the child than those offered by the local authority. Whilst it is unlikely that a court would make a guardianship order to a foster parent in a case where the local authority were opposed to the application, an application for guardianship might be worth pursuing in a case where the foster parent has been looking after an orphaned foster child for some considerable length of time,[5] and where the local authority are planning to remove the child from her care.

1   S.5(1), and see ch 1.
2   S.22(1) provides that a child is being 'looked after' by a local authority whether the child is merely being accommodated by the local authority under s.20 or is the subject of a care order under s.31. See further ch 3.
3   S.91(1).
4   S.41(6).
5   But for less than three years, otherwise the foster parents would be entitled to apply for a residence order under s.10(5)(b).

Local authorities and section 8 orders

Local authorities do not fall within the categories of persons who are entitled to apply for section 8 orders but they, like anyone else, may apply to a court for leave to apply for an order. However section 10(3) provides that section 10 is subject to the restrictions imposed by section 9, and section 9(1) and (2) impose specific restrictions on local authorities.

A court may only make a residence order with respect to a child in care

Section 9(1) provides that—

'No court shall make any section 8 order, other than a residence order, with respect to a child who is in the care of a local authority.'

Why may a residence order be made but none of the other orders? Looking first at the residence order: it is an order which goes to the source of the local authority's powers, and not to the manner in which they are exercised. The effect of a residence order is not only to settle the arrangements as to the person with whom the child is to live, it also discharges the care order.[6] It therefore brings to an end a local authority's parental responsibility for the child. By contrast, the other three orders are each directed to the manner in which a person with parental responsibility is able to exercise that responsibility, and when a child is in care such a person is the local authority. Section 9(1) therefore enshrines an important constitutional principle, namely that where Parliament has imposed duties on a local authority, and given them corresponding powers to put them into effect, courts may only interfere in the exercise of those powers and duties where Parliament has authorised this. Otherwise the only challenge which can be directed to the exercise by the local authority of their statutory functions is where the authority's behaviour has been such as to render them liable to an action in judicial review.[7]

Although a contact order cannot be made under section 8 in relation to a child in care the Act does allow for judicial interference in a local authority's decisions about contact, but it does so under section 34. Contact arrangements are a vital aspect of the relationship between a child and his parents and members of his wider family. Unless contact is allowed on a reasonably frequent basis it will normally be impossible to secure the rehabilitation of the child with his parents, and the eventual discharge of

---

6 S.91(1).
7 *A v Liverpool City Council* [1981] 2 All ER 385; *W v Hertfordshire County Council* [1985] 2 All ER 301.

the care order. Thus although orders about contact go to the manner in which a local authority exercise their powers over a child in care, contact is an issue of such importance in relation to the right of the child and his parents to enjoy one another's company that Parliament has authorised that questions about contact with a child in care may be determined by the courts.[8]

The reason for the prohibition on a court making a specific issue order, or a prohibited steps order, is because when a child is in the care of a local authority, not only do the authority have parental responsibility for the child, but also they have the power to determine the extent to which a parent or guardian may meet his parental responsibility for the child.[9] Thus the position of local authorities is different from that of others who share responsibility for a child's upbringing. It is they who can determine all matters relating to the child's upbringing.[10] Section 9(1) reflects this. It also reflects the constitutional rule that normally the day-to-day decision-making of local authorities should not be subject to review and interference by courts. If courts were permitted to make specific issue and prohibited steps orders in respect of a child in care this would give power to courts to dictate to local authorities how they should carry out the duties imposed on them by statute. Such power would conflict with orthodox principle.

A local authority may not apply for a residence or contact order

Section 9(2) provides that—

> 'No application may be made by a local authority for a residence order or contact order and no court shall make such an order in favour of a local authority.'

Why are these restrictions imposed? Why is a local authority prohibited from seeking leave to apply for either a residence or contact order, yet permitted to apply for leave to apply for a specific issue or prohibited steps order? The first point to realise is that section 9(2) is directed at those cases where a local authority do not have a care order. The purpose of the provision in relation to the prohibition against applying for a residence order is to prevent a local authority from obtaining parental responsibility for a child otherwise than through making an application in care proceedings. Without this prohibition a local authority might be tempted to by-pass making an application in care proceedings under Part IV of the

8 See ch 3.
9 S.33(3).
10 Apart from issues relating to contact; and see s.33(3) which puts other limits on the local authority's powers.

Act, and instead to seek a residence order. A local authority may not apply for a contact order for similar reasons. Such an order could enable the authority to have enforceable contact with a child other than through obtaining a supervision order in an application brought in care proceedings.

Good intentions, a genuine motive, and a different view about where a child should live, and whether he should be supervised by a social worker, are not regarded as sufficient reasons for permitting a local authority to obtain control over a child's upbringing. If a local authority wish to obtain such control, they must prove that there are sufficient grounds to justify this type of intervention. The law relating to care proceedings contains many checks and balances designed to limit state intervention in family life. Courts are empowered to order the removal of children from their homes, and to give parental responsibility to local authorities, only in those cases that can be justified on carefully formulated criteria including, among other things, proof of actual or anticipated significant harm to the child.[11] By contrast, residence and contact orders are governed solely by the application of the principle that the child's welfare is paramount.

There may, however, be some potential for the restriction in section 9(2) to be circumvented through indirect means. Many children who are being accommodated on a voluntary basis by a local authority are placed with foster parents.[12] It may be, in a particular case, that the local authority and foster parents form the view that there are insufficient grounds to institute proceedings for a care order, but that nonetheless the child's interests will best be served by remaining in foster care. Where the child, too, is strongly expressing a wish to remain where he is, this view will be compounded. In these circumstances there is nothing to prevent a local authority from consenting to the foster parents applying for leave to apply for a residence order, and supporting the foster parents in their leave application.[13] Alternatively they could encourage a child of sufficient age and understanding to see a lawyer and initiate his own application for leave to apply for a section 8 order.

There is a tension here between the interests of the individual child to have his upbringing looked into by a court on the basis of the paramountcy of his welfare, and the more general public law principle that the state should not intervene in the private family life of those with parental responsibility without sufficient cause. If, in a case like the one given above, the foster parents were to obtain a residence order, and if the local authority were to continue to make contributions towards the foster parents' costs of accommodating the child,[14] and perhaps to continue to supervise the

11 S.31(2); and see ch 3.
12 Under the accommodation provisions in s.20: see ch 3.
13 S.9(3)(a); and see above.
14 Sch. 1, para 15(1).

child on a voluntary basis too, this public/private divide could become
blurred, arguably to an unacceptable degree.

A local authority may apply for a specific issue, or prohibited steps, order

A local authority may seek a court's leave to apply for a specific issue or
prohibited steps order (except when they already have a care order, and
section 9(1) therefore applies). Why are these orders treated differently
from residence and contact orders? This question is best answered by
recalling the various philosophies which underpin the Children Act 1989.
These include the belief that it is normally in the best interests of a child
to be brought up by his own parents; that parents and state should work
in partnership to further a child's welfare; and that any state intervention
which results in the conferment of parental responsibility on a local
authority should be limited to those occasions when the child is suffering,
or is likely to suffer, significant harm. Having the freedom to apply for
leave to apply for specific issue or prohibited steps orders affords local
authorities the opportunity to seek a court's assistance to make a ruling
on one aspect of the exercise of parental responsibility, without otherwise
interfering in the day-to-day control exercised by parents, and others, over
a child's upbringing. As Johnson J accepted in *Re O (A Minor) (Medical
Treatment)*,[15] where the issue to be resolved was whether the child should
have a blood transfusion, it is wholly inappropriate for a court to make
even an interim care order where the child's parents are 'caring, committed
and capable and where only one issue arises for decision, albeit one of the
gravest significance.'[16] In *Re R (A Minor) (Blood Transfusion)*[17] the issue
to be resolved was also whether a child should have a blood transfusion.
Booth J court ruled that a local authority should make an application for
a specific issue order before a High Court judge where there was no need
for any other order to safeguard the child

Where a local authority are seriously concerned about an aspect of a
child's upbringing they must strike a proper balance between applying for
one or both of the two private law orders under section 8, and using the
public law provisions under Part IV or V. The choice is not always easy
bearing in mind the non-interventionist philosophy of the Act. In
Nottinghamshire County Council v P[18] the Court of Appeal held that a
local authority which believed a child to be at risk of suffering significant
harm should proceed by way of an application for a care or supervision

15 [1993] 2 FLR 149.
16 However, in *Re O (A Minor) (Medical Treatment)* Johnson J also ruled that the inherent
jurisdiction was the most appropriate legal framework in which to consider the issue.
17 [1993] 2 FLR 757.
18 [1993] 2 FLR 134.

order and not use the private law provisions. The court also warned against the local authority attempting to use a prohibited steps order for the purpose of controlling a father's contact with his daughters, stating that this is disallowed under section 9(2) and (5).[19] This ruling means that where a local authority take the view that it is safe to leave a child with one parent, but that the other parent presents a serious risk to the child, that they must seek to persuade the caring parent to apply for orders which will be effective to protect the child. This is likely to include orders under section 8 and under legislation which permits a court to oust a parent from the home.[20] Where the caring parent refuses, or is too frightened, to take such action, the local authority then has no alternative but to apply for an order in care proceedings. Where a local authority will not take such steps, it appears that a court is powerless to direct them to do so.[1]

The inherent jurisdiction of the High Court

The inherent jurisdiction of the High Court in children cases dates back to feudal times. Its origins lie in the duty of the king, as parens patriae, to take care of those who are not able to take care of themselves. The situations in which the court can act under its inherent jurisdiction to protect a child have never been defined. However the courts themselves, and Parliament through the enactment of the Children Act 1989, have severely curtailed the availability of the jurisdiction. The most usual way of invoking the High Court's inherent jurisdiction is by making a child a ward of court. A child becomes a ward as soon as an application is made, that is to say even before any order is made, and once a child has been warded no important step in the child's life can be taken without the court's leave. Thus the High Court takes control over the child's upbringing, but it then delegates powers to make decisions about a child to the persons who have the day-to-day care of the child.

There is nothing in the Children Act 1989 to prevent any individual who has a genuine interest in the upbringing of a child from asking the High Court to exercise its inherent jurisdiction over the child. However, one purpose of the Act is to provide a comprehensive framework within which decision-making about children may best proceed, and another is to make available a variety of orders designed to encompass all aspects of a child's upbringing. Furthermore, proceedings brought under the inherent jurisdiction fall within the definition of family proceedings, and therefore

19 See above.
20 Normally by means of an injunction under the Domestic Violence and Matrimonial Proceedings Act 1976: see ch 5.
1   See the concluding remarks of Sir Stephen Brown P in *Nottinghamshire County Council v P* [1993] 2 FLR 134.

a court is entitled to make any section 8 order when exercising its inherent jurisdiction.[2] One of the advantages of wardship is that the court retains control over the child's upbringing, but since the enactment of the Children Act 1989 such control can also be exercised through making a prohibited steps order. A prohibited steps order gives the court power to oversee what happens to the child, because the court can order that no step which could be taken by a parent in meeting his parental responsibility for a child shall be taken by any person without the consent of the court. In cases of difficulty brought under the Children Act 1989, the lower courts are empowered to transfer the proceedings upwards to the High Court.

Situations not covered by the Children Act 1989

There may be some situations in which the orders available under the Children Act 1989 do not adequately make provision for the circumstances, and where it may therefore be helpful to ask the High Court to intervene under its inherent jurisdiction. The High Court has been jealous to preserve its role to come to the assistance of children when the law is otherwise powerless or inadequate. By refusing to define the scope of the jurisdiction, the High Court has reserved to itself the power to respond to circumstances as they arise. An example might be to prevent the publication of information which could be harmful to the child, though in a case of this nature the court would need to balance the interest in freedom of information against the welfare of the child.[3] Another might be where a contract for surrogate parenthood is involved, and where there appears to be a need to throw a ring of care around the child, but where care proceedings are inappropriate.[4] In *Re X (A Minor) (Adoption Details: Disclosure)*[5] the Court of Appeal held that it was open to the High Court under its inherent jurisdiction to attach to an adoption order an order that the Registrar General should not reveal details of the adoption recorded in the Adopted Children Register without the leave of the court. The Registrar General had a mandatory duty, under section 50 of the Adoption Act 1976, to keep a register and to allow any person to search the index and to have a certified copy of any entry. The fear in this case was that the mother, who was an aggressive and violent woman, of whom the child was terrified, would discover the child's whereabouts if she had access to this information. However, in the main even the most delicate and difficult decisions, such as whether a child should be sterilised,[6] or whether a child should receive life-saving treat-

2   S.8(3).
3   *Re M and N (Minors) (Wardship: Freedom of Publication)* [1990] 1 All ER 205; *Re X (A Minor)* [1975] 1 All ER 697.
4   *Re C (A Minor) (Wardship: Surrogacy)* [1985] FLR 846.
5   [1994] 2 FLR 450.
6   *Re HG (Specific Issue Order: Sterilisation)* [1993] 1 FLR 587.

ment,[7] can be heard by High Court judges under proceedings brought under the Children Act 1989.

Because there is no statutory restriction placed on individuals on making an application to the High Court for the exercise of the inherent jurisdiction, the question arises whether an individual may seek the assistance of the High Court when other remedies under the Children Act 1989 are denied, or have been used and exhausted. While there appears to be no direct authority on this point, it can be predicted with confidence that a court would not allow the inherent jurisdiction to be used to circumvent restrictions which are included within the statutory framework. For example, if grandparents were to be refused leave to apply for a residence order in relation to their grandchild under section 10(9), it is suggested that it is inconceivable that they would be able to obtain a hearing on the merits under the inherent jurisdiction for an order to be made that the child should live with them.[8] For a court to rule otherwise would be to turn the inherent jurisdiction into an alternative code for resolving disputes about children, with its own body of case law separate and distinct from cases decided under the Act. This would seriously undermine the Act and its associated procedures.

The inherent jurisdiction and local authorities

Historically, local authorities could invite the High Court to exercise its inherent jurisdiction in wardship to make up for apparent deficiencies in the statutory child protection framework. Wardship was used to safeguard children when other procedures and remedies were unavailable, or had failed. In return, the local authority relinquished some of their control over a child to the court, and they were required to refer back to the court before they took any important step in the child's life which related to his upbringing. However, it is no longer open to local authorities to ask the High Court to exercise the inherent jurisdiction as an alternative to taking proceedings under the Children Act 1989. Section 100(2) provides that no court shall exercise the inherent jurisdiction to put a child in care, under local authority supervision, or into local authority accommodation. Nor may the jurisdiction be used for the purpose of conferring on any local authority the power to determine any question which has arisen, or which may arise, in connection with any aspect of parental responsibility for the child.[9] The court may only grant a local authority leave to apply for the exercise of the court's inherent jurisdiction if it is satisfied both that the desired result cannot be achieved by any other order for which the local

---

7   *Re R (A minor) (Blood Transfusion)* [1993] 2 FLR 757.
8   See the discussion below of *W v Hertfordshire County Council* [1985] 2 All ER 301.
9   S.100(2).

authority are entitled to apply, and that there is reasonable cause to believe that if the court's inherent jurisdiction is not exercised the child is likely to suffer significant harm.[10] The reason for this restriction is that if a local authority could invoke the inherent jurisdiction, or make a child a ward of court, this could enable them to obtain parental responsibility for a child other than by satisfying the threshold test for care proceedings.[11] The threshold test lays down a standard which, if established, allows a court to authorise the removal of children from their homes and for their placement in the care of a local authority. It is a universal standard applicable in all cases to all local authorities.

In *Devon County Council v S*[12] Thorpe J drew a distinction between a local authority seeking to have protective powers conferred upon them through resort to the inherent jurisdiction, which is prohibited by section 100(2)(d), and a local authority inviting the court to exercise its inherent powers to make an order which does not give any powers to the local authority. He held that, because of the Court of Appeal's judgment in *Nottinghamshire County Council v P,*[13] there was no jurisdictional foundation for making a prohibited steps order on an application from a local authority, where the purpose of the order was to prevent a child sex abuser from having contact with children living at home with their mother. However, the local authority could invite the court to exercise its own powers under the inherent jurisdiction in order to protect the child.

Restrictions on the power of a court to make orders in favour of a local authority either under the Children Act 1989, or under the inherent jurisdiction may sometimes present a local authority with a predicament. Section 9(1) provides that a court may not make a section 8 order other than a residence order in respect of a child in care. Yet a specific question may arise in connection with an aspect of the authority's parental responsibility where they take the view that a court should be the decision-maker rather than themselves. Examples might be where a child in care is seeking an abortion against her parents' wishes;[14] where sterilisation is believed to be in a child's best interests;[15] where a '*Gillick* competent child' is refusing consent to medical treatment;[16] or where a child and his parents are

---

10 S.100(4).

11 S.31(2); see ch 3.

12 [1994]1 FLR 355.

13 [1993] 2 FLR 134, in which the Court of Appeal ruled that a local authority could not apply for a prohibited steps order to stop contact between a father and his daughters, because this was in effect to apply for a contact order, and it would therefore be to evade the restrictions imposed by s.9(2) and (5); see above.

14 *Re B (Wardship: Abortion)* [1991] 2 FLR 426.

15 The sterilisation of a minor in virtually all cases requires the prior sanction of a High Court judge: *Practice Note* [1990] 2 FLR 530; *Re B (A minor) (Wardship: Sterilisation)* [1987] 2 FLR 314.

16 *Re R (A Minor) (Wardship: Medical Treatment)* [1991] 4 All ER 177; *Re W (A Minor) (Medical Treatment)* [1992] 4 All ER 627, see ch.1.

refusing to consent to medical treatment on religious or other grounds.[17] The strict legal position is that because the local authority are a person with parental responsibility they have the right to give the requisite consents to the medical treatment which is in issue. But these questions raise sensitive and controversial moral dilemmas, and it may be thought that a court, rather than the local authority, ought to be the final decision-maker. Indeed, in the case of sterilisation there is a practice direction to the effect that the matter must be resolved by a High Court judge.[18] Because a local authority with care of a child cannot apply for a specific issue order in relation to that child, it is in this type of case that they may properly apply for the leave of the court to apply for the exercise of the inherent jurisdiction.

More controversial is the situation when the inherent jurisdiction is invoked because an effort to protect a child is apparently being thwarted by statute. It has been seen that since the enactment of section 100 of the Children Act 1989 it is clear that the inherent jurisdiction cannot be used to replace, or supplement, a local authority's statutory powers of intervention. It is against this background that the ruling in *South Glamorgan County Council v W and B*[19] presents difficulties. During the course of care proceedings a judge made an interim care order, and gave directions under section 38(6) for the child, a girl of 15, to undergo a psychiatric examination and assessment and, if necessary, to be treated at an adolescent unit and to remain there during the assessment. Section 38(6) provides that 'if the child is of sufficient understanding to make an informed decision, he may refuse to submit to the examination or other assessment.' The girl refused to comply with the court's direction and the court found that she was competent to make an informed decision.[20] The court therefore gave leave to the local authority to bring proceedings to invoke the exercise of the court's inherent jurisdiction to authorise that the child be assessed and treated without her consent. Leave was granted because the court was satisfied that the result which the local authority wished to achieve could not be achieved through the making of any order made otherwise than in the exercise of the court's inherent jurisdiction, and for which the local authority were entitled to apply. It therefore fulfilled the requirements of section 100(5). It was put to the court that the court's power under the inherent jurisdiction, exercising the parens patriae jurisdiction, to override in a proper case the wishes of a child, and to give consent for medical treatment, had been abrogated by section 100 of the Children Act 1989. This view was rejected by the court on the ground that the court had always

---

17 *Re B (A Minor) (Wardship: Medical Treatment)* [1981] 1 WLR 1421; *Re E (A Minor) (Wardship: Medical Treatment)* [1993] 1 FLR 386.

18 *Practice Note, Sterilisation* [1993] 2 FLR 222.

19 [1993] 1 FLR 574.

20 The court expressed this in the negative, that is that it was not prepared to find that she was not competent.

been able to override the wishes of a competent child, and that it would require very clear words in a statute to take that right away.

There were compelling reasons why the child in *South Glamorgan County Council v W and B* should receive psychiatric assessment and treatment, and it is easy to appreciate why the court was determined to override her refusal. However the difficulty with the ruling is that Parliament had specifically legislated, in section 38(6), that a child with sufficient competence could refuse to comply with a direction *from a court* that she undergo such an assessment. Thus Parliament appeared deliberately to have circumscribed the powers *of a court* in the face of a refusal from the child. The ruling in *South Glamorgan County Council v W and B* allowed the inherent jurisdiction to be used to give powers to the court which were denied it by statute. The court's justification for this was that when in a particular case other remedies within the Children Act 1989 have been used, and exhausted, and found not to bring about the result desired by the court then, in these exceptional circumstances, the court could have resort to the inherent jurisdiction. In this regard the ruling in *South Glamorgan County Council v W and B* parallels the pre-Children Act rulings that the powers of the High Court should be made available to a local authority when this is deemed necessary in the interests of a child.[1] However, it seems that the inherent jurisdiction may not be used as an alternative to the statutory framework in cases involving a local authority unless the authority request this, even though the result desired by the court cannot otherwise be achieved. Certainly the Court of Appeal appears to have held this view in *Nottinghamshire County Council v P*,[2] because it held that it was powerless to compel a local authority to take care proceedings, and further held that it could not make a care order of its own motion.

It is clear that an individual who seeks to question the manner in which a local authority are exercising their statutory powers and duties over a child in care cannot do this by having resort to the inherent jurisdiction. It is fundamental that the prerogative jurisdiction may not be used to interfere in the day-to-day administration by local authorities of their statutory powers and duties, and in *W v Hertfordshire County Council*[3] the House of Lords affirmed the profoundly important principle that the High Court may not intervene on the merits when Parliament has entrusted decision-making powers about children to local authorities.[4] This ruling is reflected in section 9(1) of the Children Act 1989, which prevents courts from making

1   *A v Liverpool City Council* [1981] 2 All ER 385; *W v Hertfordshire County Council* [1985] 2 All ER 301.
2   [1993] 2 FLR 134.
3   [1985] 2 All ER 301.
4   *A v Liverpool City Council* [1981] 2 All ER 385; *W v Hertfordshire County Council* [1985] 2 All ER 301.

a prohibited steps order or a specific issue order in respect of a child in local authority care. It is clear that this statutory prohibition cannot be circumvented through resort to the inherent jurisdiction.

Who decides in children cases?

It has been seen that where a person, including a local authority, is unhappy with a decision about the upbringing of a child the question whether that decision can be reconsidered by a court turns on a variety of rules. *W v Hertfordshire County Council,*[5] which occurred before the enactment of the Children Act 1989, illustrates in compelling form the draconian consequences for individuals caught up in a dispute about a child of being refused a hearing by a court. The mother of a little girl called Sarah started to ill-treat the child. She and her husband therefore approached their local authority to ask the authority to institute care proceedings with a view to Sarah being freed for adoption in further legal proceedings. A care order was obtained, but at this stage Sarah's grandparents, and an uncle and aunt, who had never rejected the child, learnt about what had happened. The aunt and uncle wished to look after Sarah, and the grandparents to have contact with her, but the local authority were determined on the adoption plan. As the law then was, the relatives had no right to apply for a court order which would bring the care order to an end. Nor did they have any right to be heard in the proceedings which would free Sarah to be adopted outside the family. They therefore took the only step then available to them, namely to make Sarah a ward of the High Court.

In the wardship proceedings Ewbank J made an order the effect of which was that the critical decisions for Sarah's future would be taken not by the local authority, but by the court. The court would hear all interested parties, including the members of the wider family and the local authority. Crucially, the care of Sarah would henceforward be for the court to decide, and the local authority would be required to exercise their statutory powers as directed by the court. However Ewbank J's ruling was overturned, first by the Court of Appeal, and then by the House of Lords, which ruled that a court did not have jurisdiction to hear the relatives' application. Consequently the future welfare of Sarah was a matter for the local authority. It was their decision whether to consult with the relatives, and to consider their alternative proposals, before making an application for an order freeing the child for adoption outside the family.

In *W v Hertfordshire County Council* Lord Bridge, after commenting that it was a highly distressing case, concluded his speech with an appeal to the local authority. He said: 'It will not, I hope, be misunderstood if I

5   Above.

suggest that in these circumstances the local authority might well feel it appropriate to reconsider Sarah's future with an open mind and with a full appreciation of the appellant's deep and natural concern for her.'[6] Lord Brightman said:

'It is tempting to ask the question whether in the particular circumstances of this case it is likely that the interests of Sarah would best be served by upholding the order of Ewbank J, or by leaving the local authority to operate the statutory scheme .... But I do not think that the question is legitimate. Whether the case is resolved by the local authority or is resolved by the High Court, the question before the resolver is precisely the same, namely whether a home with outside adopters as envisaged by the local authority, or a home with the uncle and aunt as sought by them, or some other solution, is in the best interests of Sarah. The arbiter chosen by Parliament to make that decision is the local authority. The court cannot properly ask itself whether it considers that it or the local authority is likely to make the better arbiter, for to ask that question would be to undermine the statutory scheme.'[7]

Thus the decision-making power was vested firmly in the local authority.

How the Children Act 1989 has affected the ruling in *W v Hertfordshire County Council*

The relatives in *W v Hertfordshire County Council*, when faced with obduracy from the local authority, could hope to obtain a different decision only if the power to determine Sarah's upbringing was given to a different decision-maker, namely a court. It has been seen in this chapter that the law has moved on since the ruling in *W v Hertfordshire County Council*, and that the Children Act 1989 now allows for greater accessibility to courts in children cases. Crucially, it has been seen that persons in the position of the grandparents and the uncle and aunt in Sarah's case would now be entitled to seek the leave of the court to apply for a residence order. If such an order were to be granted, they would acquire parental responsibility and the care order would come to an end. The court would have a discretion whether to grant such leave, and would be guided in the exercise of its discretion by the criteria in section 10(9) and its attendant case law.[8]

6 [1985] 2 All ER 301 at p 308.
7 Ibid, at p 312.
8 As described above.

Assuming that leave was granted, it would be for the *court* to determine how the welfare of the child would best be served, and not the local authority. An alternative solution to Sarah's future upbringing might have been that her welfare would better be promoted if she were to be allowed to live with members of her natural family, who loved her, and wished to look after her, rather than if she were to be placed for adoption outside the family. A guardian ad litem would be appointed to examine the local authority's proposals, and those of the relatives. The guardian ad litem's role would be to represent the interests of the child. A common feature of children cases is that there are choices to be made between viable alternatives, and often there is no obviously right decision. Rather one course of action will seem preferable to one decision-maker, and different decision will seem preferable to another, for a variety of reasons. Thus who has the right to have the final word about a child's upbringing is a matter of very great importance. How local authorities and courts have determined which decision is in the best interests of a child is considered in the next two chapters.

Chapter 3

Children needing services, care or protection

Interim care orders and assessment
Which order should be made—an interim order or a final order?
The role of the guardian ad litem
The final hearing in care proceedings—how courts have interpreted the
    threshold test
The meaning of 'significant' harm
Where a relative is caring, or offering to care, for the child
Re M (A Minor) (Care Order: Threshold Conditions)
Anticipating significant harm
The harm is attributable to a lack of reasonable parental care
The harm is attributable to the child's being beyond parental control
Standard of proof where child abuse is alleged
Orders on an application made in care proceedings
The implications of making a care order
Supervision orders
Contact with a child in care
Contact with a child in care and court orders
Contact and emergency protection orders
Contact and interim care orders
Regulating contact with a child in care
Contact, the local authority's plans and the court's jurisdiction

Chapter 3

Children needing services, care or protection

Children needing services, care or protection

Many persons caring for children are unable properly to fulfil their parental responsibilities without the assistance of services. The Children Act 1989 recognises that families sometimes require help in bringing up children, and it imposes specific duties and powers on local authorities to facilitate this process. The Act also recognises that children who need care or protection may sometimes be the same children who need the provision of services. It will be seen that the guiding principle lying behind the duty to provide services is to promote the upbringing of children by their families;[1] that these services should be used to prevent children from suffering ill-treatment or neglect;[2] and that some services should be designed to reduce the need to bring care proceedings.[3] Thus the inter-relationship between providing services for children in need, and protecting children from suffering significant harm, is firmly established. The importance of this inter-relationship should not be underestimated; it influences not only the manner in which local authorities exercise their statutory powers and duties, but also the way in which courts approach care proceedings.

Part III of the Children Act 1989 is concerned with the duty of every local authority to provide support for children and their families. Much of this Part, which is developed under Part 1 of Schedule 2, is devoted to the duty of every local authority to provide services for children in need and their powers to provide services for other children. The Act itself provides only part of the legal and administrative framework within which services for children and their families are provided. A large body of regulations

---

1 Children Act 1989, s.17(1); further statutory references in this chapter are to the Children Act 1989 unless otherwise stated.
2 Sch. 2, para 4.
3 Ibid, para 7.

and guidance have been issued which give detailed instructions on how this Part (and other Parts) of the Act are to be implemented.[4]

Children in need should normally be brought up by their families

Fundamental to the thinking in Part III of the Children Act 1989 is the principle that it is normally in the best interests of children to be brought up by their own families. Section 17, the opening provision, states that—

'(1) It shall be the general duty of every local authority...—
(a) to safeguard and promote the welfare of children within their area who are in need; and
(b) so far as is consistent with that duty, to promote the upbringing of such children by their families,
by providing a range and level of services appropriate to those children's needs.'

Who are 'children in need'?

Section 17(10) provides that a child shall be taken to be in need if—

'(a) he is unlikely to achieve or maintain, or to have the opportunity of achieving or maintaining, a reasonable standard of health or development without the provision for him of services by a local authority under this Part;
(b) his health or development is likely to be significantly impaired, or further impaired, without the provision for him of such services; or
(c) he is disabled,
and "family", in relation to such a child, includes any person who has parental responsibility for the child and any other person with whom he has been living.'

Section 17(11) explains what is meant by 'disabled', 'development' and 'health'. It provides—

4   For the status of regulations and guidance, see *The Care of Children, Principles and Practice of Regulations and Guidance* (HMSO). Some details concerning the provision of services under Part III, the regulation of child-minding, private foster care, community homes and voluntary homes are beyond the scope of this book. For greater detail, see the Department of Health volumes on *The Children Act 1989 Guidance and Regulations* (HMSO, 1991). See too M D A Freeman *Children, Their Families and the Law* (Macmillan, 1992); A Bainham *Children The Modern Law* (Family Law, 1993); B Hoggett *Parents and Children* (Sweet and Maxwell, 1993).

'For the purposes of this Part, a child is disabled if he is blind, deaf or dumb or suffers from mental disorder of any kind or is substantially and permanently handicapped by illness, injury or congenital deformity or such other disability as may be prescribed; and in this Part—
    "development" means physical, intellectual, emotional, social or behavioural development; and
    "health" means physical or mental health.'

Thus it can be seen that the definition of a child in need focuses both on a child who is disabled, and on a child who is at risk of impaired health or development unless preventative steps are taken. These steps may include not only the provision of services for the child himself, but also their provision for any member of his family, if they are provided with a view to safeguarding or promoting the child's welfare.[5]

Provision of services—duties and discretion

Part III and Schedule 2 use the language of 'shall' and 'may' when specifying the nature of the services to be provided by a local authority. The difference in the words is important—'shall' means that a local authority *must* provide the service; 'may' gives them a discretion. Where a local authority fail to provide a service for a child in need which they 'shall' provide, then they are in breach of their statutory duty. However, discretion is also built into many of the 'shall' provisions; often the provision made must either be 'reasonable' or 'as is appropriate.' Because local authority social services departments are under a duty not only to provide services for children in need in their area, but also for other needy members of the community, and because they are operating with limited budgets, standards of reasonableness and appropriateness may sometimes be low.[6] Limited budgets may also affect the ability of local authorities to make full use of their powers under section 17(6) to give assistance in kind or in exceptional circumstances in cash.

A local authority 'shall' provide day care for pre-school and other children in need; they 'may' provide such care for other children.[7] They 'shall' provide accommodation for specified children in need, including a child who has reached the age of 16 whose welfare is otherwise likely to be seriously

---

5   S.17(3).
6   Hence the frequent complaint that the principles in Part III are excellent, but that the resources to implement them have not been provided. See too *R v Royal Borough of Kingston upon Thames, ex p T* [1994] 1 FLR 798, where the local authority were unable to accommodate two Vietnamese sisters together, partly because of resource constraints.
7   S.18; this is qualified by 'as is appropriate'.

prejudiced; they 'may' provide accommodation for other children.[8] They 'shall' provide family centres in relation to children within their area[9] where the child, his parents, any person with parental responsibility and any other person who is looking after him may attend for occupational, social, cultural or recreational activities; advice, guidance and counselling; and where such a person may be provided with accommodation while he is receiving such advice, guidance or counselling.[10] In relation to children in need who are living with their families, a local authority 'shall make such provision as they consider appropriate' for the following services: advice, guidance and counselling; occupational, social, cultural or recreational activities; home help (which may include laundry facilities); facilities for, or assistance with, travelling to and from home for the purpose of taking advantage of any other service provided under the Act or of any similar service; and assistance to enable the child concerned and his family to have a holiday.[11] They 'shall' also take reasonable steps designed to prevent any children within their area suffering ill-treatment or neglect, and to reduce the need to bring care or other legal proceedings with respect to such children.[12] Where it appears that a child is suffering, or is likely to suffer, ill-treatment at the hands of another person who is living on the same premises the local authority 'may' assist that person to obtain alternative accommodation, and such assistance may include the provision of cash.[13]

There are many children in need, and a local authority may not have the resources to provide a service which has been requested; or they may have other reasons for failing or refusing to provide a service. Each local authority is required to establish a procedure for considering any represent-ations, including any complaint, made to them by certain specified persons. Where such a person is dissatisfied with the provision offered by the local authority he or she should make use of this procedure. A complainant will not be given leave to pursue an action in judicial review unless this remedy has first been exhausted.[14]

Co-operation between different authorities

The effective provision of services for children and their families may require inter-departmental collaboration within a local authority at all levels. The Act promotes a structure which not only requires different local

---

8   S.20(1), (3), (4), (5).
9   Not merely children in need.
10   Sch. 2, para 9; qualified by 'as they consider appropriate'.
11   Ibid, para 8.
12   Ibid, paras 4 and 7.
13   Ibid, para 5.
14   *R v Royal Borough of Kingston upon Thames, ex p T* [1994] 1 FLR 798.

authorities to assist one another, but also requires different bodies within the same local authority to co-operate with one another, to assist the local social services department to fulfil their general duty to provide services for children in need. Section 27 provides that a local authority may request help in the exercise of any of their functions under Part III from any local authority, local education authority, local housing authority, health authority or National Health Service trust, or any other authorised person. An authority whose help is so requested 'shall' comply with the request 'if it is compatible with their own statutory or other duties and obligations and does not unduly prejudice the discharge of any of their functions.'[15]

The policy of the Act is to encourage corporate arrangements and clear procedures with respect to inter-departmental collaboration. Guidance issued under the Act clearly contemplates that a social services department within a local authority can request help from another department within the same local authority.[16] At one stage this policy appeared to have been severely undermined by *R v Tower Hamlets London Borough Council, ex p Byas*,[17] which concerned a request made by a social services department for assistance from the housing department of the same local authority in providing housing for some children in need, and their parents. The Court of Appeal ruled that section 27 applies only to requests for help from other local authorities, and that a local authority cannot request help from itself under that section. However, this restricted construction of section 27 appears to have been wrong. In *R v Northavon District Council, ex p Smith*,[18] where a similar request had been made under section 27 by a county council to a district housing authority, Lord Templeman said, 'the present appeal concerns two authorities...Where one and the same authority is both housing authority and social services authority, the same problems of the interaction of the two statutory codes would arise as between the housing department and the social services department of that authority.'[19] Their Lordships do not appear to have had their attention drawn to the ruling in *R v Tower Hamlets London Borough Council, ex p Byas*, and strictly Lord Templeman's statement is obiter only. However, it is suggested that his statement must be right, and that the Court of Appeal's construction of section 27 was wrong.[20]

15 S.27(2).
16 *The Children Act 1989 Guidance and Regulations* Vol 2, para 1.13.
17 [1993] 2 FLR 605; see too *R v Oldham Metropolitan Borough Council, ex p Garlick* [1993] AC 509. For comment on these and other cases on the link between the Children Act 1989 and the Housing Act 1985 see Gilbert *Housing for Children* (1993) 5 JCL 166.
18 [1994] 3 All ER 313.
19 Ibid, at p 318.
20 The language of s.47(9)-(12) is similar, though not identical, to that used in s. 27. S. 47 is concerned with inter-agency co-operation where there is a suspicion of child abuse. The crucial wording in s.27(3) which refers to any local authority and any local housing authority is identical with that in s.47(11). It is inconceivable that the duty to co-operate

Clearly there are difficult issues for both social services departments and housing authorities where children and their parents are threatened with homelessness. In *R v Northavon District Council, ex p Smith*, the housing authority decided that the applicant and his wife were homeless, and in priority need because they had five children, but that they had become homeless intentionally within section 60(1) of the Housing Act 1985. The housing authority therefore declined to provide accommodation for the applicant and his family in response to a request made under section 27 by the social services department. The House of Lords ruled that section 27 did not enable a local authority to require a housing authority to exercise its powers to provide housing. Instead it imposed a duty of co-operation between social services and housing authorities, both of which had together to do the best they could to carry out their respective responsibilities for children and housing.[1]

Provision of accommodation for children

It has been seen that the primary purpose of the provision of services under Part III is to keep children and their families together. However, sometimes this may not be possible and a child may need instead to live away from home. Local authorities have a duty to provide accommodation for certain children. Section 20(1) provides—

'Every local authority shall provide accommodation for any child in need within their area who appears to them to require accommodation as a result of—

(a) there being no person who has parental responsibility for him;

(b) his being lost or having been abandoned; or

(c) the person who has been caring for him being prevented (whether or not permanently, and for whatever reason) from providing him with suitable accommodation or care.'

Subsection (4) provides—

'A local authority may provide accommodation for any child within their area (even though a person who has parental responsibility

---

under s.47 is imposed only when two separate local authorities are involved; such a construction would entirely defeat the requirement that agencies in the same authority work together in matters relating to child protection. It is suggested that not only should the same reasoning apply to children in need of services, but also that, for consistency, ss.27 and 47 should be construed in the same manner.

1   The issue of homelessness is further discussed in ch 5.

for him is able to provide him with accommodation) if they consider that to do so would safeguard and promote his welfare.'[2]

It can be seen that a range of children are covered by those for whom there is a duty to provide accommodation, but that they all must fall within the definition of a 'child in need'. The discretion to accommodate a child arises when the local authority consider that to do so would safeguard and promote his welfare. The influence of the notion that the child himself should be involved in important decisions which are made about his upbringing can be seen in section 20(6), which requires a local authority to take reasonable steps to ascertain the child's wishes and feelings on the matter, and to give them due consideration having regard to his age and understanding. Clearly, whilst the child may have strong negative wishes and feelings about whether he should be accommodated at all, the practicalities of his situation may appear to leave room for no alternative. It is in this regard that attempts to involve members of the child's extended family who have not previously been looking after him may be of great importance in preserving the child's family links, and in keeping him out of foster care or a residential home. Where this cannot be arranged, it is important that the child's views on the type of accommodation to be provided for him are also taken into account.

The voluntary nature of accommodation

The philosophy of Part III is to encourage local authorities to work in partnership with parents and persons with parental responsibility, and to promote mutual confidence and trust. The thinking is that parents and others should be able to turn to local authorities for positive help and support in bringing up their children, and that they should not have cause to fear that they may lose their children into state care if they take advantage of the services provided. Such fear may be very real in a case where a person with parental responsibility is encouraged to agree to his child being accommodated under section 20, because he or she thereby loses a measure of control over the child's upbringing. Reassurance is provided by subsections (7) and (8) which together make it clear that accommodation under section 20 may only be provided, or continue to be provided, if the persons with parental responsibility for the child are willing to agree.

Section 20(7) provides that—

---

2 Accommodation for certain children aged over 16 and up to the age of 21 may also be provided under sub-ss.(3) and (5).

'A local authority may not provide accommodation under this section for any child if any person who—
(a) has parental responsibility for him; and
(b) is willing and able to—
(i) provide accommodation for him; or
(ii) arrange for accommodation to be provided for him, objects.'

It can be seen that section 20(7) does not require a local authority to obtain the consent of persons with parental responsibility before a child is received into accommodation. Such a provision would prove unworkable for the practical reason that it may not always be possible to contact such persons. However, where there is a positive objection from a person with parental responsibility, the local authority may not accommodate the child where the objecting person can make his own arrangements for the child.

It is not clear how suitable the accommodation arrangements offered by the objecting person with parental responsibility must be. Where the local authority take the view that they are entirely unsuitable, the question then arises whether the authority are entitled to accommodate the child in the face of such an offer. It is suggested that the local authority are not so entitled. The accommodation provisions in section 20 are built around the principle that the arrangement is voluntary. Should the local authority go ahead and accommodate the child in the face of an objection from a person with parental responsibility, there is nothing to prevent the objecting person from removing the child immediately. In this regard, section 20(8) gives a person with parental responsibility an unqualified right to remove the child. It provides that—

'Any person who has parental responsibility for a child may at any time remove the child from accommodation provided by or on behalf of the local authority under this section'.

It is therefore suggested that the same voluntary principle applies to section 20(7), and that the local authority are not entitled to accommodate a child where they disapprove of the accommodation arrangements proposed. Where the local authority are unhappy with this outcome, and where they have reasonable cause to believe that the child is likely to suffer significant harm if he is not accommodated by them, or if he is removed from accommodation which they are providing, they should take steps to obtain the authority to keep the child by applying for an emergency protection order, or for an order in care proceedings.[3]

3   See below.

Exceptions to the voluntary principle

The uncompromising language in which subsections (7) and (8) are couched makes it clear that the accommodation arrangements made under section 20 are entirely voluntary. However, there are three qualifications to this principle: the subsections only apply to persons with parental responsibility; they do not apply where a residence order, or an order under the High Court's inherent jurisdiction, has been made; and they do not apply when the child concerned is 16.

The unmarried father

The first of these exceptions places an unmarried father in a vulnerable position because he is usually a parent without parental responsibility.[4] An unmarried father has no enforceable right to object to his child being accommodated, and he is not entitled to remove his child from accommodation at any time. However, the position of the unmarried father may not be as bleak as the one which is sometimes painted.[5] The general duty of a local authority is to promote the upbringing of children by their families,[6] and they are not required to receive the child into accommodation when a family member is offering to look after the child. In a case where the child is already being accommodated they can bring the accommodation arrangement to an end, or where they continue to accommodate the child,[7] they 'shall' make arrangements to enable an accommodated child to live with a parent unless that would not be reasonably practicable or consistent with his welfare. Thus an unmarried father should only find himself in conflict with the local authority when placement with him appears to the authority to be against the interests of the child. Where this is the case, the father's remedy would be to apply for a residence order.[8] In determining the merits of his application, the court would give paramount consideration to the welfare of the child, but normally it would give considerable weight to the fact that a parent was offering to provide a home for a child in a case where the alternative offered was foster care, or accommodation in a residential home.[9]

---

4   See ch 1.
5   See A Bainham *Children: The New Law* (Family Law, 1990) para 4.25; A Bainham *Children The Modern Law* (Family Law, 1993) pp 345-7.
6   S.17(1), above.
7   Under s.23(6).
8   He is entitled to apply by virtue of s.10(4)(a): see ch 2.
9   On the application of the welfare principle generally, see ch 4.

Where there is a residence order, or an order made by the High Court

A parent with parental responsibility is placed in a similar position to an unmarried father where there is a residence, or other, order settling the arrangements as to the person with whom the child is to live. Section 20(9) provides that—

> 'Subsections (7) and (8) do not apply while any person—
> (a) in whose favour a residence order is in force with respect to the child; or
> (b) who has care of the child by virtue of an order made in the exercise of the High Court's inherent jurisdiction with respect to children,
> agrees to the child being looked after in accommodation provided by or on behalf of the local authority.'

Where more than one person has the benefit of a residence order all such persons must agree.[10]

The thinking lying behind subsection (9) is that it is the voice of the person who has had the benefit of the residence order which should prevail in dealings with the local authority. Where there has been an estrangement between parents, between parents and others, or where some other reason has led to a residence order being made, a court must have decided that it is better for the child to make a residence order than not to make an order.[11] The thinking is that it is normally in the interests of the child that the person with the residence order should be able to make arrangements about where the child will live, including placing him with a local authority, despite the fact that a parent or other person with parental responsibility objects.

Subsection (9) has been the subject of criticism on the ground that it undermines the notion of continuing parental responsibility. It has been said that the purpose of a residence order is simply to regulate where the child is to live but otherwise to leave intact the full parental responsibility of both parents.[12] It is suggested that this criticism of subsection (9) is flawed because it fails to draw an analogy between a person with a residence order using local authority accommodation and that person choosing to make his own private arrangements to place the child with a relative or other person. In the latter situation, the person with a residence order is able to delegate parental responsibility, and make such an arrangement

---

10 S.20(10).
11 S.1(5): see ch 2; or the High Court has intervened in the exercise of its inherent jurisdiction.
12 A Bainham *Children the New Law* (Family Law, 1990) para 4.26; A Bainham *Children the Modern Law* (Family Law, 1993) pp 345-7.

in the confident knowledge that a parent with parental responsibility is not entitled to remove the child. Such a removal would violate the incompatibility principle in section 2(8).[13] Similarly, section 20(9) enables a person with a residence order to feel free to place the child in local authority accommodation without fear that another person with parental responsibility will be entitled to remove him. Treating local authority accommodation as different from making private arrangements is arguably to perpetuate the pejorative association between turning to the state for the provision of services for children rather than making one's own arrangements.

In fact the reality is that persons with a residence order are in a relatively weak position when approaching a local authority to accommodate a child in comparison with the situation where they make their own private arrangements. Where there is a residence order, but where a parent with parental responsibility is offering to look after the child, the local authority's position is identical to the one described where an unmarried father is offering to care for the child. The local authority are only obliged to accommodate the child where they take the view that this would be in the child's best interests. Where the local authority do so agree, a parent who is aggrieved by the decision should apply under section 10 for the discharge of the existing residence order and for a residence order to be made in his or her favour.

Where the child is 16

The third exception to the voluntary principle is where a child who has reached the age of 16 agrees to being accommodated. Section 20(11) provides that in these circumstances subsections (7) and (8) do not apply. Subsection (11) is an important example of how the law has moved towards allowing a child to determine his own upbringing in the face of objections from a parent or other person with parental responsibility. It respects the right of the competent child to be treated as an autonomous individual as established in *Gillick v West Norfolk and Wisbech Area Health Authority*,[14] and gives the decision-making power about the child's future upbringing to the child. It assumes that the child of 16 is old enough, and has reached a sufficient level of understanding, to make an informed choice about where he wishes to live.[15] In many cases this will be correct. The thinking is that a child of 16 is approaching full adulthood so that he should be entitled to

13 See ch 1.
14 [1985] 3 All ER 402.
15 For further discussion of a child's competence to make decisions about his or her own upbringing, see ch 1.

leave home and to seek assistance from a local authority in obtaining properly regulated accommodation. Where the child is already being accommodated, he should be entitled to remain with the persons with whom he has been living in the face of parental objection. Subsection (11) also assists the local authority because they need not consider instituting care proceedings to assist the mature child in a case where the persons with parental responsibility refuse to agree to the child being accommodated.

The disadvantage of subsection (11) is that it may sometimes place parents and others with parental responsibility in an intolerable position in a case where they do not wish the child to be accommodated. The fact that a child chooses to put himself into, or to remain in, local authority accommodation may be a matter of very great concern to them. Children being looked after by a local authority come from a variety of backgrounds, some of which are very disturbed. An accommodated child who comes from a 'good home' may live on premises where he or she associates with children who have been involved in prostitution, drug abuse and various types of crime. The child's desire to remain in accommodation may be because these alternative forms of life style seem attractive at an age which is notoriously associated with rebellion against parental norms. Whilst those charged with the duty of looking after older accommodated children make every effort to ensure that such children are not involved in unhealthy, dangerous and criminal forms of activity, there may be little they can do to prevent a determined child from becoming so involved. Local authorities do not have the power to restrict the liberty of delinquent children whom they are looking after unless given specific authority to do so by a court.[16]

Whilst it has been observed that, since the ruling in *Gillick*, 'children will now have, in wider measure than ever before, that most dangerous but most precious of rights: the right to make their own mistakes,'[17] it is suggested that, during a child's minority, such rights should not include those which may lead to the permanent impairment of the child's health, to imprisonment, or even death. In an extreme case of this kind, a child's desire to be accommodated is associated with reasons which an objective observer would characterise as being against the child's best interests. It would seem that the obvious solution would be for the persons with parental responsibility to apply for a residence order, as this would have the effect of overriding the child's decision to be accommodated. However, such persons are normally powerless to obtain a residence order once a child is 16. Section 9(7) provides that a court shall not make any section 8 order with respect to a child who has reached the age of 16 unless it is satisfied that the circumstances of the case are exceptional. It is suggested that a

16 S.25 enables a court to make a secure accommodation order on specified grounds for a maximum period of three months.

17 J Eekelaar *The Emergence of Children's Rights* (1986) 6 OxJLS 161 at p 182.

person with parental responsibility should either seek to persuade a court to treat the case as exceptional under section 10(7),[18] or should seek the leave of the High Court to invoke the exercise of the inherent jurisdiction.[19] Once decision-making power was taken from the child and placed in the court, the court's decision would be determined by the view it took of the child's best interests, in relation to which the child's wishes and feelings would be but one element.[20]

Accommodated children who need care or protection

Providing accommodation for a child forms part of a local authority's strategy to provide services for a child in need, to prevent him suffering ill-treatment or neglect, and to reduce the need to bring care or other proceedings about his upbringing.[1] In this regard, accommodation may be used by a local authority as an alternative to bringing care proceedings in a case where there are concerns and fears about the manner in which a child is being looked after. Whilst the voluntary nature of accommodation arrangements made under section 20 is in keeping with the partnership philosophy of the Act, in some cases subsections (7) and (8) may be difficult to reconcile with a local authority's child protection duties.

It has been seen that a local authority cannot prevent a child's removal from accommodation where they are unable to persuade a person with parental responsibility to agree to this. Where such a person is obdurate, the local authority must either release the child to that person's care or they must institute proceedings to obtain the authority to retain the child. Where the local authority have reasonable cause to believe that the child is suffering significant harm, or that he is likely to suffer significant harm if he is removed from his present accommodation, they may make an application in care proceedings for an interim care order.[2] Where the local authority have reasonable cause to believe that the child is likely to suffer significant harm if he does not remain in the place in which he is then being accommodated, and the situation is one of emergency, the authority may apply for an emergency protection order.[3] Either order will authorise the local authority to retain care of the child for a limited period[4] while an

---

18 It would probably be wise to ask a lower court to transfer the case to the High Court.
19 See ch 2.
20 See generally ch 4 on the application of the welfare principle.
1   Including criminal proceedings: Sch. 2, para 7.
2   S.38(1): see below.
3   S.44(1)(a)(ii): see below.
4   Under an interim care order the maximum period is eight weeks: s.38(4)(a); under an emergency protection order it is eight days: s.45(1).

assessment is made of whether an application for a care order should be further pursued.

In an emergency, where a person is demanding instantly to remove the child, there will be a short period between the demand to remove the child and the obtaining of an emergency protection order from a court.[5] The question then arises whether the local authority may refuse to release the child into the care of the person exercising his right of removal bearing in mind that section 20(8) states that the child may be removed 'at any time'. There is no authority on this point. It is suggested that the local authority might be protected for a brief period by section 22(3). This places a general duty on a local authority which is looking after a child to safeguard and promote the child's welfare. Alternatively it is suggested that they could rely on section 3(5). This permits a person who does not have parental responsibility for the child, but who has his care, to do what is reasonable in all the circumstances for the purpose of safeguarding or promoting the child's welfare.[6] There are overwhelming policy reasons why either section 22(3), or section 3(5), or both, should apply. If the position were otherwise, and the local authority were compelled immediately to hand the child over, the child might suffer the feared significant harm which had formed the basis of the application for the emergency protection order. This reasoning is assisted by the Court of Appeal's ruling in *F v Wirral Metropolitan Borough Council*[7] that there is no separate tort of interference with parental rights. If a local authority were to be sued for retaining a child in breach of section 20(8) the plaintiff would have the burden of establishing that a tort had been committed against the *child*, and not against the person with parental responsibility.

A separate possibility might be to involve the police. A constable has emergency powers to prevent the removal of a child from the place in which he is being accommodated where he has reasonable cause to believe that the child would otherwise be likely to suffer significant harm.[8] The advantage of invoking police powers over applying for an emergency protection order is that the police will attend at the situation and no court is involved. Whereas an application for an emergency protection order must either be made at a court, or at the home of a magistrate or judge.

The accommodation plan

Some of the difficulties outlined above might better be overcome by careful forward planning between the local authority and the persons with parental responsibility. Regulations provide that a scheme of arrangements should

---

5   In this context a court includes a single magistrate or judge to whom an application may be made outside court hours.
6   See ch 1.
7   [1991] 2 All ER 648; for a useful comment see A Bainham (1990) 3 JCL 3.
8   S.46(1).

be agreed between the local authority and a person with parental responsibility for the child whenever a child is accommodated.[9] This scheme, which
must be drawn up in writing,[10] should include details about 'the expected
duration of arrangements and the steps which should apply to bring the
arrangements to an end, including arrangements for rehabilitation of the
child with the person with whom he was living before the voluntary
arrangements were made or some other suitable person ...'[11] This type of
planning enables the local authority and persons with parental responsibility to agree in advance about any problems which might arise through
the strict enforcement of rights under section 20(8). For example, a parent
might be prepared to agree that the best interests of a child are not normally
served by a precipitate and unplanned removal from accommodation, and
that at least a brief period of notice is normally better for the child.
Furthermore, the guidance on agreements issued by the Department of
Health suggests that it should include a statement of the steps each party
should take if the other party were to decide to change the agreement. In
this context the guidance suggests that the local authority should warn
the persons with parental responsibility that the local authority would
consider applying for an emergency protection order if one of them were to
decide to take action which was harmful to the child.[12]

The advantage of this type of formal planning between a local authority
and persons with parental responsibility is that it reinforces the philosophy
that local authorities, parents and others should work together in partnership, and that each should trust the other. In this regard, warning parents
and others in a written agreement that precipitate removal might lead to
an application for an emergency protection order is honestly to reflect the
reality. It tells them in no uncertain terms that a 'voluntary' arrangement
might be transformed into a compulsory arrangement if their co-operation
is withdrawn. Injecting this note of realism into accommodation arrangements may better promote the child's sense of security with his current
carers, and the child can be reassured that his wishes and feelings will be
taken into account before there is any sudden change of plan.

The disadvantage of agreements of this kind is that terms which require
persons with parental responsibility to give a period of notice before
removing a child from accommodation[13] undermine the principle that the
arrangement is voluntary. Parliament was insistent that no notice period
should be included in section 20(8) in the face of very great pressure to
include at least a brief period.[14] Local authorities are in a much stronger

9   Arrangements for Placement of Children (General) Regulations 1991, reg.3 and Sch. 4.
10   Reg.3(5).
11   Sch. 4 para 9.
12   *The Children Act 1989 Guidance and Regulation* Vol 3, para 2.66.
13   As suggested in para 2.66 of the *Guidance*, above.
14   *House of Commons Debate, Standing Committee B*, 18 May 1989, cols 137-154; *House of Lords, Official Report,* 20 December 1988, col 1335.

position than parents when suggesting what terms should be included, and they are likely to tell parents what the arrangements will be, however much this is couched in the language of mutual agreement. There is a risk that written accommodation agreements will take on a spurious authority in the eyes of those who are party to them, so that local authorities may feel that they can 'contract out' of the law's provisions, and parents and others may feel 'bound' by the terms, and not be aware of their rights under section 20(8).

Investigating whether a child is suffering, or is likely to suffer, significant harm

It has been seen that children in need are those children who are disabled, or those children whose health or development will be put at risk without the provision of services.[15] An even more serious situation arises where there is reasonable cause to believe or suspect that a child is suffering, or is likely to suffer, significant harm. When such a suspicion is brought to the attention of a local authority they are under a duty to investigate. Section 47(1) provides—

'Where a local authority—
(a) are informed that a child who lives, or is found, in their area—
   (i) is the subject of an emergency protection order; or
   (ii) is in police protection; or
(b) have reasonable cause to suspect that a child who lives, or is found, in their area is suffering, or is likely to suffer, significant harm,
the authority shall make, or cause to be made, such inquiries as they consider necessary to enable them to decide whether they should take any action to safeguard and promote the child's welfare.'[16]

The value of different agencies working together in the early detection and prevention of child abuse is emphasised in the guidance issued under the Act.[17] Each local authority, under the auspices of their area child protection committee,[18] must draw up child protection procedures to which

15 S.17(10).
16 The local authority have the identical duty where they themselves have obtained an emergency protection order with respect to a child: s.47(2).
17 *Working Together under the Children Act 1989* (DOH, 1991); the absolute necessity for inter-agency co-operation has been demonstrated many times in the reports of official inquiries into the deaths of children where child protection procedures have failed.
18 Which are multi-disciplinary bodies.

all collaborating agencies and persons are expected to adhere. Section 47(9) and (11) emphasise the importance of inter-agency co-operation by placing a duty on specified persons to assist the local authority in conducting their inquiry.[19] The focus of the inquiry must be directed in particular towards establishing whether the local authority should initiate any court proceedings or exercise any of their other powers under the Act.[20]

The conduct of an investigation under section 47 requires not only the co-operation of other agencies, but also the co-operation of persons with parental responsibility for the child. Section 47 does not give a local authority any coercive powers. There is nothing in section 47 which empowers a local authority to enter premises, despite the fact that one of their duties when conducting their investigation is to take such steps as are reasonably practicable to obtain access to the child.[1] Rather, the local authority are reliant on the person who has care of the child allowing them to see the child. However, co-operation from such a person may be forthcoming when it is explained to him that if a person conducting an inquiry under section 47 is refused access, or denied information as to the child's whereabouts, 'the authority *shall*[2] apply for an emergency protection order, a child assessment order, a care order or a supervision order with respect to the child unless they are satisfied that his welfare can be satisfactorily safeguarded without them doing so.'[3] It is suggested that only rarely should a local authority be so satisfied without actually seeing and talking to the child. Tragically, many children who have died at the hands of those looking after them are those children to whom social workers and others have not insisted on having proper access.[4]

Once a suspicion has been raised that a child is suffering, or is likely to suffer, significant harm the local authority have a duty to consider whether some kind of continuing surveillance of the child is necessary. If, at the conclusion of their inquiries, the local authority decide not to apply for a court order in respect of the child, they must decide whether it is appropriate to review the case at a later date and, if so, set a date for the review.[5]

---

19 Unless it would be unreasonable in all the circumstances of the case, s.47(10). The persons specified are any local authority, any local education authority, any local housing authority, any health authority, and any other person authorised by the Secretary of State. Surprisingly, and arguably wrongly, the police are omitted from this list.

20 S.47(3).

1 S.47(4).

2 Emphasis added.

3 S.47(6).

4 See particularly *A Child in Mind: The Report on the Death of Kimberley Carlile*, Greenwich London Borough Council (1987). See too *A Child in Trust: Report on the Death of Jasmine Beckford*, London Borough of Brent (1988); *Whose Child: Report on the Death of Tyra Henry*, London Borough of Greenwich (1987); *Child Abuse: A Study of Inquiry Reports 1973-1981* (HMSO, 1982).

5 S.47(7).

There may be no need for legal intervention even where significant harm is discovered. Where parents and other persons caring for the child are willing to work with social workers and other professionals in addressing the concerns which have arisen, it may be decided that the child can be adequately protected if he remains at home while work with the family is attempted.[6]

Can a court prohibit a section 47 investigation?

In *D v D (County Court Jurisdiction: Injunctions)*[7] a county court judge attempted to prevent a local authority and the police from pursuing their inquiries under section 47 by issuing an injunction against both. There were proceedings before the judge for a residence order, and he was clearly incensed at the manner in which the local authority were carrying out their investigation at a time when the court was seised of matters relating to the welfare of the children. On appeal the judge was held to have exceeded his jurisdiction in issuing the injunctions. However, the Court of Appeal stated, obiter, that the judge could have made a prohibited steps order to prevent a person with parental responsibility from allowing the child to be interviewed, or examined in a way which the court thought would be detrimental to his welfare. Thus although a court has no power to prohibit an investigation by a local authority, it can frustrate it by prohibiting a parent from consenting to the child being investigated. It has been seen that the co-operation of persons caring for the child is normally needed for a section 47 inquiry to be effective. Were a court to exercise powers to prohibit such co-operation the inquiry would almost certainly have to be abandoned. Unless the court is entirely confident that it is in possession of all relevant information about the child and his family, it is suggested that it is a very risky step indeed for a court to seek to inhibit a local authority from carrying out their investigative duties. The main purpose of a section 47 inquiry is to discover whether there are grounds for initiating care or other proceedings. Without the necessary evidence, any application for an order will inevitably fail. Whilst in *D v D (County Court Jurisdiction: Injunctions)* itself the judge may have had good cause to be critical of the local authority,[8] it is suggested that the power to issue a prohibited steps order in this context should be exercised with the greatest of caution.[9]

---

6   See below about placing a child on a child protection register.
7   [1993] 2 FLR 802.
8   The Court of Appeal were divided on this.
9   *D v D (County Court Jurisdiction: Injunctions)* is also discussed in ch 2 p 58.

The power of a court to direct an investigation

One of the times when the welfare of a child may come under scrutiny is when an application is made to a court in family proceedings. A question with respect to the welfare of a child may arise in any family proceedings, but the most common occasion is when persons are divorcing. Parties to a divorce are required to provide a fairly extensive statement of arrangements about the future upbringing of any children of their family who are under the age of 16. This statement will be scrutinised by the court, and in every case the court must consider whether it should exercise any of its powers under the Act with respect to any of the children.[10] Sometimes these arrangements give rise to concern, or even alarm, and the court may take the view that the position of a child should be further investigated. One response is to request a welfare officer's report under section 7. Such a request may be made in any case where the court feels in need of assistance in determining the welfare of a child. Where there is serious concern about the upbringing of a child, such that the court takes the view that it may be appropriate to make a care or supervision order with respect to him, section 37 provides that the court may direct a local authority to undertake an investigation of the child's circumstances.

In responding to this direction, and when undertaking their investigation, the local authority must consider whether they should apply for a care or supervision order, provide services or assistance for the child or his family, or take any other action with respect to the child.[11] Because it is the court which is instigating the inquiry, it may wish to specify particular matters which it would like the local authority to look into. In *Re H (A Minor) (Section 37 Direction)*,[12] which concerned a residence order application by a lesbian couple who were looking after an eight-month-old child under what amounted to a quasi-surrogacy and backdoor adoption arrangement, Scott Baker J particularly wanted the local authority to consider the emotional and other difficulties the child was likely to face as she grew up. He asked the local authority to inform him of whether the applicants were likely to be able to handle such difficulties; what counselling or psychiatric help might be available; and if such difficulties could not be overcome with help, how these should be weighed against the possibility of removing the child from her present carers. Scott Baker J stated that a child's circumstances should be widely construed, and should include any situation which may have bearing on the child being likely to suffer significant harm in the future.

10 Matrimonial Causes Act 1973, s.41(1); in exceptional circumstances the court may direct that the decree nisi is not made absolute: s.41(2).
11 Children Act 1989, s.37(2).
12 [1993] 2 FLR 541.

Where a local authority undertake an investigation under a direction given under section 37 and decide not to apply for a care or supervision order, they must give the court their reasons. They must also inform the court of any service or assistance which they have provided, or intend to provide, for the child and his family, and of any other action which they have taken, or propose to take, in relation to the child.[13] However, it was held in *Nottinghamshire County Council v P*[14] that a court has no power to direct the local authority to initiate care proceedings where it is not satisfied with the authority's reasons for failing to do so. *Nottinghamshire County Council v P* is an example of a case where who had the final decision-making power was crucial to its outcome. On the one hand the trial judge and the Court of Appeal were in no doubt that a care order was necessary to prevent the children from suffering further significant harm; on the other hand the local authority were obdurate in their refusal to pursue an application for a care order. The decision-making power lay with the local authority and, as Sir Stephen Brown P said, 'if a local authority doggedly resists taking the steps which are appropriate to the case of children at risk of suffering significant harm it appears that the court is powerless'.[15]

Child assessment orders

It has been seen that an assessment of whether a child is suffering, or is likely to suffer, significant harm can normally only be made if the child is seen and examined and, where appropriate, interviewed. Persons with parental responsibility, and other persons caring for the child, also need to be interviewed, and their part in the cause for concern about the child needs to be explained to them. However, such persons are sometimes unco-operative in allowing access to the child; or they may prevent a proper assessment from taking place by refusing to allow the child to be medically, or otherwise, examined. Where access is denied, or the person making enquiries is denied information as to the child's whereabouts, the local authority must apply for a court order unless they are satisfied that the child's welfare can otherwise be satisfactorily safeguarded.[16] It is suggested that this latter response should be most unusual, because it is a dangerously optimistic reaction to a suspicion of abuse which has not been properly investigated. Normally the most appropriate response where access is denied is to apply for an emergency protection order.[17] Where access is

13 S.37(3); they must provide this information within eight weeks unless the court directs otherwise: s.37(4).
14 [1993] 2 FLR 134.
15 Ibid, at p 148.
16 S.47(6).
17 S.44(1)(b): see below.

allowed, but where an assessment of the child is being frustrated, the most appropriate response might be to apply for a child assessment order. The effect of this order is to place any person who is in a position to produce the child under a duty to produce him to the persons named in the order, and to comply with the court's directions.[18]

Section 43(1) provides that a child assessment order may be made if, but only if, the court is satisfied that—

'(a) the applicant has reasonable cause to suspect that the child is suffering, or is likely to suffer, significant harm;
(b) an assessment of the child's health or development, or the way in which he has been treated, is required to enable the applicant to determine whether or not the child is suffering, or is likely to suffer, significant harm; and
(c) it is unlikely that such an assessment will be made, or be satisfactory, in the absence of an order under this section.'

It can be seen that the standard of proof which must be satisfied is one of reasonable suspicion only. Because this standard of proof is relatively low, the type of intervention allowed is strictly limited. The order gives the local authority a time-limited period of a maximum of seven days in which to discover whether there is any real foundation to their suspicion.[19] It is the court which takes control over the type of assessment which should take place. The court may give such directions as it thinks fit, and the order authorises any person carrying out an assessment to do so in accordance with the terms of the order.[20] Those carrying out the assessment are limited as to where the assessment is carried out: a child may only be kept away from home where this is in accordance with directions specified in the order; where it is necessary for the purposes of the assessment; and where it is for such period, or periods, as may be specified in the order.[1] Where a child is to be kept away from home, the court must give directions about contact arrangements.[2] The voice of the child may also be determinative in a case of this kind. A child who has sufficient understanding to make an informed decision may refuse to submit to a medical, psychiatric or other assessment.[3]

It can be seen from this structure that it is up to the court to determine how far a child assessment order can be used as a 'fishing expedition' to

18 S.43(6); this person may not, of course, be a person with parental responsibility.
19 S.43(5).
20 S.43(6)(7).
1   S.43(9).
2   S.43(10).
3   S.43(7); and see above ch 2, p 99, on the power of the High Court to overrule decisions made by a competent child.

discover whether the suspicion that the child is suffering, or is likely to suffer, significant harm is soundly based. It is not clear to what extent it would be appropriate for the court to be very specific in the type of assessment it authorises, and to what extent it can leave this to the discretion of the local authority. It seems that the court is expected to be cautious about authorising removal of the child from the home. A fine balance must be struck between taking the steps which are needed to discover whether or not the local authority's decisions can be verified, and causing unnecessary distress and anxiety to a child and his parents in a case where there is nothing untoward happening. The caution surrounding the structure of child assessment orders can be partly explained by the crisis which occurred in Cleveland in the period immediately preceding the passing of the Children Act 1989. A large number of children were suspected of being sexually abused, and very many children were subjected to forms of interviewing which in some cases could properly be described as interrogations.[4] Hence the control given to courts to be very specific about the manner in which the investigation is carried out.

If on hearing an application for a child assessment order the court is satisfied that there are grounds for making an emergency protection order it may make such an order, and it must not make a child assessment order where it feels that it ought to make an emergency protection order.[5] This provision is designed to obviate the risk of children being left in a position of immediate danger because the wrong proceedings have been commenced. For the same reason, a court may treat an application for a child assessment order as an application for an emergency protection order.[6]

Protecting children in an emergency

Normally when it is believed that a child is suffering, or is likely to suffer, significant harm, a social worker, or other person, should explain to the child what steps are going to be taken to protect him. Before a child is removed from his home and familiar surroundings he should be given the opportunity to discuss this, and to come to terms with proposed changes in his upbringing before these changes are implemented. Ideally he needs to know in advance when he will be taken from his parents, and he should meet the persons who will be looking after him before any transfer to their care is made. However, sometimes there will be very great concern about the child's situation, and its urgency may therefore justify immediate steps being taken to protect him. It is in these circumstances that an application

4 *Report of the Inquiry into Child Abuse in Cleveland 1987*, Cm 412 (1988).
5 S.43(4).
6 S.43(3).

can, and indeed should, be made under section 44 for an emergency protection order.

The effect of an emergency protection order is that it operates as a direction to any person who is in the position to do so to comply with a request to produce the child. In addition, it authorises either the child's removal to accommodation provided by the applicant, or the prevention of his removal from any hospital or other place in which he is currently being accommodated.[7] Clearly an order which authorises the sudden removal of a child from his home, often without any prior warning, is a powerful order which could have a traumatic effect on the child and his parents. Other relatives of the child are also likely to be shocked, angry or distressed when an emergency protection order is obtained. Therefore there is tight legal control over when an emergency protection order may be granted, the purpose of this control being to limit the availability of the order to those circumstances which merit such urgent intervention. There is further tight control over the duration of such an order and over the powers which may be exercised in relation to the child while an order is in force.

The grounds for an emergency protection order

Section 44(1) provides that where an application is made for an emergency protection order the court may make the order if, but only if, it is satisfied that—

'(a) there is reasonable cause to believe that the child is likely to suffer significant harm if—
  (i) he is not removed to accommodation provided by or on behalf of the applicant; or
  (ii) he does not remain in the place in which he is then being accommodated;
(b) in the case of an application made by a local authority—
  (i) enquiries are being made with respect to the child under section 47(1)(b); and
  (ii) those enquiries are being frustrated by access to the child being unreasonably refused to a person authorised to seek access and that the applicant has reasonable cause to believe that access to the child is required as a matter of urgency.'[8]

---

7 S.44(4).
8 Paragraph (c) makes similar, but not identical, provisions in the case of an application made by an authorised person, presently only the NSPCC.

Paragraph (a) requires the applicant to raise the anxiety level of the court to the point where the court has reasonable cause to believe that the child is likely to suffer significant harm unless an emergency protection order is made. In doing this the applicant can put any information he wishes before the court, and the court can take it into account regardless of any enactment or rule of law which would otherwise prevent it from doing so, provided that, in the opinion of the court, it is relevant to the application.[9] The applicant must further persuade the court that there is a causative link between the harm being likely to occur and the child being removed from, or remaining in, his present accommodation. Thus, for example, if the child is reasonably believed to have suffered a serious non-accidental injury, but if the person who is suspected of having injured the child has been remanded in custody pending trial, and the person presently caring for him is not implicated in the abuse in any way, it is suggested that it is most unlikely there are grounds for making an emergency protection order. On the other hand, where the alleged abuser has moved out of the home, but where there is uncertainty about where he is living, or whether he will stay away from the child, there may be grounds for an order being made. Where the alleged abuser is still in the home, or intends to discharge the child from hospital, there are likely to be very clear grounds for making the order.

Paragraph (b) is aimed at those cases where a local authority have reasonable cause to suspect that a child in their area is suffering, or is likely to suffer, significant harm, and where they are therefore under a duty under section 47(1)(b) to make enquiries about the child in order to decide what action they should take to safeguard or promote his welfare.[10] In conducting such an enquiry, the local authority must normally obtain access to the child.[11] This provision reflects the findings made in various inquiries which have been conducted into cases where child protection procedures have failed to protect children from being killed as a result of ill-treatment and neglect. These inquiries have emphasised that it is usually imperative that access is obtained to a child where there is a suspicion that he is suffering, or is likely to suffer, significant harm.[12] Unless the child is seen, and in the case of a young child physically examined for signs of injuries, ill-treatment or neglect, and in the case of an older child spoken to in private as well, it may be very easy for a parent to conceal significant harm to the child from a concerned professional. It should be noted that when an application is made under section 44(1)(b) a court is empowered to make an emergency protection order on the basis that the

9   S.45(7).
10   On s.47 generally, see above.
11   S.47(4).
12   See particularly *A Child in Mind: The Report on the Death of Kimberley Carlile*, Greenwich London Borough Council (1987).

applicant has reasonable cause to *suspect* that the child is suffering, or is likely to suffer, significant harm and has reasonable cause to believe that access to the child is urgently required. This is a lesser standard than the requirement that the court should have reasonable cause to *believe* that such harm is likely to occur, which must be proved in relation to applications made under section 44(1)(a). Clearly, where access is being refused, it may be impossible for the applicant to obtain the evidence to substantiate a belief, and therefore a reasonable suspicion provides an adequate basis for an order being made.

Powers of entry and police powers

Sometimes an applicant for an emergency protection order may be unsure of the child's whereabouts, or be denied entry on to premises where he suspects the child to be. Sometimes he may have reasonable cause to believe that there is another child on the premises with respect to whom an emergency protection order ought to be made. In cases of this kind the applicant should apply for orders under section 48(3) and (4) which authorise him to enter premises and search for the children concerned. However, such orders do not authorise the applicant to break into premises by force; where force is needed the police must be involved and a warrant obtained under section 48(9).[13] The police have their own separate powers to remove children to suitable accommodation and to keep them there, or to prevent the child's removal from hospital or any other place. A police constable may exercise these powers where he has reasonable cause to believe that the child would otherwise be likely to suffer significant harm.[14] Section 46 provides a code of guidance on how the police should exercise their powers, and how they should inform the parents and liaise with the local authority once they have taken the child into police protection. In difficult cases, particularly where it is anticipated that those looking after the child will respond to being served with an emergency protection order with violence, police involvement is likely to be an added feature of the implementation of an emergency protection order.

Court control over emergency protection orders

In urgent child protection cases the law seeks to strike a proper balance between protecting children from suffering significant harm by authorising their immediate removal to, or retention in, a place of safety, and allowing

13 See too the Police and Criminal Evidence Act 1984, s.17(1)(e) which authorises the police to enter premises without a warrant where there is an immediate risk to life or limb.
14 S.46(1).

those who are caring for a child to have the opportunity to give an explanation for the child's condition before the child is taken from them. Clearly, because emergency protection orders are, as their title makes manifest, for emergency situations only, it is often essential that the application is made ex parte. Indeed, in some cases if the person caring for the child were to be alerted in advance to the fact that an application for an order was being made, this could expose the child to an even greater risk of suffering significant harm. Most applications for emergency protection orders are made to magistrates, and the justices' clerk has an important role in determining whether the application should be heard at an inter partes or ex parte hearing. Rule 4(4) of the Family Proceedings Court (Children Act 1989) Rules 1991 provides that an application may be made ex parte with the leave of the justices' clerk. The clerk therefore acts as a filter to which proceedings are allowed to proceed without the normal safeguard of allowing all interested parties the opportunity to be heard. An ex parte application made during court hours will normally be heard by a bench of magistrates, or a single magistrate, at the court; one made in the evening, during the night, or at a weekend will normally be heard by a magistrate at his or her home. The magistrate must supply reasons why he or she has made, or refused to make, the order.[15] Where the single magistrate, or bench of magistrates, refuse to make an order on an ex parte application they may direct that the application be made inter partes.[16]

The child, a parent, anyone with parental responsibility for the child, or any person with whom the child was living immediately before the making of the order may apply for the emergency protection order to be discharged, but not until at least 72 hours have elapsed since the order was made.[17] However, this provision does not apply in a case where such a person was given at least one day's clear notice of the hearing at which the order was made, and was present at that hearing.[18] Allowing the order to be challenged after 72 hours gives some measure of safeguard to the interests of those persons affected by an ex parte application; whereas those persons who had the opportunity to attend the hearing, and did attend it, are not further entitled to challenge the order. An emergency protection order lasts for a maximum period of eight days.[19] It can be extended for up to another seven days, but only where the court has reasonable cause to believe that the child is likely to suffer significant harm if the order is not extended, and it may only be extended once.[20]

15 Family Proceedings Court (Children Act 1989) Rules 1991, r.21(5).
16 R.4(5).
17 S.45(8)(9).
18 S.45(11); also, an application to discharge cannot be made where the order has been extended under s.45(5): see below.
19 S.45(1)(2)(3).
20 S.45(5)(6)

When making an emergency protection order the court may direct that the applicant, on exercising any powers conferred by the order, be accompanied by a general practitioner, nurse, or health visitor, if he so chooses.[1] This latter provision may assist in preventing removal of a child from the home in a case where fears about his health and safety prove to be unfounded. Section 44(5)(a) provides that the applicant shall only exercise the power to remove, or to prevent the removal of, the child in order to safeguard the welfare of the child. In a case where a doctor is willing to accompany the applicant (who will normally be a social worker) to the child's home, a medical examination of the child in the home might sometimes reveal that there is nothing to give rise to concern that the child is suffering, or is likely to suffer, significant harm. In such a case the child should be left where he is. In a case where the child has been removed or retained under an emergency protection order, and where it appears to the applicant that it is safe to return the child, or to allow him to be removed, the child must be returned or his removal must be allowed.[2]

Parental responsibility and emergency protection orders

An emergency protection order gives the applicant parental responsibility for the child.[3] However, section 44(5)(b) provides that—

> 'the applicant shall take, and shall only take, such action in meeting his parental responsibility for the child as is reasonably required to safeguard or promote the welfare of the child (having regard in particular to the duration of the order).'

Thus the applicant should not make a major decision having long-term effects on the child unless it must be made as a matter of urgency. The applicant's parental responsibility is also circumscribed by section 44(13) which requires the applicant to allow the child to have reasonable contact with his parents and other specified persons. This provision reflects the assumption which permeates the Act that maintaining contact between a child and his parents, and others who have parental responsibility for him, is normally in the best interests of the child and must therefore be permitted unless a court authorises otherwise. Such contact may not, of course, be in the interests of the child, and it is important that the applicant draws this to the attention of the court where he believes this to be the case. The court has the power to exercise control over contact arrangements

---

1   S.45(12).
2   S.44(10).
3   S.44(4)(c).

by directing what contact, if any, is or is not to be allowed between the child and any named person.[4]

An applicant for an emergency protection order may sometimes want the child to be medically or psychiatrically examined or otherwise assessed whilst the emergency protection order is in force. Without such an examination or assessment it may not be possible to establish whether the child is indeed suffering, or likely to suffer, significant harm, and to what that harm is attributable. One of the attributes of parental responsibility is the power to give permission for a child to be examined, or otherwise assessed, and therefore an applicant who has been granted an emergency protection order undoubtedly has this power. However, in 1988 the Cleveland inquiry[5] had concluded that a local authority, and the doctors concerned, had been examining and otherwise assessing children subject to place of safety orders[6] without having proper regard either for the interests and welfare of the children, or for the responsibilities of their parents. This inquiry was highly influential on parts of the Children Act 1989, and one outcome was that courts may now choose whether or not to exercise control over the medical or psychiatric examination or other assessment of children who are the subject of emergency protection orders. Section 44(6)(b) provides that where the court makes an emergency protection order it may give such directions, if any, as it considers appropriate with respect to the medical or psychiatric examination or other assessment of the child. Section 44(8) further provides that such a direction may be to the effect that there should be no such examination or assessment of the child, or no such examination or assessment unless the court directs otherwise.[7] In the face of such a direction, the parental responsibility of the applicant to permit such an examination or assessment must yield to the superior decision-making powers of the court.

Another of the attributes of parental responsibility is the power to give permission for a child to have medical or psychiatric treatment. The extent to which this power may be exercised by an applicant for an emergency protection order is not entirely clear, because of the limiting impact of section 44(5)(b). It is suggested that this section would appear to mean that the applicant should not normally arrange for the child to have any major medical or psychiatric treatment without the agreement of a parent or other person with parental responsibility, unless the child is in urgent

---

4   S.44(6)(a).
5   *Report of the Inquiry into Child Abuse in Cleveland 1987,* Cm 412 (1988), which concerned an investigation into the management of cases in Cleveland in which an exceptionally large number of children were suspected of having been sexually abused.
6   Which preceded emergency protection orders.
7   S.44(6)(b) and s.44(8). The child may, if he is of sufficient understanding to make an informed decision, refuse to submit to the examination or other assessment: s.44(7); see further ch 1.

need of such treatment. In such a case, where the parent refuses to agree to the child receiving treatment, and where to authorise the treatment would conflict with the strongly held religious or other beliefs of the parents, it has been held that the matter should be determined, wherever possible, by a High Court judge.[8]

Challenging the making of, or refusal to make, an emergency protection order

Section 45(10) provides that no appeal may be made against the making of, or refusal to make, an emergency protection order, or against any direction given by the court in connection with such an order. In *Essex County Council v F*,[9] Douglas Brown J held that section 45(10) allows no scope for the use of the appellate process, and he ruled that if magistrates act unreasonably in refusing to make an order the only possible remedy is in proceedings brought in judicial review. But of course judicial review proceedings are totally impracticable in an emergency situation; they are not designed to provide speedy relief. Douglas Brown J arrived at his ruling in *Essex County Council v F* with considerable regret because the facts 'cried out for the intervention of the court'; however he took the view that the words of the statute gave him no alternative.

It is suggested that the combined effect of section 45(10) and the ruling in *Essex County Council v F* is particularly alarming when it is recalled that applications for an emergency protection order are often heard by a single magistrate in his or her own home. It cannot be acceptable that nothing further can be done to protect a child in a case where, as in the *Essex* case, the court's decision is plainly wrong. In that case, the mother promised the local authority that she would not remove the child from her foster parents until the hearing of the application in care proceedings, which would come before the court a few days later. However, other mothers might not be so compliant, and the fact that the child was secure in the *Essex* case may have lulled the judge into a false sense of security. It is the precedent force of *Essex County Council v F* in relation to other cases which makes the decision so disturbing. A child could be put in grave danger by the wrongful refusal of a court to make an emergency protection order. He might even be badly injured or killed. It cannot be acceptable that the courts are apparently powerless to protect a child in circumstances of this kind.

---

8   See *Re O (A Minor) (Medical Treatment)* [1993] 2 FLR 149 and *Re R (A minor) (Blood Transfusion)* [1993] 2 FLR 757.
9   [1993] 2 FCR 289.

It is therefore necessary to search for possible solutions and to consider what might be done if a case of this kind arose again. One possibility might be for the local authority to make a fresh application for an emergency protection order to a judge, probably a High Court judge. However, there are obstacles to this. It seems implicit in the judgment in *Essex County Council v F* that this is not possible, for otherwise the court hearing the appeal in the *Essex* case could itself have made an ex parte emergency protection order. Also, the Children (Allocation of Proceedings Order) 1991[10] requires such applications to be made in a magistrates' court with only limited exceptions. However, it is nonetheless suggested that, where a child's safety is gravely at risk, a judge might find that he has the power to make the order requested. There is no actual precedent which prevents the judge from making such an order, and he would be likely to be very aware of his own personal responsibility for any possible tragic outcome of his refusal to do so.

Another possibility might be to make an application under the inherent jurisdiction of the High Court. It seems, on its face, that recourse to the inherent jurisdiction would be barred where the applicant is the local authority. Section 100(2) prohibits the exercise of the inherent jurisdiction so as to require a child to be placed in the care of, or to be accommodated by or on behalf of, a local authority, or to give the local authority power to determine any aspect of parental responsibility for the child. However, section 100(4) might possibly come to the assistance of the child. This allows the High Court to grant leave to a local authority to apply for the exercise of the court's inherent jurisdiction where the court is satisfied that the result which the authority wish to achieve could not be achieved through the making of any order other than in the exercise of the court's inherent jurisdiction. It is therefore suggested that the local authority might rely on section 100(4) and ask the court to make an order placing the child in the care of an individual (but not of course an order which placed the child in the care of the local authority, or in local authority accommodation, as this is prohibited). It is suggested that the court might, for example, order that the child be kept in hospital, or live with a relative or friend of the family, or possibly even with the local authority foster parents with whom he has been living, but only in their personal capacity and not as agents of the local authority. These suggestions are all devices which might be attempted in order to overcome section 45(10), and the ruling in *Essex County Council v F*. It is regrettable to be put in the position where it seems necessary to suggest the use of such devices to circumvent specific provisions in a statute. However, taking action of this kind may be essential where the safety of a child is at stake.

---

10   SI 1991/1677.

The definition of harm and standards for intervention

When a local authority, other agencies or a court are deciding whether a child is suffering, or is likely to suffer, significant harm what is it that they are looking for?[11] The Act provides a very clear meaning of the phrase. Section 31(9) provides —

> 'Harm' means ill-treatment or the impairment of health or development;
> 'development' means physical, intellectual, emotional, social or behavioural development;
> 'health' means physical or mental health; and
> 'ill-treatment' includes sexual abuse and forms of ill-treatment which are not physical.

It can be seen that the definition of harm is very wide and covers all types of conceivable harm to the child. It is qualified by the adjective 'significant' which means that not any falling off in standards of parenting causing harm to the child will fall within the definition. A resilient child, who is able to withstand forms of ill-treatment or other types of unacceptable parenting, may fall outside the scope of the meaning of 'significant harm' where the harm he is presently suffering is not serious. However, where the standards of parenting of those who are looking after him show no sign of being capable of change, so that the child will sustain the effects of poor parenting continued over a considerable period of time, it is suggested that such a child might be one whom a local authority should take steps to protect on the basis that he is 'likely' to suffer significant harm, because the harm he is presently suffering is likely to become 'considerable, noteworthy or important.'[12]

Further assistance on the meaning of significant harm is provided by section 31(10). This subsection creates a yardstick against which to make an assessment of whether a child's health or development is being significantly impaired. It states that the child's health or development 'shall be compared to that which could reasonably be expected of a similar child'. According to guidance issued under the Act, the meaning of 'similar' in this context needs to take account of environmental, social and cultural characteristics of the child.[13] It seems that a similar child is a child with

---

11 Many of the most important topics relating to child abuse and child protection, seen from a medical, legal and social work perspective, are looked at in Allan Levy QC (ed) *Re-Focus on Child Abuse* (Hawksmere, 1994).

12 See *Humberside County Council v B* [1993] 1 FLR 257 in which this dictionary definition of 'significant' was approved: see below p 154.

13 *The Children Act 1989 Guidance and Regulations* Vol 1 Court Orders, para 3.20.

similar attributes, that is a child of the same age, sex and ethnic origin. Where a child has learning difficulties he should be compared with a child with similar learning difficulties. Where the child was born prematurely the child's achievement of developmental milestones should be compared with those achieved by other premature babies. Where the child has a spurt in growth in weight and height if put into hospital or foster care, and comparison is made with a similar child, the question to be asked is would a similar child demonstrate such a growth spurt under these conditions. Where such a child would not, the question then arises whether the first child has been malnourished, or otherwise treated in an abusive manner which has led to him failing to grow and put on weight, or whether there is some organic cause for his condition.

More contentious is the question how far a disadvantaged child should be compared to a similar disadvantaged child, and how far he should be compared to a child who has benefited from greater material, social and intellectual advantages. An example might be of children living in deprived circumstances in an inner city area. It might be expected that some such children will be poorly clothed, have few toys or books, be fed on a diet which is not very healthy and not receive much intellectual stimulus from those who are caring for them. It is suggested that it could probably be maintained that a child who is looked after in this way is being treated in no worse a manner than many other children living in deprived circumstances, and that the standard of care he is receiving amounts to good enough parenting in the light of his background. However, it is suggested that deprivation and relative poverty do not provide a reasonable excuse for a child being dressed in filthy clothing, for complete lack of attention to his personal hygiene, for not seeking medical attention when he is ill, for no interest being taken in his intellectual and emotional development, or for the child running out of control and becoming involved in serious criminal activity. Decision-makers must, of course, take account of poverty, but where one or more of these conditions applies to a child, then it seems proper to conclude that the level of care has fallen below the minimum standard which is acceptable.

Children are too young and immature to protect themselves, and it is adults who must determine whether the manner in which they are living is such that they are suffering significant harm. The setting of standards by local authorities of when it is appropriate to intervene is undoubtedly the most difficult issue to be resolved, and the question of what amounts to significant harm inevitably turns on value judgments. If standards are set too high, too many children and their families may be drawn into the net of child care and protection processes. If standards are set too low, children may be forced to endure a life style which is intolerable by any objective criteria.

Likely harm

Where a child is not presently suffering significant harm, it may be even more difficult for the local authority to determine when it is appropriate to intervene on the basis that a child is likely to suffer significant harm. The main benefit of the inclusion of likely harm as a basis for taking child protection action is that it allows for intervention before any actual harm is suffered. Clearly local authorities and guardians ad litem of the child will approach legal intervention on this basis with great caution. Local authorities may sometimes be uncertain about what type of evidence will be sufficient to satisfy a court that a child is likely to suffer significant harm, and therefore whether it is appropriate to pursue a case in care proceedings. It is suggested that assistance on this can usefully be derived not only from cases which have occurred since the Children Act 1989,[14] but also from the law which preceded the Act. Under the Children and Young Persons Act 1969 it was possible for a court to make a care order on the basis of risk, but it defined the evidence which had to be adduced to substantiate that risk. Either a child had to be a member of the same household of another child for whom the grounds for care proceedings had been proved;[15] or a care order could be made where a person who had been convicted of an offence under Schedule 1 of the Children and Young Persons Act 1933 had joined, or might be going to join, the household where the child was living.[16] These provisions allowed babies to be removed at birth, siblings within a family to be protected, and orders to be made when a child abuser moved from one household to another. In the case of a Schedule 1 offender, they allowed for swift intervention even before the convicted person joined the household, for example when he was due for release from prison. It is suggested that this is exactly the type of evidence which can properly substantiate a claim under the 1989 Act that a child is 'likely' to suffer significant harm.

However, the Children Act 1989 does not impose any evidential restrictions on the establishment of likely significant harm, so there can be intervention outside this narrow range of circumstances. Professionals who engage in child protection work are aware that parents and other carers may have little appreciation of the vulnerability of babies and small children to suffering significant harm. In the case of babies a shaking which is relatively mild by adult standards may lead to disastrous consequences such as brain damage, impairment of sight, or even death. A parent with learning difficulties may not be able to be trusted always to

14 See below on how courts have approached the meaning of likely harm.
15 This wording is a paraphrase of the Children and Young Persons Act 1969, s.1(2)(b).
16 Ibid, s.1(2)(bb); the offences were offences against the person of a child, including offences involving the taking of indecent photographs: Protection of Children Act 1978, s.1(5).

test that water in which a child is bathed is of the correct temperature, yet for a child to be scalded may be fatal, or it may have permanent serious consequences for the child's appearance, health and development. When setting standards, and evaluating the risk of harm occurring to a child, the question to be resolved is: 'when should the parents and others be allowed the opportunity to demonstrate whether it is safe for the child to remain in their care, and when is it proper to intervene to prevent predicted harm from occurring?' In some cases this question arises even when no such harm has occurred already.

Local authority responses to significant harm

Determining which is the most effective response to a discovery that a child is suffering, or is likely to suffer, significant harm is not easy for local authorities. The main system which is used to protect children is to hold a multi-agency case conference. At that case conference, persons with knowledge of the child and his family pool information about the child, make recommendations for future action, and decide whether the child should be put on a child protection register. This register lists all the children in the locality for whom there is an inter-agency protection plan. The plan itemises the steps which have been agreed about what should be done to protect the child and it is for the agency representatives to decide how responsibility for implementing the various parts of the plan is to be allocated. A date for reviewing how the plan is working will be set. The child of sufficient age and understanding is encouraged to attend at the conference, though normally not to be there throughout, so that his voice about his own future is properly heard. Parents and persons with parental responsibility should also be invited to attend unless there are exceptional reasons for their exclusion.[17]

The choice for a local authority where they have reasonable cause to believe that a child is suffering, or is likely to suffer, significant harm, is either to leave the child where he is and to put resources into protecting the child at home, or to take care proceedings. In making this choice there are various issues to be balanced. Some have argued that:

'Every child must have the basic right of remaining in his own family unless there are compelling reasons which justify his removal. This presumption in favour of parental autonomy should only be rebutted by proof of some specific harm to the child or of the disruption or absence of parental ties. Even when this is proved,

---

17 A detailed account of the working of case conferences is given in *Working Together* (HMSO, 1991).

however, there should be a presumption against removal of the child from his home; such intervention should be a last resort. Removal should require a thorough investigation of alternative ways of dealing with the situation (for example by voluntary services and support) and evidence that such measures are inadequate.'[18]

The Children Act, in part, reflects this thinking. It has been seen that a local authority are under a duty to provide services for children who would otherwise be at risk of sustaining impaired health or development, and that such services must be directed to preventing the need to take care proceedings.[19]

However, the sting in the tail in the reasoning in the above quotation is in the last sentence. There is evidence that children who have suffered significant harm through sexual abuse and other forms of ill-treatment will often continue to be abused even though the adults in the family receive treatment. There is evidence that neglecting families can drift for years beyond the boundaries of acceptable parenting without a systematic assessment being made of the situation, or legal proceedings being instituted.[20] For the law to require that evidence should be produced in *all* cases to demonstrate that services and other measures are inadequate could mean that some children who are suffering significant harm will continue to suffer significant harm for some considerable period before there is legal intervention. Yet placing a child in care may not be the best solution for the child. Research has demonstrated that 'far from remedying existing deficiencies ... periods in public care have further impaired the life chances of some children and young people because of poor educational achievement, uncorrected health problems and maladjustment.'[1]

The dilemma for child protection law and procedures is how to 'ensure that a child shall not be separated from his or her parents against their will, except when competent authorities subject to judicial review determine, in accordance with applicable law and procedures, that such separation is necessary for the best interests of the child.'[2] The law must strike a proper balance between giving due weight to the right of everyone to respect for his private and family life,[3] and giving due weight to the rights and freedoms of the child. The dilemma is made more complex

18 A Morris, H Giller, E Zwed and H Geach *Justice for Children* (Macmillan, 1980) p 128.
19 S.17; Sch. 2, para 7; and see above.
20 *Protecting Children* (HMSO, 1988) p 7.
1 *Patterns and Outcomes in Child Placement, Messages from Current Research and their Implications* (HMSO, 1991) p 7.
2 See Art.9 of the United Nations Convention on the Rights of the Child.
3 A right embodied in Art.8 of the European Convention on Human Rights and Fundamental Freedoms.

because the rights and freedoms of the child are inextricably bound up with the rights and freedoms of the parents. The notion that every child has the right to be brought up by his own family is a notion which normally accords with the child's wishes and feelings, and is generally believed to promote his best interests. Yet, when taken to an extreme, such a notion may identify a child's interests too closely with his parents, and create a climate of unwillingness to remove a child from his home even when this is necessary to protect the child. It may lead to responses to significant harm failing to give adequate respect to the child's right to be treated as an autonomous individual.

Interim care and supervision orders

In some cases the local authority will conclude that in order to fulfil their responsibility to protect the child they have no alternative but to make an application in care proceedings. Section 31(2) of the Children Act 1989 contains the grounds. It provides—

'A court may only make a care order or supervision order if it is satisfied—
(a) that the child concerned is suffering, or is likely to suffer, significant harm; and
(b) that the harm, or likelihood of harm, is attributable to—
   (i) the care given to the child, or likely to be given to him if the order were not made, not being what it would be reasonable to expect a parent to give to him; or
   (ii) the child's being beyond parental control.'

When a local authority first make an application in care proceedings it would be most unusual for either the local authority, or the other parties to the proceedings, to be in a position fully to present their case. Of greater significance is the fact that the court will not have sufficient information on which to base a final order until an independent investigation of the child's circumstances has been conducted by a guardian ad litem appointed for the child. In the meanwhile arrangements must be made about where the child will live and with whom he may have contact. Sometimes the local authority will be satisfied that the child can be protected from harm if he remains living at home pending the final hearing of their application. They may, for example, be able to persuade the person whom they allege is causing significant harm to the child to move away from the premises.[4] Sometimes a relative or friend of the child will offer to look after him and

4 They may assist that person to obtain alternative accommodation under Sch.2, para 5.

this may give the child the protection he needs. In a case of this kind it may be appropriate to make a residence order to the person offering to care for the child, in which case section 38(3) provides that the court must make an interim supervision order unless satisfied that the child's welfare will be satisfactorily safeguarded without such an order being made. Sometimes the local authority will offer to accommodate the child under section 20, and his parents, and any others with parental responsibility, may be willing to comply with this arrangement. It is where voluntary arrangements of this nature cannot be agreed, or where the local authority take the view that they will not give the child sufficient protection, or where the local authority take the view that they need to have parental responsibility for the child during the period preceding the final hearing, that they are likely to make an application for an interim order.

Section 38(1) provides that where in any proceedings for a care order or a supervision order the proceedings are adjourned, or where the court gives a direction under section 37(1) that the local authority should investigate the child's circumstances,[5] the court may make an interim care order or an interim supervision order. Section 38(4) makes provision for various time limits to be imposed when an interim order is made; in essence these provide that the maximum period for the initial interim order is eight weeks and that subsequent orders may be made to last for a maximum of four weeks.[6] The temporary nature of an interim order allows the court to maintain a degree of control over the steps taken by the local authority in the interim period. Issues can be raised about how the local authority are exercising their parental responsibility under the order each time an application is made for the renewal of the order. Where the court is dissatisfied with action taken by the local authority it can refuse to make a further interim order.[7]

Interim care and supervision orders—the standard of proof

There is a gradation in the standard of proof which must be satisfied before a court may make an order under Parts IV or V of the Act. It has been seen that the standard which must be satisfied before a court may make a child assessment order is one of a reasonable suspicion only.[8] The standard of proof which must be discharged in relation to an application for an interim

---

5   See above.
6   The position is slightly more complicated than as described; however there is nothing in s.38 which prevents a number of consecutive interim orders from being made. The Family Proceedings Courts (Children Act 1989) Rules 1991 (SI 1991/1395), r.28 allows for the continuation of interim orders by consent, and without the attendance of the parties.
7   See *Re G (Minors) (Interim Care Order)* [1993] 2 FLR 839.
8   S.43(1)(a); see above. See below for the standard of proof in care proceedings.

order in care proceedings is higher. Section 38(2) provides that a court shall not make an interim care order or an interim supervision order unless it is satisfied that there are reasonable grounds for believing that the child is suffering, or is likely to suffer, significant harm. In *Re B (A Minor) (Care Order: Criteria)*,[9] Douglas Brown J held that this test means that the court does not have to be satisfied in fact that the grounds exist but simply that there are reasonable grounds for believing that they do. He also held that evidence which might not be sufficient to satisfy the court at a final hearing may be acceptable to discharge the lower standard for an interim care order. An application for an interim order is not a trial run for the final hearing, and the courts have ruled that evidence, and the cross-examination of witnesses, should be restricted to the issues which are essential at the interim stage.[10]

Interim care orders and assessment

In the period between first making an application in care proceedings and the final hearing a local authority will often need to investigate further the grounds for believing that a child is suffering, or likely to suffer, significant harm, and to evaluate the risk of him suffering further such harm. Often they will wish to carry out a careful assessment of the child, his parents, his siblings and others, such as relatives, who are important persons in his life. The purpose of this assessment is to give the local authority a clearer idea about the nature of the harm which the child is suffering, or is likely to suffer, and to whom it can be attributed. The local authority also need to give close attention to whether a care or supervision order is the most appropriate response to the child's circumstances, and to decide on the arrangements they wish to make for the future care of the child should they obtain a care order. In many cases the local authority are likely to take the view that they can only carry out a proper assessment of the child if they have all the rights and powers which are conferred under an order which gives them parental responsibility. Where this is the position the local authority are likely to apply for an interim care order.

Parents and other family members, by contrast, will probably view an application for an interim care order with apprehension, and the making of such an order as a judgment in advance on the merits of the local authority's case. Where an interim care order is made they may take the view that the court's mind is already made up. In *Re G (Minors) (Interim Care Order)*,[11] Waite LJ was keen to dispel this view. He said 'the making of an interim care order is an essentially impartial step, favouring neither

9   [1993] 1 FLR 815.
10 *Hampshire County Council v S* [1993] 1 FLR 559; *Re W (A Minor) (Interim Care Order)* [1994] 2 FLR 892.
11 [1993] 2 FLR 839.

one side nor the other, and affording no one, least of all the local authority in whose favour it is made, an opportunity for tactical or adventitious advantage.'[12] He said that in a case in which all the parties accept that the threshold requirements in section 31 are satisfied, the making of an interim care order is a neutral method of preserving the status quo.

Despite this reassurance about the function of an interim care order parents, or other persons such as a relatives, may wish the child to have his home with them in the period leading up to the final hearing while the local authority's assessment of the child and his family takes place. Difficulty may then arise whether the threshold test for care can be established when a person who has not caused the child to suffer significant harm is offering to look after the child. This difficulty manifested itself in *Re B (A Minor) (Care Order: Criteria)*.[13] Here there were reasonable grounds for believing that the child was suffering, and was likely to suffer, significant harm because there was evidence that she was being sexually abused. However it was not clear to whom that harm should be attributed, and therefore an assessment was essential so that knowledge could be obtained about the child's responses to the adults in her life, and so that her views and feelings about these adults could be discovered. An aunt who had been looking after the child, and with whom the child had been happy, was offering to look after the child during the assessment period. It was therefore argued that the threshold for care could not be established because the child was not likely to suffer significant harm if placed with the aunt. This argument was rejected by Douglas Brown J. He found that the child would remain at risk of significant harm if the assessment was not carried out because there was evidence before him that the assessment could only be carried out successfully if the child was placed with a neutral carer, and he found that the aunt's attitude to the case was not neutral. He said that if the assessment did not continue or was rendered valueless, this gave reasonable grounds for believing that significant harm would be suffered by the child, and the harm would be attributable to the care given by her aunt. He ruled that care, which is not defined by the Act, goes beyond physical care and includes the emotional care which a reasonable parent would give the child. In the case of a child who has probably been sexually abused, he said that care includes listening to the child and monitoring its words so that a professional assessment can be carried out.

The significance of the judgment in *Re B (A Minor) (Care Order: Criteria)* is that it recognises the importance of a proper assessment being allowed to proceed during the period between the original application being made in care proceedings and the final order. By holding that a reasonable parent would allow such an assessment to take place, and that frustration of the assessment process in itself allows a court to find that a child is likely to

12 Ibid, at p 845.
13 [1993] 1 FLR 815.

suffer significant harm, the judgment makes it clear that a court can exercise control to facilitate the proper assessment of the child's circumstances. Where a family member who has not caused any harm to the child offers to look after the child, and where such an arrangement would be incompatible with an assessment of the child, that allows a court to find reasonable cause to believe that the child is likely to suffer significant harm if an interim care order is not made.

Although an interim care order gives the local authority parental responsibility for the child, the court is nonetheless empowered to exercise a large measure of control over the assessment process while such an order is in force. Section 38(6) provides that the court may give such directions as it considers appropriate about the medical, psychiatric or other assessment of the child when making an interim care or supervision order. Where a court gives a direction that a child should be subjected to a specific form of assessment this is a mandatory direction with which the local authority must comply.[14] The court may also direct either that there is to be no such examination or assessment, or that there is to be no such examination or assessment unless the court directs otherwise. These directions may be given when the interim order is made, or at any time when it is in force, and an application may be made at any time for the order to be varied.[15] These provisions enabling a court to prohibit certain forms of assessment were included in the Act partly in response to matters raised in the Cleveland inquiry.[16] The report revealed that children who were suspected of having been sexually abused were subjected to repeated medical examinations and prolonged interviews which caused them a considerable degree of distress. Now the type and duration of such assessments can be strictly controlled by a court.

Where a child is of sufficient understanding to make an informed decision, section 38(6) provides that he may refuse to submit to a medical or psychiatric examination or other assessment. However, the scope of this safeguard for the child has been limited by the ruling in *South Glamorgan County Council v W and B*.[17] During the course of care proceedings a court gave directions under section 38(6) for the child, a girl of 15, to undergo a psychiatric examination and assessment and, if necessary, to be treated at an adolescent unit and to remain there during the assessment. The girl refused to comply with the court's direction, and the court found that she was competent to make an informed decision.

---

14 See *Re O (Minors) (Medical Examination)* [1993] 1 FLR 860, in which a local authority were unsuccessful in their appeal against a direction that the children should be tested to discover whether they were HIV positive. In *Re HIV Tests* [1994] 2 FLR 116 a direction was given that the question whether there should be HIV tests of children should always come before a High Court judge.
15 S.38(6)(7)(8).
16 *Report of the Inquiry into Child Abuse in Cleveland 1987*, Cm 412 (HMSO, 1988).
17 [1993] 1 FLR 574.

Leave was therefore given to the local authority to institute proceedings to invoke the exercise of the High Court's inherent jurisdiction to authorise that the child be assessed and treated without her consent. The constitutional implications of the ruling in *South Glamorgan County Council v W and B* do not appear to have been considered by the court. Section 38(6) clearly contemplates that a competent child can refuse to comply with a direction made by a court in relation to examinations and assessments. Whether the High Court, in the exercise of its inherent jurisdiction, should be able to override the right of a child to refuse to consent to an assessment directed by a court under statutory powers, raises profound issues relating to the inter-relationship between the courts and Parliament.[18]

Which order should be made—an interim order or a final order?

Decision-making about the future upbringing of a child passes from the court to the local authority once a final care order is made. It has therefore been stressed that a court should not divest itself of decision-making powers and make a final care order until it is in possession of all relevant information.[19] Where a further assessment of the situation is needed in order to determine whether it will be safe to allow the child to live with members of his family, or where, as in *Hounslow London Borough Council v A,*[20] an application for a residence order is made at a late stage in the proceedings, and the local authority and the guardian ad litem have not had the opportunity to assess the merits of the applicant's case, no final decision should be made. The child may be protected in the meanwhile by an interim order. This order may be an interim care order, an interim supervision order, or an interim residence order, and in the case of the latter two orders it can be strengthened by the imposition of conditions which afford additional safeguards for the child. The disadvantage of an interim order is that it delays proper arrangements being made for the child's future. Normally delay is prejudicial to the welfare of the child.[1] But where it is a planned and purposeful delay, designed to ensure that the correct decision is reached, then it is justifiable. At the date of the final hearing it is essential that a court has full information on which to determine what order, if any, it should make.

In *C v Solihull Metropolitan Borough Council,*[2] Ward J emphasised that just as it may be wrong for a court to make a final order giving parental responsibility to a local authority on the basis of insufficient information,

18 *South Glamorgan County Council v W and B* is more fully discussed in ch 2, pp 99–100.
19 *Hounslow London Borough Council v A* [1993] 1 FLR 702; *C v Solihull Metropolitan Borough Council* [1993] 1 FLR 290.
20 Above.
1   S.1(2).
2   [1993] 1 FLR 290.

so too it may be equally wrong for a court to make a final order which leaves the parental responsibility with the parents, unless and until it is properly satisfied that the child is not at risk of suffering further significant harm. In that case a further assessment was necessary to discover why a child had suffered a serious non-accidental injury. The court ordered that the child should be returned to her parents under an interim residence order conditional upon the parents undertaking a programme of assessment, allowing access to their home at all reasonable times, and co-operating with all reasonable requests made by the local authority.

It is clear that the court can no longer monitor the administration of a child's upbringing by a local authority once a care order is made.[3] The only way in which the court can again be involved is if an application is made to discharge the care order,[4] or if there is disagreement over contact arrangements.[5] The child's guardian ad litem has no further part to play, and a court may not direct that the guardian continues his involvement in the case.[6] What is the position where a court is satisfied that a care order is the appropriate order, but where it disagrees, or is unhappy, with aspects of the care plan which the local authority have in mind? Here the issue to be resolved is whether the court should nonetheless make a care order, or whether it should make an interim order, or orders, until satisfied that the care order is working. This was the question which arose in *Re J (Minors) (Care: Care Plan)*[7] and, as the court recognised and emphasised, it went to the heart of the division of responsibility between courts and local authorities in determining the upbringing of a child.

The reasoning of Wall J in *Re J (Minors) (Care: Care Plan)* developed as follows. Before making an application for a final order the local authority should have prepared a care plan for the child which should be explained to the guardian ad litem, and which must be presented to the court.[8] A court is not in the position to assess whether a care order will be in the child's best interests unless it is able carefully to examine the care plan, and Wall J said that local authorities should be left in no doubt that in each case the care plan will be subject to rigorous scrutiny. However, he added that the court must not engage in an over-zealous investigation into matters which properly fall within the administrative discretion of the local authority. When determining what order, if any, to make, the court must apply the welfare principle, it must consider the effect any

3 And see *Re B (Minors) (Care: Contact: Local Authority's Plans)* [1993] 1 FLR 543.
4 S.39; or if an application for a residence order is made under s.10, which if granted would discharge the care order: s.91(1).
5 S.34.
6 *Kent County Council v C* [1993] 1 FLR 308.
7 [1994] 1 FLR 253.
8 In accordance with *The Children Act 1989 Guidance and Regulations*, Vol 3, para 2.62; and see *Manchester City Council v F* [1993] 1 FLR 419n.

further delay would have, it must apply the checklist, and it must be satisfied that to make an order would be better for the child than not to make an order. Where it is not satisfied that the care plan is in the best interests of the child it may refuse to make a care order.[9] It had been suggested to Wall J in *Re J (Minors)* that he should make a series of interim care orders until he could be satisfied that the local authority's care plan was working well in practice. He rejected this suggestion. He said that a court should be wary of using interim orders to exercise a supervisory function over a local authority. He emphasised that a court has no such supervisory function. It cannot review a care order to see if it is working, and it cannot direct the local authority to make a different plan where the original care plan is not working. These are matters which Parliament has entrusted to local authorities. Rather the court's function is to entrust the execution of the care plan to the local authority and then to step back.[10]

On the other hand, an interim order may be the most appropriate way of handling the position where the local authority and guardian ad litem have recommended that a care order be made on a final application in care proceedings, but where the court has concluded that a care order is not in the child's best interests, and that the child should be rehabilitated with a parent. This was the situation in *Buckinghamshire County Council v M*.[11] The Court of Appeal held that the trial judge had been plainly wrong to make no order because, without an order, there would be no continuing proceedings to which a review of the child's position could be attached. It would also end the professional work of the guardian ad litem in relation to the child. An interim order, by contrast, would allow a structured scheme of phased rehabilitation to take place over a specified period.[12] It would be necessary to renew the interim care order every 28 days, but the renewal hearing would enable the court to determine whether the rehabilitation process was working, or whether it was floundering, in which case the court would be able to reconsider its decision.

The role of the guardian ad litem

Where an application is made in care proceedings it will often be the case that the interests of the child and the interests of the persons who are

9   In other words it must apply s.1(1)(2)(3)(4)(5). These provisions are further discussed in chs 2 and 4.
10 Despite his clear recognition of the division of functions between the local authority and the court, it is interesting that Wall J nonetheless felt sufficiently anxious about the case to urge the local authority to appoint a member of its senior management as co-ordinator in overall charge of it.
11 [1994] 2 FLR 506.
12 Three months was the suggested period.

looking after him do not coincide. Significant harm to the child, attributable to a lack of reasonable parental care, is being alleged against those persons, and a conflict of interest between the child and his carers should therefore almost always be assumed. It may not be in the best interests of the child that a care order is made even where the application for the order is unopposed. It might, for example, be better for the child if a residence order were made to a relative. However, unless there is someone who has the duty to be the voice of the child, and who has a duty to safeguard the child's interests before the court, there is a risk that the child's perspective will be inadequately represented. Because care proceedings usually involve babies and children who lack the capacity properly to instruct a lawyer, the normal safeguards afforded by separate legal representation do not assist the child to any great extent. A lawyer has only limited opportunities to make a close and independent investigation into the circumstances surrounding a child client's case, and he is likely therefore to feel obliged to support the local authority's perception of the case unless he receives instructions from someone who has the authority to make enquiries and to represent the child's position.[13] A guardian ad litem for the child is such a person. He or she is trained and experienced in social work, and has the knowledge and skills necessary to investigate the child and his family, to ask questions of other persons, and to assess the merits of the local authority's case. He or she must be independent of the local authority, or any other body concerned in the case (such as the NSPCC), and must not have been involved professionally as a social worker with the child at any time during the last five years.[14]

It is not only in relation to applications for a care order that it is important that the child's position is fully and independently examined. The dangers inherent in an unopposed application to discharge a care order being allowed to proceed without any separate investigation being conducted on behalf of the child was graphically illustrated by the tragic circumstances surrounding the death of Maria Colwell.[15] At that time no one had the duty to give an account of Maria's wishes and feelings to the court, and no one had the duty to make an assessment, independent of the one made by the local authority, of whether Maria's mother and step-father

---

13 The solicitor should nonetheless always remember that it is the child who is his client, and note the recommendation made in *A Child in Trust: The Report of the Panel of Inquiry into the Circumstances surrounding the Death of Jasmine Beckford*, London Borough of Brent (1985) (Chairman Louis Blom-Cooper QC), that a solicitor acting in care proceedings should see, and if possible talk to or play with the child. It is suggested, however, that this should only be done after consultation with the guardian ad litem; the child may already be frightened and confused by being spoken to by a number of strange adults.

14 The Family Proceedings Courts (Children Act 1989) Rules 1991, r.10(7).

15 *Report of the Committee of Inquiry into the Care and Supervision provided in relation to Maria Colwell* (1974, HMSO) (Chairman: T G Field-Fisher QC).

might ill-treat her, or otherwise cause her harm, were she to be returned to their care. Guardians ad litem for children were first introduced as a result of Maria Colwell's death, initially in respect of unopposed applications to discharge a care order. Gradually the appointment of guardians ad litem to safeguard and represent the interests of children has been extended to other proceedings. Section 41 of the Act provides that a court must appoint a guardian ad litem for the child unless satisfied that it is not necessary to do so in order to safeguard his interests in the following proceedings: on an application to make or discharge a care order including when the court is considering making a residence order with respect to a child who is the subject of a care order; on an application to make, vary or discharge a supervision order; when a direction has been made in family proceedings and the court has made, or is thinking of making, an interim care order; when an application is made with respect to contact with a child in care; in respect of any proceedings brought under Part V; and on an appeal in relation to any of the above proceedings.[16]

The duty of the guardian ad litem is to safeguard the interests of the child in a manner prescribed by rules of court.[17] The manner in which the guardian ad litem discharges his or her duty to apply the principle that delay will normally be prejudicial to the child's welfare, and applies the checklist in section 1(3) to the circumstances of the child's case, will of course turn on the individual discretion of the person concerned.[18] However, the rules direct that he must carry out such investigations as may be necessary for him to carry out his duties, and in particular he must contact or seek to interview such persons as he thinks appropriate, or as the court directs. He has a right to inspect and take copies of any local authority records and, where he thinks that they may assist in the determination of the case, he may bring them to the attention of the court. He may also obtain such professional assistance, such as a report from an expert, which he thinks appropriate, or which the court directs him to obtain.[19] In addition the guardian ad litem must appoint a solicitor to represent the child,[20] attend all directions, appointments and hearings unless excused from so doing,[1] and advise the court on various specified matters.[2] Where the local authority's care plan is adoption, the guardian ad litem has the right to

---

16 S.41(6).
17 S.41(2)(b); the Family Proceedings Courts (Children Act 1989) Rules 1991, r.11; and the Family Proceedings Rules 1991, r.4.11. For the avoidance of confusion, all references in this section are to the former rules.
18 R.11(1).
19 R.11(9).
20 Unless such a solicitor has already been appointed: r.11(2).
1 R.11(4).
2 R.11(4)(a)-(f); these include the level of the child's understanding, his wishes in relation to court attendance, the appropriate forum for the proceedings and their timing and the options available in respect of the child.

see the case record in relation to the prospective adopters even though this is normally confidential. As the Court of Appeal held in *Re T (A Minor) (Guardian ad Litem: Case Record)*,[3] unless the guardian ad litem can see this record, and include relevant information derived from it in his report to the court, he cannot properly fulfil his duties.

Occasionally the child may wish to give instructions to his solicitor which conflict with those of the guardian ad litem. This is most likely to arise where the guardian ad litem forms the view that it would be in the interests of the child if a care order were made and the child does not want to go into care. In such a case, provided that the solicitor is satisfied that the child is able, having regard to his understanding, to give instructions on his own behalf, the rules provide that the solicitor must conduct the case in accordance with the instructions received from the child.[4] The guardian ad litem will nonetheless continue to investigate the case on behalf of the child, and must perform all his duties set out in the rules other than his duty to appoint a solicitor for the child.[5] The guardian ad litem may also, with the court's leave, obtain his own legal representation.[6] These provisions are an example of how the law seeks to balance giving due weight to the child's right to be respected as an individual, and to have access to the type of legal safeguards which are given to adults, and the concern of the law to ensure that the welfare of children is afforded proper protection in proceedings designed to secure their safety and well-being.

It is undoubtedly improper for a court to refuse to appoint a guardian ad litem at the request of one party to the proceedings when the other party is acting on the assumption that such an appointment will be made. It is also improper for a court to refuse to make such an appointment in the exercise of its discretion in a case where the proceedings are strongly contested, and where the case for the child's interests being separately represented are clear. These principles are illustrated by *R v Pontlottyn Juvenile Court, ex p R*[7] which concerned two teenage boys who were in local authority care. Their mother was applying for contact with her sons but the local authority were strongly opposed to her obtaining such contact. The local authority, without informing the mother, successfully opposed the appointment of a guardian ad litem on the grounds that such an appointment would unsettle the children. In proceedings brought by the mother in judicial review, an order of certiorari was granted on the grounds that the justices had been thoroughly unreasonable and perverse when

---

3   [1994] 1 FLR 632.

4   R.12(1)(a), and see *Re H (A Minor) (Care Proceedings: Child's Wishes)* [1993] 1 FLR 440.

5   See *Re M (Minors) (Care Proceedings: Child's Wishes)* [1994] 1 FLR 749 where Wall J laid down guidelines to be followed where the views of the guardian ad litem conflict with those of the child.

6   R.11(3).

7   [1991] 2 FLR 86.

they refused to appoint a guardian ad litem. The court held that the case for someone to speak for the boys, and to investigate their views and interests with an open mind, was overwhelming. Furthermore, the court's decision had been made at a hearing at which the mother had been encouraged not to attend, in circumstances in which she had been led to believe that there was no point in issue over the appointment of a guardian ad litem. Clearly this was wrong, and the Divisional Court held that the procedure adopted by the justices had been so unfair and contrary to natural justice that their decision should therefore be quashed.

When the guardian ad litem has completed his investigation he must provide a report for the court for the final hearing. The parents and other parties must have the opportunity to read the report in advance of the hearing. This is particularly important where the guardian ad litem is supporting the local authority's application for a care order, for the persons affected are entitled to know details of the case which is being made against them, so that they can prepare their own case properly.[8]

The final hearing in care proceedings—how courts have interpreted the threshold test

It has been seen that at early stages in an investigation the court is empowered to make an order where there is a reasonable suspicion, or a reasonable belief, that the child is suffering, or is likely to suffer, significant harm.[9] At the final hearing the court must be satisfied, on the balance of probabilities, that the threshold test for care has been made out before it can make either a care or a supervision order. It must therefore be confident that the facts of the case as presented fulfil the criteria specified in section 31(2). This provides that—

'A court may only make a care order or a supervision order if it is satisfied—
(a) that the child is suffering, or is likely to suffer, significant harm; and
(b) that the harm, or likelihood of harm, is attributable to—
   (i) the care given to the child, or likely to be given to him if the order were not made, not being what it would be reasonable to expect a parent to give to him; or
   (ii) the child's being beyond parental control'.

8 *R v West Malling Juvenile Court, ex p K* [1986] 2 FLR 405.
9 The reasonable suspicion of the applicant is sufficient to justify a child assessment order; the court must have a reasonable belief that the grounds exist before an emergency protection order, or an interim care order, can be granted: see above.

The language of child care legislation must seek to avoid the pitfalls which are the hallmarks of all legislation: too precise drafting of the grounds for making an order may inadvertently create loopholes through which some children may fall leaving them incapable of being protected; too loose drafting may permit intervention where there are insufficient reasons for it. The aim of the language of section 31(2) of the Act was to strike the correct balance between these extremes. Courts, when they construe the meaning of the words in the Act, must similarly take care to avoid the pitfalls associated with the construction of child protection statutes, namely too literal or narrow an interpretation may leave some children unprotected, but too wide a construction may extend the law beyond the scope of the mischief which the law is designed to address. There is often a tension between a literal and a purposive way of construing statutory provisions, and in *Newham London Borough v AG*,[10] Sir Stephen Brown P issued a warning against courts taking a too legalistic approach to the analysis of the language of section 31(2). He said 'of course, the words of the statute must be considered, but I do not believe that Parliament meant them to be unduly restrictive when the evidence clearly indicates that a certain course should be taken in order to protect the child.'[11]

The threshold test can be broken down into parts. It will be satisfied where it is shown that the child 'is suffering' significant harm or it will be satisfied where it is shown that he is 'likely to suffer' such harm. The harm suffered must be 'significant harm'. In either case it must be shown that the significant harm is 'attributable either to a lack of reasonable parental care, or to the child's being beyond parental control'. 'Harm' means ill-treatment or the impairment of health or development; 'development' means physical, intellectual, emotional, social or behavioural development; 'health' means physical or mental health; and 'ill-treatment' includes sexual abuse and forms of ill-treatment which are not physical.[12]

The meaning of 'significant' harm

The meaning of 'significant' is not defined in the Act. In *Humberside County Council v B*[13] Booth J accepted that significant should be construed in accordance with its dictionary meaning of being either 'considerable, or noteworthy or important'. Where the question of whether harm suffered by a child is significant turns on the child's health or development, section 31(10) provides that his health and development should be compared with that which could reasonably be expected of a similar child.[14]

10 [1993] 1 FLR 281.
11 Ibid, at p 289.
12 S.31(9).
13 [1993] 1 FLR 257.
14 For criticism of the similar child concept, see M D A Freeman *Care After 1991* in D Freestone (ed) *Children and the Law* (Hull University Press, 1990).

In *Re O (A Minor) (Care Order: Education: Procedure)*[15] the meaning of significant harm, in the context of a child's intellectual, emotional, social and behavioural development was considered, and parallels were drawn with a similar child. *Re O* concerned a 15-year-old girl who had been truanting from school for three years. Considerable efforts had been made by the local education authority to secure the girl's attendance at school, but to no avail. The main thrust of the local authority's application for a care order, which was supported by the guardian ad litem, was that if the girl's absenteeism was not arrested, it would have a profound effect on her ability to cope in adult life. Although there was anxiety about her intellectual and educational development,[16] the real concern related to her emotional and social development. It was said that her refusal to go to school 'will have a major impact on her self-esteem, her self-confidence and her perception of herself....it will also seriously impair her ability to relate to peers and adults in a more formal way. This will inhibit [the girl's] development because school is, of course, not only about intellectual learning, it also provides young people with necessary social and relationship skills.'[17]

On appeal from magistrates who made a care order, Ewbank J ruled that it had been entirely open to the magistrates to come to the view that the girl's intellectual and social development was suffering, and was likely to suffer, significant harm. He said 'if a child does not go to school and is missing her education, it is not difficult to draw the conclusion that, if she had gone to school and had not truanted, she would have improved her intellectual and social development.' With regard to the comparison to be made with a similar child he said 'in the context of this type of case, "similar child" means a child of equivalent intellectual and social development, who has gone to school, and not merely an average child who may or may not be at school.'[18] Ewbank J therefore confirmed the care order, and the care plan that the girl should go to a children's home and should be taken to school from there until a pattern of attendance had been achieved, when consideration would be given to sending her home.[19]

The question whether a care order should be made where children from two different families were orphans, where no family members were available to be appointed as their guardians, and where they were being

---

15 [1992] 2 FLR 7.

16 The evidence was that the girl had in fact acquired educational skills so that, in comparative terms, she was of about average ability.

17 [1992] 2 FLR 7 at pp 11-12.

18 Ibid, at p 12.

19 For comment on, and criticism of, *Re O (A Minor) (Care Order: Education: Procedure)*, see J Fortin *Significant Harm Revisited* (1993) 5 JCL 151, in which, amongst other things, she argues that the facts did not justify removing a child from her parents, that it was wrong to use removal into state care to deal with a child's lack of self-esteem and self-confidence, and that an application for an education supervision order would have been the appropriate response. See too R White (1992) 142 NLJ 396.

accommodated by the local authority, arose in *Birmingham City Council v D and M.*[20] The local authority argued that the absence of parental responsibility in any person imperilled the children because they would not be fully empowered to deal with crises and emergencies, and that therefore the children were at risk of suffering significant harm. The application was resisted by the children's guardians ad litem, who said that the needs of orphans were addressed by the accommodation provisions in the Act.[1] Thorpe J rejected the local authority's application. He said that 'section 31 is plainly designed to protect families from invasive care orders unless there is a manifest need evidenced by a perceptible risk of significant harm ... in these cases the local authority does not seek to invade, but to protect and compensate children who have been bereft of parental support. I have every sympathy with the local authority's motives and their aims, but I must construe section 31 sensibly and realistically. If there is some shortcoming in the statutory framework it is not for me to remedy the deficiency by a strained construction of section 31, particularly in the light of the opposition of the guardians ad litem.'[2] This case is illustrative of the principle that even where the proposals made by a local authority are entirely well-meaning, and arguably in the child's best interests, they cannot be authorised by a court unless the grounds for an order are first established. Here the language of the relevant provision prevented the court from intervening, even had it wished to do so.

Where a relative is caring, or offering to care, for the child

Before a final application is made in care proceedings there is always some considerable lapse of time between the commencement of the case and the final hearing while enquiries are made on behalf of the child by the child's guardian ad litem. In the meanwhile the child will normally have lived for several weeks, and often months, with local authority approved foster parents, or on an agreed basis with relatives. Indeed, local authorities are positively charged with the the duty to place a child whom they are looking after with a member of his family unless this would not be reasonably practicable or consistent with his welfare.[3] Consequently, by the time of the final hearing, when full evidence is given to substantiate the allegation that the child is suffering, or is likely to suffer, significant harm, steps will already have been taken to protect him. Indeed the child may be positively thriving in his new environment and clearly not so suffering in a literal sense. Difficult questions about the proper interpretation of section 31(2)

20 [1994] 2 FLR 502.
1   Ss.20, 22 and 23.
2   [1994] 2 FLR 502 at pp 504-5.
3   S.23(6).

have consequently arisen in cases where a relative, or other person, is offering to care for the child, and where there is no evidence to suggest that the child would positively come to harm if cared for by that person. Can present, or likely, significant harm attributable to a lack of reasonable parental care be established in these circumstances without unduly straining the language of the section?

A fairly straightforward situation is where the court is satisfied that the relatives would be unable to protect the child from suffering further significant harm, even though the relatives themselves are caring persons. Such a situation arose in *Newham London Borough v AG*[4] where grandparents were offering to provide a home for their grandchild with the assistance of the extended family. The trial judge found that the grandparents were loving and caring persons, but that they did not show any real insight into the nature of their daughter's illness, and would find it impossible to protect the child from the serious danger that she presented. He therefore made a care order. The Court of Appeal dismissed the grandmother's appeal. It found that there was a real likelihood that the child would suffer significant harm if a care order was not made, even though the child was currently not at risk.

A similar approach was taken in *Re B (A Minor) (Care Order: Criteria)*,[5] where the language of section 31(2) came under scrutiny at an interim stage in the proceedings. The child had alleged that she had been sexually abused by her father. A consultant child psychiatrist had advised the local authority that the child should be placed with foster parents, because they would provide her with a neutral and secure placement while an assessment was carried out. The local authority were therefore seeking an interim care order until the substantive hearing. The child's aunt was seeking an interim residence order. She refused to accept the possibility that the father had abused the child. The court found that the assessment would be seriously impaired, or rendered valueless, if the child was living with her aunt. Since an assessment was crucial to the question of the attribution of the harm, or likely harm, the child would remain at risk of significant harm if it was not carried out. The court therefore found that there were reasonable grounds for believing that significant harm would be suffered by the girl unless the assessment took place, and this would be attributable to the care likely to be given to her by her aunt. It therefore concluded that an interim care order was essential to prevent the frustration of the assessment.

A more difficult situation arose in *Northamptonshire County Council v S*.[6] The court had found that the significant harm which the child was

4   [1993] 1 FLR 281.
5   [1993] 1 FLR 815.
6   [1993] 1 FLR 554.

suffering was attributable to the care provided by the mother. However, the children's grandmother was offering to look after the children and the question arose whether the court should consider the care offered by the grandmother when determining whether both limbs of the threshold condition had been proved. Ewbank J said that the answer to this was clearly 'no'. He ruled that the threshold test related only to the parent or other carer whose lack of care has caused the harm referred to in section 32(1)(a). He said that the care which other carers might give to the child only became relevant after the threshold test had been met.[7]

Cases where a relative is looking after, or offering to look after, a child not only give rise to awkward questions about the proper meaning of the language of section 31(2), they also raise fundamental issues of social policy, and go to the root of child protection practices and procedures. Essentially such cases pose the question 'when is it right for the state to be allowed to impose its own view on what would be best for the child when this view is at variance with the sincerely held wishes of members of the child's family'?[8]

Re M (A Minor) (Care Order: Threshold Conditions)

The proper interpretation of section 31(2), and the proper response of the courts when a relative is offering to look after the child, came under close scrutiny in the leading case of *Re M (A Minor) (Care Order: Threshold Conditions)*[9] which was appealed to the House of Lords. The complex issues raised in *Re M* can better be understood after the facts have been outlined in some detail. It concerned a two-year-old child. His parents were married and he had three half siblings. In October 1991, when M was four months old, his father murdered his mother in a very brutal manner in the presence of all the children. It was the police who immediately obtained a place of safety order in respect of all the children.[10] After a week the three half siblings went to live with Mrs W who was the mother's maternal cousin, and in August 1992 she obtained a residence order which gave her parental responsibility for them.[11] However Mrs W, who was a lady in her mid fifties, felt unable to care for M because he was so young and because of the special needs of the older children. M was therefore accommodated by the local

---

7   At that stage the court has a choice between making no order at all or making a care order, a supervision order, or an order under s.8: see below.

8   This is a dilemma to which social workers and other professionals are constantly exposed when discussing a child's future at a child protection case conference.

9   [1994] 3 All ER 298.

10 Under the Children and Young Persons Act 1969, s.28. That Act has since been repealed and place of safety orders have been replaced by emergency protection orders under the Children Act 1989, s.44: see above. The police have their own separate powers under s.46.

11 Children Act 1989, ss.8 and 12(2), and see ch 2.

authority and placed with a short-term foster mother. In May 1992 the local authority applied for a care order in respect of M. Members of the father's family and Mrs W separately applied for residence orders, but before the final hearing the paternal relatives had discontinued their application. The final hearing was not until February 1993. Mrs W, who had managed to care for the older children, now felt able to care for M. The local authority were also of the opinion that Mrs W could care for M. They therefore supported her application and were no longer pursuing their application for a care order. However, M's guardian ad litem recommended that a care order be made with a view to M being adopted outside the family.[12] The question therefore arose whether the grounds for making a care order had been made out, and if they had, whether such an order should be made in the light of the suggestion that the child should be adopted.[13]

Bracewell J found that the threshold conditions for making a care order had been established. In interpreting the wording of section 31(2)(a) she followed the decision of Ewbank J in *Northamptonshire County Council v S*[14] and ruled that the relevant date for deciding whether the child 'is suffering' significant harm relates to the period immediately before the process of protecting the child is first put into motion, in this case when the father deprived the child for all time of the mother. In relation to the welfare of M, she found that Mrs W who was of course presently caring for the child's three siblings, might not be able to give the child the quality of emotional care which the child, with his particular background, was likely to require. She found that the child had special needs which meant that his interests would best be served by a care order being made with a view to his adoption.

Mrs W appealed, supported by the local authority.[15] The Court of Appeal disapproved Bracewell J's interpretation of the wording of the statute; it also disagreed with her judgment for reasons of social policy. Balcombe LJ, who gave the judgment of the court, said that the choice by Parliament

12 The father, who had by now been sentenced to life imprisonment for murder, supported the guardian ad litem's recommendation.
13 A difficult feature in analysing this case is that the local authority were not seeking a care order, and although the court could make a care order on the recommendation of the guardian ad litem, she could not impose her view on the local authority on what should happen to the child if the care order was made.
14 [1993] 1 FLR 554.
15 One of the many curious features of this case is that once a care order is made it is up to the local authority, and not the court, to decide about the child's future upbringing. Therefore the local authority could have chosen to disregard the judge's opinion that the child should be placed for adoption and have placed the child in the care of Mrs W, thus obviating the necessity for an appeal. However, for reasons which are not explained, the local authority appear to have conceded their decision-making powers to the court, and to have treated Bracewell J's view that adoption would best promote the welfare of the child as a ruling which was binding upon them.

of the phrase 'is suffering' over the phrase 'has suffered' (which was in the original draft of the Children Bill) served to emphasise Parliament's intention that it is not the past but the continuous present to which attention must be directed. He concluded that it is not enough that something happened in the past which caused the child to suffer harm of the relevant kind if, before the hearing, the child has ceased to suffer such harm. In *Re M (A Minor)* the past harm to the child had been when the father murdered the mother, but since then the child had been looked after for 16 months by a foster mother, and he was no longer suffering significant harm because of the care given to him by the foster mother. The court ruled that there was therefore no evidence to satisfy the language that the child 'is suffering significant harm'.[16]

Having found that there was no evidence to suggest that the child was presently suffering significant harm, the Court of Appeal then went on to consider whether the child was 'likely' to suffer significant harm if the care order was not made. Bracewell J had found that the child had no permanent home, that the only person with parental responsibility for him was his father who was in prison for murder, and that the cousin might not be able to offer him care of sufficient quality. Of this latter finding Balcombe LJ said that 'this is a thousand miles away from saying that if M were to live with Mrs W he was likely to suffer significant harm of the relevant kind.'[17] He ruled that there was nothing in the evidence to suggest that the child would be likely to suffer significant harm attributable to the care likely to be given to him by Mrs W if he went to live with her. In relation to the social policy question of when it is proper for the state to intervene in family life, he said that the facts of *Re M* were analogous with a case where a child's parents have both been killed in a motor accident, but where relatives offer to care for the child, and said for it to be open to a court to say that the second threshold condition was satisfied on facts of this kind would amount to a form of 'social engineering'.[18] The Court of Appeal therefore concluded that there was no evidence before the court which entitled it to find that M was 'likely' to suffer significant harm 'attributable to a lack of reasonable parental care'.

The House of Lords reversed the decision of the Court of Appeal and restored the care order which had been made by Bracewell J.[19] In relation

16 See [1994] 1 All ER 424.
17 Ibid, at p 432.
18 Ibid, at p 432. It is suggested that this analogy is apposite only where the local authority intervene before any other family member provides the child with a home.
19 Somewhat curiously, the appeal to the House of Lords was pursued not by the child's guardian ad litem but by the father. It is suggested that it was wrong for anyone other than the child to have been allowed to pursue the appeal. It is suggested that the fact that the father took the same view of the child's interests as the guardian ad litem should have been treated as irrelevant. It was a classic situation where the court should have assumed that there might at some stage be a conflict of interest between parent and child.

to the issues of statutory interpretation which had been discussed at some length by the Court of Appeal, the House of Lords' approach is best summarised in the opening words of Lord Templeman's speech. He said: 'My Lords, this appeal is an illustration of the tyranny of language and the importance of ascertaining and giving effect to the intentions of Parliament by construing a statute in accordance with the spirit rather than the letter of the Act.'[20] The House condemned the Court of Appeal's apparent pre-occupation with whether the present tense drafting of the statute was satisfied at the date of the final hearing. Rather, Lord Mackay LC ruled that:

'Where, at the time the application is to be disposed of, there are in place arrangements for the protection of the child by the local authority on an interim basis which protection has been continuously in place for some time, the relevant date with respect to which the court must be satisfied is the date at which the local authority initiated the procedure for protection under the Act from which these arrangements followed. If after a local authority had initiated protective arrangements the need for these had terminated, because the child's welfare had been satisfactorily provided for otherwise, in any subsequent proceedings it would not be possible to found jurisdiction on the situation at the time of the initiation of these arrangements. It is permissible only to look back from the date of disposal to the date of initiation of protection as a result of which local authority arrangements had been continuously in place thereafter to the date of disposal'.[1]

This is not an easy passage to understand, but when it is read in the context of the remainder of Lord Mackay's speech it seems clear that he is stating that where there has been a continuum of protective measures between the first initiation of proceedings and the final hearing, the fact that the child is being currently well cared for does not preclude the making of a care order. He endorsed the view that the point of time at which the court has to consider whether a continuing situation exists is at the moment in time immediately before the process of protection is first put into motion,[2] and stated that Ewbank J's approach in *Northamptonshire County Council v S*[3] had been correct.

---

20 [1994] 3 All ER 298 at p 309; though it is suggested that this was unfair to the Court of Appeal, which was clearly seeking to understand the language and to relate it to the social policy issues.
1 Ibid, at p 305.
2 Following the House of Lords' ruling in *D (A Minor) v Berkshire County Council* [1987] 1 All ER 20 which turned on similar present tense drafting in earlier child protection legislation.
3 [1993] 1 FLR 554.

By the time the appeal reached the House of Lords the child had been living for several months with Mrs W and, because he was thriving in her care, all parties were agreed that there was no question of the child being taken from her at the present time and placed for adoption. The issue for the House of Lords, once they had resolved the jurisdiction question, was whether they should confirm the residence order to Mrs W, or restore the care order made by Bracewell J. Somewhat astonishingly, their Lordships restored the care order. Lord Mackay gave as his reason for so doing that there was a possibility in the longer term of difficulties, and the care order would enable the local authority to monitor the progress of the child. Also, a care order would give them the power to determine the extent to which the father should be allowed to meet his parental responsibility for the child.[4] Lord Templeman said that a care order would have the advantage for Mrs W that it would enable her to turn to the local authority for advice and help if necessary. He also expressed the view that it would have the advantage for the child that the local authority would be able to monitor his progress, and intervene with speed if anything went wrong.

It is regrettable that there was virtually no discussion in the House of Lords of the important and controversial social policy issues raised by the case. No attempt was made to deal with Balcombe LJ's telling analogy with a case where a child's parents have been killed in a motor accident. No comparison was made between the results which would be produced by the competing interpretations of section 31(2). At no stage did they address the question of fundamental difficulty posed by Bracewell J's ruling, namely 'when is it a proper application of the welfare principle to make an order which will result in a child being adopted when a relative is offering to care for him'? However, it was accepted by most commentators that the House of Lords' ruling on the issue of law was in accordance with the purpose of the legislation, and that it struck the correct balance between giving respect to the rights of families to make provision for children who are suffering, or at risk of suffering, significant harm, and allowing local authority and court involvement with such children.[5] The Court of Appeal's decision had given rise to considerable concern because of its impact on the powers of local authorities to protect children. Authorities were being quite properly advised that they could not normally pursue an application in care proceedings where a relative was offering to look after the child, even though they took the view that the relative would not be a suitable carer. The courts too were experiencing serious difficulties when applying the test laid down by the Court of Appeal.[6] It is suggested that a separate

4   Under s.33(3)(b).
5   A Bainham (1994) 53 CLJ 458; J Whybrow (1994) 6 JCL 177. For a contrary view, see J Masson (1994) 6 JCL 170.
6   *Re A (A Minor) (Care Order: Significant Harm)* [1994] 2 FCR 125; *Re H (A Minor) (Care or Residence Order)* [1994] 2 FLR 80.

disadvantage of the Court of Appeal's ruling was its potential to deny the child the benefit of an investigation by a guardian ad litem. Unless a local authority can institute care proceedings despite the fact that a relative is looking after, or is offering to look after, the child, there can be no independent inquiry into whether a care order is needed, or whether the alternative proposals for the child should be promoted. Thus the Court of Appeal's ruling created a very real danger that the voice of the child would not be heard about vital decisions concerning his welfare.

It is suggested that the House of Lords' ruling was unsatisfactory with respect to their Lordships' approach to the choice of orders available. They were at pains to emphasise that the fact that the threshold test for care can be established, even though satisfactory arrangements are currently in place for the child, does not preclude the court from taking these arrangements into account when deciding whether or not to make a care order. They emphasised that the conditions which must be established under section 31(2) merely confer jurisdiction on a court to make a care order; and pointed out that after applying the welfare principle, and considering the factors in the checklist in section 1(3), the court may choose to make an order under section 8 instead.[7] It is nonetheless suggested that the justification given by Lords Mackay and Templeman for making a care order was an untenable application of the welfare principle. The statement that a care order would enable Mrs W to turn to the local authority for help and advice was undoubtedly correct. But such help and advice would almost certainly have been forthcoming in any event, and even if it were not, surely its desirability cannot justify permitting the state to take over parental responsibility? In relation to the court's continuing concerns about the child, these could adequately have been alleviated by making a residence order to Mrs W, possibly with conditions attached, and coupling it with a supervision order. The supervisor would have been charged with the duty to advise, assist and befriend the child,[8] which would inevitably have involved giving help and advice to the child's carer. Moreover it was Mrs W, not the local authority, who would have responsibility for making the day-to-day decisions about the child's upbringing, but the House of Lords was expecting her to carry out this function without the benefit of a residence order, and without the parental responsibility which such an order confers. The statement that a care order would enable the local authority to determine the extent to which the father should meet his parental responsibility for the child does not bear close examination. He was serving a life sentence for murder, and had been recommended for deportation on his release. Thus he would have no part

7   Or indeed no order at all, applying the principle in s.1(5).
8   S.35(1).

to play in the child's life in the foreseeable future, if at all. Also, the child's siblings similarly needed protection from the father exercising parental responsibility at some time in the future, but it would have been inconceivable that anyone could have successfully pleaded that this would justify making a care order in respect of them too. Any problems could clearly have been dealt with by orders under section 8.[9]

Anticipating significant harm

The inclusion of 'likely' significant harm within the threshold test allows for an order to be made where no significant harm to the child has yet occurred. In an extreme case it enables a baby to be removed from her mother at birth, as in *F v Leeds City Council*[10] where the court found that the mother's dangerously egocentric behaviour posed an unacceptable risk to her child. Clearly, any removal of a baby from her mother without giving the mother the opportunity to demonstrate that she has the capacity to care for the child is a Draconian decision, and one which should only be reached where there is compelling evidence that the child is likely to suffer significant harm. In *Newham London Borough v AG*[11] the Court of Appeal held that a court should not approach the interpretation of section 31(2) on the basis that 'likely to suffer' should be equated with the balance of probabilities. Rather, the court approved the approach taken by the House of Lords in *Davies v Taylor*,[12] namely that it cannot be proved that a future event will happen on the balance of probabilities; all that can be done is to evaluate the chance. On the information before the court in *Newham London Borough v AG* there was 'a real significant likelihood' of the child suffering significant harm if the court did not make a care order, and this level of proof was found to be sufficient to satisfy the threshold test. In *Re H (A Minor) (Section 37 Direction)*,[13] Scott Baker J ventured the opinion that when considering whether facts exist to make a care or supervision order, and when looking at the likelihood of significant harm, the court is not limited to looking at the present and the immediate future. He said 'if a court concludes that a parent, or a carer, is likely to be unable to meet

9   The orders available on an application made in care proceedings are discussed in greater detail below.

10   [1994] 2 FLR 60; see also *Re A (A Minor) (Care Proceedings)* [1993] 1 FCR 824 where three children had already been removed from their mother. When a fourth child was born, the local authority immediately obtained an emergency protection order and commenced care proceedings on the basis of likely harm.

11   [1993] 1 FLR 281.

12   [1972] 3 All ER 836, which concerned a very different state of affairs, namely a claim by a widow under the Fatal Accidents Acts 1846-1959.

13   [1993] 2 FLR 541.

the emotional needs of a child in the future—even if years hence—my view is that the condition in section 31(2) would probably be met.'[14]

The harm is attributable to a lack of reasonable parental care

The second limb of section 31(2) focuses on the source of the harm. It requires proof that

> 'the harm, or likelihood of harm, is attributable to—
> (i)   the care given to the child, or likely to be given to him if the order were not made, not being what it would be reasonable to expect a parent to give to him.'

It can be seen that the test to be applied is an objective test. It is not whether the child's actual parents or carers have fallen below standards of acceptable parenting, but whether they have fallen below the standard of care which it would be reasonable to expect 'a parent' to give to the child. In a case where parents or others do not have the capacity to care for the child without the child suffering, or being likely to suffer, significant harm, the test is satisfied even though any harm to the child is entirely unintentional. This is not to say that the motive of the person who has harmed the child is irrelevant; clearly harm which is caused intentionally or recklessly will be viewed with far greater concern than harm which occurred accidentally. Rather, it is to say that the caring person's motive is only partly relevant to proof of the second limb of the threshold test. Although this may seem harsh, it is suggested that any test which would always require some kind of intentional, reckless or negligent behaviour on the part of the person who had caused the child significant harm could put the child at serious risk. It would mean that a child could not be protected from persons with serious physical incapacities, serious or unpredictable mental illness or severe learning difficulties.

The harm is attributable to the child's being beyond parental control

Occasionally a child may be suffering, or be likely to suffer, significant harm not because of a failure of reasonable parental care, but because he is beyond parental control.[15] An example might be where a child has become

14   He did not need to resolve the question because no application had been made for a care or supervision order. The case concerned an application by a lesbian couple for a residence order in respect of a baby girl. Scott Baker J ordered the local authority to undertake an investigation under s.37(1).
15   S.31(2)(b)(ii).

addicted to drugs, or is sexually promiscuous, or has developed anorexia nervosa, and where the parents are powerless to influence the child's behaviour. An example arose in *M v Birmingham City Council*[16] where the child, aged 13, was very seriously disturbed and behaving in an uncontrollable fashion, such that she was posing a serious risk to herself and those around her. It is suggested, however, that those initiating care proceedings, and courts when determining an application brought in care proceedings, should be wary of improper reliance being placed on the beyond control provision. Where parents, or others, have truly tried their best to make reasonable arrangements for the child's upbringing it is right that they should not be stigmatised as causing the child to suffer, or to be likely to suffer, significant harm because the care they have given the child, or are likely to give the child, is not what it would be reasonable to expect a parent to give to him. However, it is equally stigmatising for the child to be found to be beyond parental control in a case where the fault lies with those who have brought him up. Such a finding is likely to influence the arrangements which are made about how the child will be looked after if a care order is made, or the types of activities in which the child will be required to take part if a supervision order is made.

Justice to a child requires that he should only be labelled as beyond control where there is cogent evidence to support this allegation. Where a child is badly behaved, or otherwise apparently out of control, it may be comparatively easy to prove that the child is bringing harm upon himself. It may be far harder to prove wrongdoing or other failure by a parent which has led to the child coming to harm, or to be likely to come to harm. It seems likely that there is a risk that the attribution of harm to the child, rather than the parent, might sometimes be selected as the basis for bringing proceedings, or making an order, because it is easier to prove. However, just as it is wrong to label a parent as having caused his child to come to harm unless there is evidence to substantiate this, so too it is wrong to label a child as being beyond parental control if the true cause of his coming to harm is because his parents, or others, have failed to give him reasonable parental care.

Standard of proof where child abuse is alleged

The standard of proof in children cases is the civil standard of the balance of probabilities. However, the courts have said that the degree of probability

---

16 [1994] 2 FLR 141. The case arose after the Court of Appeal decision, but before the House of Lords' decision, in *Re M (A Minor) (Care Order: Threshold Conditions)* [1994] 3 All ER 298, above. Since the House of Lords' ruling, the point of law about when the extent of parental control should be assessed is no longer in issue.

required in any particular context may vary and must be 'commensurate with the occasion' or 'proportionate' with the subject matter.[17] Applying this approach to children cases, the Court of Appeal ruled in *Re W (Minors) (Sexual Abuse: Standard of Proof)*[18] that the more serious the allegation which is made against a parent by a child the more convincing must be the evidence to establish the truth of what is alleged. The court held that where an allegation is made that a parent has sexually abused his child, the stigma and disgrace to the parent is such that the level of proof to substantiate this allegation is a very high standard, though not necessarily as demanding as the criminal standard. A similar approach to the standard of proof was adopted in *Re M (A Minor) (No 2) (Appeal)*[19] in which the trial judge justified his finding that the child's mother and her cohabitee had not seriously injured and otherwise ill-treated the child on the ground that 'given the seriousness of the nature of the allegation and the person- alities and relationships involved, it is a proportionately higher standard of probability than otherwise for less serious allegations'. The Court of Appeal confirmed the judge's approach.[20]

It is suggested that this approach to the standard of proof in children cases is entirely misconceived. As one critic has said:

'The consequence of finding that the parents nearly killed their child when they did not will be that the child will be removed from them. The consequence of finding that they did not do it when they did is likely to be the refusal to make a care order, and the child being returned to the people who nearly killed her. In this context, [this theory] about the standard of proof is worse than just not sensible: it is actually perverse. In practice it means that the worse the danger the child is in, the less likely the courts are to remove her from it.'[1]

In the earlier case of *Re G (No 2) (A Minor)*[2] Sheldon J had drawn a distinction between the degree of probability which must be established to satisfy a court that a child has been sexually abused, and the degree of probability required to discharge the burden of proving that a child has been sexually abused by her father. In the case of the former he said that 'any tilt in the balance suggesting that [the child] had been the victim of

---

17 Adopting the approach of Denning LJ (as he then was) in *Bater v Bater* [1951] P 35.
18 [1994] 1 FLR 419; see too *Re H (A Minor); K v K (Minors) (Child Abuse: Evidence)* [1989] 2 FLR 313.
19 [1994] 1 FLR 59.
20 Though it expressed the test slightly differently. See too, *Re P (A Minor) (Care: Evidence)* [1994] 2 FLR 751.
1   See J R Spencer (1994) 6 JCL 160.
2   [1988] 1 FLR 314.

sexual abuse would justify a finding to that effect.' However, in relation to whether the child's father was the perpetrator of the abuse he said 'a higher degree of probability is required to satisfy the court that the father has been guilty of some sexual misconduct with his daughter.'[3] In *Re W (Minors) (Sexual Abuse: Standard of Proof)*[4] the Court of Appeal expressed no view on whether this dichotomy is generally correct. However, it held that where there is only one person who could be the abuser of the child, so that a finding of abuse inevitably leads to a finding on the identity of the perpetrator, the standard to be applied must be the higher standard.

Decision-making in children cases not only looks backwards to make findings of fact about what has occurred in the past, it also looks forward to what is likely to happen to the child in the future. Indeed, it has been seen that the threshold test for care allows an order to be made solely on the ground that the child is likely to suffer significant harm. It may be in a particular case that an allegation of past sexual abuse, or other forms of abuse, cannot be substantiated to the high standard of proof required by the authorities. However, despite this, it seems that a court may be entitled to find that the threshold test for care is nonetheless proved. Prior to the Children Act 1989, in wardship proceedings in *Re H (A Minor); K v K (Minors) (Child Abuse: Evidence)*,[5] Butler-Sloss LJ said that a judge may have come across circumstances which constitute a high degree of concern about the child but which he cannot say amounts to actual abuse. On the other hand he may have:

> 'sufficient evidence of concern about past care for the child to be satisfied that the child was in a potentially abusing situation without having sufficient evidence to be satisfied as to the extent of the abuse in the past or the identity of the abuser. He has to assess the risks and, if there is a real possibility that the child will be at risk, he will take steps to safeguard the child.'[6]

She continued 'the assessment of possibilities is crucial at this stage' but added that 'the court can only act on evidence. Otherwise the judge would be dispensing palm tree justice.'

The approach in *Re H (A Minor); K v K (Minors) (Child Abuse: Evidence)* would appear to allow a court to intervene to protect a child when significant harm in the form of sexual or other abuse is feared even though past abuse cannot be proved. It is not clear to what extent this thinking has survived the enactment of the Children Act 1989. It is plain that the court must be satisfied that the threshold test for care is established before it can

3 Ibid, at p 321.
4 [1994] 1 FLR 419.
5 [1989] 2 FLR 313.
6 Ibid, at p 325.

intervene. However, when in *Newham London Borough v AG*[7] the Court of Appeal was invited to give a strict construction to the meaning of 'is likely' to suffer significant harm, so that the test is satisfied only if it is proved on the balance of probabilities, or to a very strong degree, the court resisted this invitation. Sir Stephen Brown P ruled that 'likely to suffer' should not be equated with the balance of probabilities. Rather, all that can be done is to evaluate the chance.[8] On the information before the court there was 'a real significant likelihood' of the child suffering significant harm if the court did not make a care order and that, the court ruled, was sufficient to satisfy the threshold test.

It is suggested that it should be possible to accommodate both proper weight being given to a child's right to be protected, and proper respect being given to an adult's right not to be identified as a perpetrator of child abuse except where this is established by cogent evidence proved to a high standard. As Waite J acknowledged in *Re W (Minor) (Child Abuse: Evidence)*,[9] cases of this kind are exceptionally difficult because 'they bring into contrast two stark principles which everyone would acknowledge as fundamental to our society. One is the basic requirement of justice that nobody should have to face a finding by any court of serious parental misconduct without the opportunity of having the allegations against him clearly specified and cogently proved. The other is the public interest in the detection and prevention of parental child abuse as conduct which is liable, if persisted in, to do serious damage to the emotional development of the victim and to his or her capacity to form stable and satisfying relationships in adult life.' It is suggested that Sheldon J's approach in *Re G (No 2) (A Minor)*,[10] in which he proposed that a lower standard should be applied to proof that a child has been abused than the high standard required to establish who is the abuser, should be followed. If this approach is applied to applications made on the basis that a child is suffering, or is likely to suffer, significant harm, this would allow proper weight to be given to both principles enunciated by Waite J. However, this separation of proof of abuse from proof of who is the abuser has been undermined by the Court of Appeal decision in *Re W (Minors) (Sexual Abuse: Standard of Proof)*.[11] Whilst the logic of the Court of Appeal's ruling that where the alleged abuser is the only possible perpetrator a high standard of proof applies is acknowledged, it is nonetheless suggested that this was a mistaken decision which could have very serious consequences for children

---

7   [1993] 1 FLR 281.
8   It was in this context that Sir Stephen Brown P expressed the hope that courts would not be invited to perform in every case a strict legalistic analysis of the statutory meaning of s.31(2): see above p 154.
9   [1987] 1 FLR 297 at p 298.
10 [1988] 1 FLR 314.
11 [1994] 1 FLR 419; and in *Re M (A Minor) (No 2) (Appeal)* [1994] 1 FLR 59.

who may be the victims of abuse. Sexual abuse in particular is notoriously difficult to prove, and proving the identity of the abuser can be almost impossible because of the child's fears of what may happen to him if he reveals the 'secret' between himself and the abuser.

It may often be the case that there is only one possible perpetrator, but for the court then to elevate the standard of proof to a very high standard, commensurate with the seriousness of the allegation, has the paradoxical consequence that the more grave the risk of harm to the child, the harder it is to prove. When a court is considering how to balance risk to a child against wrongfully intervening in the child's family life, surely the more serious the harm to the child if the risk should materialise the more ready the court ought to be to take steps to protect him. It is suggested that it should be possible for a court to find that a child is being abused, or is likely to be abused, on the balance of probabilities even though on a higher standard it cannot be satisfied that the evidence is sufficient to establish that the only possible perpetrator has carried out the abuse. One standard is about child protection, the other is about casting grave imputations on a parent or other person. It is suggested the two can and should be kept separate. The courts might best achieve this by finding on the balance of probabilities that a child is likely to suffer significant harm, applying the more flexible approach and real likelihood test taken in *Newham London Borough v AG*.[12]

Orders on an application made in care proceedings

The grounds for instituting care proceedings are commonly referred to as the 'threshold test' for care because, once established, they allow the court to make a care order. But proof of the grounds is permissive only. It by no means follows from proof of the grounds for care that a care order will always be in the child's best interests, and the court has a choice between a variety of orders. It may of course make a care order, in which case parental responsibility for the child is given to the local authority. Or it may decide that a supervision order will afford the child sufficient protection against suffering further significant harm, and that to allow him to remain in his present home will best promote his interests. In some cases the court may determine that no useful purpose will be served by the local authority continuing to have involvement with the child, and that it is better for the child if no order at all is made. Sometimes a residence order may be thought to be the most appropriate response, particularly where a relative is offering to look after the child. A residence order can be made subject to conditions, or it could be coupled with a supervision order where

12 [1993] 1 FLR 281.

this seems necessary for the purpose of protecting the child.[13] A family assistance order may be a helpful adjunct to a residence order, particularly where there may be difficulties about contact arrangements with the child.[14] Such an order, which requires either a probation officer or an officer of the local authority to advise, assist and befriend any person named in the order, may only be made with the consent of any adult named in the order, and only in exceptional circumstances. It lasts for six months unless a shorter period is specified.[15] A specific issue order might afford the child sufficient protection against further harm, for example where the issue precipitating the care proceedings relates to the child receiving medical treatment, and where the court authorises such treatment to take place without the consent of the parents.[16] Or a prohibited steps order might suffice, where a specified person is prohibited from having any contact with the child. However, it has been made clear that a prohibited steps order cannot be used to order a parent to leave home,[17] or to prevent parents from having contact with each other.[18] Should the court wish to order that an unmarried father should have parental responsibility for his child, without wishing to grant him a residence order, it can do so only on the father's application. It does not have own motion powers in this regard. Similarly, where a child has no parent with parental responsibility, it may only order that a person is appointed guardian of the child if an application is made by an individual.[19]

Whatever the court chooses, its decision must be governed by the principle that the child's welfare is its paramount consideration. It is bound to apply the checklist in section 1(3), and it must be satisfied that to make an order or orders will be better for the child than making no order at all.[20] Even when parties to the proceedings agree about which order is most suitable, the decision is nonetheless one for the court to make. The parties might, for example, all agree that the threshold for care is established but that the child can be adequately protected by a supervision order. The court, on the other hand, might be unhappy with this arrangement, and take the view that a care order is the only order which will properly safeguard the child from suffering further significant harm. In these circumstances it should make a care order. Similarly, the court can refuse to make a care order even though the guardian ad litem recommends that this order should be made. However, where a court departs from a

13 *Re DH (A Minor) (Child Abuse)* [1994] 1 FLR 679.
14 See *Leeds City Council v C* [1993] 1 FLR 269.
15 S.16(1)(3)(5). On family assistance orders generally, see ch 2.
16 Cf *Re E (A Minor) (Wardship: Medical Treatment)* [1993] 1 FLR 386.
17 *Nottinghamshire County Council v P* [1993] 2 FLR 134.
18 *Croydon London Borough Council v A (No 1)* [1992] 2 FLR 341.
19 On guardianship orders generally, see ch 1.
20 S.1(5).

recommendation made by the guardian ad litem it must give particularly full and clear reasons for reaching a different decision.[1]

The implications of making a care order

Where a court makes a care order it may also make an order in relation to contact with the child under section 34, otherwise the court must step back and allow the local authority to take over. When making the care order, the court cannot attach any conditions to it, or ask the guardian ad litem to report back on how the order is working, for this would amount to an attempt to regulate the manner in which a local authority exercise their powers under the order.[2] Once the order is made, parental responsibility lies with the local authority and all decision-making powers about the child are henceforth vested in the local authority and taken from the court.[3] The court will only become involved in further litigation about the child where an application is made which would have the effect of discharging the care order,[4] or where an application is made for a contact order under section 34.

The court therefore needs to have a clear idea of the nature of the local authority's plans for the child before it transfers decision-making powers to the authority.[5] In *Manchester City Council v F*[6] Eastham J stated that the local authority should submit a care plan which should accord, so far as possible, with guidance on the format and content of such a plan which has been issued by the Department of Health.[7] In *Re J (Minors) (Care: Care Plan)*[8] Wall J said that, wherever possible, evidence to support the care plan should be provided, though he acknowledged that the extent and nature of the evidence will vary from case to case, and that the local authority may have been inhibited from formulating long-term plans until

---

1   *S v Oxfordshire County Council* [1993] 1 FLR 452; *Leicestershire County Council v G* [1994] 2 FLR 329.
2   *Kent County Council v C* [1993] 1 FLR 308; *Re B (A Minor) (Care Order: Review)* [1993] 1 FLR 421; *Re T (A Minor) (Care Order: Conditions)* [1994] 2 FLR 423.
3   Once a care order is made it lasts until the child reaches 18 unless it is brought to an end earlier by order of a court: s.91(12).
4   As when a direct application is made to discharge the care order under s.39; where an application is made for a residence order, which, if made, would have the effect of discharging the care order: s.91(1); or in adoption proceedings, when a freeing order or an adoption order is made: Adoption Act 1976, ss.12 and 18; see ch 4.
5   This sometimes gives rise to the question whether the court is in a position to make a final order or whether it should make an interim order: see above.
6   [1993] 1 FLR 419n.
7   *Guidance and Regulations*, Vol 3, para 2.62; this paragraph is reproduced in its entirety in *Re J (Minors) (Care: Care Plan)* [1994] 1 FLR 253 at p 259.
8   Above.

sure of obtaining a care order.[9] Where the court disagrees with the care plan it can refuse to make a care order, though of course this gives rise to the dilemma that unfettered parental responsibility will therefore remain with those who already have it, and this too may be an unsatisfactory outcome.[10]

Parents and guardians do not lose their parental responsibility when a care order is made because parental responsibility is not lost solely because some other person subsequently acquires it.[11] However, section 33(3)(b) provides that the local authority have the power to determine the extent to which a parent or guardian of the child may meet his or her parental responsibility for the child.[12] Thus it can be seen that local authority and parents are not equal holders of parental responsibility; decision-making has been firmly vested by statute in the local authority. However, the local authority do not have an unfettered discretion on whether they continue to involve parents in the upbringing of their children. Part III creates a framework in which local authorities are expected to work in partnership with parents where this is consistent with the welfare of the child. Section 22(3) imposes a general duty on a local authority in relation to a child whom they are looking after to safeguard and promote the child's welfare, and section 22(4) imposes on the authority the more specific duty to consult with the child and his parents, so far as is reasonably practicable, before making any decision about the child. When choosing the child's placement, the local authority 'shall' make arrangements to enable him to live with a parent, a person with parental responsibility, the holder of a residence order immediately before the care order was made, or a relative, friend or other person connected with the child. They must also seek to secure that the child is accommodated near his home and that siblings are accommodated together. Understandably, these requirements are subject to the proviso that they should be followed only when to do so would be reasonably practicable and consistent with the child's welfare.[13]

It can be seen that a child is able to live at home with his parents despite the fact that he is in the care of the local authority. Indeed, a significant proportion of children in care live at home with their parents for all or

9   For example, they are unlikely to arrange a potential adoption placement until certain that they will obtain a care order, but they could give the court some idea of how easy such an arrangement would be to make.
10 Parental responsibility could be given to a third party under s.8, and control over the exercise of parental responsibility by parents could be imposed by other s.8 orders, but there are no administrative mechanisms for ensuring that the court's orders are obeyed.
11 S.2(6).
12 There are some limits imposed on the exercise of parental responsibility by a local authority in s.33(6)-(9) which relate to maintaining the child's religious upbringing, giving consent to adoption, appointing a guardian, changing the child's surname and removing him from the United Kingdom.
13 S.23(4)-(7); see too Sch.2 Part II and *Guidance and Regulations*, Vol 4.

part of the time, where the local authority's purpose is to rehabilitate the child with his family. Clearly, where it was the parents who caused, or failed to protect, the child from suffering, or being likely to suffer, significant harm, safeguards are needed to ensure the safety of the child when this arrangement is made. There are special regulations about such placements which impose stringent requirements on the local authority to be sure that the placement of the child is the most suitable way of performing their duty to safeguard and promote the child's welfare,[14] to make proper inquiries, to ensure all interested persons are notified of the placement and to supervise the placement at regular intervals.[15] The child should, if possible, be seen alone when visited,[16] and the local authority are under a duty to remove the child immediately if the child's welfare or safety is at risk.[17] Because the local authority have parental responsibility, it is they who are accountable for ensuring that the child receives an upbringing which secures his safety and promotes his welfare. However, where the local authority are alleged to have failed to exercise their responsibility in a manner which amounts to negligence or breach of statutory duty, this does not give the child a cause of action in damages.[18]

Supervision orders

When the only practical choice for the court is between making a care order or a supervision order, the question to be resolved is whether a supervision order will afford the child sufficient protection. A supervision order gives a local authority far less power in relation to the child than a care order, and correspondingly imposes a far less onerous duty on the authority. The duty of the supervisor is to advise, assist and befriend the child and to take such steps as are reasonably necessary to give effect to the order.[19] A supervision order does not require the supervisor to keep the child safe; such a requirement would be unreasonable because the supervisor does not have the powers and resources to do this, and it is misguided to think of a supervision order as 'a sort of watered-down version

14 S.22(3).
15 Placement of Children with Parents etc. Regulations 1991 (SI 1991/893).
16 Reg.9; the importance of seeing and talking to the child alone has been stressed in a number of inquiries where children have been killed or come to harm when being cared for by parents or foster parents, see particularly *A Child in Mind: The Report on the Death of Kimberley Carlile*, Greenwich London Borough Council (1987), *A Child in Trust*, London Borough of Brent (1988).
17 Reg.11.
18 *X v Bedfordshire County Council; M v Newham London Borough* [1994] 1 FLR 431; at the time of writing leave to appeal against these rulings has been given by the House of Lords.
19 S.35(1)(a).

of care.'[20] A supervisor cannot enforce compliance with the order, but where the order is not wholly complied with, or where it appears no longer to be necessary, the supervisor must consider whether an application should be made to vary or discharge the order.[1] Clearly, if the supervisor becomes anxious that supervision is not enough to protect the child from suffering significant harm, he should set in motion the process which will lead to a fresh application in care proceedings being made, this time for a care order. In an emergency, steps should be taken to obtain an emergency protection order.

Provisions within Schedule 3 enable a highly-structured supervision order to be made which may afford the child adequate protection without the need to give parental responsibility to the local authority. A supervision order can be supplemented and strengthened by giving the supervisor additional powers. He may require the supervised child to comply with directions about where the child is to live, places he should go to, persons he should meet and activities in which he should take part. These directions can be given to the child without the child's consent; indeed it will only be in the case of an older child that his willingness to comply with such directions will be a relevant consideration.[2] The order may also require the child to submit to medical or psychiatric examination and treatment.[3] In the large majority of cases the child will be too young to control his own upbringing in any way and to express a view on the directions and requirements imposed. Directions are likely to include such matters as that the child should go to a day nursery, attend a clinic and go to a family centre on specified days. Co-operation from the persons looking after the child is therefore normally essential if the supervision order is to work. Consequently, there is power to impose obligations on a 'responsible person'[4] to ensure that the supervised child complies with the directions imposed and any examination or treatment ordered. The order may also include a requirement that the responsible person complies with any directions given by the supervisor that he attends at certain places for the purpose of taking part in specified activities. However, these obligations can only be imposed if the responsible person consents. But even where he does, the supervisor has no powers to make him comply. The supervisor's only 'sanction' in the case of non co-operation is to consider seeking variation or discharge of

---

20 *Re S(J) (A Minor) (Care or Supervision Order)* [1993] 2 FLR 919 at p 950, per Judge Coningsby QC; see too *Leicestershire County Council v G* [1994] 2 FLR 329.

1   S.35(1)(c).

2   This may be particularly relevant where the significant harm is attributable to the child's being beyond parental control.

3   The usual proviso about the competent child agreeing to such examination or treatment applies: Sch. 3, paras 4(4) and 5(5).

4   A responsible person means any person who has parental responsibility for the child and any other person with whom the child is living: Sch. 3, para 1.

the order.[5] It is therefore entirely inappropriate for a supervision order to be made where it is the court's intention that the local authority should be able to control the situation.[6]

In *Re H (Supervision Order)*,[7] the children concerned were living with their mother and having contact with their father. He had served a sentence of imprisonment for sexual assaults on his step-child. He was anxious to receive treatment for his behaviour and therefore readily agreed to attend at a specialist clinic. It was agreed by all parties, and by the court, that a supervision order was appropriate. But the mother, father and guardian ad litem sought an order under Schedule 3 that the local authority should direct the father to attend a particular course of treatment at the clinic. The local authority contended that the court had no power to make such a direction. Bracewell J upheld the local authority's contention. She drew a contrast between the power of the court to direct that the child submit to a medical or psychiatric examination or treatment, and its powers to make orders in respect of a responsible person. She held that requirements as to treatment of the child are wholly the responsibility of the court, and must be specified in the order itself. However, she held that the imposition of obligations on a responsible person fell into a wholly different category, namely that such directions are solely a matter for the supervisor, and that it is not open to the court to order the local authority to give any such directions. Clearly, if a court were entitled to impose such an obligation on a local authority, this would amount to a form of court control over local authority expenditure. Services provided by clinics of this kind are an expensive resource, and therefore it is for the local authority, rather than the court, to decide whether use should be made of such services as part of the authority's child protection strategy.

The choice for the court is whether a supervision order will afford the child adequate safeguards against coming to harm. In *Re D (A Minor) (Care or Supervision Order)*[8] Ewbank J held that where a local authority take the view that a care order would undermine working co-operatively with parents, that this is not a proper reason for making a supervision order rather than a care order where a supervision order would not afford the child sufficient protection. On the other hand, in *Re M (A Minor) (No 2) (Appeal)*[9] Ward J justified declining to make a supervision order on the ground that confidence between the parents and the local authority had been 'irredeemably destroyed'. He reached this conclusion despite having found that the mother, by failing to obtain medical attention for the child, had caused the child to suffer, and to be likely to suffer, significant harm,

5   S.35.
6   *Re R and G (Minors) (Interim Care or Supervision Orders)* [1994] 1 FLR 793.
7   [1994] 2 FLR 979.
8   [1993] 2 FLR 423.
9   [1994] 1 FLR 59.

and that the child was dangerously ill by the time she was taken to hospital.[10] It is suggested that the approach in *Re D (A Minor) (Care or Supervision Order)* is preferable. Unless a local authority are authorised to make regular checks on a child's progress, there are real dangers that the child may slip through the net of child protection procedures.

Contact with a child in care

Generally speaking a child is likely to find it easier to cope with living away from his parents and wider family if he believes that these persons are concerned about his upbringing, and wish to see him on a regular basis. Furthermore, unless the child maintains regular contact with his parents and wider family it is unlikely that he will be rehabilitated home again. The encouragement of contact between a child in care with his parents and other persons is therefore of the greatest importance. The public law part of the Children Act 1989 is built around the notion that contact between a child in care and his family is in his interests. Paragraph 15(1) of Schedule 2 positively promotes the maintenance of contact by providing that—

'Where a child is being looked after by a local authority, the authority shall, unless it is not reasonably practicable or consistent with his welfare, endeavour to promote contact between the child and—

(a) his parents;

(b) any person who is not a parent of his but who has parental responsibility for him; and

(c) any relative, friend or other person connected with him.'

Other provisions in the Act reinforce this general principle: local authorities are required to make efforts to secure that a child is accommodated near his home;[11] parents and persons with parental responsibility should be told where the child is living;[12] and it is recognised that parents, relatives and friends of a child in care may be too poor to afford the travelling costs

10 *Re M (A Minor) (No 2) (Appeal)* is a highly disturbing case in which the Court of Appeal confirmed the finding of the trial judge that a child aged five had not been seriously non-accidentally injured, beaten and sexually abused. The child became hysterical on being told that she was to be returned to her parents, and the professionals and the child's grandparents were convinced that the child had been the victim of serious and repeated abuse. For critical commentary, see J R Spencer (1994) 6 FLR 160, and the editorial by M Hayes in the same issue.

11 S.32(7).

12 Unless, in the case of a child in care, this would prejudice the child's welfare: Sch. 2, para 15(2)(3)(4).

involved in visiting the child, and the local authority have a discretion to make payments towards defraying these and other expenses.[13] More generally, the guidance to local authorities issued under the Act encourages them to work in partnership with parents, to share parental responsibility with them and to seek to ensure that contact between the child and his family is maintained in a positive manner.[14] The guidance emphasises that the first weeks during which a child is looked after by a local authority are likely to be particularly crucial to the success of contact because it is at this time that patterns of behaviour are set.[15]

Contact with a child in care and court orders

Because contact is of such significance to both the child and his family, there is a framework of provisions in Parts IV and V of the Act within which those who are caring for the child must operate. The law takes as its starting point the rule that a child must be allowed to have reasonable contact with his parents and other important persons in his life even though he has been removed from their care.[16] However, whilst the maintenance of contact between a child and his family is normally regarded as beneficial to the child, in some cases it is in the interests of the child that contact between him and his family should be heavily restricted, or even denied. It is in cases of this kind, where the child needs protection from contact with his family, or where there is disagreement between interested persons such as the local authority, the child, his parents and others over contact with a child in care, that the courts become involved.

Contact and emergency protection orders

The first occasion where a question about contact arrangements is likely to arise is when a court makes an emergency protection order under section 44.[17] Section 44(13) provides that a successful applicant for an emergency protection order must allow the child to have reasonable contact with certain specified persons.[18] The applicant, who can be anyone, but who is almost always the local authority, does not have the power to refuse contact unless the court authorises this by an order made under section 44(6)(a).

13 Sch. 2, para 16.
14 *Guidance and Regulations*, Vol 3, para 6.10.
15 Ibid, para 16.
16 S.34(1); see below.
17 Emergency protection orders are discussed above.
18 These are: parents, persons with parental responsibility, persons with whom the child was living, persons with a contact order, and persons acting on behalf of the above persons.

This provision states that the court may give such directions (if any) as it considers appropriate with respect to the contact which is, or is not, to be allowed between the child and any named person. Emergency protection orders are made either ex parte or at an inter partes hearing. In the case of the former, the court (which will normally be a single magistrate) is likely to make no order about contact and to leave the question of what amounts to reasonable contact to be decided at the discretion of the local authority. However, where the local authority wish to deny contact altogether they must obtain a direction from the court permitting them to do so at the time the order is made. Where an emergency protection order is made at an inter partes hearing, parents and others may wish to raise questions about how much contact they should be permitted to have with their child, and whether it must always be supervised. In a case of this kind, where parents disagree with what the local authority are proposing, the court may give more specific directions about contact.[19]

Contact and interim care orders

The next occasion when an issue may arise about contact with a child is when an application has been made in care proceedings, where no final order has yet been made, and where the child is being looked after under an interim care order. In such a case the local authority must allow reasonable contact between a child and his parents and other specified persons.[20] What amounts to 'reasonable contact' is not the same as contact at the discretion of the local authority. In *Re P (Minors) (Contact with Children in Care)*,[1] Ewbank J stated that 'reasonable' implies contact which has been agreed between the local authority and the parents, or, if there is no such agreement, contact which is objectively reasonable. Clearly, this will vary according to the child's particular circumstances, but must be in accordance with the local authority's general duty to promote contact and must take account of the wishes and feelings of the child and his parents.[2] Where the local authority and the parents, or other specified persons, cannot agree over contact arrangements an application can be made under section 34 for the court to determine the matter. Guidance was given in *A v M and Walsall Metropolitan Borough Council*[3] on how courts should approach such an application. Ewbank J ruled that contact should not

---

19 Emergency protection orders are in any event of only limited duration. They last initially for a maximum period of eight days (s.45(1)), but can be extended for a further period of up to seven days (s.45(5)).
20 S.34(1).
1 [1993] 2 FLR 156.
2 S.22(4).
3 [1993] 2 FLR 244.

normally be terminated at an interim stage in care proceedings, rather, he said, contact should be maintained save in circumstances of exceptional and severe risk. Thus where the child can be kept safe, for example by the contact being supervised, then contact should be permitted, for any other conclusion anticipates the decisions to be made at the final hearing of the application for the care order, and to do this is premature at an interim stage.

Regulating contact with a child in care

Once a care order has been made the general principle that courts are not permitted to intervene in a local authority's day-to-day plans for the upbringing of a child in care is tempered by the rival principle that any major intervention in a person's family life should only be authorised after a judicial hearing at which the rights and interests of all the persons concerned are properly represented.[4] The starting position in relation to contact with a child in care is stated in section 34(1). This prevents a local authority from exercising an unrestrained discretion over contact arrangements by providing that—

'Where a child is in the care of a local authority, the authority shall (subject to the provisions of this section) allow the child reasonable contact with—
(a) his parents;
(b) any guardian of his;
(c) where there was a residence order in force with respect to the child immediately before the care order was made, the person in whose favour the order was made; and
(d) where, immediately before the care order was made, a person had care of the child by virtue of an order made in the exercise of the High Court's inherent jurisdiction with respect to children, that person.'

At the time when an application is made for a final care order, the local authority's attitude towards contact between the child and his parents will normally form part of their care plan for the child. Section 34(11) provides that before making a care order the court must consider the contact arrangements which the local authority have made, or propose to make, and must invite the parties to the proceedings to comment on those arrangements. The court is empowered at this stage to make any order it

4 See too the European Convention on Human Rights, Arts.6 and 8.

thinks appropriate in relation to contact, either on the application of one of the parties, or in the exercise its own motion powers.[5] Generally speaking a court is unlikely to make a contact order at the time when it makes a care order because contact is normally a matter to be arranged by agreement between the local authority, the child, the parents and other interested persons. However there may be occasions when an order about contact may be appropriate right at the outset of a care order. In *Re SW (A Minor) (Care Proceedings)*,[6] Booth J held that justices were correct to exercise their own motion powers to order no contact between a child and his mother in circumstances where there was no realistic chance that the child would return to live with her, where the local authority's plan was to find a permanent substitute family for the child, and where the guardian ad litem supported this plan.

Where the question whether contact should be denied arises at the outset of the operation of a care order a balance must be struck between allowing time for the parents to explore with the local authority whether the rehabilitation of the child with his family will be attainable under the changed circumstances of a care order, and recognising that any delay in determining a question about the child's upbringing is likely to prejudice the welfare of the child.[7] Where the long-term plan for the child is to place him for adoption, the more swiftly any questions about contact are resolved, the sooner steps can be taken to place a child with potential adoptive parents.[8] When it is believed that the child needs the security of a settled placement, the difficulty is to know how much opportunity, if any, should be given for alternative arrangements which continue to involve the parents to be attempted before an order authorising the reduction or termination of contact is made.

Questions about contact may arise at any time while a child is in the care of a local authority. Because any decision by the authority to refuse contact between a child and the persons specified in section 34(1) is a judgment of such major importance to both the child and those persons, section 34(6) provides that it cannot be implemented without the authority of a court order, except in a case of urgency, and then only for up to seven days.[9] Where the authority wish to bring contact to an end they must apply to the court under section 34(4). Similarly, where agreement cannot be reached on what amounts to reasonable contact, the child, the local

5 S.34(2)(3)(4)(5)(10).
6 [1993] 2 FLR 609.
7 S.1(2).
8 Research informs us that the chances of an adoption being successful start to diminish the older the child becomes, see J Fratter, J Rowe, D Sapsford and J Thoburn *Permanent Family Placement* (BAAF, 1991).
9 S.34(6).

authority and the persons specified in section 34(1) are each entitled to apply for a contact order.[10]

Decisions about contact are governed by the principle that the child's welfare must be the court's paramount consideration. In *Birmingham City Council v H (No 3)*[11] the question arose as to how the court should apply the paramountcy of the child's interests when the child, and the mother of the child, were both children. The Court of Appeal took the view that a court must approach the question of their welfare without giving one priority over the other, and refused to allow the local authority to deny the mother contact. The House of Lords allowed the local authority's appeal. It ruled that the child for the purposes of section 34 was the child in care in respect of whom an order was being sought. It was that child who was the subject of the application, the question to be determined related to that child's upbringing and it was that child's welfare which must be the court's paramount consideration.[12]

Any other person who is aggrieved about the amount of contact, if any, which he is allowed with a child in care may apply to a court for a contact order. However, in some cases it could clearly be disruptive and damaging to the child if anyone was entitled to apply for contact; thus a non-entitled person must first obtain the leave of the court to make the application.[13] Somewhat surprisingly, there are no specific criteria which the court must apply to the leave decision. In the light of the ruling in *Re A (Minors) (Residence Order)*[14] that an application for leave is not a substantive application concerning the upbringing of a child to which the welfare principle must therefore apply, this leaves a vacuum of principle against which to test whether or not leave should be granted.[15]

Contact, the local authority's plans and the court's jurisdiction

Any decision by a court to order contact against the wishes of a local authority is likely seriously to interfere with the authority's plans for the

10 However, where a court in earlier proceedings has ordered that there should be no contact between a child and his parent, if an application is later made under s.34 a court is entitled to act robustly and to dismiss the application without hearing oral evidence: *Cheshire County Council v M* [1993] 1 FLR 463.
11 [1994] 1 FLR 224.
12 In relation to the risk of harm to the child, the paramountcy principle and contact, see *Re N (Minors) (Care Orders: Termination of Parental Contact)* [1994] 2 FCR 1101. This decision, and the decision in *Birmingham City Council v H*, above, is discussed in ch 4.
13 S.34(2)(3); thus the structure is similar to that in s.10: see above ch 2.
14 [1992] 3 All ER 872.
15 In *Re B (Minors) (Care: Contact: Local Authority's Plans)* [1993] 1 FLR 543 Butler-Sloss LJ stated, obiter, that there is no statutory requirement to have particular regard to the local authority's plans for the child's future on a leave application. However, it is suggested that these plans will nonetheless be highly relevant to the determination of the merits of many such applications.

child's future upbringing. It was acknowledged by the Court of Appeal in *Re B (Minors) (Care: Contact: Local Authority's Plans)*[16] that such a decision therefore raises profound questions about the inter-relationship between the plans of the local authority, the jurisdiction of the court and the proper exercise of the court's discretion. The fundamental principle that courts have no reviewing power over how local authorities exercise their discretionary powers when carrying out their statutory functions remains intact.[17] However, in *Re B (Minors),* and subsequently in *Re E (A Minor) (Care Order: Contact),*[18] the Court of Appeal unhesitatingly rejected the argument that the court cannot go behind the long-term plans of the local authority unless they were acting capriciously, or were otherwise open to scrutiny by way of judicial review. In *Re B (Minors)* Butler-Sloss LJ said that it is clear that the discretion to refuse to allow contact, or otherwise to determine what contact is reasonable, is firmly vested in the courts and not in the local authority.[19] She said that the proposals of the local authority, based on their appreciation of the best interests of the child, must command the greatest respect and consideration from the court, but that the duty to decide is in the court. 'Consequently' she said 'the court may have the task of requiring the local authority to justify their long-term plans to the extent only that those plans exclude contact between parent and child.' It is for the court to determine whether such a plan is in the best interests of the child.[20] However, it is also plain that orders about contact should not be made where their purpose is to enable the court to review the implementation by the local authority of its care plan. At this point the judge would be 'straying into the forbidden territory of supervising the administration of the local authority's arrangements for rehabilitation.'[1]

When the converse position applies, so that it is the court which wishes to prevent contact between a child and his parent, or another person, in a case where a local authority are content to allow such contact to continue, the position is more complex. It is clear that a court has power to order that no contact should take place.[2] However, regulations allow the terms of any order made under the section to be departed from by agreement between the local authority and the person in relation to whom the order has been made.[3] Thus, theoretically at least, a court could make a no contact

---

16 Above.

17 *A v Liverpool City Council* [1981] 2 All ER 385.

18 [1994] 1 FLR 146.

19 Butler-Sloss LJ said that her own earlier judgment in *Re S (A Minor) (Access Application)* [1991] 1 FLR 161 should be read 'with considerable caution'. *West Glamorgan County Council v P (No 2)* [1993] 1 FLR 407 in which Rattee J had applied an even more stringent test was disapproved in both *Re B (Minors) (Care: Contact: Local Authority's Plans)* and *Re E (A Minor) (Care Order: Contact)* above.

20 See too the emphasis on the scrutinising role of the court in *Re E (A Minor)* above.

1 *Re S (A Minor) (Care: Contact Order)* [1994] 2 FLR 222, per Simon Brown LJ at p 226.

2 S.34(2), and see *Kent County Council v C* [1993] 1 FLR 308.

3 S.34(8) and the Contact with Children Regulations 1991 (SI 1991/891), reg.3.

order on one day and the local authority could, with the agreement of the person concerned, depart from such an order the following day. Clearly it is wrong that a court is put in the position that an order which it has made on the merits is overridden by a decision made subsequently by agreement between the person concerned and the local authority, and therefore in *Kent County Council v C*,[4] Ewbank J said that a court ought not in the ordinary way make an order for no contact between parent and child.

It can be seen that there are subtle distinctions in the provisions in section 34 relating to the interplay between a court's powers to make orders about contact and a local authority's powers to make decisions about a child's upbringing free from supervision by the courts. These can be summarised as follows. Only a court has the power to authorise a local authority to terminate contact with the persons specified in section 34(1). A court may exercise this power either on an application made by the local authority or in the exercise of its own motion powers. Where the court believes that it is in the best interests of a child that contact should be refused or terminated it may authorise the local authority to do so, but it cannot compel the authority to do so. Therefore a court would be unwise to make a no contact order using its own motion powers without first ascertaining whether the local authority would welcome it. Similarly, where the court makes an order under section 34(2) regulating contact arrangements between the child and a specified person, these can only be altered by the local authority where the person affected by the contact order agrees. However, an order of the court can be overridden where such an agreement is made. When a court is determining the merits of a contact application it must apply the principle that the child's welfare is its paramount consideration. The manner in which courts have approached the welfare principle is considered in the next chapter.

4   [1993] 1 FLR 308.

Chapter 4

Approaches to welfare in children cases

Chapter 4

Approaches to welfare in children cases

Civil child law proceedings and welfare

Where a child is directly or indirectly involved in legal proceedings the law, and procedures associated with the law, are likely to impinge on the child's welfare. During the second half of this century increasing respect and regard has been given to the rights and interests of children who are caught up in the civil process and this is reflected both in the development of various aspects of the substantive law and in the processes which are designed to resolve family and other disputes.[1] Giving consideration and weight to the welfare of the child sometimes gives rise to tension in those cases where the child's welfare appears to conflict with principles which also command high regard. Sometimes the child's welfare must be treated as the paramount consideration, but at other times there is no statutory or common law principle which states what importance should be given to welfare considerations. In this chapter the weight given to the welfare of the child is considered in a variety of contexts. It commences with the vexed question whether certain types of conflicts involving children should ever come before the courts, or whether they are better handled outside the court system through private ordering.

Agreed arrangements are normally in the child's best interests

Before a court can make an order in family proceedings it must be satisfied that it would be better for the child than making no order at all.[2] This principle reflects an increasing realisation that courts are not always the

---

1 This is also being reflected in criminal proceedings where a child is a witness. Some attempts have been made to reduce the trauma this causes by allowing a child to give evidence in court shielded by screens, or by allowing the child's evidence to be recorded on video tape from a separate room.
2 Children Act 1989, s.1(5).

most appropriate forum within which decisions about the upbringing of children should be made. This is particularly true in those cases where the persons in dispute are the parents and where there is no issue about whether the state should intervene to protect the child. In cases of this kind the law seeks to promote a climate in which parents and others are encouraged to take steps to find their own solution to the matter in dispute. The thinking behind this approach is that if parents are able to agree about the child's upbringing they are more likely to abide by their agreement, and therefore an agreed outcome will better promote the child's welfare than a solution imposed by a court. But when parents are quarrelling, and where they are grappling with the myriad of feelings which usually accompany relationship breakdown, they often may not be capable of reaching agreement about the upbringing of their children without the assistance of a third party.

Sometimes the third party will be a lawyer, and intervention by lawyers on behalf of their clients often leads to an agreed outcome. When parents instruct separate lawyers they become involved in a process of negotiation: they tell their lawyers about what they want to achieve, and whether and how they are prepared to reach a compromise. This process, in which the parties are kept at arm's length, and in which the lawyers act as inter-mediaries, may achieve a satisfactory outcome for all, including the child. But there is a risk that lawyers will use their skills in such a way that the quality of the parents' relationship is further undermined, and so that the chances of them maintaining a reasonable association with one another in the future is further diminished. Certainly, if negotiation fails and the case comes before a court, even the most sensitive and careful of lawyers, who is mindful that an aggressive and point-scoring approach is usually unhelpful, must nonetheless present his client's case in a manner which is favourable to the client's position.[3] This usually involves not only promoting the client's strengths, but also emphasising the opposing party's weaknesses and seeking to discredit him or her as a parent. As Sir Thomas Bingham has said, it is 'notorious that, when marriages break down and problems arise affecting the children, resolution of these problems through the ordinary processes of adversarial litigation often leads to exaggerated accusations and counter-accusations with, in consequence, an exacerbation of feelings and a heightening of tension'.[4] Thus the legal process may sometimes aggravate existing hostilities, store up trouble for the future and give rise to further litigation. When this occurs, the aim of the legal process to conclude the dispute in the interests of the child is defeated.

Where the parties cannot reach a solution with the assistance of their lawyers, and where the matter is then placed before a court, the court will normally impose a solution on the parties by making an order. But children

3 The Solicitors Family Law Association operate a code of practice which encourages lawyers to approach family cases in a constructive and non-aggressive manner.
4 *Re D (Minors) (Conciliation: Disclosure of Information)* [1993] 2 All ER 693 at p 695.

cases are different from most other types of civil litigation in which court orders provide a remedy for wrongs which have occurred in the past. By contrast, the majority of court orders in children cases are not concerned with the past, but state what arrangements must be made for the child in the future. But of course whilst courts can anticipate what is likely to happen in relation to the child and his parents they cannot know what will happen. Yet it is inevitable that the personal circumstances of the parents and their children will alter.[5] Sometimes these changes in circumstances will mean that a solution imposed by court order, which was acceptable to all at the time it was made, suddenly becomes unacceptable to one of the parties, or to the child.[6] When this occurs, a major disadvantage of a court-imposed order is likely to become apparent, namely the order is probably inflexible and incapable of making provision for the altered circumstances. Consequently, where the parents cannot agree on alternative arrangements, the party who wants the arrangements to be changed must apply to the court for the original order to be varied, and thus the parents and the child become embroiled in further litigation about the child's upbringing. Such a process can rarely be in the child's best interests, and in many cases it may be positively harmful to the child.

Conciliation and mediation

A recognition that the legal process is often not the most appropriate system for resolving conflict about the upbringing of children has, in recent years, led to a growing movement to encourage parents to make use of conciliation and mediation services.[7] Conciliation and mediation do not form part of the legal process but as a matter of practice they are becoming an important tool in the procedure of many courts.[8] Proponents of these services explain that often it is only after a parent in a failed relationship has been able to voice his or her anger, anxiety, distress and fears within a safe and non-judgmental environment that he or she becomes capable of making sensible decisions about the upbringing of the children. Proponents also explain that parties to a broken relationship are often unable to communicate with one another about their children because of the level of misunderstanding and mistrust which has grown up between them, and that an

5   The mere fact that the children grow older may make a court order inappropriate or unenforceable.
6   This problem usually arises in cases concerning contact arrangements.
7   For an account of the development of conciliation as a recognised process, see University of Newcastle Conciliation Project Unit *Report to the Lord Chancellor on the Costs and Effectiveness of Conciliation in England and Wales* (1989). See too, G Davis *Partisans and Mediators* (1988, Oxford University Press); J M Eekelaar and R Dingwall (eds) *The Development of Conciliation in England*, in *Divorce Mediation and the Legal Process* (1988, Clarendon Press).
8   See *Practice Direction: Conciliation – Children* [1992] 1 FLR 228.

invaluable aspect of the service provided by conciliation and mediation is that it facilitates parents to communicate with one another.[9] Conciliation and mediation provide a structured setting in which parents, and sometimes the children and other relatives,[10] meet with an independent third party and explore whether they can reach an agreement. Sometimes it is only where spouses and partners have been able to work through their feelings about the ending of their relationship that they are capable of negotiating reasonable contact arrangements for the children.

Marriage or relationship breakdown often precipitates one or both of the parties into a state of emotional turmoil, which varies in its intensity, and the parties may not have the energy to concentrate on the emotional needs of their children. When suffering the pain and anger associated with relationship breakdown, some parents behave in ways which they would not normally contemplate. They may regress into child-like behaviour which includes an aggressive determination to pursue their own personal needs. Disputes over contact can give rise to some of the most bitter and difficult conflicts over the upbringing of children, and the warring of the adults is often at the expense of their children. Consequently the process of conciliation may be particularly suited to resolving contact issues. The process is designed to empower those using the service to arrive at their own solution, and in this way the responsibility for making decisions about the upbringing of children stays where it belongs, with the parents and children themselves.

Conciliation also provides a process in which people can resolve their differences without feeling under pressure of time, and without feeling that unless they agree the court may impose an unacceptable arrangement on them.[11] For this reason some take the view that the provision of conciliation and mediation services under a court-directed system, with persons being pressured into making use of these services, could be self-defeating, because an agreement reached under these conditions might not be one to which the parties had freely given their consent. It also could be unfair to one of the parties. On the other hand it is said that there is evidence that many parents who reach a mediated agreement, and who then check the arrangements with their own solicitor in order to obtain reassurance that it is fair and appropriate, abide by the decision they have reached. This is clearly for the benefit of all parties.

9   Although conciliation services must carefully be distinguished from services which are designed to assist spouses and unmarried couples to explore whether they can be reconciled, reconciliation is sometimes the outcome of conciliation because, through using the process, the couple start to speak to one another about matters which go to the heart of their relationship.

10 For example, grandparents seeking contact with their grandchildren.

11 For example, where people arrive at an agreement 'at the door of the court' under some pressure from their counsel, solicitor and sometimes from the judge himself.

The notion that parents are free to arrive at their own decision within a process assisted by a third-party conciliator has, however, been doubted. This notion pre-supposes that the conciliator is neutral, and does not seek to impose his or her views on the parties. But, as has been pointed out, all such arrangements are arrived at 'within the shadow of the law'[12] and it has been asserted that 'the conciliator is clearly not neutral but the purveyor of certain ideologies and practices';[13] and that 'the common thread of an idea can be almost lost through the speed with which it is modified to suit the purposes of practitioners in different fields.'[14] Currently there is anxiety about divorce reform proposals emanating from the Lord Chancellor's Department, which appear to require the majority of divorcing parents to resolve their problems about their children through the process of conciliation, and which would deny them access to legal aid to pursue an application in relation to their children in the courts.[15]

Which courts hear children cases?

Family proceedings arise in the High Court, county court and magistrates' court and are widely defined.[16] In a family proceedings case the court hearing the substantive application may also make orders in relation to the children.[17] The courts also exercise a concurrent jurisdiction in relation to freestanding applications brought under the Act, and questions then arise concerning which court is the most appropriate forum for hearing particular cases. The Children (Allocation of Proceedings) Order 1991 provides that care and other public law proceedings should normally commence in the magistrates' court.[18] However, that court has power to transfer any such proceedings upwards, and should do so where this would obviate delay, or where the proceedings are exceptionally grave, important or complex and for other specified reasons.[19] It has been held that magis-

---

12 A famous phrase first coined by R Mnookin and L Kornhauser in *Bargaining in the Shadow of the Law: The Case of Divorce* (1979) 88 Yale Law Journal 950.
13 A Bottomley *Resolving Family Disputes: A Critical View* in *State, Law and the Family: Critical Perspectives*, ed. M D A Freeman (1984, Stevens).
14 G Davis *Mediation in Divorce: A Theoretical Perspective* [1983] JSWL 131.
15 See ch 6.
16 Children Act 1989, s.8(3)(4).
17 S.10(1) empowers it to make any order under s.8. The orders available are fully described in ch 2.
18 Art.3.
19 Art. 7; examples of particular circumstances are included in the article. Directions are sometimes given that certain decisions should always be made by a High Court judge; see for example, *Re HIV Tests* [1994] 2 FLR 116.

trates should transfer a case to the county court where there is conflicting evidence, or where the case involves a very difficult assessment of risk to the child.[20] That court can in turn decide whether the case is more suited to be heard by a High Court judge. Private law proceedings, by contrast, can commence in any court. Where they are started in the magistrates' court they can be transferred to the county court, and in *R v South East Hampshire Family Proceedings Court, ex p D*[1] it was held that when a magistrates' court is determining whether to transfer a case its main function is to consider which court is most appropriate, and what would be in the interests of the child. It is not limited to transferring cases solely where this would prevent delay.

Evidence in children cases and welfare

Before a court can make a decision it must first be supplied with information upon which to base its ruling. In children cases this information may come from a variety of sources. Parents, relatives and other persons with a personal interest in the child may give evidence about past incidents relating to the child and what each of them has to offer the child in the future. Other persons may give evidence in support of one of the parties. An expert witness may be asked to give his or her opinion; this may be about a contested issue of fact, such as whether injuries to a child were caused deliberately or whether they could have occurred accidentally, or it may be about which course of action the witness, in his or her professional judgment, thinks would best promote the child's welfare. In a contested private law case a court is likely to request a court welfare officer to make enquiries into the child's present circumstances, to interview the parties and other relevant persons and to supply the court with a report on his or her findings. The courts are highly dependent upon this investigative service; without it they would often lack the necessary material upon which to make an informed decision. In public law cases where a local authority is a party to the proceedings a guardian ad litem for the child will normally have been appointed and he or she will provide a report for the court, and will often give oral evidence too. During the course of the hearing the court may itself take the view that it needs more information before it arrives at its decision. It may find out what it needs to know simply by putting questions to the witnesses, or it may adjourn the case for further inquiries to be made, or for an expert witness to be approached to assist the court.

---

20 *C v Solihull Metropolitan Borough Council* [1993] 1 FLR 290; *S v Oxfordshire County Council* [1993] 1 FLR 452.
1 [1994] 2 All ER 445.

Court control over evidence which can be adduced

Parties to proceedings about the upbringing of a child often wish to obtain a report from an expert or experts about the child's health or development. This gives rise to a risk that a child might be exposed to unnecessary and upsetting medical, psychiatric or other assessments for the purpose of legal proceedings, particularly where such an assessment would include an intimate physical examination. This risk, and the realisation that some children were seriously harmed in Cleveland during the period when there were intensive investigations into allegations of child sexual abuse,[2] have led to rules being made which prevent such examinations and assessments being conducted without the court's leave.[3] Where such an examination or assessment does take place without leave first being obtained, no evidence arising from it may be adduced without the leave of the court.[4] These rules are a major invasion into the normal right of a litigant to prepare his or her case in the manner which the litigant regards as most appropriate, and they apply uniquely to children cases. It is suggested that they can be justified on the basis that it is the child who is the subject matter of the proceedings even though he or she is not a party to them, and therefore there must be procedural safeguards which protect the child's rights and interests. As the court's inquiry is focused on what decision will advance the child's welfare the court is empowered to control the preparation of a party's case where it appears to conflict with the child's welfare.

The parties must submit witness statements and other documentary evidence supporting their case well in advance of the hearing, the actual timing being as directed by the court.[5] In a case where a guardian ad litem has been appointed, once he completes his investigation he must file a written report advising on the interests of the child which must be served on the parties to the proceedings at least seven days in advance of the hearing.[6] These time periods are intended to afford all parties to the proceedings the opportunity to deal with any allegations made in witness statements, in the guardian ad litem's report, in experts' reports and in reports prepared by the local authority, either by arranging to call witnesses in rebuttal or by taking other steps. If these rules are not complied with, and if an adjournment is refused, an aggrieved party might have grounds for proceeding in judicial review on the basis that he has been denied a fair hearing because he has not received sufficient notice of the case.[7]

---

2   *Report of the Inquiry into Child Abuse in Cleveland 1987*, Cm 412 (1988).
3   Family Proceedings Courts (Children Act 1989) Rules 1991, r.18(1); Family Proceedings Rules 1991, r.4.18. The rules are virtually identical and reference will therefore be made to the former rules only, unless otherwise stated.
4   R.18(3).
5   R.17.
6   R.11(7).
7   *R v West Malling Juvenile Court, ex p K* [1986] 2 FLR 405.

Expert evidence

The evidence of an expert differs from that of an ordinary witness of fact because he may give opinion evidence. The role of the expert is not to promote a particular cause or point of view; such an approach is to advance an argument and not an opinion. Rather, the court looks for objectivity and impartiality in an expert witness and for his expression of opinion to be properly researched so that the court can place reliance on it. In some cases this may mean that an expert may find that he has to give an opinion adverse to his client.[8] Fundamentally, it is the duty of an expert not to mislead the court. As Cazalet J said in *Re R (A Minor) (Experts' Evidence)*[9] 'an absence of objectivity may result in a child being wrongly placed and thereby unnecessarily put at risk.' In *Re M (Minors) (Care Proceedings) (Child's Wishes)*[10] Wall J emphasised the non-adversarial nature of children's proceedings, and stressed the vital importance of expert evidence in assisting the judge to arrive at the correct decision. Wall J has also given extensive guidance on the preparation of cases for trial when expert witnesses are involved.[11]

The court must be satisfied that the expert has the appropriate qualifications and experience to be accepted as an expert in the field of expertise relevant to his testimony. Where the expert does not satisfy these requirements his opinion evidence is liable to be discounted. Sometimes so-called 'experts' give evidence based on no properly conducted research and on no clinical information, and courts and lawyers need to be very wary of this. Thus in *Rochdale Borough Council v A*[12] Douglas Brown J was dismissive of the testimony of the expert witness called by the local authority in relation to allegations of child sexual abuse, including satanic abuse, because, he said 'she is not a child psychologist, she is a clinical psychologist,

8 See the detailed guidance given to experts by Cazalet J in *Re R (A Minor) (Experts' Evidence)* [1991] 1 FLR 291n; and by Wall J in *Re M (Minors) (Care Proceedings: Child's Wishes)* [1994] 1 FLR 749. See generally, J R Spencer and R Flin *The Evidence of Children* (Blackstone Press, 2nd edn, 1993); C Keenan and C Williams *Expert Witnesses in Child Sexual Abuse Cases* (1993) 1 Me Law Int 57; D Ormerod *Expert Witnesses in Children's Cases* (1992) 4 JCL 122; and the opposing views of M N Howard and J R Spencer [1991] Crim LR 98 and 106.
9 [1991] 1 FLR 291n.
10 [1994] 1 FLR 749.
11 *Re M (Minors) (Care Proceedings) (Child's Wishes)* above; *Re DH (A Minor) (Child Abuse)* [1994] 1 FLR 679; *Re M and TD (Minors) (Time Estimates)* [1994] 2 FLR 336; *Re G (Minors) (Expert Witnesses)* [1994] 2 FLR 291.
12 [1991] 2 FLR 192 at p 216; contrast his approach to the testimony of this witness with his acceptance of the evidence of another witness whom he described as very experienced in the field; see too *Re E (A Minor) (Child Abuse: Evidence)* [1991] 1 FLR 420 in which a police surgeon admitted in evidence that he had neither the knowledge nor experience to reach a definite conclusion that a child had been anally penetrated.

dealing mainly with adults. She has had no experience of ritual or satanic abuse, and bases her views almost entirely on her understanding on writings on the subject.'

A witness may sometimes be asked to give an opinion about a child's mental state and whether the child has a propensity to fantasise, or otherwise invent information which is presented to the court as an accurate statement of fact. In *Re S and B (Minors) (Child Abuse: Evidence)*[13] the Court of Appeal held that a fine line must be drawn between an expression of opinion about whether what the child has said to the witness is credible, which it held could lie within the scope of the witness's professional competence, and an expression of opinion that the child is telling the truth and not lies, which is a matter for the court and not the witness. In other words it is for the court to assess the credibility of what the child has said, and not for the expert, and a witness crosses that line and trespasses on the function of the court if he ventures the opinion that 'there is little doubt that the accounts given to me by the child are accurate.'

Legal professional privilege

When a person who is a party to legal proceedings asks an expert witness to prepare a report for actual or contemplated legal proceedings usually that person will want to rely on the report at the hearing. However, sometimes the expert's report, far from assisting the person who has commissioned it, may in fact be adverse to his case. The general rule relating to civil litigation is that the report is covered by legal professional privilege and therefore only the party concerned can waive the privilege and choose whether to disclose the information to other parties to the proceedings. The reason for this privilege is to encourage experts to give their opinions fully and frankly to the persons who engage them, and to enable them to comment on the case, with all its strengths and weaknesses, without fear that the other side will be able to take advantage of this openness.

In relation to children cases the arguments in favour of privilege are overriden by other, stronger, policy considerations. The thinking which justifies treating children cases differently is that courts should not decide such cases in ignorance of material facts. It was made clear in *R v Hampshire County Council, ex p K*[14] that local authorities do not have the benefit of legal professional privilege in respect of expert's reports in care proceedings. They are obliged to disclose to all parties all relevant

13 [1990] 2 FLR 489.
14 [1990] 2 All ER 129.

documents and experts' reports which are in their possession. In *Oxfordshire County Council v M*[15] this principle was extended to the other parties to care proceedings. The Court of Appeal ruled that children cases fall into a special category in which the welfare of the child is the court's paramount concern. It said that if a party was able to conceal, or withhold from the court, important matters relevant to the future of the child, there would be a risk that the welfare of the child would not be promoted as the Children Act 1989 requires. The court therefore concluded that the court has power to override legal professional privilege in relation to experts' reports in care proceedings when it gives leave to the parties to obtain them.[16]

The Court of Appeal did not expressly cover the question whether counsel has a duty to make voluntary disclosure of an expert's report on which he is not intending to rely. This issue has yet to be resolved. It is a matter of fundamental principle that there should be confidence between a client and his advocate, and it would normally be regarded as an extremely serious breach of professional practice if a lawyer were to disclose material which was against his client's interests, and contrary to instructions. Nonetheless, in *Essex County Council v R*[17] Thorpe J said: 'For my part I would wish to see case law go further and to make it plain that the legal representatives in possession of such material relevant to determination but contrary to the interests of their client, not only are unable to resist disclosure by reliance on legal professional privilege, but have a positive duty to disclose to the other parties and to the court.' And in *Re DH (A Minor) (Child Abuse)*,[18] Wall J stated (obiter): 'In my judgement ... the answer is that the client needs to be told authoritatively at an early stage in the relationship that whilst the advocate has a duty to present the client's case to the best of his or her ability, the advocate has a higher duty to the court and to the child whose interests are paramount to disclose relevant material to the court even if that disclosure is not in the interests of his client.' He concluded that practitioners should therefore be under a duty to disclose all material, unless and until the Court of Appeal rules otherwise.[19]

---

15 [1994] 2 All ER 269, following the ruling of Thorpe J in *Re R (A Minor) (Disclosure of Privileged Material)* [1993] 4 All ER 702.
16 The full scope of this decision is not entirely clear: Sir Stephen Brown P appeared to apply the principle to all children cases; Steyn LJ to care proceedings only; and Kennedy LJ took the view that leave to consult an expert can be made conditional on disclosure of the report, a view which Steyn LJ rejected.
17 [1993] 2 FLR 826 at p 828.
18 [1994] 1 FLR 679 at p 704.
19 Wall J dealt with some of the practical difficulties this approach can cause, ibid, at p 704; he also said that the letter of instruction to an expert is not privileged, and should therefore be disclosed.

Confidential information

The rule that there should be full disclosure of reports and statements is qualified where public interest immunity will justify withholding specific information. Public interest immunity arises where confidentiality cannot be waived because this would be against the public interest. Local authorities must be able to carry out their statutory child care functions without fear that they will be forced to divulge highly sensitive information. Consequently, where the public interest in ensuring that all relevant information is disclosed comes into conflict with the public interest that children are protected from suffering significant harm, the former may have to yield to the latter. Thus in *D v National Society for the Prevention of Cruelty to Children*[20] the House of Lords ruled that if a local authority were to be forced to name the person who has passed information about a child to the NSPCC, this might deter others from coming forward to give information on a confidential basis. It can be seen here that the broader principle that the law should safeguard the welfare of all children prevailed against the claim of an individual litigant to obtain access to material information relating to proposed litigation.[1]

The courts are extremely wary of extending the notion of confidentiality in children cases to situations where a court welfare officer, or a guardian ad litem, wishes to place information before the court, but asks that the contents of that information should not be disclosed to the parties to the proceedings. It is a fundamental principle of natural justice that persons should be informed of the nature of any allegations made against them. A court should not make a decision in reliance on information which is adverse to one of the parties unless that party has been given the opportunity to challenge it, or to address the court about it. However, occasionally a situation arises when an application is made that information before the judge should not be disclosed to the parties because it is alleged that it will be harmful to the child. Here the principle that there should be full disclosure must be balanced against the interests of the child.

The leading case on confidentiality within proceedings is the House of Lords' ruling in *Official Solicitor to the Supreme Court v K*,[2] which was a case heard in wardship. The principles in that case have since been extended to proceedings brought under the Children Act 1989.[3] In *Re B (A*

---

20 [1977] 1 All ER 589.
1 See too *Re D (Minors) (Wardship: Disclosure)* [1994] 1 FLR 346, in which it was said that social work case notes, medical records and other documents in the possession of the local authority, and health authority, probably attracted public interest immunity.
2 [1965] AC 201.
3 *Re C (A Minor) (Irregularity of Practice)* [1991] 2 FLR 438; *Re B (A Minor) (Disclosure of Evidence)* [1993] 1 FLR 191; *Re M (Minors) (Disclosure of Evidence)* [1994] 1 FLR 760.

Minor) (Disclosure of Evidence)[4] the Court of Appeal confirmed that a court
has power in a children case to act on evidence adduced by one party, or
given by a welfare officer, which is not disclosed to the other party. However,
it stated that this power should only be exercised in most exceptional
circumstances, and only where the court is satisfied that the disclosure of
the evidence would be so detrimental to the welfare of the child as to
outweigh the normal requirements for a fair trial. In *Re G (Minors) (Welfare
Report: Disclosure)*[5] the Court of Appeal reinforced this approach in a case
where a welfare officer had given a promise of confidentiality to certain
informants, wished to place what the informants had said before the court,
but for that information not to be disclosed to the parties. The Court of
Appeal stated that the court welfare officer was not entitled to protect her
sources of information; it is only the judge who can decide whether
information should be treated as confidential. It further emphasised that
the evidence of the welfare officer is compellable, and that once she had
put documentary evidence before the court she was not in the position to
be able to withdraw that evidence. The evidence is compellable unless the
witness can properly claim privilege, and that is for the court to decide.

In *Re M (Minors) (Disclosure of Evidence)*[6] the question arose whether
an addendum to a report from a court welfare officer about the wishes and
feelings of the children could properly be treated as confidential to the
court. In *Re M (Minors)* the children had expressed fears and reservations
to the welfare officer about their mother's reaction if she saw the contents
of the report, and had asked that it be revealed to the judge alone. The
judge acceded to this request holding that a 'real significant risk of harm'
to the children would be occasioned were the addendum to be disclosed.
The Court of Appeal held that whilst a court does have the power to order
that evidence should not be disclosed to a party, it must be sure that such
disclosure would be so detrimental to the child as to outweigh the normal
requirement for a fair trial that all evidence is fully disclosed, so that all
parties can consider it and, if necessary, seek to rebut it.[7] Following the
House of Lords ruling in *Official Solicitor to the Supreme Court v K*,[8] the
Court of Appeal held that the welfare of the children was paramount, but
that to withhold evidence is an exceptional procedure, and that a judge
should not conclude that the paramount interests of the child outweigh
the right of a properly interested party, particularly a parent, to disclosure
of information submitted to the judge save where he is satisfied that 'real

4   Above.
5   [1993] 2 FLR 293.
6   [1994] 1 FLR 760.
7   See *Official Solicitor to the Supreme Court v K* [1965] AC 201; *Re C (A Minor) (Irregularity
    of Practice)* [1991] 2 FLR 438; *Re B (A Minor) (Disclosure of Evidence)* [1993] 1 FLR 191;
    Re G (Minors) (Welfare Report: Disclosure) [1993] 2 FLR 293.
8   Above.

harm to the child must otherwise ensue'. It pointed out that this is a far more stringent test than the test of whether there was a 'real significant risk of harm'. Thus it is clear that the courts, when applying the welfare principle, will nonetheless exercise their discretion to withhold information from parties to the proceedings only where the circumstances are most exceptional, because any other approach undermines the basic principle of natural justice that parties to proceedings must know the case which they have to meet.[9]

Evidence given in wardship proceedings must be treated as confidential by the parties, and any breach of this rule is a contempt of court.[10] A similar rule applies to proceedings brought under the Children Act 1989.[11] The purpose of these rules is to encourage witnesses to give their evidence fully and frankly, and without fear that doing so could be used against them. However, the preservation of confidentiality in wardship or Children Act proceedings is not absolute; the court may grant leave for such information to be disclosed. In *Re Manda*[12] a child had been made a ward of court when he was 12 because it was suspected that he had been sexually abused, and had been committed to the care of a local authority. Evidence had been given in the wardship proceedings by a consultant paediatrician who had examined the child. Subsequently the boy was returned to his parents and the wardship was discharged. The parents, who had always vehemently denied abusing their son, wished to institute proceedings on his behalf in negligence or trespass to the person.[13] The parents' solicitors had in their possession papers relating to the wardship proceedings, and the parents sought leave to disclose these documents to solicitors acting on their child's behalf in the proposed civil action. Thus a conflict existed between the interests of the particular child who wished to pursue litigation, and the general public interest in preserving confidentiality in relation to wardship proceedings.[14] In this case the interests of the child litigant prevailed. The Court of Appeal ruled that the public interest in seeing that he had available to him all relevant information outweighed the public interest in preserving witness confidentiality. Balcombe LJ also gave a warning to professionals giving evidence in children cases that they should not assume that this evidence would always be treated as confidential.

---

9 Secrecy may also prevent material information being fully canvassed and so possibly prevent a decision being arrived at which would truly be in the interests of the child.
10 Administration of Justice Act 1960, s.12(1)(a).
11 Family Proceedings Rules 1991, r.4.23.
12 [1993] 1 All ER 733.
13 The child himself reached majority during the course of the litigation and would therefore be able to pursue his own claim.
14 It was a matter of importance that although the litigation was unlikely to succeed, it was not bound to fail.

Similarly, in *Re K (Minors) (Disclosure)*[15] a father sought leave to disclose at his trial for rape evidence adduced in proceedings brought under the Children Act 1989. The court, granting him leave, held that while it had to have regard for the interests of the children concerned, it had to balance the importance of confidentiality and frankness in children proceedings against the public interest in ensuring that persons receive a fair trial and that the interests of justice are properly served. It was in the interests of justice that the defendant in a criminal trial should have available all relevant and necessary material for the conduct of his defence.[16]

Statements made in conciliation proceedings

The courts have taken the view that statements made in the course of conciliation proceedings should be treated as confidential and privileged and may not be adduced without the consent of both parties. Here the public interest in encouraging parties to a dispute about their children to come to their own arrangements outweighs any right of one party to rely on concessions and admissions made during the course of conciliation in any subsequent litigation. In *Re D (Minors) (Conciliation: Disclosure of Information)*[17] the Court of Appeal held that statements made by one or other of the parties in the course of meetings held, or communications made, for the purpose of conciliation may not be used in evidence in any proceedings brought under the Children Act 1989. Because otherwise 'it is plain that the parties will not make admissions or conciliatory gestures, or dilute their claims, or venture out of their entrenched positions unless they can be confident that their concessions and admissions cannot be used as weapons against them if conciliation fails and full-blooded litigation follows.'[18] The only exception to this rule is where the maker of the statement has said something which indicates that he has caused, or is likely to cause, serious harm to the child. Where this is the case, it is for the judge to determine whether the evidence can be admitted.

Hearsay

The normal rule in civil proceedings is that evidence given by one witness of a statement made by another person, which is tendered to prove the

15 [1994] 1 FLR 377; following *Re D (Minors) (Wardship: Disclosure)* [1994] 1 FLR 346.
16 See too, *Re F (A Minor) (Disclosure: Immigration)* [1994] 2 FLR 958 in which leave was given for the disclosure to the special adjudicator in immigration proceedings, of documents used, and a transcript of the evidence given, in proceedings which had been brought under the Children Act 1989.
17 [1993] 2 All ER 693.
18 Ibid, per Lord Bingham MR at p 695.

truth of the statement, is inadmissible. However, this rule has been relaxed in children cases. Section 96(3) of the Children Act 1989 empowers the Lord Chancellor to make provision for the admissibility of evidence which would otherwise be inadmissible under any rule of law relating to hearsay, and Article 2 of the Children (Admissibility of Hearsay Evidence) Order 1991[19] provides that—

'In civil proceedings before the High Court or a county court and in family proceedings in a magistrates' court, evidence given in connection with the upbringing, maintenance or welfare of a child shall be admissible notwithstanding any rule of law relating to hearsay.'

Thus Parliament has taken the view that cases 'in connection with the upbringing, maintenance or welfare of a child' should be treated differently from other civil cases because it is in the interests of children that all possible relevant information should be placed before the courts. The scope of this provision came under scrutiny in *Re C (Minors) (Hearsay Evidence: Contempt Proceedings)*.[20] Here it was alleged in contempt proceedings that a father had breached a non-molestation injunction. The mother wished to introduce in evidence statements made by the children of the family about the alleged breach which were contained in a court welfare officer's report, and which were therefore hearsay. Whilst the Court of Appeal held that hearsay evidence could be introduced in contempt proceedings, it ruled that the courts would only allow this where a substantial connection between the proposed evidence and the welfare of the child had been established, and that this will be a matter of fact in each case. In this case the connection was held to be insufficiently substantial.

It is suggested that this ruling was unduly narrow even within the context of contempt proceedings, which traditionally have been surrounded by stringent safeguards because the penalty for contempt may be imprisonment. In *Re C (Minors)* the children's statements would have pointed to breaches of an injunction by the father not to enter the former matrimonial home in which the children were living with their mother. It seems unhelpful to draw a distinction between cases in which the injunction is designed to protect the child himself, and one in which it is designed to protect the parent with whom the child is living, which distinction was drawn by the Court of Appeal. Furthermore, the Order does not state that a 'substantial' connection must be established between the hearsay evidence and the welfare of the child; it is drafted in far more neutral terms. It is suggested that this judicial gloss on the wording of the order may lead to

19 SI 1991/1115.
20 [1993] 4 All ER 690.

hearsay evidence being inappropriately excluded in cases concerning children, and that it was a strange finding of fact in *Re C (Minors)* that the children would not be affected by any breaches of the injunction.[21]

The dilemma for the court in those cases where the Order does apply is not whether a hearsay statement can be admitted, because article 2 states that it *shall* be admissible, but how much weight should the court give to this type of evidence. A first-hand account from a witness of what he saw, heard or otherwise experienced can be given significant probative weight because it can be tested for its veracity. By contrast, a hearsay statement has two major disadvantages which tend to diminish its probative value: it cannot be tested in cross-examination, and the person reporting what the maker of the statement has said may do so inaccurately, or even deliberately falsely.[1] It is suggested that very little, or no, probative weight should be given to a prejudicial hearsay statement when the statement was made by an adult who could be called as a witness. For example, if a social worker were to give evidence that a teacher told her that she, the teacher, saw the child's mother beat the child such a statement is prejudicial because it appears to establish that the child has been beaten. But where the mother is denying beating the child, such a statement clearly needs to be tested in cross-examination, and the only way in which this can be done is if the teacher herself is called to give evidence. Unless this happens, it is suggested that no probative weight can properly be given to a statement of this kind.

It is nevertheless almost inevitable in children cases that hearsay information will be presented by witnesses as true accounts of what has occurred. For example, a consultant paediatrician may give a clinical description of a child's physical condition when first admitted to hospital, and of changes observed in the child's growth and development whilst under his care. Parts of this information will come from the paediatrician's own observations, and his own examination of the child, but other parts are likely to have been taken from notes compiled by other medical personnel such as nurses and more junior doctors. Similarly a social worker who is called as a witness by a local authority may have taken over the child's case from a previous worker. He may be called upon to give an historical account to the court of incidents involving the child and his family which have given rise to professional concern, and of action taken by the local authority in response to these incidents. His source of information will be the file kept on the child, and conversations with other persons. In

---

21 In the light of this ruling it would also seem wise for a parent who is the subject of domestic violence to seek an injunction which embraces the children as well as herself where appropriate.

1 See, for example, *Re E (A Minor) (Child Abuse: Evidence)* [1987] 1 FLR 269, where the court found that oral evidence of an interview bore little resemblance to the video recording of the same interview, and that the expert witness's conclusions bore no relationship with the actual questions asked.

either case, the paediatrician, or the social worker, is relying on reports and findings made by others, he does not have first-hand knowledge of the facts he is recounting. Normally no problem arises with the hearsay element in the witness's statement where the facts recounted are non-controversial. It is when facts are disputed, or when an account is given of actions and statements made by the child which is challenged by a party to the proceedings, that difficulties arise about how much weight and probity should be given to hearsay evidence.

Statements made by a child

A child can be treated as a competent witness in civil proceedings even though he or she does not, in the opinion of the court, understand the nature of the oath.[2] Section 96(2) provides that—

> 'The child's evidence may be heard by the court if, in its opinion—
> (a) he understands that it is his duty to speak the truth; and
> (b) he has sufficient understanding to justify his evidence being heard.'

However, it is extremely rare for a child to give evidence in a civil child case because it is the generally held view that it is an ordeal for a child to appear in court as a witness.[3] Consequently, someone else will tell the court what the child has said about his experiences. But the court's task in assessing a child's credibility is not made easier by the fact that any statements from the child presented to the court will therefore almost invariably be in the form of hearsay. There is guidance in *Re W (Minors) (Wardship: Evidence)*[4] in relation to the weight to be given to remarks made by children, and reported to the courts by adults. A note of caution was sounded by Neill LJ when he said 'this evidence and the use to which it is put has to be handled with the greatest care and in such a way that unless the interests of the child make it necessary, the rules of natural justice and the rights of parents are properly observed.' He said that a court 'will be very slow indeed to make a finding of fact adverse to a parent

2   S.96(1).
3   This ordeal for the child cannot be avoided in criminal proceedings where the hearsay rule still applies (though see s.23 of the Criminal Justice Act 1988). There is some amelioration of the process through the use of live TV-link evidence and video recorded evidence: Criminal Justice Act 1988, ss.32 and 32A. The use of screens to shield the child in court is governed by the common law: see *R v X, Y and Z* (1989) 91 Cr App Rep 36. See generally JR Spencer and R Flinn *The Evidence of Children* (Blackstone Press, 1993), *The Pigot Report* (HO, 1989).
4   [1990] 1 FLR 203, decided in wardship. Hearsay evidence was admissible in wardship prior to it becoming admissible in all children cases.

if the only material before it has been untested by cross-examination.'[5] McCowan LJ expressed similar caution when he said 'it would be wrong for a judge to find sexual abuse proved against a particular person solely on the basis of hearsay evidence.' However he continued 'what he can do, however, is to have regard to hearsay evidence to assist him to form a view as to the degree of risk involved for the future in permitting children to return to their parents.'[6] Thus it can be seen that only rarely will the unsupported statements of a child be sufficiently cogent and reliable to satisfy a court that the person the child identifies as a perpetrator of abuse against him is in fact such a perpetrator.[7]

Video taped interviews

Making a video recording of interviews with the child is one way of overcoming some of the disadvantages and difficulties which arise where otherwise the only evidence adduced of what the child has said is hearsay evidence. Clinicians experienced at working in the field of child abuse have pointed out that the value of video taped recordings may be diminished by poor technology.[8] They have also expressed anxiety about judges interpreting interviews, a task which traditionally has been the exclusive territory of experts.[9] Nonetheless, in *Re M (Child Abuse: Evidence)*[10] Latey J explained why courts much prefer this evidence. Not only can the court see and hear the child's responses to questions, and detect changes in the child's vocal inflection, it can also observe the child's non-verbal responses such as body movements and gestures. This reasoning was reinforced in the Cleveland Report, which includes amongst the points to be observed in conducting interviews with children the requirement that there must be careful recording of what the child says, whether or not there is a video recording.[11] Furthermore, the advantage of a video taped recording is that the court can see and hear for itself whether the child discloses information about abuse spontaneously, or whether he is pressurised by the interviewer into responding in a particular way.[12] As Butler-Sloss LJ said in *H v H and C; K v K (Child Abuse: Evidence)*:[13]

---

5   Ibid, at p 228.
6   Ibid, at p 222.
7   See too *Re M (A Minor) (No 2) (Appeal)* [1994] 1 FLR 59.
8   E Vizard *Interviewing Young Sexually Abused Children* (1987) 17 Fam Law 28.
9   E Vizard, A Bentovim and M Tranter *Interviewing Sexually Abused Children* (1987) 11 Adoption and Fostering 20.
10 [1987] 1 FLR 293n.
11 Report of the Inquiry into Child Abuse in Cleveland 1987, Cm 412, para 12.34.
12 See *Re E (A Minor) (Child Abuse: Evidence)* [1991] 1 FLR 420.
13 [1989] 3 All ER 740 at p 752.

'The conduct of the interviews would inevitably have a marked effect on the weight to be attached to the evidence adduced. Frequent repetitive interviews with young, suggestible children, reminding them of what they had previously said, would be likely to have decreasing evidential value. The spontaneous statements of a child at an early stage have far greater impact ... The pressure or absence of pressure upon the child can be seen by the observer, including the judge'.

Identifying the welfare of the child

The principle that the child's welfare must be the court's paramount consideration in children cases is not new. Equity adopted this approach towards the end of the last century, and the paramountcy of the child's welfare was given formal statutory recognition in section 1 of the Guardianship of Infants Act 1925. Thus courts have long been grappling with the difficult task of determining what decision will best promote the child's interests. However, whilst the principle is long-established, responses to it have altered radically as succeeding generations have applied different norms and values to the choices to be made. Growth in knowledge about human development, and how certain experiences have affected that development, means that comments made by judges applying the welfare principle in the early part of this century may be viewed with amazement by later generations.

An illustration arose in *Re W (Infants)*[14] which concerned two children who had been looked after for many years by a couple who were seeking to adopt them. Their application was opposed by the children's father, and the issue for the court was whether the children would be positively harmed if taken from the care of the potential adopters and returned to their father's care. *Re W (Infants)* came before Cross J in 1965. Similar facts had come before Eve J in 1925 in *Re Thain*,[15] in which the child's mother had died and the child had been brought up for many years by her uncle and aunt, Mr and Mrs Jones. Her father was seeking to recover her care. Restoring the child to her father, Eve J said 'it is said that the little girl will be greatly distressed and upset at parting from Mr and Mrs Jones. I can quite understand it may be so, but, at her tender age, one knows from experience how mercifully transient are the effects of partings and other sorrows and how soon the novelty of fresh surroundings and new associations effaces the recollection of former days and kind friends.' Cross J, commenting on these words in *Re W (Infants)*, in which he ordered that the children should remain with the potential adopters, said:

14 [1965] 3 All ER 231.
15 [1926] All ER Rep 384, which was emphatically approved by the Court of Appeal.

'When I was called to the Bar some 35 years ago, it was not, as I remember, usual to have medical evidence as to the effect which the order of the court would be likely to have on the infant .... But child psychiatrists who give evidence in these cases nowadays, though they do not always agree in detail, all emphasise the risks involved in transferring young children from the care of one person to another....while as to the views of Eve J, Dr S,[16] when they were put to him, plainly regarded them much as Thomas Huxley would have regarded the suggestion that the world came into being in the manner set out in the first chapter of Genesis.'[17]

Precedent and the welfare principle

When a court determines what decision will best promote the welfare of the child it is expressing a preference which is likely to be founded on a variety of norms. It may be that a case with similar facts has already come before the courts, and that the Court of Appeal has given a ruling on how such facts should be approached. The question then arises whether such a ruling can ever set a precedent which must be followed. Strictly the answer to this question is 'no'. Every child case is unique and therefore one case cannot be a precedent for another. As Stamp LJ has said 'although one may of course be assisted by the wisdom of remarks made in earlier cases, the circumstances in infant cases and the personalities of the parties concerned being infinitely variable, the conclusions of the court as to the course which should be followed in one case are of little assistance in guiding one to the course which ought to be followed in another case.'[18] However, there may be situations in which an approach to a similar problem has become so firmly established that it appears to take on precedent force. Thus in *Belton v Belton*[19] the Court of Appeal ruled that the trial judge had erred when he formed the view that it was not in the child's welfare to grant her mother leave to remove her from the jurisdiction because the child would thereby lose contact with her father and paternal relatives. Purchas LJ stated that the judge had failed to appreciate 'the force of the authorities' in which leave had been granted, and added that 'these authorities are quite clear in the course the court must take'. But affording such weight to earlier case law decided on the welfare principle is unusual, and the Court of Appeal is generally loth to give precedent force to a particular view about the factors which will serve a child's best interests.

16 The child psychologist who had interviewed the children.
17 [1965] 3 All ER 231 at pp 248-9.
18 *Re K (Minors) (Wardship: Care and Control)* [1977] 1 All ER 647 at p 649.
19 [1987] 2 FLR 343.

An example arose in *Re A (A Minor) (Custody)*[20] in which the trial judge, apparently following what he thought to be precedent, namely a statement made by Butler-Sloss LJ in *Re S (A Minor) (Custody)*,[1] had taken as his starting point that it is natural for a mother to have the care of a six-year-old daughter. Butler-Sloss LJ disapproved this approach stating that:

'There is no starting point that the mother should be preferred to the father and only displaced by a preponderance of evidence to the contrary ... The welfare of the child is paramount, and each parent has to be looked at by the judge in order to make as best he can the assessment of each, and to choose one of them to be the custodial parent. In so far as the judge appears to have started with the proposition that little girls naturally go to their mothers, the judge was in error and applied the wrong test.'[2]

The role of the appeal court

The precedent value of a children case cannot properly be ascertained unless the role of an appeal court in children cases is also understood. Because the determination of welfare is a decision which turns on the exercise of judicial discretion, an appellate court is not entitled to interfere with the ruling of the trial court unless the grounds for appeal fall within the scope of the principles laid down by the House of Lords in *G v G*.[3] The fact that the trial court has reached a decision with which the appellate court might reasonably disagree is not enough. In order to intervene, the appellate court must be satisfied that the trial court has taken account of matters it ought not to have taken into account, has failed to take account of matters it ought to have taken into account, or that the decision was so plainly wrong that the only legitimate conclusion is that the court has erred in the exercise of its discretion.[4]

Re J (A Minor) (Contact)[5] provides an example of how this principle operates. The trial judge had ordered that there should be no order on the father's application for contact with his son because of the mother's implacable hostility to the father, and her vehement opposition to contact

20 [1991] 2 FLR 394.
1 [1991] 2 FLR 388 at p 390.
2 [1991] 2 FLR 394 at p 400.
3 [1985] 2 All ER 225; an appeal court is reluctant to interfere with a trial court decision because it is the judge who has seen and heard the witnesses and he who has formed an opinion of their truthfulness, strengths and weaknesses. It is recognised that impressions of the personalities of the contenders for a child can be a highly material influence on the exercise of discretion in a child case.
4 See too, *Re F (A Minor) (Wardship: Appeal)* [1976] Fam 238.
5 [1994] 1 FLR 729.

taking place. The father appealed. The Court of Appeal confirmed that the principles which should be applied to cases of this kind are well established, namely that 'contact with the parent with whom the child is not resident is the right of the child, and very cogent reasons are required for terminating such contact.' Balcombe LJ went on to state that 'it was undoubtedly open to the judge to have made an order for contact, and there are ... strong policy reasons for saying that a recalcitrant parent should not be allowed to frustrate what the court considers the child's welfare requires. Had the judge made such an order, I do not see how the mother could successfully have appealed from it'.[6] However, the trial judge in the exercise of his discretion had concluded that the making of a contact order would cause the child harm, and the Court of Appeal, applying the ruling in *G v G*, was unable to say that he was plainly wrong within the *G v G* principle. The father's appeal was therefore dismissed.

This example demonstrates how the determination of the precedent force of a Court of Appeal ruling can be extremely complex. It would clearly be wrong to treat *Re J (A Minor)* as a precedent for saying that where one parent is implacably hostile to the other parent having contact, and where that contact may cause harm to the child, that contact will therefore be denied. On the contrary, Balcombe LJ stated that had the trial judge made a contact order the Court of Appeal would have felt equally unable to intervene. Furthermore, he was at pains to point out that courts should be very reluctant to allow parental hostility to deter courts from making contact orders. But nevertheless in *Re J (A Minor)* the mother won, and the father was denied contact, and to that extent it is a precedent for saying that a judge will not be plainly wrong if he refuses contact on the grounds that it will cause the child harm. It is suggested that the value of *Re J (A Minor)* is as much to reaffirm the precedent force of *G v G* as it is on giving guidance on how courts should approach contact cases. The case illustrates the vital importance of the first instance ruling in children cases, and how an appellate court may reluctantly dismiss an appeal even where it takes the view that one parent has suffered an injustice at the hands of the other parent.

It can be seen from this analysis that it is not easy to state with confidence how much weight should be given to previous case law when advising on cases which turn on the welfare principle. The task is made harder because previous cases are often relied on by the higher courts to support and justify their rulings, despite the fact that precedent does not determine the course to be followed. It is undoubtedly true to say that it is essential to be familiar with the up-to-date approach of courts to the welfare principle in a similar context, because of course advising on the law is a predictive exercise, and the best guide to the future is what the courts

6   Ibid, at p 735.

have done already. Where the courts, and particularly the Court of Appeal, have adopted a consistent approach to similar facts a lawyer can feel fairly confident, though not certain, that the same approach will be adopted in relation to the child case on which he is giving advice.

Research studies

The study of child development is a growing science and this, coupled with studies on the impact of marriage and relationship breakdown on children, has led to a better understanding of the types of upbringing which best advance a child's physical, intellectual, emotional and social development. But of course legal proceedings are usually concerned with circumstances in which the child's upbringing cannot be ideal, and applying the welfare principle often means choosing the least damaging alternative for the child. Here too research studies can assist.[7] However, research studies should always be viewed with caution. Flawed research is dangerous because it deceives. In some studies the researcher's methodology is beyond reproach, but in others the researcher may arrive at conclusions which are scientifically invalid, and which ignore contradictory research.[8] Even greater caution should be exercised where there is reason to believe that the researchers hold a particular ideological theory about the upbringing of children which they wish to advance. Sometimes this leads them, either consciously or unconsciously, to extrapolate findings from their own and others' research which are not supported by the data that has been collected.[9] The risk created by research which is methodologically unsound is that it may lead to misguided judgments being made about what decisions will serve a child's best interests. On the other hand, where well-conducted research is referred

---

7 They may, for example, throw light on the likely impact on a child of separating her from the adults who have cared for her for many years; or they may give guidance on the advantages or disadvantages of seeking to preserve contact between a child and the parent with whom he is not living after divorce. Useful research material is referred to in C Piper *'Looking to the Future' for Children* (1994) 6 JCL 98.

8 See the review by J Kelly and R Emery in (1989) 19 Fam Law 489 of Wallerstein and Blakeslee *Second Chances: Men, Women and Children a Decade after Divorce* (Bantam Press, 1989); see too Elliott et al *Divorce and Children: A British Challenge to the Wallerstein View* (1990) 20 Fam Law 309.

9 This has occurred in the area of trans-racial adoption where some researchers have alleged that the adoption of white children by black parents is harmful to the children, despite the fact that this conclusion is unsupported either by the researchers' own findings or by the findings of other researchers: see E Bartholet *Where Do Black Children Belong? The Politics of Race Matching in Adoption* (1991) 139 University of Pennsylvania Law Review 1164; P Hayes *The Ideological Attack on Transracial Adoption in the USA and Britain* (1995) 9 IJLF 1.

to in evidence by a highly qualified expert, this may have a very persuasive impact on the outcome of a case.[10]

Courts must give reasons for their decisions

The determination of what decision will best promote a child's welfare cannot be a science because the decision revolves around the behaviour and personalities of the child, the parents, and any other persons who are offering to care for the child. Essentially, therefore, the determination of welfare is a matter of personal preference. However there are mechanisms which are designed to ensure that such a determination is arrived at in a structured way. One such mechanism is the requirement that courts give reasons for their decisions.[11] A court must make findings of fact and articulate the values which are informing its ruling. It must indicate the nature of the evidence which supports its findings and the conclusions which it draws from these findings. Where evidence is presented which is rejected by the court as unproved, irrelevant or unconvincing, it must explain why it arrived at this conclusion.[12] The requirement to give reasons therefore naturally exerts a discipline on decision-making. It is mandatory and any failure to observe the rule vitiates the decision.[13]

The welfare principle

The welfare principle is the golden thread which runs through decision-making by courts in children cases. Section 1 of the Children Act 1989 provides that—

'When a court determines any question with respect to
(a) the upbringing of a child; or
(b) the administration of the child's property or the application of any income arising from it,
the child's welfare shall be the court's paramount consideration.'

This simple statement means that a court must give overriding weight to the welfare of the child when determining any question with respect to

---

10 See, for example, the research studies on lesbian mothers cited in *B v B (Minors) (Custody, Care and Control)* [1991] 1 FLR 402 at p 406.
11 The Family Proceedings Court (Children Act 1989) Rules 1991, r.21; The Family Proceedings Rules 1991, r.4.21.
12 See, for example, *Leicestershire County Council v G* [1994] 2 FLR 329.
13 *W v Hertfordshire County Council* [1993] 1 FLR 118; *Re W (A Minor) (Contact)* [1994] 1 FLR 843. It is suggested that this is a particularly valuable new requirement in the case of magistrates, who are lay persons and unaccustomed to having to justify their judgments.

the child's upbringing.[14] But the very simplicity of the welfare principle conceals two often highly complex problems. The first is which questions are questions 'with respect to the upbringing of a child'. It has been explained elsewhere that the welfare principle does not apply to applications made under section 10 of the Children Act 1989 for leave to apply for a section 8 order;[15] to orders for financial and property provision made under section 15 and Schedule 1 of the Act;[16] or to applications for ouster orders,[17] and it will be seen below that other disputes involving the upbringing of children are not governed by this principle either. The second problem faced by courts is how is the goal of promoting the child's best interests best achieved, and it is to this question that attention is now turned.

The 'checklist'

A mechanism leading to the controlled exercise of discretion and structured decision-making is the requirement that courts consider a 'checklist' of factors before giving judgment. Section 1(4) provides that where a court is considering whether to make, vary or discharge a section 8 order, and the making, variation or discharge is opposed by any party to the proceedings, or where the court is considering whether to make, vary or discharge an order under Part IV of the Act, the court must have regard to a list of factors before arriving at its decision. Section 1(3) provides that—

'In the circumstances mentioned in subsection (4), a court shall have regard in particular to—
(a) the ascertainable wishes and feelings of the child concerned (considered in the light of his age and understanding);
(b) his physical, emotional and educational needs;
(c) the likely effect on him of any change in his circumstances;
(d) his age, sex, background and any characteristics of his which the court considers relevant;
(e) any harm which he has suffered or is at risk of suffering;
(f) how capable each of his parents, and any other person in

---

14 For a useful and oft-quoted description of the meaning of 'paramount' see Lord MacDermott's speech in *J v C* [1970] AC 668 at p 710. In *Birmingham City Council v H* [1994] 1 All ER 12, the House of Lords ruled that when both the parent and the parent's child are children, the welfare principle applies only to the parent's child because it is that child who is the subject of the application; see too *F v Leeds City Council* [1994] 2 FLR 60.
15 See ch 2.
16 See ch 8.
17 See ch 5.

relation to whom the court considers the question to be relevant, is of meeting his needs;

(g) the range of powers available to the court under this Act in the proceedings in question.'

This checklist seeks to ensure that judicial preferences are properly informed, and that judicial rulings are based on reasoning which takes account of all relevant considerations. Witnesses in children cases often give evidence in a self-serving and highly persuasive manner. Were such evidence to be received within a completely free and unstructured discretionary framework it could add to the risk, which is inherent in all discretionary decision-making, that a particular ideology, an idiosyncratic point of view, or a feeling of sympathy for an adult witness, could be given more weight than is merited, and lead to the court making a decision in which the child's welfare has become subordinated to other values. The advantage of the checklist is that it focuses the attention of the court on those factors which are widely accepted to be relevant to the promotion of a child's welfare. It is a mechanism which is designed to achieve balanced decisions after the court has consciously weighed all the factors which it ought to take into account.

Where all, or most, of the factors in the checklist point in one direction the decision on what will best promote the child's welfare may be relatively straightforward, and indeed a court ruling is unlikely to be necessary. However the complexity of children cases often turns on the fact that the matters listed in the checklist are pulling the courts in different directions. For example, the age and sex of a child may point to an order being made that she should live with her mother rather than an older relative, but there may be evidence to suggest that the mother might cause the child to suffer harm. The court must then determine whether the factor specified in paragraph (d) should be given greater weight than the factor specified in paragraph (e) and in this it must be guided by the factors in the other paragraphs, which again are likely to conflict, and to point to different outcomes. Thus opinion evidence may have been given that the child is likely to be badly affected by a change in her circumstances, which raises the considerations in paragraphs (b) and (c), but that if she were to remain with the mother it is unlikely that the mother could meet some of her needs, which raises paragraph (f).

An analysis of case law assists in the prediction of how a court is likely to approach the resolution of a case where the factors in the checklist point to different outcomes. Whilst each child case is unique, the majority of children cases can nonetheless be divided into loose categories. The analysis below discusses how courts have approached cases within different contexts.

Residence and welfare

When a marriage breaks down, and where parents no longer live together, both may wish to provide the children with a home. In many cases each parent is perfectly capable of caring for the children (paragraph (f)), neither parent is likely to harm the children (paragraph (e)), and when parents part there is inevitably a change of circumstances for the children (paragraph (c)), though if one parent remains in the former matrimonial home, he or she has a clear advantage under that head. But because each parent can usually provide a reasonable standard of care for the child, the decision about which parent will better provide for the child's welfare often turns on considerations relating to the child's physical, emotional and educational needs (paragraph (b)), and the child's age, sex, background and any characteristics of his which the court considers relevant (paragraph (d)). Courts, when choosing between parents, are therefore inevitably drawn into making value judgments about the roles of mothers and fathers, about different lifestyles, and about which factors make the most important contribution to a child's well-being.[18]

During this century, society has gained increasing insight into the physical and psychological needs of children and how provision can best be made for these needs. Studies of children whose parents have divorced or separated reveals that children are usually deeply saddened by their parents' parting and wish that they had remained together; that those who suffer most are those whose parents remain in conflict; but that those who suffer least are those who are able to retain a good relationship with each parent.[19] One commentator at least has therefore suggested that where both parents are able to provide the child with a reasonable upbringing, the child's welfare will normally best be served if he lives with the parent who will most encourage the continuing role of both parents as parents after divorce, and who will foster the child's links with his wider family.[20] This approach was reflected by Butler-Sloss LJ, when in *Re A (A Minor) (Custody)*[1] she said that the approach of a parent to contact is highly relevant to the determination of whether the child should live with him or her.

---

18   See, for example, *May v May* [1986] 1 FLR 325 where the welfare officer said that the conflict was not as to the competence of either of the parents, it was a conflict of different values and she concluded that she was confident that the children would be well cared for by either party.

19   A Mitchell *Children in the Middle: Living through Divorce* (Tavistock, 1985); M P M Richards and M Dyson *Separation, Divorce and the Development of Children: A Review* (DHSS, 1982). For an up-to-date account of the literature, see C Piper 'Looking to the Future' for Children (1994) 6 JCL 98.

20   M P M Richards *Joint Custody Revisited* (1989) 19 Fam Law 83.

1   [1991] 2 FLR 394 at p 400.

Shared residence

Many parents recognise that their children need to maintain positive links with each of them and some are able to organise their lives so that care of the children is shared between them. Where such an arrangement breaks down, or where parents cannot agree over with whom the children will live, and where their disagreement leads to an application for a residence order being made to a court, the court normally makes a residence order in favour of one of the parties and a contact order in favour of the other.[2] However, the parent who is most likely to obtain contact rather than residence may find this unsatisfactory and may wish to share providing the child with a home with the other parent. Prior to the Children Act 1989 the Court of Appeal had ruled in *Riley v Riley*[3] that it was not open to a court to make a joint care and control order. However this ruling has since been overtaken by section 11(4) which specifically contemplates a residence order being made to both parents despite the fact that they are living apart. It provides—

> 'Where a residence order is made in favour of two or more persons who do not themselves all live together, the order may specify the periods during which the child is to live in the different households concerned.'

Although courts have acknowledged that they now have power to make orders in which a child's residence is shared, they have stated that such orders are unusual, and that there must be some positive benefit to the child before such an order is made.[4] Courts have taken the view that where parents cannot agree, it is not in the child's best interests to make a shared residence order because of the difficulties which such an arrangement can cause. The nature of the concern about the effect of shared residence on the welfare of the child orders was illustrated in *Re J (A Minor) (Residence)*.[5] Here residence was strictly divided between the parents. However, the child was playing one parent off against the other, and was developing such a degree of anxiety and stress as to lead the court welfare officer to recommend that the child should spend the greater part of the week with one parent and a smaller proportion with the other. In *Re H (A Minor) (Shared Residence)*[6] Purchas LJ took the view that the establishment of

---

2   Provided that the court is satisfied that to make an order will be better for the children than to make no order at all: s.1(5); see ch 2.
3   [1986] 2 FLR 429.
4   *A v A (Minors) (Shared Residence Order)* [1994] 1 FLR 669.
5   [1994] 1 FLR 369.
6   [1994] 1 FLR 717.

two competing homes only leads to confusion and stress and is contrary to the paramount interests of the child, and he stated that such an order 'would rarely be made and would depend upon exceptional circumstances'. In the same case Cazalet J said that there may be circumstances in which a shared residence order is appropriate because it may reduce the differences between the parties, but that, where there are differences between them, a child should normally make his settled home with one parent.

In *A v A (Minors) (Shared Residence Order)*[7] the conflict was not over the amount of time which the children should spend with their mother and their father, that had already been agreed. For the previous 12 months the children had spent the school week with their mother and divided their weekends and holidays between their parents. However, the parents had great difficulty in communicating with one another, and when the father applied for a shared residence order the mother strongly opposed this. The issue for the court, therefore, was whether the children should continue to see their father under the auspices of a contact order or under the auspices of a shared residence order. The trial judge confirmed the existing arrangements and made a residence order in favour of each parent. Dismissing the mother's appeal, the Court of Appeal found that the judge had not exceeded the generous ambit within which reasonable disagreement is possible, and therefore there was no evidence that he had been plainly wrong.[8] However, Butler-Sloss LJ disagreed with Purchas LJ's approach in *Re H (A Minor) (Shared Residence)* in so far as he had imported a general test of 'exceptional circumstances' into the interpretation of section 11(4), and emphasised that each case must be decided on its own facts.[9] She stated that a shared residence order is an unusual order which should only be made in unusual circumstances, but that a judge should exercise his discretion in accordance with the checklist. Giving guidance on where a shared order would *not* be appropriate, she said:

> 'A shared residence order would, in my view, be unlikely to be made if there were concrete issues still arising between the parties which had not been resolved, such as the amount of contact, whether it should be staying or visiting contact or another issue such as education, which were muddying the waters and which were creating difficulties between the parties which reflected the way in which the children were moving from one parent to another in the contact period.'[10]

7   [1994] 1 FLR 669.
8   *G v G* [1985] 2 All ER 225. On the role of the appeal court, see above p 207.
9   [1994] 1 FLR 669 at p 678.
10 Ibid, at p 677.

Should the children live with their mother or their father?

Although the law does not favour mothers over fathers in the sense that there is no presumption that a child should live with his mother, surveys of practice reveal that mothers retain care of the children far more often than fathers.[11] These surveys were carried out prior to the Children Act 1989; however there does not appear to be any evidence to suggest that patterns have undergone any marked alteration. In the past judges felt able to express a bias towards women using language which would not be acceptable today. Thus in *M v M*,[12] when comparing the claim of the father against the mother to look after their four-year-old daughter, Stamp LJ stated 'I would entertain no doubt whatsoever that this little girl of four and a half years old ought to be brought up by her mother that *nature has ordained* should look after her own little girl.'[13] He added, 'however good a man [the father] may be, he cannot perform the functions which a mother performs by nature in relation to her own little girl.' Whilst Ormrod LJ expressed the opinion that '[the mother] can give up work much more easily than the father can if the child is ill.'

It is suggested that it is inconceivable that the Court of Appeal would speak of the role of a mother in this manner today. The present approach of the Court of Appeal was articulated by Butler-Sloss LJ in *Re S (A Minor) (Custody)*[14] where she said 'it is natural for young children to be with their mothers but, where it is in dispute, it is a consideration but not a presumption.' She subsequently elaborated on what she meant by this in *Re A (A Minor) (Custody)*.[15] She explained that where a young child has lived throughout with the mother in an unbroken relationship, such a relationship is very difficult to displace unless the mother is unsuitable to care for the child.[16] However, she distinguished the situation where there has been a continuum of care by the mother from that where mother and child have been separated, and where the mother seeks the return of the child. She said that in these circumstances other considerations applied, and there is no starting point that the mother should be preferred to the father and only displaced by a preponderance of evidence to the contrary. She emphasised that there is no presumption which requires the mother, as mother, to be considered as the primary caretaker in preference to the father.

11 J A Priest and J C Whybrow *Custody Law in Practice in the Divorce and Domestic Courts* Supplement to Law Com WP No 96 (HMSO, 1986).

12 (1978) 1 FLR 77.

13 Emphasis added.

14 [1991] 2 FLR 388 at p 390.

15 [1991] 2 FLR 394.

16 Thus, in this regard, Butler-Sloss LJ was confirming the approach that mothers have an inherent advantage in relation to young children, but using more moderate language than in *M v M*.

It is clear that a mother has a clear advantage over a father in a case where a baby or young child is involved. In *Re W (A Minor) (Residence Order)*,[17] the Court of Appeal held that while there is no presumption of law that a child of any given age is better off with one parent there is a rebuttable presumption of fact that a baby's interests are best served by being cared for by his mother. As Balcombe LJ said, 'it hardly requires saying that a baby of under four weeks old would normally be with his or her natural mother.' Furthermore the court emphasised the risks of delaying a decision while full welfare reports are prepared. In *Re W (A Minor)* the baby had been separated from her mother and was in the care of her father. A judge had ordered that the status quo be maintained pending the preparation of reports. Allowing the mother's appeal, the Court of Appeal substituted an interim residence order in favour of the mother.[18]

A parent's sexual orientation

Occasionally questions have arisen about the relevance of a parent's sexual orientation to the welfare of the child.[19] In *C v C (A Minor) (Custody: Appeal)*[20] the court had to choose between parents of a six-year-old girl who both clearly loved the child and could give her good physical care. The father had remarried and was living with his new wife, the mother was living with a lesbian partner. The trial judge gave the care of the child to the mother, holding that her lesbian relationship was not a matter to put into the balancing exercise since its impact on the child would be much the same whether she visited her mother from time to time or lived with her permanently. Allowing the father's appeal and remitting the case for a fresh hearing the Court of Appeal ruled that the judge had been plainly wrong to engage in the balancing operation as if there were no lesbian relationship. Balcombe LJ stated that a judge must not allow his subjective views to affect his decision on what a child's welfare requires when approaching sensitive issues on which different views are held, rather he

17 [1992] 2 FLR 332.
18 See too the unusual facts of *Re P* [1987] 2 FLR 421 where a mother of five-month-old twins had entered into a private surrogacy arrangement but refused to hand the babies over to the commissioning couple. Although the couple could offer the children an advantageous upbringing in terms of intellectual stimulus, material benefits and a two-parent household, these factors did not outweigh the advantage of preserving the children's link with their mother to whom they were bonded.
19 Cases of this nature have tended in the past to lead to less than temperate language being used by the judges, see Lord Wilberforce's speech in *Re D (An Infant)* [1977] AC 602 at p 609 where he refers to children, at critical ages, being exposed to homosexual ways of life which may lead to 'severance from normal society, to psychological stresses and unhappiness and possibly even to physical experiences which may scar them for life'. Surely the same could be said for heterosexual encounters too?
20 [1991] 1 FLR 223.

should apply the moral standards which are generally accepted in society. Taking this approach, he said:

> 'It is still the norm that children are brought up in a home with a father, mother and siblings (if any) and, other things being equal, such an upbringing is most likely to be conducive to their welfare. If, because the parents are divorced, such an upbringing is no longer possible, then a very material factor in considering where the child's welfare lies is which of the competing parents can offer the nearest approach to the norm. In the present case it is clearly the father.'

Later he added 'if her home was to be with the father that would be a normal home by the standards of our society; that would not be the case if the home were with the mother.'[1] Glidewell LJ expressed the same view in even stronger language. He said 'despite the vast changes over the past 30 years or so in the attitudes of our society generally to the institution of marriage, to sexual morality, and to homosexual relationships ... a lesbian relationship between two adult women is an unusual background in which to bring up a child.' He continued:

> 'The judge had no evidence, and thus we have none, about the effect on a young child of learning the nature of a lesbian relationship and of her friends learning about it. Nevertheless, it seems the judge accepted, and it is certainly my view, that this child should learn or understand at an early age the nature of her mother's relationship .... Moreover, he seems to have disregarded the effect on [the child] of her school friends learning of the relationship. If or when they do, she is bound to be asked questions which may well cause her distress or embarrassment.'[2]

It is suggested that much of the reasoning in *C v C (A Minor) (Custody: Appeal)* relied on assertions about what is 'normal' stemming from a narrow perspective of normality, and was based on speculation about how living with a lesbian parent is likely to affect a child. There was neither empirical nor research evidence to support the judges' assertions, and there was no evidence before them on the impact which a lesbian upbringing would be likely to have on the child's relationship with her peers, or on the development of her own sexuality.[3] It is suggested that where a parent's sexual orientation is homosexual or lesbian he or she might be well advised

1 Ibid, at pp 231 and 232.
2 Ibid, at pp 228-9.
3 Which was another matter of concern to the court. It is interesting to note that when the case was reheard by a Family Division judge that he ordered that the child should live with her mother: see F Tasker and S Golombok *Children Raised by Lesbian Mothers* (1991) 21 Fam Law 184.

to adduce expert evidence that this will not harm the child. Evidence of this nature was very persuasive in *B v B (Minors) (Custody, Care and Control).*[4] Here a highly qualified expert witness was able to assure the court that there is no increased incidence of homosexuality amongst the children of homosexual parents. In relation to stigmatisation and reputation, the witness was further able to reassure the court that children tend to be teased about matters about which they show sensitivity relating to them personally, and that it was very rare for children to show an interest in the background of other children. There is nonetheless a body of authority to the effect that a parent's sexual orientation is a relevant matter in the assessment of a child's welfare, and that, all other things being equal, a child will benefit more from being brought up in a heterosexual household.[5]

Continuity of care

Paragraph (c) directs courts to consider the likely effect on the child of any change in his circumstances, and where present arrangements are working it is unlikely that a court will be willing to alter the status quo.[6] Continuity of care is generally regarded as desirable for a child because it assists in giving him a sense of security at a time when he is feeling vulnerable and threatened by his parents' separation. Courts are reluctant to interfere with established arrangements because bonds are likely to exist not only between the child and the parent with whom he is living, but also between the child and other members of the household, neighbours, friends and companions at school.[7] This means that the parent who keeps the children in the immediacy of marriage breakdown is the parent who is most likely, all other things being equal, to obtain a residence order. It is in cases of this kind that a father has tended to be successful in obtaining an order that the care of young children should remain with him.[8] Furthermore, the status quo position is reinforced when a court requests the preparation

---

4   [1991] 1 FLR 402.
5   *Re P (A Minor) (Custody)* (1983) 4 FLR 401; *S v S (Custody of Children)* (1978) 1 FLR 143. In *Re H (A Minor) (Section 37 Direction)* [1993] 2 FLR 541 a lesbian couple applied for a residence order in respect of a baby girl whom they had been looking after for eight months. There were various serious concerns about the suitability of the applicants, including about the impact on the child of being brought up in a lesbian household, and the court directed that an investigation under s.37(1) of the Children Act 1989 take place: see ch 3.
6   For a pre-Children Act 1989 example, see *D v M* [1982] 3 All ER 897. Retention of the status quo is also highly relevant to paragraphs (b) and (e). Where a child has formed settled relationships, to move the child may be positively harmful to his or her future mental health and ability to relate normally to people: see, for example, *Re JK (Adoption: Transracial Placement)* [1991] 2 FLR 340 which is discussed below.
7   See the comments by Ormrod LJ in *Dicocco v Milne* (1983) 4 FLR 247.
8   *Re A (A Minor) (Custody)* [1991] 2 FLR 394; see too *Stephenson v Stephenson* [1985] FLR 1140.

of reports in order to assist it in arriving at its decision. Owing to the pressures on court welfare officers it is unlikely that a report will be prepared in less than two months, and three months is a more common minimum preparation time.[9] In addition, although children cases take priority in court listing arrangements, the pressure on courts also leads to delay in the hearing of cases. Therefore the parent who has care of the child in the meantime inevitably has a built-in advantage, because by the time the case is heard, the status quo will have assumed even greater importance.

It is suggested that parents seeking legal advice should be made fully aware of this bias towards the status quo. In particular a father or mother, who might otherwise be willing to leave the matrimonial home pending divorce, needs to appreciate the implications of doing so in relation to the children. However, a short period of separation from the children may not be problematic. Where the parties have separated fairly recently the status quo argument does not carry the same weight, and a court is more likely to be willing to order a transfer of residence.[10]

'Snatching' and ex parte applications

Courts are anxious to prevent children from becoming pawns in a battle between their parents, particularly where this develops into a situation where parents are literally pulling the child from one home to the other. Married parents, of course, enjoy equal parental responsibility and, in the absence of a court order, each is entitled to exercise all aspects of that responsibility. But in *Re B (Minors) (Residence Order)*[11] the Court of Appeal made it clear that this does not mean that a parent is free to take the children away from their settled home. Nor does it mean that a parent is entitled to refuse to return a child after a contact visit where the child's home is with the other parent.[12] The courts have expressed grave displeasure at behaviour of this kind, and are likely to counter it by making an interim order restoring the child to the parent who had de facto residence pending a fuller investigation and the preparation of welfare reports.[13]

In *W v D*[14] a father had refused to return his daughter aged four to her mother after a contact visit. The mother applied for an order restoring the

9   The National Standards For Probation Service Family Court Welfare Work (Home Office, 1994) states at para 4.28 that a report should normally be filed within 10 weeks of the receipt of the relevant papers from the court.
10   *Allington v Allington* [1985] FLR 586.
11   [1992] 3 All ER 867.
12   *Re H (A Minor) (Interim Custody)* [1991] 2 FLR 411.
13   *Jenkins v Jenkins* (1978) 1 FLR 148.
14   (1979) 1 FLR 393; although this case preceded the implementation of the Children Act 1989 by a decade it is suggested that the approach of the Court of Appeal has not altered.

child to her care, but the judge adjourned the case pending the preparation of a welfare report, and ordered that the child should stay in her father's care pending the final hearing. Allowing the mother's appeal, the Court of Appeal ruled that against the background of snatch the principles are these: where a child of tender years has spent her life in the care of her mother then, unless it appears on credible evidence that there is something so prejudicial to the life of the child flowing from the care of the mother so that it would be dangerous to restore the pre-existing situation, the court should order that the child is restored to the situation that existed before the snatch.[15] In *Re R (Minors) (Interim Custody Order)*[16] Balcombe J criticised the use of the word 'principle' in this context, pointing out that the only principle to be applied in children cases is the paramountcy of the child's welfare. But in *Townson v Mahon*[17] the Court of Appeal reasserted the approach that a judge making an interim order ought to restore the status quo in the absence of particular reasons to the contrary. As Wood J pointed out, one of the arguments which had been put for the father at the hearing before the judge was that the child had settled with him after he had wrongfully kept her after a contact visit. Thus when the judge had dismissed the mother's application to have the child returned to her forthwith, the effect of that was to consolidate the position created by the father's wrongdoing.

Where allegations are made by the 'snatching' parent against the residential parent the court may adopt a less rigorous approach to snatching. In *Re J (A Minor) (Interim Custody: Appeal)*[18] the snatching father had made allegations against the mother in relation to her care of the child in swiftly heard inter partes proceedings, and the trial judge had concluded that the child should stay with her father during the short period pending a fuller hearing. Dismissing the mother's appeal, Butler-Sloss LJ emphasised that there was no principle that where a child has been retained beyond the agreed time that the court should automatically order that the child be returned pending a final decision. However, and by contrast, in *Re H (A Minor) (Interim Custody)*[19] Butler-Sloss LJ reproved the trial judge for making an order in ex parte proceedings transferring the care of a child from the mother to the father. The father had alleged that the child had been non-accidentally injured by being kicked by her mother's partner, and had supported this allegation with opinion evidence to that effect from a doctor who had examined the child. Butler-Sloss LJ said that she deprecated the use of an ex parte order for changing the child's home from

15 The court asserted these principles on the assumption that the child had been snatched from the mother; it is not clear whether it would have adopted the same approach if the mother had snatched a young child from the father.
16 (1980) 2 FLR 316.
17 [1984] FLR 690.
18 [1989] 2 FLR 304.
19 [1991] 2 FLR 411.

one parent to another unless the circumstances were very exceptional. She drew an analogy with a case where a local authority wished to obtain an emergency order to protect a child from immediate danger, and said that unless the facts justified such an order the court should not transfer the child from one parent to the other until after an urgent inter partes hearing.

It is suggested that the analogy drawn with an application by a local authority for an emergency order[20] was not apt to proceedings involving parents. When an emergency protection order is made the child is taken from home and placed in unfamiliar surroundings and parental responsibility is given to the applicant, who is usually a social worker. This is traumatic for the child and involves state interference in family life which must be carefully controlled for reasons of broad policy.[1] By contrast, when a non-residential parent takes, or retains, care of a child, the child will not be moving to a strange environment where he is cared for by people whom he does not know. Rather, he will be with a parent who enjoys de jure, or at least de facto, parental responsibility for him, and with whom he is familiar. Whilst it may be upsetting for the child, the child may well be unaware of what is taking place because he is merely staying longer with a known and trusted adult. Where, as in *Re H (A Minor)*, a general practitioner gives evidence that there is a prima facie case of child abuse, and the non-abusing parent is wanting to care for the child, it is suggested that the welfare of the child should normally point to the child being transferred to that parent for a very short period while further enquiries are made, this being the safest alternative for the child. It is suggested that the approach taken in *Re H (A Minor)* may sometimes fail to serve a child's welfare, and that a judge, in the exercise of his discretion, should not feel inhibited from ordering that a child's residence is *temporarily* transferred from one parent to another in ex parte proceedings where there is an allegation of child abuse, while further investigations take place.[2]

Where the choice is between a parent and a third party

The principle that the child's welfare must be the court's paramount consideration can sometimes exist uneasily alongside the principle that it is parents who enjoy parental responsibility, and it is they who have the right to bring up their own children. Where a child is being cared for by a

20 In *Re H (A Minor) (Interim Custody)* Butler-Sloss LJ drew an analogy with an application for a place of safety order under the Children and Young Persons Act 1969. This has since been replaced by the emergency protection order under the Children Act 1989, s.44.

1 See ch 3.

2 See too *Re B (Minors) (Residence Order)* [1992] 3 All ER 867.

parent, and where he is well looked after and happy, it would be most unusual for a court to order that the child should live with someone else, even his other parent, because courts are quite properly reluctant to disturb an arrangement which is working well. However, where a third party such as a relative, friend or foster parent is bringing up a child within a loving and stable environment, and where that third party is seeking to retain care of the child against the opposition of the child's natural parents, a real tension can arise. In a case of this kind the court is often faced with a choice between leaving the child in the care of persons whom he loves, and with whom he has formed bonds of attachment, and returning him to parents who usually live in more disadvantaged circumstances, and to whom the child's attachment links may have been weakened. Thus the welfare principle and the principle that parents have a right to bring up their own children may sometimes be pulling in different directions.

The principle to be applied in such a situation is clear: the child's welfare must be the court's paramount consideration. In 1969 the House of Lords ruled in *J v C*³ that just as the paramountcy principle applies between parent and parent, so too it applies to disputes between parents and strangers. Lord MacDermott's speech provides helpful guidance on the practical application of this principle. The issue in *J v C* was whether a 10-year-old Spanish boy should be returned to the care of his natural parents or whether he should remain with his English foster parents, with whom he had spent most of his childhood. In this regard Lord MacDermott stated that the rights and wishes of the parents must be assessed and weighed as to their bearing on the welfare of the child in conjunction with all other factors relevant to that issue. He added that 'such rights and wishes, recognised as they are by nature and society, can be capable of ministering to the total welfare of the child in a special way, and must therefore preponderate in many cases.' However he stated that there is no rule of law that the rights and wishes of unimpeachable parents must prevail, and that experience shows that serious harm can sometimes be occasioned to children by moving them from one home to another. He added that a child's future happiness and sense of security are always important factors, and that the effect of such a change will often be worthy of close and anxious attention.

The weight to be given to the wishes and feelings of parents came under further scrutiny from the House of Lords in 1988 in *Re KD (A Minor) (Ward: Termination of Access)*.⁴ Here a local authority had applied to terminate contact between a child and his mother so that they could place the child for adoption. The issue to be resolved was whether the welfare principle applied to the termination of contact between a child and his

3   [1969] 1 All ER 788.
4   [1988] 1 All ER 577.

parent, or whether such an approach was inconsistent with the European Convention on Human Rights and Fundamental Freedoms, to which the United Kingdom is a party. Article 8 of the Convention provides—

'1. Everyone has the right to respect for his private and family life, his home and his correspondence.
2. There shall be no interference by a public authority with the exercise of this right except such as is in accordance with the law and is necessary ... for the protection of health or morals, or for the protection of the rights and freedoms of others.'

The House of Lords ruled that there is no conflict between the Convention and giving paramountcy to the child's welfare. Lord Oliver stated that pronouncements made by the European Court of Human Rights[5] and the principles laid down by the House of Lords in *J v C* could be reconciled, and that:

'Such conflict as exists is, I think, semantic only and lies in differing ways of giving expression to the single common concept that the natural bond and relationship between parent and child gives rise to universally recognised norms which ought not to be gratuitously interfered with and which, if interfered with at all, ought to be so only if the welfare of the child dictates.'

Lord Oliver was at pains to point out that 'parenthood, in most civilised societies, is generally conceived as conferring on parents the exclusive privilege of ordering, within the family, the upbringing of children of tender age, with all that that entails'. But he added 'it is a privilege circumscribed by many limitations imposed both by the general law, and, where the circumstances demand, by the courts or by the authorities on whom the legislature has imposed the duty of supervising the welfare of children and young persons'.[6]

Like Lord Oliver, Lord Templeman found no difficulty in reconciling the paramountcy principle with Article 8 of the Convention. He said:

'In my opinion there is no inconsistency of principle or application between the English rule and the convention rule. The best person to bring up a child is the natural parent. It matters not whether the parent is wise or foolish, rich or poor, educated or illiterate, provided the child's moral or physical health are not endangered .... In terms of the English rule the court decides whether and to

5   *R v United Kingdom* [1988] 2 FLR 445, E Ct HR.
6   [1988] 1 All ER 577 at p 588.

what extent the welfare of the child requires that the child shall be protected from harm caused by the parent, including harm which could be caused by resumption of parental care after separation has broken the parental tie. In terms of the Convention rule the court decides whether and to what extent the child's health or morals require protection from the parent and whether and to what extent the family life of parent and child has been supplanted by some other relationship which has become the essential family life for the child.'[7]

Whilst the guiding principles are undoubtedly clear, the cases where the conflict over the child is between a parent and a third party are undoubtedly the most difficult for the courts to resolve. There is often a strong tension between having regard to the wishes and feelings of the parents and giving paramountcy to the child's welfare. An example arose in *Re K (A minor) (Custody)*.[8] The child had gone to live with his uncle and aunt, Mr and Mrs E, after the suicide of his mother. When the child's father sought to recover the care of his son the trial judge asked himself the question: 'who would provide the better home for the child, the father or Mr and Mrs E?' and decided that Mr and Mrs E would do so. Reversing the judge's decision, Fox LJ said that this approach had been wrong. The question was not where the child would get the better home. The question was: 'was it demonstrated that the welfare of the child positively demanded the displacement of the parental right.'[9] Waite J stated that the speeches in *Re KD (A Minor)* 'make it plain that the term "parental right" is not there used in any proprietary sense, but rather as describing *the right of every child*, as part of its general welfare, to have the ties of nature maintained wherever possible with the parents who gave it life.'[10]

In *Re K (A Minor) (Wardship: Adoption)*,[11] the Court of Appeal warned against a court making an order which could offer the child an advantageous style of upbringing with substitute parents where this would prevent the natural parents caring for their child themselves. The case concerned a child of seven months whose mother was being treated for heroin addiction and who, with her husband, was seeking to recover the child from a couple to whom the mother had handed her over when she was six weeks old. Reversing the trial judge's decision to leave the child in a 'warm and loving family who are currently caring for her admirably and wish to continue to do so' and where 'if she moves there will be inevitable upheaval and upset

7   Ibid, at p 578.
8   [1990] 2 FLR 64.
9   Fox LJ acknowledged that the word 'right' was not accurate in so far as it might connote something in the nature of a proprietary right, which, he emphasised, it is not.
10   Ibid, at p 70, emphasis added.
11   [1991] 1 FLR 57.

for the child,' Butler-Sloss LJ said 'the mother must be shown to be entirely unsuitable before another family can be considered, otherwise we are in grave danger of slipping into social engineering.'[12]

It is suggested that if the courts maintain their recent antipathy to social engineering it is unlikely that a court would again make a ruling like the one in *Re H (A Minor: Custody)*[13] in which a 'warm and loving' Indian mother was unable to regain the care of her son from her brother-in-law and sister-in-law. In *Re H* the child aged seven and a half had been placed with these relatives by his father, and they had looked after him for the last two and a half years. During this time the mother had had regular contact with her son, apart from a period of nine months at the outset, when the father very improperly cut off contact. The case is illustrative of how the considerations in the checklist which relate to the child's sense of security, and its link with the status quo, may point in one direction, and the claim of a parent to bring up her own child may point in another. The child was living in a secure and stable environment, and had settled well at school, and the court was unwilling to upset this arrangement even though nothing could be said against the mother as a mother. However, the ruling in *Re H* was disturbing because of the manner in which the claims of the mother to care for her own child, and the interests of the child to be brought up by his own mother, were so readily displaced.

The two decisions in *Re K (A minor) (Custody)*[14] and *Re K (A Minor) (Wardship: Adoption)*[15] were interesting developments of thinking in this area. By labelling the notion that a child should be brought up by his parent as the 'right of the child', and by stating that the court must beware of 'social engineering', the courts were able to give considerable weight to the parents' claims to bring up their own children without appearing to come into conflict with the paramountcy of the child's welfare. However, there are dangers in taking a rights approach to the welfare principle. A child's right to family life is separate and independent of that of his parents, and the child may, or may not, agree with the characterisation of his right to family life as the 'right to be brought up by the parents who gave birth to him'. The child's views are likely to be coloured by the strength of his attachment to his 'natural' parents and the strength of his attachment to those who have been caring for him as substitute parents. Where he has little attachment to his natural parents, and where he is much loved by

---

12 Ibid, at p 62. However, care must be taken over the weight to be given to this authority: the couple caring for the child were not themselves entirely suitable as carers because of their age, and they had attempted to circumvent the safeguards surrounding the placement of children for adoption.

13 [1990] 1 FLR 51.

14 [1990] 2 FLR 64.

15 [1991] 1 FLR 57.

his substitute parents and they have been making very considerable provision for his physical, emotional and educational needs, the child may have reservations, or even strong negative views, about the perceived advantages of his returning to live with his natural parent against his remaining with his substitute 'psychological' parents'.[16] He certainly may not regard it as his 'right' to be brought up by his parents, who, to him, may be the strangers rather than his substitute parents whom he regards as his family. Thus the definition of what is meant by 'family' or 'parents' turns on whether the blood tie defines the relationship, or whether the child's experience, wishes and feelings define it. In a case where the dispute is between parents and third parties what a court is often doing is determining whether the parents are capable of providing the child with a good enough standard of parenting; where they can, the court must find strong reasons for preventing the parents from providing that care. Where the child has formed strong attachment bonds, the question for the court is whether returning the child to the parents is likely to cause him psychological harm. Where it is, such a finding is likely to justify leaving the child where he is.[17]

It is suggested that when a decision is characterised as one which upholds the rights of the child this can tend to inhibit discussion about the thinking which is informing the decision. It would be preferable if it were more openly acknowledged that courts are applying ideologies and values when choosing between parents and strangers, because such an acknowledgment would better encourage debate about whether these ideologies and values command widespread acceptance. It might aid clarity if courts found it easier to state that parents do indeed have 'rights' as part of their parental responsibility, and that for a court to interfere in these rights without good cause would be to implement a dangerous social policy amounting to unwarranted state interference in private family life. It seems undoubtedly to be the case that where a court takes as its starting point that it is the right of the child to be brought up by his parents, and that a court should turn its face against social engineering unless there are good reasons, it is applying norms which command international acceptance.[18]

---

16 A phrase first used by J Goldstein, A Freud and A Solnit in their highly influential book *Beyond the Best Interests of the Child* (Collier Macmillan, 1973).

17 As in *J v C* [1969] 1 All ER 788; see too *Re N (A Minor) (Adoption)* [1990] 1 FLR 58 and *Re A (A Minor) (Cultural Background)* [1987] 2 FLR 429 (which concerned a dispute between a grandmother and third parties). Both are discussed below.

18 It is suggested that this approach is consistent with Arts.5, 9 and 18 of the United Nations Convention on the Rights of the Child. The Convention was adopted, without a vote, on 20 November 1989.

Placement with a parent or placement for adoption

Conflict between the principle that the welfare of the child is paramount, and the principle that it is normally the responsibility of the parent to bring up his or her own child, may arise where one parent wishes the child to be given up for adoption, and the other wishes to look after the child. In *Re M (A Minor) (Custody Appeal)*[19] the Court of Appeal adopted a very different approach to that of Lord Templeman in *Re KD (A Minor) (Ward) (Termination of Access)*,[20] and gave very considerable weight to the perceived advantages to a child of being brought up by strangers rather than by his own family. In *Re M* the mother and father were at school and aged 16 and 17 when the child was born. The mother decided that the child should be adopted so the father, supported by his parents, applied for custody of the child.[1] The trial judge found that the father's application was sincere and that the grandparents could provide the child with a good home, but he nonetheless concluded that it would be in the child's best interests to be placed for adoption. The reasons given for refusing the father custody were speculative and based on a particular view of 'normal' family life and the behaviour of young men. Nothing was said against the father or grandparents which suggested that they were unfit to care for the child, indeed the grandparents were described as 'excellent'. In relation to the father's claim to bring up his own child, the trial judge had said 'I do not give particular weight to the blood tie, although I take it into account, but I do not think it should be the decisive factor.'[2]

It is suggested that this was a case which gives cause for considerable unease. The approach taken in *Re M (A Minor) (Custody Appeal)* to the paramountcy of the child's welfare was far removed from Lord Templeman's strictures in *Re KD (A Minor)* that a natural parent is the best person to bring up his or her own child, and that the natural bond between parent and child should only be interfered with where the child's moral or physical health is endangered. By contrast, the trial judge in *Re M* appeared intent on optimising the child's position by means of adoption by a two-parent family. Perhaps the greatest cause for unease is that the father's appeal was dismissed not simply for the usual reasons, namely that the matter was one for the trial judge in the exercise of his discretion, and that the

---

19 [1990] 1 FLR 291.
20 [1988] 1 All ER 577.
1   The modern equivalent would be to make an application for a residence order.
2   Virtually no weight at all appears to have been given to the notion of extended family rights and the claim of the grandparents to be involved in the upbringing of their grandchild; contrast with the approach in *Re L (A Minor) (Care Proceedings: Wardship) (No 2)* [1991] 1 FLR 29 in which grandparents were offering to care for their grandchild. Judge Willis, sitting as a deputy High Court judge, stated 'adoption should only be the last resort when no-one in the wider family is available and suitable to look after a child'.

appellant had failed to establish that he had been plainly wrong. Rather, in *Re M* the Court of Appeal fully endorsed the trial judge's approach and said that, had the decision been for the Court of Appeal to make, it would have arrived at the same conclusion.

Subsequently the Court of Appeal have reverted once more to the approach taken in *Re KD (A Minor)*, and in *Re K (A minor) (Custody)* and *Re K (A Minor) (Wardship: Adoption)*. In *Re O (A Minor) (Custody: Adoption)*[3] Butler-Sloss LJ used the phrase 'social engineering' to describe the authorisation of adoption in a case where a parent was offering to care for the child. In *Re O* a married woman had conceived in the course of an adulterous relationship. She became reconciled with her husband and, after much heart-searching, she placed her child with an adoption agency with a view to his adoption. The child's father was seeking to look after the child, but the mother, who was very hostile to the father, strenuously opposed his application. The trial judge made an order in favour of the father giving him the care of the child, and the Court of Appeal dismissed the mother's appeal. Butler-Sloss LJ said that the test to be applied was whether the father was a fit and suitable person to care for his son, and that if he was adoption did not arise. She stated that no distinction should be drawn between the married and the unmarried father because, so far as the child was concerned, he was the other parent, and added 'the judge quite correctly posed to himself the test that if the mother and father were married and the mother could not care for the child, would one say that the child should not go to the father? Quite simply, the answer would be that one could not say that.'

However, it is suggested that just as *Re M (A Minor) (Custody: Adoption)*[4] gives cause for unease so too *Re O (A Minor) (Custody: Adoption)*, in which the contrary decision was reached, also gives cause for unease. This time the anxiety arises because of the manner in which the mother's strongly held views were discounted by the court. In *Re M* there was no suggestion that the natural parents were hostile to one another, or that the father had behaved badly towards the mother. By contrast, whilst the court did not accept all the mother's allegations against the father in *Re O*, it found as a fact that the mother felt very strongly that the father had behaved dishonourably towards her, and that she was vehemently opposed to the father bringing up her child. It is suggested that *Re O* has serious implications for any unmarried mother who is considering placing her child with an adoption agency. It seems essential that she should be warned that her wish that the child should be brought up by an adoptive couple who can offer the child a two-parent family may be frustrated by an application for a residence order from the father. Where she is passionately

3   [1992] 1 FLR 77.
4   Discussed above.

opposed to the father having care of her child, she also needs to know that, in the light of *Re O,* her opposition is unlikely to prevent an order being made in the father's favour.

Re O (A Minor) (Custody: Adoption) poses the broader question whether courts would be wise to treat all unmarried fathers in an identical fashion to married fathers where the mother wishes the child to be adopted, or whether they would be better to adopt the approach taken in *Re M (A Minor) (Custody: Adoption).* It is suggested that there *is* a distinction between married and unmarried parenthood. When a man and a woman marry, they agree implicitly to share parental responsibility for any child of their union. When an unmarried woman becomes pregnant by a man there is no such implicit agreement; how the mother sees the father's role in the child's life is likely to turn on the length and quality of her relationship with the father. Where that relationship has been relatively fleeting, and where she feels betrayed or otherwise ill-used by the father, she is unlikely to want him to have sole responsibility for the upbringing of their child. If courts too readily make residence orders in favour of unmarried fathers in cases where the mother wishes the child to be adopted by third parties, the knowledge that such an order could be made is likely to deter some unmarried mothers from placing their children for adoption. It seems likely that some mothers will not be prepared to risk the fathers obtaining a residence order. If this results in more babies being brought up by single mothers who would otherwise prefer that their children are adopted, it can be questioned whether this promotes the general welfare of children.

A child's ethnic origin

When making plans about a child's welfare, virtually all local authority social services departments take the view that it is self-evident that the child's interests are best served if he has his home with persons of the same ethnic origin.[5] The Children Act 1989 itself makes reference to religious, racial and cultural matters,[6] and guidance on the implementation of the Act provides that 'it may be taken as a guiding principle of good practice that, other things being equal and in the great majority of cases, placement with a family of similar ethnic origin and religion is most likely to meet a child's needs as fully as possible and to safeguard his or her welfare most effectively.'[7] The guidance adds the proviso that this principle

5   Including when the local authority are acting as adoption agency.
6   S.22(4) and (5)(c) provide that before making any decision with respect to a child whom they are looking after, or proposing to look after, a local authority must take into consideration the child's religious persuasion, racial origin, and cultural and religious background.
7   *Children Act 1989 Guidance and Regulations*, vol 3, Family Placements, para 2.40.

should be applied with proper consideration for the circumstances of the individual case, and that there may be circumstances where placement with a family of a different ethnic origin may be the best choice for a particular child. It gives as examples where a child has formed strong links with prospective foster parents, or where he is related to them; where siblings who have different ethnic origins need to be placed together; where the child needs to remain close to his family, school and friends; or where he has special needs. However, the guidance takes it as axiomatic that placement in a family which reflects as nearly as possible the child's ethnic origins is likely to be the best choice in most cases. Indeed, it goes so far as to advise that, when exploring a child's wishes and feelings on the matter, 'responsible authorities should be ready to help the child with any confusion or misunderstandings about people of different ethnic groups which may have arisen through previous family or placement experience. Children of mixed ethnic origin should be helped to understand and take pride in both or all elements of their cultural heritage and to feel comfortable about their origins.'[8] In relation to the selection of persons to care for children, the guidance states that carers must be able to provide children with such help.

This view on child rearing, which is presented in the guidance in terms of having a universal and objective value,[9] has been highly influential not only on the manner in which local authorities select foster parents and adoptive parents, but also in the manner in which they, and the courts, have approached litigation about a child who is already living with a family of a different ethnic origin. Several highly contentious cases have come before the courts in which the child's ethnicity has been treated by one of the parties as an issue of great importance.

In *Re A (A Minor) (Cultural Background)*[10] a Nigerian child was sent to live with her grandmother in England. For various reasons relating to her work and her health the grandmother was unable to care for the child so she placed her with foster parents who were white. For the next five and a half years the child lived with the foster parents and their daughter, with whom she formed a very close relationship, and she came to look upon

---

8   Ibid, para 2.42.
9   Despite the fact that several studies have consistently found that trans-racial adoption has a long-term aggregate success rate similar to the success rate of adoption in general. There is a brief analysis of the relevant studies by J Thoburn in *Review of Adoption Law - A Consultation Document* (DOH, 1992). There appear to be no research studies to say whether a black child placed with a black family is better able to withstand discrimination and racial prejudice than a black child placed in a white family. This may be the case, but until research establishes this, it is merely a matter of opinion. Yet it is presented as authoritative: see, for example, J Triseliotis (1989) 13 Adoption and Fostering 21. For a critique, see P Hayes *The Ideological Attack on Transracial Adoption in the USA and Britain* (1995) 9 IJLF 1.
10 [1987] 2 FLR 429.

them as her family. The grandmother visited the child from time to time, and after one such visit, when the child was nine, she sought to recover the care of the child. The child was adamant that she wished to stay with her foster parents and so the matter came before the court in wardship. The case for the grandmother was that for a Nigerian child to be brought up by a white English family stored up trouble for the child in the future. A senior social worker, with extensive experience of the fostering and placement of children from Africa, gave evidence as an expert witness. She expressed the view that 'any child of West African background, regardless of the length of time that a child has been in an alternative family, must be placed back with a West African family.' Indeed, she went so far as to say that although she had not examined the details of the care which would be provided for the child if she were to return to live with her grandmother 'she felt so strongly that a Nigerian child should be returned to her own family that she would be quite sure that the arrangements would be satisfactory.' The case for the foster parents was that the child was happy and contented living with them and that they loved her as if she was their own daughter. A social worker who knew the child well gave evidence that she thought it would be catastrophic if the child was removed from the care of her foster parents. In arriving at his judgment, Swinton Thomas J stated that he had to balance the need of the child to have stability, love and security against the loss to her of her Nigerian culture and background and her own family. He found that to remove the child from the family with whom she had lived for so long would have a devastating effect on her, and that the best prospect for the child was for her to enjoy a happy and secure childhood leading to a well-adjusted adulthood. He therefore concluded that the child should remain in the care of the foster parents and that her grandmother should continue to have contact with her.

Analysing *Re A (A Minor)*, it can be seen that the court was presented with totally divergent views on what factors would serve the child's best interests. It is suggested that the opinion of the expert witness that great weight should be given to the child's ethnicity when identifying the child's long-term needs, and that, save in extreme circumstances, this should outweigh other considerations, is illustrative of the powerful hold which a particular ideological approach to the upbringing of children has over some persons who work for local authorities in the child-care field. The court, by contrast, took a more balanced approach, and whilst it gave weight to the child's origins, it weighed this factor against the likely harmful effect on the child of bringing about a change in her circumstances, and it gave respect to the child's wishes and feelings.

Similar opinion evidence about the importance to a Nigerian child of living with persons of the same ethnic origin, and that black children should not be brought up by white parents, was placed before Bush J in *Re N (A*

Minor) (Adoption)[11] in a case where a father was seeking in wardship proceedings to recover the care of his black daughter aged four and a half who had been living with the same white foster parents since she was a baby. An application by the foster parents to adopt the child was also before the court. In a powerful judgment, Bush J resoundingly rejected the emphasis on colour rather than cultural upbringing in the assessment of the welfare of a child stating that such an approach was 'highly dangerous'. After commenting that he had been 'bombarded with a host of theories and opinions by experts who derive their being from the political approach to race relations in America in the 1960s and 1970s' which had persuaded most local authorities not to place black children with white foster parents, Bush J said that other expert evidence presented to the court had pointed out that there is little real evidence, other than anecdotal, that black-white fosterings are harmful. He pointed out that some local authorities 'even go in for what one advocate described as colour co-ordination, that is if the child is three parts white and one part black, then you try to get the same combination in foster parents.' He added 'I have only to cite this doctrine to show the ridiculous nature of a dedication to dogma.' He concluded that to separate the child from her foster parents would be cruel to the child and likely to cause her serious psychological damage both at present and in the future. He therefore ordered that she should remain living with them. However, he gave weight to Nigerian cultural patterns when considering whether the child should be adopted. He found that in the father's culture adoption was regarded as a form of slavery and that the father would feel shame and distress if such an order were made. Furthermore, he found that the father had an important part to play in the child's life in the future, when she was likely to seek out her cultural roots. Balancing these factors against the security which an adoption order would give to the child, Bush J concluded that it would not be in the child's interests to make an adoption order.

The single-mindedness with which some local authorities pursue same race policies for the children whom they are looking after was further illustrated in *Re JK (Adoption: Transracial Placement)*.[12] A local authority had placed a Sikh child with short-term white English foster parents soon after her birth while they looked for adopters of the same ethnic origin. Three years later the child was still living with the foster parents because they had been unable to find a suitable matching placement. Meanwhile the child had become deeply attached to her foster parents, who asked to be considered as prospective adoptive parents. They were rejected as such a proposal was contrary to the local authority's same race policy. When the local authority decided to move the child to a bridging family until

11 [1990] 1 FLR 58.
12 [1991] 2 FLR 340.

suitable adopters could be found the foster parents issued wardship proceedings and sought care of the child. The issue for the court was whether three years' settled attachment, or racial and cultural considerations, should determine where the child should live until adulthood.[13] Evidence was given by a child psychiatrist that in the depths of her being the child understood the foster parents as having been her parents all her life. He expressed the firm view that to move the child at this stage from the only home she had ever known would be likely to cause her irreparable psychological damage and that she would probably never trust anyone again. He said 'the separation from a much loved home at the age of three will always leave a profound pining for the rest of the child's life.' In the light of this evidence the court committed the child to the care of the foster parents with a view to her adoption by them.[14]

Re A (A Minor), Re N (A Minor) and *Re JK (Adoption: Transracial Placement)*, although they preceded the implementation of the Children Act 1989, are illustrative of the value which the checklist may have in preventing one consideration in the matters itemised in the checklist being given undue weight. Paragraph (d) requires a court to consider the child's background and any characteristics of his which the court considers relevant, and it seems clear that considerations relating to a child's ethnic origin fall within its scope. Where considerations relating to a child's background and characteristics dominate planning for a child, there is a danger that other equally important factors will be ignored or undervalued. By requiring a court to consider all factors which are relevant to the welfare of the child, the checklist acts as a safeguard against this occurring.

Contact and welfare

Litigation over contact normally centres around whether any contact at all should take place and, if so, when, where and how often this should be. Disputes arise not only about the frequency and venue of contact, but also over whether the child should stay overnight with the non-residential parent (a form of contact which is often referred to as 'staying' contact),

13 The local authority were investigating three families as possible adoptive families; all were Asian, two were Hindus, the third was Roman Catholic. Yet the child's religious heritage was Sikh. It is hard to see how such an arrangement would have paid regard to the child's religious and cultural heritage. There is evidence in the cases that the same race policies operated by some local authorities are related to colour, and are otherwise crude: see Bush J in *Re N (A Minor) (Adoption)* [1990] 1 FLR 58 at p 63.

14 Cf *Re P (A Minor) (Adoption)* [1990] 1 FLR 96 where the trial judge sanctioned the removal of a black child aged 16 months from white foster parents where he was thriving. The Court of Appeal held that he had been entitled to conclude that the advantages of bringing up a child of mixed race in a black family outweighed the importance of maintaining the status quo for the child.

and over whether contact visits should be supervised by a third party. The disadvantage of an order in which contact arrangements are closely defined is that it is rigid, and unable to respond flexibly to changing circumstances. Therefore contact provisions which are responsive to the child's developmental needs, and to the needs of the parties, are normally preferable.[15]

Contact is the right of the child

For more than two decades the courts have emphasised that contact with a parent is the right of the child. In *M v M (Child: Access)*[16] the Court of Appeal affirmed the principle that no court should deprive a child of contact with either parent unless it is wholly satisfied that it is in the interests of the child that contact should cease.[17] It held that a court should be extremely slow to arrive at such a conclusion. Courts have taken the view that the companionship of a parent is of such immense value to a child that there is a basic right in him to such companionship. In *Re R (A Minor) (Contact)*[18] Butler-Sloss LJ stated that this principle has been repeatedly stated by the appellate courts, that it is endorsed in the Children Act 1989, and that it is underlined in the United Nations Convention on the Rights of the Child. The principle applies whether the court is deciding whether contact should cease or whether it should be reintroduced. In the latter situation it was held in *Re H (Minors) (Access)*[19] that the court should *not* ask the question whether any positive advantages were to be gained by the resumption of contact. Rather, the test to be applied is whether there are any cogent reasons why a child should be denied the opportunity to have contact with a parent.

Where the residential parent is implacably opposed to contact

The principle that contact is the right of the child has been highly influential on the manner in which courts have approached cases where the residential parent is implacably opposed to contact taking place with the other parent.

---

15 Prior to the Children Act 1989 it was normal for courts to make orders for reasonable contact in favour of the non-residential parent, and the courts left it to the parties to negotiate what was reasonable. However, s.1(5) requires the court to be satisfied that making an order will be better for the child than making no order at all, and as a result the automatic making of reasonable contact orders has mainly fallen out of use.

16 [1973] 2 All ER 81.

17 The importance of the ruling was its emphasis on depriving *the child* of contact with the parent, rather than the parent of contact with the child.

18 [1993] 2 FLR 762.

19 [1992] 1 FLR 148.

Thus in *Re E (A Minor: Access)*[20] the mother and her new husband had made their hostile feelings towards the child's father known to the child, thereby causing the child unnecessary suffering and conflict, which had manifested itself in disturbed behaviour at school and at home. The Court of Appeal nonetheless held that contact should continue. It took the view that the fact that the attitude of the mother and step-father had led to distress on the child's part could not of itself render inimical an order which was made in the child's best interests.

A similar approach to contact in the face of the mother's implacable hostility was taken in *Re W (A Minor) (Contact)*.[1] Here contact between the father and the child of the marriage had been a constant source of difficulty, and after the mother remarried she made a conscious and deliberate decision to prevent the child from having contact with his father. The boy, who was aged four, was being brought up to believe that his step-father was his father. The mother and step-father had stated that they would rather go to prison than obey a contact order. The trial judge, relying on the no order presumption in section 1(5), refused to make a contact order on the ground that it would cause harm and destabilising unhappiness for the child. In this the Court of Appeal found the judge to have been plainly wrong. It emphasised that contact with his parent was the fundamental right of the child, that the mother had no right whatsoever to deny the child contact with his father, and that the judge was therefore under a positive duty to make an order despite the obduracy of the mother. The court added that it was an abdication of judicial responsibility to decline to make an order simply on the basis that the mother would not obey it. A court could not simply allow a parent to defy an order of the court.[2]

However, despite the determination of the courts to prevent a parent's obduracy from being an obstacle to contact they are faced with an extremely difficult dilemma where the hostility between the parents makes contact a very stressful experience for the child. A child is able to benefit from visiting the other parent where a parent conceals his or her negative feelings about contact arrangements. But where the occasion of visits is accompanied by tension, anger and tears on the part of the residential parent, a child will normally wish to avoid precipitating these emotions. In *Re J (A Minor) (Contact)*[3] the 10-year-old child's experience of contact arrangements was associated with acrimony, recrimination and family upset. The boy told the court welfare officer that he did not wish to see his father again, and she concluded that it would not be in the child's best interests to be forced into a situation which was fraught with anxiety and

20 [1987] 1 FLR 368.
1   [1994] 2 FLR 441.
2   See too *Re S (Minors: Access)* [1990] 2 FLR 166.
3   [1994] 1 FLR 729.

insecurity for him. The trial judge said that the mother's hostility to contact was about as great as he had ever come across, and that she would continue to communicate this implacable hostility to her son. He therefore concluded that 'for me to make a contact order would cause such disturbance and distress within this boy's home and such disturbance and distress for the boy himself that it is not possible for me to say that it is in the best interests of the boy ... that such an order be made. I come to the conclusion with the utmost reluctance.' He added 'if I am satisfied, as I am, that this child would be caused deep disturbance by my making the order then I must not make it.' The Court of Appeal refused to upset the judge's decision. It said that there were no grounds for finding that the judge had been plainly wrong in how he had balanced the harm caused by making an order against the harm which would be caused to the child by being deprived of contact with his father. However, Balcombe LJ made the general observation that courts should be very reluctant to allow the implacable hostility of one parent to deter them from making a contact order where they believe the child's welfare requires it.[4]

Where contact is likely to destabilise the child's present family unit

Where a child has never known his father, and where his mother has formed a secure family unit with another partner, the normal notion that maintaining contact with both natural parents is in a child's best interests may not apply. The court has been anxious not to destabilise the family unit of mother, step-father and child where the child concerned is very young, has no comprehension of relationships and where the step-father is acting as a father to him or her. In *Re H (A Minor) (Parental Responsibility)*[5] the step-father of a two-year-old boy wrote to the natural father saying that his marriage to the mother would be put at risk if the father continued to have contact with the child. The court therefore refused contact on the ground that the child's welfare would not be served if he lost his present home and security because his mother's marriage broke down. In *Re W (A Minor) (Access)*[6] an intermittent relationship between the parents had ended before the child was born, and the father had enjoyed only a brief

---

4   *Re D (A Minor) (Contact: Mother's Hostility)* [1993] 2 FLR 1 is an example of where there were cogent reasons why the child should not have contact with his father in the light of the mother's hostility. The mother had left the father before the child was born because of his violence, dabbling with drugs and excessive drinking. He had behaved in an intimidating manner to the mother and her parents and his past conduct had left an indelible impression on them. The fact that the father had not seen the child since his birth was another matter which the court took into account.
5   [1993] 1 FLR 484. However, the court did make a parental responsibility order.
6   [1989] 1 FLR 163.

period of contact shortly after the child's birth. Meanwhile the mother was living with another man whom she planned to marry. The child, who was two, had grown up in the belief that his mother's partner was his father. Magistrates made a contact order to the father, but their decision was reversed by Heilbron J. She found that the magistrates should have considered whether contact would have a destabilising effect on the family unit and on the marriage of the mother and step-father. She said they should have considered the confusion and disturbance which the child would probably feel. She found that the child was presently developing well both physically and emotionally, said that his life should be kept free from conflict as far as possible, and ruled that no contact should therefore be allowed between the child and his father.

The fear that contact would destabilise the mother's marriage was also highly influential on Sir Stephen Brown P in *Re SM (A Minor) (Natural Father: Access)*.[7] The facts were similar to those in *Re W (A Minor) (Access)*, but were more favourable to the father because he had enjoyed contact once a month until the child was 22 months old. The mother stopped contact when she resumed her relationship with her former husband, whom she intended to remarry. The court welfare officer stated in her report that 'experience shows that if [contact] is established while the child is still young, it can become an accepted and pleasurable part of life and a good relationship formed with the absent parent. Disruption is more likely to occur if the child learns the truth at a later date.' She recommended that contact take place and the magistrates made a contact order. Allowing the mother's appeal, Sir Stephen Brown P said that the welfare officer and the magistrates had applied the theoretical general principle that contact was beneficial to a child without considering the particular facts of the case. He found that the only bonds the child had were with her mother and step-father, and held that the magistrates had failed to take account of the risk of destabilising this family unit, and causing the child confusion, if the natural father were reintroduced into the child's life.

Concealing a child's true paternity

Where the mother has had a relatively fleeting relationship with the father of her child, and where she has subsequently married another man, she may choose to conceal the child's true paternity from the child so that the child believes that his step-father is his father. This was the position in both *Re SM (A Minor) (Natural Father: Access)*[8] and in *Re W (A Minor) (Access)*[9]. It is suggested that a disturbing feature of these cases is the way

7   [1991] 2 FLR 333.
8   Above.
9   [1989] 1 FLR 163.

in which the courts appeared to connive at the continuance of this fantasy. They appeared to be supporting the view that it would be confusing for young children to be brought up knowing the truth, and that they should be left in ignorance of their true paternity until some later date. During the course of her judgment in *Re W (A Minor) (Access)*, Heilbron J said:

> 'The court should consider [the child's] welfare not only now and in the short term but in the long term, as, for instance, how will he begin to understand these matters at such an early age, and how will he explain to himself and to his friends that he has a living-in as well as a visiting father with whom he has, and can only have, a very tenuous relationship.'[10]

This appears to imply that the child would wish to conceal his parentage from his friends, almost as if this was a matter for embarrassment. But surely this was a very unhealthy attitude to foster? It is very hard for a child to cope with a feeling that he is different from others, and even harder if it is implied that his situation is in some sense shameful. It is suggested that it is far better for a child if he is brought up to realise that many children are conceived in similar circumstances to his own, and if he is encouraged to feel confident about his origins. The literature on adopted children suggests that those who grow up in the knowledge that they are adopted right from the start are the children who make the most comfortable transition into adulthood. It is those children who learn about their birth parents at a later stage who become emotionally disturbed. Heilbron J surmised that the mother might need to seek psychiatric or psychological help when it became appropriate for the child to know who his true father was at some time in the future. Yet it is inevitable as a child grows up that he will learn that his step-father is not his father, and it is suggested that when courts collude at the concealment of a child's origins, and take no steps to discourage a step-father from passing himself off as the child's natural father, as distinct from his psychological father, they may themselves be creating the child's need for future professional assistance.[11]

However, there are recent indications that courts are becoming unhappy about the concealment from a child of his or her paternity. In *Re W (A Minor)(Contact)*,[12] Sir Stephen Brown P commented 'it is disturbing to read in the report which has been made available to us, that [the child] has apparently regarded Mr C, the second husband of the mother, as his father and refers to him as "daddy".' He added that a child and adolescent

10 Ibid, at p 172.
11 The problems such concealment can cause is illustrated in *Re R (A Minor) (Contact)* [1993] 2 FLR 762, which is discussed below.
12 [1994] 2 FLR 441, which concerned a four-year-old child whose parents had divorced shortly after his birth, whose mother had remarried, and where the court made a contact order despite the mother's implacable hostility: see above.

consultant psychiatrist had pointed out that difficulty now arose as to how to explain to the child that his step-father was not his father and that his sister was his half sister. This was a rather different approach to the one which Sir Stephen Brown P had taken in *Re SM (A Minor) (Natural Father: Access)*, in which the little girl was being brought up to believe that her step-father was her father. He had voiced no criticism in that case of the mother's decision to conceal from her child the truth about her paternity for the time being.[13]

Re R (A Minor) (Contact)[14] illustrates the difficulties which can arise if a child is not told who her real father is from a very young age. It concerned an application by a divorced father for contact with his five-year-old daughter who was living with her mother and step-father. The mother had refused to allow the father to have contact with his daughter on the basis that this would destabilise the new family unit, and because the child had been brought up to believe that her step-father was her father. The mother could not bring herself to tell her daughter the truth about her paternity. The court welfare officer had expressed the view that to reintroduce the child to her father was potentially seriously disruptive of the child's settled environment and welfare and that it might go so far as to wreck the family unit. The judge had concluded that the child could not see her father for the time being without considerable risks and therefore he had denied contact at the present time. The Court of Appeal approved that part of the judge's ruling denying the father contact in the present circumstances. However, Butler-Sloss LJ emphasised that it was the right of the child to have contact with her father and therefore that she ought to be informed about her true parentage soon. She was anxious, too, that the child might accidentally discover that her step-father was not her father, and was not prepared to leave the decision about when the child should be told the truth to the mother. Instead she joined the child as a party to the proceedings and invited the Official Solicitor to become her guardian ad litem. She invited the Official Solicitor to instruct a child psychiatrist to assess the family and to assist the mother to inform the child of her true paternity. If that proved impossible she requested that the psychiatrist tell the child if he or she thought this was appropriate. She also asked the Official Solicitor and the psychiatrist to advise the court on the best way to implement a period of renewed contact between the father and his daughter, or to give any reasons why such contact should not take place.

It is suggested that the lengths to which the Court of Appeal was prepared to go in order to ensure that the child discovered her father's

13 One explanation for this difference may have been the difference in the ages of the children; in *Re SM (A Minor)* the child was aged two and three quarters, in *Re W (A Minor) (Contact)* he was just four years old. Another may have been that in *Re SM* the parents had never been married, whereas in *Re W* they had.

14 [1993] 2 FLR 762.

true identity were quite remarkable bearing in mind that the function of the court is to act as an appellate jurisdiction. These lengths were illustrative of the seriousness with which the court viewed the right of the child to know her own father, and of a growing antipathy by some judges towards the concealment from a child of his or her true origins.

Contact where a parent has caused harm to the child

Paragraph (e) of the checklist directs a court to consider any harm which the child has suffered, or is at risk of suffering, before making an order. Where the risk to the child is from a parent who has sexually abused the child the court must balance the importance to the child of maintaining a relationship with the parent against the risk to the child if contact takes place. The harm caused to a child as a result of sexual abuse has often resulted in a parent being denied any form of contact with the child. In *Re R (A Minor) (Child Abuse: Access)*[15] the Court of Appeal were firmly of the view that any benefit to the child of maintaining the blood tie had no weight against the risk to her of being further sexually abused. In *S v S (Child Abuse: Access)*[16] the trial judge made a finding that a father had sexually abused the eldest of his three daughters. He therefore refused the father contact with that daughter but allowed him supervised contact with the younger children. Allowing the mother's appeal, Fox LJ ruled that the father should be denied contact with all three girls. He found that an order which distinguished between the children would be destructive of family cohesion and likely to cause tensions in the household.

It was proposed on behalf of the fathers in *Re R (A Minor) (Child Abuse: Access)* and *S v S (Child Abuse: Access)* that strictly supervised contact would resolve any risk of further sexual abuse of the children. However, as the Court of Appeal pointed out, limited contact under supervised conditions has the disadvantage that it takes place infrequently and in artificial surroundings. Furthermore, at some stage a child is likely to enquire why contact is taking place under these conditions, and if given the true answer could suffer psychological damage. However, courts are so strongly of the view that contact with a parent is normally of benefit to a child that, despite the reservations expressed in *Re R (A Minor)* and *S v S*, they have nonetheless made supervised contact orders. In *Re H (Minors) (Access: Appeals)*[17] the Court of Appeal confirmed the decision of a trial judge to allow two successive periods of contact between a father and his daughters before making a final decision as to what was in the best interests

15 [1988] 1 FLR 206.
16 [1988] 1 FLR 213.
17 [1989] 2 FLR 174.

of the children; and in *L v L (Child Abuse: Access)*[18] the Court of Appeal upheld a contact order to a father who had abused his daughter despite the opposition to it from both the mother and the supervising local authority. The court found that there was a close bond between the child and her father, that she enjoyed contact visits, that she was socially well adjusted and that she showed no disturbance after the abuse. It therefore concluded that contact was in her best interests.

In *Re H (Minors) (Access: Appeals)* and *L v L (Child Abuse: Access)* the courts acknowledged the strongly held feelings of the mothers against contact taking place but they were not persuaded by these feelings to deny contact between the children and their abusing fathers. Indeed, the mother in *L v L* was severely criticised for breaking the court's order and refusing the father contact pending the appeal. It is suggested that the courts failed to appreciate the level of fear, disgust and repulsion that mothers are likely to feel at the thought of their children having contact with fathers who have sexually abused them. Sexual abuse is such a serious betrayal of a child's trust that the notion that a child will benefit from having further contact with the abuser is likely to be totally alien to the majority of residential parents. It may be that some courts are failing to recognise the magnitude of the distress suffered by the non-abusing parent when sexual abuse is discovered, and the impact any contact order will have on her and therefore on her ability to relate properly to the child. An anxious and distressed residential parent, who is fearful for her child's safety, is unlikely to be able to give an abused child the balanced and calm care which such a child needs. It is suggested that courts should exercise great caution before making orders which conflict with the fundamental values of the parent who is called upon to allow contact, particularly where, as in *L v L*, the local authority are also of the view that contact should not be allowed.[19]

Refusing contact with a child in care

A local authority must allow parents to have reasonable contact with their child in care, and may only refuse such contact where they have been given the power to do so by a court.[20] A local authority are most likely to seek to terminate contact where there is a risk of harm to the child. The presumption that contact with parents is in the best interests of the child is displaced where the child is likely to be injured by the parent. In such a case, the local authority may decide to abandon any attempt to rehabilitate the child with his or her family, and adoption may be their long-term plan

18 [1989] 2 FLR 16.
19 See generally on child sexual abuse cases, I Weyland *The Response of Civil Courts to Allegations of Child Sexual Abuse* (1989) 19 Fam Law 240.
20 S.34: see ch 3. See below on the link between contact orders under s.34 and adoption.

for the child. In *Birmingham City Council v H*[1] the mother of the child was herself a child in the care of the local authority. She had very serious behavioural problems, and her behaviour towards her baby caused great anxiety about his safety. Connell J concluded that it was very unlikely that the mother would make significant progress in her ability to care for the child, and that it was important that he should be adopted as soon as possible and given a stable long-term home. He therefore authorised the local authority to refuse contact. The case raised the point of law as to whose welfare was paramount where both parent and child were children. The House of Lords ruled that it was the welfare of the baby which must be the court's paramount consideration. Applying the paramountcy test to the facts, their Lordships concluded that Connell J had given due weight to the fact that an order prohibiting contact between a mother and a young child should rarely be made, and that it was impossible to say that he had erred in the exercise of his discretion when authorising the refusal of contact.

Terminating contact is a Draconian decision and one which courts will not make lightly. It is recognised that contact is for the benefit of children in care because by retaining a link with their biological parents, children sustain a continuing knowledge of their parents as real people rather than as figments of their memory or imagination. However, the courts also recognise that contact must not be allowed to destabilise or endanger the local authority's plans for a child. As Thorpe J said in *Re N (Minors) (Care Orders: Termination of Parental Contact)*[2] 'it is always tempting to keep doors open against possible developments in an uncertain future, but the future must be surveyed in terms of probabilities and not low possibilities.' The three children concerned had suffered very severe significant harm at the hands of their parents, and as a consequence had special needs and would be difficult to place with long-term foster or adoptive parents. Thorpe J found that the search for a permanent new family would be made more difficult if the children continued to have a relationship with their parents in the interim. He therefore concluded that the need for an order authorising the refusal of contact had been plainly established.

Authorising the child's removal from the jurisdiction

If a child is taken out of the jurisdiction by a parent or some other person it is almost inevitable that the child will be unable to enjoy regular contact with the other parent. Moreover, where the child is young it is likely that contact will be brought to an end entirely, or at least until he or she is old

---

1   [1994] 1 FLR 224.
2   [1994] 2 FCR 1101 at p1107.

enough to travel long distances alone. The most serious risk to a parent is that the child will be taken out of the country without either his or her knowledge or agreement. The Child Abduction Act 1984 provides a measure of safeguard against this occurring. It is a criminal offence under the Act for a person to take or send a child out of the United Kingdom without 'the appropriate consent'.[3] This safeguard means that before such removal is legal, either all persons with parental responsibility for the child must have consented to the child's removal, or the leave of the court must first have been obtained. Section 13(1)(b) of the Children Act 1989 reinforces this safeguard by providing that—

'Where a residence order is in force with respect to a child, no person may—
(b) remove [the child] from the United Kingdom;
without either the written consent of every person who has parental responsibility for the child or the leave of the court.'

However, families commonly travel abroad for holidays, and the stringent nature of this provision could prove very disruptive and inconvenient for the parent with whom the child is living. Section 13(2) therefore contains some amelioration by providing that a person with a residence order may take the child out of the jurisdiction for a period of up to one month without first obtaining such consents or the court's leave. Also, when making the residence order, the court may grant the leave required by section 13(1)(b), either generally or for specified purposes.[4] Where a parent is anxious that his child will be permanently removed if allowed to travel abroad he or she is also entitled to apply under section 10 for a prohibited steps order[5] under which the court could either prohibit the child's removal absolutely, or it could control when and to where the child was taken by the imposition of conditions in the order.[6]

The decision to remove a child from the jurisdiction is undoubtedly a matter which concerns the child's upbringing; the welfare principle therefore applies, and the likely effect on the child of this change in his circumstances falls squarely within paragraph (c) of the checklist. *Poel v Poel*[7] is the leading case on how courts should approach an application for leave by one parent which is opposed by the other parent. Although decided 20 years before the implementation of the Children Act 1989 it is nonetheless highly influential on current practice. In *Poel v Poel* the Court of Appeal ruled that a child of two, who had been enjoying regular contact

3   Defined in s.1(3).
4   S.13(3).
5   Under s.8.
6   S.11(7).
7   [1970] 1 WLR 1469.

with his father, should be allowed to emigrate to New Zealand with his mother and step-father. Sachs LJ reasoned as follows:

'Once custody is working well, the court should not lightly interfere with such reasonable way of life as is selected by that parent to whom custody has been rightly given ... The way in which the parent who properly has custody of the child may choose in a reasonable manner to order his or her way of life is one of those things which the parent who has not been given custody may well have to bear.'

He explained the connection between this approach and the welfare principle by saying that any such interference 'may produce considerable strains which would not only be unfair to the parent whose way of life is interfered with but also to any new marriage of that parent. In that way it might well in due course reflect on the welfare of the child.'

Subsequently, a body of case law has grown up in this area in which the courts have followed and developed the *Poel v Poel* line of reasoning.[8] Indeed, in *Belton v Belton*,[9] when reversing the decision of the trial judge to refuse leave for the time being to a mother and step-father to emigrate to New Zealand with the three-year-old daughter of the mother's previous marriage, Purchas LJ said that the judge, by refusing leave:

'had misapplied the authorities and the law which dictate that the hard and difficult decision which must be made once it is established that the custodial parent genuinely desires to emigrate and, in circumstances in which there is nothing adverse to be found in the conditions to be expected, those authorities are quite clear in the course that the court has to take, whatever the hardship and distress that may result.'[10]

The thinking which has informed the approach since *Poel v Poel* is that the welfare of children is best served by bringing them up in a happy and secure family atmosphere. Where, after divorce, a parent remarries, the children then become members of a new family and it is on the happiness and security of that family that their security will depend. But a parent and step-parent would be likely to feel frustrated and resentful were the courts to refuse them leave to emigrate and this sense of resentment could spill over on to the children. Moreover, it might sometimes put the stability

8 *Nash v Nash* [1973] 2 All ER 704; *Chamberlain v De La Mare* (1982) 4 FLR 434; *Lonslow v Hennig* [1986] 2 FLR 378; *Re F (A Ward) (Leave to Remove Ward Out of the Jurisdiction)* [1988] 2 FLR 116; *P (L M) v P (G E)* [1970] 3 All ER 659.
9 [1987] 2 FLR 343.
10 Ibid, at pp 349-50.

of the second marriage at risk which clearly would be harmful to the children.[11] Therefore, if the decision to leave is in itself reasonable, the court must take account of how the unhappiness, distress or even bitterness which the parent and step-parent are likely to feel if refused permission will rebound upon the child.[12]

A striking feature of the cases in which leave has been granted is that the mother was the applicant and she had either remarried or was planning to do so.[13] By contrast, leave has been refused in three cases in which the mother was living as a single parent.[14] In *Tyler v Tyler*[15] the mother applied for leave to take her two sons to Australia where she had been brought up and where her parents and extended family lived. Her ex-husband had enjoyed frequent contact with the boys who were aged six and eight and there was a close bond between them and their father. The trial judge found that the mother's desire to emigrate was genuine and not motivated by spite, or a desire to take the children away from their father without herself having any reasonable wish to emigrate. However, he nonetheless was persuaded that the mother should be refused leave to take the children to Australia because of the warm and loving relationship between the father and his sons, and because they would leave behind their roots in the family farm where the father lived and where they had been brought up. The judge therefore took the view that the mother's desire to remove the boys from the jurisdiction at this age was not reasonable. The judge also considered whether the undoubted bitterness and frustration of the mother would have an adverse effect on the boys. He found that she would cope with the decision and would not allow her feelings about it to destroy her relationship with boys, or between the boys and their father. The Court of Appeal held that there were no grounds for upsetting the judge's ruling.

In *K v K (A Minor) (Removal from Jurisdiction)*[16] the mother who was born in the USA applied to take the child of the marriage, who was nearly four, to the USA so that she could pursue postgraduate education. Thorpe J held that the principles to be applied were established in *Poel v Poel*, namely the approach of the court was to sanction the realistic proposals of the residential parent unless these proposals was inconsistent with the child's welfare. He found that the mother would feel despair or disenchantment if not allowed to return to the USA with her daughter, but that she had an underlying resilience which would enable her to cope. He

11 See Griffiths LJ in *Chamberlain v De La Mare* (1982) 4 FLR 434 at p 445.
12 See Kerr LJ in *Re F (A Ward) (Leave to Remove Ward Out of the Jurisdiction)* [1988] 2 FLR 116.
13 *Re F (A Ward) (Leave to Remove Ward Out of the Jurisdiction)* was an exception; the mother had not remarried in that case.
14 *Tyler v Tyler* [1989] 2 FLR 158; *K v K (A Minor) (Removal from Jurisdiction)* [1992] 2 FLR 98; *M v A (Wardship: Removal from Jurisdiction)* [1993] 2 FLR 715.
15 Above.
16 Above.

refused the mother leave on two grounds. First and foremost, he found that the continuation of the relationship between the child and her father was of very great importance and that to reduce contact to annual visits would be a retrograde step. Secondly, he refused leave on the ground that the mother's proposals were ill thought out, and because she had paid insufficient attention to the practicalities of pursuing postgraduate studies in the USA.

In *M v A (Wardship: Removal from Jurisdiction)*[17] a mother who wished to return to Canada with her sons aged 12 and 9 was similarly refused leave. She had lived with the boys' father for many years, and after the parties separated they had shared the care of the children, though their principal home remained with the mother. The boys themselves loved both homes and wished to remain in England. Bracewell J said that although the test remained the same as in *Poel v Poel*, the Children Act 1989 had increased the emphasis to be placed on the wishes of the children where they were of sufficient age and understanding to be able to express their own views. She found that the mother's plans were ill thought out and little researched and that they were not reasonable because they did not accommodate the needs and wishes of the children.[18]

It is suggested that courts have been too ready to indulge the selfish feelings of mothers and second husbands in those cases where they have granted them leave to take the children of a previous marriage out of the jurisdiction. By granting leave, the courts have deprived the children of contact with their natural fathers, yet time and again courts have emphasised that contact is the *right* of the child as well as being in the child's best interests. A large number of marriages end by divorce whilst the children are young, and many children live in reconstituted families. It is suggested that one of the many responsibilities of parenthood is to put the interests of the children first, and that this often requires parents and step-parents to negate their own wishes and feelings. A woman who marries again cannot simply substitute her second husband as father for her children and expect the children to have no need or desire to know their natural father. A man who marries a woman who already has children knows that she has responsibilities to those children, and that they have a father with whom they have a relationship which ought to be maintained. If the second husband is a foreign national that in itself should not entitle him to take another man's children out of the jurisdiction simply because he has married their mother. It is suggested that a parent and step-parent are not entitled to feel bitter, frustrated and resentful if they cannot live in the country of their choice during the minority of the children. These

17 Above.
18 See too *M v M (Minors) (Jurisdiction)* [1993] Fam Law 396 where an Israeli mother was refused leave to take her children permanently to Israel because they did not want to be uprooted from their father, schools and this country.

are natural responses, but they are also self-indulgent emotions and ones which should not be countenanced by courts unless the circumstances are exceptional.[19] Restrictions on mobility should simply be regarded as one of the burdens of bringing up children, and a recognition that the parental responsibility of the natural parents is shared throughout the children's minority. Childhood passes rapidly, and when the children are old enough to express an informed opinion they can be asked whether the benefits of visiting a loved parent outweigh the opportunities offered by moving to a new country.[20]

The child's wishes and feelings

The first paragraph in the checklist, which states that a court must have regard to the ascertainable wishes and feelings of the child concerned (considered in the light of his age and understanding), recognises that children are entitled to be treated as persons in their own right and not merely as the subject matter of legal proceedings in which only the adults have a voice. It recognises that children have an appreciation of their own situation, that they have views about what should happen to them, and that such views should be accorded respect when the child's welfare is determined. A child is not a party to private law proceedings, unless a court orders otherwise, and therefore he is not entitled to independent legal or other representation. How then are the child's views to be made known to the court? Normally a court welfare officer is asked to undertake the task of ascertaining the child's wishes and feelings. He or she is usually a probation officer, and the court may ask the officer 'to report to the court on such matters relating to the welfare of the child as are required to be dealt with in the report.'[1] Whilst a report from one person about the wishes and feelings of a different person suffers from the disadvantages inherent in all hearsay information, namely that it may be incomplete, inaccurate and cannot be tested in evidence, the alternative is for children to appear before courts and give evidence themselves, or to see the judge, or magistrates, in private. However, it is generally regarded as highly

19 It is suggested that if the marriage were to break down because leave was refused such a marriage would in any event be likely to collapse if some other stress was placed upon it.
20 It is salutary to note that the children wished to maintain their relationship with their father in those cases where they were old enough to express a view. It is suggested that the approach of the trial judge in *Belton v Belton* [1987] 2 FLR 343, in which he adjourned the application until the child was five so that real bonds between her father and extended family could be established before the child left was wise, and that it truly gave paramount consideration to the child's interests.
1 S.7. Alternatively, the court may ask a local authority to arrange for an officer of the authority, or some other appropriate person, to report to the court.

undesirable to expect children to give evidence, or for them to be interviewed in private, because of the stress, and sometimes distress, such an experience is likely to cause them. This practice is discouraged in the case of judges[2] and is positively frowned upon in the case of magistrates.[3] Using a court welfare officer to transmit the child's wishes and feelings to the court provides an alternative system which appears to operate in an acceptable and reliable manner. Any questions about the child's strength of feeling, or reasons for it, can be put to the court welfare officer.

Where proceedings are brought under Parts IV and V of the Children Act 1989 the child's voice is afforded greater protection because the child is a party to the proceedings. However, most children are not capable of safeguarding their own interests before a court, and therefore a guardian ad litem for the child will normally be appointed whose duty it is to safeguard the child's interests in the manner specified in the court rules.[4] This includes the duty to advise the court about the child's wishes and feelings, and to appoint a solicitor for the child.[5] The solicitor must represent the child in accordance with instructions received from the guardian ad litem unless the child wishes to give instructions which conflict with those of the guardian ad litem. In such a case the rules provide that where the solicitor considers that the child is able, having regard to his understanding, to give instructions on his own behalf, the solicitor must conduct the case in accordance with the instructions he receives from the child, and not the guardian ad litem.[6] In *Re H (A Minor) (Care Proceedings: Child's Wishes)*,[7] Thorpe J stated that the court should apply the rules in a manner which ensures that 'not only is the professional voice of the guardian heard through an advocate's presentation, but that also the wishes and feelings of the child, however limited the horizon, should be similarly presented.'[8]

The weight given to the child's wishes and feelings

Section 1(3)(a) is drafted cautiously. It refers to the *ascertainable* wishes and feelings of the child concerned because, of course, a very young child

2 *B v B (Minors) (Interviews and Listing Arrangements)* [1994] 2 FLR 489.
3 *Re M (A Minor) (Justices' Discretion)* [1993] 2 FLR 706; *Re W (A Minor) (Contact)* [1994] 1 FLR 843 in which Wall J said 'in my judgment, there have to be unusual circumstances before any tribunal interviews any child.'
4 S.41; and see ch 3.
5 The Family Proceedings Court (Children and Young Persons) Rules 1991, r.11.
6 R.12(1)(a).
7 [1993] 1 FLR 440.
8 Ibid, at p 450. He ruled on the facts that the level of understanding that enables a child to make an informed decision whether to refuse to submit to a psychiatric examination is in all practical senses a much higher level of understanding than is required to enable him to give instructions to a solicitor on his own behalf.

is unable to articulate these. Nonetheless, even in the case of a baby it may be possible to ascertain the child's feelings in an indirect manner. For example, an expert witness might be called to give factual evidence about the child's behaviour, appearance and body language when in the presence of an adult, and opinion evidence about what, in the expert's view, this means in terms of the child's feelings.[9] An older child may have no difficulty in expressing a point of view, but may not fully appreciate the significance of what he or she is saying. Paragraph (a) puts the child's wishes and feelings into the context of his age and understanding, and greater weight is likely to be given to the child's point of view where he has the maturity properly to understand what the outcome would be if his wishes and feelings were allowed to influence the court's decision in a particular direction.

But even children who are very close to adulthood may be found not to have sufficient comprehension fully to understand what it will mean if their wishes and feelings are allowed to prevail. In *Re E (A Minor) (Wardship: Medical Treatment)*,[10] the 'child' was a youth aged 15 years and 9 months who was suffering from leukaemia and very likely to die unless he received a transfusion of blood or blood products. He and his parents were devout Jehovah's Witnesses and it was contrary to the tenets of their faith to permit transfusions of blood. Ward J found that whilst the youth was of sufficient intelligence to be able to make decisions about his own well-being, and that he knew that he might die as a result of his decisions, he was nonetheless not fully able to grasp the implications of the views he was expressing. Even when a child has the intelligence and understanding to make his own decision about the matter in question this does not mean that the child's wishes and feelings will be allowed to dominate the court's ruling; the child's wishes and feelings and the child's welfare may pull in opposite directions and where this happens the child's welfare must be the court's paramount consideration, and welfare is for the court, not the child, to determine.[11] However, the Court of Appeal has emphasised that the court should always listen to the child and has stated that a mature child's views will be given very considerable weight.[12]

Courts have expressed considerable caution about the weight to be given to a young child's wishes and feelings because they have doubts about the reliability of what the child is saying. Whilst they have probably moved away from the thinking that persuaded the Court of Appeal to state in

9 Thus a paediatrician might describe a child's face as being in a state of 'frozen awareness' when in the presence of a particular adult and interpret this to mean that the child is in fear of that adult.
10 [1993] 1 FLR 386.
11 See *Re R (A Minor) (Wardship: Medical Treatment)* [1991] 4 All ER 177; *Re W (A Minor) (Medical Treatment)* [1992] 4 All ER 627, which are discussed in ch 1. See too *Re S (Minors) (Access: Religious Upbringing)* [1992] 2 FLR 313.
12 *Re P (A Minor) (Education)* [1992] 1 FLR 316, in which the wishes of a boy of 14 about where he should be educated had a crucial influence on the court's determination.

1981 that 'cases that come to this court show only too well that children of tender years are apt to express their wishes upon no truly reasonable grounds'[13] they are nonetheless likely to be anxious as to whether a child has been put under pressure by a parent to express a particular point of view, particularly the parent with whom the child is currently living.[14] Sometimes a child may choose to live with the parent whom the child thinks needs him most, or because his siblings are living with the other parent and the child therefore feels sad and anxious about the parent who will be living on his or her own. In *Guery v Guery,*[15] the Court of Appeal said that it would be dangerous to give decisive weight to the wishes of a boy of 12, because at that age a child can be extremely suggestible, reluctant to upset a parent and very protective towards him or her. The courts have therefore been careful about giving significant weight to the views of children.

However in *M v M (Transfer of Custody: Appeal)*[16] a strong-minded child, who was determined in her views about the parent with whom she wished to live, effectively forced the court to make an order which was against its own perception of the child's best interests. *M v M* provides an example of a sense of realism by courts in their approach to older children. Where a child disagrees with the court's ruling he or she is likely to disobey it, or to cause so much trouble, or to become so unhappy, that the order becomes unworkable. Furthermore the courts are increasingly aware of the requirement to pay heed to the wishes and feelings of the children. As Butler-Sloss LJ said in *Re P (Minors) (Wardship: Care and Control)*[17] 'in all family cases it is the duty of the court to listen to the children, ascertain their wishes and feelings and then make decisions about their future having regard to but not constricted by those wishes.' Similarly, in *Re A (A Minor) (Cultural Background)*[18] Swinton Thomas J stated that although it is important that decisions about a child's future should not be dictated by the child herself, the views of a nine-year-old child expressed to an experienced court welfare officer were nonetheless of considerable importance, and where the child was adamant about where she wished to live any court would be bound to hesitate very long before it made an alternative placement. In *Re F (Minors) (Denial of Contact),*[19] the Court of Appeal held that the trial judge had rightly given the views of boys aged 12 and 9

13 *Cossey v Cossey* (1980) 11 Fam Law 56.
14 See *Doncheff v Doncheff* (1978) 8 Fam Law 208; *M v M* (1976) 7 Fam Law 17. It is submitted that the thinking in these, and the other pre-Children Act 1989 cases cited below, carry equal force today because the anxieties about the veracity of what the child is saying remain the same.
15 (1982) 12 Fam Law 184.
16 [1987] 2 FLR 146.
17 [1992] 2 FCR 681.
18 [1987] 2 FLR 429.
19 [1993] 2 FLR 677.

very considerable and not disproportionate weight when determining not to make a contact order in favour of their father, who was a transsexual. The boys were steadfast in their present wish not to see their father and the judge was not prepared to force them to do so.[20]

Despite the growing recognition of the importance of heeding the wishes and feelings of the child, young children who cannot control their own destiny are still vulnerable to having their strongly held wishes and feelings discounted or ignored by courts. In *Re M (A Minor) (No 2) (Appeal)*[1] the trial judge had declined to make a care order in respect of a child aged six because he did not believe that the mother and her partner had beaten and sexually abused the child.[2] The local authority appealed and asked leave to call further evidence relating to the child's hysterical reaction on being told that she was going to go back to live with her mother. The Court of Appeal refused to allow this evidence to be called on the ground that it only tended to confirm that the child had ambivalent feelings about returning home and that 'the only way to the true feelings of this troubled child is through the experienced eyes of the trial judge who saw and heard over a long period the numerous witnesses.' However, as a critic of this approach to the wishes and feelings of the child has pointed out:

'It seems impossible to justify the Court of Appeal's refusal to hear evidence of the child's extreme reaction to the judge's order. To say, as they did, that assessing the child's true feelings is a matter for the trial judge who has heard the evidence is quite illogical. This was an important piece of evidence which the judge never heard and could not possibly have heard, because the incident had not yet happened.'[3]

Whilst it is generally accepted that it is right that children should be consulted when decisions are being made which will intimately affect their future, court welfare officers, guardians ad litem and other professionals working with children, and the courts themselves, are anxious about the burden of responsibility which an insensitive handling of section 1(3)(a) could sometimes place on children.[4] Research tells us that many children

---

20 See too *M v A (Wardship: Removal from Jurisdiction)* [1993] 2 FLR 715 and *M v M (Minors) (Jurisdiction)* [1993] Fam Law 396, discussed above. The wishes and feelings of the children were strongly influential on the outcome of both of these cases.

1 [1994] 1 FLR 59.

2 He had nonetheless found the threshold test for care proved because the mother did not seek medical attention for her daughter until a very late stage, and by the time the child was admitted to hospital with a very severe haemotama and other bruising she was dangerously dehydrated.

3 See J R Spencer *Evidence in Child Abuse Cases – Too High a Price for Too High a Standard?* (1994) 6 JCL 160.

4 See *B v B (Minors) (Interviews and Listing Arrangements)* [1994] 2 FLR 489.

blame themselves for the breakdown of their parents' marriage, and for the fact that their parents are in dispute about their upbringing, and that they suffer badly from unwarranted feelings of guilt and shame. Most children love each of their parents and do not like to have their loyalties divided. Therefore there is a risk that a provision which expects a court welfare officer to ask a child to voice his or her wishes and feelings about, for example, residence and contact arrangements could increase the child's sense of personal responsibility for what has happened, cause the child pain and add to his or her feelings of guilt. Indeed, it has been argued that one of the rights of a child in this context is the right not to make a decision.[5] There is also a danger that children will be asked to express their wishes and feelings in circumstances where the chances that the court will be able to give weight to their expressed preferences are remote because they are unrealistic in the light of other evidence. For example, if a child is asked whether he or she wants to leave local authority care and return home in a case where the parent is so ill, or so disturbed, that this is an impossibility, such a question may simply add to the child's sense of loss and rejection. A delicate balance must therefore be struck between taking proper account of the child's wishes and feelings and burdening the child with choices which should be made on his or her behalf by adults.

International child abduction and welfare

When a marriage between persons of different nationalities breaks down the adult who is living in the 'foreign' country may wish to return to his or her country and to take the children as well. It has been seen already that it is an offence for a child to be taken from the United Kingdom for more than a month without either the consent of all persons with parental responsibility or the leave of the court.[6] However, this provision may not deter a determined parent from leaving the United Kingdom with the children. Equally a United Kingdom citizen who is living in a foreign country may return to this country with his or her children in breach of that country's domestic laws. Or a parent may agree to a child spending time in a foreign country with the intention that the child's stay should be temporary only. But when the time comes for the child to return to his country of habitual residence, the persons looking after the child in the foreign country may retain him there. The United Kingdom is a signatory to two international Conventions which are designed to achieve a common response to cases of this nature where a child is wrongfully removed or

5   *M v M* (1976) 7 Fam Law 17, per Sir George Baker P, referring to law reform proposals in Canada.
6   Child Abduction Act 1984, s.1, see above p 244.

retained. The Child Abduction and Custody Act 1985 gives force of law to both the Convention on the Civil Aspects of Child Abduction, hereinafter referred to as the 'Hague Convention', and the European Convention on Recognition and Enforcement of Decisions concerning Custody of Children and on the Restoration of Custody of Children, hereinafter referred to as the 'European Convention'. The purpose of the Hague Convention is to secure the return of children wrongfully removed or retained in any contracting state whether or not a judgment has been given by a court. The purpose of the European Convention is to secure the recognition or enforcement of judgments concerning custody of children, and only applies where there has been a court order. Where both Conventions apply, an application under the Hague Convention takes precedence over one made under the European Convention.[7]

The Hague Convention

The philosophy informing the Hague Convention is contained in Article 1 which provides that its objects are—

'(a) to secure the prompt return of children wrongfully removed to or retained in any Contracting State, and
(b) to ensure that rights of custody and access under the law of one Contracting State are effectively recognised in other Contracting States.'

With this purpose in mind, each contracting state has established a central authority which is charged with the duty to take measures to secure the prompt return of children and to achieve the other objects of the Convention.[8] Thus if, for example, a child has been wrongfully removed from England, a request for assistance can be made to the central authority for England and Wales. The authority will approach the Central Authority of the country to which the child has been taken and that authority should take steps to secure the child's immediate return to England. Alternatively, an approach may be made directly to the central authority of the country to which the child has been taken. Similarly, if a child is retained in England in breach of the Convention, the central authority for England and Wales will take steps to secure the return of the child to the country in which the child was habitually resident before the wrongful retention.

Article 3 provides that—

'The removal or retention of a child is to be considered wrongful where—

7   Child Abduction and Custody Act 1985, s.16(4)(c).
8   Art.7.

(a) it is in breach of rights of custody attributed to a person, an institution or any other body, either jointly or alone, under the law of the State in which the child was habitually resident immediately before the removal or retention; and

(b) at the time of removal or retention those rights were actually exercised, either jointly or alone, or would have been so exercised but for the removal or retention.

The rights of custody mentioned in sub-paragraph (a) above may arise in particular by operation of law or by reason of a judicial or administrative decision, or by reason of an agreement having legal effect under the law of that State'.

Article 5(a) provides that—

'rights of custody' shall include rights relating to the care of the person of the child and, in particular, the right to determine the child's place of residence.

'Rights of custody'

An English court must look to the law of the country in which the child was habitually resident[9] immediately before the removal or retention to determine whether the case before it is in breach of 'rights of custody'. Where the abduction violates an existing court order there is no difficulty in establishing unlawfulness under Article 3. However, a child may be taken abroad before any order has been made, or it may not be customary to make court orders about children at the time of marriage or relationship breakdown,[10] or the parents may be unmarried and the father may not have any rights unless, or until, they are granted by court order. In each of these circumstances there may be difficulty in establishing a breach of Article 3. Unless there is such a breach, the court is not able under the Convention to return the child to the requesting state.[11]

The leading case on Article 3 is the House of Lords' ruling in *Re J (A Minor) (Abduction: Custody Rights)*.[12] The mother and father were not married and lived together with their child in Australia. The mother brought the child to England. After she left, the father obtained an order in the Family Court of Western Australia giving him sole custody and

9 In relation to the meaning of 'habitual residence', and to the nature of the enquiry needed to determine the child's habitual residence, see *Re B (Minors) (Abduction)* [1993] 1 FLR 993 at pp 994-5 and 998, per Waite J.

10 As is the position now in England in the light of the Children Act 1989, s.1(5).

11 It may, however, be able to order the return of the child relying on common law principles: see below.

12 [1990] 2 AC 562.

guardianship of the child. The House of Lords held that the mother had not unlawfully removed the child when she took him from Australia because, under Western Australian law,[13] she alone had the legal rights of custody, and included in those rights was the right to decide where the child will live. Although the unmarried father had been sharing de facto custody of the child he had no legal rights of custody at the time that the child was removed from the jurisdiction. Furthermore, it ruled that the child's retention outside the jurisdiction had not been wrongful because the mother had come to England with the settled intention of remaining here, and therefore the child had ceased to be habitually resident in Australia before the order conferring custodial rights on the father had been made.

This strict ruling has, however, been ameliorated to some small extent by the Court of Appeal's subsequent decision in *Re B (A Minor) (Abduction)*.[14] The parents of a six-year-old boy were unmarried and living in Australia. In April 1992 the mother, who was a heroin addict and living a chaotic existence, left Australia and returned to England. The child was left in the care of his father and maternal grandmother and by February 1993 the father was providing the majority of the child's care. The grandmother wished to take the child to England for a holiday, but the father would not agree to the child leaving Australia for longer than six months. He arranged for a consent order to be drawn up, including one term giving him sole custody of the child, and another that the child would be returned to Australia by a specified date in January 1994. This document was posted to the mother, she signed it but it was misdirected and never received by the father's solicitor. A second copy was sent to the mother for her signature, but by this time the grandmother was anxious to leave with the child for England. The father and mother spoke on the telephone and the mother assured the father that she had signed the second document. The grandmother deposited a sum of money with the father's solicitor and signed an authority that it could be used by the father to take any action required to recover custody of the child. Persuaded by the mother's assurance and the grandmother's bond that they were sincere, the father allowed the child to leave in August 1993. The second signed document was subsequently received by the father and eventually approved by the court in Adelaide in January 1994. The mother resiled on her agreement, made the child a ward of court and refused to return him to Australia. The father therefore made an application for the child's immediate return under Article 12.[15]

The crucial question in *Re B (A Minor) (Abduction)* was did the father have 'rights of custody' at the date of the child's removal from Australia? Under Australian law he had no rights at the time of the child's removal,

13 Family Law Act of Western Australia 1975-1979, s.35.
14 [1994] 2 FLR 249.
15 See below.

and no order by a court had yet been made in his favour. The question therefore arose whether the father's position was distinguishable from that of the father in *Re J (A Minor) (Abduction: Custody Rights)*. The Court of Appeal ruled by a majority that it was.[16] It stated that the issue to be determined was whether the concept of 'rights of custody' was confined to rights propounded by law or conferred by court order, or whether the concept was capable of describing the inchoate rights of a person who had been acting as a parent without the benefit of either official status or a court order. It stated that the authorities established that the Convention must be construed broadly as an international agreement according to its general tenor and purpose, without attributing to any of its terms a specialist meaning which the word, or words, in question may have acquired under the domestic law of England.[17] It ruled that where, before the child's abduction, the aggrieved parent was exercising parental functions in the requesting state, it must in every case be a question for the court of the requested state to determine whether these amounted to 'rights of custody' within the terms of the Convention.[18] The majority concluded that the expression 'rights of custody' should be construed in the sense which will best accord with the purpose of the Convention and that in most cases this will involve giving the term the widest sense possible. They therefore held that inchoate rights could properly be called 'rights of custody' in the Convention sense in those cases where a court in the requesting state would be likely to uphold them in the interests of the child concerned, at least to the point of not allowing them to be disturbed without due opportunity to consider issues relating to the child's welfare. The majority therefore confirmed the ruling of Connell J that, in the case of this father, he had acquired 'rights of custody' first through his active role in the care of the child, second through the status which the mother and grandmother had themselves accorded to him, and third through the rights recognised or accorded to him when the mother signed the second document. Of this latter document, Staughton LJ said, 'it seems to me highly probable that the law of Western Australia attributes some effect of some kind to an agreement between parents as to custody or guardianship'.[19]

16 Waite and Staughton LJJ; Peter Gibson LJ dissented.
17 See *Re C (A Minor) (Abduction)* [1989] 1 FLR 403; *Re J (A Minor) (Abduction: Custody Rights)* [1990] 2 AC 562.
18 Waite LJ gave as examples, at one end of the scale a transient cohabitee of the sole custodial parent whose status and functions would be unlikely to qualify for recognition as 'rights of custody' within the terms of the Convention, and at the other a relative or friend who had assumed the role of a substitute parent in place of the legal custodian, where the opposite would be true.
19 And see the crucial wording in the last paragraph of Art.3, which Waite and Staughton LJJ did not explicitly discuss, but the generous interpretation of which was implicit in their judgments. In relation to whether the father had 'consented' to the child's removal, the court found that it was not a true consent because it had been obtained by a cruel deceit.

Article 12

Where a court is satisfied that the case before it is a Convention case then, under the provisions of Article 12, it *must* order the return of the child forthwith provided that the application was brought within 12 months of the child's unlawful removal or retention. The essence of the jurisdiction is peremptory. The English court must cede jurisdiction to hear the merits of the case to the country of the child's habitual residence in the interests of international co-operation and comity. The Convention is built on the assumption that the courts of all of its signatories are equally capable of handling the case, and that they will apply proper procedures and principles to its resolution. Arguments that peremptory return may be against the best interests of the particular child concerned are therefore to no avail.[20]

Article 12 further provides that the court must order the return of the child even where proceedings are commenced more than a year after the child's removal or detention 'unless it is demonstrated that the child is now settled in its new environment'. The burden is on the abducting parent to establish such a settlement. In *Re N (Minors) (Abduction)*[1] the court was asked to determine the meaning of 'now'. Did it mean the 'date of the hearing' or the 'date of commencement of proceedings'? Bracewell J ruled that it meant the latter, otherwise any delay in hearing the case might affect the outcome. She held that 'settlement' involved a physical element of being established in the community and environment, and an emotional constituent denoting security and stability. In relation to the degree of settlement which must be demonstrated, she ruled that it meant that the present position imports stability when looking at the future, and is permanent. She held that the word 'new' encompassed place, home, school, people, friends, activities and opportunities, but not the relationship with the abducting parent which had always existed in a close, loving attachment.

Article 13

The absolute nature of Article 12 is tempered by Article 13. This provides three grounds for releasing the court or administrative authority of the requested state from its duty to order the return of the child. Under Article 13(a) the court is given discretion whether to order the child's return where the person who opposes the child's return establishes that—

> 'the person, institution or other body having care of the person of the child was not actually exercising the custody rights at the time of removal or retention, or had consented to or subsequently acquiesced in the removal or retention.'

20 *Re N (Minors) (Abduction)* [1991] 1 FLR 413; *Re L (Child Abduction) (Psychological Harm)* [1993] 2 FLR 401.
1 Above.

Thus prior consent or subsequent acquiescence allows the court to refuse to return the child. It can be active consent or acquiescence signified by express words or conduct, or it can be passive and inferred from inactivity or silence on the part of the parent from whose custody the child has been wrongfully removed. If the acceptance is active, it must be in clear and unequivocal words or conduct, and the other party must believe that there has been an acceptance.[2] Thus where the language and behaviour of the person alleged to be consenting is ambivalent, or where the abducting parent does not believe that the other parent is acquiescing, the ground cannot be established.[3]

Where a parent delays in bringing proceedings this may amount to acquiescence because it is conduct which is inconsistent with seeking an order for the summary return of the child. In *W v W (Child Abduction: Acquiescence)*[4] a father took no steps for 10 months to secure his son's return after learning of the mother's decision not to return him to Australia and this was held to amount to acquiescence in his unlawful retention. However, where an aggrieved parent's inactivity arises because he has been given erronous legal advice this will negative any inference of acquiescence.[5] But a parent does not have to know his precise legal rights in order to acquiesce. In *Re A (Minors) (Abduction: Acquiescence)*[6] Stuart-Smith LJ stated that:

> 'A party cannot be said to acquiesce unless he is aware, at least in general terms, of his rights against the other parent. It is not necessary that he should know the full or precise nature of his legal rights under the Convention: but he must be aware of the factual situation giving rise to those rights, the court will no doubt readily infer that he was aware of his legal rights, either if he could reasonably be expected to have known of them or taken active steps to obtain legal advice.'[7]

In *Re A (Minors) (Abduction: Acquiescence)* the majority of the Court of Appeal ruled that where there has been clear acquiescence a subsequent change of mind cannot alter the position. They stated that acquiescence is not a continuing state of affairs, and that once it has been given it cannot be withdrawn.[8]

2 See Stuart-Smith LJ in *Re A (Minors) (Abduction: Acquiescence)* [1992] 2 FLR 14.
3 *Re A (Minors) (Abduction)* [1991] 2 FLR 241.
4 [1993] 2 FLR 211.
5 *Re S (Minors) (Abduction: Acquiescence)* [1994] 1 FLR 819.
6 [1992] 2 FLR 14.
7 Ibid, at p 26; see too Waite J in *W v W (Child Abduction: Acquiescence)* [1993] 2 FLR 211 at p 217.
8 However, in a strong dissenting judgment, Balcombe LJ stated that this was to give 'acquiesced' far too technical a meaning in the context in which it was used, and that it undermined the purpose of the exceptions contained in Art. 13, which are directed to the interests of the children, and not those of the parents.

In *Re B (Minors) (Abduction) (No 2)*[9] an English father and German mother came to England from Germany for a holiday, and during this period the father issued proceedings for the dissolution of the marriage and for a residence order in family proceedings. He also obtained an ex parte order restraining the removal of the children from England. The mother made a cross-application in family proceedings and consented to an order prohibiting the removal of the children pending the hearing in family proceedings. On the same day she also made an application under the Hague Convention for the immediate return of the children to Germany. Dismissing the claim of the father that it was not he who had retained the children in England, but the order of the court, Waite J said:

'The Convention is not, in my view, an instrument to be construed semantically but purposively. Full and sensible effect can only be given to it if the term "retention" is construed as wide enough to comprehend not only acts of physical restraint on the part of the retaining parent but also juridical orders obtained on his initiative which have the effect of frustrating a child's return to the jurisdiction of its habitual residence.'[10]

Waite J was similarly dismissive of the father's claim that, by consenting to the order prohibiting the removal of the children until the family proceedings hearing, the mother had acquiesced to their wrongful detention. He held that the mother's consent to the direction given for trial of the case in England could be relied on only for the purpose of demonstrating that she had so far, and without prejudice to any issue of forum conveniens[11] which might arise in the future, agreed that the courts in England would be the forum in which issues about the children would be tried, and that her agreement to this could not possibly be interpreted as consent on her part to the children remaining in the meantime in England. As Waite J explained:

'Parents should ... be encouraged ... to proceed as rapidly as possible with family welfare proceedings designed to settle the children's future at the earliest achievable date. It would be very injurious to that encouragement if a parent's participation in family proceedings involved the risk of depriving him or her of a right to the children's return in the meantime, which would otherwise be theirs under the terms of the Convention'.[12]

9   [1993] 1 FLR 993.
10 Ibid, at p 1000.
11 That is the place of jurisdiction appropriate for the purposes of determining the merits of the case.
12 Ibid, at p 999. The reference to the issue of forum conveniens is puzzling. The whole thinking informing the Convention is that it is the country of the child's habitual residence

Article 13(b) allows the court discretion not to return the child where:

'there is a grave risk that his or her return would expose the child to physical or psychological harm or otherwise place the child in an intolerable situation.'

It is in the context of Article 13(b) that issues relevant to the welfare of the child can legitimately be advanced. However, it must be understood at the outset that the child's welfare is *not* the court's paramount consideration. A *grave* risk of physical or psychological harm must be established, or the child must be placed in an *intolerable* situation. Lord Donaldson MR acknowledged in *Re C (A Minor) (Abduction)*[13] that a child caught up in a case which involves operating the machinery of the Convention is bound to suffer some psychological harm if he or she is returned. But he said that it is the concern of the state to which the child is returned to take steps to minimise or eliminate this harm, and in the absence of compelling evidence to the contrary the courts should assume that this will be done. In *Re C (A Minor) (Abduction)* the mother said that she would refuse to accompany the child if he was returned to Australia and she asserted that the child would therefore suffer severe psychological harm. The Court of Appeal rejected this contention stating that the parent could not create a psychological situation and then seek to rely on it.[14]

The courts have been extremely wary of accepting the claim that a child will suffer psychological harm if his or her return is ordered because by doing so they could rapidly undermine the whole purpose of the Convention. As Bracewell J said in *Re N (Minors) (Abduction)*,[15] 'it is plain that it is not a trivial risk and it is not a trivial psychological harm which is envisaged and which has to be justified and, furthermore, I am satisfied that the intolerable situation envisaged has to be something extreme and compelling'. In *P v P (Minors) (Child Abduction)*[16] the mother claimed that if the court ordered the return of the children to the USA she would at once become a deeply unhappy person, and that an unhappy mother means unhappy children. Of this claim Waite J said:

'Arguments of this kind are commonly raised within this jurisdiction. They are really, however, beside the point. That is not

---

which should determine the merits of the case. And see the even more puzzling, and indeed almost certainly wrong, decision in *H v H (Child Abduction: Stay of Domestic Proceedings)* [1994] 1 FLR 530 in which Thorpe J, despite making a finding of wrongful retention, nonetheless ordered that the merits of the case should be investigated in England.

13 [1989] 1 FLR 403.

14 See also, *Re L (Child Abduction) (Psychological Harm)* [1993] 2 FLR 401.

15 [1991] 1 FLR 413 at p 419; see also, *Re C (A Minor) (Abduction)* [1989] 1 FLR 403.

16 [1992] 1 FLR 155; see also, *B v B (Abduction)* [1993] 1 FLR 238 in which the severity of the harm, and high degree of intolerability, is emphasised.

because the jurisdiction is inhumane. On the contrary there is a humane purpose underlying it in ensuring that children are not subjected to disruption through arbitrary movement by one parent or the other. The reason why evidence of that kind is beside the point at this stage is the underlying assumption of the Con-vention ... that the courts of all its signatories are equally concerned to ensure, and equally capable of ensuring, that both parties receive a fair hearing, and that all issues of child welfare receive a skilled, thorough and humane evaluation.'[17]

An objecting parent may be fearful about the manner in which she and the children will be treated by the other parent and the foreign legal system if the court orders the return of the children to the requesting state. In *Re A (Minors) (Abduction: Acquiescence)*[18] the mother declared that if she and the children were to return to Australia they would have no home and no financial support from the father. She contrasted this situation very unfavourably with the support she was receiving from her family in England. The Court of Appeal found that the mother would be eligible to claim Australian state benefits and therefore it held that this assertion came nowhere near to establishing what the Convention meant by an 'intolerable' situation. In *Re O (Child Abduction: Undertakings)*[18a] the mother expressed the fear that the Greek courts would never allow her to bring the children to England if they were returned to Greece. Singer J ruled that reliance could be placed on this consideration under Article 13(b), but only if it were established in relation to a given country that there was some fixed embargo on allowing the removal of children to another country, or precluding the removal of children by a parent who had once wrongly removed them. A method often used by courts to handle these and other fears is to obtain undertakings from the applicant, which are binding promises made to the court, breach of which is punishable by fine or imprisonment. The efficacy of this method of protecting the returning parent and children is not clear because undertakings are, of course, only enforceable in the jurisdiction in which they are given. However, courts have generally been satisfied that they afford sufficient safeguards for the respondent.[19]

Article 13 also provides that—

17 [1992] 1 FLR 155 at p161; see also, *Re L (Child Abduction) (Psychological Harm)* [1993] 2 FLR 401; *Re O (Child Abduction: Undertakings)* [1994] 2 FLR 349.
18 [1992] 2 FLR 14.
18a [1994] 2 FLR 349.
19 *Re C (A Minor) (Abduction)* [1989] 1 FLR 403; *Re G (A Minor) (Abduction)* [1989] 2 FLR 475; *G v G (Minors) (Abduction)* [1991] 2 FLR 506; *P v P (Minors) (Child Abduction)* [1992] 1 FLR 155; *Re O (Child Abduction: Undertakings)* [1994] 2 FLR 349; *Police Comr of South Australia v Temple (No 2)* [1993] FLC 92.

'The judicial or administrative authority may also refuse to order the return of the child if it finds that the child objects to being returned and has attained an age and degree of maturity at which it is appropriate to take account of its views.'

This provision allows children a voice in the proceedings.[20] It does not lay down any age below which a child is to be treated as too immature to voice an opinion, and therefore it is for the judge to determine whether the child objects, and to decide whether the child has attained the age and degree of maturity at which it is appropriate to take account of his or her views.[1] It is also a matter for the judge whether to authorise an investigation into the child's views and to determine how such an investigation should be carried out; but the courts have held that it is contrary to the purpose of the Convention if such an investigation is allowed to delay the prompt return of the child to any significant extent.[2] If, on the other hand, the child has already made his objection apparent, as in *Re M (A Minor) (Child Abduction)*,[3] then the matter should be investigated before such a return is ordered.[4] In *S v S (Child Abduction)*,[5] the Court of Appeal ruled that the child's objection is an entirely separate matter from paragraph (b) of Article 13, and that there is no need to establish that the child will be at risk of physical or psychological harm before the discretion comes into play.[6]

Exercise of discretion under Article 13

Once the mandatory requirement in Article 12 has been relaxed by a finding under Article 13 the court has a discretion whether to order the child's return or whether to permit the merits of the case to be heard in England. The question then arises whether, at this stage, the court can take account of the interests of the child, and if so, how much weight can be given to his or her interests. The final paragraph provides that—

'In considering the circumstances referred to in this Article, the judicial and administrative authorities shall take into account the information relating to the social background of the child provided

20 Art.12 of the UN Convention on the Rights of the Child contains a similar provision.
1 See *Re G (A Minor) (Abduction)* [1989] 2 FLR 475; *S v S (Abduction)* [1992] 2 FLR 492.
2 *P v P (Minors) (Child Abduction)* [1992] 1 FLR 155; *Re G (A Minor) (Abduction)* above.
3 [1994] 1 FLR 390.
4 In *Re M (A Minor) (Child Abduction)* above the Court of Appeal ruled that the wording of Art.13 does not inhibit the objection of a child to returning to a parent rather than to a country.
5 [1992] 2 FLR 492.
6 It said that the extra gloss put on the word 'object' in *Re R (A Minor) (Abduction)* [1992] 1 FLR 105 at pp 107-8 had been unwarranted.

by the Central Authority or other competent authority and the child's habitual residence'.

Clearly if a court finds that to order the child's return would expose the child to a grave risk of physical or psychological harm or otherwise place the child in an intolerable position it is extremely unlikely that it would ever order that the child should nonetheless be restored to his or her country of habitual residence. However, where the child has expressed a wish to remain in this country the court must decide how much weight to give to the child's views bearing in mind the purpose of the Convention. In *S v S (Child Abduction)*[7] the court was alert to the danger that Article 13 could be interpreted in a manner which would undermine the notion that it is normally in the best interests of children that they should be promptly returned to the country from which they have been wrongfully removed. Thus Balcombe LJ stated that:

'If the court should come to the conclusion that the child's views have been influenced by some other person, eg the abducting parent, or that the objection to return is because of a wish to remain with the abducting parent, then it is probable that little or no weight will be given to those views. Any other approach would be to drive a coach and horses through the primary scheme of the Hague Convention.'[8]

In *Re R (Minors) (Child Abduction)*[9] the Court of Appeal emphasised that in exercising the discretion, the policy of the Convention, and its faithful implementation by the courts, should always be a weighty factor to be brought into the scales. On the other hand the weight to be attached to the views of the child would clearly vary with his age or maturity: the older the child the greater the weight, the younger the child the less weight.[10] It is however clear that where the court finds the child has valid reasons for his or her objections to being returned then it may refuse to make an order, as in *S v S (Child Abduction)* itself, where the child aged nine had given strong and independent reasons why she did not want to return to France.[11]

7   [1992] 2 FLR 492.
8   Ibid, at p 501.
9   (1994) Times, 5 December.
10 The court took account of the wishes of boys aged seven and a half and six to stay in England with their mother, but exercising its discretion, ordered that they be returned to Illinois.
11 See too, *Re A (Minors) (Abduction: Acquiescence)* [1992] 2 FLR 14; *Re M (Minor)* (25 July 1990, unreported) in which the court refused to order the return of three children aged 11, 9 and 8 to America. In *Re M (A Minor) (Abduction)* [1994] 2 FLR 126 the dispute was

It is less clear what approach the court should take where a parent has consented or acquiesced in the child's otherwise wrongful removal but where he or she is requesting that the child should nonetheless be returned, and for the merits of the case to be heard in the country from which the child was taken. In *Re A (Minors) (No 2) (Abduction: Acquiescence)*[12] the question arose whether the court can take account of the welfare of the child at this stage. The Court of Appeal ruled that the final paragraph of Article 13 makes it clear that it is appropriate for the court to consider the welfare interests of the child at this stage. However, the court added that the court need not treat the welfare of the child as paramount. In *W v W (Child Abduction: Acquiescence)*[13] Waite J itemised various matters which appeared to him to be relevant to the exercise of his discretion, including the emotional effect on the child in ordering his peremptory return, and the extent to which the purpose and philosophy of the Convention would be at risk of frustration if a return order were to be refused. Another factor which has influenced the courts is whether the children are likely to be removed back to their country of habitual residence only for that court to order that they should be allowed to leave again.[14]

The European Convention

The aim of the European Convention is to ensure the mutual recognition and enforcement of decisions relating to the custody of children between contracting states.[15] It may be invoked where a child has been improperly removed across an international frontier in breach of a decision relating to his or her custody. Application for the recognition or enforcement of a decision is made to the central authority in the relevant contracting state which is then under a duty to take all appropriate steps, if necessary by instituting proceedings before its competent authorities, in order—

'(a) to discover the whereabouts of the child;
(b) to avoid, in particular by any necessary provisional measures, prejudice to the interests of the child or of the applicant;
(c) to secure the recognition or enforcement of the decision;

---

between a 13-year-old boy and his mother who was seeking his return to Ireland under the Convention. The boy was made a party to the proceedings and in the light of his allegations of ill-treatment and the validity of his objections the court refused to order his return to Ireland.

12   [1993] 1 FLR 396.
13   [1993] 2 FLR 211.
14   See Staughton LJ in *Re A (Minors) (No 2) (Abduction: Acquiescence)* [1993] 1 FLR 396; *W v W (Child Abduction: Acquiescence)* above.
15   Art.7.

(d) to secure the delivery of the child to the applicant where enforcement is granted;

(e) to inform the requesting authority of the measures taken and their results.'[16]

A person with custody rights conferred by another contracting state may apply under section 16 of the Child Abduction and Custody Act 1985 for the decision to be registered in an appropriate court in the United Kingdom. Once registered, section 18 provides that the court in which it is registered shall have the same powers for the purpose of enforcing the decision as if it had been made by that court. It is a mandatory requirement that a subsisting decision relating to custody which is enforceable in its country of origin should be registered, recognised and enforced in England. However, recognition and enforcement may be refused on various limited grounds specified in Articles 9 and 10. Article 10(1)(b) provides that registration or enforcement may be refused:

'if it is found that by reason of a change in the circumstances including the passage of time but not including a mere change in the residence of the child after an improper removal, the effects of the original decision are manifestly no longer in accordance with the welfare of the child.'[17]

Article 15(1) provides that before reaching a decision under Article 10(1)(b), the court or administrative authority

'shall ascertain the child's views unless this is impracticable having regard in particular to his age and understanding.'

The meaning of 'the effects of the original decision are manifestly no longer in accordance with the welfare of the child' was considered by Latey J in *Re K (A Minor) (Abduction)*.[18] The child concerned was aged seven, she had a Belgian mother and an English father who were unmarried. The father was violent towards the mother and the parties separated, the mother taking the child. Shortly afterwards the father abducted the child to England. The mother obtained a custody order in a Belgian court and 16 months later she applied to have the order registered and enforced in the High Court under the Child Abduction and Custody Act 1985. The mother was not responsible for the delay in taking these proceedings. The father defended the action under Article 10(1)(b). Evidence was given that the child had settled happily in England, was progressing well at school,

16 Art.5.
17 See too Art.10(1)(d) and how it was applied in *Re M (Child Abduction) (European Convention)* [1994] 1 FLR 551.
18 [1990] 1 FLR 387.

that she was being very well cared for by her father and enjoyed the company of her paternal grandparents. Evidence was also given that the mother was a very good and loving mother who could offer the child a happy home surrounded by members of the wider family. The issue for the court was whether the effects of the decision of the Belgian court to award custody to the mother were manifestly no longer in accordance with the child's welfare. Latey J said that this test was not the same as whether it was in the child's best interests for the order to be enforced. Moreover, it was a question which required a speedy resolution without the type of full investigation which was necessary where the welfare of the child was paramount.[19] The length of time the child had spent in England was an important consideration; however the evidence suggested that the child would adjust well if she returned to Belgium. Latey J therefore made an order recognising, registering and enforcing the order of the Belgian court.

In *Re L (Child Abduction: European Convention)*[20] the parents were Irish, married and lived in Ireland with their three children. The mother, who had brought two of the children from Ireland to England in breach of an Irish court order giving custody to the father, asked the court to exercise its discretion under Article 10(1)(b), relying on the fact that the children had lived with her since she left the matrimonial home. She also sought an adjournment to enable the court to exercise its powers under Article 15 to ascertain the views of the children. Booth J rejected both of the mother's applications and ordered the registration and enforcement of the order of the Irish court. She emphasised that proceedings under the Act should be taken swiftly, that decisions should be made by courts expeditiously, and that the court should only exercise its discretion not to comply with the spirit and terms of the Convention in a very clear case. She added that a very high burden of proof rests on the party who seeks to satisfy the court that Article 10(1)(b) applies.

Thus it can be seen that the attitude of the courts is firmly to reinforce the purpose of the Convention by making summary orders without engaging in prolonged enquiries into the position of the children. However, where the child's views are known, and where the child objects to the enforcement of the order, it may then be manifestly no longer in accordance with the welfare of the child for the order to be enforced. In *Re H (A Minor) (Foreign Custody Order)*[1] the Court of Appeal held that recognition and enforcement should be interpreted disjunctively, and that enforcement does not automatically follow recognition where the provisions of Article 10(1)(b) apply.[2]

19 Latey J did however state that, had the welfare of the child been the paramount consideration, the court would have concluded that she should return to Belgium.
20 [1992] 2 FLR 178.
1   [1994] 1 FLR 512.
2   Thus although an order providing for a 13-year-old girl to have staying access with her father in Belgium was registered under s.16 of the Child Abduction and Custody Act 1985, the court applied Art.10(1)(b) and refused to enforce it as this would have been manifestly no longer in accordance with the welfare of the child.

Child abduction in non-Convention cases

Where a child is abducted to England from a non-Convention country the question then arises whether an English court should determine issues relating to the child's upbringing or whether it should order the child's immediate return to the country of the child's habitual residence. In *Re F (A Minor) (Abduction: Jurisdiction)*[3] and *G v G (Minors) (Abduction)*[4] the Court of Appeal, adopting the view that it is in the interests of all children that parents and others should not abduct them from one jurisdiction to another, decided that the general principles of the Hague Convention should be applied in non-Convention cases too. However, the Court of Appeal sounded a note of caution in *D v D (Child Abduction)*,[5] in which the trial judge had applied the principles and Articles in the Convention to the facts of the case and had not considered the welfare of the children separately from this. Of this approach Butler-Sloss LJ said:

> 'The courts have always set their face against condoning the abduction of children from their rightful homes and have for many years provided a summary procedure to determine whether to return them. Nonetheless it is important to remember that the Articles of the Convention are not to be applied literally in the wardship jurisdiction and the court retains discretion to consider the wider aspects of the welfare of the wards.'[6]

Balcombe LJ expressed a similar caveat when he said:

> 'His judgment is open to criticism in that [the judge] appears to have sought to apply the detailed provisions of the Convention to a non-Convention case....However, I should stress that, in a non-Convention case, the welfare of the children remains the paramount consideration, and the principles of the Convention are applicable only to the extent that they indicate what is normally in the interests of the children.'[7]

---

3   [1991] 1 FLR 1.
4   [1991] 2 FLR 506.
5   [1994] 1 FLR 137.
6   Ibid, at p 140.
7   Ibid, at p 144. The court nonetheless ruled that the trial judge had been right to apply the general principles of the Convention to the case before him. However, the mother's situation had changed by the time of the appeal, and the Court of Appeal held that the welfare of the children now required that their future should be decided by an English court.

There may however be cause for concern that the courts are too readily applying Convention principles to non-Convention cases.[8] The Convention is built around administrative structures which are designed to achieve mutual co-operation between states parties, including in particular rights of access,[9] and these will not be in place where children are returned to a non-Convention country. There are also grounds for anxiety that a child may be returned to a country where the principles governing the resolution of children cases are significantly different from the welfare principle as operated by the English courts. Of this fear Lord Donaldson MR said in *Re F (A Minor) (Abduction: Jurisdiction)*[10]

> 'Which court should decide depends ... on whether the other court will apply principles which are acceptable to the English courts as being appropriate, subject always to any contra indication such as those mentioned in Article 13 of the Convention, or a risk of persecution or discrimination, but prima facie the court to decide is that of the state where the child is habitually resident immediately before its removal.'

In *Re S (Minors) (Abduction)*,[11] Balcombe LJ stated that the general principles of the Hague Convention should apply in an 'appropriate' non-Convention case, and added 'an appropriate non-Convention case is one where there is no reason to suppose that the courts in the other jurisdiction will apply an approach to the question of the case of the child significantly different to that of the English court'. In the light of that general principle it is suggested that the ruling in *Re S (Minors) (Abduction)* is worrying because of the approach taken by the Court of Appeal to what other systems are 'appropriate'. The case concerned whether children of Muslim parents should be returned to Pakistan. Their mother, although born in Pakistan, had been brought up in England, but had gone to live in Pakistan after marrying, and had had three children there. Later she brought the two younger children to England without the father's knowledge or consent and he sought their return to Pakistan. Expert evidence was given that although the Pakistani courts would apply a similar welfare principle to the determination of the upbringing of the children, the attitude of the Pakistani courts towards the welfare of the children would differ consid-

---

8   See too, *S v S (Child Abduction: Non-Convention Country)* [1994] 2 FLR 681 where the court ordered the return of a child to South Africa even though the mother's removal was not in breach of the father's custody rights, and therefore Art.12 would not have applied had the case been a Convention case.

9   Arts. 7 and 21.

10 [1991] 1 FLR 1 at p 5. Cf *C v C (Abduction: Jurisdiction)* [1993] Fam Law 185 in which Cazalet J refused to return a child to Brazil because of the delay which would occur before the merits of the case would be tried in the Brazilian courts.

11 [1994] 1 FLR 297.

erably from an English court. The Pakistani court would try to give effect to the children's welfare from a Muslim point of view and this point of view would exclude a Muslim mother from entitlement to bring up her children in certain specified circumstances. Of this approach to welfare, Nolan LJ said:

> 'that seems to me to be neither surprising nor, in the circumstances of these children, objectionable. They are the children of Muslim parents who are part of a Muslim family.... . In my judgment, [the trial judge] was fully entitled to take the view that, for Muslim children of Muslim parents whose home hitherto has been in Pakistan, the principles of Pakistani law are appropriate by English standards.'[12]

Thus the Court of Appeal was prepared to order children aged three and seven, who were living with their mother and grandmother in England, to be returned to a country where, according to the expert evidence, the law would allow the children to be deprived of the care of their mother if she concluded a subsequent marriage, or formed a liaison with another man other than a close relative to the children; or if she was deemed to be unsuitable, for instance if she had a way of life which the court would consider unIslamic. It is suggested that the general justification relied on for this approach, namely that these were children who were being alienated from their background, home, school, friends and relations[13] was not borne out by the facts.[14] A child of three has no sense of country and nationality. A little girl of seven would be far more likely to wish to remain in the same country as her mother and maternal family rather than experience the further upheaval of returning to her original home country. If the child were to learn that there was a possibility that she would be deprived of her mother's care if she returned to Pakistan it is surely inconceivable that she would wish to return there. The underlying assumption of the Convention is that 'the courts of all its signatories are equally concerned to ensure, and equally capable of ensuring, that both parties receive a fair hearing, and that all issues of child welfare receive a skilled, thorough and humane evaluation.'[15] However, although the Court of Appeal claimed that it was acting in the best interests of the children, in *Re S (Minors) (Abduction)* it was allowing them to return to a system which would take account of matters which an English court would regard as incompatible with the welfare principle. What in reality it was doing when

12 Ibid, at pp 304-5.
13 See Buckley LJ in *Re L (Minors) (Wardship: Jurisdiction)* [1974] 1 WLR 250 at p 264.
14 Indeed, it is suggested that this justification for the approach of the Hague Convention does not survive close examination in the case of young children.
15 *P v P (Minors) (Child Abduction)* [1992] 1 FLR 155 per Waite J at p 161.

it applied the Hague Convention philosophy in this non-Convention case was preserving comity between nations, giving respect to a different judicial system, giving respect to the tenets of a non-Christian religion, and deterring parents wishing to return to England after a failed marriage from bringing their children to this country. Furthermore, it was ordering the return of children with none of the safeguards built into the system as it operates between contracting states. In particular Article 19 makes it clear that a decision under the Convention concerning the return of the child must not be taken to be a determination of any custody issue. A non-Convention state on the other hand might well be influenced by the English court's order when adjudicating on the merits.[16]

Adoption and welfare

Adoption applications can raise complex questions relating to the welfare of children. When an adoption order is made it ends the status relationship between the child and his or her natural parents. The child is treated by law as the child of the adopters, and as if he or she had been born to them in lawful wedlock even where the child is adopted by a single person.[17] This conceptual framework applies to all adoptions irrespective of the factual circumstances of the child, the natural parents and the adopters. Adoption is traditionally associated with the early transfer of parental responsibility for a baby from the child's unmarried mother to married adoptive parents. Adoption continues to make provision for such children, but the number of babies available for adoption has undergone a rapid decline. On the other hand adoption is one of the options open to a local authority when planning the upbringing of a child in care, and there has been an increase in the adoption of older children, and children with special needs. Furthermore, the growth in the number of children born outside marriage, and the increase in the number of divorces which are followed by remarriage, has led to a steady demand from step-parents to be able to adopt the children of a previous relationship. Thus many children for whom adoption is considered as the most appropriate way of giving them a secure childhood have existing links with their natural parents, and sometimes it may be thought important to preserve these links. In the context of adoption difficult questions can then arise in relation to whether the

16 It is suggested that, at the very least, expert evidence should be obtained on this point.
17 Adoption Act 1976, s.39. S.39(4) specifically states that the section prevents an adopted child from being illegitimate. S.12(3) provides that the making of an adoption order operates to extinguish any previously held parental responsibility, any order under the Children Act 1989, and any maintenance obligation made by agreement or court order. All statutory references hereafter in this section are to the Adoption Act 1976, unless otherwise stated.

complete severance of the relationship between the child and his or her natural family necessarily promotes the child's welfare. This section concentrates on various contentious aspects of adoption which directly impinge upon the welfare of the child.

The welfare test in adoption

Section 6 of the Adoption Act 1976 states that—

> 'In reaching any decision relating to the adoption of a child a court or adoption agency shall have regard to all the circumstances, first consideration being given to the need to safeguard and promote the welfare of the child throughout his childhood; and shall so far as practicable ascertain the wishes and feelings of the child regarding the decision and give due consideration to them, having regard to his age and understanding'.

This provision should be contrasted with the principle enshrined in section 1 of the Children Act 1989 which provides that when a court determines any question with respect to the upbringing of a child the welfare of the child shall be the court's *paramount* consideration. In the case of adoption the child's welfare is the court's *first* consideration; this means that whilst it is of first importance it does not always and necessarily override all other considerations and determine the course to be followed. The reason why the child's welfare is not paramount is because the welfare test in adoption is bound up with the question whether the objection of a parent to his or her child being adopted can ever be reasonable. Clearly if a court is satisfied that adoption would otherwise be in the best interests of the child, and if the child's welfare is paramount, the fact that a parent is objecting to the adoption would not be a reason for refusing to make the order.[18]

Unfortunately for the child, the first consideration test has the disadvantage that, even where the parents' agreement to the child's adoption is forthcoming, it is still the case that neither the court nor the adoption agency is required to treat the child's welfare as paramount. However, it is suggested that this disadvantage is more theoretical than practical, and that adoption agencies and courts do in practice give paramount consideration to the child's welfare where the question of dispensing with agreement is not in issue. The law of adoption is currently undergoing review, and the inter-departmental working group recommended in their consultation

18 See the *Report of the Departmental Committee on the Adoption of Children (The Houghton Committee)* (1972) Cmnd 5107, HMSO.

document that the welfare principle in adoption cases should be brought into line with that in the Children Act 1989. However the review recognised that if the principle of paramountcy were to apply where a parent's agreement was not forthcoming 'the court would be able to override completely a parent's wishes, which we would consider unacceptable in relation to an order which irrevocably terminates a parent's legal relationship with a child'. The review therefore recommended that the child's welfare should not be the court's paramount consideration when the court is determining whether to make an adoption order without the agreement of the child's parent.[19]

'Open adoption', contact and welfare

In the past adoption tended to be shrouded with secrecy and the notion that it could be in the interests of the child to maintain links with his or her birth parents was alien to what was essentially a secretive arrangement. Currently the view is taken that more openness is needed in the adoption process. It was stated in the *Review of Adoption Law* that:

'For many years now, there has been an increasing recognition that a child's knowledge of his or her background is crucial to a formation of positive self-identity, and that adoptive families should be encouraged to be open about the child's adoptive status and the special nature of the adoptive relationship. There has also been a move towards enabling some children to maintain contact with their birth families'.[20]

This thinking is influencing the selection of adopters by adoption agencies, and has started to influence the courts' decisions when they are assessing whether adoption without contact will best promote the welfare of children. Where adoption will lead to a denial of contact with a parent the court may take the view that it will not serve the child's long-term interests.[1] However, in *Re C (A Minor) (Adopted Child: Contact)*[2] the court was not persuaded by arguments extolling the value of openness in adoption to allow courts to provide a forum in which these alleged advantages could be explored. Thorpe J refused a birth mother leave to apply for contact

19 *Review of Adoption Law* (1992) DoH, para 7.1. This has been followed by a White Paper on adoption law *Adoption: The Future* (1993) Cm 2288.
20 Ibid, para 4.1. For a comparative survey, see C Bridge *Changing the Nature of Adoption: Law Reform in England and New Zealand* (1993) 13 LS 81; see too C Bridge *Adoption and Contact: the Value of Openness* (1994) 6 JCL 147.
1   See *Re E (A Minor) (Care Order: Contact)* [1994] 1 FLR 146, discussed below.
2   [1993] 2 FLR 431.

with her adopted child under section 8 of the Children Act 1989. He emphasised that adoption orders are intended to be permanent and final. He said that 'a fundamental question such as contact, even if confined to the indirect, should not subsequently be reopened unless there is some fundamental change in circumstances.'

On the other hand, a contact order may be made at the same time as an adoption order. Section 12(6) of the Adoption Act 1976 enables a court to attach such terms and conditions to an adoption order as the court thinks fit. In *Re C (A Minor) (Adoption: Conditions)*[3] an application was made by foster parents to adopt a girl aged 13 who was in the care of the local authority. Her younger brother was also in care and the girl was very attached to him and had contact with him. The applicants to adopt recognised the value to the girl of continuing her relationship with her brother after adoption. However the lower courts took the view that they had no power to make an adoption order with a condition of contact.[4] The House of Lords held that this was wrong, and that it was possible to make an adoption order with a condition of contact where such a condition was in the child's best interests. It therefore ruled that the case should be remitted to the High Court with a direction that an adoption order should be made with a condition of reasonable contact between the girl and her brother. However, Lord Ackner, who made the main speech, emphasised that in normal circumstances there should be a complete break between the child and his natural family. He added:

> 'The court will not, except in the most exceptional case, impose terms or conditions as to access to members of the child's natural family to which the adopting parents do not agree. To do so would be to create a potentially frictional situation which would be hardly likely to safeguard or promote the welfare of the child.'[5]

Selection of adopters and placement of a child for adoption

Every local authority is under a duty to establish and maintain an adoption service within their area. Local authorities themselves act as adoption agencies and provide the requisite services, or they secure that they are provided by approved adoption societies.[6] Adoption agencies have exclusive

3 [1988] 1 All ER 705.
4 The case was further complicated by the fact that the mother was refusing to agree to the adoption because it would weaken the relationship between the children. The lower courts took the view that she was therefore being reasonable in withholding her agreement. The mother's refusal to agree to the adoption was no longer reasonable once contact could be preserved, and the House of Lords dispensed with it.
5 [1988] 1 All ER 705 at p 712.
6 S.1.

responsibility for selecting adopters and placing children for adoption. Private adoption placements are illegal except where the prospective adopter is a relative of the child, or where the placement is made in pursuance of a High Court order.[7] Section 11(1) provides that no person other than an adoption agency shall make arrangements for the adoption of a child. However, section 13(2) allows a court to make an adoption order where the child has not been placed with the applicants by an adoption agency, but where the child has had his home with the applicants at all times during the preceding 12 months. This provision is essential, for otherwise it would be impossible for a court to make an adoption order where the child had been illegally placed, even though such an order would be manifestly in the best interests of the child.[8]

In the case of agency placements there are few legal restrictions relating to a person's eligibility to adopt a child. The Adoption Act 1976 imposes lower age limits, requirements relating to domicile, and in the case of adoption by two persons states that the parties must be married.[9] Adoption agencies, on the other hand, operate very specific criteria when determining eligibility to adopt which are neither laid down in the primary legislation nor in the associated Regulations.[10] Agencies specifically exclude certain persons from being chosen as adopters. They all impose upper age limits, and many reject would-be adopters for reasons such as that they already have natural children, because they follow the wrong religion, or have no religion, or are the wrong race or colour to adopt the child in question, or because they smoke or are obese, or are undergoing fertility treatment. Agencies apply these and other criteria to the selection process because they take the view that such factors relate to the welfare of the children who are available for adoption.

Where persons are rejected as prospective adopters there is no formal appeal system available to them. The complaints procedure established under section 26(3) of the Children Act 1989 does not apply to prospective adopters. However, it may be that a local authority would be willing to allow this procedure to be used even though there is no obligation on the

---

7   S.11.
8   See *Re ZHH (Adoption Application)* [1993] 1 FLR 83 where Booth J held that the fact that an illegal placement is a criminal offence did not preclude the court from making an adoption order. It is also a criminal offence under s.57 for certain payments to be made in connection with adoption in order to prevent trafficking in children both in this country and in children from abroad. And see *Re C (A Minor) (Adoption Application)* [1993] 1 FLR 87 where Booth J held that for a court subsequently to authorise such payments would amount to the court ratifying the sale of children for adoption. Breaches of ss.11 and 57 raise difficult questions and the case law is not always consistent. It is most usefully summarised by S M Cretney in (1993) 23 Fam Law 276.
9   Ss.14 and 15.
10 The Adoption Agencies Regulations 1983, regs.10(1)(c) and 11(1) simply require that the agency is satisfied about the suitability of the prospective adopter and that she would be a suitable adoptive parent for a particular child.

authority to make it available.[11] Otherwise the only way of challenging the agency's decision would be in judicial review. This is a jurisdiction which enables the High Court to review the behaviour of a public authority where it has acted illegally, with procedural impropriety or irrationally. It is a jurisdiction which is exercised with great caution. Courts are generally extremely reluctant to intervene in the way in which public authorities carry out their duties and powers. Furthermore, the court does not have an appellate function, it is confined to determining whether there has been an abuse of power.

Illegality might be established if it could be shown that the adoption agency have fettered their discretion by adopting a rigid policy which allows for no exceptions. The agency is entitled to follow a general policy, but they must consider each case on its merits.[12] However, it is likely to be extremely difficult to satisfy the court that a rigid policy has been adopted. Thus in *R v Lancashire County Council, ex p M*[13] foster parents sought to challenge the decision of the local authority to reject them as suitable adopters for a foster child who had lived with them from shortly after his birth until he was two years old. The foster parents alleged that the primary reason for moving the child from their care was to implement a rigid policy, namely that children ought to be placed with families of the same cultural or ethnic background as the child. It was further alleged that the authority had taken account of matters which it ought not to have taken into account, and had refused or neglected to take account of matters which it ought to have done, and therefore that they had come to a decision which no reasonable authority could have arrived at. Refusing to grant the adopters leave to bring an action in judicial review, the Court of Appeal stated that they had failed to establish that the authority's decision was so unreasonable that no authority could ever have come to it. It emphasised that judicial review proceedings are not concerned with what the court would have done had it been applying the welfare principle. In the context of judicial review the role of the court was simply to determine whether the authority had acted in such a way as to be almost perverse. Thus decision-making about the choice of adopters is vested firmly in adoption agencies, and it is most unlikely that a successful challenge could be mounted against a refusal to select a person or couple as suitable where the child is not living with them.

Removal of a child from prospective adopters

Parents who arrange for their child to be placed for adoption by an adoption agency may subsequently change their mind and seek the return of the

---

11 Unpublished research presently in progress at Sheffield University reveals this to be the case.
12 Cf *R v Lewisham London Borough Council, ex p P* [1991] 2 FLR 185.
13 [1992] 1 FLR 109.

child. Until an adoption order is made the natural mother, and sometimes the natural father, have parental responsibility for the child and, prima facie, this entitles them to recover the care of the child from prospective adopters or the adoption agency.[14] The Act therefore contains various provisions which are designed to protect the child from the disruptive and possibly harmful effects of precipitate removal by a parent. It also contains provisions which give the prospective adopters a measure of security against the child being taken from them by the local authority or adoption agency against their will.

Section 27(1) provides that—

'While an application for an adoption order is pending in a case where a parent or guardian of the child has agreed to the making of an adoption order ... the parent or guardian is not entitled, against the will of the person with whom the child has his home, to remove the child from the home of that person except with the leave of the court'.

This protection only arises where agreement has been given. In *Re T (A Minor) (Adoption: Parental Consent)*[15] the Court of Appeal held that such agreement could be given orally or in writing, and that in either case the agreement falls within the scope of section 27(1). It is the institution of legal proceedings which triggers the protection from removal; thus where applicants to adopt are fearful that the parent will change her mind, they can make an application for an adoption order at an early stage. It is suggested that whether they are well-advised to do so depends on all the circumstances of the case, but particularly on whether the court is likely to regard the application as premature, such as where the child has been with the applicants for only a relatively short time. Where foster parents or relatives have looked after a child for some considerable length of time, and where the parent has needed some persuasion to agree to the making of an adoption order, it would normally seem wise to make a swift application for an order so that the protection afforded by section 27(1) immediately comes into play. It should however be realised that although the protection afforded by this section arises only when agreement has been given, in those cases where parental agreement is not forthcoming the child is often in local authority care. The child is therefore protected against removal from the prospective adopters because of the effect of the care order.

Where a parent has not agreed to the child being adopted, the child is vulnerable to being taken by a parent at any time from the home of the

---

14 Whether the father has parental responsibility depends on his status or whether he has a parental responsibility agreement or order: see ch 1.

15 [1986] 1 All ER 817.

persons who have been caring for him, and who would like to adopt him. Once a child has been taken from the home of the applicants to adopt it is inevitable that they will fail to satisfy section 13 which requires that the child should have lived with them for a specified period during the weeks or months preceding the making of the adoption order.[16] Section 28(1) affords some protection to the child in circumstances of this kind. It provides that while an application for an adoption order is pending, and where the child has had his home with the applicants for the five years preceding the application, no person is entitled to remove the child from the applicants' home against the will of the applicants except with the leave of the court.[17] However, five years is a considerable length of time before the protection arises, and it is the initiation of adoption proceedings which operates as the trigger to prevent removal. Unless and until an adoption application has been made, there is nothing in the Adoption Act 1976 to prevent the child from being taken by the parents from the prospective adopters' care.

However, it should be remembered that the child is afforded protection against precipitate removal from a settled home under section 10 of the Children Act 1989. Any person with whom the child has lived for a period of at least three years is entitled to apply for a residence order.[18] Furthermore, where persons have looked after the child for a lesser period they can seek the leave of the court to apply for a residence order.[19] However, this will only assist persons who are seeking an adoption order if they are able to obtain a residence order, or an order restraining the child's removal under section 29(2), before the child is taken from their home.[20] Once the child has gone, even if he is restored to the potential adopters' care by a court, it seems that they will no longer be able to fulfil the requirements of section 13, and therefore no adoption order can be made, at least for the time being.

It may not only be parents who wish to remove a child from persons who wish to adopt him. For example, where the child is in the care of a local authority the authority may have plans for the child which do not include continuing care by the foster parents who are currently looking after the child. Section 28(2) imposes additional restrictions on the removal

---

16 S.13(1) states that the child must have had his home with the applicant for the preceding 13 weeks where the application is made by a parent, step-parent or relative, or where the child was placed by an adoption agency, or in pursuance of a High Court order. S.13 (2) states that in any other case the child must have had his home with the applicant during the preceding 12 months.

17 'Or under authority conferred by any enactment or on the arrest of the child'. This proviso also applies to s.28(2) below.

18 Children Act 1989, s.10(5)(b) and (10).

19 Unless they are local authority foster parents to whom special rules apply: see ch 2.

20 Where a child has been removed in breach of ss.27 and 28, a court may order the person who has removed the child to return the child: s.29.

of the child where a person has provided a home for a child for at least five years. It provides—

> 'Where a person ("the prospective adopter") gives notice to the local authority within whose area he has his home that he intends to apply for an adoption order in respect of a child who for the preceding 5 years has had his home with the prospective adopter, no person is entitled, against the will of the prospective adopter, to remove the child from the prospective adopter's home, except with the leave of the court or under authority conferred by any enactment,... before—
> (a) the prospective adopter applies for the adoption order, or
> (b) the period of three months from the receipt of the notice by the local authority expires,
> whichever occurs first.'

This prohibition safeguards the child against removal by anyone, including the local authority, without the leave of the court once notice of intention to adopt has been given. However, the applicants must apply for an adoption order before three months expire or they lose this protection.[1]

In *Re H (A Minor) (Adoption)*[2] it was held that the court ought not to exercise its discretion under the adoption legislation to refuse a local authority leave to remove the child where the applicant's purpose was to frustrate the local authority's plans. However, it is suggested that the court mistakenly applied the principle in *A v Liverpool City Council*[3] in this case and that it therefore should not be followed. Section 28(2) contemplates a situation where the decision-making function on the merits of removal is clearly vested in the court, and since the implementation of the Children Act 1989 the courts have been careful to preserve their powers where it is they, and not the local authority, who have the right to determine the case on the merits.[4]

Further provisions preventing the child's removal from his present home by either an adoption agency or a local authority without the leave of the court are contained in sections 30 and 31. The placing adoption agency is charged with the duty of ensuring that the child's placement is in the interests of the child. Sometimes the agency may form the view that the child should not be allowed to remain in his present placement. Where this is the position, section 30(1) provides—

1   A fresh notice of intention to adopt cannot be issued until 28 days have elapsed after the expiry of the original notice: s.28(6).
2   [1985] FLR 519.
3   [1981] 2 All ER 385.
4. *Re C (A Minor) (Adoption)* [1994] 2 FLR 513, see below; see too on this general principle, *Re B (Minors) (Termination of Contact: Paramount Consideration)* [1993] 1 FLR 543.

'Subject to subsection (2), at any time after a child has been placed with any person in pursuance of arrangements made by an adoption agency for the adoption of the child by that person, and before an adoption order has been made on the application of that person in respect of the child—

...

(b) the agency may cause notice to be given to that person of their intention not to allow the child to remain in his home'.

Subsection (2) provides—

'No notice under paragraph (b) of subsection (1) shall be given in respect of a child in relation to whom an application has been made for an adoption order except with the leave of the court to which the application has been made'.

Again it should be noted that it is the application for an adoption order which brings section 30(2) into play. Where no such application has been made, the agency may issue a notice under section 30 requiring the return of the child within seven days without the leave of the court. Where this occurs, it seems that the prospective adopters have no means of challenging the agency's decision. In *Re W (A Minor) (Adoption Agency: Wardship)*[5] prospective adopters who received such a notice thereupon made the child a ward of court. Discharging the wardship without considering the merits of the prospective adopters' application for care and control of the child, the court ruled that the principle in *A v Liverpool City Council*[6] applied, namely that the court had no power to intervene in wardship proceedings to review the merits of an adoption agency's decision made in pursuance of its statutory powers.

Section 31 makes provision for those cases where a child has not been placed for adoption by an adoption agency. It provides that section 30 shall apply as if the child had been placed in pursuance of such arrangements:

'Where a person gives notice in pursuance of section 22(1) to the local authority within whose area he has his home of his intention to apply for an adoption order in respect of a child—

(a) who is (when the notice is given) being looked after by a local authority'.

The effect of this provision is to prevent a local authority who are looking after the child from giving notice of their intention not to allow the child to

5   [1990] 2 FLR 470.
6   [1981] 2 All ER 385.

remain in the applicant's home without the leave of the court. This is a significant provision, because where a local authority are looking after a child under a care order it is normally the local authority who are entitled to make all decisions about the child, including the decision to remove the child from his present foster parents and to place him elsewhere. Local authority foster parents are not entitled to challenge the decision in the courts unless the child has been living with them for at least three years.[7] However, foster parents who wish to be considered as a child's adopters may be assisted by the combination of provisions in section 13(2), section 22(1) and section 31. Section 13(2) provides that an adoption order can be made where the child has had his home with the applicants at all times during the preceding 12 months; section 22(1) states that the applicants to adopt must notify the local authority of their intention to apply for an adoption order at least three months before the date of the order; and section 30(1) prevents the child being removed from the home of applicants who have notified the local authority under section 22(1) without the leave of the court.

This combination of provisions has a critical impact on what is often the key question in children cases, namely whether it is the local authority, or the court, which has the final word about who can look after the child. This was illustrated in *Re C (A Minor) (Adoption)*.[8] A foster mother had been rejected by the local authority as either a long-term carer or adopter of a child who had been living with her since he was a few days old, and who was now aged two years and four months. The local authority were in the process of moving the child away from her home to other adoptive parents when the foster mother served notice of intention to apply to adopt under section 22(1) and issued the adoption application. The effect of the foster mother's action was to halt the move of the child to his new home. The local authority therefore applied for leave to serve notice on the foster mother of intention to remove the child from her home under sections 30(2) and 31.

There were two issues for the court to resolve when considering the leave application: first, whether the welfare test in section 6, which required the court to give first consideration to the welfare of the child, applied to applications for leave to remove a child under Part III of the Act; and second, if it did, whether the court had a free discretion when considering the welfare of the child, or whether it must limit its function to interfering with the local authority's plans only if the authority were acting perversely. The trial judge found that the court should not take steps which were tantamount to a review of the adoption agency and local authority's powers and decisions, and granted the local authority leave to serve the notice of

7   See ch 2.
8   [1994] 2 FLR 513.

removal. Allowing the foster mother's appeal, the Court of Appeal ruled that an application by a local authority for leave under section 30(2) was 'a decision relating to the adoption of a child' and therefore that section 6 applied.[9] In relation to how much weight should be given to the local authority's plans for the child, Butler-Sloss LJ said that they had to be given the weight they deserved and that the court was entitled to assume that the local authority had the welfare of the child to the forefront of their thinking when making plans for the child. However, she said:

> 'A court determining a section 30(2) application must give most careful consideration to the plan of the local authority but it has the task to decide whether that plan should go ahead or whether the child should remain with its existing carer even if the consequence of its decision may be to frustrate the local authority's arrangements. It is never the task of the court to rubber stamp the local authority. Either it has no duty to interfere or it has the duty to decide.'[10]

The court stated that where the application by the foster parent was a genuine one, with reasonable prospects of success, it was in the best interests of the child that it should be determined by a full hearing and not brought to a premature conclusion without a proper investigation.

Agreement to adoption

Normally an adoption order cannot be made unless each parent agrees to the child being adopted. For adoption purposes, 'parent' means any parent who has parental responsibility for the child under the Children Act 1989, thus the agreement of an unmarried father is not necessary.[11] There are two methods of obtaining parental agreement to adoption: under section 18, through a procedure known as 'freeing' the child for adoption; and under section 16, where the parent agrees to a specific adoption order being made, whether or not she knows the identity of the applicants.

---

9   It distinguished *F v S (Adoption: Ward)* [1973] 1 All ER 722 and *Re A (Residence Order: Leave to Apply)* [1992] 2 FLR 154 (see ch 2) on the grounds that they were applications to initiate proceedings, whereas the application by the foster parent had already triggered the procedure to be followed under the adoption legislation.
10 [1994] 2 FLR 513 at 522-3. Butler-Sloss LJ added that a guardian ad litem can be appointed in a case of this kind under the Adoption Rules 1984, r.47(8).
11 Adoption Act 1976, s.72; the position of the unmarried father is explained below.

Freeing for adoption

Under the freeing procedure an application is made by an adoption agency for an order declaring the child free for adoption. The parents must consent to the application being made and, under section 18(1)(a), the court must be satisfied that each parent:

'freely, and with full understanding of what is involved, agrees generally and unconditionally to the making of an adoption order'.

On the making of a freeing order, parental responsibility for the child is given to the adoption agency until the child is adopted. The parents lose their parental responsibility, and therefore have no subsequent entitlement to withhold their agreement to the child's adoption.

The freeing procedure has advantages for the child, the parents and the potential adopters. Because all issues about agreement are resolved at an early stage, it means that the child can be placed with applicants to adopt without any risk that the birth parent will change her mind and seek the return of the child. This has undoubted advantages for the child, who will be able to form attachments to his adoptive family without any danger of these being broken through his removal from the adopters and return to his birth mother. It also may take some of the strain of the adoption process away from the parent who has decided that her child should be adopted. Freeing allows a parent to make a relatively speedy decision, and it may make her experience of giving up her child for adoption less distressing than under the alternative process which takes considerably longer. The mother of a new-born baby is given special protection against making such a momentous decision at a time when she may not be in a proper mental and physical state to arrive at an informed choice; at least six weeks must elapse after the child's birth before her consent can be effective.[12] But once this period has elapsed, a mother can relinquish her parental responsibility for the child to the adoption agency, and thus from any further involvement in the arrangements for the child. The advantage for the potential adopters is that the child is not normally placed with them until all matters relating to agreements to adoption have been resolved. Consequently they are free from the outset of the fear that the mother may wish to have the child restored to her care, and able to feel secure in their relationship with the child as soon as the child is placed. In cases where there are issues over whether there are grounds for dispensing with a parent's agreement to the child's adoption, these can be dealt with in the context of freeing

---

12 S.18(4). This does not prevent the child being placed for adoption before he or she is six weeks old.

proceedings, which means that the adoption agency bears the costs of legal proceedings rather than the applicants to adopt.

A freeing application is sometimes used to determine whether adoption by strangers, or present foster carers, will be for the welfare of the child or whether the child should continue to maintain his links with his natural family. The fact that an adoption agency has decided that adoption is in the child's interests and has applied to the court for a freeing order does not mean that the court is bound to make the order; it must first consider under section 6 whether adoption would safeguard and promote the interests of the child throughout his childhood. The court should only make a freeing order where it is satisfied that the child's welfare will be served by adoption. Thus in *Re U (Application to Free for Adoption)*[13] the adoption agency wished the child to be freed for adoption by strangers. The paternal grandparents wished themselves to adopt the child. The court, applying section 6, decided that the paternal grandparents would make suitable adopters and it therefore rejected the adoption agency's application for a freeing order. However, because adoption proceedings are family proceedings for the purposes of the Children Act 1989,[14] the court could choose to make a section 8 order under that Act rather than a freeing order, and here the court made a residence order in favour of the paternal grandparents with the purpose of eventually enabling them to apply for an adoption order.

Applying for an adoption order

The alternative procedure for giving agreement to adoption is where a parent agrees to a specific adoption order being made. Section 16(1) provides that—

> 'An adoption order shall not be made unless—
> (a) the child is free for adoption by virtue of an order made—
>   (i) in England and Wales, under section 18;
>   ....; or
> (b) in the case of each parent or guardian of the child the court is satisfied that—
>   (i) he freely, and with full understanding of what is involved, agrees unconditionally to the making of an adoption order (whether or not he knows the identity of the applicants)'.

Under this procedure the court must be satisfied at the time that it makes the adoption order that each parent agrees to the order being made.

---

13 [1993] 2 FLR 992.
14 See ch 2.

Inevitably there is some time lapse between the child being placed for adoption and the adoption hearing. In all adoptions the child must be at least 19 weeks old and at all times during the preceding 13 weeks have had his home with the applicants, or one of them.[15] In practice the time gap between the child's placement and the adoption hearing is likely to be much longer, because health and other reports must be prepared, and the relationship between the child and the applicants to adopt scrutinised, in order to ensure that adoption will be for the welfare of the child.

The advantage of this procedure over the freeing procedure is that the child can be placed as soon as the parent has given her preliminary agreement, and this means that the attachment links between the child and the prospective adopters can be established from an early stage which is clearly in the interests of the child. It allows the birth mother a longer period of reflection before she finalises her agreement to her child's adoption, and thus provides safeguards against her making a decision which she later regrets. Also, the parent gives her agreement in the knowledge that suitable adopters have been chosen, and she can have the reassurance of knowing that the professionals dealing with the child are satisfied that the adoption placement will serve the child's best interests. However, the requirement that parental consent should be forthcoming at the time that the adoption order is made can be stressful for all parties: the birth parent may be asked on several occasions whether she agrees to her child being adopted and this may compound her pain;[16] a child who is old enough to understand the process will not be certain whether the adoption will take place; and the potential adopters may find that parental agreement is withdrawn at the last minute.[17]

The unmarried father and agreeing to adoption

It is only where an unmarried father has parental responsibility that his agreement to his child's adoption is required, or must be dispensed with, before an adoption order can be made.[18] However, the interests of a father who has forged links with his child are afforded protection in freeing proceedings by section 18(7). This states that before a court makes a freeing

15 S.13(1).
16 It is the duty of the reporting officer, who must be appointed in all cases where parental agreement is forthcoming, to ensure that consents have been freely given: Adoption Rules 1984, r.17. Notice of the hearing must be served on the parent, but she is not required to attend: r.21(1). Once the application has been made and the parent has agreed to the child being adopted, the child cannot be taken from the potential adopters pending the adoption hearing: Adoption Act 1976, s.27; see above.
17 Cf *Re G (A Minor) (Adoption: Parental Agreement)* [1990] 2 FLR 429.
18 See the definition of parent in s.72. A court may make a parental responsibility order even where it is inevitable that the father's agreement to adoption will be dispensed with: see *Re H (Illegitimate Children: Father: Parental Rights) (No 2)* [1991] 1 FLR 214.

order the court shall satisfy itself in relation to any person claiming to be the father that he has no intention of applying for either a parental responsibility order or a residence order, or that if he did make any such application it would be likely to be refused.[19] Also, if the father is liable by virtue of any order or agreement to contribute to the child's maintenance he must be made a respondent to freeing and adoption proceedings, he is entitled to attend the hearing, and he is entitled to be heard on whether an adoption order should be made.[20] Furthermore, the court has a general discretion to add any person as a party to freeing and adoption proceedings, and may exercise this in favour of the unmarried father.[1] In any event the court is likely to obtain information about the father in the report supplied by either the adoption agency or local authority covering matters specified in paragraph 2 of Schedule 2 of the Adoption Rules 1984. Schedule 2 states that, so far as is practicable, this report shall include information about each natural parent's wishes and feelings in relation to the adoption, 'including where appropriate the child's father who was not married to the child's mother at the time of his birth.'[2]

However, unless the father is entitled to be a respondent to the proceedings, these safeguards of the unmarried father's position may not always assist him. In *Re B (A Minor) (Adoption)*[3] a county court judge refused to allow an unmarried father to be joined as a party to adoption proceedings. The Court of Appeal held that there was no presumption that the father should be made a party where he had no right to be a party, and that it was a matter for the court's discretion whether it allowed him to be joined.

In *Re L (A Minor) (Adoption: Procedure)*[4] the mother of a child was very anxious that the unmarried father did not discover that the child existed. She had placed the child with a local authority in their capacity as an adoption agency. The child had been placed with potential adopters and they had applied for an adoption order. During the course of the adoption proceedings the judge directed that the father be discreetly interviewed to ascertain his wishes and feelings. The local authority appealed against this direction, because they feared that the mother might withdraw her agreement to the adoption if the father was told of the child's existence. Allowing the appeal, the Court of Appeal held that the words 'where appropriate' in Schedule 2 were highly significant. It held that they were

---

19 It is suggested that the father will fulfil the requirement that he would be likely to obtain a parental responsibility order in any case where he has had a relationship with the child. Cases on parental responsibility orders are analysed in ch 1.
20 Adoption Rules 1984, rr. 4(1)(f),10(1),15(2)(h) and 23(1).
1 R.15(3).
2 In *Re Adoption Application (No 2) 41/61* [1964] Ch 48 it was held that no one has a duty positively to seek out the father.
3 [1991] Fam Law 136.
4 [1991] 1 FLR 171.

intended to confer a discretion upon the adoption agency preparing the report whether to include particulars of the unmarried father. Furthermore, it held that this discretion was that of the adoption agency alone, and that the court had no power to interfere unless it had been improperly exercised. As the local authority were convinced that adoption was in the child's best interests, and as they were concerned that it should not fall through because of an approach to the father which the mother did not want, it was impossible to say that they had improperly exercised their discretion. Thus whether the father learns of the adoption application is a matter for the adoption agency and not for the court.

It is suggested that the decision in *Re L (A Minor) (Adoption: Procedure)* is worrying. Unless the court is told why no details about the father have been provided it is lacking a piece of information which may be relevant to its assessment of whether the child's welfare will be served by adoption. Whilst it is clear from the rules that the decision whether to pursue enquiries about the father is one for the agency, the court's duty under section 6 of the Act is to be satisfied that adoption is for the welfare of the child, and it is suggested that it should not arrive at this finding on the basis of incomplete knowledge. The scope of the Court of Appeal's ruling is not clear, but if it is taken to mean that a court should make no enquiries as to why information about the father has been omitted from the Schedule 2 report that is surely to leave too much power in the hands of the agency. Whilst in the particular case the mother's reasons for denying the father knowledge of his paternity may have been valid, in other cases she may have improper motives of which the court should be aware. It is suggested that fresh consideration should be given to whether it should be the adoption agency, or the court, which finally determines whether a father who can be identified and traced should nonetheless be excluded from being involved in the adoption proceedings.

Dispensing with agreement to adoption

Section 16(1) of the Adoption Act 1976 enables a court to dispense with a parent's agreement to the making of the adoption order where it is satisfied that one of the grounds in section 16(2) has been established. Similarly, the court may dispense with the parent's agreement to adoption in a freeing application brought under section 18. The grounds are:

'that the parent or guardian—
(a) cannot be found or is incapable of giving agreement;
(b) is withholding his agreement unreasonably;
(c) has persistently failed without reasonable cause to discharge his parental responsibility for the child;

(d) has abandoned or neglected the child;
(e) has persistently ill-treated the child;
(f) has seriously ill-treated the child.'

Paragraphs (c) to (f) are each concerned with fault on the part of the parent, and in practice are rarely relied upon. Paragraph (a) is concerned with those cases where a parent cannot be traced or where he or she lacks the mental capacity to give agreement. The provision which is almost always relied on in practice is paragraph (b) and the discussion below concentrates on that provision.[5]

The parent is withholding his or her agreement unreasonably

Unlike paragraphs (c) to (f), paragraph (b), which allows a court to dispense with parental agreement on the ground that it is being unreasonably withheld, contains no built-in standards of behaviour which have been breached. The meaning of the phrase has been the subject of much judicial exposition. The classic statement is contained in Lord Hailsham's speech in *Re W (An Infant)*[6] and it needs to be quoted extensively in order to capture the essence of the test which the courts must apply. Lord Hailsham approved as authoritative the passage from the judgment of Lord Denning MR in *Re L (An Infant)*[7] in which he said:

'In considering the matter I quite agree that: (1) the question whether she is unreasonably withholding her consent is to be judged at the date of the hearing; and (2) the welfare of the child is not the sole consideration; and (3) the one question is whether she is unreasonably withholding her consent. But I must say that in considering whether she is reasonable or unreasonable we must take into account the welfare of the child. A reasonable mother surely gives great weight to what is better for the child. Her anguish of mind is quite understandable; but it may still be unreasonable for her to withhold consent. We must look to see whether it is reasonable or unreasonable according to what a reasonable woman in her place would do in all the circumstances of the case.'

Lord Hailsham said:

'From this it is clear that the test is reasonableness and not anything else. It is not culpability. It is not indifference. It is not

5 For an account of the case law on the other provisions see the *Inter-Departmental Review of Adoption Law, Discussion Paper No 2, Agreement and Freeing* (DoH, 1991).
6 [1971] 2 All ER 49.
7 (1962) 106 Sol Jo 611: see ibid, at p 55.

failure to discharge parental duties. It is reasonableness and reasonableness in the context of the totality of the circumstances. But although welfare per se is not the test, the fact that a reasonable parent does pay regard to the welfare of his child must enter into the question of reasonableness as a relevant factor. It is relevant in all cases if and to the extent that a reasonable parent would take it into account. It is decisive in those cases where a reasonable parent must so regard it'.[8]

Later in his speech Lord Hailsham said:

'...it does not follow from the fact that the test is reasonableness that any court is entitled simply to substitute its own view for that of the parents. In my opinion, it should be extremely careful to guard against this error. Two reasonable parents can perfectly reasonably come to opposite conclusions on the same set of facts without forfeiting their right to be regarded as reasonable. The question in any given case is whether a parental veto comes within the band of possible reasonable decisions and not whether it is right or mistaken. Not every reasonable exercise of judgment is right, and not every mistaken exercise of judgment is unreasonable. There is a band of decisions within which no court should seek to replace the individual's judgment with his own'.[9]

When considering the question of the reasonableness of the parental veto it should be remembered that the Adoption Act 1976 imposes two conditions which must be complied with before an adoption order can be made. The first is under section 6, which requires that the court be satisfied before making an adoption order that adoption will safeguard and promote the welfare of the child throughout his childhood. It is only after the court has made a positive finding in favour of adoption that the court moves to the second consideration, namely whether the parental veto to adoption falls within or outside the band of possible reasonable decisions. It is solely where the veto falls outside this band that the court may dispense with the parent's agreement, despite the fact that the court has already determined that adoption would be in the interests of the child. How the test of reasonableness should be applied has been considered in a number of contexts.

An influential factor in determining whether the parent is unreasonable in withholding his or her agreement to adoption is what the consequences for the child will be if an adoption order is refused. In baby adoption cases the normal outcome will be that the child will return to the care of his or

8 Ibid, at p 55.
9 Ibid, at p 56.

her mother; in step-parent adoptions the child will normally remain with the parent and step-parent regardless of whether an adoption order is made; in cases involving children in care who are enjoying contact with their birth families reasonableness is likely to revolve around contact arrangements, and whether a form of 'open adoption' is thought desirable. It is therefore suggested that care should be taken before statements made in one context are extrapolated and applied in a different context.

Baby adoptions and dispensing with agreement

It has been seen that delay is built into the adoption process and that adoption orders under section 16 are not normally made until several months, and often as much as a year, after the placement of the child with the prospective adopters. Where a mother of a baby agrees to her child's adoption the law indicates that she can withdraw her agreement at any time until the adoption order is made. However, once the mother sets the adoption process in motion her action has an impact not only on herself, but also on the child and the applicants to adopt. The difficulty facing the courts is that the child, in the time between his placement and the adoption hearing, will almost certainly have formed close bonds of attachment with the prospective adopters. Expert opinion evidence is likely to be given that to remove the child from the only home he has ever known and to place him with his mother, who is a stranger to him, is likely to cause him serious psychological damage, particularly where there are unstable features about the mother's household, as was the situation in *Re W (An Infant)*[10] itself. The adopters too will have had their hopes and expectations raised, and as Lord Reid said in *O'Connor v A and B*[11] 'the adopting family cannot be ignored either. If it was the mother's action which brought them in in the first place, they ought not to be displaced without good reason.' Thus although the mother has in no sense been culpable in her behaviour towards her child it may nonetheless be unreasonable for her to change her mind and to seek to recover the care of her child. The dilemma in a case of this kind is how to balance the welfare of the child against the prima facie reasonableness of the mother's decision to bring up her own child herself.

In circumstances where the child's welfare positively demands that he be adopted the House of Lords ruled in *Re W (An Infant)* that a reasonable mother may be expected to put aside her own anguish of mind and to agree to the child's adoption. In *Re H (Infants) (Adoption: Parental Consent)*[12] Ormrod LJ pointed out that 'it ought to be recognised by all

10 [1971] 2 All ER 49.
11 [1971] 2 All ER 1230 at p 1232.
12 [1977] 2 All ER 339n at p 340.

concerned with adoption cases that once formal consent has been given, or perhaps once the child has been placed with adopters, time begins to run against the mother and, as time goes on, it gets progressively more and more difficult for her to show that the withdrawal of her consent is reasonable.' The fact that the mother has vacillated in her intentions is not conclusive that she is being unreasonable but it is a further factor which weighs against her.[13]

However, the majority of contested baby cases were decided some time ago, when the pendulum then had swung markedly in favour of giving considerable weight to the child's welfare. For example, in *Re P (An Infant)*[14] the Court of Appeal considered the quality of the mother's lifestyle, compared it unfavourably with the opportunities offered to the child by the adopters and concluded that the mother was withholding her agreement unreasonably. Since then the Court of Appeal has stated that there must be a limit to this shift towards the prioritising of the child's welfare, and the indications are that it is swinging back towards giving greater consideration to the parent's position. Thus in *Re E (A Minor) (Adoption)*[15] the mother of two children accepted that adoption was in the best interests of her younger child who had been taken into care, but nonetheless opposed it. Allowing the mother's appeal against the decision of the trial judge to dispense with her agreement, the Court of Appeal said that he had failed to consider properly what weight the hypothetical reasonable parent would give to the interests of her other child, who had a loving relationship with his half brother. Furthermore, the fact that two witnesses, a teacher and a social worker, held the view that the mother was capable of looking after the child was something she was entitled to take into account when reaching her decision, as was the fact that although the local authority had prospective adopters in mind, the placement had not, as yet, been tested. The court therefore concluded that the mother's refusal to consent to the adoption was within the band of possible reasonable decisions. 'She may have been wrong, she may have been mistaken, but she was not unreasonable.'[16]

It is not clear how far this approach would be applied in a case where the mother initially agrees to her child being adopted and subsequently changes her mind. A crucial factor in this type of case is that the child, in the meanwhile, has formed strong attachment bonds with the prospective adopters, and the issue for the court is likely to focus on whether severing these bonds will cause him psychological damage. By contrast, in *Re E (A Minor) (Adoption)* the child was in foster care, and had not forged links with an alternative family. However, there is evidence to suggest that the

13 *Re P (Adoption: Parental Agreement)* [1985] FLR 635; *Re G* [1990] 2 FLR 429.
14 [1977] 1 All ER 182.
15 [1989] 1 FLR 126.
16 Ibid, per Balcombe LJ at p 133.

courts are more sympathetic towards parents who wish to retain links with their children, and less prepared to give considerable weight to the child's welfare.[17]

Is adoption by a step-parent in the child's interests?

Many children live in families with a birth parent and a step-parent. This situation arises where the mother or father has had children by a previous unmarried relationship, or where an earlier marriage has ended by divorce, or where the mother or father of the children has died. Sometimes couples who already have children by different partners marry and thus each spouse is both a birth parent and a step-parent. Where the birth parent and step-parent wish for their family relationship to be cemented through the process of adoption they must apply jointly for an adoption order. If the step-parent were the sole applicant an adoption order to him would sever the child's legal relationship with both his birth parents, and not merely the parent he was replacing.[18] The question whether adoption by step-parents is normally in the best interests of children is controversial. In step-parent cases there is no issue about whether the child will continue to have his home with his parent and step-parent; and in an opposed case the court does not face the difficulty that the child will be removed from the applicants if an adoption order is not made. The welfare question revolves around the key question whether altering the child's status relationship with his natural parent and his step-parent will be of more benefit to him than retaining the status quo.

The advantages of adoption are mainly in the intangible consequences of the order on the emotional links between the parties. A step-parent who adopts is committing himself to a relationship with the child which has as much to do with putting into legal form the expression of his love for the child, and of the child's love for him, as it has with altering the parties' status. Adoption is also an expression of commitment to the marriage, and it may be seen by the spouses as a method of publicly affirming the permanence of their relationship and of the viability of their family as a unit. A consequence of adoption may therefore be an improvement in the relationships between members of the family because they feel more secure as a result of the step-parent's de facto commitments having been legally recognised. A more practical benefit flows from the legal consequence that the child's name can be changed to that of the step-parent. Research reveals

---

17 See too *Re H; Re W* (1983) 4 FLR 614.
18 The *Review of Adoption Law*, para19.3, recommends that a new order should be available only to step-parents which does not make the birth parent an adoptive parent.

that the lack of a common surname is important to the majority of those seeking step-parent adoption orders.[19]

Anxieties that step-parent adoption orders may not promote the welfare of the child relate to concerns about the impact on the child of the severance by law of his ties with his birth parent and one half of his natural family. Thus where a child is adopted by his step-father not only does he lose a birth father and acquire an adoptive father, he also loses his legal relationship with his paternal grandparents and other paternal relatives.[20] In the Adoption Law Review, the opinion is expressed that:

> 'Where the prime motivation behind an adoption application is the wish to cement the family unit and put away the past, this may be confusing and lead to identity problems for the child, especially if (as is statistically not unlikely) the new marriage breaks down. It is also possible that the step-parent's family has little or no involvement or interest in the adopted child, so that the child loses one family without really gaining another'.[1]

Other anxieties relate to the reasons why the parent and step-parent are applying to adopt. So, for example, the child's guardian ad litem and the court are likely to wish to discover whether they are making the application in order to conceal a previous failed marriage, or the fact that a child was born when the mother was unmarried, or to cut the birth father out of the child's life, rather than because they take the view that the child will benefit from the change in status.[2] The impact of the Child Support Act 1991 has created a different ground for concern about motives, namely whether the natural father's agreement to his child's adoption is influenced by the financial consideration that his support obligation will come to an end, and not because he no longer is interested in the child.

The court is specifically directed in section 6 to consider the wishes and feelings of the child and to give due consideration to them before making an adoption order. The question whether the child has sufficient age and understanding to appreciate what he is being asked takes on a special significance in the context of step-parent adoptions because of the far-

---

19 J Masson, D Norbury and S G Chatterton *Mine, Yours or Ours? A Study of Step-Parent Adoption* (1983, HMSO). On change of name see the Children Act 1989, s.13(1)(a). After divorce a parent is not entitled to change a child's surname without the agreement of the other parent or the leave of the court and the courts have been very reluctant to grant such leave, *W v A (Child: Surname)* [1981] 1 All ER 100; *Re F (Child: Surname)* [1993] 2 FLR 837n.

20 Whether in practice these are lost will depend on whether the adoptive parents are willing to maintain these links for the child, at least until the child is old enough to make his own decisions.

1 Para 19.2.

2 *Re S (Infants) (Adoption by Parent)* [1977] 3 All ER 671.

reaching effects of an adoption order. Thus in *Re S (Infants) (Adoption by Parent)*[3] the views of three children aged between six and 11 were largely discounted because they were thought to be too young to understand the full effects of adoption.

Dispensing with agreement to a step-parent adoption

Where after divorce and remarriage a parent and step-parent apply to adopt, and where the application is opposed by the other parent, it is very unlikely that the court will find that adoption will promote the child's welfare. The order extinguishes for ever the father's parental responsibility for the child and cuts him out of the child's life and it is therefore almost invariably against the child's interests. As Cumming-Bruce LJ said in *Re B (A Minor) (Adoption: Jurisdiction)*:[4]

> 'Where there has been a divorce and the parent...has married again, and seeks with her new husband by adoption to extinguish the relationship between the children and their father, against the will of the father who honestly wishes to preserve his relationship, and who is not said to be culpable, it is likely to be difficult to discover any benefit to the child from the adoption commensurate with the probable long-term disadvantages'.

He continued 'it is quite wrong to use the adoption law to extinguish the relationship between the protesting father and the child, unless there is some really serious factor which justifies the use of the statutory guillotine'.

It is only where the court decides that adoption by a parent and step-parent is in the child's interests that the question arises whether the parent is being unreasonable in withholding his agreement. In *Re S*[5] the husband had deserted his wife before the child was born so that the child had never known his father, the mother was living in a stable relationship with the step-father and they applied to adopt the child. The husband refused his consent. The Court of Appeal said that the question to ask was 'would a reasonable father who had not seen the child at all, apart from a short visit when the child was three weeks old, withhold his consent to adoption, the adoption being plainly to the advantage of the child'. Ormrod LJ took the view that just as Lord Denning in *Re L (An Infant)*[6] had said that a reasonable mother gave great weight to what was best for her child, so too a reasonable father would surely give great weight to the nature of the

3   Above.
4   [1975] 2 All ER 449 at p 461.
5   (1978) 9 Fam Law 88.
6   (1962) 106 Sol Jo 611.

relationship existing between him and the child, and what it was likely to be in the future. He held that if that test was applied to the facts of the case there was only one answer: the father was unreasonably withholding his agreement.

Adoption, contact and children in care

The question whether it is for the welfare of a child in care to be adopted is normally inextricably linked with the question whether it is in his interests to continue to have contact with his parents.[7] In the latter situation, a long-term foster placement may provide the child with the security he needs without severing the links with his natural family. The determination of whether fostering or adoption will better serve the child's welfare is further complicated by the fact that there are differing views on whether 'open adoption', which allows for some kind of continuing contact between the child and his natural parents, is a desirable outcome. It may not be realistic to think that prospective adopters will be found who will encourage such contact. Some adopters may be prepared to countenance a form of open adoption, but many find continuing parental contact inconsistent with the concept of adoption itself, and they are not willing to offer themselves as adopters unless the arrangement is exclusive. Thus the continuation of parental contact may undermine the adoption process itself because suitable applicants are not forthcoming.[8]

In some cases the question whether a child in care should have contact with his parents is determined at the time when the care order is made. The local authority may take the view that rehabilitation with the parents will not be possible, and that adoption will therefore be the best arrangement for the child, in which case they should state this in their care plan. Where this is the local authority's position they may seek an order authorising them to terminate contact with the parents at the same time as they apply for the care order.[9] Where the children have suffered serious harm, as in *Re N (Minors) (Care Orders: Termination of Parental Conduct)*[10] the court may decide that the case is one which requires 'robust management', and that the interests of the children dictate that there should be an immediate termination of contact. However, in most cases a local authority will initially attempt to rehabilitate a child with his parents. But where attempts at rehabilitation fail, the authority may then conclude

7   Under s.34 of the Children Act 1989 a local authority are normally under a duty to allow the child reasonable contact with his parents.
8   See Butler-Sloss LJ in *Re A (A Minor) (Adoption: Contact)* [1993] 2 FLR 645 at pp 649-50.
9   Children Act 1989, s.34(4).
10 [1994] 2 FCR 1101.

that contact should be terminated, their purpose being to end the child's family links so that adoption can be considered as the long-term plan for the child.

In *Re B (Minors) (Care: Contact: Local Authority's Plans)*[10a] Butler-Sloss LJ said that:

> 'The presumption of contact, which has to be for the benefit of the child, has always to be balanced against the long-term welfare of the child and particularly where he will live in the future. Contact must not be allowed to destabilise or endanger the arrangements for the child and in many cases the plans for the child will be decisive of the contact application.'

However, in a significant ruling on the division of responsibility for decision-making between the courts and local authorities, she stated that the denial of contact is a decision for the court and not the local authority, and that a court is not bound to make an order which is consistent with the local authority's plan that the child should be adopted. Where the court takes the view that the benefits of contact outweigh the disadvantages of the disrupting the local authority's plan that the child should be adopted it must refuse the authority's application to terminate contact.

This was the position in *Re E (A Minor) (Care Order: Contact)*.[11] The local authority, in an agreed application for a care order, applied at the same time for an order authorising them to refuse the children contact with their parents. Their plan was that contact should gradually be reduced and finally terminated when the children were placed with prospective adoptive parents. However, the guardian ad litem took the view that the children would benefit from continuing face-to-face contact with their parents, and that the parents would not undermine the children's placement whether it was in an adoption setting or a long-term fostering setting. The trial judge held that the court should not make an order which was incompatible with the local authority's care plan unless the children's welfare demanded otherwise. The Court of Appeal, following *Re B (Minors) (Care: Contact: Local Authority's Plans)* ruled that this approach was incorrect, and that the decision to terminate contact was one for the court to make after considering the merits of the application. It held that section 34 of the Children Act 1989 created a strong presumption in favour of continuing parental contact, and that the onus was on the local authority to show why it should be discontinued. It held that it was premature for the court to authorise the termination of contact until the local authority had made some positive efforts to find prospective adopters who would

10a [1993] 1 FLR 543 at p 551.
11 [1994] 1 FLR 146.

accept some form of parental contact with the children. It added that it was not enough for the local authority to dismiss the likelihood of obtaining suitable adopters who were prepared to entertain an open adoption on the basis that there were none on the register at the time. In relation to the value to the children of continuing parental contact when adoption was planned, Simon Brown LJ said:

> 'Even when the section 31 criteria are satisfied, contact may well be of singular importance to the long-term welfare of the child: first, in giving the child the security of knowing that his parents love him and are interested in his welfare; secondly, by avoiding any damaging sense of loss to the child seeing himself abandoned by his parents; thirdly, by enabling the child to commit himself to the substitute family with the seal of approval of the natural parents; and fourthly, by giving the child the necessary sense of personal and family identity. Contact, if maintained, is capable of reinforcing and increasing the chances of success of a permanent placement, whether on a long-term fostering basis or by adoption.'[12]

Where the parents will not agree to the child being adopted and wish to maintain contact, difficulty sometimes arises as to how the matter should proceed. Should the authority take steps to free the child for adoption and seek an order dispensing with the parents' agreement, or should they first apply for an order authorising the termination of contact? In *Re E (Minors) (Adoption: Parental Agreement)*[13] the Court of Appeal held that until the question of contact had been decided it was premature to issue a freeing application. This approach was reaffirmed in *Re C (Minors) (Adoption)*[14] in which Balcombe LJ stated 'with all the emphasis at our command' that where children are in care, but are enjoying beneficial contact with a parent, it is premature to make an application for a freeing order until the issue of contact is first determined. He further stated that it is wholly inappropriate to assert that a parent who seeks to continue such contact at the date of the freeing application is unreasonably withholding her agreement to an order freeing the child for adoption. Subsequently Butler-Sloss LJ in *Re A (A Minor) (Adoption: Contact)*[15] held that these cases have been overtaken now that it is possible under the Children Act 1989 to attach a contact order to a freeing order. However the sentiments expressed in the cases on the association between contact and the appropriateness of adoption

---

12 Ibid, at pp 154-5. It is unclear whether these assertions by Simon Brown LJ are supported by empirical studies. For a review of research findings relating to adoption, see the analysis by J Thoburn in *The Review of Adoption Law* (DoH, 1992) appendix C.

13 [1990] 2 FLR 397.

14 [1992] 1 FLR 115.

15 [1993] 2 FLR 645.

continue to be applicable. Procedurally it is now deemed to be appropriate for a freeing application to be heard concurrently with an application to terminate contact.[16]

It is therefore the case that the question whether it is in the interests of a child in care to continue to have contact with his parents is highly relevant when a court is determining whether it is reasonable for a parent to refuse to agree to the child's adoption. In *Re H; Re W (Adoption: Parental Agreement)*[17] Purchas LJ said that the chances of a successful reintroduction to, or continuance of contact with, the natural parent is a critical factor in assessing the reaction of the hypothetical reasonable parent. In *Re E (Minors) (Adoption: Parental Agreement)*[18] a mother of children in care had done everything within her limited power to preserve contact with her children. However, the local authority terminated contact and the magistrates' court adjourned the mother's contact application pending the outcome of the local authority's application to free the children for adoption.[19] The Court of Appeal held that the mother was not unreasonable if she withheld her agreement to her children being freed for adoption until issues relating to contact had been resolved, and until she had had a proper opportunity to demonstrate that continuing contact with her children would benefit them. It was further held that since the prospective adopters had stated that they would not abandon the children if they could not adopt them that this was also a factor which a reasonable parent could take into account. A similar approach to contact was taken by the Court of Appeal in *Re C (Minors) (Adoption)*.[20] It held that where a child in care was enjoying beneficial contact with a parent it was wholly inappropriate to assert that a parent who was showing a keen interest in continuing having such contact at the date of the freeing application was unreasonably withholding his agreement. In *Re E (A Minor) (Adoption)*[1] a mother of a child in care refused to agree to her child's adoption because his elder brother was devoted to him and had regular contact with him. The Court of Appeal held that was not being unreasonable. As Balcombe LJ said 'she may have been wrong, she may have been mistaken, but she was not unreasonable.'

16 In *G v G (Adoption: Concurrent Applications)* [1993] 2 FLR 306 Cazalet J, following *Re G (A Minor) (Adoption and Access Applications)* [1980] FLR 109, held that where there were competing contact and adoption applications both applications should be heard concurrently so that all available options were open to the court when it was making its decision as to what the child's welfare required. The case concerned an application by a mother and step-father to adopt, and where the unmarried father sought contact.

17 (1983) 4 FLR 614.

18 [1990] 2 FLR 397.

19 The mother's application was made under s.12C of the Child Care Act 1980, which preceded the Children Act 1989. It is not clear whether a local authority can continue to refuse contact under s.34(6) of the Children Act 1989 once an application is pending in the court.

20 [1992] 1 FLR 115.

1 [1989] 1 FLR 126.

In *Re A (A Minor) (Adoption: Contact)*[2] the Court of Appeal took a fresh look at the reasonableness of a parent's refusal to agree to a freeing application made in respect of her child in care in the light of changes in the law brought about by the Children Act 1989. Applications had been made by the local authority for a freeing order and for leave to terminate contact between the child and his mother.[3] Both applications were heard together. At the hearing the guardian ad litem advised the judge that the child should be freed for adoption, but that continuing contact between the child and his mother and other family members was in the child's best interests. The judge found that there was no prospect of the child being rehabilitated with his natural family, that long-term fostering was a less suitable option for the child than adoption, and that adoption would still be in the child's best interests even if the adopters chosen for him could not tolerate any contact with the mother. He found that a reasonable mother would recognise that adoption was the right decision for her son and he therefore made an order freeing the child for adoption, and dispensed with the mother's agreement on the grounds that it was being unreasonably withheld. However, in addition he exercised powers under section 8 of the Children Act 1989 to order that the child should have monthly contact with his mother until the adoption took place.

The mother appealed against the freeing order arguing that continuing substantial contact and freeing were inconsistent and therefore that her refusal to agree to the freeing application was reasonable. The Court of Appeal held that since the implementation of the Children Act 1989 a court has the opportunity not only to free a child for adoption, but also to preserve contact between the child and his natural family pending adoption by making a contact order under section 8. It therefore held that all issues relating to contact did not have to be resolved before a freeing order was made, and that the judge had been correct to dispense with the mother's agreement. Butler-Sloss LJ made it clear that the contact order would not survive the making of an adoption order, but stated that, in theory at least, a section 8 contact order could be imposed on the adopters when the adoption order was made.[4] She added that in the adoption proceedings, although the mother would no longer have parental responsibility she would have the right to be heard on whether she should have continuing contact after the adoption order was made.

It is suggested that the decision in *Re A (A Minor) (Adoption: Contact)* to use Children Act 1989 powers to make a contact order in freeing proceedings, when the local authority did not already have potential

2   [1993] 2 FLR 645.
3   The father too was involved, but the issues taken on appeal concerned the mother only.
4   She said that this would be an alternative to making an adoption order with conditions under s.16 of the Adoption Act 1976. However, she foresaw dangers in different judges being involved in future applications concerning the adoption and the continuance of contact, and said that steps should be taken to guard against different courts arriving at different decisions.

adopters who were prepared to enter into an open adoption, did little to promote the welfare of the child. Indeed the contact order appears to have been positively counter-productive in furthering the adoption plans for the child. The general principle enshrined in section 1(2) of the Children Act 1989 is that any delay in determining a question about a child's upbringing is likely to prejudice the welfare of the child. In the case of a young child who needs to form permanent attachments as soon as possible, such delay may be extremely damaging.[5] Yet eight months after the freeing order a suitable adoptive family had not been found for the child, and evidence was given that this was because of the effect of the contact order on the willingness of prospective adopters to put themselves forward. Sections 18(5) and 12(3)(a) of the Adoption Act 1976 state that parental responsibility is given to the adoption agency on a freeing order being made, and that the order operates to extinguish the parental responsibility which any person has for the child immediately before the order was made. It is suggested that for a court to free a child for adoption and at the same time to make a contact order under section 8 should normally be regarded as being inconsistent with these provisions unless it knows that there are adopters who are willing to accept the child on these terms.

A similar problem arose in *Re P (Adoption: Freeing Order)*[6] where the trial judge combined a freeing order, in which he dispensed with the mother's agreement, with a contact order. However, the case differed from *Re A (A Minor) (Adoption: Contact)* because the judge not only found that it was in the interests of the children for contact with their mother to continue but, crucially, he also found that the mother would not be unreasonable in withholding her agreement to the adoption if it meant that she would lose contact with her children. Allowing the mother's appeal against the freeing order, Butler-Sloss LJ held that a court cannot guarantee that adoption with contact will be possible at the time that it makes a freeing order. She therefore held that the judge had been wrong to dispense with the mother's agreement where he had concluded that he did not have grounds to do so unless contact would continue. She said that the judge had:

> 'fallen between two stools in not saying either "adoption in any event although contact is highly desirable", or leave it to the adoption application where the mother can fight her corner as to whether or not at that stage the adopters should be accepting contact or there should not be an adoption order.'[7]

5 In *Re A (A Minor) (Adoption: Contact)* the child concerned was three.
6 [1994] 2 FLR 1000.
7 Ibid, at p 1004.

Thus it is clear from *Re P (Adoption: Freeing Order)* that a court should not free a child for adoption against the wishes of the parent where it takes the view that adoption should only be authorised on the condition that contact with the parent continues to take place. Moreover, as Butler-Sloss LJ pointed out, the effect of the freeing order had been to tie the local authority's hands as to the persons they could select as adopters for the children. Although optimism had been expressed at the original hearing that suitable adopters would be forthcoming, seven months after the judge's order such adopters had not been found. The ruling also illustrates the difficulties faced by local authorities when planning for children in care. The Court of Appeal recognised that the children were difficult to place for adoption because there was a history of serious mental illness in the family. It also recognised that adopters might be found for the children who could accept the risk of the children developing mental illness, but who would not be able to tolerate continuing contact with the mother. But, in a case of this kind, unless a court makes an unconditional freeing order, the decision whether contact is more important than adoption is delayed until the application to adopt is made. This in itself may make it difficult to obtain prospective adopters for children who are continuing to have contact with their natural parents. Adopters may not be prepared to put themselves forward unless they are satisfied that questions relating to consent, and to contact, have been resolved. Yet, at the same time, it may be in the interests of the children to have contact with their natural mother until an alternative family is found, and perhaps after it has been found. And a parent may not be unreasonable in withholding her agreement to adoption unless and until such an alternative family is found. Thus the problem can become circular, and identifying at which point the circle should be broken may be an extremely difficult decision to make. Stating that the welfare of the child should be treated as paramount is easy. Determining how to give effect to that principle can sometimes demand a degree of wisdom and foresight with which the best-intentioned of decision-makers are not necessarily endowed.

Chapter 5

Personal protection and regulating the occupation of the matrimonial home

Chapter 5

Personal protection and regulating the occupation of the matrimonial home

The law's response to domestic violence

One of the most dangerous symptoms of conflict in personal relationships is when it escalates into domestic violence. According to studies the incidence of such violence is high and 'spouse killings were found to occur almost exclusively against a background of severe marital discord'.[1] Domestic violence occurs between people of all social classes, amongst all racial and religious groupings and in all age groups.[2] Crime and other statistics provide only a rough estimate of the nature and extent of the suffering which is endured by families behind closed doors, but there can be no doubt that parents and children living in households in which assaults take place are damaged by this behaviour, both physically and emotionally. Victims of domestic assaults often do not complain of violence, either through fear of being further assaulted, or because they are too embarrassed and ashamed to reveal their plight to professionals who might be able to assist them. Wife beating is not regarded with the same revulsion as child beating; indeed, until recently, it was not identified as a social problem which required addressing by agencies concerned with the welfare of families. It was during the late 1960s that the pernicious nature of domestic violence started to exercise the minds of law reformers,[3] but not

1 See A Wallace *Homicide: The Social Reality* Research Study No 5, Bureau of Crime Statistics and Research, NSW Attorney General's Department (1986). See generally, R Graycar and J Morgan *The Hidden Gender of Law* (The Federation Press, 1984), ch 11; M D A Freeman *Violence in the Home* (1979) Farnborough, Saxon House.
2 See M Russel *Taking Stock: Refuge Provisions in London in the late 1980s*, Southwark Council (1989); United Nations Centre for Social Development and Humanitarian Affairs *Violence against Women in the Family* (1989).
3 Who were stimulated into taking action by such pioneering women as Erin Pizzey who opened the first women's refuge in Chiswick, and who subsequently published a dramatic account of the horrors of domestic violence and the failure of the law to provide safeguards for its victims in *Scream Quietly or the Neighbours Will Hear*, Harmondsworth (Penguin Books, 1974).

until the 1970s that the political will was found to create a legislative framework designed to meet the needs of battered women.[4] Of course women are not the only victims of domestic assaults; men, children and the elderly are vulnerable to domestic violence too. However, there is an abundance of evidence to show that it is women and children who are the main victims. Children who themselves suffer violence at the hands of a parent are in the main protected by the state through child protection procedures.[5] The remedies provided by the civil law are therefore generally used to obtain protection for an adult victim. But where that victim is looking after children, any orders or injunctions which she obtains will normally assist the children too. For children to witness violence is undoubtedly a damaging experience, and it will be seen that the welfare of such children may influence the courts in the exercise of their discretion.

The role of the criminal law

Domestic assaults are criminal offences and a man who has attacked his wife can be prosecuted for his actions. He may be charged with one or more of various offences against the person,[6] including the offence of rape.[7] However, victims of domestic violence may be reluctant to become involved in the prosecution process for a number of reasons. These include the realisation by the victim that the matter is no longer under her control once she has reported an attack to the police. It will be up to the police to decide whether and how they wish to investigate her complaint, and it will be the decision of the Crown Prosecution Service whether or not to go ahead and press charges. This loss of control acts as a disincentive to women to report incidents of violence, as they may well fear the consequences of their action if the police and Crown Prosecution Service fail, as they see it, to respond in an appropriate fashion. In the past the police have been unwilling to intervene in cases of domestic violence, and to prosecute offenders. This perception of the police as unwilling to come to the assistance of victims of domestic assaults is still evident today, even though

4   House of Commons Select Committee on Violence in Marriage *Report, Minutes of Evidence and Appendices* (HMSO, 1974-5). In the reported case law on domestic violence the woman is virtually always the complainant, and the use of the personal pronouns 'he' and 'she' in this chapter reflects this fact.
5   See ch 3.
6   See the major textbooks on criminal law for details of these offences.
7   It was not until 1991 that the House of Lords ruled that a man could be convicted of the offence of rape when the victim was his wife: see *R v R (Rape: Marital Exemption)* [1991] 4 All ER 481. The House took a far more radical approach than the Law Commission which, somewhat timidly and conservatively, had recommended that such a change in the common law would require legislation; see Law Commission Working Paper No 116 *Rape Within Marriage* (1989).

domestic violence is taken much more seriously by the police than in the past, and even though police practices in many areas have changed radically in favour of the victim.[8]

Other factors which may deter a woman from becoming involved in the criminal process include the fear of further, and perhaps more vicious, assaults on her person in retaliation for her action; anxiety about the financial hardship which the family would suffer if the man were to lose his job; and a more general reluctance to be instrumental in the man gaining a criminal record, and perhaps being sent to prison. Although a woman may wish to take steps to stop a man from assaulting her, such steps may not include taking the risk that the man (who is often the father of her children) will be sent to prison. Furthermore, the criminal law is concerned with identifying and punishing criminals, whereas what the victim of domestic violence needs is protection against further assaults once the punishment process has come to an end.

Criminal injuries compensation

The question whether a woman might be entitled to receive criminal injuries compensation is an important factor which should be taken into account when advising a woman whether to press for the prosecution of her assailant. Any victim of an assault is potentially able to make a claim under the criminal injuries compensation scheme. However, where the victim lives in the same household as the perpetrator, as a member of the same family, she can only claim compensation if she satisfies certain conditions.[9] Amongst these conditions there is one stating that the perpetrator of the violence must either have been successfully prosecuted for the offence, or the Criminal Injuries Compensation Board must be satisfied there are good reasons why such a prosecution has not taken place. Clearly the amount of compensation the woman would be likely to receive if her application to the Board were successful, and what amounts to good reasons for the Board's purposes, should influence any advice given.

Personal protection orders and non-molestation injunctions

The solution offered by the civil law to the brutality of domestic violence and to other forms of personal molestation is the personal protection order

---

8 See generally A Sanders *Personal Violence and Public Order: The Prosecution of 'Domestic' Violence in England and Wales* (1988) 16 Int J Soc L 359.
9 See the 26th Report of the Criminal Injuries Compensation Board, Cm 1365, 1990, App C.

or the injunction. Personal protection orders are made by magistrates who exercise a local jurisdiction which is easily accessible. Injunctions are granted by circuit judges and designated district judges sitting in county courts. In fact the majority of applications for protection against violence and other forms of molestation are made to the county courts for reasons which are explained below. Personal protection orders and injunctions are aimed at providing a speedy remedy for the victim which can be enforced through contempt proceedings, or through police involvement.

Personal protection orders

Magistrates/married couple only. — violence —

The jurisdiction of magistrates to make personal protection orders extends to married couples only. Magistrates have no power to make personal protection orders where the parties are unmarried either in relation to the parties themselves, or in relation to any children living with them. Magistrates are empowered to make orders where the respondent has used, or threatened to use, violence and where an order is necessary for the protection of the applicant or a child of the family. Section 16(2) of the Domestic Proceedings and Magistrates' Courts Act 1978 provides that—

> 'Where on an application for an order under this section the court is satisfied that the respondent has used, or threatened to use, violence against the person of the applicant or a child of the family and that it is necessary for the protection of the applicant or a child of the family that an order should be made under this subsection, the court may make one or both of the following orders, that is to say—
> (a) an order that the respondent shall not use, or threaten to use, violence against the person of the applicant;
> (b) an order that the respondent shall not use, or threaten to use, violence against the person of a child of the family.'

Early on in the life of the 1978 Act it was established that violence was confined to violence of a physical nature only. In *Horner v Horner*[10] magistrates had originally granted an order because of the husband's violence. Subsequently the husband started to harass his wife in a non-physical way. However it was held that she was unable to bring proceedings for breach of the order because the language of section 16 did not extend to the husband's non-violent behaviour.[11] At the time when the Act was

10 [1982] 2 All ER 495.
11 Instead she applied for an injunction under the Domestic Violence and Matrimonial Proceedings Act 1976: see below.

originally drafted this restriction on magistrates' powers was deliberately included; it was argued that adjudicating on allegations of psychological damage is very difficult and might involve magistrates making an assessment of evidence given by psychiatrists.[12] The Law Commission, having raised this probably baseless fear, then commented: 'This is a highly skilled task which we do not think can appropriately be placed on magistrates.'[13] It is suggested that it is somewhat anomalous that both then, and now, magistrates are entrusted with the task of adjudicating on evidence given by psychiatrists and other expert witnesses in applications brought in care proceedings to protect a child from suffering significant harm, yet the view is taken that they cannot be so trusted in domestic violence proceedings.

Where the actual or threatened violence is made against a child the child must be a 'child of the family'.[14] Such a child is a child of both parties to the marriage, or any other child (apart from a foster child) who has been treated by both parties as a child of their family.[15] Whilst this definition will cover most children living in households where the parents are married, it is suggested that its limitations do give rise to the risk that some vulnerable children could be excluded from the Act's protective scope. For example, where a woman already has a child by another man prior to her marriage, or where she has a child during the course of the marriage because of an adulterous relationship, it is suggested that such a child is more at risk of violence in a case where the husband has refused to treat him as a child of the family than in a case where the husband has so treated him.

There is no guidance in the Act itself as to when magistrates should deem an order to be 'necessary' for the protection of the applicant or a child of the family. In *McCartney v McCartney*[16] it was held that in considering whether or not to grant an exclusion order, the magistrates must assess whether the 'danger' of violence, which section 16(3) requires, is objectively observable, rather than merely subjectively feared by the complainant. By analogy, therefore, it is arguable that magistrates must, themselves, fear for the safety of the wife or child if the application for an order for personal protection is to be successful. However, despite granting a personal protection order in *McCartney v McCartney,* neither the magistrates, nor the appeal court, adverted to what test should be applied.

---

12 Many women complain of psychological abuse, and indeed find it harder to bear: see E Malos and G Hague *Domestic Violence and Housing: Local Authority Responses to Women and Children escaping Violence in the Home* Women's Aid Federation and School of Applied Social Studies, University of Bristol (1993). Contentious evidence from psychiatrists is not often given in court proceedings for domestic violence injunctions.
13 (1976) Law Com No 77, para 3.12.
14 For a more detailed account of obligations owed to a 'child of the family' see ch 8.
15 Domestic Proceedings and Magistrates' Courts Act 1978, s.88.
16 [1981] 1 All ER 597.

The magistrates did appear to have the same objective fear for the wife, as they granted her a personal protection order, with a power of arrest attached, 'in order to enable the parties to live in the same household fairly peacefully' despite the accepted good behaviour of the husband over the last four months.[17]

Emergency courts and expedited orders for personal protection

One of the main reasons for giving magistrates powers to make personal protection orders was to provide an emergency remedy for wives which is local and easily available. Section 16 makes provision for both emergency courts and expedited orders. Emergency courts can be convened to hear an application either for a personal protection order or an order excluding the respondent from the home.[18] These courts do not have to conform to the standard regulations concerning the composition of the court; whereas normally the court should consist of at least one member of each sex, for an emergency court all the members can be of the same sex. Furthermore, the restriction that each member of the court should be a member of the family panel does not apply.

An expedited personal protection order can be made against a husband who has either not been served with a summons, or has not been given reasonable notice of the proceedings. Consequently, an application for an expedited order will usually be heard ex parte, and may be heard by a single member of the family panel.[19] It is, of course, a very exceptional step for a court to make an order affecting a party's rights without his knowledge, and without giving him the opportunity to be heard. Hence the court can only make an expedited order where the wife or child is in 'imminent danger of physical injury',[1] and the order must be made for the shortest possible time.[2] Furthermore, the court has no power to make an expedited ouster order.

These limits on the courts' powers raise the question whether an expedited personal protection order, on its own, gives the wife the type of protection that she normally requires. The advantage of having a personal protection order is that if it is broken it can be enforced. The husband can be arrested for breach and either fined a maximum of £5,000, or imprisoned

---

17 The case was sent back for a rehearing on appeal for a number of reasons, including the fact that the magistrates had been prepared to make a finding about danger of injury in the future without having heard oral evidence from the husband.
18 S.16(5).
19 Family Proceedings Courts (Matrimonial Proceedings etc.) Rules 1991, rr. 2(1) and 25(a).
1 S.16(6).
2 See *Practice Direction* [1978] 1 WLR 925; *Ansah v Ansah* [1977] 2 All ER 638; *G v G (Ouster: Ex Parte Application)* [1990] 1 FLR 395.

for a maximum period of two months.[3] However, although that may be of some consolation to the wife, what she requires from a court order is not the husband's punishment for breach, but protection against further assaults in the future. If the making of a personal protection order is sufficient to deter the husband from attacking the wife, then its existence is clearly of value. But the wording of section 16(6) requires that she, or the child, must be in *imminent* danger before an expedited order can be made. The remedy therefore looks to be inadequate in those cases where the husband and wife are still living together, or where the wife is living in the matrimonial home. She needs an ex parte ouster order too; however, she cannot obtain such an order in the magistrates' court.

It has been recognised that the law in relation to personal protection orders is in urgent need of reform.[4] The jurisdiction of magistrates differs from that of judges granting non-molestation injunctions, with judges having more extensive powers. Furthermore, magistrates have recently lost their powers to make orders in relation to periodical payments for children, because enforceable child maintenance has been taken over by the Child Support Agency. This has resulted in a diminution of the already low number of applications for personal protection orders being made to magistrates.[5] Yet the whole purpose of giving jurisdiction to magistrates was to provide a speedy local jurisdiction. It is suggested that unless and until magistrates are given the same powers as judges in relation to responding to complaints of molestation, lawyers will continue to advise their clients to apply to the county courts for relief.

Non-molestation injunctions

It has been seen that magistrates may only make personal protection orders where there has been actual or threatened violence. By contrast, orders in the county court can be made against 'molestation'. Section 1(1) of the Domestic Violence and Matrimonial Proceedings Act 1976 provides that—

'Without prejudice to the jurisdiction of the High Court on an application by a party to a marriage a county court shall have

---

3 Magistrates' Courts Act 1980, s.63(3).
4 As is that relating to non-molestation injunctions. For reform proposals made by the Law Commission see Working Paper No 113 and Law Com No 207 *Domestic Violence and Occupation of the Family Home;* see further below.
5 The number of applications has been dropping steadily over a number of years, from 5,960 in 1987 to 2,260 in 1992; see Home Office Statistical Bulletin, Issue 26/93. A solicitor's choice of court is also strongly influenced by the rules relating to the provision of legal aid, which at present favour an application to the county court rather than the magistrates' court in cases of this kind.

jurisdiction to grant an injunction containing one or more of the following provisions, namely,—

    (a) a provision restraining the other party to the marriage from molesting the applicant

    (b) a provision restraining the other party to the marriage from molesting a child living with the applicant.'

Although section 1(1) refers to an application by a 'party to a marriage' this phrase is widened in section 1(2) to include persons who are 'living with each other in the same household as husband and wife'. This phrase is intended to include those couples who are living together 'on a stable basis.'[6] Prior to the 1976 Act unmarried women suffering violence at the hands of their partners could only bring an action in tort, which they rarely did, and which remedy was not without its difficulties.[7] Parliament recognised that such women are just as vulnerable to violence as married women and therefore included them within the remit of the legislation.[8] Subsequently difficulties have arisen over the meaning of this phrase, and unless the applicant falls within its scope she cannot use the 1976 Act to assist her.[9] However, once the applicant has established that she has the requisite status to make an application under the Act, the fact that she is not married to the respondent has no bearing on the court's decision.

'Molestation' covers the obvious case where the victim is subject to an assault or battery which could give rise to criminal proceedings. But, despite the reference to 'violence' in the title of the Act, it is clear that the court is not limited to granting injunctions in cases where violence or threats of violence occur. 'Violence is a form of molestation, but molestation may take place without the threat or use of violence and still be serious and inimical to mental and physical health.'[10] Any conduct which is a sufficient harassment of the victim as to call for intervention of the court can be the subject of an injunction.[11] Harassment can take a variety of forms. In *Horner v Horner*[12] the molestation by the husband took the form of handing the wife upsetting notes, and intercepting her on her way to the station. In *Spencer v Camacho,*[13] after a series of other activities for which the woman

6   Official Report (HC) Standing Committee F, 30 June 1976, col 5, Jo Richardson MP.

7   See S Maidment *The Law's Response to Marital Violence in England and the USA* (1977) 26 ICLQ 403.

8   See the Report of the Select Committee on Violence in Marriage HC 553 (1974-5).

9   See below for the difficulties to which this definition sometimes gives rise. Where the applicant falls outside its scope her only remedy lies in bringing an action in tort: see further below.

10   *Davis v Johnson* [1978] 1 All ER 1132, per Viscount Dilhorne at p 1144.

11   See generally Judge Nigel Fricker QC *Molestation and Harassment after Patel v Patel* (1988) 18 Fam Law 395.

12   [1982] 2 All ER 495.

13   (1984) 4 FLR 662.

had obtained non-molestation orders, riffling through her handbag was held to be sufficient conduct to amount to molestation. Other activities that have given rise to injunctions have included writing abusive letters and shouting obscenities,[14] and following the applicant around and making a 'perfect nuisance' of oneself.[15] The actual wording of the injunction will clearly be tailored to the needs of the particular case, but a usual form of wording is that the respondent is restrained from 'assaulting, molesting, annoying or otherwise interfering with the applicant or any child living with the applicant'.

It is suggested that any conduct which has the express purpose of harassing another family member should be subject to regulation by the law if sufficiently serious, and that the very wide definition of molestation is to be welcomed. However, in *Johnson v Walton*[16] the court was of the opinion that molestation involving harassment includes an *intent* to cause distress or harm. It is suggested that any restriction which requires that the conduct must be intentional would be unfortunate. It is certainly the case that where the respondent is physically violent towards the applicant an order can be granted regardless of intention, as demonstrated in *Wooton v Wooton*,[17] where the respondent only became violent during epileptic episodes. The Court of Appeal were clear that it was the actual violence, and the consequences suffered by the applicant, which were the important factors to be considered, and that the court therefore had jurisdiction to grant an injunction in such a case. There seems to be no reason in principle why the same should not apply to non-violent behaviour. A husband who, perhaps due to mental illness, is behaving in such a way that the court would normally intervene, may be causing just as much distress as if he were acting out of spite. Whilst concern and compassion should always be extended to the mentally ill, nonetheless, if the victim is finding the behaviour intolerable she should be just as much entitled to the protection of the law as the victim of intended action. Of course in cases where the respondent is so ill that he is incapable of understanding the nature and consequences of an injunction it ought not to be granted. The injunction would not have a deterrent effect because the respondent would not be capable of complying with it, and any breach could not be subject to effective enforcement proceedings since the respondent would have a clear defence to an application for committal for contempt, as in *Wookey v Wookey*.[18]

Normally a woman who is seeking a non-molestation injunction on the grounds of violence, or other serious misbehaviour, will also be seeking an

14 *George v George* [1986] 2 FLR 347.
15 *Vaughan v Vaughan* [1973] 1 WLR 1159.
16 [1990] 1 FLR 350.
17 [1984] FLR 871.
18 [1991] 3 All ER 365.

injunction which gives her exclusive occupation of the matrimonial home for a temporary period. However, this will not necessarily be the case. Sadly it is a fact that people get locked into destructive relationships and find it enormously difficult to break free from them. Some people, mainly but not exclusively women, wish to stay with their partner even though they are the victim of persistent violence. They may, therefore, still wish to remain living in the same household as their partner, but be seeking an order from the court to restrain any further violence being committed upon them. In *F v F (Protection From Violence: Continuing Cohabitation)*[19] it was held by judge Nigel Fricker QC[20] that an injunction cannot be granted to an applicant who is living, and intends to continue living, in full cohabitation with the respondent. The judge thought that Parliament cannot have intended that injunctions should be used to direct conduct between cohabiting couples under the threat that disobedience would amount to contempt of court. However, there is nothing in the wording of the Act to limit the jurisdiction to grant injunctions in this way and it is suggested that the decision was wrong. Many women continue to live with their violent partner. They should be afforded the protection of an injunction.[1]

Non-molestation of a child

An important protective element in the injunction which restrains the other 'party to the marriage' from molesting a child is that the child merely has to be living with the applicant.[2] There is no requirement that the child has to be one of the family, indeed he need not have any defined relationship at all with either the applicant or the respondent. Thus children such as foster-children are afforded protection under the 1976 Act.[3] Bringing all such children into the scope of the Act recognises that a child who is living with the applicant and who has not been treated as part of the family is liable to be a child most at risk. Jealousy and anger directed at a child who has no blood relationship with the man living in the household has led to tragedy in a number of well-known cases.[4] However, the drafting of section

---

19 [1989] 2 FLR 451. This is a rare example of a county court judgment being reported, rather than an appeal from such a judgment.
20 Who is an acknowledged expert on domestic violence injunctions and who has written extensively in this field.
1   For a critique of *F v F* see R Stevens *Protection or Not?* (1989) 19 Fam Law 464.
2   Domestic Violence and Matrimonial Proceedings Act 1976, s.1(1)(b).
3   In contrast to the position under the Domestic Proceedings and Magistrates' Courts Act 1978: see above.
4   See for example the reports into the deaths of Jasmine Beckford *A Child in Trust* (London Borough of Brent, 1985), and Kimberley Carlile *A Child in Mind* (London Borough of Greenwich, 1987), both of whom were killed by their step-fathers.

1(1)(b) may nonetheless prove to be seriously defective. If the woman has moved out of the home, perhaps because of the man's violence, and is now living elsewhere, and if the children remain living with the man, it could be argued that the woman cannot apply for an injunction on behalf of the children, even though she may fear for their safety, because they are no longer living with her. Whilst such an argument would probably fail in a case where the woman immediately takes proceedings on behalf of her children,[5] it seems that it would be almost bound to succeed if the alleged molestation of the children were to occur at some considerable time after the woman had left.

One solution to this problem would be to enable the child himself to apply for an injunction where he is the victim of molestation. It is well known that many women who are the victims of domestic violence feel powerless to protect themselves and their children, and it could be useful if steps could be taken on behalf of the child by interested persons who could act as the child's next friend.[6] Taking injunction proceedings might sometimes avoid the necessity to institute care proceedings on behalf of a child who is suffering, or who is likely to suffer, significant harm, and help to keep such a child safe within his own home.[7]

Tort and personal protection

Some groups of people, such as divorcees and ex-cohabitees, do not fall within the scope of the domestic violence legislation. The difficulty for such women, seeking an injunction to restrain conduct directed against them, is that they must ally their application for an injunction with an action for an established tort.[8] A woman can clearly bring an action for assault or trespass in cases where the man has physically assaulted her. However, conduct which falls within the definition of 'molestation' under the 1976 Act does not necessarily amount to a tort, and in *Patel v Patel*[9] the Court of Appeal confirmed that there is no such tort as the tort of harassment. Thus an ex-boyfriend who follows a woman around, writes upsetting notes to her, or persists in making constant unwanted telephone

---

5   This situation is analogous with where a woman is able to establish that she is living with her partner as husband and wife even though she has left him: see below.
6   See the Law Commission's proposals in Law Com No 207.
7   See ch 3 for when care proceedings can be taken to protect children from harm.
8   An action in tort has disadvantages. It is slower and less appropriate in cases where an emergency remedy is required, and the scope of injunctions is narrower: see below.
9   [1988] 2 FLR 179. The Court of Appeal upheld an order that the plaintiff's son-in-law should not assault or molest him, or trespass on his property. However, it confirmed that an injunction restraining the defendant from coming within 50 yards of the house had been correctly discharged by the judge, as such action did not consitute an actionable wrong.

calls to her is not necessarily guilty of tortious conduct. However, recent decisions have shown a willingness on the part of the courts to develop the law of tort in the areas of trespass and nuisance, and have opened the way for possible future developments.

In the old decisions of *Wilkinson v Downton*[10] and *Janvier v Sweeney*[11] it was established that lies or threats which the speaker knows are likely to cause physical harm, including through shock, are actionable. This aspect of the tort of trespass has been developed in the recent decision of *Burnett v George*.[12] The plaintiff complained of harassment by the defendant in a number of different ways after their relationship broke up. She was granted an injunction which restrained the defendant from 'assaulting, molesting or otherwise interfering with her.' On appeal the Court of Appeal stated that molestation and interference are not actionable wrongs, and it was therefore not just to grant an injunction to restrain them. However, they went on to say that where there was evidence that the health of the plaintiff was being impaired by such actions, and when those actions were calculated to create such impairment, then relief would be granted by way of an injunction to the extent that it would be necessary to avoid that impairment of health. In similar fashion in *Pidduck v Molloy*[13] an injunction simply not to speak to the plaintiff was held to be too wide. However, when the defendant had spoken to the plaintiff in the past it was usually for the purpose of 'intimidating, threatening or abusing her, all of which are capable of amounting to crimes or torts'.[14] The injunction was therefore modified to read 'not to speak to the plaintiff in an intimidatory, threatening or abusive manner'. The feature of both cases is that an injunction could be granted when the plaintiff suffered injury to her health caused by the defendant's behaviour. Commenting on these decisions, Judge Nigel Fricker QC has proposed that in future 'personal injury by molestation' would be the most appropriate name for the *Wilkinson v Downton* tort recognised in *Burnett v George*.[15]

The tort of nuisance is based on the right of an occupier to the peaceful use and enjoyment of his land. A cause of action in nuisance, therefore, has always lain at the instance of any person who has an interest in the land, but has been confined to such plaintiffs. However, in *Khorasandjian v Bush*[16] the Court of Appeal moved away from this limitation and opened

10 [1897] 2 QB 57.
11 [1919] 2 KB 316.
12 [1992] 1 FLR 525. For an interesting discussion of the ramifications of this decision see Judge Nigel Fricker QC *Personal Molestation or Harassment* (1992) 22 Fam Law 158. See also M Brazier *Personal Injury by Molestation — An Emergent or Established Tort?* (1992) 22 Fam Law 346.
13 [1992] 2 FLR 202.
14 Ibid, at p 205.
15 See Judge Nigel Fricker QC *Personal Molestation or Harassment* (1992) 22 Fam Law 158.
16 [1993] 3 All ER 669.

up the possibility of future developments. The plaintiff was a young woman whose friendship with the defendant had ceased. Since the end of their relationship the defendant had, amongst other acts, persecuted both her, and also her mother and current boyfriend, with telephone calls. The defendant conceded that the mother could complain about the persistent telephone calls made to the parental home if she had a freehold or leasehold interest in the property, as such conduct would fall within the tort of private nuisance. However he claimed that as the plaintiff was a mere licensee in her mother's property, with no proprietary interest, she did not fall within the scope of the law. In a robust judgment Dillon LJ commented: 'To my mind, it is ridiculous if in this present age the law is that the making of deliberately harassing and pestering telephone calls to a person is only actionable in the civil courts if the recipient of the calls happens to have the freehold or a leasehold proprietary interest in the premises in which he or she has received the calls.'[17] He then went on to approve the wording of the injunction granted by the judge which prohibited the defendant from 'using violence to, harassing, pestering or communicating with' the plaintiff.

The decision in *Khorasandjian v Bush* has been widely welcomed by commentators, but at the same time it has aroused considerable speculation and debate as to its extent.[18] There are undoubtedly questions which will require future clarification. Dillon LJ argued that if the wife of the owner of land was entitled to sue, then there was no reason why a child living at home should not do likewise. But, this inevitably raises the question as to who else might qualify? Is the remedy limited to members of the family, or can it be extended to other people living on the premises? If telephone calls are made not simply to the home, but also to the plaintiff's place of work, or mobile phone, are these calls subject to the same injunctive powers, and if so on what basis? These, and other queries, will undoubtedly give rise to problems in the future, and the scope of the decision is as yet unclear. However, whatever the scope of the action it is suggested that it is to be heartily endorsed. As one commentator has written:

> 'For too long harassment of women has been treated as part of the "rough and tumble" of male/female relationships. If a woman complains of sexual or other forms of harassment she is told not to take it seriously; it is a sign of "affection". This case suggests a greater sensitivity to the real harm that is done by such harassment

17 Ibid, at p 675.
18 See S M Cretney [1993] All ER Annual Review 231; A Mullis [1993] All ER Annual Review 473; E Cooke *A Development in the Tort of Private Nuisance* (1994) 57 MLR 289; J Ford *Squaring Analogy with Principle, or Vice Versa* (1994) 53 CLJ 14; J Murphy *The Emergence of Harassment as a Recognised Tort* (1993) 143 NLJ 926; M Noble *Harassment – A Recognised Tort?* (1993) 143 NLJ 1685; J Bridgeman and M A Jones *Harassing Conduct and Outrageous Acts* (1994) 14 Legal Studies 180.

and in so doing provides women not protected by the 1976 Act with a legal remedy. [There] is, as the majority recognised, a pressing social concern that needs redressing; a new tort of unreasonable harassment would go some way to doing that.'[19]

The jurisdiction to regulate the occupation of the matrimonial home

The breakdown of a personal relationship often occurs over a long period of time and it may be punctuated by incidents of violence and molestation. Victims of domestic assaults do not necessarily want their relationship with their spouse or partner to come to an end, rather they may want it to continue but for the violence and threatening behaviour to cease. Or they may decide that the position has become so unbearable that the only solution is to end the relationship. In the case of a married victim she may decide to institute divorce proceedings. In the case of an unmarried victim she may start to take steps to sort out the parties' personal affairs. In either situation, a spouse or partner who is being assaulted, harassed, threatened or otherwise abused and molested may reach the stage where she can no longer tolerate living under the same roof with the man. Indeed, many victims of domestic violence are forced to flee the home because of the risks to which they are exposed. The question of whether an order can be obtained to oust one of the parties from the home and, where one party has been driven from the home, an order obtained which will entitle her to return and live on the premises unmolested, then arises as a matter of real urgency. This is particularly true where the parties have few assets and a relatively low income; in a case of this kind the parties often cannot agree about who should stay in the home and who should leave, because the person who leaves may have nowhere suitable to go. Where there are children, a spouse or partner may insist on remaining in the home because he takes the view (probably correctly) that to leave would prejudice any chance he has of obtaining a residence order in respect of the children.[20] Where violence is alleged against one of the parties (usually against the man) he may refuse to leave the home because he may take the view that to do so would amount to an admission of his guilt.

It has been seen that non-molestation injunctions and personal protection orders can be granted which focus solely on the person of the victim, but these may have little value if the perpetrator of an assault (or other form of molestation) is living in the same household as the victim. The law therefore makes provision for the temporary ousting of one of the parties from the home irrespective of that person's property rights.

19 A Mullis [1993] All ER Annual Review 473, at pp 473-4.
20 On residence orders and the status quo, see ch 4.

The statutory framework

A spouse can make an application for an order or an injunction regulating the occupation of the matrimonial home under three different Acts: the Matrimonial Homes Act 1983; the Domestic Violence and Matrimonial Proceedings Act 1976; and the Domestic Proceedings and Magistrates' Courts Act 1978. Couples who are unmarried can only turn to the Domestic Violence and Matrimonial Proceedings Act 1976 for relief. Where children are involved, it may also be possible to obtain an order concerning occupation of the home under the inherent jurisdiction of the High Court, and under the Children Act 1989.

The reasons for this plethora of legislation are historical. Prior to the enactment of the Domestic Violence and Matrimonial Proceedings Act 1976 there were many unsatisfactory features of the civil law relating to domestic violence and ouster from the home. In particular a wife who wished to obtain an injunction ousting her husband from the home had first to take proceedings for divorce or judicial separation; injunctions were rarely enforced; and an unmarried 'wife' had no right to apply for an injunction ousting her 'husband' from the home in which he had a proprietary right of occupation. Furthermore, provisions in the Matrimonial Homes Act 1967, which was the only Act then on the statute book which dealt with the regulation of the occupation of the matrimonial home, were held by the House of Lords in *Tarr v Tarr*[1] not to encompass the power to prohibit a husband with a proprietary right from occupying the matrimonial home, even for a temporary period.[2] These defects in the law's response to domestic violence were highlighted in the Report of the Select Committee on Violence in Marriage.[3] Parliament's response was to amend the Matrimonial Homes Act 1967;[4] to insert provisions into the Domestic Proceedings and Magistrates' Courts Act 1978, giving magistrates power to make personal protection and exclusion orders; and to enact new legislation, the Domestic Violence and Matrimonial Proceedings Act 1976, which, amongst other things, extended the protection of the civil law to couples who are living together as husband and wife.

---

1   [1972] 2 All ER 295.
2   *Tarr v Tarr* is one of those cases where the House of Lords had the opportunity to interpret the wording of a statute in a manner which would have afforded protection to weaker members of society who were being oppressed by immoral persons with greater physical strength, in this case women who were being battered in their homes by men. Their Lordships failed to grasp this opportunity; indeed, they gave a highly restrictive and legalistic interpretation of the meaning of 'to regulate' with scant consideration for the social policy implications of their ruling. Cf *Davis v Johnson* [1978] 1 All ER 1132, discussed below.
3   HMSO (1974-5).
4   Now the Matrimonial Homes Act 1983.

Regulating the occupation rights of spouses under the Matrimonial Homes Act 1983

All spouses have a personal right to occupy the matrimonial home, and since 1967 they have been able to protect this right against third parties through the registration system.[5] The nature of this personal right is described in section 1(1) of the Matrimonial Homes Act 1983, which provides that a spouse who is not entitled to occupy the home by virtue of a beneficial estate or interest or contract or by virtue of any enactment shall have the following 'rights of occupation'—

'(a) if in occupation, a right not to be evicted or excluded from the dwelling house or any part thereof by the other spouse except with the leave of the court given by an order under this section;
(b) if not in occupation, a right with the leave of the court so given to enter into and occupy the dwelling house.'

Section 1(2) makes provision for the regulation of each spouses' right to live in the matrimonial home. It states—

'So long as one spouse has rights of occupation, either of the spouses may apply to the court for an order—
(a) declaring, enforcing, restricting or terminating those rights, or
(b) prohibiting, suspending or restricting the exercise by either spouse of the right to occupy the dwelling house, or
(c) requiring either spouse to permit the exercise by the other of that right.'

Alternatively where each spouse has a legal right of occupation, section 9 provides that—

'... either of them may apply to the court, with respect to the exercise during the subsistence of the marriage of the right to occupy the dwelling house, for an order prohibiting, suspending or restricting its exercise by the other.'

Curiously, only a small body of case law has been developed on these provisions. Practitioners have developed the habit of applying for ouster orders in other proceedings,[6] and appear rarely to make use of the 1983

---

5   Now under the Matrimonial Homes Act 1983; the registration provisions were first enacted in the Matrimonial Homes Act 1967. For further details, see ch 7.
6   It is suggested that the main reason for this was the House of Lords' ruling in *Tarr v Tarr* [1972] 2 All ER 295 in which it was held that a spouse with a right to occupy (as distinct

Act, despite the pressure placed on them to do so in the House of Lords' ruling in *Richards v Richards*.[7] Instead, case law mixes together the law relating to the 1983 Act with the case law relating to applications for ouster injunctions under the Domestic Violence and Matrimonial Proceedings Act 1976. This entanglement makes it difficult to write with confidence about the role of the 1983 Act in regulating the occupation of the matrimonial home, particularly as the main statements of principle about ouster from the home have been made in cases brought under the 1976 Act. However, it is suggested that it may sometimes be correct for applications made under the 1983 Act to be treated differently from applications made under the 1976 Act. It will be seen that ouster injunctions under the 1976 Act are normally limited in time to a maximum period of three months. It may be that orders under the 1983 can last for a longer period, or that a 1983 Act order can be made after a 1976 Act injunction has run its course, particularly if divorce proceedings are pending.[8] Certainly it is arguable that the provisions of the 1983 Act allow scope for more flexible orders than under the 1976 Act. Section 1(3)(b) enables the court to order the occupying spouse to make periodical payments to the other in respect of that occupation; and section 1(3)(c) allows the court to impose on either spouse obligations as to the repair and maintenance of the dwelling house or the discharge of any liabilities in respect of the dwelling house. The inclusion of all or some of these provisions in an order excluding one spouse from the home could help to obviate any unfairness to the excluded spouse.[9] Section 1(3) specifies the criteria which a court must take into account when making an order under section 1(2); these criteria and their related case law are discussed below.

Ouster from the home under the Domestic Proceedings and Magistrates' Courts Act 1978

Magistrates have power to make an order requiring a spouse to leave the matrimonial home, or an order prohibiting him or her from entering the matrimonial home. Section 16(3) of the Domestic Proceedings and Magis-

---

from a right of occupation) could not be evicted under the provisions of the Matrimonial Homes Act 1967. The Act was subsequently amended, by the Domestic Violence and Matrimonial Proceedings Act 1976, but practitioners got into the habit of using other proceedings and appear not to have changed this habit.

7 [1983] 2 All ER 807, see Lord Hailsham at p 815, and Lord Brandon at p 829. *Richards v Richards* is discussed below. For a commentary on this pressure, see P Parkinson *The Domestic Violence Act and Richards v Richards* (1986) 16 Fam Law 70.

8 See *Galan v Galan* [1985] FLR 905 where such a possibility was canvassed. Such a two-stage approach was suggested in *Davis v Johnson* [1978] 1 All ER 1132.

9 There appears to be no case law on this point.

trates' Courts Act 1978 provides that a court has power to make one or both of these orders—

'Where on an application for an order under this section the court is satisfied—
(a) that the respondent has used violence against the person of the applicant or a child of the family, or
(b) that the respondent has threatened to use violence against the applicant or a child of the family and has used violence against some other person, or
(c) that the respondent has in contravention of an order made under subsection (2) above threatened to use violence against the person of the applicant or a child of the family,
and that the applicant or a child of the family is in danger of being physically injured by the respondent (or would be in such danger if the applicant or child were to enter the matrimonial home) the court may make one or both of the following orders, that is to say—
(i) an order requiring the respondent to leave the matrimonial home;
(ii) an order prohibiting the respondent from entering the matrimonial home.'

Subsection (4) provides that where the court makes an order under subsection (3) it may make a further order—

'requiring the respondent to permit the applicant to enter and remain in the matrimonial home'.

These tightly drafted provisions limit the power of magistrates to intervene to those cases where there has been actual violence or, where violence has been threatened, to those cases where the applicant already has a personal protection order. Furthermore, the applicant must prove in addition that either she, or a child of the family, is in danger of being physically injured by the respondent. There appears to be only one reported case on section 16(3). In *McCartney v McCartney*,[10] where there had been a gap of four months between the date of the last incident of violence and the date of the hearing before the magistrates, the magistrates took the view that the danger to the applicant must be immediate before an exclusion order could be made. On appeal it was made clear that the magistrates had been wrong to take this view, and that it was sufficient for the wife to establish that if the parties were to carry on living together under the same roof an attack of violence would almost undoubtedly follow.

10 [1981] 1 All ER 597.

However, it was also made clear in *McCartney v McCartney* that it is for the court to be satisfied there is an objectively observable danger; it is not enough for the wife simply to establish she herself is in fear.

Thus whilst magistrates do indeed provide a local and readily accessible jurisdiction, that jurisdiction is violence-based and hedged around with restrictions which make it unattractive both to practitioners and to their clients.[11] It has already been seen that magistrates do not have the power to make an expedited exclusion order.[12] On the other hand they are empowered to attach a power of arrest to some of their orders, provided that strict criteria are satisfied.[13] The attachment of a power of arrest may have distinct advantages for the battered wife and provides a sound reason for applying for an order under the 1978 Act rather than for an order under the Matrimonial Homes Act 1983. However, a power of arrest can also be attached to an injunction granted in the county court under the Domestic Violence and Matrimonial Proceedings Act 1976, and injunctions obtained under that Act have additional advantages over orders made under either the 1983 Act or the 1978 Act. It is therefore not surprising that the majority of applications for orders designed to regulate the occupation of the matrimonial home are made under the 1976 Act, and it is to that Act that attention will now be turned.

Ouster and other injunctions under the Domestic Violence Act 1976

The main reason for the enactment of the Domestic Violence and Matrimonial Proceedings Act 1976 was to enable the civil law to respond with urgency to the pernicious nature of domestic violence. In addition to the court's powers under section 1(1) to grant injunctions against molestation,[14] the court has the following powers to grant injunctions in relation to the matrimonial home—

'(c) a provision excluding the other party from the matrimonial home or a part of the matrimonial home or from a specified area in which the matrimonial home is included;

(d) a provision requiring the other party to permit the applicant

---

11 In 1992 only about 2,300 applications were heard by the magistrates; see Home Office Statistical Bulletin Issue 26/93. Magistrates' courts have the further disadvantage of unpredictability. Practitioners soon become familiar with the type of response they can expect from their local district judges; the composition of a magistrates' bench, by contrast, may have a strong influence on the way in which a case is handled, and that composition will not be known to the practitioner in advance.

12 See above.

13 The power of arrest is fully considered below.

14 See above.

to enter and remain in the matrimonial home or a part of the
matrimonial home;
whether or not any other relief is sought in the proceedings.'

There are several advantages to a wife in seeking an injunction under
the 1976 Act rather than an order under either the 1983 Act or the 1978
Act. First the court can throw a ring around the matrimonial home and
order that the husband does not come within its vicinity. Thus in *Tuck v
Nicholls*[15] the order stated that the respondent should not enter 'that area
of King's Lynn in which lies the matrimonial home.'[16] Such an injunction
confers considerable additional protection on a battered wife who can take
action to have her husband brought before the court for breach of the court's
order before he comes near enough to attack her. Thus if he is hanging
around in the road outside the house, or threatening her when she goes to
the shops, or harassing her when she goes to collect the children from
school, and an injunction is in force prohibiting him from being in that
area, she can have him brought back before the court for contempt.
Secondly, an application can normally be heard after a minimum notice
period of four days,[17] and in an urgent situation after only two clear days'
notice;[18] and in extreme circumstances she can be granted an injunction
in ex parte proceedings. Thirdly, in serious cases, the court may attach a
power of arrest to an injunction thereby involving the police in the civil
protection afforded to the battered woman.[19]

It is the case that in extreme circumstances an applicant can be granted
an injunction in ex parte proceedings. However, it has been stressed that
ex parte applications should only be made, and injunctions only granted,
in an emergency, where there is 'real immediate danger of serious injury
or irreparable damage'.[20] Such cases will be rare. The type of case where it
might be appropriate is where the wife is frightened that the husband
may have a violent reaction to the actual service of the proceedings. Where
an injunction is granted it should be strictly limited in time until a full
hearing can be arranged.[1] In *G v G (Ouster: Ex Parte Application)*[2] Lord

---

15 [1989] 1 FLR 283.
16 The order was in fact discharged on appeal, but for other reasons. In *Vaughan v Vaughan*
    [1973] 1 WLR 1159 (which arose under the inherent jurisdiction) the husband was warned
    by the judge not to travel on the same bus, or enter the wife's neighbourhood.
17 CCR Ord 47, r.8(3).
18 CCR Ord 13, r.1(1)(b); see *Ansah v Ansah* [1977] 2 All ER 638. Furthermore application
    can be made for abridgement of time for service where even a delay of two days is too
    long; see CCR Ord 13, r.4(1) and FPR 1991, r.4.14(2)(b). By contrast, under the
    Matrimonial Homes Act 1983 the notice period is 21 days; see CCR Ord 3, r.4 and Ord 7,
    r.10(5).
19 See below.
20 See *Practice Direction (Matrimonial Causes Injunction)* [1978] 1 WLR 925.
1   *Ansah v Ansah* [1977] 2 All ER 638.
2   [1990] 1 FLR 395.

Donaldson MR expressed the general hostility of the court to such ex parte orders, and stated that setting a hearing date seven weeks hence was completely unjustifiable. He went on to comment that as the wife, against whom the order was sought, was readily available for service, there was no reason why the judge could not simply have granted an ex parte non-molestation order, which could have been served on the wife at the same time as notice of an inter partes hearing for ouster. It may be that in *G v G* the husband was sufficiently able to defend himself from the acts of violence by his wife for this to be justified.[3] However, it is suggested that the court should be cautious in taking the view that where a violent reaction to service of the summons is feared a widely couched non-molestation injunction will be sufficient protection for the wife. In highly volatile domestic situations fear of being in breach of an injunction is unlikely to deter many respondents from assaulting their spouse, and an ex parte order for ouster is also necessary.

The Court of Appeal has a similar antipathy to courts granting ouster injunctions solely on the basis of affidavit evidence. Stringent conditions were laid down in *Whitlock v Whitlock*[4] where it was said:

> 'It needs to be emphasised that this is a Draconian type of order involving the expulsion from his home of one of the parties. It should never lightly be made, and it certainly should not be made where there is a conflict on affidavit, save in cases where the court can safely accept evidence on affidavit justifying the order without further investigation.'[5]

Jurisdiction where the parties live in the same household as 'husband and wife'

The only persons who are entitled to apply for injunctions under the Domestic Violence and Matrimonial Proceedings Act 1976 are spouses and 'a man and a woman who are living with each other in the same household as husband and wife'.[6] Prior to the enactment of the 1976 Act, the unmarried 'wife' who wished to bring civil proceedings could only obtain an ouster order where she alone had a proprietary right to occupy the 'matrimonial home' and where her 'husband' had no such right. The 1976 Act was passed in direct response to the Report of the Select Committee on Violence in

---

3 Although in his evidence the husband stated that recently the wife had been inviting a 'gentleman' to the house, of whom the husband was so frightened that on one occasion he had jumped out of a first floor window.
4 [1989] 1 FLR 208; see also *Shipp v Shipp* [1988] 1 FLR 345.
5 [1989] 1 FLR 208, per Russell LJ at p 210.
6 Section 1(2).

Marriage,[7] which revealed that there were grounds for serious disquiet about the lack of protective safeguards for women abused by their violent spouses or partners. Section 1(2) of the Domestic Violence and Matrimonial Proceedings Act 1976 provides—

> 'Subsection (1) above shall apply to a man and a woman who are living with each other in the same household as husband and wife as it applies to the parties to a marriage and any reference to the matrimonial home shall be construed accordingly.'

This requirement means that there is an issue of jurisdiction when the parties are unmarried. The court will only be able to adjudicate if the parties fall within the meaning of this provision. The phrase 'living together as husband and wife' has given rise to difficult questions of interpretation. Given a strictly literal interpretation, the phrase would deny a remedy to the women who are probably the most in need, because in cases of extreme violence the woman has usually fled the home.

At one stage the Court of Appeal doubted whether a woman who had fled the home due to violence was still living with the man for the purposes of the subsection, and therefore whether she fell within its scope.[8] Fortunately the House of Lords adopted a realistic approach to the present tense drafting of the section in *Davis v Johnson*[9] and ruled that it did not prevent a woman who had physically removed herself, or who had been removed from the premises, from applying for an injunction under section 1(1). The law was further clarified in the Court of Appeal ruling in *O'Neill v Williams*[10] which stated that the proper test of jurisdiction is to ask whether it has been established that the parties were living together as husband and wife at the date of the violence complained of. In *O'Neill v Williams* the woman was forced to leave the home in August but did not bring proceedings until the following March. Despite the time lag, the court held that it still had jurisdiction to hear the case.[11] On the other hand, the woman fell outside the scope of the subsection in *McLean v Burke*.[12] After the breakdown of the parties' relationship she moved out of the 'matrimonial home'. Subsequently she moved back in, but she occupied a separate bedroom and ceased to have any form of communal living with her ex-partner. Her sole purpose in returning to the home was to protect her interest in the property. About five months later the man locked the

---

7   HC 553 (1974-5).
8   *B v B* [1978] 1 All ER 821.
9   [1978] 1 All ER 1132, affirming the decision of the Court of Appeal on this point.
10 [1984] FLR 1.
11 However it will be seen below that the lapse of time led the court, in the exercise of its discretion, to refuse to grant an injunction to the woman.
12 (1982) 3 FLR 70.

applicant out. She immediately brought proceedings to be allowed to re-enter and to evict him. The Court of Appeal held that the Act did not supply her with a remedy since it was the fact of being locked out that had prompted her to bring the complaint, and at that time she was not living as husband and wife.[13]

In *McLean v Nugent*[14] the parties had had a relationship which resulted in the birth of a child. Subsequently the woman moved into accommodation away from the man because she did not want to continue her association with him. However the man found her and forced his way in. He then treated her with violence and, on her account, raped her.[15] After three months the woman left. The Court of Appeal held that the court did have jurisdiction to hear her application.[16] It ruled that the parties had been living together as husband and wife because 'there can be no doubt in fact, as I think, that willy nilly she was living with him as husband and wife in the same household.'[17] Clearly this decision was aimed at granting the woman a remedy in very needy circumstances, and on that basis it is to be applauded. However, it is suggested that it poses serious difficulties to state that a woman who is being forced against her will to live with a man who is also raping her, is living in the same household with him as 'husband and wife'. It is perhaps best to rationalise the decision by stating that one of the crucial factors in deciding whether the statutory wording applies is to ask whether at least one of the parties possesses the intention to live together with the other. Provided that this test is satisfied at the relevant date, it seems that this should be sufficient to bestow jurisdiction upon the court.

This rationalisation of *McLean v Nugent* assists in the explanation of another difficult case, *Tuck v Nicholls*.[18] After the birth of their child the parties, who had never lived together, obtained council housing. The man moved in first and did some decorating. The woman spent one or two nights there with him, and then went back to her parents. The following day she went round and found him with another woman. A violent dispute took

13 It is not difficult to envisage facts which are far more borderline than *McLean v Burke* and which may be difficult to resolve. If one party simply moves out of one room and commences occupying a separate bedroom, how soon after the parties have started occupying separate bedrooms can it be said that they are no longer living together as husband and wife? If the woman continues to supply other 'domestic services' to the man, are they still living together as husband and wife? For a discussion of whether married couples who have adopted such living arrangements are 'living apart' for the purposes of divorce law, see *Mouncer v Mouncer* [1972] 1 All ER 289; and ch 6.

14 (1980) 1 FLR 26.

15 Ormrod LJ, ibid at p 28, says: 'He treated her with some violence. He forced her to have intercourse, she says against her will, from time to time.'

16 In *McLean v Nugent* the woman was in fact seeking a non-molestation injunction, rather than an order for ouster.

17 Ibid, at p 31.

18 [1989] 1 FLR 283.

place, and since then she had not lived with him. On appeal the Court of Appeal held that the question that must be asked was whether she had moved into the house because, if she had not, section 1(2) did not apply and the court did not have jurisdiction. This, the court ruled, was a question of fact which must be properly decided, and as the issue had not been properly addressed at first instance the case should be remitted for a rehearing. Tying this decision in with that of *McLean v Nugent,* if what must be established is simply the intention to live together it appears that the length of the cohabitation is not of the essence. Once cohabitation has commenced the court has jurisdiction.

Once cohabitation ends, however, the court's jurisdiction also ends. At this stage the applicant can no longer rely on her status to seek an ouster order under the 1976 Act. Instead she must rely on what rights, if any, she has in the property. However, it seems that the courts will not come to her assistance despite the fact that she has a right to live in the property where the man has a right to live there too. This was the situation which arose in *Ainsbury v Millington.*[19] The man and woman were joint tenants of a council house. The man was sent to prison for burglary, and during the period of his imprisonment the woman married someone else and gave birth to his child. On his release, the man moved back into the home and drove the couple and child out of the home into overcrowded and unsatisfactory conditions. The court refused to come to the assistance of the couple. As the man and woman were no longer living with each other in the same household as husband and wife, the provisions of the Domestic Violence and Matrimonial Proceedings Act 1976 did not apply. Therefore the woman was only entitled to an injunction if she could establish a legal right which would give the court power to grant her an injunction.[20] But, ruled the Court of Appeal, she was one of joint tenants of a council house, accordingly she and the respondent had equal rights to occupy the property, and neither had the right to occupy it to the exclusion of the other.

The ruling in *Ainsbury v Millington* placed the applicant in an impossible situation. It was clear that one or other of the parties could not live in the house. It was a council house, so there was no property which could be sold. Its value to each of the parties was its occupation value. It is absurd for the courts to refuse to adjudicate on which co-owner should leave and which should be entitled to remain where it is clearly intolerable for both parties to live under the same roof. It is suggested that such a refusal is an abdication of judicial responsibility. Furthermore, it leads to the consequence that the more aggressive and powerful co-owner is the one who gains long-term occupation of the premises. This is what occurred in *Ainsbury v Millington.*

19 [1986] 1 All ER 73.
20 By virtue of the Supreme Court Act 1981, s.37 as applied in the county court by the County Courts Act 1984, s.38

This was also the outcome in *O'Neill v Williams*.[1] Here the court decided that it had jurisdiction under the 1976 Act to grant an ouster order because the parties were living together as husband and wife at the time when the incident of violence drove the woman from the home. However, it refused to exercise its jurisdiction. Six months had elapsed between the man's assault on the woman which led her to flee the home, and her application for him to be ousted coming before the court. Ruling that it was now too late to grant the woman the short-term relief which the 1976 Act was designed to provide,[2] the Court of Appeal made no attempt to determine whether the woman, who with the man was a tenant of their flat, and therefore had a proprietary right to live there, could be assisted on the basis of common law principles. But surely the law should enforce the woman's right to return to premises from which she has been wrongfully evicted by a violent partner, and in which she has a proprietary interest, whatever the lapse of time. If the only way of doing this is for the man to be evicted, then so be it.[3] It is entirely unacceptable that a violent co-owner can evict his partner and for the courts merely to stand by and do nothing simply because the parties do not fall within the scope of the domestic violence legislation.

The criteria governing orders regulating the occupation of the matrimonial home

No specific guidance is included in the Domestic Proceedings and Magistrates' Courts Act 1978 to assist magistrates to determine whether they should order a man to leave, or should prohibit him from entering, the matrimonial home. However, it has been seen that the jurisdiction of magistrates to make such orders is dependent on proof of violence, or threats of violence in breach of a personal protection order, coupled with proof of danger of further physical injury.[4] Thus the criteria which a magistrates' court must apply is implicit within the provisions which are the source of its powers.

When a court is making an order which regulates the occupation of the matrimonial home under section 1(2) of the Matrimonial Homes Act 1983, guidance on how the court should exercise its discretion is provided in section 1(3). The Domestic Violence and Matrimonial Proceedings Act 1976 is totally silent on the matters which a court should take into account

1 [1984] FLR 1.
2 The court did not totally exclude the possibility of a successful late application, and they hypothesised the case where the woman had been seriously injured and had to spend time in hospital. In those circumstances they considered that she might successfully apply to have the man ousted on her release from hospital.
3 Cf *Gurasz v Gurasz* [1969] 3 All ER 822.
4 Domestic Proceedings and Magistrates' Courts Act 1978, s.16(3); see above.

when determining whether to grant one or more injunctions. Clearly injunctions against molestation of the applicant, or any child living with her, will not be granted unless there is proof that such molestation has occurred or is threatened.[5] However, no guidance is given on when a court should exclude one of the parties from the matrimonial home or from its vicinity, or when it should require one party to permit the other party to enter and remain in the matrimonial home or a part of the matrimonial home.

This lack of guidance initially caused problems; indeed it led to an almost complete breakdown in the doctrine of precedent in domestic violence cases, with differently constituted Courts of Appeal applying different principles to ouster cases.[6] The different strands of reasoning being operated by the courts, and the conflicting guidance offered by the Court of Appeal, came to a head in the landmark decision in *Richards v Richards*.[7] The House of Lords was clearly horrified by the anarchical position which had been reached, and their Lordships ruled that the criteria which courts must apply to ouster and related injunctions under the Domestic Violence and Matrimonial Proceedings Act 1976 are the same criteria as those which apply to orders made under the Matrimonial Homes Act 1983, namely the criteria specified in section 1(3). In *Lee v Lee*[8] the Court of Appeal confirmed that the criteria are also applicable to applications by unmarried partners, despite the fact that the Matrimonial Homes Act 1983 does not apply to them. Whilst this ruling imposed some order on the chaos which had been emerging, arguably it created as many problems as it resolved. In particular, no heed appears to have been given to whether it is proper always to treat an unmarried 'wife' with no property rights in the 'matrimonial home' in the same way as a spouse with a statutory right of occupation.

The universal guiding principles for the exercise of the court's powers are those contained in section 1(3) of the Matrimonial Homes Act 1983, which provides that—

'On an application for an order under this section, the court may make such order as it thinks just and reasonable having regard to

---

5   Though whether it is proper for a court to make a non-molestation injunction in relation to a child where the only evidence of molestation relates to attacks on the applicant is not clear.
6   One line of cases adopted an essentially pragmatic approach, whereby applications were treated as issues of housing. If it was found that a woman needed a home for herself and the children she would be allowed to stay in the house and the husband would be ousted. Little attention was paid to the merits of the application: see, for example, *Spindlow v Spindlow* [1979] 1 All ER 169; *Samson v Samson* [1982] 1 WLR 252. The other approach was very different. Before an order would be granted the court would require evidence that it was impossible for the spouses to remain together under the same roof: see, for example, *Elsworth v Elsworth* (1978) 1 FLR 245; *Myers v Myers* [1982] 1 WLR 247.
7   [1983] 2 All ER 807.
8   [1984] FLR 243.

> the conduct of the spouses in relation to each other and otherwise, to their respective needs and financial resources, to the needs of any children and to all the circumstances of the case.'

Thus there are four matters to which the court must have regard in deciding whether or not to make an order regulating the occupation of the matrimonial home: conduct; needs and resources; the needs of the children; and all the circumstances of the case. Furthermore, the overall aim of the court must be to make an order which is just and reasonable.[9] In *Richards v Richards*[10] the trial judge found that Mrs Richards had no reasonable grounds for refusing to return to live with her husband in the matrimonial home,[11] and he commented: 'I think it is thoroughly unjust to turn out this father, but justice no longer seems to play any part in this part of the law'.[12] The husband appealed, but the Court of Appeal dismissed his appeal on the ground that the needs of the children were paramount. In allowing the husband's appeal, the House of Lords ruled that each of the factors specified in section 1(3) should be given equal weight, and that the welfare of the children should not be the court's paramount consideration.[13] As a result of this decision there is a continuing tension in the law between those cases where, after balancing all the factors, decisive weight is given to whether the respondent's conduct has been sufficiently serious to justify making an order ousting him from the home, and those cases where the needs of the applicant and her children appear to demand an order requiring the husband to leave. The analysis which follows examines how this tension has been handled.

Analysis of the exercise of the discretion to oust

Since *Richards v Richards* the Court of Appeal has inserted its own gloss on the language of section 1(3) by insisting that ouster orders are 'Draconian orders' which require strong justification. Thus in *Reid v Reid*[14] the court

9 Though whether this type of wording in a statute should be included is debatable; courts are hardly likely to wish to make orders which are unjust and unreasonable, and where they do they are likely to be reversed on appeal!

10 [1983] 2 All ER 807.

11 Indeed, a reading of the facts in *Richards v Richards* reveals that any 'misconduct' by one of the spouses had been on the part of the wife, not the husband. For a comment raising the question whether orders regulating the occupation of the matrimonial home should be made morally neutral, see M Hayes *The Law Commission and the Family Home* (1990) 53 MLR 222.

12 See Lord Hailsham' s speech [1983] 2 All ER 807 at p 811.

13 Lord Scarman gave a short but powerful dissenting speech on this statement of principle, see [1983] 2 All ER 807 at pp 819-21.

14 (1984) Times, 30 July, which was the first reported Court of Appeal decision after *Richards v Richards*.

ruled that ouster is a very serious order which should be made only where the judge is satisfied that no lesser measure will suffice to protect the wife and children. In *Summers v Summers*,[15] the trial judge had found that the repeated loud quarrels between the parents were frightening and adversely affecting the children. In deciding to oust the husband the judge included in his considerations the fact that 'at this time it might be beneficial for there to be a break for a while. It may be a forlorn hope but might ease a reconciliation.'[16] On appeal he was criticised for taking the prospect of reconciliation into account, and for failing to take into account the 'Draconian' nature of an ouster order.[17] Subsequently the statement that ouster orders are Draconian has been repeated in a number of cases;[18] and in *Burke v Burke*[19] an ouster order was described by Lloyd LJ as 'a drastic order and an order which should only be made in cases of real necessity. It must not be allowed to become a routine stepping-stone on the road to divorce on the ground that the marriage has already broken down and that the atmosphere in the matrimonial home is one of tension.'

Conduct

This approach to ouster orders has led courts to concentrate their attention on the respondent's conduct, and on whether anything he has done justifies ordering his eviction from the home. Although, in 1988, the Court of Appeal ruled in *Wiseman v Simpson*[20] that it is not necessary to prove violence or other adverse behaviour to the applicant or a child living with the applicant in order to be granted an ouster injunction, it is disturbing to note that the Law Commission pointed out in 1989[1] that there appeared to be no reported cases in the Court of Appeal since *Richards v Richards* of ouster in circumstances other than violence, although before that time there had been several. In *Wiseman v Simpson* itself the Court allowed an appeal against the making of an ouster order, and sent the case back for a retrial, Ralph Gibson LJ stating that 'it can only be "just and reasonable" to make an ouster order if the case of the party claiming the order is not only stronger on those matters than the other party's case but is such as to justify making an order that a man or woman be ousted from his or her home.'[2] Since

---

15 [1986] 1 FLR 343.
16 Ibid, at p 347.
17 The case was sent back for retrial by another judge; the outcome of the proceedings is not known.
18 See especially *Wiseman v Simpson* [1988] 1 All ER 245; *Shipp v Shipp* [1988] 1 FLR 345; and *Blackstock v Blackstock* [1991] 2 FLR 308, which is analysed in detail below.
19 [1987] 2 FLR 71 at p 73.
20 [1988] 1 All ER 245.
1 *Domestic Violence and Occupation of the Family Home,* Law Com Working Paper No 113 at p 22.
2 [1988] 1 All ER 245 at p 251.

then, there have been cases in which ouster orders have been made without proof of violence, but the courts have continued to emphasise the drastic nature of the order.[3]

The Court of Appeal's tendency to focus on misconduct, coupled with a determination that trial courts should discover which of the parties is responsible for the misconduct, is highlighted in *Blackstock v Blackstock*.[4] The trial judge accepted that there had been an 'horrendous' incident of violence, and that both parties had had severe injuries inflicted upon them.[5] The wife had left home with the three children and since then they had been living in highly unsatisfactory accommodation. The wife applied for an ouster order so that she and the children could return. The judge refused her application on the ground that he was unable to say which party was to blame for the incident and, in view of that lack of finding, he could not justify the making of an ouster order. He accepted that the children were living in unsatisfactory accommodation, but found that they were in no danger from the husband and did not need any protection from him if they were living under the same roof. The husband offered to give an undertaking not to molest the wife, and the judge found that such an undertaking would be sufficient to protect her.[6] On appeal it was argued on behalf of the wife that the high level of violence justified her staying away, irrespective of where the fault might lie. The Court of Appeal refused to accept this argument. It ruled that the court could not ignore the source of the violence; that the burden had been on the wife to prove culpability on the part of the husband; and that she had failed to discharge this burden. The court therefore concluded that an order should not be granted, since it was not clear who was responsible for the initiation of the violence, and because there was a real possibility that the wife herself might have been its instigator.

It is suggested that the Court of Appeal's approach in *Blackstock v Blackstock* was dangerously misguided.[7] It is normally the case that violence in the home is not witnessed by outsiders and therefore, where both spouses have injuries, it is easy for each to accuse the other of being the main assailant. Even if it had been established that it was the wife who had instigated the violence it was clearly extremely risky for the parties to continue to live together under the same roof. The notion that the giving

3 See the recent example of *Brown v Brown* [1994] 1 FLR 233.
4 [1991] 2 FLR 308. See too *Shipp v Shipp* [1988] 1 FLR 345, where it was hotly contested as to who was responsible for the one serious incident of violence. The Court of Appeal criticised the trial judge for granting a short-term ouster order in proceedings on the basis of affidavit evidence without having explored in depth who was to blame for the incident.
5 The wife sustained a fracture of the shaft of the ulna of the right forearm. The husband suffered scalding and a broken cheekbone with pinning through the nose.
6 A factor influencing the judge in reaching this decision was that he was not satisfied that this was a marriage in which there had been a long history of violence.
7 And to a lesser extent in *Shipp v Shipp* [1988] 1 FLR 345.

of an undertaking not to be violent provides adequate protection where serious violence has already occurred flies in the face of all the evidence about the recidivist nature of domestic assaults. It is suggested that it should be the role of the civil law to afford protection in cases of domestic violence by contrast with the role of the criminal law, which is to apportion blame and to punish. Therefore, in a case of this kind, it is suggested that one of the parties *must* be evicted from the home regardless of who was responsible for initiating the assaults. An ouster order is in the interests of the personal safety of each of the parties. In relation to the children, the fact that they are not physically at risk does not mean that the violence has no impact upon them. It cannot be in the interests of children to live in a household where the parents have attacked one another in the manner in which they did in *Blackstock v Blackstock*. Such children would clearly be vulnerable to serious psychological damage were they to witness such violence. Because the children were living with their mother it is suggested that the father should have been ousted regardless of the merits relating to the question who had first assaulted whom.

The Court of Appeal's decision in *Scott v Scott* [8] is in marked contrast to that in *Blackstock v Blackstock*. Here there was no evidence that the husband had treated his wife with violence, or had behaved with any other misconduct towards her. Rather, the wife's complaint was that her husband could not accept that their marriage had irretrievably broken down, and that he was constantly pressing her to resume their relationship, despite the fact that she had obtained a decree nisi of divorce. This difference between the parties as to the state of their marriage had been in existence for some considerable time, and in earlier proceedings the husband had given undertakings not to interfere with his wife, which had been followed by an injunction to this effect. Eventually the trial judge took the view that the only way of enforcing the court's injunction was to make an order under section 9 of the Matrimonial Homes Act 1983, excluding the husband from the house which they jointly owned. The Court of Appeal clearly found the judge's approach difficult to reconcile with existing principles. As Glidewell LJ said, having considered the criteria in section 1(3) apart from conduct, and having reminded himself that ouster orders are Draconian orders:

'The final question is, is this conduct sufficiently serious to justify the making of an ouster order? This has greatly troubled me, because I take the view that it is wrong that ouster injunctions should be used too widely or too commonly, and I think there is a risk that they are. I recognise the force of the previous decisions of this court to the effect that they are only to be used in cases of real

8   [1992] 1 FLR 529.

necessity. In the end I am persuaded that, knowing as he did all about the history …., the judge was justified in concluding that he had to keep these parties apart if that injunction was not going to be broken in the future, and this was the way in which he could do it. Therefore I cannot say that the judge was wrong to reach the conclusion to which he came.'[9]

It is suggested that *Scott v Scott* is an important decision because of its essentially pragmatic approach. It recognised the reality that marriages are often brought to an end by the unilateral decision of one of the parties. One spouse wants to be free of the relationship, and to move on, the other clings to what has been between the parties, and is unable to accept that the marriage has irretrievably come to an end.[10] Where this is the case, the question then arises whether the court is entitled to treat reconciliation overtures made by the spouse who cannot accept that the marriage is finished as a form of molestation. In *Scott v Scott* the trial judge was prepared to treat such overtures in this way and to accept undertakings and to make orders against further such reconciliation attempts. When the husband persisted, the judge was prepared to enforce the court's order by evicting the husband from the home, and the Court of Appeal was not willing to find that he had been plainly wrong. The ruling is in marked contrast with the Court of Appeal's desire in *Blackstock v Blackstock* to discover who was to blame for the violence which, in that case, had erupted between the parties. In *Scott v Scott* the court was not concerned to allocate blame; indeed, in relation to blame Glidewell LJ said 'of course, the rights and wrongs are not all on one side and [not on][11] the other. It is the conduct of both parties that has led to the breakdown of the marriage.'[12] It is suggested that it was a radical decision to allow a court to be used to assist a wife to avoid having to listen to her husband's repeated requests for a reconciliation. It is suggested that it was even more radical to enforce the court's order by evicting the husband from his home even before the decree nisi had been made absolute. If, instead, contempt proceedings had been instituted, it may have been difficult to prove that the husband's behaviour amounted to contempt, bearing in mind the court's concession that the husband's behaviour arguably 'did not go so far as molestation.'[13]

9 Ibid, at pp 536-7.
10 Glidewell LJ himself adverted to this at the end of his judgment when he attempted to offer the husband sympathetic and constructive advice. It is suggested that the courts will be faced with similar moral dilemmas if the Law Commission's proposals for divorce reform are implemented. Under these proposals the courts will be empowered to make orders regulating the occupation of the home during the one-year period of consideration and reflection: see ch 6.
11 Authors' insertion.
12 [1992] 1 FLR 529 at p 536.
13 Ibid.

Needs and financial resources

In *Richards v Richards*[14] the House of Lords was at pains to emphasise that all the factors specified in section 1(3) of the Matrimonial Homes Act 1983 should be given equal weight. Thus the needs and financial resources of the parties are of major importance, particularly the need of both parties to be adequately housed. However, it is abundantly clear that ouster orders are not to be regarded simply as housing matters. In *G v J (Ouster Order)*[15] Purchas LJ commented:

> 'The decision which the judge made would appear to most people to be fair and sensible if the task of the court was to decide who, in fairness, between the man who is going to work and the woman who has the care of the child, should have the flat to live in. As a matter of housing policy the judge's answer may well be right. But the court has no power to decide such a case simply as a matter of housing policy. The jurisdiction is given by the Domestic Violence and Matrimonial Proceedings Act 1976 and the question is whether the order can be sustained under the provisions of that Act.'

Thus the ability of the man to rehouse himself is by no means a guarantee that the court will make an order ousting him from the home, even though the court may accept that it is impossible for the two parties to carry on living together under the same roof. In *Shipp v Shipp*[16] the wife had made a successful application for ouster in proceedings based on affidavit evidence only. Allowing the husband's appeal, the Court of Appeal took account of the possible practical impact of a temporary ouster order on the husband, and stated that ouster for a period of two months 'might make it practically impossible for the husband to reverse the arrangements which he would be bound to make in the intervening period and go back to live in the matrimonial home, if it was held at the adjourned hearing that he should be allowed to do so.'[17] In the result, the husband was left living alone in the three-bedroomed house, whilst the wife and child were living in very cramped conditions at the house of her sister.

On the other hand, if the respondent actually has suitable accommodation available to move into the court may more readily grant the order, as in *Scott v Scott,*[18] where the husband, who was a property developer,

---

14 [1983] 2 All ER 807.
15 [1993] 1 FLR 1008 at pp 1015-6.
16 [1988] 1 FLR 345.
17 Per Nourse LJ at p 347. Why it would be 'practically impossible' to 'reverse' any arrangements is not explained, nor was it explained why the respondent husband could not simply seek a short tenancy of two months' duration.
18 [1992] 1 FLR 529. The fact of the alternative accommodation almost undoubtedly influenced the court in taking a less rigorous attitude than is usual towards conduct.

owned another house as well as the matrimonial home. Similarly in *Baggott v Baggott*[19] the Court of Appeal confirmed the decision to oust the husband, commenting that it was obvious that he was in a position to find himself a home or somewhere to live because he had put in the forefront of his case an offer to raise £20,000 in order to provide a fund to enable either himself, or the wife, to live elsewhere.[20]

In some instances it may be that the husband might offer to share the accommodation. The 1983 Act provides for this possibility by empowering the court to 'restrict' a person's occupation of the home,[1] and the 1976 Act provides for the respondent to be excluded from 'a part of the matrimonial home'.[2] The husband might propose that the parties carry on living under the same roof, but not as husband and wife, and with him being allowed only to use certain rooms. Where there has been no violence on his part, and the house is sufficiently large, this is a proposal to which the court might give a sympathetic hearing, particularly in view of the general approach that ouster orders are Draconian orders. It is suggested that it may also make sense on the part of the wife to accept such an offer, as the difficulties in gaining an ouster order are such that parties are frequently left living together. To have an order restricting occupation may be better than no order at all.[3] However, where there are children involved it is suggested that the court should think very carefully about how it might affect them. Where there has been violence sufficient to justify ouster then it is suggested that the court ought not normally to take up this option in view of the risk to the wife. In *E v E (Ouster Order)*,[4] despite accepting the evidence of the wife that her husband had attempted to rape her, the Court of Appeal confirmed the trial judge's decision simply to exclude the husband from one of the two bedrooms in the house. In her evidence-in-chief the wife had said: 'separate rooms would help, yes. I don't necessarily want him to go. I want my safety and peace. I don't want any more aggravation.' The Court of Appeal considered that normally it should be expected that

---

19 [1986] 1 FLR 377.
20 In view of the fact that the court has no property adjustment powers when dealing with unmarried couples, it could be the case that the criteria relating to needs and financial resources should be applied differently, according to the status of the couple, as all that the unmarried woman can normally obtain, at best, is a temporary breathing space. However, *Richards v Richards* did not make any such distinction, and neither has the subsequent case law. However, in *Hennie v Hennie* [1993] 1 FCR 886 the Court of Appeal did suggest that the provision of alternative accommodation and a wife's right of occupation might affect the decision whether or not to oust a man differently according to whether an application is made under the 1983 Act or under the 1976 Act. (See the comments of Connell J at p 894.)
1 Section 1(3).
2 Section 1(1)(c).
3 See for example *G v J (Ouster Order)* [1993] 1 FLR 1008, where the man successfully appealed against an ouster order despite allegations of violence. He originally offered to live separately from the woman under the same roof.
4 [1994] 2 FCR 773.

an ouster order would follow where the judge finds allegations of rape or attempted rape proved. However, the evidence of the wife, coupled with other factors,[5] indicated that it was not possible for them to say that the judge had been plainly wrong in the exercise of his discretion. However, despite *E v E,* it is suggested that the smaller the accommodation the less possibility there should be of such an order being made. In *Anderson v Anderson*[6] an order to share the property had been made at first instance despite the fact that the parties lived in a two-bedroomed flat, the wife was pregnant, they already had a two-year-old child, and there was a history of violence. This was overruled on appeal, where it was held that the trial judge had been wrong to put the onus on the wife to establish that it would probably be disastrous for the couple to stay under the same roof.

Where the parties live in accommodation provided by a local authority the court is likely to be influenced by the authority's housing policies in determining whether or not to make an ouster order. Where the court is satisfied that suitable alternative accommodation will be provided for the husband the decision to evict him from the home then becomes less Draconian. However, if ousting the husband will render him homeless this is an extremely serious matter. In *Freeman v Collins*[7] the parties were unmarried and the tenancy of their council house had been granted to the 'husband' only. Therefore the 'wife' had no long-term right to remain in the property. The court made an order ousting the husband, but only for one month. The court took the view that this would be a sufficient period of time to enable the housing authority to consider the woman's application for rehousing. In *Wooton v Wooton*[8] the court found that if the man were to be ousted he would become homeless and the local authority would be under no obligation to rehouse him,[9] whereas if the woman and her children were to leave they would be treated by the local authority as in priority need for rehousing. Consequently, as the court felt that there was no urgent need to protect the applicant, they refused to oust the man, who was the sole tenant. By contrast, in *Thurley v Smith*[10] the man was ousted for a period of three months, even though he would be rendered homeless as a consequence. His position as a single man was contrasted with that of the woman and her eight-year-old son. The man was a violent alcoholic, whom

5   A living pattern whereby the parties were not in the house together very often, no children, and the wife's uncertain immigration status, which meant she might be reluctant to bring divorce proceedings.
6   [1984] FLR 566.
7   [1984] FLR 649.
8   [1984] FLR 871.
9   Although they were probably incorrect in this view, as the man appeared to fall within the definition of priority need, now found in the Housing Act 1985, s.59(1)(b), as he was suffering from epilepsy which was difficult to control.
10 [1984] FLR 875.

the court felt could be justly condemned to a substantial extent for his conduct. The woman was living in wholly unsuitable accommodation, and though the court thought that she had a prospect of eventually being granted more satisfactory local authority accommodation, they also recognised that it was likely that it would not approach the standard afforded by the matrimonial home because of severe pressures on the authority's housing resources.

The needs of the children

Where children are living in a household where one or both of the adults is alleging that it is impossible for the parties to remain together under the same roof, the court must determine how much weight to give to the interests of the children when deciding what orders, if any, to make. In *Richards v Richards*[11] the House of Lords rejected the argument that any orders regulating the occupation of the matrimonial home should be governed by the welfare principle.[12] Rather, it ruled that the welfare of the children should be given the same weight as the other factors specified in section 1(3). In *Gibson v Austin*[13] an attempt was made to reopen this issue and to argue that the decision in *Richards v Richards* had been overruled by the Children Act 1989. However this argument was firmly dismissed by the Court of Appeal. As Nourse LJ stated, 'that argument is a hopeless one. It is quite clear that *Richards v Richards* has not been overruled by the 1989 Act.'[14]

In the 1979 case of *Hopper v Hopper*[15] the wife was appealing against an order which ousted the husband from the home, but which was not to take effect for one month. She claimed that 24 hours would have been sufficient time for her husband to find alternative accommodation. The wife stressed that her daughter was presently suffering very severely; she was living in very cramped conditions, and having to sleep on a camp bed. The child's situation was made very much worse by the fact that she was suffering from a broken arm. In relation to this Stamp LJ commented: 'I cannot think that the harm that may be done to this girl by having to sleep on a camp bed with a broken arm after being in hospital can possibly outweigh the undesirability of driving her step-father out of the home at very short notice.'[16]

11 [1983] 2 All ER 807. But note Lord Scarman's dissenting speech.
12 Which gives paramountcy to the interests of the children: see ch 4.
13 [1992] 2 FLR 437.
14 Ibid, at p 441.
15 [1979] 1 All ER 181.
16 Ibid, at p 183.

It is difficult to evaluate how far this unsympathetic attitude to children still prevails in the Court of Appeal. Certainly in *Lee v Lee*[17] it took a more generous stance. The wife had left the home and was unable to find accommodation for herself and her children all to live together as a family. It was held that the needs of the children to be together, and to be with their mother, were sufficient to establish the necessity for an order. On the other hand the Draconian nature of an ouster order was emphasised in *Tuck v Nicholls*[18] despite evidence that the child may have been at risk living with the wife at the home of her parents. The couple were unmarried,[19] and the trial judge had made an ouster order on the basis of affidavit evidence alone on the grounds that it was unsafe to leave the parties together, because of allegations that the woman's father might be a child sex abuser, and because the reason why the couple had been granted a council tenancy was because they had a young baby. Allowing the man's appeal, the Court of Appeal ruled that although 'nobody would wish to leave a baby in circumstances where that child might be at risk' this evidence had been produced in an affidavit at the last moment, and nothing had been done to alert the husband in advance to the allegations made against the wife's father. For this and other reasons the court therefore discharged the ouster injunction and remitted the case for a fresh hearing.[20]

It is suggested the Court of Appeal adopted a rigid and uncompromising position in *Tuck v Nicholls* and that it gave far too little weight to the interests of the mother and her child. Of course it would be Draconian to oust the man, but the woman had left the home and she needed a proper roof over her head for herself and her baby. It is understandable that courts are reluctant to base orders on affidavit evidence only, and even more reluctant to do so where the contents of the affidavit have not been served in advance on the other party. But ouster orders are often sought in an emergency, and where the applicant has left the home, either she or the man will suffer the Draconian consequences of being out of the home pending a hearing at which oral evidence can be tested in cross-examination. One party will always suffer temporary inconvenience in cases of this kind, yet it is suggested that the Court of Appeal is refusing to recognise that the woman out of the house has an equal claim to live in it pending a full hearing as does the man. It is suggested that the woman's claim to be restored, and for the man to be ousted, should be treated as overwhelming

17 [1984] FLR 243.
18 [1989] 1 FLR 283.
19 A crucial aspect of the appeal was whether the court had jurisdiction to make an order which turned on whether they were 'living with each other in the same household as husband and wife' within the scope of s.1(2) of the Domestic Violence and Matrimonial Proceedings Act 1976: see above.
20 The issue as to whether the woman's father really was an abuser was never properly examined in the case.

where she has children whom she says are at risk of harm in their present accommodation. If her allegations prove to be groundless, the man will eventually be restored to the property. If there is a choice between an adult or a child suffering in the interim period, surely it should be the adult.

However, the Court of Appeal has declined to adopt this approach. In *G v J (Ouster Order)*[1] it was unwilling to give decisive weight to the interests of the child where the merits of the case were evenly divided between the adult parties. The trial judge had adopted the approach that if the needs of the child combined with the needs of the mother together added up to a greater need than that of the father, then an order for ouster could be justified. He found as a fact that neither party was significantly more to blame than the other for the break-up in the relationship. In the end what 'tipped the balance' in favour of ousting the man was 'the primacy of J's [the child's] interest. Not primacy in the sense of overriding other considerations, but the combination of needs of [the mother] and J in my view indicates that the balance is in favour of them residing in the house.' However, the Court of Appeal ruled that this 'tipping of the balance' approach was not the correct test and fell short of what is required to justify the making of a Draconian order.

Cases in which it is said that the parties' present living circumstances are having a detrimental effect on the child tend to be based on assertions and counter-assertions made by the parties, and these have little evidential force. In *Wiseman v Simpson*[2] the mother claimed that the continual arguing between the parents was retarding the development of the child, then aged 18 months. She brought no evidence from a doctor, or other expert, to support her allegation. Although the Court of Appeal accepted that expert evidence was not necessarily essential before a finding on such a matter could be reached, it considered the wife's assertions to be a most uncertain basis for making a finding that the child's development was being retarded by the circumstances in the home. It is suggested that it would therefore seem wise for an applicant to bring medical, or other, evidence to substantiate any allegation that the child is suffering harm.[3]

Where parents are in dispute about with whom the child will live the question then arises whether the residence issue should first be resolved, before any order is made ousting one of the parties from the matrimonial home. In *Re T (A minor); T v T (Ouster Order)*[4] it was held that normally the court should decide first who is to be the parent with whom the children

---

1   [1993] 1 FLR 1008.
2   [1988] 1 All ER 245.
3   Similarly, if the wife has been driven out of the home and is now living in highly unsuitable accommodation, and the poor living conditions are such as either to cause, or aggravate, illness or disability in the child, she would be well advised to bring the appropriate evidence to substantiate her case.
4   [1987] 1 FLR 181.

are to have their home, and then go on to decide whether or not to oust the other parent. If the issue of occupation of the home arises at the same time as an application for a residence order the applicant must couple her application for residence with an appropriate application for ouster under either the 1983 or the 1976 Act. If she does not the court has no power to make an ouster order.[5]

All the circumstances of the case

As the Law Commission have commented[6] it is difficult to know what other matters may be thought relevant under the head 'all the circumstances of the case'. In *Baggott v Baggott*[7] it was pointed out that the matters to be considered by the judge in exercising his discretion are couched in the widest possible terms, and that 'the judge is not required to set out a series of questions and answers in giving his judgment. It is a discretion which he has to exercise under those very wide powers.' Certainly excluding the husband in order to allow the dust to settle has been disapproved.[8] Likewise, it should not be used as a threat to bring a man to his senses.[9] If the home is owned and/or lived in by other persons as well as the husband and wife, this clearly could be a relevant factor, as in *Chaudhry v Chaudhry*.[10] Here the wife was seeking an order permitting her to re-enter the home, but the house was partly occupied by the husband's relatives. The court therefore refused to make an order, as this would create an impossible situation. It is suggested that other factors which it might be appropriate for a court to consider under this head could include the fact that one of the parties is disabled and the property is specially adapted for him or her, or the fact that one party works from home.[11]

5   Although this may be rectifiable on appeal: see *Re M (Minors) (Disclosure of Evidence)* [1994] 1 FLR 760. In *Re M* the Court of Appeal shared the concern of the trial judge as to the extreme effect of the conduct of the mother on the children, and the urgent need to protect them. Thus although the father had not originally applied for an ouster order they confirmed the judge's decision to oust the mother. They were satisfied that the judge had been fully apprised of all the relevant criteria, and since the appropriate application had now been made, they could, without risk of injustice, make their own decision and exercise their own discretion.
6   Working Paper No 113 at p 27.
7   [1986] 1 FLR 377 at p 379.
8   See *Summers v Summers* [1986] 1 FLR 343.
9   *Burke v Burke* [1987] 2 FLR 71.
10 [1987] 1 FLR 347, where four members of the husband's family lived in the property, and he and his father were the joint owners of the house.
11 Although it could be maintained that these factors fall under the heading 'needs and financial resources' in any event.

The 'Draconian order' principle

It is suggested that a disturbing feature of the above analysis is that it reveals that a new 'principle' has been allowed to take root since the House of Lords' decision in *Richards v Richards,*[12] namely that ouster orders are 'Draconian' orders which should only be made in exceptional circumstances. Yet in *Richards v Richards* itself the court stated that all four of the criteria should be considered, none of them being pre-eminent. Lord Hailsham LC in giving the leading judgment of the majority stated:

> 'The facts in matrimonial proceedings are so varied in their nature that courts should be extremely careful before reading into judgments which are uttered in the context of a particular case universal principles which may have the virtue of simplicity but which if so treated are at variance with the fuller and more appropriate criteria prescribed by Parliament, and in particular with the requirement that the total result should be just and reasonable.'[13]

This was a clear exhortation to be cautious in extracting general principles from the cases. Yet *Burke v Burke*[14] lays claim to the idea that an order should only be made in a case of 'real necessity' although there is nothing in section1(3) which forces such an interpretation.[15] The section simply states that the order must be one that is 'just and reasonable', which is by no means the same thing. Of course there is force in the argument that an order requiring one of the parties to leave the home should not be made lightly, and it is probably the case that the pendulum had swung too far in cases like *Richards v Richards* in which, at first instance, the judge found that Mrs Richards had no reasonable grounds for refusing to return to live with her husband in the matrimonial home, and in which he commented 'I think it is thoroughly unjust to turn out this father, but justice no longer seems to play any part in this part of the law'.[16] However, it seems that the pendulum has now swung back too far in the other direction.

It is suggested that there is a very real danger in normally requiring proof of some type of serious misconduct, usually violence, on the part of the husband before he can be ousted. It is arguable that such an approach creates the risk that a wife who is determined to leave her husband, but who has nowhere to go, may feel forced to take steps to goad him into

12 [1983] 2 All ER 807.
13 Ibid, at p 817
14 [1987] 2 FLR 71.
15 This approach has been repeated time and again; see particularly *Tuck v Nicholls* [1989] 1 FLR 283; *Shipp v Shipp* [1988] 1 FLR 345; *Blackstock v Blackstock* [1991] 2 FLR 308; and *G v J (Ouster Order)* [1993] 1 FLR 1008.
16 [1983] 2 All ER 807 at p 811.

assaulting her. This could have serious consequences for both parties. The wife could be badly injured, and the husband could acquire a criminal record. Furthermore, requiring the wife to prove that the husband is at least equally, if not more, to blame for the violence element within the relationship, as the Court of Appeal did in *Blackstock v Blackstock*,[17] is to give greater priority to the conduct element in the criteria than to the welfare of the children. From the point of view of the children it matters not who is the instigator of violence between the parents. Their concern is to have a safe and comfortable roof over their heads. They need to be living in a household where they are not subjected to scenes of violence between their parents. Violence not only has the potential to be extremely damaging to the mental well-being of any children, but also exposes them to the risk of becoming personally involved, if they feel the need to try and step in to protect one of their parents, as in *Jordan v Jordan*.[18]

It is suggested that in determining whether an ouster injunction is a Draconian order it should be incumbent on the court to consider the practical consequences on both parties of making, or refusing to make, an order. Giving minimal weight to the fact that the woman has felt compelled to leave home and to live in highly unsuitable accommodation, often with the children, is to ignore the Draconian consequences of refusing to make an order. The living circumstances of the applicant surely merit just as much attention as those of the respondent. Yet when, for example, the approach of the Court of Appeal in *Summers v Summers*[19] is contrasted with its approach in *Shipp v Shipp*[20] there are grounds for suggesting that the Court of Appeal is far more concerned about the impact of an ouster order on the husband than it is about the refusal to make an order on the wife and children. In *Summers v Summers* if the husband were to be ousted from his home he would be reduced to sleeping on the settee at the home of his grandmother. Clearly this would have a major impact on him, and the court commented sympathetically on these 'difficult' living conditions. By contrast, in *Shipp v Shipp* the court had very little empathy for the wife's position. It merely stated that it was up to her to decide whether she wished to return to the matrimonial home with her child, under the protection of an undertaking given by the husband that he would not molest her, or whether she and the child would continue living with her sister in very cramped conditions. However, it may be that the mood of the Court of Appeal is altering. In the recent decision of *Brown v Brown*[1] the Court of Appeal confirmed a decision to oust the husband where there had been no

17 [1991] 2 FLR 308.
18 [1993] 1 FLR 169.
19 [1986] 1 FLR 343.
20 [1988] 1 FLR 345.
1 [1994] 1 FLR 233.

violence. The recorder had considered the fact that the wife and child had been driven to sleep in sleeping-bags on the floor a highly important factor.

It is suggested that an approach which concentrates on proof of misconduct penalises those spouses and partners whose relationships have broken down but who do not attack or otherwise molest one another. It is suggested that it is absurd for a court to arrive at the conclusion that it is impossible for the parties to remain together under the same roof, but to refuse to assist them to part, as it did in *Wiseman v Simpson*.[2] Parties often cannot engage in self-help and negotiate an agreed arrangement in cases of this kind. Where each has an interest in remaining in the property they are likely to need an independent arbitrator to determine who should go and who should be allowed to remain, at least for the time-being.[3]

It is suggested that the ruling in *Summers v Summers*[4] that 'allowing the dust to settle', in the admittedly forlorn hope of effecting a reconciliation, fell outside the scope of the criteria in section1(3) was narrow and excessively legalistic. The court is specifically required to consider 'all the circumstances of the case', and the trial judge, after evaluating the witnesses and the evidence, clearly thought that these factors were relevant in this particular case. Indeed, if a short-term ouster order had succeeded in achieving the judge's purpose this would have been of positive benefit both to the parties and to their children.[5] It is suggested that courts should be encouraged to take the prospect of achieving a reconciliation into account in appropriate cases rather than being castigated for it.

Duration of ouster orders

Although the courts apply the same criteria when exercising their discretion to grant injunctions under the Domestic Violence and Matrimonial Proceedings Act 1976 whether the applicant is married or unmarried, the duration of the order may be influenced by the applicant's status. A spouse has a right of occupation in the matrimonial home and is entitled to be protected in the exercise of that right. By contrast, an unmarried partner has no right to live in the 'matrimonial home' flowing solely from her status; thus where she has no proprietary interest in the home, any injunctive relief she obtains will authorise her to live in property belonging entirely to someone else. It was for this reason that the House of Lords in *Davis v*

2   [1988] 1 All ER 245.
3   See further M Hayes *The Law Commission and the Family Home* (1990) 53 MLR 222.
4   [1986] 1 FLR 343.
5   Contrast the obiter dicta of Glidewell LJ in *Scott v Scott* [1992] 1 FLR 529 at p 537 in which he recognised that an order requiring one of the parties to leave the home can sometimes give rise to a positive outcome in respect of their relationship.

Johnson[6] was at pains to emphasise that ouster injunctions are intended to provide 'first-aid but not intensive care.' Subsequently, a *Practice Note*[7] was issued which stated that the normal maximum length for an ouster injunction should be three months. This direction applies to both spouses and unmarried partners.

Duration of ouster orders where the parties are married

Despite the length of time the Domestic Proceedings Magistrates' Courts Act 1978 has been in force, no general guidance has been issued stipulating for how long an ouster order should last. However, it is unlikely that the order will last for longer than a maximum of three months,[8] in common with applications under the 1976 Act.[9] This time limit conforms with the general purpose of the violence provisions of the Act, and ties in with the other domestic violence legislation. The idea behind giving jurisdiction to magistrates was to provide the wife with immediate protection. It enables the parties to consider their position. It gives the husband the opportunity to 'cool down', or the wife time to go on to make further applications. It is certainly the case that magistrates do not have any jurisdiction to interfere in the long-term property interests of spouses. Magistrates should not, therefore, interfere in the spouses' use and enjoyment of the property, except on a temporary basis.

There is very little case law discussing the duration of ouster orders under the Matrimonial Homes Act 1983, and no guidelines have been laid down by the court. Section 1(4), on its face, gives the court an unfettered jurisdiction. It provides—

'Orders under this section may, in so far as they have a continuing effect, be limited so as to have effect for a period specified in the order or until further order.'

In *Davis v Johnson*[10] Viscount Dilhorne considered the relationship between the Matrimonial Homes Act 1967[11] and the Domestic Violence and Matrimonial Proceedings Act 1976. He stated that an injunction under the 1976 Act was intended as a temporary measure, designed to give the applicant

6   [1978] 1 All ER 1132, per Lord Salmon at p 1152.
7   [1978] 2 All ER 1056.
8   This was the length of time of the exclusion order in *Widdowson v Widdowson* (1982) 4 FLR 121, one of the very rare reported decisions of the magistrates.
9   In Fricker et al *Family Courts: Emergency Remedies and Procedures* (Jordan Publishing, 1993) p 370, it is stated that the family proceedings courts follow the practice of the county courts and make orders for relatively short terms.
10 [1978] 1 All ER 1132. See also *O'Neill v Williams* [1984] FLR 1.
11 As it then was; now the 1983 Act.

some breathing space, and could be followed up by an application under the 1967 Act. In particular Viscount Dilhorne commented that after an order had been granted under the 1976 Act:

'It might be followed by an application under the Matrimonial Homes Act 1967 and it may be that a county court judge ... would grant an injunction until further order and would make it clear that it would lapse if no application was made under the 1967 Act and, if such an application was made, only continued until an order had been made under it.'[12]

This opened the door to more long-term regulation of the occupation of the home in an application under what is now the 1983 Act. More generally the 1983 Act is specifically designed to regulate rights of occupation in the matrimonial home in a variety of different circumstances. It would seem correct, therefore, that a court should be left with a great deal of discretion in determining the duration of an order.

Nonetheless, it appears that orders made under the Matrimonial Homes Act 1983 tend to be limited in time in line with the approach taken under the Domestic Violence and Matrimonial Proceedings Act 1976, and the three month practice direction. It would certainly be most unusual for a court to make an order which was unlimited in time because it would, in effect, amount to an order settling the property on the wife, and this is a power which only exists in ancillary proceedings under the Matrimonial Causes Act 1973.[13] It seems that such an order is a possibility for those rare cases where the wife is in need of an extreme remedy.[14] But even then, the court would be likely to give the ousted spouse liberty to bring the matter back to court should the circumstances alter. However, where a party to ouster proceedings brought under the Matrimonial Homes Act 1983 is also applying for a decree of divorce or judicial separation, the existence of the court's power to make a property adjustment order on the grant of a decree may influence the court in making its decision about the length of the ouster order. Faced with a wife who is also petitioning for divorce, the court might consider it proper to make the order to last pending the outcome of the divorce proceedings, when a final property adjustment order can be made. This could be considered appropriate even though the divorce is several months away.[15] The same approach could also be applied in proceedings for judicial separation.[16]

12 [1978] 1 All ER 1132, at p 1146.
13 S.24; and see generally ch 7.
14 In *Galan v Galan* [1985] FLR 905 the wife was granted just such an order, although under the Domestic Violence and Matrimonial Proceedings Act 1976. The parties were joint owners of the property, and the court expressed its disappointment that earlier applications had not been made under s.9 of the 1983 Act.
15 *Baggott v Baggott* [1986] 1 FLR 377.
16 *Anderson v Anderson* [1984] FLR 566.

Local authority tenancies and spouses

An order ousting one of the spouses from local authority owned property of which they are joint tenants, or of which the person ousted is the sole tenant, could have serious implications if the order were to be made unlimited in time. Under the Housing Act 1985, a spouse acquires rights under the 'right to buy' provisions.[17] Furthermore, under section 87 one spouse is normally entitled to succeed to a secure tenancy if the other spouse dies. However, to succeed to these rights he must be residing in the property as his 'only or principal home' at the time when the right accrues. It is suggested that where an ouster order is stipulated to last without limit of time, that once the order takes effect the husband can no longer claim the property as his only or principal home, as he is forbidden to reside there. Thus as from that date he loses any accrued rights.[18] However, this is not such an extreme, or serious, an outcome as first appears. The husband is only entitled to his rights under the Housing Act 1985 in his capacity either as the tenant, or as a spouse. Once he is divorced he loses his rights as a spouse in any event. If the tenancy is transferred, he loses his rights as a tenant.

A woman who has instituted divorce proceedings is entitled to apply under Schedule 1 of the 1983 Act for the tenancy to be transferred into her sole name.[19] In the meantime she is entitled to pay the rent whether or not she is the tenant.[20] Of course the local authority may have their own view of the matter, and indeed may not wish the tenancy to be transferred, and therefore provision is made for the local authority to be heard in such property adjustment proceedings.[1] In *Buckingham v Buckingham*[2] it was held that, faced with an objection to a transfer from the local authority, the court must engage in a balancing exercise, weighing the hardship to the wife if the property were not transferred against the disruption which would be caused to the local authority's housing policy if it were to be transferred. It would be unusual for an objection by the local authority to succeed. The court has no powers to terminate the tenancy altogether, and the powers of the local authority to terminate a tenancy are heavily circumscribed by the provisions of the Housing Act 1985.[3] Thus one or other of the spouses will remain in occupation in any event. An example of

---

17 Found in Parts IV and V.

18 Where the ouster order is lengthy, but limited in some way, the position is unclear.

19 See paras 1 and 2.

20 Matrimonial Homes Act 1983, s.1(5). This right of a spouse to pay any outgoings in respect of the matrimonial home is an important safeguard. She should be advised to take steps to ensure that rent or mortgage arrears do not accrue, as this could result in her losing possession of the property.

1 Sch.1, para 8(1).

2 (1979) 129 NLJ 52.

3 The grounds for terminating a tenancy are found in Housing Act 1985, Sch. 2.

violence perpetrated by the woman to consider it necessary to oust her from the home, but had they been it would seem that they might well have decided to oust her until the property issues had been finally resolved either by agreement or by proceedings taken under section 30.

Unfortunately sale will by no means always supply a satisfactory solution for the woman. It is not unusual for a woman to find herself in the same situation as the woman found herself in *G v J (Ouster Order)*.[13] Here the court recognised that the parties could no longer live together, and thought sale the obvious answer. However, there was a negative equity in the house. The court therefore advised that the 'parties will have to reach some other suitable solution.'[14] What other solution they had in mind they did not indicate, but the situation would seem to be a desperate one. The parties will obviously not wish to sell and be left with a large debt and no housing. It might be possible for one of them to agree to buy the other one out. However, this would not appear to be feasible in all but the most unusual of cases, as it would mean one person either having, or raising, a large sum of capital. Clearly that person would not be able to raise the money on mortgage, so his only other option would be to raise the money from some other source, where he is liable to be charged a very high rate of interest. Another possibility would be to negotiate with the mortgage lender and try and arrange a transfer of the mortgage to two separate properties. Quite apart from the difficulty of persuading the mortgage lender that this is a practical proposition, the parties would inevitably end up very considerably out of pocket if they could secure such an arrangement. They would still be the owners of property with a negative equity, and may well subsequently find that they are not in fact able to afford to finance such an arrangement. There therefore appears to be no obvious solution to the problem where there is a negative equity.

Local authority tenancies and parties living together as husband and wife

If a local authority tenancy is in the unmarried woman's name alone the answer to the problem of occupation is the same as that for owner-occupied property. The woman is entitled to demand that the man leave the property. In view of this the court should feel free to make an order to last without limit of time if requested. Similarly, if the tenancy is in the man's name alone the order to oust him will only last for a very limited period, just sufficient to enable the woman to find alternative accommodation.[15] However, because the woman is being forced out of council accommodation,

13 [1993] 1 FLR 1008.
14 Ibid, at p 1019.
15 *Fairweather v Kolosine* (1983) 11 HLR 61 was an exceptional case, where the woman not only got an order for ouster, but it was granted for a period of five years. However, the

she is likely to be looking to the council for alternative housing. The court is therefore also likely to consider the current local authority housing situation and policies. This may influence them both in deciding for how long to oust the man, and whether or not to oust him at all.

Where the parties are joint tenants of property provided by a local authority the situation is once again extremely unsatisfactory as regards the victim of violence. An early decision, *Spencer v Camacho*,[16] suggested that in extreme cases a lengthy ouster order should be made to protect a joint tenant who was suffering violence. In that case the woman had to come back repeatedly to court for further orders. It was therefore held appropriate to make the ouster to last 'until further order'. Unfortunately, however, although this case was followed by a number of decisions building upon it, they were based upon a fundamentally flawed assumption, perhaps stemming from the decision in *Davis v Johnson*[17] where the House of Lords had to consider the position of a cohabitee joint tenant. In ousting the very violent man their Lordships assumed that during the three months of ouster the local authority might be prepared to terminate the joint tenancy and regrant it in the sole name of the woman. At the time this was a reasonable assumption, and there was nothing to prevent the local authority from so doing. However, subsequently the Housing Act 1980, now the Housing Act 1985, has given security of tenure to council tenants. It is no longer possible to terminate any tenancy except for one of the reasons specified under the Act, and these reasons do not include domestic violence.[18] As a result the local authority, or court, are simply unable to terminate the joint tenancy, however much sympathy they may have for the woman and however much they may wish to help her.[19] It was not until *Wiseman v Simpson*[20] in 1988 that the inability of either the local authority or court to transfer the

court relied heavily on *Spindlow v Spindlow* [1979] 1 All ER 169, a decision which was severely criticised by the House of Lords in *Richards v Richards* [1983] 2 All ER 807. It is therefore suggested that such a ruling is highly unlikely to be repeated.

16   [1984] FLR 662.
17   [1978] 1 All ER 1132.
18   Housing Act 1985, Sch. 2.
19   Unfortunately the cases immediately following *Spencer v Camacho* do not seem to have taken account of the change in the law. Thus in *Lee v Lee* [1984] FLR 243 the order was expressed to last until further order, but the Court of Appeal appear to have been heavily influenced in their decision by a misunderstanding of the law. For, in making the order, they stressed that this was not intended to be permanent, and they suggested that the tenancy could be transferred into the sole name of the woman. In similar fashion in *Thurley v Smith* [1984] FLR 875 the decision to oust the man for only three months seems to have been influenced by what it was thought would happen to the tenancy in the meantime. The man brought a letter to court which had been sent to him by the local authority. The letter stated that if he was ousted a sole tenancy would be granted to the woman. Legally the local authority could not transfer the tenancy, but nonetheless everyone appears to have acted on the basis that that was what was going to happen.
20   [1988] 1 All ER 245.

tenancy was judicially recognised, and the Court of Appeal stated that there was a gap in the law.

Ending the joint tenancy

It clearly is a serious gap when the law does not permit a woman joint tenant suffering from domestic violence to gain anything other than very short-term relief. There is a potential self-help remedy available to women, but unfortunately this remedy is not itself without considerable problems. The solution stems from the decision of *Greenwich London Borough Council v McGrady,*[1] in which it was held that where one joint tenant gives notice to quit to the local authority, without either the knowledge or consent of the other, that is nevertheless sufficient to terminate the tenancy. A battered woman can therefore simply terminate the tenancy, and either apply to be rehoused if she wishes to get away from the man or conceal her address from him, or request that the tenancy be regranted in her sole name. Unfortunately this simple solution becomes more complex on consideration. Perhaps the most worrying of all the practical difficulties arising out of this solution is the possible reaction of the man on discovering that he has lost his right to the tenancy. Research into the problems of domestic violence and homelessness reveals that housing officers, in various authorities, have stated that where a woman has taken advantage of the ruling in *Greenwich London Borough Council v McGrady* this has sometimes seriously jeopardised her safety.[2] The reason for this is because it was she who was instrumental in causing her ex-partner to lose his accommodation. If the net result of advising a woman to serve notice to quit is to precipitate further violence between the parties this is not a solution to be advocated.

This solution is also not devoid of legal problems. It is possible that the woman's action could be considered to constitute a breach of trust on her part. Under normal equitable principles both joint tenants hold property on trust for each other. Thus if one joint tenant destroys the other party's interest in the property she will be in breach of trust. This point was adverted to in the House of Lords' decision in *Hammersmith and Fulham London Borough Council v Monk,*[3] where Lord Browne-Wilkinson, in an obiter comment, briefly stated his opinion that he thought this would not be a breach, but without elaborating on his reasons.[4] If the view of Lord

1 (1982) 6 HLR 36.
2 See E Malos and G Hague *Domestic Violence and Housing: Local Authority Responses to Women and Children escaping Violence in the Home* (1993) Women's Aid Federation and School of Applied Social Studies, University of Bristol at p 73.
3 [1992] 1 All ER 1 at p 11.
4 Unfortunately the cases he cited in support of his view do not actually cover the situation, and cannot really be said to be authorities on the point.

Browne-Wilkinson is correct the problem is solved. But if on reflection it was held to be incorrect some awkward consequences flow from the breach. One consequence could be an action for breach of trust. In view of the likely financial status of the woman this worry is perhaps more theoretical than real. However, of more significance is a straightforward application of basic trust law. If the woman remained in the home as sole legal tenant she would be profiting from her breach of trust. Basic trust law will then operate to say that she holds the equitable estate, which includes the right to physical enjoyment of the property, not only for herself, but for the man as well on a constructive trust.[5] The woman has thereby come full circle and the problem has not been solved.

A further problem which has to be addressed is that there is no way of telling what a local authority will do faced with a woman wishing to terminate the tenancy. They must, of course, accept her notice to quit. However, what action they will take thereafter is not clear cut. Initially the local authority may have no way of telling whether the story the woman is telling is true. They may well be reluctant, therefore, simply to regrant the tenancy to the woman, or to grant her another tenancy. It is even conceivable that they could deem her intentionally homeless.[6] They may also be worried about their duties concerning the man, and want to investigate whether they would be under any duty to rehouse him. All these problems would need to be sorted out with the local authority before a woman took any action.

Ouster after divorce

Where a marriage has been ended by divorce, any questions relating to the occupation of the home are normally settled during the course of the matrimonial proceedings.[7] However, there are instances where no agreements or orders have been made, and where the husband and wife continue to live under the same roof. At this stage they are not eligible to apply for orders and injunctions relating to the occupation of the home because the legislation applies only to spouses, and to persons who are living with each other in the same household as husband and wife. Consequently, an applicant's ability to obtain an ouster order will be dependent either on

5　For more detailed consideration of this difficulty, see C Williams *Ouster Orders, Property Adjustment and Council Housing* (1988) 18 Fam Law 438.
6　See below for a brief outline of the homelessness provisions.
7　Under the Matrimonial Causes Act 1973, ss.23-25: see ch 7. The courts have the same financial provision and property adjustment powers when granting a decree of nullity, or of judicial separation. The marriage will not be finally terminated until decree absolute: see ch 6. The Matrimonial Homes Act s.1(3) will therefore still apply after decree nisi: see *P v P (Ouster: Decree Nisi of Nullity)* [1994] 2 FLR 400.

the status of the parties' interests in the matrimonial property, or on whether there are any children living at home. In *Pearson v Franklin*[8] Thorpe J, when determining whether a divorced woman was entitled to an ouster order, considered nine decisions of the Court of Appeal since *Richards v Richards*[9] in chronological order. He said that where a woman is a former spouse, her rights are determined by *Webb v Webb*,[10] *Wilde v Wilde*[11] (following and applying *Quinn v Quinn*[12]), *Lucas v Lucas*[13] and *Hennie v Hennie*.[14] Thorpe J reconciled all these decisions, which had been said by counsel to be in some respects inconsistent and irreconcilable.[15] Each is discussed below in the light of his judgment.

Ouster where there are children still living at home

Thorpe J said where there are still children living in the home then, according to *Quinn v Quinn*,[16] the court is able to oust the ex-husband from the home solely on the basis of protection of the interests of the children. In his leading judgment in *Quinn v Quinn* Ormrod LJ stated:

> 'I would have thought that it is perfectly clear that, where children are involved, the court's inherent jurisdiction to intervene to protect the interests of children of course subsists. It has always subsisted and the court has always exercised the jurisdiction to exclude one parent, no matter what the proceedings, if that was desirable in the interests of the children.'[17]

This approach was subsequently followed in *Wilde v Wilde*.[18] Here the parties had continued living in the matrimonial home maintaining separate

8   [1994] 2 All ER 137.
9   [1983] 2 All ER 807.
10 [1986] 1 FLR 541.
11 [1988] 2 FLR 83.
12 (1983) 4 FLR 394. This was a pre-*Richards* decision.
13 [1992] 2 FLR 53.
14 [1993] 1 FCR 886.
15 In commenting on the nine decisions he felt that *M v M (Custody Application)* [1988] 1 FLR 225 was the only case which did not fall comfortably within the rationalisation. *M v M* was a case involving ex-spouses which he considered had wrongly been held to be governed by the decision of *Ainsbury v Millington* [1986] 1 All ER 73, rather than that of *Quinn v Quinn* (1983) 4 FLR 394. For a detailed consideration of the attempted rationalisation of the cases in *Pearson v Franklin,* and of the use of the inherent jurisdiction generally, see Judge Nigel Fricker QC *Inherent Jurisdiction, Ouster and Exclusion* (1994) 24 Fam Law 629.
16 (1983) 4 FLR 394.
17 Ibid, at p 395.
18 [1988] 2 FLR 83.

households for some months after decree absolute. Ancillary proceedings for the final disposition of the property were still on foot, but in the meantime the wife applied to have the husband ousted. She had left the home with the two children and was now living in accommodation which was overcrowded, and which was a long way from the children's schools, personal possessions and friends. This was held to be sufficiently serious as to justify excluding the husband in the interests of the children. The Court of Appeal held that there is an inherent jurisdiction in the court to ensure the protection of the children's interests without any need on the part of the applicant to establish any infringement, or threatened infringement, of a legal right. Nor was there any need to make the children wards of court.

Ouster where there are no children still living at home

A woman who does not have any children whose interests she is seeking to protect is in a much more vulnerable position. Wherever any proceedings between the parties have either been commenced, or are in the process of being commenced, she is able to seek an injunction by virtue of the power contained in the Supreme Court Act 1981, section 37(1)[19] which provides that—

> 'The High Court may by order (whether interlocutory or final) grant an injunction ... in all cases in which it appears to the court to be just and convenient to do so.'

However, despite the apparently very wide wording of the section, it was established in *Richards v Richards*[20] that the court only has jurisdiction to grant injunctions for the purpose of protecting a legal or equitable right.[1] As a result, a woman is able to make an application for an injunction only in a case where she has an interest in the property. Furthermore, before the jurisdiction can be exercised the applicant must establish that the relief that she is seeking bears some appropriate relation to the subject matter of the relief claimed in the proceedings.[2]

Where the parties have still not reached any final arrangement concerning the disposition or occupation of the matrimonial home, this can provide

---

19 See also County Court Act 1984, s.38.
20 [1983] 2 All ER 807.
1   Where an injunction is sought relating to the occupation of land the county court now has the same jurisdiction as the High Court. The jurisdiction used to be limited to cases where the net annual value for rating of the property did not exceed the county court limit.
2   See *Des Salles D'Epinoix v Des Salles D'Epinoix* [1967] 1 WLR 553.

sufficient nexus to the main proceedings to enable one of them to bring an injunction application under section 37(1). After considering a number of past authorities, in *Lucas v Lucas*[3] the Court of Appeal had concluded that the divorce court had jurisdiction under section 37(1) to entertain an application by a former spouse for an injunction to exclude the other spouse from the property wherever she has a proprietary interest in the former matrimonial home. However, the court went on to point out that it would be quite inappropriate for divorce proceedings to be used for the purpose of making a claim to an injunction long after decree absolute, and where there were no other relevant interests to be protected (such as those of children). In *Lucas v Lucas* the decree absolute had been granted only two months previously, the wife could point to continuing molestation by the husband, and the husband was claiming an interest in the property although the wife was the sole tenant. In addition, there was a child of the family living in the house. In these circumstances the Court of Appeal felt that it was highly desirable for the issue of who was entitled to possession of the former matrimonial home to be determined within the divorce proceedings. It was not an issue which could be satisfactorily resolved in an ordinary action for possession. Indeed the court ruled that it was preferable that the tribunal resolving other ancillary matters should also determine who should be in possession of the home. It held that it was therefore correct for the judge to entertain on its merits the wife's application for an injunction to exclude the husband from the property.

An ex-spouse who has no property interest in the matrimonial home is afforded no protection by section 37(1). She is unable to obtain an injunction, even though she may have commenced proceedings for a property adjustment order under the Matrimonial Causes Act 1973,[4] for unless and until she has obtained an order in those proceedings she has no property interest to which she can attach her injunction application. This situation arose in *Hennie v Hennie*.[5] Here it was the ex-husband who was seeking an order for re-entry into the former matrimonial home. The wife had purchased the property, and she and her daughter were its joint legal and beneficial owners. The Court of Appeal were clear that the husband had no rights to be protected in the absence either of the involvement of any children, or of any proprietary right in the property.

The Children Act 1989 and ouster

Attempts have been made to use the Children Act 1989 in order to oust a parent from the home. Applications have been sought using the section 8

3 [1992] 2 FLR 53. See also *Webb v Webb* [1986] 1 FLR 541.
4 See ch 7.
5 [1993] 1 FCR 886.

orders of both a prohibited steps order, and a specific issue order, but these have proved unsuccessful. However, the door has been left open for future applications under section 15 and Schedule 1.

The orders sought

In *Nottinghamshire County Council v P*[6] the children were suffering significant harm due to sexual abuse by their father. The local authority took the view that it was in the best interests of the girls if they remained living in the home with their mother. They concluded that it was unnecessary to apply for a care order if the father could be ousted from the home. They therefore applied for a prohibited steps order in order to achieve this purpose. Counsel for the local authority argued that to drive local authorities to apply for a care order might well be an excessive intervention in the life of a family where an order ousting a parent from the home would suffice to protect the children. However the Court of Appeal were of the opinion that the route chosen by the local authority was wholly inappropriate, and that they should use the provisions of Part IV of the Act in cases where children are suffering, or are likely to suffer, significant harm. Furthermore, Sir Stephen Brown P commented: 'it is very doubtful indeed whether a prohibited steps order could in any circumstances be used to "oust" a father from a matrimonial home.'[7]

In *Pearson v Franklin*[8] a second attempt was made to use provisions in the Children Act 1989 in order to oust a parent from the home. The parents of young twins were unmarried. They were joint tenants of a tenancy granted by a housing association. The relationship broke down, and the mother moved out with the babies and went back to live with her parents, whilst the father remained in the home. Some months later the mother applied for a specific issue order that she be allowed to reside in the property with the children, in the absence of the father.[9] Confirming the judge's refusal to grant the order, the Court of Appeal was quite clear that Parliament did not intend that an ouster order should be capable of being made under the guise of a specific issue order. However, the Court of Appeal did suggest that the appropriate action for the woman to take was to apply for a property adjustment order under section 15 and Schedule 1. Under

6   [1993] 3 All ER 815.
7   Ibid, at p 825. However, see *Re S (Minors) (Inherent Jurisdiction: Ouster)* [1994] 1 FLR 623 in which Connell J ousted a man from the home at the request of a local authority under the inherent jurisdiction of the High Court.
8   [1994] 2 All ER 137.
9   Presumably she was unable to make an application under the Domestic Violence and Matrimonial Proceedings Act 1976 because of the lapse of time between her ceasing to cohabit with the man and bringing her application.

these provisions the court is empowered to make an order requiring a parent to transfer property to the other parent for the benefit of their child.[10] The Court were of the opinion that once a section 15 application has been lodged, the court seised of the issue could then control the use of the premises pending final determination of the issue by injunctive orders. There was no discussion of the criteria which would apply to the grant of an ouster injunction in these circumstances. It is suggested that the likelihood is that a court would look to the criteria in section 1(3) of the Matrimonial Homes Act 1983. In matters relating to ouster courts have consistently taken the view that the welfare of the child is not the paramount consideration, and that *Richards v Richards* prevails.[11]

Enforcement of orders and injunctions

When an application is made to a court for a non-molestation injunction, in practice it is frequently the case that the application is compromised, with the respondent giving an undertaking to the court not to molest the applicant. Similarly, when faced with an application for ouster, the respondent will often agree to leave the home, thus obviating the necessity for the court to make an order. An undertaking is a promise given to the court. Theoretically, the protection afforded by it is as effective as a court order, and breach of an undertaking can give rise to proceedings for contempt. It is often to the man's advantage to give such an undertaking because the court will not make any findings of fact about his alleged behaviour. It is also to his advantage because there is evidence to suggest that undertakings are not viewed as seriously as injunctions by either the courts or the police.[12] Even when the court does make the requisite findings of fact against the man, it may still deal with his case by accepting an undertaking from him not to repeat the behaviour. Where an undertaking is broken, and the issue is brought back to court, in some cases the court will simply accept a further undertaking from the man. Or it may grant an injunction in the same or similar terms to the undertaking, rather than commit the man for breach.[13] Women who are subjected to violence may well come under pressure to accept an undertaking, rather than to proceed

---

10 See ch 8 for a fuller discussion of these powers.
11 [1983] 2 All ER 807. See *Gibson v Austin* [1992] 2 FLR 437. However, where a couple have lived together unmarried, and where the man has treated the woman's child as his own, the provisions in Sch. 1 will not assist the child. The concept of the 'child of the family' applies only to couples whose marriage has broken down: see *J v J (A Minor: Property Transfer)* [1993] 2 FLR 56.
12 It is also not possible to attach a power of arrest to an undertaking.
13 See J Barron *Not Worth the Paper: the effectiveness of legal protection for women and children experiencing domestic violence* (Women's Aid Federation, 1990).

to a full court hearing. By doing this they may put themselves at greater risk of further violence than if an injunction had been granted. It is suggested that the court should adopt a far more rigorous approach to breach of undertakings, and treat them with the same degree of seriousness as breach of an injunction.[14]

Even when an injunction has been granted, it is only of value if it is obeyed. A person who assaults his spouse or partner in the privacy of the home is unlikely to be deterred from repeating his behaviour by a court order, unless the order is backed up by swift and effective enforcement procedures. Similarly, where the court issues an injunction excluding a spouse or partner from the matrimonial home, or from a specified area in which the home is included, or requiring him to permit the applicant to enter and remain in the matrimonial home,[15] such an injunction only has 'teeth' if steps can readily be taken to enforce it should the respondent choose to ignore it.[16]

Contempt of court

Breach of an injunction is a contempt of court and can be punished accordingly. The sanctions that may be imposed are a fine or imprisonment.[17] Imprisonment for contempt may well afford some protection for the wife, but in *Ansah v Ansah*[18] Ormrod LJ stated that committal orders are remedies of last resort, particularly in family cases. He observed that they could damage the complainant spouse almost as much as the offending spouse, for example by alienating the children. *Ansah v Ansah* has proved to be a highly influential case. Since *Ansah v Ansah* there has been a general reluctance on the part of the courts to use imprisonment as a sanction. Nonetheless, counsel for the contemnor in *Jones v Jones*[19] failed in his attempt to persuade the Court of Appeal to lay down the principle that imprisonment should not be imposed on a first breach. Russell LJ made it clear that each case depended on its own individual facts, and no such general principle could be extracted from the observations of Ormrod LJ.

---

14 Unfortunately the Law Commission failed to address the issue of undertakings in their report on domestic violence, Law Com No 207.
15 These are the main injunctions available under s.1(1) of the Domestic Violence and Matrimonial Proceedings Act 1976.
16 The general principle in cases of ouster is that a period of two to three weeks is sufficient time to allow someone to move out of the home with some degree of urgency; see *Burke v Burke* [1987] 2 FLR 71; *Chadda v Chadda* (1980) 11 Fam Law 142.
17 Contempt of Court Act 1981, s.14(1). The maximum fine is currently £5,000 and the maximum sentence two years.
18 [1977] 2 All ER 638.
19 [1993] 2 FLR 377.

Contempt of court is a civil matter and the Court of Appeal has made it clear that a court should only exercise its powers in a manner that reflects the gravity of the contempt, and not go on to punish any criminal offence that may have been committed.[20] In view of this, expressions of remorse on the part of the contemnor have played a significant part in the attitude of the Court of Appeal to the use of committal to prison as a sanction. Thus in *Jones v Jones,*[1] the Court of Appeal, despite the fact that it recognised that it was faced with a 'blatant and aggravated contempt by a man who had been told over and over again of the possible consequences if he defied the order of the court,' nonetheless reduced the contemnor's period of imprisonment from six to three months because of the husband's 'contrition and remorse'. Similarly in *Jordan v Jordan,*[2] where on appeal it was stated that 'this is about as bad a case as it is possible to imagine, short of any permanent injury being caused to the wife,'[3] the Court of Appeal nevertheless ordered that the husband's period of imprisonment should be reduced to three months, as this would not only reflect the gravity of the offence but also the husband's expressions of remorse.

Committal proceedings for contempt are hedged round with procedural technicalities.[4] Where there has been a breach of these technicalities the appeal court has a number of options. First, it can uphold the appeal and release the alleged contemnor. In view of the fact that the liberty of the subject is at stake the courts have taken a very strict line in this area and have released the man on a number of occasions. For example, in *B v B (Contempt: Committal)*[5] it was stated by the Court of Appeal that where there is a blatant error it would need to be a wholly exceptional case for the court to cure the error, despite the fact that the court is satisfied that the man ought to be serving the remainder of an appropriate sentence for contempt. Alternatively, it can reverse or vary the decision of the court below and make such order as it considers to be just.[6] Thus where the effect on the contemnor has been slight, as in *Mason v Lawton,*[7] the court will be prepared to correct the error. Finally, it is possible to order a retrial, by virtue of section 13(3) of the Administration of Justice Act 1960. This power was used for the first time in *Duo v Osborne*[8] where the Court of Appeal was satisfied that the partial sentence already served by the husband would be inadequate if the wife's allegations were made out.

20 *Smith v Smith* [1991] 2 FLR 55.
1   [1993] 2 FLR 377.
2   [1993] 1 FLR 169.
3   Per Lord Donaldson MR at p 171.
4   For a detailed account of applications for committal see Fricker et al *Family Courts: Emergency Remedies and Procedures* (Jordan Publishing, 1993).
5   [1991] 2 FLR 588.
6   Administration of Justice Act 1960, s.13. See *Linnett v Coles* [1987] QB 555.
7   [1991] 2 FLR 50.
8   [1992] 2 FLR 425.

It is suggested that the Court of Appeal's ruling in *Duo v Osborne* is to be welcomed. It is highly offensive that a man who has been committed for contempt should be released on a technicality, as in *B v B (Contempt: Committal)*, where there is clear evidence that he is a wife batterer. Whilst it is of course essential that proper procedures are followed where the liberty of the subject is at stake, the remedy for failure to observe these procedures should also take account of the effect it will have on the victim. It is suggested that an order for a retrial best balances and protects the rights and interests of both parties.

The power of arrest

Civil courts often do not have sufficient personnel available to enforce their orders, and to bring a man before the court for contempt. Normally the man must be served personally with notice of an application to commit him for breach.[9] He may only be arrested by officers of the court, but they of course go home in the evenings and at weekends. Yet these are exactly the times when domestic violence is most likely to occur. This gap in the enforcement process was recognised by the Select Committee on Violence in Marriage, and they recommended that the police should become involved in the enforcement of domestic violence injunctions, despite the fact that injunctions are orders made in civil proceedings. Clearly, where a crime has been committed, or where a man is threatening to assault and batter a woman, the police have powers of arrest under the Police and Criminal Evidence Act 1984.[10] However, historically the police have sometimes been reluctant to become involved in domestic violence cases (because of the difficulties they face in mounting a successful prosecution). Furthermore, in some cases, the powers of the police do not encompass the behaviour which has been forbidden by injunction.

The solution to some of these enforcement difficulties lies in the power of the courts to attach a power of arrest to certain specified injunctions. Section 2(1) of the Domestic Violence and Matrimonial Proceedings Act 1976 provides that—

'Where, on an application by a party to a marriage, a judge grants an injunction containing a provision (in whatever terms)—
(a) restraining the other party to the marriage from using violence against the applicant, or
(b) restraining the other party from using violence against a child living with the applicant, or

9   CCR Ord 29, r.1(4) and r.1(7).
10 Ss.24 and 25.

(c) excluding the other party from the matrimonial home or from a specified area in which the matrimonial home is included,

the judge may, if he is satisfied that the other party has caused actual bodily harm to the applicant or, as the case may be, to the child concerned and considers that he is likely to do so again, attach a power of arrest to the injunction.'

If the respondent is in breach of the injunction a constable may arrest him without a warrant.[11] In this way the normal powers of the police are considerably extended. Section 18(1) of the Domestic Proceedings and Magistrates' Courts Act 1978 contains similar, but not identical provisions, which enable magistrates to attach a power of arrest to personal protection orders, and orders prohibiting the respondent from entering the matrimonial home.[12] It was held in *Lewis v Lewis*[13] that if a woman seeks an injunction in any other proceedings, such as divorce proceedings, or proceedings under the Children Act 1989,[14] a power of arrest can be attached to the injunction, providing that the applicant falls within the provisions of section 2(1) of the 1976 Act. However delay in bringing proceedings may disqualify an unmarried woman from the protective scope of this decision. In *Harrison v Lewis; R v S*[15] the respective applicants had brought proceedings in tort, and under the Guardianship of Minors Acts 1971 and 1973. As neither applicant was currently living with the man as husband and wife the Court of Appeal held that they could not attach a power of arrest to the injunctions, because neither woman fell within the provisions of section 2(1).[16]

A power of arrest can only be attached where the respondent has caused 'actual bodily harm' to the applicant or to the child concerned. This phrase encompasses not just physical violence directed towards the person, but also psychological violence.[17] In *Kendrick v Kendrick*[18] the Court of Appeal held that actual bodily harm can be established provided that there is clear evidence that the person assaulted has suffered real psychological damage, causing a real change in her condition. However, the test is a

---

11 S.2(3). The phrase 'a party to a marriage' includes a man and a woman who are living with each other in the same household as husband and wife.

12 Somewhat extraordinarily, magistrates cannot attach a power of arrest to an order requiring the respondent to leave the matrimonial home. Therefore care should always be taken that an ouster order from magistrates also includes a provision which prohibits entry to the home.

13 [1978] 1 All ER 729.

14 At the time the injunction could have been sought under the existing children legislation.

15 [1988] 2 FLR 339.

16 Because, of course, s.2(1) only applies to parties who are living together as husband and wife.

17 This is in line with the meaning of the phrase for the purposes of the criminal law.

18 [1990] 2 FLR 107.

stringent one, and in that particular case merely being very frightened of the husband was held to be insufficient. Furthermore, in *Bowen v Bowen*[19] the Court of Appeal held that where a power of arrest has been attached to an injunction if the husband then molests the applicant in a way which does not amount to violent molestation the power of arrest cannot be exercised. Finally, a battered wife cannot have a power of arrest added solely because her husband has attacked her in the past; she must also establish that he is likely to do so again.

Shortly after the Domestic Violence and Matrimonial Proceedings Act 1976 came into force the Court of Appeal held in *Lewis v Lewis*[20] that attaching a power of arrest to an injunction should not be a routine remedy. The court stated that it was quite plainly intended for the exceptional situation 'where men or women persistently disobey injunctions and make nuisances of themselves to the other party and to others concerned.'[1] This set the pattern for the approach in subsequent cases, and the courts have consistently stated that the power of arrest should only be attached in exceptional circumstances.[2] It is suggested that this approach fails to recognise the very dangerous nature of domestic violence, and that tacit within it is the assumption that victims of assaults within the privacy of the home can be expected to put up with this type of immoral behaviour unless it is extremely serious. It is suggested that this is unacceptable, and that the approach taken in *Lewis v Lewis* and subsequent cases is wrong. Such an approach fails to afford battered women adequate protection and is far too solicitous of the civil liberties of their assailants. What would be wrong with giving a court the authority to attach a power of arrest to any injunction which prohibited physical violence? The man could only be arrested if he were to breach the injunction. And as any such breach would be a crime, why should he not therefore be vulnerable to arrest?

Where the applicant succeeds in having a power of arrest attached to the injunction it is suggested that a lawyer advising a battered woman should always ensure that a copy of the injunction, with its power of arrest,

---

19 [1990] 2 FLR 93.
20 [1978] 1 All ER 729. Similarly, in *Widdowson v Widdowson* (1982) 4 FLR 121, it was held that magistrates should only attach a power of arrest where it is really necessary, and they should specifically state their reasons for so doing.
1   Ibid, at p 731. This wording also suggests that a power of arrest should only be attached to an injunction where there has already been a breach. Where a man has been exceptionally violent there does not seem to be any reason in principle why a power of arrest should not be attached to the original injunction.
2   See *Harrison v Lewis; R v S* [1988] 2 FLR 339. In *McLean v Nugent* (1980) 1 FLR 26 it was stated that a power of arrest should not be attached unless the respondent has been forewarned of the application, because he might not otherwise bother to turn up at court if he thinks that only an injunction is going to be made, whereas he might well do so if he thinks that a power of arrest is to be attached.

is sent to her local police station, with a letter explaining exactly what powers the court's order confers on a constable. The lawyer should also ensure that the woman has her own copy of the injunction so that she can show it to a constable should she need to seek the constable's assistance.

Where a court attaches a power of arrest to an injunction it must consider for how long that power should last. The period should not exceed three months unless the judge is satisfied that a longer period is necessary in a particular case.[3] An application may be made to extend the duration of the order if danger is still apprehended when the three months is due to expire. Any breach of the injunction must be dealt with very swiftly in a case where the man is arrested. The 1976 Act states that he must be kept in custody and brought before a judge within 24 hours, excepting Christmas Day, Good Friday or any Sunday.[4] He must then be dealt with immediately, either by being committed to prison for contempt, or by being released. The court has no power either to remand him in custody or to release him on bail.[5] A difficulty may arise where the man is arguing that he is not in breach and wishes to call witnesses to prove it. It could well be impossible for him to organise his witnesses within 24 hours. In these circumstances it was held by the Court of Appeal in *Roberts v Roberts*[6] that the proceedings should be adjourned 'to a convenient date a short way further on' and in the meanwhile the man should be released. It is suggested that this was unduly lenient towards the contemnor. Whilst it may have given him plenty of time to arrange his witnesses, it gave very little protection to the wife. It is suggested that a more satisfactory course would have been to direct an adjournment to the earliest date possible, with the court imposing a very tight limit on the amount of time given to either party to gather information or to contact witnesses.

Homelessness

Persons who are victims of domestic violence, or who otherwise have been driven from their homes, may turn to their local housing authority for assistance. Under the Housing Act 1985, a local authority are obliged to provide accommodation for certain categories of person whom the law deems to be 'homeless'. The legislation is accompanied by a code of practice.[7] In order to qualify for the provision of emergency accommodation, the

---

3 *Practice Note* [1981] 1 All ER 224.
4 S.2(4); see too s.18(3) of the Domestic Proceedings and Magistrates' Courts Act 1978.
5 *Practice Direction* [1988] Fam Law 240.
6 [1991] 1 FLR 294.
7 *Homelessness – Code of Guidance for Local Authorities* Department of the Environment (1992, HMSO).

applicant must establish that she has no reasonable home to go to, that she is in priority need, and that she is unintentionally homeless.[8]

Under the Housing Act 1985, section 58(2A)—

> 'A person shall not be treated as having accommodation unless it is accommodation which it would be reasonable for him to continue to occupy.'

Under section 58(3) a person is deemed to be homeless if he has accommodation but:

> '(a) he cannot secure entry to it, or
> (b) it is probable that occupation of it will lead to violence from some other person residing in it or to threats of violence from some other person residing in it and likely to carry out the threats.'

Thus the Act makes provision both for the woman who has been locked out of the home, and for the woman who is too frightened either to stay in the home,[9] or to return there. The woman who takes shelter in a refuge is nonetheless homeless.[10]

Priority need

If a woman is regarded as homeless under the criteria in section 58 she must then show that she is in priority need of accommodation. Section 59(1) provides—

> 'The following have a priority need for accommodation—
> (a) a pregnant woman or a person with whom a pregnant woman resides or might reasonably be expected to reside;
> (b) a person with whom dependent children reside or might reasonably be expected to reside;
> (c) a person who is vulnerable as a result of old age, mental illness or handicap or physical disability or other special reason, or with whom such a person resides or might reasonably be expected to reside;

---

8 The homelessness provisions are complex and have given rise to a considerable body of case law, the analysis of which is beyond the scope of this book. The outline below provides merely a brief overview.
9 See *R v Broxbourne Borough Council, ex p Willmoth* (1989) 22 HLR 118.
10 *R v Ealing London Borough Council, ex p Sidhu* (1982) 80 LGR 534.

(d) a person who is homeless or threatened with homelessness as a result of an emergency such as flood, fire or other disaster.'

'Dependent child' is not defined in the Act, but the *Code of Guidance* suggests that it should cover children under 16, and those aged 16-18 who are still in full-time education or training, or who are unable to support themselves and live at home.[11]

'Vulnerable' is also undefined. The *Code of Guidance* gives advice as to how it is to be interpreted. It states that it is good practice for a local authority to 'secure wherever possible that accommodation is made available for men and women without children who have suffered violence at home or are at risk of further violence if they return home.'[12] This leaves it to the discretion of a local authority whether or not to classify a woman without dependent children as being in priority need. Research has found that local authority policy and practice is variable, and that whereas some authorities operate a generous interpretation of this provision, other authorities are very restrictive when considering a single woman's application for housing.[13]

It may also be possible for a woman to establish that she is in priority need under the category of vulnerability where she has a child living with her, but that child is now over 18 years, if the child himself is vulnerable. Where the child is severely handicapped he may not be able to make an application for housing on his own behalf, as he may be considered to lack the capacity to do so.[14] However, section 59(1)(c) also encompasses the carer of a vulnerable person. Provided that her homelessness is not intentional, she will qualify for an offer of accommodation which will enable her to continue looking after her vulnerable child.

Intentional homelessness

If the woman is found to be homeless and in priority need a local authority must then assess whether or not she is intentionally homeless. Where her homelessness is unintentional, the authority are under a duty to secure that accommodation becomes available for her occupation.[15] If, however, the local authority decide that she is intentionally homeless their duty is limited to securing her some temporary accommodation, simply in order

11 Para 6.3.
12 Para 6.17.
13 See E Malos and G Hague *Domestic Violence and Housing: Local Authority Responses to Women and Children escaping Violence in the Home* (1993) Women's Aid Federation and School of Applied Social Studies, University of Bristol, at para 3.16.
14 *Garlick v Oldham Metropolitan Borough Council* [1993] 2 All ER 65.
15 S.65(2).

to enable her to have a reasonable opportunity of securing her own accommodation, and to furnishing her with advice and assistance.[16] The relevant date for determining whether or not homelessness is intentional is the date a person leaves the accommodation, and the cause of homelessness must be assessed as at that date.[17]

Local authorities are, of course, anxious to preserve scarce resources for those who cannot make provision for themselves. Research reveals that some authorities will not assist a woman unless she has taken her own steps to secure an exclusive right to occupy her present accommodation. They put pressure on the woman, and will not classify her as being homeless unless she has taken such steps.[18] If a woman fleeing violence is offered accommodation, but rejects it as being unsuitable, she may then find that the local authority classify her as being intentionally homeless. When offering accommodation, the local authority must comply with the terms of section 69 and make her an offer of 'suitable' accommodation. Where the local authority consider that they have fulfilled their duty under section 69, the woman may find it very difficult to challenge their decision that she is now intentionally homeless.[19]

Where a woman has dependent children and is driven from the home by domestic violence, she does not automatically qualify for assistance if the local authority take the view that her complaint of violence has not been substantiated. In *R v Westminster City Council, ex p Bishop*[20] the applicant had a 10-year-old daughter living with her. She claimed that she had been driven from the home by her partner's violence, but was nonetheless classified by the local authority as being intentionally homeless. However, the mother successfully challenged the council's decision in judicial review on the grounds that they had never properly addressed the position of the daughter. The Court of Appeal commented that the position of the daughter was of 'great significance'. This welcome ruling suggests that it would be most unwise for a local authority to deem a woman to be intentionally homeless where she has dependent children living with her, except where they have strong evidence, and unless they have considered the position of the children with great care.

In *Garlick v Oldham Metropolitan Borough Council*,[1] the parents had been declared intentionally homeless by their local authority. The parents

16 S.65(3).
17 *Din v Wandsworth London Borough Council* [1983] 1 AC 657.
18 *R v Westminster City Council, ex p Bishop* [1993] 2 FLR 780. See further *E Malos and G Hague* ch 5; R Thornton *Homelessness Through Relationship Breakdown: The Local Authorities' Response* [1989] JSWL 67.
19 *R v Lewisham London Borough Council, ex p D* [1993] Fam Law 277; *R v London Borough of Brent, ex p Awua* (1994) 26 HLR 539.
20 [1993] 2 FLR 780.
1 [1993] 2 All ER 65.

therefore used the device of making their children the applicants for accommodation on the basis of homelessness and priority need. The children were then aged four. The local authority refused to accept the children's application, so an action was then brought in judicial review to compel them to do so. The application was dismissed on the basis that the provisions in the Housing Act 1985 were not intended to confer any rights to housing directly upon dependent children. The House of Lords ruled that the intention of the legislation was that the parents of children, or those looking after them, would provide the children with accommodation, and it was to those carers that any offer of accommodation should be made. In dismissing the application, Lord Griffiths commented: 'I wish however to point out that there are other provisions of our social welfare legislation that provide for the accommodation and care of children and of the duty of co-operation between authorities in the discharge of their duties.'[2]

However, these provisions do not directly overcome the difficulties experienced by families who have been declared intentionally homeless. The provisions to which his Lordship was referring are sections 20 and 27 of the Children Act 1989.[3] Section 27 states that a local authority may request another authority to assist them in the exercise of any of their functions under Part III of the Act.[4] In *R v Northavon District Council, ex p Smith*[5] the House of Lords ruled that where a local housing authority have turned down a request for housing on the grounds that the applicants are intentionally homeless, the authority cannot be required to supply such housing in response to a request made by the social services department of the local authority under section 27. The two authorities had different responsibilities, one being responsible for children and the other for housing. They should co-operate for the benefit of the children, but, the House of Lords ruled, it was up to them to decide what form that co-operation would take.

Proposals for reform

In 1989 the Law Commission published a working paper for discussion.[6] Their Report was published in 1992.[7] The proposals are wide-ranging in

2   Ibid, at p 70.
3   Which are discussed in ch 3. S.20 is concerned with a local authority's duty to accommodate children, but not their parents.
4   This Part is mainly concerned with the provision of services for children in need and other children.
5   [1994] 3 All ER 313.
6   No 113 *Domestic Violence and Occupation of the Family Home.*
7   Law Com No 207. A draft Bill is included in the Report.

scope, and contain some radical changes.[8] The Government intend introducing legislation to implement the bulk of the proposals, although they have rejected some of the suggested reforms.

The aims of the reform proposals are stated by the Law Commission to be threefold:

> 'The first is to remove the gaps, anomalies and inconsistencies in the existing remedies, with a view to synthesising them, so far as possible, into a clear, simple and comprehensive code. Secondly, we have taken it for granted that any reform should not reduce the level of protection which is available at present and might wish to improve it. Thirdly, however, it is desirable, and consistent with our work on children and divorce, to seek to avoid exacerbating hostilities between the adults involved, so far as this is compatible with providing proper and effective protection both for adults and for children.'[9]

In seeking to achieve these aims the major proposal is that there should be a single consistent set of remedies, available in all courts having jurisdiction in family matters, although accepting that there may have to be some limitation on the powers of magistrates.[10]

The Commission specifically excluded certain areas from their deliberations. They did not include aspects of criminal law relating to domestic violence. They also largely did not include issues of public housing law which relate to occupation of the family home on the breakdown of a relationship.[11] Their reason for so doing was because this issue was under consideration by a Department of the Environment Working Party.[12]

In formulating their new proposals the Commission state that in principle there must be a distinction between an order not to be violent towards, or to molest, another family member, which can be obeyed without prejudice to the interests of the person concerned, and an order to leave or stay away from the home, which obviously does prejudice those interests, albeit temporarily. They therefore recommend that the new scheme should provide for two distinct kinds of remedy: a non-molestation order and an

8   For a critique of these proposals, see M Hayes *The Law Commission and the Family Home* (1990) 53 MLR 222; and M Hayes and C Williams *Domestic Violence and Occupation of the Family Home: Proposals for Reform* (1992) 22 Fam Law 497.

9   Law Com No 207, para 1.2.

10 Magistrates would be required to transfer a case upwards where a dispute over the nature or existence of an interest in the property had arisen, unless it was unnecessary for this to be resolved before dealing with the matter.

11 Although some of the recommendations take account of some of the problems which arise out of public housing issues.

12 The Relationship Breakdown Working Party. Representatives of the Law Commission participated in this working party.

occupation order, each with its own criteria, but being capable of combination one with the other, and with other family law remedies where appropriate.

Non-molestation orders

The Commission recommend that, as now, the term 'molestation' should remain undefined, there being no evidence that lack of a statutory definition has caused problems in practice.[13] In deciding whether or not to grant an order the Commission propose that the criteria, to be applied in all courts, should be that it is 'just and reasonable, having regard to all the circumstances including the need to secure the health, safety or well-being of the applicant or a relevant child.'[14]

In deciding who might be protected by the new proposals the Commission considered three possibilities: limiting applications to those people who are presently covered by the legislation, with minor amendments; opening the jurisdiction to all persons who wish to apply; and having a defined list of 'family' applicants. They favoured the last of these options and recommend that a non-molestation order be capable of being made between people associated with one another in any one of the following ways:

(i)   they are or have been married to each other;

(ii)   they are cohabitants or former cohabitants;

(iii) they live or have lived in the same household, otherwise than merely by reason of one of them being the other's employee, tenant, lodger or boarder;

(iv)   they are within a defined group of close relatives;

(v)   they have at any time agreed to marry each other (whether or not that agreement has been terminated);

(vi)   they have or have had a sexual relationship with each other (whether or not including sexual intercourse);

(vii) they are the parents of a child or, in relation to any child, are persons who have or have had parental responsibility for that child (whether or not at the same time);

(viii) they are parties to the same family proceedings.[15]

The Government have accepted all these categories of people, except those in categories (v) and (vi), which they felt did not have the same domestic link as the others, and would involve considerable extension of the specialised jurisdiction of civil injunctions for domestic violence. The Government legislation will therefore be based on the accepted categories.

13 Para 3.1.
14 Para 3.7.
15 Para 3.26.

A defined list of potential applicants inevitably has inherent problems. As the Commission themselves recognised this can give rise to strange results. They give the example of four friends sharing a flat. If they are all joint tenants a remedy may be available to any one of them. Yet where one of them took the tenancy and then sublet to his friends, the remedy would not be available to him. It seems unfortunate to legislate knowing in advance the difficult problems that are liable to arise, if those difficulties can be avoided. It is suggested that unfair and absurd results could flow from formulating the proposals in this way, and it would have been better for the Commission not to have attempted to draw up a list of defined applicants. Instead it is suggested that a simple, accessible remedy available to all who are subject to molestation, not just to those in a 'familial' relationship, should have been proposed.[16]

Occupation orders

The Commission propose that in relation to the occupation of the home the courts should have the power to make an occupation order. This would be either declaratory, declaring, conferring or extending occupation rights, or regulatory, controlling the exercise of existing rights. Potential applicants for such an order would fall into two categories: 'entitled applicants', that is those persons who are entitled to occupy the home by virtue of a legal or beneficial estate or interest or a contractual or statutory right; and 'non-entitled applicants', that is those persons not so entitled.

'Entitled' applicants would be able to apply for an occupation order against any person who falls within the defined list of persons against whom a non-molestation order could be made. The Commission recommend that there should be no maximum time limit for an occupation order, but rather it should be capable of being made for a fixed period, or until further order. In view of this they also recommend that the court should have power to make ancillary orders relating to the property, and to the possession or use of its contents. Whilst these proposals incorporate a great deal of flexibility, the limitation that orders may only be sought as against people within the defined list of associated persons for a non-molestation order could once again give rise to anomalous results. For example, whereas a wife might seek an order against her spouse's uncle, who merely visits the house, she might not be able to do so if she shares her house with her cousin and one of them is the sole owner of the property.[17] It is suggested

---

16 For a more detailed criticism of this aspect of the Law Commission's proposals see M Hayes and C Williams *Domestic Violence and Occupation of the Family Home: Proposals for Reform* (1992) 22 Fam Law 497 at p 498.

17 The uncle would come within the defined group of close relatives under head (iv), see draft Bill cl.27, but the cousin would not. If sharing the house with a cousin the wife might fall foul of the limiting provisions contained under head (iii). See further M Hayes and C Williams (1992) Fam Law 497 at p 499.

that where a dispute arises over the occupation of the home the court should be able to resolve the issue with an occupation order wherever it seems appropriate.

The Commission recommend that 'non-entitled' applicants should be able to apply for an occupation order, but only as against a former spouse, cohabitant or former cohabitant. The justification for allowing them to do so is the overriding need for short-term protection in cases of domestic violence, or for short-term accommodation for themselves and their children when a relationship breaks down. In considering an application from a non-entitled applicant, the Commission recommend that the court should be required to consider three qualifying criteria: the nature and duration of the relationship between the parties, and whether they have children; the length of time since their relationship ended; and the existence of pending proceedings between them.[18] The effect of an occupation order in favour of a non-entitled applicant would be to bestow rights, similar to those obtained by a spouse under the Matrimonial Homes Act 1983, for the duration of the order. However, these rights would be personal only, and not capable of registration. As a result the owner of the property would be free to sell or mortgage the property during the period of the order, unless the court granted an injunction to the applicant prohibiting such action. An order could last for a period of up to six months in the first instance, with the possibility of renewal for up to six months at a time.

Criteria to be applied when making an occupation order

In formulating the proposed new criteria the Commission did not find it easy to balance two tests: that of the balance of hardship between the parties, and the paramountcy of the welfare of the children.[19] The suggested criteria takes as its basis the balance of hardship test, but also cleverly incorporates the welfare of the children. The Commission propose that the court should have regard to all the circumstances including: (i) the respective housing needs and resources of the parties and of any relevant child; (ii) the respective financial resources of the parties; and (iii) the likely effect of any order, or of any decision by the court not to make an order, on the health, safety and well-being of the parties and of any relevant child.[20] However, they add the requirement that the court should have an overriding duty to make an order if it appears that the applicant, or any

18 Despite being described as qualifying criteria the applicant does not have first to obtain the leave of the court to apply. These are extra criteria, over and above those considered in the generality of cases.

19 Paras 4.20-4.35.

20 A 'relevant child' is discussed in para 3.27. In essence it would include any child living, or who might reasonably be expected to live, with either party, plus any other child the court considers relevant.

relevant child, is likely to suffer significant harm if an order is not made, and that the harm will be greater than the harm which the respondent or any relevant child will suffer if the order is made.

This test helpfully incorporates criteria found in the Children Act 1989[1] with which the courts are becoming increasingly familiar. It aims to strike a fair balance between the interests of children and those of adults, where children are involved, yet it is equally responsive to the differing needs between the adults. The Commission comment: 'We believe that this approach will enable the courts to cater properly and fairly for the wide range of cases in which occupation orders may be sought.'[2] It is to be hoped that this belief will be fully justified.

Other proposals

The Commission make two interesting proposals in relation to the inter-relationship between domestic violence and the activities of the police. They propose that wherever there has been actual or threatened violence the court should be required to attach a power of arrest, unless satisfied the applicant or any child will be adequately protected without such a power. They also propose that where the police have been involved in an incident of molestation or violence they should have the power to apply for a civil remedy on behalf of the victim. This latter proposal, however, has not been accepted by the Government. The Home Affairs Select Committee in its *Report on Domestic Violence*[3] recommended that this suggestion should be rejected. They felt that the police should not be required to decide on the basis of a particular incident whether or not to seek an order. This would be to impose significant and unaccustomed responsibilities upon the police, for which the service has neither the resources nor the expertise.

Although the Commission do not deal at length with the housing law problems which arise on relationship breakdown, they do deal with one extremely important issue, namely the inability of either the court or the local authority to transfer a tenancy between unmarried partners.[4] This causes real difficulties, not just for the applicant but for local authorities as well. In recommending that the provisions of the Matrimonial Homes Act 1983 should be extended to cover unmarried partners, whether the parties are joint tenants, or whether one party is sole tenant and the other is non-entitled, their conclusions were largely influenced by the fact that most affected tenancies are joint tenancies of a family size home, granted by the local authority as a home for the couple and their children. They

1   S.31 requires proof of significant harm to a child.
2   Para 4.34.
3   1993, HMSO.
4   For the difficulties see above.

also recommend that new statutory criteria should be introduced for such an application, directing the court to have regard to certain matters. These are: the circumstances under which the tenancy was granted; the various needs and resources of the parties; and their respective suitability as tenants. It is clear that there is an urgent need for reform of the law in this area, and these are radical proposals which, if enacted, will have a major impact on the law relating to unmarried partners.

Another welcome proposal is that the Children Act 1989 should be amended in order to give the court power to make a short-term ouster order for the protection of children. This power would be a supplement to an emergency protection order, or an interim care order, and could therefore only be made if the criteria for making either order was met. There should therefore be a two-stage process: the court should first consider whether or not the relevant order should be granted; it should then go on to consider whether or not the criteria for ouster had also been fulfilled. These criteria would cover two main areas: the order should only be made where the likelihood of significant harm to the child will not arise if a named person is removed from the home; and another person in the household must be willing and able to provide reasonable care for the child.

The recommendations of the Law Commission, when enacted, will greatly widen the scope of the legislation relating to domestic violence and occupation of the matrimonial home. Many more applicants in need of a remedy will be able to turn to the law for the assistance which they urgently require. As such, these proposals are warmly to be welcomed.

Chapter 6

Ending a marriage by decree

Chapter 6

Ending a marriage by decree

The law of nullity—void marriages

The law of nullity stems from the Canon law administered by the Ecclesiastical courts prior to the Reformation. At that time, annulment was the only means by which a marriage could be brought to an end; divorce was then unheard of. Even after divorce was introduced, the law of nullity remained. The conceptual base of nullity differs from divorce. Divorce is concerned with the breakdown of marriage, and a decree must be granted to bring the marriage to an end. Nullity, by contrast, is built around the notion that there is an impediment to the marriage which prevents it coming into existence. In the eyes of the law there is no marriage. Parties to a void marriage are therefore free to marry someone else whenever they please, and neither needs to apply for a decree to annul their 'marriage' before remarrying. Because there is no legally recognised union to annul, it may seem curious that a decree of nullity can nonetheless be obtained in respect of a void marriage. This is justified on the basis that a decree resolves uncertainty. It is a judgment in rem, and therefore binding on future courts. Nullity decrees can be granted not only to the parties to the 'marriage' themselves, but also to third parties who have an interest in whether or not the marriage is a valid marriage.[1] Third parties can challenge the validity of a marriage even where the 'spouses' are dead. Thus it can be seen that there is a need for a legal framework within which the validity, or otherwise, of a particular marriage can be clarified. The remedy could, of course, simply be a declaration as to the status of the parties. The advantage to the 'spouses' of the availability of a nullity decree is that the court's powers to make financial provision and property adjustment orders on the grant of a decree of divorce are equally available on the grant of a decree of nullity. This is an important safeguard, for a

---

1   This is most likely to arise in a dispute involving succession rights.

void marriage may last for many years, and children may be born. One, or sometimes, both parties to a void marriage may be completely unaware that their marriage is an invalid marriage, and as such either of the parties may need to be able to resort to a property adjustment framework when the invalidity of their union is exposed.

Section 11 of the Matrimonial Causes Act 1973 provides that—

'A marriage celebrated after 31 July 1971 shall be void on the following grounds only, that is to say—
(a) that it is not a valid marriage under the provisions of the Marriage Acts 1949 to 1986 (that is to say where—
   (i) the parties are within the prohibited degrees of relationship;
   (ii) either party is under the age of sixteen; or
   (iii) the parties have intermarried in disregard of certain requirements as to the formation of marriage);
(b) that at the time of the marriage either party was already lawfully married;
(c) that the parties are not respectively male and female;
(d) in the case of a polygamous marriage entered into outside England and Wales, that either party was at the time of the marriage domiciled in England and Wales.
For the purposes of paragraph (d) of this subsection a marriage may be polygamous although at its inception neither party has any spouse additional to the other.'[2]

Each of these grounds go to the very root of the existence of the concept of marriage in the eyes of English law, which is why they render it void from the outset.

Marriage within the prohibited degrees of relationship

English law prohibits marriage between certain blood relations; this is known as a relationship of consanguinity.[3] Thus a marriage between a person and his or her parent, grandparent, child, grandchild, sibling, aunt or uncle, niece or nephew is not a valid marriage. However, cousins are entitled to marry because the blood tie link is sufficiently distant. The prohibition on marriage between persons related closely by blood is founded on both biological considerations and social and moral reasons. The biological reasons are based on genetic factors: inherited disorders are

2   Whether or not a marriage is polygamous may involve difficult issues of the conflict of laws, which are beyond the scope of this book.
3   Part I, Sch. 1, of the Marriage Act 1949 lists the prohibited degrees of relationship of consanguinity.

more liable to arise within the same genetic pool. It is for this reason that an adopted child may not marry his or her natural relatives who fall within the prohibited degrees of relationship. An adopted child also may not marry his or her adoptive parents for social and moral reasons; but there is no prohibition on marriage between a child and siblings to whom he or she is related through adoption. Clearly there is no genetic reason why such a marriage should not take place, and because adoption arises in a variety of contexts, it could be unduly restrictive if adoptive siblings were unable to marry.[4] The reasons of morality and social policy which forbid certain marriages relate closely to what is acceptable to public opinion. These reasons are therefore not susceptible to proof that they are 'right' or 'wrong'. People have a strong sense of taboo about sexual relationships taking place between persons who are closely related, even though they fall outside of the scope of the criminal law of incest. Thus on relationships of consanguinity, the Law Commission posed the question: 'would public opinion tolerate or object to marriages between uncle and niece or nephew and aunt? ... There are some matters of conviction on which men hold strong feelings of right and wrong though they cannot place their fingers on any particular reason for this conviction.'[5]

There is also a prohibition on marriage between certain persons who are related through marriage, this is known as a relationship of affinity.[6] The historical basis of the prohibition is that, by marriage, a relationship becomes equivalent to a relationship by blood. Whilst this thinking is no longer one which holds sway, the rule that certain marriages should be prohibited turns on the notion that such unions are morally wrong, and therefore that they should not be permitted. When the Law Commission produced their Report on Nullity of Marriage in 1970, they concluded that there should be no change in the law relating to the prohibited degrees of affinity as there was no evidence that public opinion had altered since the question had last been canvassed in 1955.[7] The Commission found that the almost unanimous view of those who had commented on their Working Paper[8] was that the law should remain as it was. Somewhat surprisingly, therefore, the law was made less restrictive than hitherto by the Marriage (Prohibited Degrees of Relationship) Act 1986. It is now permissible for a man to marry his step-daughter, that is the daughter of his former wife, if, but only if, both parties are over 21, and provided that he has never treated her as a child of the family before she reached the age of 18. He may also marry his son's former wife if, but only if, both parties are over 21 and both his son, and the mother of his son, have died.[9] Should a man wish to

4   On adoption generally, see ch 4.
5   Law Com No 33, Report on Nullity of Marriage, 1970, at p 24.
6   Parts II and III, Sch. 1, of the Marriage Act 1949 list the prohibited degrees of affinity.
7   See the Report of the Royal Commission on Marriage and Divorce, 1956, Cmd 9678.
8   Law Commission Working Paper No 20.
9   Marriage Act 1949, s.1(5)(b).

marry his mother-in-law, this is permitted only if his former wife, and the father of his former wife, are both dead.[10] These prohibitions are clearly based on social policy considerations designed to discourage sexual relationships within the family which cut across taboos of what is generally regarded as acceptable behaviour. But the law of marriage cannot, of course, prevent a man from having sexual intercourse with his step-daughter before she reaches the age of 21, or committing adultery with his daughter-in-law. All that the law can do is to refrain from putting any kind of stamp of approval on the relationship through the orthodoxy of marriage.[11]

Marriage under the age of 16

Under English law, a person only acquires the capacity to marry when he or she reaches the age of 16. The view has been taken that it is 'essential that the minimum age for marriage and the age of consent for sexual intercourse should be the same.'[12] It is a criminal offence to have sexual intercourse with a girl aged under 16. The notion that a man should nonetheless be entitled to have sexual intercourse with a girl under the age of 16, under the cloak of marriage, offended law reformers when the age of marriage was raised from 12 for girls, and 14 for boys, in 1929, and it continues to cause similar offence today. There are social reasons too for discouraging marriage between young persons. There is evidence to suggest that the youthfulness of parties to a marriage may lead to it breaking down, and it is generally thought advisable for persons to delay the commitment which marriage entails until they have acquired greater maturity. Before producing their Report on Nullity, the Law Commission considered whether an under-age marriage should be voidable rather than void, because of the hardship which the rule rendering it void might cause. They concluded that, on balance, the arguments against this proposal were the more compelling.[13]

Failure to observe certain formalities

The formal requirements for entering into a valid marriage are contained in the Marriage Act 1949. Because English law recognises both civil and religious ceremonies of marriage, the law relating to the civil and religious preliminaries, and to the solemnisation of the marriage itself, is involved

10 Ibid, s.1(5)(a). The equivalent provisions apply to a woman.
11 For further discussion, see S M Cretney and J M Masson *Principles of Family Law* (5th edn, Sweet and Maxwell, 1990) ch 2.
12 *Report of the Committee on the Age of Majority*, the Latey Committee (1967) Cmd 3342, para 177.
13 *Report on Nullity of Marriage*, Law Com No 33, paras 16-20.

and somewhat puzzling.[14] However, despite there being an abundance of rules to be observed, failure to observe them may have no impact on the validity of the marriage. Thus, for example, the consent of parents is needed where the parties to the marriage are aged under 18.[15] But where the parties succeed in evading this restriction, and marrying without obtaining the requisite consents, their marriage is a valid marriage. Other defects render the marriage void, but only where the parties 'knowingly and wilfully intermarry'.[16] Thus it is impossible innocently to contract a marriage which is void for lack of formality.

Bigamous marriages

Where a person marries whilst he or she is already validly married to someone else, the marriage will be bigamous, and therefore void. The crucial date for determining whether a marriage is bigamous is the date of the marriage, and thus the supervening death of the first spouse will not validate the second 'marriage'. The marriage is void even though the bigamous party held an honest and reasonable belief that the first marriage had been lawfully terminated at the time of the second 'marriage', or that the first spouse was dead.[17] The bigamist will also be committing a criminal offence, and is liable to punishment, including being sentenced to a term of imprisonment.[18] Whether the criminal law should concern itself with the bigamist is a debatable point. The victim of the offence may well need the remedy of some sort of financial provision or property adjustment order, which she can indeed obtain both for herself, and for any children of the union.[19] However, her position, and that of the first wife, will not be assisted, and may in fact be harmed, by jailing the offender. The rationale for involving the criminal law lies in the general public policy that society is entitled to express its disapproval of such behaviour.[20] Where bigamy

---

14 For details, see major texts on family law.
15 Marriage Act 1949, s.3.
16 Ibid, s.25 in respect of marriages according to the rites of the Church of England; s.49 in respect of civil marriages by superintendent registrar's certificate.
17 This will, however, provide a defence to the crime of bigamy: see *R v Gould* [1968] 1 All ER 849.
18 Offences Against the Person Act 1861, s.57.
19 Matrimonial Causes Act 1973, ss.23 and 24. In *Whiston v Whiston* [1994] 2 FCR 529, in ancillary proceedings, the 'husband' argued that his bigamous 'wife' should not be entitled to ancillary relief on the basis that she was asserting rights directly arising from the commission of a crime. However, this argument was roundly rejected.
20 The traditional rationale was stated by Cockburn LJ in *R v Allen* (1872) LR 1 CCR 367, at pp 374-5: 'It involves an outrage on public decency and morals, and creates a public scandal by the prostitution of a solemn ceremony, which the law allows to be applied only to a legitimate union, to a marriage at best but colourable and fictitious, and which may be made and too often is made, the means of the most cruel and wicked deception.'

results in grave social consequences it can be argued that there is still a place for the criminal law to operate. However, beyond that it is suggested that the criminal law no longer has any place. As one commentator has written:[1] 'The only anti-social consequences that are necessarily involved in the mere celebration of a bigamous marriage are (1) the falsification of the State records, and (2) the waste of time of the Minister of Religion or Registrar.'[2]

Decree of presumption of death and dissolution of the marriage

A difficult situation arises where a spouse completely disappears, where the other spouse does not know whether he or she is alive or dead, and where that spouse wishes to marry again. If the second marriage goes ahead, it will be void where the first spouse is still alive. In a case of this kind, a spouse can be assisted by the decree of presumption of death and dissolution of the marriage. Section 19 of the Matrimonial Causes Act 1973 provides that—

'(1) Any married person who alleges that reasonable grounds exist for supposing that the other party to the marriage is dead may present a petition to the court to have it presumed that the other party is dead and to have the marriage dissolved, and the court may, if satisfied that such reasonable grounds exist, grant a decree of presumption of death and dissolution of the marriage.

(2) In any proceedings under this section the fact that for a period of seven years or more the other party to the marriage has been continually absent from the petitioner and the petitioner has no reason to believe that the other party has been living within that time shall be evidence that the other party is dead until the contrary is proved.'

The court can grant the decree before the seven years have elapsed, but any shorter period does not raise the presumption that the absent person has died. Consequently the evidential burden on the petitioner is considerably higher. The decree both presumes death and dissolves the marriage.

1 Glanville Williams *Language and the Law* (1945) 61 LQR 71, at pp 77-78.
2 Recently, in sentencing a farm labourer who had pleaded guilty to two counts of bigamy, to eight months' imprisonment, the judge called him a 'cad', and one of his victims described him as a 'silver-tongued Romeo' (see (1994) 144 NLJ 1349). Without knowing any further details of the case it is difficult to comment on the decision. However, if the extent of his villainy is expressed in the two descriptions given of him, it is perhaps fortunate for the system of criminal justice that not all 'cads' and 'silver-tongued Romeos' are hauled before the court!

Thus, if the missing person should reappear after the second marriage has taken place, his reappearance has no effect on the validity of the second marriage. In *Chard v Chard*[3] the court held that, before a decree can be granted, the petitioner must establish that there are persons who would be likely to have heard from the missing spouse during the seven-year period; that those persons have not heard from him or her; and that all due enquiries appropriate to the circumstances have been made.

The parties are not male and female

Because under English law marriage can only take place between a man and a woman, the requirement that the parties be respectively male and female seems, at first sight, to be self-evident. However, difficulties arise when the gender of one of the parties is unclear, because he or she is a transsexual. A transsexual is a person who has many of the fundamental characteristics of one sex, gonadal, chromosomal and genital, and who will thus have been registered as a member of that sex as a baby. However, he or she will function psychologically as a member of the opposite sex. Such a person may then undergo operative and hormonal treatment to enable him or her to function totally, to all outward appearances, as a member of his or her psychological sex. If such a person wishes to marry, the question then arises as to whether or not the marriage can be classified as a valid marriage. Three celebrated cases have tested the issue of classification of sex, both in the English courts and in Europe.[4] The conclusion in each instance has been that, under English law, the sex that is recorded on a birth certificate cannot be altered subsequently.[5] Consequently any marriage is not valid.

The leading case is that of *Corbett v Corbett*[6] in which it was determined that a person's biological sex is fixed at birth at the latest, on the basis of the gonadal, chromosomal and genital biological criteria, and that whatever artificial means are subsequently taken to alter the situation, this cannot take effect so as to alter the registration of a person's birth. Accordingly, as the respondent was registered as a male at birth, the marriage she entered into with the petitioner 'husband' was void. This decision was subsequently challenged in the European Court of Human Rights in *Rees v United*

3   [1956] P 259.
4   *Corbett v Corbett* [1971] P 83; *Rees v United Kingdom* [1987] 2 FLR 111; and *Cossey v United Kingdom* [1991] 2 FLR 492.
5   Except in cases where there has been 'a clerical error, or where the apparent and genital sex of the child was wrongly identified or in a case of biological intersex': see *Cossey v United Kingdom* [1991] 2 FLR 492 at p 498. This is not what is claimed in the case of a transsexual.
6   [1971] P 83.

Kingdom[7] and *Cossey v United Kingdom.*[8] In both cases the complainant argued that the British Government was in breach of articles 8 and 12 of the Convention for the Protection of Human Rights and Fundamental Freedoms. Article 8 provides—

'Everyone has the right to respect for his private and family life, his home and his correspondence.'

Article 12 provides—

'Men and women of marriageable age have the right to marry and to found a family, according to the national laws governing the exercise of this right.'

In both instances the complainant was living a life as a member of his or her psychological sex, having undergone both hormonal and operative treatment. Both had changed their names by deed poll, and both had acquired various documents which established their new identity.[9] In essence the only differences between the two complainants was that one of them was now a man, Mr Rees, and one a woman, Miss Cossey;[10] and Mr Rees had no partner whom he wished to marry, whereas Miss Cossey had intended to marry a man at the time of her application to the European Commission, and had subsequently purported to undergo a ceremony of marriage with a different man. This latter distinction between the two complainants was held by the European Court of Human Rights to be of no legal relevance, as articles 8 and 12 are not dependent on the existence, or otherwise, of a willing marriage partner. In dismissing the applications the court held that, as regards article 8, the refusal to alter the register of births, or to issue a new, altered, birth certificate was not an interference with a person's private life; that what the applicant was arguing was not that the State should abstain from acting, but simply that the State should take steps to modify its existing system. As regards article 12, it was argued that a person in the position of the applicants would be completely unable to marry. However, it was held that their inability to marry a person of the opposite biological sex to the one to which each applicant had been assigned at birth did not stem from any *legal* impediment. It therefore could not be said that the right to marry was impaired as a consequence of domestic law. Further, the court ruled that the criteria adopted by English law with

7   [1987] 2 FLR 111.
8   [1991] 2 FLR 492.
9   By acquiring new names by deed poll, these names could thereby be used in documents such as driving licences, car registration books, national insurance cards, medical cards, tax codings and social security papers.
10 This was of no legal relevance.

regard to marriage was in conformity with the concept of marriage to which the right guaranteed by article 12 referred, that is the traditional marriage between persons of the opposite biological sex. Therefore as the applicants were not of the opposite *biological* sex to any actual or potential marriage partner, article 12 did not afford them any rights which could be protected.

The result of these decisions is that transsexuals are unable to marry without the marriage being a nullity. If a female transsexual wishes to marry a man, any marriage will be void, because the female was born a male and therefore the parties will be held not to be of the opposite sex. In the highly unlikely event of a female transsexual wishing to marry a woman, any marriage would clearly be voidable on the ground of 'his' incapacity to consummate it. English law conforms with that of many other countries in refusing to recognise the validity of the marriage of a transsexual. However some countries, states, and provinces have adopted a different attitude, and have afforded transsexuals full legal recognition of change of status, including the ability to marry.[11] It is suggested that it is time that English law also changed and that the rulings in these cases were unfortunate. Where a person has undergone the radical hormonal and operative treatment that is necessary to bring about a change of sex it is inhumane not to allow such a person to enter into a valid marriage.[12] It has been argued that, in any event, the biological test propounded by Ormrod J in *Corbett v Corbett*[13] was not medically correct.[14] To the non-scientist the terms biological and psychological sex appear to be two entirely different things. Psychology is to do with the functioning of the mind, whereas biology is to do with the make-up of the body. However, it has been argued that psychological sex, psycho-sexuality and behaviour is hormone determined and consequent upon the sex of the brain, and is therefore biological.[15] Research by scientists has been done on the sex differentiation of the brain. Experts in the field have written:

'Infants are not blank slates on whom we scrawl instructions for sexually appropriate behaviour. They are born with male or female minds of their own. A male foetus will have enough male hormones to trigger a development of male sex organs though they may not be able to push the brain into the male pattern. This being so, his brain will stay female so that he could be born with a female brain in a male body.'[16]

---

11 For example Denmark, South Australia and New Jersey.
12 Indeed, a court has held that the fact that a woman has an artificial vagina does not prevent the natural act of sexual intercourse taking place: see *S Y v S Y* [1963] P 37.
13 [1971] P 83.
14 Interestingly, Ormrod J practised medicine before he became a lawyer.
15 See C M Armstrong and T Walton, *Transsexuals and the law* (1990) 140 NLJ 1384.
16 A Moir and D Jessell *Brain Sex* (Michael Joseph Ltd, 1989).

If this statement is valid, the arguments in favour of altering the law become all the more compelling.[17]

Children of void marriages

The status of a child of a void marriage is determined by section 1(1) of the Legitimacy Act 1976, which provides that—

> 'The child of a void marriage, whenever born, shall ... be treated as the legitimate child of his parents if at the time of the insemination resulting in his birth, or where there was no such insemination, the child's conception (or at the time of the celebration of the marriage if later) both or either of the parties reasonably believed that the marriage was valid.'

The child will be treated as a legitimate child notwithstanding that the belief that the marriage was valid was due to a mistake as to the law; furthermore, there is a presumption that one of the parties reasonably believed that the marriage was valid.[18] Where the child of a void marriage wishes to establish his legitimacy he may apply to a court for a declaration of legitimacy.[19] The burden of proof is on the person seeking to establish his or her status. In *Re Spence*[20] the Court of Appeal held that section 1 of the Legitimacy Act 1976 applies only where the parents have entered the void marriage before the birth of the child. Where, after the birth of their child, unmarried parents marry, but their marriage is a void marriage, the child will not be legitimated whatever their belief about the validity of the marriage. It is suggested that it is unfortunate that legitimacy turns upon the reasonableness, or otherwise, of the beliefs of a person's parents. If one of them honestly, but unreasonably, believes that the marriage was valid, it appears harsh that the child should be adversely affected. In similar vein, in *Re Spence* Nourse LJ thought it was not easy to see why Parliament should have legislated to discriminate against the child whose parent reasonably believes that he or she has contracted a marriage which, if valid, would legitimate a pre-marital child.

---

17 The authors are neither medical practitioners nor scientists, and are therefore not in a position either to comment on the research, or the force of the arguments, presented by A Moir and D Jessell.

18 Legitimacy Act 1976, s.1(3)(4). Sub-s.(4) applies in relation to a child born after s.28 of the Family Law Reform Act 1987 came into force.

19 Family Law Act 1986, s.56.

20 [1990] 2 All ER 827.

Voidable marriages

A voidable marriage is a valid, subsisting marriage unless and until a decree of nullity is obtained. It can only be annulled during the lifetime of both parties, and the parties to the marriage are the only parties who are able to petition. In common with a void marriage, on a decree being granted all the court's powers are available as if the marriage had been terminated by divorce. Section 12 of the Matrimonial Causes Act 1973 provides that a marriage shall be voidable on the following grounds only —

'(a) that the marriage has not been consummated owing to the incapacity of either party to consummate it;

(b) that the marriage has not been consummated owing to the wilful refusal of the respondent to consummate it;

(c) that either party to the marriage did not validly consent to it, whether in consequence of duress, mistake, unsoundness of mind or otherwise;

(d) that at the time of the marriage either party, though capable of giving a valid consent, was suffering (whether continuously or intermittently) from mental disorder within the meaning of the Mental Health Act 1983 of such a kind or to such an extent as to be unfitted for marriage;

(e) that at the time of the marriage the respondent was suffering from venereal disease in a communicable form;

(f) that at the time of the marriage the respondent was pregnant by some person other than the petitioner.'

Thus the grounds for avoiding a marriage have a similar conceptual base to the void marriage, namely that there is an impediment to the marriage which prevents it from coming into being. However, in the case of a voidable marriage, the impediment has a subjective dimension. For example, many people may enter into a marriage in the full knowledge that one of the parties is incapable of having sexual intercourse. It would be appalling if this lack of capacity were to render such a marriage void. Sexual intercourse between spouses is essentially an entirely personal and private matter between the couple themselves. There is no public interest in whether or not marriages are consummated, thus there is no question of such a marriage being rendered void. Yet equally, non-consummation of a marriage may cause a considerable amount of anguish and distress to one or both of the parties to the marriage. A sexual relationship is what marks out marriage from the other forms of intimacy which people bring to their personal relationships. Where that sexual relationship is lacking in a marriage, for some couples there will be a real sense that their relationship does not amount to a marriage. It may also be important to such persons that their marriage is brought to an end by annulment, rather than by divorce, for spiritual reasons. Many faiths recognise annulment as an acceptable way of withdrawing from a marriage which has never, in the eyes of the particular faith concerned, properly come into existence.

Incapacity and wilful refusal to consummate

For the purposes of consummation, sexual intercourse must be 'ordinary and complete, and not partial and imperfect'.[1] The courts have concentrated entirely on whether there has been a physical union between the parties. Thus a marriage is consummated where there is coitus interruptus,[2] or where the husband is incapable of ejaculation.[3] The use of contraceptives does not prevent consummation occurring,[4] and the fact of intercourse is the sole issue, not whether it is qualitatively satisfactory.[5] In *S v S (Otherwise W) (No 2)*,[6] as the wife was willing to undergo an operation to enable her vagina to be artificially extended, making penetration possible, the husband's petition based on her incapacity to consummate was dismissed.[7] This strict, and somewhat technical, approach to consummation is in keeping with its canonical origins. However, there is no need to prove that the spouse who has failed to consummate the marriage is incapable of having sexual intercourse with anyone; it need only be established that he or she is incapable of sexual intercourse with his or her spouse. This

1   *D_E v A_G* (1845) 1 Rob Eccl 279, per Dr Lushington at p 298. This should be contrasted with the law of rape, and adultery, in which sexual intercourse occurs where the penis makes the slightest penetration of the vagina.
2   That is, where the husband withdraws before ejaculation. See *White v White* [1948] 2 All ER 151; *Cackett v Cackett* [1950] 1 All ER 677. (But see contra, *Grimes v Grimes* [1948] 2 All ER 147).
3   *R v R (Otherwise F)* [1952] 1 All ER 1194.
4   *Baxter v Baxter* [1947] 2 All ER 886. The decision leads to a difficult question: what would be the position if one party is only willing to consummate the marriage if contraceptives are used, and the other is only willing if they are not. Has either party wilfully refused to consummate the marriage?
5   *S v S (Otherwise W) (No 2)* [1962] 3 All ER 55. If the husband is incapable of sustaining an erection this may not amount to consummation: *W (Otherwise K) v W* [1967] 3 All ER 178n.
6   Above.
7   At common law relief would only be granted where the impotence of the party was incurable. *S v S (Otherwise W) (No 2)* imports the same notion into the word incapacity. How far this notion can be taken is not clear. If the respondent refuses to undergo any treatment the petitioner should be able to plead either incapacity or wilful refusal. But what if it is the petitioner who refuses treatment? Where this will involve the petitioner in risky, or highly speculative, medical intervention there would be no reason to deny the petitioner a remedy. But where the treatment is relatively minor, and has a high success rate, it might be argued that the petitioner cannot then complain.

accords with medical science in that non-consummation may well have a psychological, rather than a physical, cause.

Where wilful refusal to consummate is being relied upon, 'a settled and definite decision not to consummate without just excuse' must be established.[8] It is this requirement that led to the failure of the wife in *Potter v Potter*[9] to have the marriage annulled on the basis of her husband's wilful refusal to consummate it. After the parties married in October 1969 they attempted to consummate the marriage on many occasions. Unfortunately the wife had a physical defect which made her unable to have sexual intercourse. In August 1970 she had an operation curing this defect, and the husband again attempted to consummate the marriage. However he failed once more, not due to unwillingness on his part, but principally due to the wife's emotional state. Thereafter he refused to make another attempt. On the wife's petition on the ground of her husband's wilful refusal to consummate, the trial judge found that the failure to consummate was due to the husband's loss of ardour, which was something that had happened naturally, not deliberately. Accordingly the wife failed to establish wilful refusal on his part.

Clearly, incapacity to consummate, and wilful refusal to consummate, are very closely linked even though, conceptually, the two grounds are quite different. Incapacity is a pre-existing condition which exists at the date of the marriage, whereas wilful refusal, by its very definition, cannot arise until after the celebration of the marriage. However, where a petitioner wishes to plead that the marriage has not been consummated, he or she may well be unsure which of the two grounds is the relevant one, and may indeed plead them in the alternative.[10] However, in the case of incapacity to consummate, the impotent spouse may present a petition in reliance on his or her own lack of capacity. By contrast, wilful refusal can only be pleaded by the 'innocent' spouse, a petitioner cannot rely on his or her own wilful refusal to consummate the marriage.[11] It has been argued

8   *Horton v Horton* [1947] 2 All ER 871. This test was applied in *Ford v Ford* [1987] Fam Law 232 where the marriage took place after the respondent husband was imprisoned. The husband lacked any reasonable opportunity to consummate the marriage, but by his conduct showed an unswerving determination not to consummate the marriage, or to live with the petitioner as husband and wife. The petitioner successfully pleaded wilful refusal.

9   (1975) 5 Fam Law 161.

10 In the Green Paper on divorce *Looking to the Future: Mediation and the Ground for Divorce* (1993, HMSO) one of the questions asked in the consultation exercise is whether wilful refusal to consummate should cease to be a ground for nullity.

11 Prior to the 1971 Act, the common law operated a bar whereby a petitioner could not plead his own impotence when he knew of it, and concealed it from the respondent; see *Morgan v Morgan* [1959] 1 All ER 539. It is suggested that when the old common law bars were swept away with the introduction of the Act this requirement also disappeared, and a petitioner can plead incapacity despite having deceived the respondent as to his sexual capacities.

that wilful refusal to consummate should not be available as a ground for nullity because it offends against the principle that the impediment to the marriage should exist at the date of the marriage, and not arise subsequently. However, the fact that the petitioner may not know whether it is by reason of incapacity, or wilful refusal, that the marriage has not been consummated is a powerful reason for retaining it as a ground for nullity.

It is particularly in the area of arranged marriages that questions have arisen as to whether the reason why a marriage has not been consummated is due to incapacity or wilful refusal on someone's part. In relation to marriages other than those celebrated in accordance with the rites of the Church of England, it is often the practice that the civil ceremony of marriage is followed by an appropriate religious ceremony. For persons of many faiths it is only after the religious ceremony has taken place that the marriage is deemed to exist, and that consummation should take place. It will normally, therefore, amount to wilful refusal if one party either refuses to go through with the religious ceremony,[12] or refuses to make the religious arrangement when it is his duty to do so,[13] or postpones the religious ceremony indefinitely.[14] Such behaviour has been held to amount to wilful refusal to consummate the marriage, because, in all three instances, the defaulting party knows that, by failing to fulfill the requisite religious requirements, that in effect he is refusing to have sexual intercourse.

Young people of a different ethnic origin, who have been brought up in England, and been subject to English schooling, culture and traditions, may find it difficult to conform to an expectation on the part of their parents that they will be parties to an arranged marriage. Cases have arisen in which such a young person has gone through a ceremony of marriage, but has subsequently failed to consummate the marriage. The question has then arisen whether such failure arose from incapacity to consummate, or whether it arose from wilful refusal. It is only in the former case that the petitioner can rely on his or her own failure to consummate. The test for incapacity was established by the Court of Appeal in *Singh v Singh*.[15] It is a rigorous test, requiring the petitioner to establish an invincible repugnance to the respondent due to a psychiatric or sexual aversion. The difficulty faced by a petitioner in satisfying such a test was illustrated by the facts of *Singh v Singh* itself. The wife had never seen the husband until the day of the civil ceremony. Although she went through with it, she then went back to her parents' house, and thereafter refused to take part in a Sikh religious ceremony. She did not see the husband again, or go near him. She petitioned for a decree of nullity on two grounds, one of

12 *Jodla v Jodla* [1960] 1 WLR 236.
13 *Kaur v Singh* [1972] 1 WLR 105.
14 *A v J (Nullity Proceedings)* [1989] 1 FLR 110.
15 [1971] 2 All ER 828.

which was her incapacity to consummate due to her invincible repugnance for the husband. Her petition was dismissed. The court found that it was understandable that the wife did not want to have sexual intercourse with her husband, as she did not wish to marry him. However, the court held that this was a very long way away from having an invincible repugnance to sexual intercourse.

In *D v D*,[16] by contrast, the evidence was much stronger. The wife had had a very restricted upbringing, and was only allowed to leave home unaccompanied when going to school. She had been subjected to violence from her father and was very frightened of him. When she was shown a photograph of her husband-to-be she protested, but was prevented from leaving her room until she agreed to marry him. All the rest of the family supported the marriage. She went through both a civil ceremony and a Hindu religious ceremony. She stayed living with her parents, the husband moving in to join them, but the marriage was never consummated. After two months she ran away to a refuge and only returned on being told her husband had gone. On finding that he was still there she subsequently escaped again. She was granted a decree of nullity on grounds of incapacity due to her invincible repugnance.

It has been seen that the mere fact that the marriage has not been consummated, does not mean that a petitioner will be granted a decree, despite the fact that the relationship is so bad that he or she feels compelled to petition for nullity.[17] A more liberal approach would permit the grant of a decree simply on the basis that the marriage has not been consummated. However, the argument against such a proposal is that it has the potential to place more marriages at risk; it could be unjust to the respondent; and that it strikes at the root of those marriages entered into for companionship only. However, it is suggested that there is considerable merit in such a suggestion, for it is up to the spouses to decide whether the marriage should continue or not. If one of them decides it should not, this is no different from the situation in divorce. Certainly the respondent cannot be protected from the emotional consequences of a nullity decree. But refusing the petitioner a decree is not aimed at mending the marriage, and will not do so except, perhaps, in the most extraordinary of cases. The respondent can be protected from the financial consequences of a decree in ancillary proceedings. Unfairness as between the parties can arise where non-consummation connotes fault on the part of one of them. However, a simple, non-judgmental, finding that the marriage has not been consummated would avoid the distasteful and fault-orientated approach to nullity which persists under the present law.[18] Where appropriate, a decree could always

16 (1982) 12 Fam Law 150.
17 See *Singh v Singh* [1971] 2 All ER 828; *Potter v Potter* (1975) 5 Fam Law 161; *S v S (otherwise W)(No 2)* [1962] 3 All ER 55.
18 See particularly *Potter v Potter* (1975) 5 Fam Law 161.

be denied under the bar in section 13(1) if injustice would otherwise be caused.[19]

Lack of consent

Where a person marries under duress, or by mistake, or is of such unsoundness of mind that he or she does not understand the nature of marriage, in each case there is no consent to the marriage. Lack of consent goes to the root of a marriage, and at common law made the marriage void. Conceptually this was correct. However the Law Commission recommended that such a marriage should become voidable only. They reached this conclusion because of the need for certainty. Such a marriage cannot, in practice, be treated as void without the court first investigating the circumstances, and being satisfied that there was indeed no consent. The law was therefore changed in 1971 to make such a marriage voidable only.

People sometimes marry out of fear, or because they are subjected to enormous pressure from others. The issue then arises as to what degree of duress is sufficient to vitiate consent. In *Szechter v Szechter*[20] in deciding whether a decree should be granted, Simon P applied the following test:

'In order for the impediment of duress to vitiate an otherwise valid marriage, it must, in my judgment, be proved that the will of one of the parties thereto has been overborne by a genuine and reasonably held fear caused by threat of immediate danger (for which the party is not himself responsible), to life, limb or liberty, so that the constraint destroys the reality of consent to ordinary wedlock'.[1]

He thus laid down three requirements for a petition to be successful: reasonable fear, innocence of the petitioner, and danger to life, limb or liberty. However, it is questionable whether any of the three requirements are necessary to establish duress. In *Buckland v Buckland*[2] Scarman J had similarly found that the fear of the petitioner must be reasonably entertained. However, this requirement was contrary to the very old decision of *Scott v Sebright*,[3] where a young woman of some means was induced to marry through fear of bankruptcy, brought about by her villainous suitor. In setting aside the marriage, Butt J commented:

19 See below.
20 [1970] 3 All ER 905.
1 Ibid, at p 915.
2 [1967] 2 All ER 300.
3 (1886) 12 PD 21.

'whenever from natural weakness of intellect or from fear—whether reasonably entertained or not—either party is actually in a state of mental incompetence to resist pressure improperly brought to bear, there is no more consent than in the case of a person of stronger intellect and more robust courage yielding to a more serious danger.'[4] When considering duress, the Law Commission were clear that the test of whether the will was overborne is a subjective one, and does not depend on whether the fear was reasonably entertained.[5] It is suggested that this is the preferable view. Provided that the party does indeed marry out of fear, its reasonableness or otherwise should not be an issue. The petitioner has clearly demonstrated that he or she does not truly consent to the marriage, and his or her will has been overborne.

The 'innocence' of the petitioner raises more difficult questions. This issue arose in *Buckland v Buckland*. The petitioner was falsely accused of seducing a young girl in Malta. He was strongly advised by his solicitor to marry the girl or face two years' imprisonment. In granting a decree on the ground of duress, Scarman J stated: '[fear] will not vitiate consent unless it arises from some external circumstance for which the petitioner is not himself responsible.'[6] In their report, however, the Law Commission recognised the basic principle that marriage should be absolutely voluntary.[7] However, and perhaps unfortunately, they failed to go on to state unequivocally that threats to expose a party's misdeeds should inevitably lead to a successful petition, as they felt that the decisions that had so far been reached on duress 'seem to be about right.' They confirmed 'illegitimate' threats as including those whereby a false charge is made against the person threatened. Some 'legitimate' threats they felt would not vitiate consent, such as mere exposure to, or legal proceedings against, a man who has made a girl pregnant. However, they felt that some threats of exposure could vitiate consent. They gave as an example: 'we doubt ... whether any court would hold that it is a legitimate threat not capable of vitiating consent for an employer to tell the office-boy who has robbed the till that unless he marries the employer's ex-mistress he will be prosecuted.' They concluded that 'any attempt to define duress with the precision appropriate to a statute would, in our view, be likely to do more harm than good. We think that the courts can safely be left to deal with each case on its merits.'[8]

A number of authorities have established that the fear to which the petitioner is exposed must be real and grave, and that there must be an

4   Ibid, at p 24.
5   Law Com No 33, para 62(b).
6   [1967] 2 All ER 300 at p 302.
7   Para 64.
8   Para 65.

immediate threat to life, limb or liberty.[9] This approach has also been applied in cases involving arranged marriages. So in *Singh v Singh*[10] where the wife was put under pressure to enter into an arranged marriage, this was held to be insufficient to amount to duress. In *Singh v Kaur*,[11] where a young man petitioned on the ground that the pressure put upon him by his parents was so great that his consent had no validity, the Court of Appeal made it clear that, even if they were not bound by precedent, they would not wish to see the test watered down. Thus, despite expressing considerable sympathy for the petitioner, Ormrod LJ commented that there were many arranged marriages in this country, and this meant that a rigorous standard must be applied. However, in *Hirani v Hirani*,[12] the most recent decision of the Court of Appeal, a different test was applied. The wife, an Indian Hindu, formed an association with an Indian Muslim. Her parents were horrified and arranged for her to marry a man whom none of them had met. The wife subsequently petitioned for nullity on the ground of duress. She claimed she was wholly dependent on her parents, and that they had threatened to throw her out of the house if she did not go through with the marriage. The Court of Appeal held that a threat to life, limb or liberty was not necessary. The crucial question was 'whether the threats, pressure or whatever it is, is such as to destroy the reality of consent and overbear the will of the individual.'[13] As they thought the parents had clearly overborne the girl's will, her consent was held invalid.

There is now no clear decision one way or the other as to the correct test, as both *Singh v Kaur* and *Hirani v Hirani* are decisions of the Court of Appeal. However, there has been some recent litigation in Scotland. In *Mahmud v Mahmud*[14] the petitioner claimed that pressure from his family over a period of years, including holding him responsible for the stroke which killed his father, had finally forced him to go through with the marriage. In the Court of Session, Lord Prosser said it was clear that the greatest pressure upon him related to the shame and degradation which would afflict his mother and family if he persisted in his refusal. The court accepted that arranged marriages did not necessarily involve an over-bearing of the will, and that if a child did change his mind and consent, albeit resentfully, the marriage was valid. But, if there was no genuine change of mind, then they held the marriage would be invalid. It is suggested that *Hirani v Hirani* and the recent Scottish decision are the better decisions, and the ones to be preferred. The threat of matters such

---

9 See, for example, *Szechter v Szechter* [1971] P 286; *Singh v Kaur* (1981) 11 Fam Law 152; *Singh v Singh* [1971] 2 All ER 828; *Buckland v Buckland* [1967] 2 All ER 300.
10 Above.
11 (1981) 11 Fam Law 152.
12 (1982) 4 FLR 232.
13 Ibid, per Ormrod LJ at p 234.
14 1994 SLT 599. See also *Mahmood v Mahmood* 1993 SLT 589.

as social degradation, financial ruin, total rejection by the family, or ostracism by the community are all immensely powerful threats, well capable of completely overbearing a person's will.[15]

Some marriages are entered into expressly for an ulterior motive, for example to evade immigration laws, or to be allowed to leave another country. Generally speaking the motive of the petitioner is irrelevant. Provided that there is a real intention to marry, the marriage is valid. However, such a marriage may also take place because of duress. *Szechter v Szechter*[16] provides a compelling illustration. The respondent divorced his wife and married the petitioner in order to effect her release from prison where she would almost certainly have died. All three parties then managed to escape from Poland and come to England. The nullity petition was presented so that the respondent could remarry his first wife. In *Szechter v Szechter* there was a real intention on the part of the petitioner to marry, so that she could benefit from the consequences of the marriage. It was by this means that she could escape a worse fate. However, it was held that the reality was that the marriage was not entered into freely at all, and that there was no true consent. However, where there is a free consent then, according to the House of Lords in *Vervaeke v Smith*,[17] such a marriage is perfectly valid. The petitioner in that case married in order to escape being deported from England. The parties had no intention of ever living together, the reason for the marriage was simply to enable the petitioner to apply for British citizenship. Where such a 'sham' marriage is held to be valid it gives rise to the particular problem that two different areas of English law operate in conflicting ways. Immigration laws will dictate that where a marriage is a sham a party to such a marriage may be deported. Yet so far as family law is concerned, the parties are validly married. This mismatch of domestic law could well lead to difficult problems in the conflict of laws, as well as to acute personal difficulties. Also, the dividing line between where there is a real intention to marry, and where there is not, may be perilously difficult to draw. For example, where an asylum seeker marries in an attempt to avoid deportation to a country where he reasonably fears that he will be imprisoned, probably tortured, and even killed, is this a sham marriage, or a marriage entered into as a result of duress?

Mistake can take one of two forms: it can relate to the identity of the other person, or to the nature of the ceremony. It is important to distinguish

15 In *Mahmud v Mahmud* above, the court was clear that there is no basis for the general view that arranged marriages involve an inherently forceful imposition of the will of the parents. Also, that both the age and the sex of the person consenting is important, but does not justify any generalisation. It is interesting to note that in a number of cases the petitioner has been a young man.

16 [1970] 3 All ER 905. See also *H (Otherwise D) v H* [1953] 2 All ER 1229.

17 [1982] 2 All ER 144.

between making a mistake as to the identity of a person, and as to the attributes of that person. Only a mistake as to the former will invalidate the marriage. However, it is not always easy to distinguish between a person's identity and his attributes. In the New Zealand decision of *C v C*,[18] the respondent pretended that he was a well-known boxer, and the petitioner married him under this erroneous belief. It was held that she was simply mistaken as to his attributes, and that she intended to marry the man who stood in front of her. Yet in the recent English decision of *Militante v Ogunwomoju*[19] the petitioner married believing the respondent to be Richard Ogunwomoju, whereas in fact he was Anthony Osimen, an illegal immigrant. Her marriage was declared a nullity.[20] It is difficult to discern any real difference between the two cases, and it is arguable that either case could have been decided the other way. Where the petitioner does not realise that the ceremony is a marriage ceremony, as in *Mehta v Mehta*,[1] where the wife thought the marriage ceremony was one of conversion to the Hindu religion, the marriage could be annulled on the ground of mistake.[2]

A person who is of unsound mind, such that he or she is unable to understand the nature of the contract of marriage, and the duties and responsibilities it creates, cannot consent to the marriage.[3] This is a protective measure. For example, in the case of the elderly it means that those who have lost their mental capacity, and who have married 'fortune hunters' not realising what they were doing, may have their marriage annulled.[4] However, because such a marriage is voidable rather than void, it means that third parties, such as relatives, cannot take steps to have it annulled. However, with the leave of the court, it is possible for a third party to institute nullity proceedings as the insane person's next friend, and it is also possible for the Court of Protection to direct that matrimonial proceedings be brought on behalf of a patient.

---

18 [1942] NZLR 356.
19 [1993] 2 FCR 355.
20 The judge himself made a fundamental mistake, as he declared that where a person marries another under a mistake 'then that marriage is void.' He should, of course, have stated that such a marriage is voidable.
1   [1945] 2 All ER 690.
2   See also *Hall v Hall* (1908) 24 TLR 756, where the petitioner who married in a registry office thought that she was putting her name down to be married in church in the future; and *Valier v Valier* (1925) 133 LT 830, where an Italian gentleman, of limited intelligence, had no idea that he was getting married.
3   *Re Park's Estate* [1954] P 112.
4   See (1987) 137 NLJ 538 where a news item reported that on 13 May 1987, the marriage of 83-year-old Mr Frank Yarwood to his housekeeper Mary was annulled on the ground that he did not validly consent to it. He was senile and remembered nothing of the ceremony, at which there had been no flowers or family witnesses, and which had not been followed by any celebration drink.

Mental disorder rendering a person unfitted for marriage

A marriage can be annulled where, at the time of the marriage, either party is so mentally ill as to be 'unfitted' for marriage. This was defined in *Bennett v Bennett*[5] as arising where the illness renders a person 'incapable of carrying out the ordinary duties and obligations of marriage.' It is distinguishable from unsoundness of mind in that the party is capable of giving a valid consent, but the state of his or her mental health is such that it would be right to annul the marriage. The illness must be present at the date of the marriage. If it arises subsequently, divorce is the remedy. A petitioner may rely on his or her own mental disorder when applying for a nullity decree.

Venereal disease

A marriage is voidable where the respondent was suffering from venereal disease in a communicable form at the time of the marriage. The basis of this ground clearly ties in with the non-consummation grounds, as it is looked upon as an impediment to sexual intercourse. It is difficult to know what to make of this ground in the 1990s. When it was first introduced in 1937, antibiotics were not available. At that time venereal disease could be an extremely serious complaint. The two most important diseases were gonorrhoea and syphilis. Gonorrhoea was undoubtedly unpleasant, and could have serious consequences, such as resulting in a woman becoming infertile. It was not, however, a fatal disease. Syphilis was more serious as it could lead to debilitating illness, or even death.[6] After the Second World War, penicillin, and other antibiotics, became widely available, and thereafter venereal disease became treatable, if not curable. In 1970 the Law Commission wisely recommended the abolition of epilepsy as a ground for nullity. (Previously epilepsy had existed as one of the grounds of mental disorder). They said: 'whatever the medical position in 1937, to-day epilepsy responds to treatment and can be kept under control.'[7] The same could be said of venereal disease. Presumably, therefore, it was the fundamental basis of the ground which was the reason for its retention,[8] namely that it was still looked upon as an impediment to sexual intercourse.[9]

5   [1969] 1 All ER 539.
6   However, it was clearly not the consequences of venereal diseases that led to the ground being introduced since, if that was the rationale, other equally serious diseases would have allowed the marriage to be avoided. For example, tuberculosis was widespread in the 1930s, and it was undoubtedly fatal in some instances.
7   Law Com No 30, para 73.
8   There is no discussion of this ground in the Law Commission report. It is simply stated that venereal disease will continue to be a ground.
9   The infertility consequence of gonorrhoea could still arise in the 1970s, as indeed it can today, as a woman might be irreparably damaged before she was treated for the disease.

Since 1970 there have been many medical advances and changes. One of these is that medical practitioners no longer even talk about 'venereal diseases'. No longer are there venereology clinics. The modern equivalent are clinics dealing with sexually transmissible diseases. That immediately raises a problem of classification. What nowadays is meant by the phrase 'venereal disease'? Does it mean the same thing as a sexually transmissible disease? If it does, should that still represent a ground for nullity? The range of sexually transmissible diseases varies enormously. Pubic lice are transferred sexually. Such a disease can be fully treated, with no adverse consequences whatsoever. Should it therefore be possible to petition for nullity if the spouse is found to be suffering from pubic lice? At the other end of the scale what about a disease such as AIDS? One of the ways that AIDS can be transmitted is through sexual intercourse. This raises an acute moral and ethical issue which needs to be addressed. If a person gets married knowing that he or she is infected with AIDS, and that this is transmissible by sexual intercourse, but conceals this information from his or her partner, should the marriage be voidable at the instance of the 'innocent' party? It would certainly appear to conform with the fundamental ethos underlying the law of nullity that it should, as it is undoubtedly an impediment to sexual intercourse.[10] It may be controversial, but it seems logical to suggest that AIDS, or any other disease which is sexually transmissible, should in principle be a ground for nullity.[11]

Pregnancy by another man

Where, at the time of their marriage, the wife conceals from her husband the fact that she is pregnant by another man, he can subsequently seek an annulment. However, the petition must be presented within three years of the date of the marriage.[12] If the wife keeps the child's true paternity secret for more than three years, the marriage cannot be annulled on this ground. The Law Commission's explanation for this ground was that a husband who marries in these circumstances has given conditional consent only to the marriage. The ground therefore appears to rest on one of two bases. Either the husband has married a woman knowing her to be pregnant and believing that he is the father of the child, in which case he might

---

However, the chances of the other highly unpleasant, or debilitating, consequences of venereal disease had by then been radically reduced.

10 Another particular disease, unfortunately prevalent in the 1990s, which would also spring to mind as being in the category of an impediment is hepatitis B.

11 A further demonstration of how medically absurd the position has become is if the issue of a person being HIV positive is considered. Such a person is in the incubation period of the disease AIDS, but does not as yet have the disease. Is such a person then suffering from venereal disease?

12 S.13(2) see further below.

then argue that, but for the pregnancy, he would not have married her. Alternatively, he might argue that he was marrying a woman who was chaste, but the lack of chastity has self-evidently been demonstrated. Whichever of these two bases applies, it is suggested that such thinking has no place in the law today. In 1937, when the ground was first introduced, men might well be forced to marry if they were believed to be responsible for the pregnancy of a woman.[13] This would not normally be the case in the 1990s. But, if it was, the ground of duress might apply. The chastity basis is not relevant or sensible in today's society. It is suggested that there are other forms of behaviour by a spouse which could just as easily be said to strike at the fundamental root of a marriage, in the sense that a spouse is giving conditional consent to the marriage. For example, the woman who marries a man not knowing that he is a convicted rapist, or paedophile, could claim her consent to the marriage should be characterised as conditional. However, her escape route is to use the law of divorce. It is suggested that similarly divorce is a more appropriate response in the case of pregnancy by another man.

Nevertheless, bringing an alien child into the marriage undoubtedly strikes at the heart of the marriage. A man is undoubtedly entitled to say that he certainly would not have married his wife had he known she was carrying another man's child. But a woman might equally state that she would not have married her husband if, at the time of the marriage, she had known that another woman was pregnant by him. It is suggested that the law should treat spouses in an equal manner in this regard. Whilst pregnancy by another man remains as a ground for nullity, rather than evidence of irretrievable breakdown of marriage, it is surely arguable that a woman should similarly be able to obtain a nullity decree where another woman is pregnant by her husband at the time that she marries him.[14]

Bars to relief where the marriage is voidable

At common law a petitioner could be denied a decree if she had either approbated, that is accepted, the marriage, or colluded in the presentation of grounds for the decree.[15] Additionally, public policy could operate as a bar even though the parties themselves would suffer no injustice if a decree

---

13 In the American 'shot-gun' wedding case *Lee v Lee* 3 SW 2d 672 (1928) it was stated that 'if there had not been a wedding there would have been a funeral.'

14 The Law Commission pointed out that this was the position under the Law of New Zealand, but commented that it had been criticised.

15 The principle behind refusing a decree in such a case was expressed in *G v M* (1885) 10 App Cas 171, per Lord Watson at pp 197-8: 'In a suit for nullity of marriage there may be facts and circumstances proved which so plainly imply, on the part of the complaining spouse, a recognition of the existence and validity of the marriage, as to render it most inequitable and contrary to public policy that he or she should be permitted to go on to challenge it with effect.'

were to be granted. However, this was altered when the law was reformed in 1971, when statutory bars to relief were introduced. These are now contained in section 13 of the Matrimonial Causes Act 1973. A petition for nullity must be instituted within three years of the date of the marriage unless the petitioner is relying on incapacity, or wilful refusal, to consummate the marriage.[16] Furthermore, where the grounds relied upon are venereal disease, or pregnancy by another man, the petitioner must be ignorant of the true facts at the date of the marriage.[17] A general bar applies to all nullity petitions. Section 13(1) provides that—

> 'The court shall not ... grant a decree of nullity on the ground that a marriage is voidable if the respondent satisfies the court—
> (a) that the petitioner, with knowledge that it was open to him to have the marriage avoided, so conducted himself in relation to the respondent as to lead the respondent reasonably to believe that he would not seek to do so; and
> (b) that it would be unjust to the respondent to grant the decree.'

The use of the word 'shall' means that the court has no discretion if facts giving rise to the bar are established; it must not grant a decree. However, the burden of proof is on the respondent, who must also raise the question whether the bar applies. If the respondent does not raise the bar, the court must grant the decree, even if it thinks that the bar would apply.[18] Furthermore, the conduct of the petitioner can only give rise to the bar provided that he or she knows that the marriage is potentially avoidable and yet behaves in a way to affirm the marriage.[19] Public policy can no longer be raised as a bar.[20]

Behaviour which could give rise to the bar is illustrated in *D v D (Nullity)*[1] where the marriage had never been consummated owing either to the incapacity, or to the wilful refusal, of the wife to consummate it.[2] Nine years after the date of the marriage the parties adopted two children, but

16 S.13(2). This is subject to s.13(4), whereby the period may be extended where a petitioner has suffered from a mental disorder during the three years, and it is just to do so.
17 S.13(3).
18 In *D v D (Nullity)* [1979] 3 All ER 337, Dunn J failed to take this into account, although he did grant a decree of nullity on the basis that it would not be unjust to the respondent wife. The wife had originally raised the bar, but subsequently withdrew it and the case came on for hearing undefended.
19 So if a man is not originally aware that the child his wife has given birth to is not his, and it is only on discovering this that he petitions for nullity, his wife cannot rely on his treatment of the child prior to the discovery as giving rise to the bar.
20 See Dunn J in *D v D (Nullity)* [1979] 3 All ER 337, at p 343, where he said: 'the common law rules are abrogated and replaced by the statutory bar, and therefore I would be prepared to hold on the ordinary natural meaning of the words of the statute, that public policy has no place in the statutory bar.'
1   [1979] 3 All ER 337, which appears to be the only reported case on this area of law.
2   The husband pleaded the two grounds in the alternative.

one year later the husband left in order to live with another woman, and subsequently presented his petition. Dunn J held that the husband knew that it was open to him to have the marriage annulled, and that by agreeing to the adoption had so conducted himself as to lead the wife to believe he would not seek to do so. However, he went on to grant the decree as he held that it would not be unjust to the wife to do so. It is this requirement of injustice to the respondent which makes it most unlikely that any respondent will be able to establish the requirements of the section. All the court's powers are available to the parties in ancillary proceedings on the granting of a decree of nullity, and even if unable to obtain a decree of nullity, the petitioner will almost certainly be able to obtain a decree of divorce. There would therefore seem to be little point in failing to grant the original petition. Indeed there has been no case reported since the inception of the Act where the bar has been successfully pleaded.

Reform of the law relating to voidable marriages

The law relating to voidable marriages is relied on in very few cases, largely because of the ease with which it is now possible to obtain a divorce. In many cases the spouses have already separated when the nullity proceedings are heard. They need only to have lived apart for a period of two years to obtain a divorce based on consent.[3] Many spouses find it preferable to rely on this ground for divorce, rather than to rely on the grounds of incapacity, or wilful refusal, to consummate the marriage, which found the majority of nullity petitions. Is it therefore sensible to retain the law of nullity in respect of voidable marriages? It would be possible to abolish the concept of the voidable marriage altogether, and to require parties to rely on the facts as evidence of the breakdown of their marriage.[4] This was recognised by the Law Commission when they reviewed the law. However, arguing for its retention, the Law Commission put forward a number of propositions.[5] They felt that the conceptual bases of the different decrees were quite different. A decree of nullity recognised an impediment to the marriage, which prevented it from being an effective marriage. Divorce recognised that a valid marriage had come into being, and that a cause to terminate it had arisen since the celebration of the marriage. They commented that the church drew a distinction between divorce and nullity, and would not welcome any attempt to abolish nullity. For some people, not necessarily members of the church, there is a stigma associated with divorce, whereas for some of the nullity grounds, such as mental illness, and some cases of incapacity to consummate, no stigma can be attached.

3　Matrimonial Causes Act 1973, s.1(2)(d), see below.
4　Voidable marriages have been abolished in Australia: Family Law Act 1975, s.51.
5　Law Com No 30, para 24.

And, finally, there was no advantage to anyone in abolishing the voidable marriage, whereas there would undoubtedly be disadvantages.

In favour of abolishing the voidable marriage it could be counter-argued that the view that there is a fundamental conceptual difference between the two decrees cannot be sustained for a number of reasons. For example, wilful refusal to consummate the marriage must arise after the marriage has taken place, it cannot be a pre-existing impediment. Furthermore, as a nullity decree has prospective, but not retrospective, effect,[6] it appears odd to say that the impediments prevent the marriage coming into existence. Also, the bar in section 13 enables spouses to attempt a reconciliation without necessarily losing their ground to petition. Yet the concept of reconciliation is not consistent with the concept that the marriage is fatally flawed by a fundamental defect. Moreover, it is arguably anomalous that the action of individual parties can somehow overcome a defect in respect of a voidable marriage, and raise a bar to the marriage being annulled, when they clearly cannot do so in the case of a void marriage.[7] In relation to the issue of stigma, whilst some of the grounds for nullity may not have stigma attached to them, that certainly cannot be said for all of them, and conversely whilst some grounds for divorce do have adverse connotations, some do not. There is stigma attached to a finding that a person has, for example, wilfully refused to consummate the marriage, or deceived a man into marrying by concealing the true paternity of a baby. There is no stigma attached to a finding that parties have lived apart for two years. As regards the position of the church, it can be said that this is in an increasingly secular society, and the religion of many members of society is not Christian. Why, therefore, should the church have any say in the law relating to marriage, when only a minority of the population attend organised Christian worship?

The last argument presented by the Law Commission in favour of retaining the concept of the voidable marriage is a formidable one: namely, that there is no advantage to be achieved in abolishing the concept, but to do so would undoubtedly have disadvantages for some persons. Where a mechanism exists which can terminate a marriage which has fundamentally failed why do away with that mechanism? Whilst it is undoubtedly the case that certain aspects of the law relating to voidable marriages are unsatisfactory, this does not mean that, should the process be amended, the concept should be abolished.

---

6   S.16.
7   If a 'wife' discovers her 'husband' is a bigamist she can be as reconciled with him as much as she wishes but that will not override the fundamental defect in the marriage.

The law of divorce

It is a curious feature of the law relating to divorce that those who have not studied, or practised, family law assume that family law is 'all to do with divorce'. There is, therefore, a natural assumption that the law relating to the actual obtaining of a divorce must be a crucial area of study. The reality is quite different. Since the mid-1970s[8] divorce has been obtainable under the 'special procedure', the objectives of which are 'simplicity, speed and economy'.[9] By this means, wherever a case is undefended the need to give evidence in court is dispensed with. A district judge, sitting in private, scrutinises the divorce application, and where satisfied that the ground is made out, issues a certificate to that effect.[10] The divorce is then formally granted in open court by a judge. Neither the parties, nor their representatives, need appear in front of either the district judge in private, or the judge in open court. The advent of the 'special procedure', which is now far from being special but is in fact the norm,[11] has had a profound bearing on the extent to which the court can make an effective enquiry into an undefended suit. Furthermore, the cost of litigation makes it impossible, in the vast majority of cases, for a respondent to defend the suit in a contested hearing, particularly in view of the fact that legal aid will not normally be granted where it is clear that the marriage has irretrievably broken down.[12] As a consequence, problems relating to the interpretation of the law of divorce almost never arise in practice, and in recent years there have been very few reported cases. However, it is of course necessary to understand the substantive law, because it is of relevance not just in those few defended cases which arise, but also because the petitioner must make out a case that falls within the ground for divorce when presenting her[13] petition under the special procedure.[14]

Divorce has only been generally available as a means of terminating a marriage for a relatively short period of time. It was not until the Matrimonial Causes Act 1857 that a statute applicable to the public at

8   1973 for all cases based on the ground of two years' separation, 1977 for all other undefended petitions.
9   *R v Nottingham County Court, ex p Byers* [1985] 1 All ER 735, per Latey J at p 737.
10 Family Proceedings Rules 1991, r.2.36.
11 See *Report of the Matrimonial Causes Procedure Committee* (HMSO, 1985) (hereinafter the Booth Report), under the chairmanship of The Hon Mrs Justice Booth, para 2.8.
12 See the Booth Report, para 2.16. Legal aid is not available for undefended divorces: Legal Aid (Matrimonial Proceedings) Regulations 1977.
13 In practice over 70% of divorces are granted to wives. For ease of writing, therefore, it will be assumed that the petitioner is the wife unless otherwise stated.
14 Advice and assistance is available to the parties under the Green Form Scheme. Under this scheme a solicitor may do nearly all the preparatory work on the documentation to be presented to the district judge: Legal Aid Act 1988; Legal Advice and Assistance Regulations 1989.

large was passed.[15] This Act, and the subsequent legislation up until 1969, was strictly fault based.[16] However in 1956 a Royal Commission, the Morton Commission,[17] published a report advocating changes in the law of divorce including introducing the concept of a no-fault divorce. Ten years later a group appointed by the Archbishop of Canterbury published their report, *Putting Asunder*, which advocated that divorce should be based on a single concept, namely that of the breakdown of the marriage. The report recommended that, in every case, there should be a judicial enquiry to ensure that a breakdown had really occurred, and that no abuse of the system had taken place. This was followed by a discussion paper issued by the Law Commission,[18] which similarly advocated breakdown as a basis for dissolving a marriage, but as an additional ground rather than as the sole ground for divorce. As a result of these deliberations the law was amended in 1969 by the Divorce Reform Act 1969, which represented a compromise between the two reports.

It was felt to be wrong to liberalise the divorce law without at the same time ensuring that dependent spouses could be protected from suffering some of the more serious economic consequences of divorce. Therefore, legislation was introduced, the Matrimonial Proceedings and Property Act 1970, which gave the courts wide powers to make financial provision and property adjustment orders on the grant of a decree.[19] Implementation of the 1969 Act was delayed and the two Acts came into force together. They were subsequently consolidated in the Matrimonial Causes Act 1973, which provides the legal framework for all matrimonial proceedings today.

Encouragement to reconcile

One of the criticisms of the pre-1969 law was that it discouraged, rather than encouraged, any attempts at reconciliation.[20] For example, where one spouse committed adultery, and the other spouse attempted to make the marriage work, and ostensibly forgave the adulterous behaviour, this act of forgiveness meant that he or she had condoned the adultery, and

---

15 Prior to that it was possible to obtain a divorce, but this could only be done by private Act of Parliament. For a fascinating and very detailed account of the history of the law of divorce, see L Stone *Road to Divorce* (1991, OUP). See also S M Cretney and J M Masson *Principles of Family Law* (5th edn, 1990, Sweet and Maxwell); P M Bromley and N V Lowe *Bromley's Family Law* (8th edn, 1992, Butterworths).
16 See the Matrimonial Causes Act 1923; the Matrimonial Causes Act 1937.
17 *Royal Commission on Marriage and Divorce* Cmd 9678.
18 *Reform of the Grounds of Divorce: the Field of Choice* Cmd 3123.
19 See ch 7.
20 See *The Field of Choice* para 28. If the parties attempted a reconciliation they ran the risk of raising the bar of condonation.

therefore could no longer rely on it for divorce purposes. Clearly this bar operated as a barrier to reconciliation. By contrast, the underlying purpose of the Divorce Reform Act 1969 was:

'(i) to buttress, rather than to undermine, the stability of marriage; and
(ii) when, regrettably, a marriage has irretrievably broken down, to enable the empty legal shell to be destroyed with the maximum fairness, and the minimum bitterness, distress and humiliation.'[1]

Provisions were introduced which were designed to assist parties to remain together and to resolve their differences. Parties are no longer barred from petitioning if they live together after adulterous, or other, behaviour which would enable them to obtain a decree.[2] The provisions of section 6 of the Matrimonial Causes Act 1973 also give some encouragement to parties to consider reconciliation rather than proceeding to a divorce. A solicitor acting for the petitioner is obliged to file a certificate stating whether or not he has discussed reconciliation with his client, or given the client names and addresses of people qualified to help.[3] Further, the court may adjourn the proceedings at any time if it appears that there is a reasonable prospect of successful reconciliation.[4] However there is no requirement to discuss reconciliation. A solicitor is at liberty simply to state that he has not discussed it. As a result, there is evidence which reveals that the provisions in section 6 have proved to be of limited value.[5]

Irretrievable breakdown must be evidenced by one of five facts

The Divorce Reform Act 1969 introduced a single ground for divorce, that the marriage of the parties has irretrievably broken down. This provision was re-enacted in section 1 of the Matrimonial Causes Act 1973 and is the law today. However, although there is only the one ground, in order to petition successfully for divorce it is necessary to prove one of five facts. Section 1(2) provides:

---

1 Ibid, para 15.
2 See now the Matrimonial Causes Act 1973, s.2; though in relation to adultery see s.2(1), which does raise a bar where the parties live together for longer than six months after the discovery of the adultery.
3 S.6(1).
4 S.6(2).
5 See the Booth Report, paras 4.42-4.43; Law Com No 170, para 3.9; G Davis and M Murch *Grounds for Divorce* (1988, Clarendon Press) ch 4.

'The court hearing a petition for divorce shall not hold the marriage
to have broken down irretrievably unless the petitioner satisfies
the court of one or more of the following facts, that is to say—

(a) that the respondent has committed adultery and the petitioner
    finds it intolerable to live with the respondent;
(b) that the respondent has behaved in such a way that the
    petitioner cannot reasonably be expected to live with the
    respondent;
(c) that the respondent has deserted the petitioner for a continuous
    period of at least two years immediately preceding the present-
    ation of the petition;
(d) that the parties to the marriage have lived apart for a contin-
    uous period of at least two years immediately preceding the
    presentation of the petition ... and the respondent consents to
    a decree being granted;
(e) that the parties to the marriage have lived apart for a contin-
    uous period of at least five years immediately preceding the
    presentation of the petition.'

If a party to a divorce cannot bring her case within one of the five facts
she cannot obtain a divorce, even though it is undoubtedly the case that
the marriage has irretrievably broken down. This is illustrated by *Stringfellow v Stringfellow*,[6] where the husband and wife had been married for
six years and had two children. The husband suddenly announced he no
longer loved his wife, and ceased showing any interest whatsoever in her
or the family. Shortly afterwards he left home, and three months later the
wife petitioned under section 1(2)(b), that the respondent had behaved in
such a way that she could not reasonably be expected to live with him. The
petition was undefended. A decree of divorce was nonetheless refused on
the basis that the petition showed nothing more than the breakdown of a
marriage, and desertion by the husband, for which the wife could only
petition after two years had elapsed. *Stringfellow v Stringfellow* provides
a clear example of the fact that whilst it is legally correct to state that
there is only one ground for divorce, the irretrievable breakdown of the
marriage, the breakdown of a marriage does not necessarily mean that
there is the basis for a divorce decree. Here the marriage had indeed
irretrievably broken down, but because the wife could not bring herself
within one of the five facts she could not successfully petition for divorce.[7]

The converse of this is that provided the petitioner can prove one of the
five facts she need not prove it was that fact which caused the marriage to

6   [1976] 2 All ER 539.
7   See also *Birch v Birch* [1992] 1 FLR 564; *Buffery v Buffery* [1988] 2 FLR 365; *Richards v
    Richards* [1972] 3 All ER 695.

break down irretrievably. An illustration arose in *Stevens v Stevens*,[8] where the court was satisfied that it was due to the petitioner's own behaviour that the marriage had irretrievably broken down. However, as the petitioner succeeded in establishing that the respondent's behaviour was now such that she could not reasonably be expected to live with him, she was granted a decree. Even where the marriage has undoubtedly irretrievably broken down, and where the petitioner can establish one of the five facts, a petition for divorce cannot be presented within the first year of marriage.[9] This is an absolute bar. It matters not how extreme a petitioner's case may be, she has no option but to wait one year from the date of the marriage. However, she may rely on the respondent's behaviour which occurred during that one-year period when she presents her petition.

Adultery

There are two distinct elements that a petitioner must prove on presentation of a petition for divorce based on adultery: that the respondent has in fact committed adultery and that the petitioner finds it intolerable to live with the respondent. It is not enough simply to allege adultery. However, under the special procedure there is no requirement that the petitioner need state why she finds it intolerable.[10] Thus although theoretically her mere assertion should not suffice,[11] in practice it almost invariably will. Adultery is the voluntary act of sexual intercourse[12] between a married spouse and another person not being married to him or her, who is of the opposite sex, and who may or may not be married. Homosexual intercourse does not, therefore, come within the definition.[13] The requirement that the act of intercourse be voluntary excludes the rape victim from the definition.[14] More difficult questions could arise if a woman was so drunk or drugged at the time of the act of sexual intercourse that she was either incapable of giving her consent, or only consented due to the influence of the intoxicant. Where the spouse has an excuse for being intoxicated it would appear that this will negative her consent.[15] However, where the

8 [1979] 1 WLR 885.
9 S.3(1).
10 A petitioner is simply required to answer the question: 'Do you find it intolerable to live with the respondent?' Family Proceedings Rules 1991, Appendix 1.
11 See *Cleary v Cleary* [1974] 1 WLR 73; *Roper v Roper* [1972] 3 All ER 668.
12 Which must involve some penetration of the female by the male: *Dennis v Dennis* [1955] 2 All ER 51. Artificial insemination would not therefore amount to adultery.
13 Although a spouse who wished to divorce her partner because of his homosexual activities would normally be able to petition under s.1(2)(b) instead. See below.
14 Sadly, in some communities, the victim of a rape may be ostracised by other members of the community, and looked upon as being a guilty party.
15 See dicta in *Goshawk v Goshawk* (1965) 109 Sol Jo 290.

intoxicant was consumed voluntarily with knowledge of its 'liberating' effects it seems that the spouse will be guilty of adultery.

Proof of adultery

Adultery may be established to the satisfaction of the court in a number of ways. The acknowledgment of service forms used in relation to petitions based on adultery asks the question: 'Do you admit the adultery alleged in the petition?'[16] If the respondent answers 'Yes', and signs the form, that is sufficient proof. Where the respondent does not admit the adultery, and fails to file an answer, the petitioner will have to prove the adultery by other evidence. This could be established by evidence such as that the respondent is living with another person as husband and wife. Other evidence could be that the respondent and the alleged co-respondent had both the inclination and the opportunity to commit adultery, such as where they spent the night in the same room.[17] An admission by the wife that a child is not her husband's child, despite the husband being named as father on the birth certificate, clearly amounts to an admission of adultery.[18] A conviction of the husband for rape means that adultery has taken place, even though his victim's part in the act of sexual intercourse was non-consensual. A finding by a court that the husband is the father of a non-marital child conceived after the marriage establishes his adultery.

As proceedings for divorce are civil proceedings it could be expected that the level of standard of proof for adultery would be the normal civil standard, that is on the balance of probabilities. However, the standard of proof has never been formally established,[19] and in view of the special procedure is never likely to be. In *Serio v Serio*[20] the Court of Appeal declared that a mere balance of probabilities was not sufficient, the burden of proof must indicate a standard commensurate with the seriousness of the issue involved. This judgment is perhaps a reflection of a tendency in the past to treat adultery as akin to the criminal offence, and therefore to require a higher standard, closer to the criminal standard of beyond all reasonable doubt. The judgment in *Serio v Serio* does not sit easily with the law relating to legitimacy. The Family Law Reform Act 1969, section 26, provides:

16 Family Proceedings Rules 1991, Appendix 1.
17 By virtue of the Family Proceedings Rules 1991, r.2.7(1), it is no longer necessary to cite the name of the person with whom the respondent is alleged to have committed adultery. Where a person is named they will be made a co-respondent to the petition.
18 *R v King's Lynn Magistrates' Court, ex p M* [1988] 2 FLR 79.
19 In *Blyth v Blyth* [1966] 1 All ER 524 the House of Lords were divided in their obiter views as to the correct standard.
20 (1983) 4 FLR 756.

'Any presumption as to the legitimacy ... of any person may ... be rebutted by evidence which shows that it is more probable than not that that person is illegitimate.'

Thus in relation to illegitimacy, the standard of proof is on the balance of probabilities. The logical result of the decision of *Serio v Serio,* coupled with section 26, is that a woman might be held not to have committed adultery, as the high standard of proof could not be established, yet her child might be held to be illegitimate on the basis of the lower standard. This is patently absurd. It is suggested that there is no reason in principle why the standard of proof for adultery should be anything other than the normal civil standard, and should the issue ever arise in practice, it seems likely that the court would so hold.

The petitioner must find it intolerable to live with the respondent

The test whether the petitioner finds it intolerable to live with the respondent is subjective rather than objective.[1] Accordingly once it is found that the petitioner is telling the truth that is sufficient, regardless of whether a reasonable person would find it intolerable.[2] Initially there was some doubt as to whether the adultery and the intolerability needed to be causally linked. This matter was resolved in *Cleary v Cleary*[3] where it was held that the adultery and the intolerability need have nothing whatsoever to do with each other.[4] On its face this was a curious decision, which could lead to some very odd results. Where a petitioner finds her spouse intolerable to live with it may be purely fortuitous that he also happens to have committed adultery. Indeed, she may be entirely indifferent to his adultery. However, despite her indifference, she is now able to base her petition on the adulterous behaviour. It is also difficult to square the

1   *Goodrich v Goodrich* [1971] 2 All ER 1340.
2   Thus, theoretically, if the wife alleges that her husband blows his nose too often and she finds this intolerable, providing that the court accepts that this is truly the case it is bound to find this part of her petition made out. See the comments of Faulks J in *Roper v Roper* [1972] 3 All ER 668 at p 670.
3   [1974] 1 All ER 498. In *Cleary* the wife had committed adultery. The husband forgave her, and she went back to live with him. However, subsequently she continued to correspond with the man, she kept going out at night, and she finally left and went back to live with her mother. The husband petitioned for divorce as 'there was no future in the marriage at all.' It was clear that it was the behaviour post the adultery that he found intolerable. The husband was held entitled to a decree, the Court of Appeal holding the Act must be interpreted literally, the two factors not being linked.
4   And see *Carr v Carr* [1974] 1 All ER 1193 where a differently constituted Court of Appeal reluctantly followed the decision of the Court in *Cleary.* They suggested that the matter ought to go to the House of Lords finally to be resolved.

decision in *Cleary v Cleary* with the provisions in section 2(2). This provides that where the parties continue cohabiting for a period of up to six months after the discovery of the adultery, this should be disregarded in determining whether or not the petitioner finds it intolerable to live with the respondent. The rationale of the provisions in section 2 is to encourage attempts at reconciliation by the parties, by allowing a period of time for them to try and resolve their problems. However, section 2(1) provides that where parties live together for a period in excess of six months after the discovery of the adultery, that this operates as a complete bar to the presentation of a petition. This clearly suggests that it is the adultery which has led to the petitioner finding it intolerable, rather than any other behaviour.

However, despite these objections, it is suggested that the Court of Appeal were correct in concluding that the two clauses are not linked. First because on a natural reading of the wording of the section they are not linked. Secondly, because Parliament did not intend there to be any linkage. In Parliamentary debates surrounding the section, an attempt to link the two clauses with the addition of the words 'by reason of which' was rejected.[5] Thirdly, one of the objections to the non-causal approach is that it could appear very unjust to the respondent, particularly where adultery is just an isolated act, perhaps in response to the distress that the behaviour of the petitioner is causing to the respondent. However, the law is no longer concerned, as such, with justice between the parties, but with irretrievable breakdown. If the petitioner does indeed find it intolerable to live with the respondent, albeit that an objective outsider might consider she is in fact far more to 'blame' for the breakdown of the marriage, she satisfies the requirements of the section and is entitled to gain a decree. Finally, the aims of the Act were to try and remove the bitterness, distress and humiliation from divorce. If the two factors are linked enquiry must then be made as to whether it is actually the adultery which has made the marriage intolerable. Dissection of the marriage must therefore take place to find out the answer. This is not in keeping with the fundamental objectives of the law.

Behaviour

The fact that 'the respondent has behaved in such a way that the petitioner cannot reasonably be expected to live with the respondent' is used more often in divorce petitions than any of the other four facts.[6] This is highly

5   See Hansard (HL), Vol 303, cols 1222-1249.
6   In 1991 46.4% (73,266) of all divorces were granted on the basis of behaviour. Of these 9,937 petitions were granted in favour of the husband and 63,329 in favour of the wife. See *Marriage and Divorce Statistics* Office of Population and Censuses Surveys (HMSO).

regrettable. The policy of terminating the marriage with the minimum bitterness, distress and humiliation is undermined where either party sets out to prove the behaviour fact. Furthermore, petitions based on this fact give rise to difficulties more often than petitions based on any of the other facts. One reason for this is that petitions frequently contain a catalogue of incidents relied on by the petitioner in support of the allegation, because it may be that no one incident, on its own, is sufficiently serious to establish the fact. Therefore, in order to ensure that a decree is granted, as many incidents as possible are dredged up, all of which have to be considered to see if, cumulatively, they add up to sufficient behaviour to establish the fact. Because of its pejorative connotations, a petition based on behaviour may be hotly contested.[7] As the Booth Committee commented:

> 'We are satisfied that the bitterness and unhappiness of divorcing couples is frequently exacerbated and prolonged by the fault element in divorce and that this is particularly so where the fact relied upon is behaviour, whether or not the suit is defended. Great hostility and resentment may be generated by the recital in the petition of allegations of behaviour, often exaggerated and some-times stretching back over many years, to the extent that no discussion can take place between the parties or any agreement be reached on any matter relating to their marriage or their children.'[8]

Behaviour by the respondent

Section 1(2)(b) is often shortened, colloquially, to 'unreasonable behaviour'. This shorthand is unfortunate, as it suggests that the subsection is only about blameworthy behaviour. However this is incorrect. The behaviour need be neither unreasonable nor blameworthy. What section 1(2)(b) requires is that, as regards this particular petitioner, it is not reasonable to expect her to continue living with this particular respondent. This is a far more flexible test than the incorrect shorthand. Unfortunately, on occasions in the past, the courts have fallen into the trap of applying the shorthand test, rather than the correct wording of the statute, and by so doing have affected the way that petitions are presented. In the early decision of *Archard v Archard,*[9] both parties were originally of the Roman Catholic faith. The wife was medically advised not to become pregnant for two years and, having lost her faith, she insisted that the husband use contraceptives. Due to his religious convictions he refused, and was advised

7 It is normal human behaviour to deny prime responsibility for the breakdown of a marriage.
8 Booth Report, para 2.10.
9 (1972) Times, 19 April.

by his priest that the way to resolve the dilemma was to stop sleeping with his wife. The wife's petition for divorce was refused on the basis that the husband was not behaving unreasonably. It is undoubtedly the case that the husband, because of his religious beliefs, was acting perfectly reasonably. However, it is suggested that had the correct test been applied, namely whether the wife could reasonably have been expected to continue to live with the husband, that she should then have been granted a decree.[10]

Other early cases under the Act adopted a similar approach and appeared to require 'bad' behaviour on the part of the respondent.[11] In *Pheasant v Pheasant*[12] the only allegation by the husband was that the wife was unable to give him the spontaneous, demonstrative affection which he said his nature demanded and for which he craved. It was held that he had failed to prove behaviour, as the wife had not been guilty of any breach of the obligations of marriage. The case thus supplied a clear invitation to petitioners to prove fault. By considering whether or not the wife had been in 'breach' of her 'obligations' of marriage, rather than concentrating on whether the husband could be expected to live with her, the emphasis of the section became concentrated on the nature of the behaviour. It is suggested that the early cases thereby encouraged petitioners to drag up as many incidents as possible to ensure that the behaviour fact was established, and thereby affected behaviour petitions to the detriment of the underlying purpose of the Act, namely to avoid bitterness, distress and humiliation.[13]

In some cases a single incident of behaviour may be sufficient to establish the petitioner's case; for example, a serious assault leading to medical treatment. Furthermore, in some circumstances conduct which is not actually directed at the marriage itself, but has a serious effect on the

10 Equally, the husband could not reasonably be expected to live with the wife. They were both reasonable in their views, but, it is suggested, neither could reasonably be expected to live with the other.

11 See *Stringfellow v Stringfellow* [1976] 2 All ER 539; *Dowden v Dowden* (1977) 8 Fam Law 106. However, in *Bannister v Bannister* (1980) 10 Fam Law 240, the trial judge was criticised on appeal for falling into the 'linguistic trap' of speaking of unreasonable behaviour and dismissing the wife's petition. Accordingly where the wife alleged that the husband had not taken her out for two years, did not speak to her except when it was unavoidable, stayed away for nights giving her no idea where he was going, and had been living an entirely independent life ignoring her completely, it was found to be behaviour that she could not reasonably be expected to live with.

12 [1972] 1 All ER 587.

13 The reality, in many instances, will be that both parties have contributed significantly to the breakdown of the marriage. The Law Commission, in their examination of the law in 1990, recognised that in the vast majority of cases the court does not conduct an enquiry into the truth of the facts alleged, and that the fault-based facts can therefore be intrinsically unjust: Law Com No 192 paras 2.8-2.14. See too, G Davis and M Murch *Grounds for Divorce* (1988, Clarendon Press) ch 5, for a compelling account of the difficulties encountered and exacerbated by the presentation of a behaviour petition.

petitioner, could also give rise to a successful petition. Thus conviction for a very serious criminal offence, such as murder or rape, would undoubtedly give a wife grounds to petition. More minor violence, such as shoves, pushes and slaps, will require more than one incident to satisfy the section. Behaviour such as drunkenness, alcoholism and drug addiction is frequently relied upon by a petitioner. Other types of behaviour have included boorishness and constant criticism adhered to over a long period of time;[14] deliberate persecution of the wife;[15] and in *O'Neill v O'Neill*,[16] behaviour causing so much stress to the petitioner that her health suffered. The final straw for the wife had been when the husband embarked on prolonged renovation work on their bungalow. This involved mixing cement on the living-room floor, and having no door on the toilet for eight months.[17] In *Carter-Fea v Carter-Fea*[18] the wife complained that the husband was incapable of managing his own affairs, and she was faced with mounting debt due to his failure to take any action to respond to his financial difficulties. She was held entitled to a decree because of the evidence she brought as to the effect that the stress was having on her health. However, somewhat unsympathetically, Lawton LJ commented that it would be a sad day when wives thought they could come to court just because their husbands conducted their financial affairs in way which upset them. It is suggested that this comment displays a distressing lack of sensitivity to the very considerable strain that financial profligacy, or incompetence, imposes on a family. For many living under the shadow of debt, the stress of living in highly straitened circumstances due to a person's behaviour is every bit as worthy of the court's sympathy as other forms of behaviour.

Where the respondent refuses to live with the petitioner, logically it could be argued that this is behaviour such that the petitioner cannot reasonably be expected to live with the respondent. However, in *Stringfellow v Stringfellow*[19] it was held that such an allegation simply amounts to an allegation of desertion by the husband, and nothing more, and that the petitioner must therefore wait the requisite two years to petition under the desertion fact. The court held that to find differently would render the desertion fact otiose, because all cases would be subsumed under the behaviour head.

It is sometimes the case that the petition is based on the sexual incompatibility of the parties. In such cases petitions may allege forms of

14 *Livingstone-Stallard v Livingstone-Stallard* [1974] 2 All ER 766. The husband was apparently 'rude, boorish and critical' of the wife even during their honeymoon.
15 *Stevens v Stevens* [1979] 1 WLR 885.
16 [1975] 3 All ER 289.
17 The husband had also written to the wife's solicitors casting doubt on the paternity of the couple's two children, which incident the Court of Appeal thought in itself was enough to ground the fact.
18 (1987) 17 Fam Law 131.
19 [1976] 2 All ER 539.

conduct which are deemed to amount to sexual perversions; or that one party is making excessive sexual demands on the other. This is obviously an extremely hurtful and damaging area, usually for both parties. It is also a very difficult matter on which to require a court to pass judgment, because whether or not the behaviour was reasonable will depend on so many different factors. In *Mason v Mason*[20] the husband alleged that the wife refused to have sexual intercourse more than once per week over a particular period of time. His petition was refused. Considerable evidence was presented in court as to the reasons for the wife's reluctance to engage in sexual intercourse, and as to the various contraceptive issues which were relevant to the parties. That the court should get involved in such intimate details of other people's sexual lives seems nothing other than distasteful and damaging. However in *Mason v Mason* Ormrod LJ expressed the opinion that: 'where refusal of sexual intercourse is the main ground alleged in support of a petition under section 1(2)(b), in my judgment it requires very careful investigation by the court into the allegations on both sides and into the reasons on both sides.'[1] It is suggested that this statement is perhaps reflective of the times, and that should such a petition be defended today the court should endeavour to concentrate its efforts on discovering whether or not the marriage has indeed irretrievably broken down because of sexual problems, rather than trawling through the parties' sexual history.

The test for behaviour is both subjective and objective

The test for deciding whether the ground has been established is a mixture of both the objective and the subjective. The test is clearly objective in the sense that the court has to decide whether the petitioner can *reasonably* be expected to live with the respondent. However, the essence of the subsection is subjective. The question that must be asked is: 'can this particular petitioner be expected to live with this particular respondent?'[2] The respondent's knowledge of the damaging effect of his behaviour on the petitioner will therefore be a relevant factor to take into account. When considering the subsection in *Ash v Ash*,[3] Bagnall J stated that the question the court must ask is:

> 'Can this petitioner, with his or her character and personality, with his or her faults and other attributes, good and bad, and having regard to his or her behaviour during the marriage reasonably be expected to live with the respondent?'

20 (1980) 11 Fam Law 143.
1   Ibid, at p 144.
2   *Birch v Birch* [1992] 1 FLR 564.
3   [1972] 1 All ER 582.

In elaborating on this he expressed the view that

> 'a violent petitioner may reasonably be expected to live with a
> violent respondent; a petitioner who is addicted to drink can
> reasonably be expected to live with a respondent similarly addicted;
> a taciturn and morose spouse can reasonably be expected to live
> with a taciturn and morose partner; a flirtatious husband can
> reasonably be expected to live with a wife who is equally susceptible
> to the attractions of the other sex; and if each is equally bad, at
> any rate in similar respects, each can reasonably be expected to
> live with the other'.[4]

In *Livingstone-Stallard v Livingstone-Stallard*[5] Dunn J formulated the
test rather differently. He said:

> 'I ask myself the question: would any right-thinking person come
> to the conclusion that this husband has behaved in such a way
> that this wife cannot reasonably be expected to live with him, taking
> into account the whole of the circumstances and the characters
> and personalities of the parties?'[6]

It is suggested that the elaboration in *Ash v Ash* was unfortunate and the
better formulation is that of Dunn J in *Livingstone-Stallard v Livingstone-
Stallard*. In *Birch v Birch*,[7] the Court of Appeal quoted with approval the
following passage from a leading practitioner's text:

> 'Allowance will be made for the sensitive as well as for the thick-
> skinned; ... conduct must be judged *up to a point*[8] by the capacity
> of the complaining partner to endure his or her spouse's conduct
> ... the court would consider to what extent the respondent knew
> or ought reasonably to have known of that capacity.'[9]

A similar approach was adopted in *Stevens v Stevens*,[10] where the behaviour
of the wife had led to the irretrievable breakdown of the marriage, and the
husband had subsequently set out to be deliberately unpleasant to the
wife. Although the wife could not complain simply because he reacted to
her behaviour, when his behaviour went beyond that, she was entitled to a
decree. It is suggested that where, for example, one spouse attacks the

4   Ibid, at pp 585-6.
5   [1974] 2 All ER 766.
6   Ibid, at p 771.
7   [1992] 1 FLR 564.
8   Emphasis added.
9   *Rayden on Divorce* (15th edn), vol 1, p 255.
10 [1979] 1 WLR 885.

other with a kitchen knife, whether the other's response is to flee in terror, or to pick up the nearest handy implement to attack back, should not be regarded as the relevant issue, despite what was said in *Ash v Ash*. The 'right-thinking' person would surely conclude that the victim of such an attack should not be expected to live with the attacking spouse. In such a case the parties are a danger to each other, and neither can reasonably be expected to live with the other.

Behaviour arising through illness

Cases involving illness, particularly mental illness, have posed problems for the courts, who have grappled with the difficulty of when to grant a decree against a spouse who is not morally responsible for his behaviour. Whilst it is generally accepted that marriage entails the taking on of certain obligations, including the burdens of illness, it is nonetheless recognised that the toll that mental illness can exact from a spouse can be very severe. The courts have made it clear that the granting of a decree does not necessarily involve blameworthiness. In *Thurlow v Thurlow*,[11] Rees J held that the court must take into account

'all the circumstances including the disabilities and temperaments of both parties, the causes of the behaviour and whether the causes were or were not known to the petitioner, the presence or absence of intention, the impact of it on the petitioner and the family unit, its duration, and the prospects of cure or improvement in the future.'

Clearly in some cases the behaviour is so damaging the petitioner must be granted a decree, such as where one spouse attacks the other. Thus in *Katz v Katz*[12] a decree was granted because, even after making allowances for the husband's mental illness (he suffered from manic-depression) his behaviour, and its impact on the wife, was sufficiently serious to warrant granting her a decree. The wife was so distressed by the situation she found herself in that she made a very serious suicide attempt. However, the courts have adopted a fairly strict interpretation of the law where illness is involved. Thus in *Richards v Richards*[13] where the husband was very moody, sat staring into space, and had assaulted the wife on two occasions, although one incident was very trivial, the court found that, after taking into account the fact of the husband's mental illness, the wife had not established sufficient cause for granting her a decree.

11 [1975] 2 All ER 979, at p 988.
12 [1972] 3 All ER 219. See also *White v White* [1983] 2 All ER 51.
13 [1972] 3 All ER 695.

A more difficult problem of statutory interpretation arises where the respondent's behaviour is passive. Establishing the ground may be hard in view of the wording of the section which requires 'behaviour' on the part of the respondent. It was established in *Katz v Katz*[14] that conduct may take the form of either an act or an omission, but that some type of behaviour must take place. Baker P commented: 'behaviour is something more than a mere state of affairs or a state of mind ... in this context [it] is action or conduct by one which affects the other.' In *Thurlow v Thurlow*[15] the issue of negative and positive behaviour, and the illness of one of the spouses, was considered in considerable detail. Rees J commented that spouses may often, but not always, be expected to tolerate more in the way of inactivity than activity. However, he went on to say that he considered that the contrast between positive and negative conduct was not a helpful distinction, and that an omission, in most cases, is at the same time a commission.[16] He said that the petitioner's health may be gravely affected by certain kinds of negative behaviour, which may be due to the respondent's mental or physical illness, or an injury, and which may be involuntary. He concluded that 'negative' as well as 'positive' behaviour is capable of forming the basis of a decree and he expressly disapproved of the decision of *Smith v Smith*,[17] where a decree was refused to the husband as the wife's cabbage-like existence was due solely to pre-senile dementia. Rees J also went on to raise, but not to answer, the hypothetical question of whether it is possible to divorce a spouse who becomes a 'human vegetable'. His view was that a petitioner might face very considerable difficulties in establishing that there was any, or any sufficient, behaviour, or alternatively that to draw the conclusion that the petitioner could not reasonably be expected to live with the respondent would be hard to justify.

Living together after the behaviour

Where a petitioner continues to live with her spouse for a period of up to six months after the date of the last incident relied on in her petition brought under section 1(2)(b), this period must be disregarded by the court when determining whether she can reasonably be expected to live with

---

14 [1972] 3 All ER 219, at p 223.
15 [1975] 2 All ER 979. In *Thurlow v Thurlow* the husband complained of both negative and positive behaviour on the part of the wife. The negative behaviour alleged was that the wife gradually became a bedridden invalid. She was unable to perform the role of a wife in any way, and became unfitted even to reside at home. The positive behaviour alleged was that she became very bad tempered, threw things, burnt various objects, and wandered around the streets causing her carers alarm and stress.
16 In so doing, Rees J quoted with approval the decision of the Court of Appeal in *Gollins v Gollins* [1963] 2 All ER 966, a case decided under the old law requiring proof of cruelty.
17 (1973) 118 Sol Jo 184.

him.[18] The idea of this provision is to facilitate reconciliation between the parties. No party should be put under pressure to reject reconciliation overtures for fear that by so doing she will lose her right to petition. Where the period exceeds six months the court must take it into account, but this does not provide an automatic bar to the granting of the petition, the court must look at each case individually. In *Bradley v Bradley*[19] the trial judge had refused the wife a decree where she had continued living in a four-bedroomed council house with her husband and seven children. The Court of Appeal held that she should be entitled to prove that it was unreasonable for her to continue living with her husband. The decision of the Court of Appeal was a vital recognition of the grave difficulties that many women find themselves in. Housing issues may well force a couple to stay together unwillingly. Unless the petitioner also applies for an ouster order, both parties are entitled to continue residing in the matrimonial home. It may well be that neither party has anywhere else to go and, in any event, both spouses may wish to stay in the home in order to share in the care of the children. It is therefore commonplace for a petitioner to argue that she had no choice in the matter but to continue living together under the same roof.[20]

Desertion

In order to establish desertion, the petitioner must show that the respondent has deserted her for a period of at least two years immediately preceding the presentation of the petition. This fact is rarely relied on, as normally in such a case the parties will use the fact of two years' separation with consent.[1] There will only be a need to use this fact where the deserting spouse refuses to consent to a divorce, has not behaved in such a way as to enable the petitioner to avail herself of the provisions of section 1(2)(a) or (b), and the petitioner either does not wish to wait for five years, or wishes to ensure that the respondent cannot avail himself (or more likely herself) of the provisions in sections 5 or 10 to oppose, or delay, the granting of the decree absolute.[2]

The straightforward situation where desertion occurs is where one spouse abandons the other, leaving the home with the intention of not returning. Where there is no agreement to part this still gives rise to desertion, even though the one deserted is thoroughly glad to see the other

---

18 S.2(3).

19 [1973] 3 All ER 750.

20 See ch 5 on regulating the occupation of the matrimonial home for a discussion of the housing difficulties that may arise.

1 Just 1,082 divorces, 0.685%, of all divorces granted in 1991 were based on this ground.

2 See ch 7 for a consideration of ss.5 and 10.

go. It is also possible for one party to desert the other whilst still living under the same roof.³ In *Pulford v Pulford*⁴ desertion was described as 'not the withdrawal from a place, but from a state of things.' Thus where there is a total cessation of cohabitation between the parties, although they remain living under the same roof, desertion can occur.⁵ Where the parties are either forcibly absent from one another, for example because the husband is in prison, or on a posting abroad, or where the parties agree to separate, that will not normally amount to desertion, unless evidence can be brought to show that the husband intended to have nothing more to do with the wife. In *Nutley v Nutley*⁶ the wife originally left the home to look after her aged and ailing parents with the consent of the husband. Some time after that, whilst her parents were still alive, she formed the intention never to return, but did not inform the husband. After the deaths of her parents she still did not return home, and the husband petitioned on the ground of her desertion. The issue therefore arose as to the date from which her desertion commenced. It was held by the Court of Appeal that communicating the intention never to return was not essential. However, because the husband had continued to consent to the wife's absence, no desertion could have taken place. The court recognised that had the wife communicated her intention then perhaps things would have been different, and the husband would not have continued to consent to her withdrawal. However, until he no longer consented, desertion had not occurred.

The intention to desert

In order to establish desertion the intention to desert is a necessary element. This may be difficult to establish where the respondent suffers from mental illness or incapacity. For example, the amnesiac who disappears for two years cannot be held to have formed the intention to desert if he has no memory that he has a wife to return to. The onus of proof is on the petitioner to establish that she has been deserted. However, by virtue of section 2(4):

> 'the court may treat a period of desertion as having continued at a time when the deserting party was incapable of continuing the necessary intention if the evidence before the court is such that, had the party not been so incapable, the court would have inferred that his desertion continued at that time.'

3 *Naylor v Naylor* [1961] 2 All ER 129; *Hopes v Hopes* [1948] 2 All ER 920.
4 [1923] P 18, per Lord Merrivale at p 21.
5 See further below on the meaning of the phrase 'living apart'; *Hopes v Hopes* [1948] 2 All ER 920; *Naylor v Naylor* [1961] 2 All ER 129.
6 [1970] 1 All ER 410.

Where the respondent is suffering from mental delusions he must be treated as if the delusions are true in assessing whether he is in desertion. So in *Perry v Perry*,[7] where the wife believed that the husband was trying to murder her, she was held not to be in desertion. Clearly if the delusions were true she would have been entitled to leave.

Sometimes behaviour by a spouse is such that the other is entitled to leave. In that event the departing spouse will not be in desertion. The test for deciding whether a departure is justified was originally described by Lord Penzance in *Yeatman v Yeatman*[8] as being where the behaviour of one party is so 'grave and weighty' as to entitle the other to leave. In *Hall v Hall*[9] a more modern wording of the test was expressed as 'whether the conduct of this husband was sufficient to justify his wife in leaving him and saying that she finds it impossible to live with him.' An interesting example arose in *Quoraishi v Quoraishi*.[10] The parties had validly entered a potentially polygamous marriage in Pakistan. They had lived in England for a number of years, and were educated people, both being doctors. The husband wished to marry a second wife, but the wife steadfastly protested against him so doing. When he did marry another woman the wife left. The Court of Appeal held that the onus was on the petitioner to establish desertion without just cause. An English court must apply English law, and therefore even if a Muslim woman has no ground for complaint under Islamic law it does not follow that she may not have just cause for leaving. Whether a wife has reasonable grounds for leaving is a matter of considering all the circumstances. In each case what must be considered is the particular husband and wife, the law of their marriage and personal lives, and most importantly their personal circumstances. Here the wife had consistently protested against her husband taking a second wife. This justified her in leaving and she was not in desertion.

Where a spouse has left home with the intention never to return and is not in desertion she could herself plead constructive desertion. This has been recognised since 1864[11] and arises where the reason why one spouse leaves is because she has been driven out by the other. This can occur either when a wife has been physically forced out, or when she has felt compelled to leave because of her husband's actions. In order to establish constructive desertion, the petitioner must show that the respondent's behaviour has been sufficiently grave to drive her out.[12] A petition based on constructive desertion could also, therefore, give rise to a petition under

---

7 [1964] 1 WLR 91.
8 (1868) LR 1 P & D 489.
9 [1962] 3 All ER 518, per Ormrod LJ at p 523.
10 [1985] FLR 780.
11 See *Graves v Graves* (1864) 3 Sw & Tr 350.
12 *Hall v Hall* [1962] 3 All ER 518. See for example *Lang v Lang* [1955] AC 402, where the husband had assaulted and abused the wife, and where (as a court would recognise today) he had raped her.

section 1(2)(b).[13] Thus it is suggested that, had it been the wife who petitioned for a divorce in *Quoraishi v Quoraishi*, she could have succeeded on the ground of her husband's behaviour.[14] Should a petitioner fail on presentation of a petition based on behaviour she will not be able to plead constructive desertion in the alternative, because the conduct will not be sufficiently grave for her to have left. In *Morgan v Morgan*,[15] where the only allegation against the husband was that he had ordered the wife to leave, it was held that 'simple desertion or an order to go' should be considered under fact (c) only and could not amount to constructive desertion. This is a similar approach to that adopted in *Stringfellow v Stringfellow*.[16]

Termination of desertion

Because desertion must be shown to have occurred for a continuous period of not less than two years it is possible that it may be brought to an end before the two years is up. Termination of desertion can arise in different ways. Most obviously this will occur where the parties resume cohabitation with each other. However, provision is made in section 2(5) that a period of up to six months' cohabitation for reconciliation purposes shall not terminate the desertion, but that period of failed reconciliation shall be added on to the two years required to establish desertion. Desertion will also come to an end where both parties agree to separate. If the deserting spouse makes a genuine offer to resume cohabitation desertion on his part ceases. Furthermore, if the wife refuses to accept this offer then, unless she has good grounds for refusing the offer, because, for example, the husband has committed adultery in his absence, she will then put herself in desertion.[17]

Two years separation with consent, and five years separation

The recognition that parties can agree that their marriage has irretrievably broken down established a real change in the law of divorce. Section 1(2)(d)

---

13 The wording of the test in *Hall v Hall,* above, bears a strong resemblance to the requirements of the fact of s.1(2)(b).
14 *Quoraishi v Quoraishi* demonstrates that where a member of an immigrant community objects to behaviour, which other members of the community find an ordinary incident of their lives, there is no reason in principle to treat that person any differently from any other divorce petitioner or respondent.
15 (1973) 117 Sol Jo 223.
16 [1976] 2 All ER 539.
17 *Everitt v Everitt* [1949] 1 All ER 908.

permits divorce by consent, something which was completely forbidden prior to 1969,[18] and makes divorce available simply on the basis that the parties have lived apart for at least two years. At the time the measure was introduced, it was the hope of law reformers that it would become the main fact relied on for divorce, it being a simple, non-judgmental situation, with no allegations of any kind being required. Unfortunately this has not proved to be the case. The fact has never accounted for more than 27 per cent of all divorces, and in 1991 accounted for just 18.6 per cent.[19]

Consent is a positive requirement of subsection (d), mere passive non-objection is not sufficient.[20] However a respondent can refuse to consent unless he or she does not have to pay costs.[1] This clearly could give one party a better bargaining position if the other is desperate for a divorce. Costs of the actual divorce are not very high, because of the special procedure, but where there are limited resources costs can still operate as a significant factor. The respondent cannot, however, refuse to pay the costs of ancillary proceedings, for example over the children, or property adjustment orders. Consent must be freely given with understanding of what it entails,[2] and it can be withdrawn at any time before a decree nisi is pronounced.[3] After decree nisi the respondent has a limited opportunity to apply to withdraw his consent. Section 10(1) provides that on an application the court may, if it is satisfied that the petitioner misled the respondent, either intentionally or unintentionally, about any matter which the respondent took into account in deciding to give his consent, rescind the decree.[4] The discussion as to the meaning of certain phrases in section 1(2)(d) is also applicable to section 1(2)(e). This also requires the parties to have been living apart for a period of time, but does not require the consent of one of the parties.

Section 1(2)(e) provides that either spouse may present a petition for divorce where the parties have lived apart for a period of at least five years. This fact was the other radically new method of obtaining a divorce

18 In fact if the parties colluded in a divorce it was an absolute bar to proceedings. Thus, pre-1969, the more both parties wanted a divorce the less chance they had of obtaining one, a state of affairs to which only Lewis Carroll could probably do justice!

19 The Law Commission in *Facing the Future* Law Com No 170 published the figures for the years 1971-1986 in Appendix B. The peak year was 1979, when 26.7% of all divorces were granted under fact (d).

20 In *McG (formerly R) v R* [1972] 1 All ER 362 it was argued that a letter from the husband's solicitors amounted to consent. It read: '[the husband] is not in the least concerned with the procedural problems that have arisen. [The husband] simply wants this affair to be brought to finality as soon as possible.' The court held that although this might be an indication that the husband did not object, there was nothing in the letter which amounted to consent by the husband.

1 *Beales v Beales* [1972] 2 All ER 667.

2 See s.2(7) and the Family Proceedings Rules 1991, r.2.10(1).

3 Family Proceedings Rules 1991, r.2.10(2).

4 See ch 7.

introduced by the Divorce Reform Act 1969. At the time it was highly controversial as it permits divorce against someone's will despite him having done nothing 'wrong'. It is of particular significance to those who are opposed to all divorce on religious grounds. Such a person is now helpless to prevent a divorce.[5] The requirements are identical to those of section 1(2)(d) except that the period is much longer, a full five years, and no consent is required. By not requiring consent this fact supplies the ultimate 'escape' for those petitioners who cannot establish any of the other facts. For example, where a spouse becomes insane during the marriage it is likely that he will not be able to give a valid consent to a two-year decree, and where the insanity takes a very passive form it may be that the petitioner will have difficulty in establishing 'behaviour'.[6] The five-year ground may then operate as a last resort for a petitioner married to such a person. This fact could also be used to divorce a spouse who is reduced to a 'human vegetable'.[7] A difficulty might arise in establishing that the parties have 'lived apart' for any period of time if the competent spouse continues looking after the incapacitated one. However, it is suggested that in such a situation the wise course would be to lodge a formal declaration of the intention to live apart with, for example, a solicitor. The fact that the parties then continue living under the same roof, with one supplying a variety of services to the other, should not prejudice the obtaining of a divorce, as the parties would not be living with each other as husband and wife.[8]

Living apart

A crucial issue under section 1(2)(d) and (e) is the meaning of the phrase 'living apart'. This is defined in section 2(6), which states that the husband and wife—

> 'shall be treated as living apart unless they are living with each other in the same household.'

Where parties are still living under the same roof it is nonetheless possible that they may still be classified as living apart. The issue the court has to resolve is whether all form of common life between the parties has ceased.[9] Only where it has can the parties be held to be living apart. This can drive

---

5   Unless able to raise a defence to a petition under s.5, which requires a respondent to establish grave financial or other hardship. Such a defence is highly unlikely to succeed: see ch 7.
6   See above.
7   The example given in *Thurlow v Thurlow* [1975] 2 All ER 979.
8   *Fuller v Fuller* [1973] 2 All ER 650, and see below.
9   This is the same test as in desertion.

parties to living in a very unnatural manner, and the difficulties this requirement can lead to were illustrated in *Mouncer v Mouncer*.[10] The husband and wife were on very bad terms and, dating from November 1969, slept in separate bedrooms. They continued to eat meals cooked by the wife, often together, and in the company of one or both of their children. They shared the cleaning, but the wife no longer did any washing for the husband. The only reason that the husband stayed was because he wished to live with, and help with, the children. He eventually left in May 1971, and petitioned for a divorce in November 1971. The petition was dismissed on the basis that the parties were not living apart until May 1971. In *Hollens v Hollens*,[11] by contrast, the husband and wife continued living in their two-bedroomed council house, but had not spoken or eaten together since a violent quarrel more than two years previously. Neither party had done anything for each other since the quarrel. In this case the petition was granted, as the parties were held to be living apart.

It is suggested that it is somewhat ironic that the more civilised the parties, and the more willing to behave well and co-operate one with the other, and to share the care of their children, the less chance there is of them obtaining a divorce. Many couples, through financial constraint, simply cannot afford for one of them to move out of the home. Until arrangements are made for a financial and property settlement after the divorce they are in effect forced to continue living under the same roof. The ruling in *Mouncer* has the effect of driving the parties to use fact (a) or (b) in order to ensure a divorce can be granted and appropriate orders made.[12]

Despite the decision in *Mouncer* there may be the occasional exceptional case where the parties are living under the same roof, where one spouse provides 'services' for the other, but where they can still be held to be living apart. An example arose in *Fuller v Fuller*[13] where the parties had separated and the wife commenced living with another man. Subsequently the husband became ill and unable to look after himself. He then moved in with the wife and the other man. The wife looked after him by cooking, cleaning and washing for him. However, the husband lived in the house as a lodger, paying a weekly rent and occupying his own bedroom, whilst the wife and her partner occupied another bedroom. The Court of Appeal held that the words 'living with each other' mean 'living with each other as

10 [1972] 1 All ER 289.
11 (1971) 115 Sol Jo 327.
12 See Law Com No 192, para 2.12, where the Commission comment: 'It is unjust and discriminatory of the law to provide for a civilised "no-fault" ground for divorce which, in practice, is denied to a large section of the population. A young mother with children living in a council house is obliged to rely upon fault whether or not she wants to do so and irrespective of the damage it may do.'
13 [1973] 2 All ER 650.

husband and wife.' It was manifest from these facts that he was not living with the wife as a husband, but as a lodger, and had therefore satisfied the living apart fact.

In order to facilitate attempts at reconciliation section 2(5) permits the spouses to resume living together for one or more periods totalling up to six months without this being taken into account in assessing whether the parties have lived apart for the requisite period. This period of cohabitation does not count as part of the two years but must be added on to it. Thus, for example, where parties have attempted a reconciliation lasting in total for five months they can seek a divorce after two years and five months have elapsed. If they stay together for longer than six months the time must start to run again if they subsequently separate.

The mental element

Parliament did not intend there to be any mental element to living apart; an amendment to this effect was defeated in the House of Lords.[14] However, there was an early landmark decision in *Santos v Santos*[15] where the Court of Appeal held not only must there be a physical separation, but there must also be a mental element on the part of at least one of the spouses of wishing to live apart, for the fact to succeed. Where spouses agree to separate the mental element is obviously present. But where spouses are physically separate due to reasons such as illness, prison, or an overseas posting it means they are not living apart until the mental decision to live apart is taken, and it is only then that time begins to run. It was held in *Santos v Santos* that the mental decision need not be a mutual one, it can be unilateral, and furthermore the party taking the decision need not communicate the decision either by word or deed. However failure to communicate could clearly lead to evidential difficulties. Sometimes it will be possible to determine the mental element by external factors such as a cessation of visits to an ill or imprisoned spouse, or cohabitation with a third party, but if there is no such evidence it would appear that some sort of corroboration of the petitioner's assertion will be required.[16]

In view of the express wish of Parliament not to include a mental element in the definition of 'living apart' the reasons given in *Santos v Santos* for holding that such an element should be included need to be examined.

---

14 Hansard (HL), Vol 304, col 1082-1130.
15 [1972] 2 All ER 246.
16 However this requirement is perhaps more theoretical than real with the advent of the special procedure. Where a petitioner states that she has formed the intention for the requisite period it is difficult to imagine how that statement will be subjected to close scrutiny.

Sachs LJ gave five reasons. First he said that a survey of Commonwealth statutes, and decisions on similar provisions to the ones contained in the Divorce Reform Act 1969, revealed that the stream of authority ran uniformly and clearly in favour of mere physical separation not constituting 'living apart'. Secondly, that English decisions on other statutes, concerning the meaning of the phrase, had also uniformly reached the same decision.[17] This prima facie led to the conclusion that the phrase meant something more than mere physical separation, and that there must be good reasons for holding differently. Thirdly he said absurdities could arise if a mental element was not an integral element of living apart. He gave as an example the case of a man who came home on leave for less than 20 per cent of the two to two and a half years immediately preceding the filing of the petition, who would be able to satisfy the fact even though the parties had been on excellent terms until they had a row on the last day of his leave. As petitions under fact (d) are normally undefended there would be no evidence to rebut the presumption of irretrievable breakdown. Of this Sachs LJ said: 'Unless—contrary to our view—the Act intended to permit divorce by consent simpliciter such a result would be absurd. On the contrary the tenor of [section 1(2)][18] is to ensure that under heads (c), (d) and (e) breakdown is not to be held irretrievable unless and until a sufficiently long passage of time has shown this to be the case.'[19] Fourthly, that the requirements of section 2(6) did not drive the court to conclude that only physical separation counts. The subsection merely makes it clear that where parties are living in the same house then, as regards living apart, a line is to be drawn in accordance with the views of Denning LJ[20] in *Hopes v Hopes,*[1] and they are to be held to be living apart if not living in the same household. Finally, that petitions founded on heads (d) and (e) needed careful judicial scrutiny. It was not correct to say that the object of the Act was to make divorce easy. It was designed to assist maintenance of marriages other than those reduced to a mere shell.

It is suggested that the Court of Appeal reached an unfortunate decision in *Santos v Santos*, and the better interpretation of the law is that no mental element is required. It was disingenuous to argue that a mental element should have been included because of the decisions of Commonwealth countries and pre-1969 English cases. Those drafting the legislation would have been well aware of those decisions, and yet chose not to include any wording importing a mental element. Although absurdities, as the

17 He mentioned the Larceny Act 1916, and also said that two revenue statutes had been cited to him.
18 At the time s.2(1) of the Divorce Reform Act 1969.
19 [1972] 2 All ER 246, at p 255.
20 As he then was.
1 [1948] 2 All ER 920.

Court of Appeal saw it, could arise if there is no mental element,[2] they could equally arise if there is a mental element. Sachs LJ himself pointed out some of the difficulties, particularly in cases involving mental illness.[3] Consider, too, the following alternative example of what would look like an absurdity to most people if a mental element must be established. Suppose a couple are separated for five years on the husband being sent to prison. The wife decides to stand by her husband. She sees very little of him, as the prison is at a great distance from the home. Almost immediately on his release the wife realises that there is no possibility of resuming the relationship. Both parties have changed radically during the five years. She has become independent, and he has been damaged by his prison experience. Now suppose the husband will not agree to a divorce. If a mental element is required she will have to wait a further five years before she can obtain a divorce. Finally, the advent of the special procedure, radically affects Sachs LJ's last reason. There simply is not the judicial scrutiny of divorce petitions which he envisaged. However, even at the time of the decision, when the special procedure did not exist, it was possible to criticise this reason. To encourage the dissection of a marriage on a petition based on consent is counter to the whole ethos of the Act that marriages should be dissolved with the minimum bitterness, distress and humiliation.

The decrees nisi and absolute

Being married gives a person status which is not just of relevance to the particular individual, but is also of importance to other individuals and to the state. The status of being married gives rise to both rights and obligations. A married person may, for example, have the right to a pension as a surviving spouse, or to inherit when his or her spouse dies intestate. He or she may have the obligation to provide financial support for a spouse. The point at which the marriage is terminated could therefore be of crucial

2   Although the example they gave is arguably not as absurd as they suggest. The fact that the parties have actually gone ahead and petitioned for a divorce would suggest that there must have been something radically wrong with the marriage in any event. It is difficult to imagine that any couple would petition for divorce on the basis of one quarrel, when it is going to involve them in all the complications that a divorce inevitably entails. It is also to be hoped that any solicitor faced with a member of such a couple would at the very least discuss the possibility of reconciliation, and supply a list of people able to help, in accordance with the provisions of s.6; see above.

3   See for example p 254 where he says: 'How, for instance, does a judge in practice discharge the unenviable task of determining at what time the wife of a man immured long-term in hospital or one serving a 15-year sentence changes from a wife who is standing by her husband … to one who realises the end has come but visits him merely from a sense of duty arising from the past?' He gives another example of a difficult case, where both spouses have been of unsound mind for more than five years, at p 256.

importance. When hearing a defended case a decree nisi of divorce will be pronounced at the end of the hearing. Where the special procedure has been invoked, the judge will pronounce the decree nisi in open court for all the cases he has on his list. The decree nisi does *not* terminate the marriage, it is of a purely provisional nature. It is not until decree absolute has been granted that the marriage finally comes to an end. This can be granted six weeks after decree nisi on the application of the party in whose favour the decree nisi was pronounced.[4] If no application has been made after 12 months, the court may require the applicant to provide evidence accounting for the delay. The court then has a discretion whether to make the decree absolute, or to rescind it altogether.[5]

The two-stage process

The importance of the two-stage process was graphically illustrated in *Re Collins*.[6] In 1978 Mrs Collins married a man with an exceptionally violent nature. However, not long after marrying him she left because of his violence, and was given leave to petition for a divorce within three years of the date of the marriage on the ground that this was a case of exceptional hardship or exceptional depravity.[7] She was granted a decree nisi, but died before the decree was made absolute. She had two children, an illegitimate daughter and a son of the marriage, who were taken into care by the local authority. The son was subsequently adopted. Mrs Collins died intestate, leaving an estate worth a net total of about £27,000. Under normal intestacy rules, Mr Collins was entitled to the whole of her estate as a surviving spouse. Some months after the son was adopted an application was made under the Inheritance (Provision for Family and Dependants) Act 1975 on behalf of the children for their reasonable financial provision. An order for a lump sum of £5,000 was made in favour of the daughter, but the son received nothing. The reason he received nothing is because the effect of an adoption order in law is that the child becomes the child of the adopters, and not the child of any other person.[8] Mr Collins, of course, ended up scooping most of the pool. He received the bulk of the money, gaining £22,000. Had the decree been made absolute, so that Mr Collins was no longer Mrs Collins' widower, the daughter would have inherited

4   The respondent may apply for the decree to be made absolute three months later: see s.9(2).
5   See *Court v Court* [1982] Fam 105.
6   [1990] 2 All ER 47. It also reveals how the change of status brought about by adoption may have financial implications.
7   At that time it was not possible to petition for a divorce within the first three years of marriage unless exceptional hardship or depravity could be established in addition to one of the facts evidencing irretrievable breakdown of marriage.
8   Adoption Act 1976, s.39.

her mother's entire estate, which is surely what Mrs Collins would have preferred. However, she would also probably have wished her son to inherit too. Thus the case also illustrates the enormous importance of each spouse making a will when their marriage has broken down, so that the inheritance rights of family members are not governed by the vagaries of the intestacy laws, or as happened in this case, by a change of status brought about by adoption, rather than by their own wishes.

Judicial separation

Some spouses whose marriage has effectively come to an end may wish to separate from each other. They may need to sort out financial and property matters, and make arrangements about the children. However they may have conscientious objections to petitioning for a divorce.[9] For such people some other remedy is a necessary provision. A decree of judicial separation can be obtained based on exactly the same facts as those for divorce.[10] Unlike divorce, these facts supply the *grounds* for a decree of judicial separation. The reason for this is that there is no requirement that the marriage should have irretrievably broken down.[11] This is because the decree does not terminate the marriage, and can indeed be rescinded. There is therefore no necessity to establish irretrievable breakdown.[12] The special procedure applies in the same way as it does for divorce and the vast majority of petitions will be dealt with in this way. Where a party wishes to contest the application it will be heard in open court. The court must then enquire into the facts pleaded to see if they can be made out, but will not be concerned with irretrievable breakdown. The provision of legal aid is based on exactly the same principles as in divorce, and will therefore not normally be granted. Most cases will be dealt with under the green form scheme.

If one of the grounds is made out the court must grant the decree, which comes into effect immediately.[13] There is no two-stage process as in divorce because, unlike divorce, the parties' status as a married couple does not

9   Most commonly this will arise where divorce is contrary to the individual's religious beliefs. Perhaps the best known example where this might happen will be where someone is of the Roman Catholic faith.

10   A petition may be presented under s.17. Prior to the Divorce Reform Act 1969 the main grounds for judicial separation were the same as those for divorce, but not all the grounds were exactly the same.

11   See s.17(2).

12   The provisions of s.6, which deal with the requirements placed on solicitors and the courts in considering the question of reconciliation, are applicable to such applications.

13   Provided the provisions of s.41 of the Matrimonial Causes Act 1973, as amended by the Children Act, Sch. 12, para 31, are satisfied. Exceptionally a decree can be withheld where the court is concerned about the arrangements made for any children.

alter. It is not possible to raise a defence of grave financial or other hardship as section 5 does not apply, and neither does section 10, which makes provision for the rescission or withholding of a decree where the petitioner has misled the respondent.[14] In addition the bar which prevents a party presenting a petition for divorce within the first year of marriage[15] does not apply, so the petition can be presented at any time.

The consequences of the decree

A decree of judicial separation has a number of important consequences. One of its principal effects is that it relieves the spouses from the duty of cohabitation with each other. Consequently, once a decree has been obtained, neither party will be in desertion for refusing to live with the other party. Another effect is that it enables the court to exercise its ancillary powers to make orders relating to finances and property,[16] and to the upbringing of the children.[17] The court is also able to grant injunctions during proceedings for judicial separation. However the court will not necessarily exclude a spouse from the home once a decree has been granted. The petitioner may therefore wish to bring separate proceedings under the Domestic Violence and Matrimonial Proceedings Act 1976, or under the Matrimonial Homes Act 1983.[18] A further effect of the decree is to alter the parties' rights of succession on an intestacy. By virtue of the provisions of section 18(2) of the Matrimonial Causes Act 1973 the parties are treated as if they have pre-deceased one another. They are therefore not entitled to succeed to any property on intestacy.[19] However, the position is different to that of divorce where the parties have made wills. On divorce any gift to a spouse in a will automatically lapses,[20] but it will not do so on judicial separation; the spouse will continue to benefit.

Either party is entitled to petition for divorce after a decree of judicial separation has been granted.[1] Where it is the same person petitioning on each occasion, he or she will normally plead the same facts as those supplying the ground for the earlier decree. These facts should then prove to be sufficient to establish the ground. In addition, the petitioner will now also have to prove irretrievable breakdown, but this is unlikely to give rise to any difficulty. If the respondent to the decree of judicial

14 See ch 7.
15 S.3(1).
16 Under ss.23 and 24, see ch 7.
17 Pursuant to s.41.
18 See ch 5 for a full discussion of ouster orders.
19 Although they are, of course, still entitled to make an application for reasonable financial provision under the Inheritance (Provision for Family and Dependants) Act 1975.
20 Wills Act 1837, s.18A.
1   Matrimonial Causes Act 1973, s.4(1).

separation is the person petitioning for a divorce, he or she will need to establish one of the facts independently. However, the one fact it will be impossible to allege will be that of desertion.

Reform of the law of divorce

Discussion documents and proposals aimed at reforming the current law of divorce have been in the public arena since 1988. In that year the Law Commission published a paper, *Facing the Future: A Discussion Paper on the Ground for Divorce.*[2] In the light of the responses they received, they published proposals for reform in *Family Law: The Ground for Divorce.*[3] Subsequently the Lord Chancellor's Department published their own Green Paper *Looking to the Future: Mediation and the Ground for Divorce,* inviting rapid responses.[4] In December 1994 the Lord Chancellor announced that he hoped to bring out a White Paper in the spring of 1995.

The ground for divorce

The aims of the law of divorce were expressed in both Law Commission papers as being encapsulated in four major propositions. First, to support those marriages capable of being saved; secondly, to enable those not so capable to be dissolved with the minimum of avoidable distress, bitterness and hostility; thirdly, so far as possible to encourage the amicable resolution of practical issues relating to the couple's home, finances and children, and the proper discharge of their responsibilities to one another and their children; and fourthly, to minimise the harm the children of the family may suffer, both at the time of the divorce and in the future, and to promote, so far as possible, the continued sharing of parental responsibility for them. The Law Commission discussion paper contained three possible models for reform: a mixed system with both fault and no fault as currently, but with some modifications; divorce after a fixed minimum period of separation; and divorce after a fixed minimum period for reflection and consideration, known as 'process over time', the proposal they preferred. As a result of responses to their consultation exercise the Law Commission recommended a 'process over time' model in their final report. The Green Paper emanating from the Lord Chancellor's Department similarly took as its preferred model the 'process over time' model proposed by the Law Commission.

2   Law Com No 170.
3   Law Com No 192.
4   1993, HMSO.

In their introduction to the Green Paper the Government's objectives in relation to the law and procedure surrounding the dissolution of marriages are expressed rather differently from those expressed by the Law Commission. They state their objectives as being: (i) to support the institution of marriage; (ii) to include practicable steps to prevent the irretrievable breakdown of marriages; (iii) to ensure that the parties understand the practical consequences of divorce before taking any irreversible decision; (iv) where divorce is unavoidable, to minimise the bitterness and hostility between the parties and to reduce the trauma for the children; and (v) to keep to the minimum the cost to the parties and the taxpayer. The objections to the current law, and the reasons for wishing for change, are spelt out in some detail.[5] The present system allows divorce to be obtained quickly and easily without the parties being required to have regard to the consequences; the system does nothing to save the marriage; the system can make things worse for the children; the system is unjust and exacerbates bitterness and hostility; the system is confusing, misleading and open to abuse; the system is discriminatory; the system distorts the parties' bargaining positions.

Looking to the Future lists nine possible options for reforming the law, the preferred option appearing to be the Law Commission model, that the sole ground for divorce should be the irretrievable breakdown of the marriage which is to be proved by the passage of time. During this time, the parties are to use the allotted period, which is suggested to be one year, as an opportunity for consideration and reflection. If implemented, this proposal would mean the end of divorce based on different 'facts', and the abolition of fault as a relevant concept in the obtaining of a decree.[6]

Mediation

Mediation is the central focus of *Looking to the Future*. As the paper comments, separation and divorce constitute a painful process, and this affects all family members, particularly the children. It therefore proposes the introduction of a comprehensive system of mediation in order to try and lessen the present harmful effects of divorce. The overall objective of mediation is seen to be to 'help separating couples reach their own

5   See *Looking to the Future*, ch 5. A more detailed analysis of the defects in the current system is provided in both Law Commission papers.
6   Although this appears to be the preferred model in the Green Paper, press reports indicate that the cabinet as a whole may not be in full agreement, see the *Observer*, 6 February 1994, '"No-fault" divorce plan to be dropped'. Subsequently this has been denied by the Lord Chancellor, see *The Times*, 28 March 1994, 'Divorce Plan Defended'. See R Smith *Forwards and backwards* (1994) 144 NLJ 326; A Bainham *Divorce and the Lord Chancellor: Looking to the Future or Getting Back to Basics* (1994) 53 CLJ 253.

agreements about the future, to improve communications between them, and to help them co-operate in bringing up their own children.'[7] Law and procedures which are essentially adversarial in nature are said to be completely out of step with the mediation process, which offers an alternative system. 'It offers couples a constructive framework for using the period between the initiation of the divorce process and the grant of the divorce for consideration and reflection—whether that period is 12 months as recommended by the Commission or a longer period.'[8]

It is suggested that there should be a single first port of call for everyone wishing to initiate the divorce process in order to ensure that all those contemplating divorce are well informed about the law, procedures and consequences of divorce, and are directed to services appropriate to their needs. This would involve a personal interview during which essential legal information, but not advice, would be given. The paper estimates that the initial interview, which would be attended by either the initiating spouse or the couple, would last for an average of about one hour. One of the major aims of the initial interview would be to offer the parties every encouragement to use mediation. During the interview the spouse(s) would be offered information about marriage guidance; receive an inform-ation pack, including legal information about the divorce process; be offered information about mediation services and the role of lawyers and the courts; be advised on costs; be advised on eligibility for state funding for those seeking the help of mediators and lawyers; and receive an explanation of the system of means testing.[9] The paper sees the person conducting the initial interview as performing a vital role in the process, and considers the options as to who might best fulfil it.[10] Family court welfare officers are felt to be inappropriate as their primary function is reporting on the welfare of children rather than family mediation, and asking them to take on another role would risk confusing their responsibilities to their clients and the court. Similarly asking local mediation services to take on a new role is thought not to be appropriate as it might lead to a conflict of interests. It is therefore suggested that a new independent organisation be allocated the task, who would be responsible for employing suitably qualified and trained staff.

An additional role is also suggested for the initial interviewer, that of being the person responsible for allocating the resources available for the public funding of mediation and legal services, and of reporting to the court on the parties' reasonableness where a question as to making an order as to costs arises. The criteria for the grant of assistance is that it should be subject to a means test; that where it can be afforded a recipient

7   Para 7.7.
8   Para 7.10.
9   Para 8.12
10 Para 8.10.

should pay a contribution; a recipient should behave reasonably; and where money, or property, in dispute is ultimately recovered it should be subject to a charge to cover some, or all, of the costs.[11] The ability of the initial interviewer to affect the parties' financial position is considerable. The paper states: 'Where one person is behaving unreasonably in the conduct of the case—for example, where he or she refuses even to contemplate mediation or provide information—that person, if he or she has the money, could be required to bear all the costs of the legal process that has been necessary as a result.'[12] Where a person is privately funded, and an application for a costs order is made against an uncooperative spouse, the initial interviewer could then report to the court about the reasonableness of the parties' approach. Where a person is publicly funded, the assistance would be withdrawn, just as legal aid can currently be withdrawn.

Where a couple indicate that they wish to seek mediation, the person conducting the initial interview would help arrange an appointment. The paper estimates that the usual period for mediation is one to three sessions for child issues, and three to seven sessions for comprehensive mediation,[13] and assumes that this will also be the case under the new system. Where the parties reach total, or limited, agreement through mediation, this could then either remain a private agreement enforceable as a contract, or be approved as a consent order. In either event most couples would need the help of a lawyer in drawing up the agreement. The paper makes it clear that the costs of public funding need to be strictly controlled,[14] and indicates that mediation is to be preferred to legal advice and assistance as it is seen to be considerably cheaper. It is estimated that the likely average cost of comprehensive mediation is £550 per case, children-only mediation is estimated to cost £180-£200 per case, whereas the average cost of a matrimonial bill paid out of legal aid was £1,565 in 1992/3.[15] The aim of the proposed new system is stated to be to ensure that couples receive a better service, but generally that this should be at less cost both to themselves, and to the taxpayer, than at present. The fundamental principle underlying Government assistance is that the cost of dissolving a marriage should be borne by the couple themselves, but where this leads to a disparity of bargaining positions, or where it would put the interests of children at risk, there is a clear case for public assistance with the costs.[16]

11 Para 9.8.
12 Para 9.22.
13 That is, covering money and property issues too.
14 The use of legal aid in matrimonial proceedings is increasing year by year. In 1983/4 the net cost was £105 million, in 1988/9 it had risen to £122 million and by 1993/4 to £180 million (all at 1992/3 prices). See para 9.6.
15 Paras 9.28 and 9.30. In ch 10 it is made clear that the current legal aid system would continue to apply in cases of domestic violence, wardship and public law cases under the Children Act 1989.
16 Para 9.7.

The paper very briefly confirms that a party who has been subjected to domestic violence would be entitled to apply for legal aid under the current system. However the objective is to separate the divorce process from other matters such as molestation and violence. Thus it is suggested that the jurisdiction to grant injunctions ancillary to divorce proceedings should be removed, and that in future such injunctions should be granted as 'free-standing' orders under the relevant domestic violence and family homes legislation.

The procedure

The procedure for setting in motion the divorce process is suggested as being the one constructed by the Law Commission.[17] Briefly, it is proposed that there should be a change of terminology to encourage a non-adversarial approach to the process. For example the spouses should be referred to as 'husband' and 'wife' rather than 'petitioner' and 'respondent'. The initiation of the period of consideration and reflection would be brought about by a statement that the matrimonial relationship has broken down, although not irretrievably, which should be lodged at court. Accompanying this should be a statement of circumstances concerning the children, home, other property, income and other resources. At the time of lodging the statement, both parties would be supplied with a comprehensive information pack. A minimum period between the making of the statement of breakdown and applying for an order would then elapse during which time the period of consideration and reflection would take place.[18] The court would have the power to direct spouses to attend a preliminary interview in order to have the possibilities of mediation outlined to them. Furthermore, the court would have the power to adjourn the hearing of any proceedings connected with the breakdown to enable the spouses to participate in mediation.

No later than 12 weeks from the statement of breakdown the court would hold a preliminary assessment in order to monitor progress, and make any orders, or exercise any necessary powers. The court would be under a specific duty to consider certain matters as part of this assessment, including whether it should exercise any of its powers under the Children Act 1989. The court would also be able to adjourn and reconvene the assessment. During the period of consideration and reflection either on an application, or using its own motion powers, the court would have power to make orders relating to children, financial provision and property

17 An outline of the proposals is set out in Appendix D. A detailed explanation of the proposals is found in Law Com No 192.
18 In the Law Commission proposals this would be a period of 11 months for consideration and reflection, after which application for an order could be made, which would be granted after one month, making a total of 12 months minimum.

adjustment,[19] and could exercise its powers under the domestic violence legislation to protect any person from violence, or to regulate occupation of the home. It would be possible to extend the period for consideration and reflection in appropriate circumstances. These circumstances cover situations where it would be desirable to do so because issues had arisen relating to children, lack of proper financial arrangements, lack of capacity of one spouse, delay in the service of documents leading to possible prejudice, or where the hardship bar had been raised. The period of consideration and reflection would be automatically suspended where both spouses notified the court of their desire to attempt a reconciliation. The process would then be restarted by either spouse notifying the court. If no notification was received after 18 months the application would lapse, as it would if the spouses jointly withdrew the statement of breakdown. An order for divorce would not be made automatically, but only where an application had been made. This could be made by either spouse, not simply the initiating spouse.

It would still be possible to prevent a divorce altogether by raising the bar of grave financial or other hardship. Rather surprisingly, this bar would be retained as a bar despite the fact that it is extremely rare for the defence to be invoked, and even more rare for it to prove successful.[20] The reasons for keeping the defence were explained by the Law Commission in their final report.[1] They recognised that there is still a considerable economic imbalance between spouses, particularly where there are children. They thought that the existence of the bar, coupled with the five-year fact, may well have affected the couple's bargaining position whichever of the five facts evidencing breakdown under the present law was finally relied upon. Therefore, they took the view that the fact that the defence is very rarely relied on was by no means proof that it is ineffective. Furthermore, because there is no means of dividing occupational pensions on divorce, the hardship involved cannot be mitigated. Thus to remove the bar would be to remove what may be a substantial protection for the economically weaker spouse. Finally, it would not be possible for either spouse to apply for an order under any circumstances until the parties had been married for at least one year. As a consequence, in a case where a marriage broke down very quickly, perhaps because of violence or adultery, it would be impossible for a spouse to obtain a divorce until the marriage had lasted for a minimum period of two years. It is only after the application has been made that the period of consideration and reflection can commence.

19 Whereas orders for financial provision would be capable of taking effect during the period, final property adjustment orders would only be made where the court was satisfied there were special circumstances making it appropriate.
20 See ch 7.
1   Law Com No 192, paras 5.72-5.77. The arguments against this were considered in para 5.74. The benefits of retaining the bar were felt to outweigh the disadvantages.

Criticisms of the proposals for reform

Some of the proposals for reform require some clarification. The requirement that a spouse wishing to initiate a divorce be required to attend an
initial interview raises questions. It is not made clear what the exact
position of a spouse who does not attend the initial interview will be. Will
he or she be given a further opportunity to attend an initial interview, or
will this be denied on the basis that the spouse should have attended the
original interview? If a spouse is permitted to attend at a second interview,
will there be sufficient resources, both in terms of manpower and finance,
to meet the extra demand? Also, the relationship between the initial
interview and the formal act of registration of marital breakdown is not
spelled out. The implication is that registration follows the initial interview.
Will this always be the case, or will there be circumstances where a party
will be entitled to register first?

The role of the interviewer

These are minor points which need clarification, but there are more serious
and fundamental objections which can be raised against the proposals.
The requirement to attend the initial interview, in itself, could be highly
oppressive in some instances. In others it could be a futile exercise, which
simply needlessly consumes time and money. The role of the person
undertaking the initial interview encompasses a wide variety of tasks and
skills. He or she must provide information, assess financial entitlement
and encourage the parties to consider reconciliation. These are wide-
ranging duties, and it is suggested that no one person could, or should, be
expected to undertake all of these tasks. The situation will commonly arise
where one spouse will have taken the momentous decision to initiate divorce
proceedings, whilst the other will not wish to be divorced, but will be at
the interview.[2] One, or both, of the recipients of these services is liable to
be in a highly volatile and emotional state. In order to fulfil the various
tasks allotted to the interviewer, he or she will need to be able to gain the
confidence and trust of both of the spouses. He or she will also need the
ability to describe how mediation works, although it is known that when
in distress people can find it enormously difficult to comprehend even the
most basic of information.[3] Having such wide-ranging powers also raises

2 See D Burrows *Marriage Breakdown and the 'Initial Interview'* (1994) 24 Fam Law 274.
   The writer questions whether the first appointment can be conducted more effectively
   by an initial interviewer rather than by a solicitor under the green form scheme.
3 Doctors have long appreciated that, after breaking bad news to patients and their families,
   at a later date they are liable to be accused of omitting vital pieces of information. This
   accusation may be levelled against them despite their having clearly explained the

the spectre of the possible manipulation and coercion of the parties at a time when they are at their most vulnerable.

The suggestion that legal aid be rationed by the newly created 'authority figure'[4] at the initial interview, who will consider the willingness of the parties to behave 'reasonably', raises serious questions. What is meant by reasonableness? Does it mean the same thing to all people? How likely is it that a lawyer and a mediator would operate by the same definition; and if they would not, why should the decision-maker be the person conducting the initial interview? He or she will not know about the case in depth, and may not possess certain necessary legal knowledge or mediation skills. If legal aid is to be rationed, could this lead to a two-tier system of justice in divorce, those who can afford it, or who are publicly funded, getting a better service than those who are ineligible for legal aid? Any legal system which sets out to restrict access to lawyers is opening up the possibility of creating one law for the rich and powerful, and another for the vulnerable. When divorce occurs it is often the case that one party is 'powerful' whilst the other is 'vulnerable'.[5]

Attending mediation

Mediation is seen to play a pivotal role in the proposed reforms, with the aim being that mediation will become the norm rather than the exception. However, it is worrying that there has been no large empirical study which demonstrates that mediation will be able to operate successfully in the way envisaged. Currently there is no way of knowing whether it will command the respect of the parties, large numbers of whom may be extremely unwilling to engage in mediation, rather than negotiate through solicitors. Furthermore, a false dichotomy is presented between a non-adversarial system of mediation, as opposed to an adversarial system involving lawyers. Many solicitors would argue that they go to great lengths to try to ensure that their clients do not enter into bitter adversarial

---

situation, and even having written it down. The reason for this is not due to malice, or any other wrongful motive, on the accuser's part. Many people in great distress simply cannot take in what they are being told, and often need to be given the information on several occasions before they can fully grasp what is being said.

4 An apt description of the initial interviewer given by G Davis in *Mediation and the Ground for Divorce: A New Era of Enlightenment or an Orwellian Nightmare?* (1994) 24 Fam Law 103. Davis, whilst supporting the basic principle of a simple period of notice, mounts an impressive critique of the proposals, in particular those relating to the mediation process. He suggests that the Government has striven to do three things: (1) to 'sell' divorce by notice; (2) to give a huge boost to mediation; and (3) to cut the matrimonial legal aid bill.

5 See (1994) 24 Fam Law 179, where a summary of the conclusions and recommendations of the Solicitors Family Law Association's response to the Green Paper is given.

disputes. Many state that they strive to persuade their clients to negotiate sensibly. Mediation will not necessarily be able to resolve the bitter conflicts which arise over property, money and children in divorce proceedings, any more than using lawyers is currently able to do so. The question therefore arises whether parties, going through the consideration and reflection process, should be entitled to choose the method they prefer to resolve any conflicts between them, without being placed under pressure to use mediation. Many people might well prefer to choose a lawyer to assist them. Vulnerable clients may need someone who knows about the complexities of the law, understands the way the system works, and who will be partisan on their behalf.[6] The paper appears to offer mediation as a complete alternative to the use of legal advice, except in so far as it is suggested that lawyers would be used in drawing up the final agreement between the parties. This again creates false alternatives. Mediation should not be seen as a substitute for legal advice, but should be seen as offering a complementary system. Lawyers can help clients through the mediation process, offering advice as to the wisdom, or otherwise, of any proposals the client or his or her spouse puts forward. A solicitor might well be necessary to protect a client from negotiating a very unfair settlement.

Divorce mediation is a service that is currently offered to parties in different parts of the country in a number of different ways. There is, however, no large-scale system of mediation. A whole new system will therefore need to be created. Whereas persons who currently act as mediators may well be highly professional and successful in carrying out this role, a wholesale increase in numbers brings with it the attendant likelihood that far fewer able people will be appointed. This throws doubt on the estimated number of interviews which the Green Paper suggests will be needed to resolve matters through the use of mediation. Because the costings in the paper are based on the expert skills of committed mediators, the estimated figures for the cost of nationwide mediation may be unreal-istic. Research shows that in the pilot projects which have been taking place, from which the average costings have been extrapolated, mediation was subsidised by both mediators and lawyers, who offered their services at a reduced rate.[7] The researchers doubt whether people would be willing to work at such low rates in the long term. The employment of inexper-ienced, or not so competent, mediators is in any event likely to increase overall costs above the estimated figures.

---

6   See S Roberts *Divorce Reform Green Paper: A Coherent and Radical Vision* (1994) 24 Fam Law 204; and the SFLA response, above.

7   See J Walker, P McCarthy and N Timms *The making and remaking of co-operative relationships* The Relate Centre for Family Studies, Newcastle upon Tyne, funded by the Joseph Rowntree Foundation.

Domestic violence

Whilst the Green Paper seeks to alleviate fears that persons subject to domestic violence will not be treated in the same way as other parties seeking a divorce, the emphasis of the whole paper on the use of mediation, and the cost-cutting aim, sits uneasily with the protection afforded to victims of violence.[8] The statement that parties who refuse to contemplate mediation could be faced with a report to the court by the initial interviewer on the reasonableness of their attitude,[9] could put pressure on a victim to agree to mediation for fear of being branded unreasonable. Similarly, although parties are stated to be able to seek legal aid, they may well fear the withdrawal of legal aid on the advice of the initial interviewer. This fear could be compounded by the statement that 'some separating partners might seek to exploit allegations of molestation and violence in order to avoid considering the merits of mediation and thereby gain access to publicly funded legal services.'[10] This gives the impression that mediation should always be at least considered, despite violence having been inflicted by the other partner.

With the emphasis in the new procedure being to look constructively to the future, rather than destructively to the past, this might also raise problems for a victim in gaining public funds. The Green Paper recognises that where there is an unacceptable disparity between the bargaining positions of the two parties that public funding should be available.[11] However, if the victim does not reveal the violence she has endured at the initial interview the disparity between the parties might not be uncovered. A victim will no longer be able to give a statement of the facts relied on for divorce, and thus the issue of violence may simply get lost in the mediation process. Many victims find it extremely difficult to admit to the life they have had to endure, and may never do so if swept up in the effort to encourage a forward rather than backward-looking approach to marriage breakdown.

The basis for divorce

The Law Commission proposals were subjected to extensive commentary and criticism both at the time of the original discussion paper, and when

---

8   For a detailed consideration of the issue of domestic violence, see F Kaganis and C Piper *Domestic Violence and Divorce Mediation* [1994] JSWFL 265; F Kaganis and C Piper *The Divorce Consultation Paper and Domestic Violence* (1994) 24 Fam Law 143.

9   Para 9.22-3.

10 Para 10.2.

11 Para 9.7.

their final proposals for reform were published.[12] Some commentators took the view that the proposals were fundamentally flawed because they abandoned the fault basis of divorce altogether. Some saw this as completely unacceptable.[13] However, the majority of commentators supported the Law Commission's approach in principle. But, whilst supporting the broad aims of the proposals, the measures have nonetheless been subjected to questioning. Irretrievable breakdown is stated to be the sole ground for divorce. However, the Law Commission themselves admitted that, in effect, the proposals will allow unilateral divorce on demand. The period of notice of 12 months may only amount in practice to an administrative mechanism.[14] The rhetoric surrounding the process over time proposal is that it allows a time for consideration and reflection; the reality amounts to divorce by repudiation.[15] It has been argued that the alternative model of divorce after a period of separation, in similar fashion to the models existing in Canada, Australia and New Zealand, is preferable.[16] The argument made is that separation is the natural indicator of whether a marriage has broken down. 'Divorce in the abstract is very different from the day-to-day cycle of loneliness, lack of funds, lack of help with chores and children, and lack of emotional support. It is only when separation has been tried and tested and found preferable that divorce touches reality.'[17]

The reforms cannot eliminate the sense of injustice which is said to be one of the major criticisms of the current system. A spouse who behaves cruelly towards the other will now be able to obtain a divorce against the other's wishes. To say, for example, to the wife that she can now use a period of time for constructive consideration and reflection is hardly likely to assuage her feelings of anger, grief and bitterness. Despite sometimes quite appalling conduct directed towards them, some people nonetheless wish to remain married for a variety of reasons. A spouse may have religious objections to divorce; or societal pressures may have a strong bearing, particularly where divorce may lead to ostracism within the community.

12 See for example a number of articles in Family Law: G Davis (1989) 182; G Brown (1991) 128; M Mears (1991) 231; S M Cretney (1992) 472; C Davies (1993) 331; P Grose-Hodge (1993) 418; R Schuz (1993) 580, 630. See also G Davis (1988) 138 NLJ 913; J Montgomery (1988) JSWL 342; R Deech (1990) 106 LQR 229.

13 See G Brown (1991) 21 Fam Law 128 who comments: 'There are now clear signs of national moral decay and the aim of divorce law must be to buttress the stability of marriage.' It is the proponents of this view in the Government who are said to be holding up the plans to implement the reforms: see R Smith *Forwards and backwards* (1994) 144 NLJ 326. See also the paper of Conservative MP David Willetts *The Family*, W H Smith, Contemporary Papers No 14, where he suggests that, where children are involved, the divorce should be more exacting, with longer delays before it is possible.

14 Or such other period that the Government decides.

15 See S M Cretney *Divorce — A Smooth Transition?* (1992) 22 Fam Law 472.

16 See C Davies *Divorce Reform in England and Wales: A Visitor's View* (1993) 23 Fam Law 331.

17 Ibid, at p 332.

Divorce may also involve some spouses in considerable financial loss, and it seems ill-considered to allow unilateral divorce on demand until the problem of pension provision is resolved.[18] There is also the danger that the period of consideration and reflection could be used tactically by one of the parties to manipulate and exploit the other party, by applying for an extension of time, or for interim orders, or by requesting further and better particulars.

There is no suggestion that agencies skilled at assisting persons with marital difficulties should receive funding to come to the aid of large numbers of couples. Furthermore, whilst parties are being invited to reflect on their marriage, and to consider whether reconciliation might be possible, court processes will be running in parallel. The parties will be required to supply certain information to the court at the time when the initial application is made, after 12 weeks, and thereafter if the court of its own motion, or on an application, wishes to exercise any of its powers. This gives a very mixed message to the couple. At the same time as they may possibly still be living together, and reflecting on whether the breakdown is indeed irreparable, they are also being required to value their assets with a view to divorce. It can be seen that whilst the proposed reforms have much to commend them, the inescapable fact of life is that, whatever system is in place, divorce remains a painful process.

18 See ch 7.

Chapter 7

Money and property on marriage breakdown

Chapter 7

Money and property on marriage breakdown

Provision for a spouse in the immediacy of marriage breakdown

During marriage spouses normally live together in the same home and, as time goes by, they are likely to accumulate possessions for their joint and separate use. The income of the household, which may be derived from earnings, investments or both, will be provided by one or both of the spouses. When neither is employed, the means for their support usually comes from state benefits. Where there are children of the family the home, possessions and income are used for the children's benefit as well. When families are functioning harmoniously such an informal arrangement works well. The fact that the spouses' rights, interests, responsibilities and claims have become tangled together, without resort to any of the formalities which usually accompany transactions between strangers involving property and money, is not a problem. However, when a marriage breaks down informal arrangements no longer work; the tangle must be untangled. Suddenly it becomes essential to identify the nature of the financial obligations, if any, which each spouse owes to the other, and to the children of their family. Suddenly it becomes important to know what rights each spouse has in relation to the matrimonial home and its contents; whether one or other can continue to live there, or whether it must be sold; and whether a dependent spouse can continue to receive the benefit of the other's income and future earnings.

Provision for periodical payments

On marriage breakdown a spouse may be in need of immediate financial assistance in the form of periodical payments.[1] She may also need a lump

1   Where her only source of income is state benefits she may also be under pressure from the Department of Social Security to institute proceedings for a periodical payments

sum to enable her to pay existing debts and to reimburse her for other expenditure. A spouse seeking periodical payments during the subsistence of the marriage has a choice of proceedings open to her: she can apply to the family proceedings court under the Domestic Proceedings and Magistrates' Courts Act 1978, section 1, for an order to be made for periodical payments and/or a lump sum not exceeding £1,000.[2] She can apply to a county court, or to the High Court, under the Matrimonial Causes Act 1973, section 27, for an order for secured or unsecured periodical payments, and a lump sum, unlimited in amount. On presentation of a petition for divorce, nullity or judicial separation, she can apply in the county court or High Court for maintenance pending suit under the Matrimonial Causes Act 1973, section 22.

The family proceedings court may be the most appropriate forum in a case when the applicant believes that the breakdown of the marriage may prove to be only temporary, and where she is reluctant to institute divorce proceedings at this stage. Research reveals that, with rare exceptions, parties to proceedings brought under the Domestic Proceedings and Magistrates' Courts Act 1978 have low incomes. Research also tells us that, in the past, the majority of orders made in family proceedings courts were for small sums and mainly for the benefit of any children of the family.[3] The advent of the Child Support Act 1991 has resulted in the role of the family proceedings court being substantially reduced. The Act prevents a court making an order for periodical payments for a child of the family except in very limited circumstances, so reducing the role of the courts. The impact of the Act means that the majority of spouses will approach the Child Support Agency where an agreement over how much the absent parent should pay to the parent with care of the children cannot be negotiated by agreement. However, a spouse can apply in his or her own right to the family proceedings court for financial support for himself or herself, whether or not there are children requiring maintenance.[4]

Section 1 of the Domestic Proceedings and Magistrates' Courts Act 1978 provides—

'Either party to a marriage may apply to a magistrates' court for an order under section 2 of this Act on the ground that the other party to the marriage—

---

order, because such an order will lead to the reduction, or elimination, of the burden of her support from state funds.

2 The order would be made under s.2. However, where the parties agree that a financial provision order should be made, the application should be brought under s.6.

3 See O R McGregor, L Blom-Cooper and C Gibson *Separated Spouses* (Duckworth, 1970); S Garlick *Judicial Separation: A Research Study* (1983) 46 MLR 719; C Smart *The Ties that Bind* (Routledge and Kegan Paul, 1984).

4 For ease of writing, henceforth it will be assumed that the applicant is the wife unless otherwise stated.

    (a) has failed to provide reasonable maintenance for the applicant; or

    (b) has failed to provide, or to make a proper contribution towards, reasonable maintenance for any child of the family; or

    (c) has behaved in such a way that the applicant cannot reasonably be expected to live with the respondent; or

    (d) has deserted the applicant.'

In practice it is unlikely that the respondent will litigate over whether grounds for making an order exist. Instead he is likely to concede one or more of the grounds, and any contest will be over whether an order should be made in the light of the parties' respective financial circumstances and, if so, how it should be quantified. In relation to failure to provide reasonable maintenance for the applicant, this is relatively easy to establish in a case where the wife has no income, or only a limited income, of her own. There is an obligation on spouses to maintain one another during marriage, and even where a respondent has no source of income from which he can pay his wife maintenance, such as where he is unemployed and living on state benefits, the ground of failure to provide reasonable maintenance can nonetheless be established. The family proceedings courts have a long-standing tradition of making nominal orders, for example for 10 pence per annum, in favour of wives in cases where their husbands lack the means to make reasonable financial provision for them.[5] The advantage to the wife of a nominal order is that it recognises that the husband has an obligation to maintain her, and it is an order which can be varied upwards should his circumstances subsequently improve. Paragraph (b) has been rendered virtually obsolete because the Child Support Act 1991 prevents a court making an order in favour of a child.[6] Behaviour such that the applicant cannot reasonably be expected to live with the respondent has the same meaning as it has for divorce purposes.[7] Desertion too has the same meaning as for divorce, but there is no minimum period for which the respondent must have deserted the applicant before an order can be made, and consequently the intricacies of the law of desertion are most unlikely to be raised.

Where the grounds for making an order are established the court, in deciding whether to exercise its powers and, if so, in what manner, must have regard to all the circumstances of the case, give first consideration to the welfare while a minor of any child of the family, and have regard to the several matters which are listed in section 3. These are virtually the same matters as those to which a court must have regard in the exercise of

5   See, for example, *Chase v Chase* (1983) 13 Fam Law 21.

6   Child Support Act 1991, s.8. On the Act, and financial and property provision for children generally, see ch 8.

7   See ch 6.

financial provision and property adjustment powers on the grant of a decree of divorce, nullity or judicial separation.[8] The differences are that, because the parties are still married, the clean break principle does not apply, and the spouses' mutual obligation to maintain one another continues. Also, of course, there is no need to consider benefits which might be lost by reason of the marriage being terminated. The powers of the family proceedings court are also much more circumscribed than those of the divorce court. The family proceedings court may only order unsecured periodical payments and/or a lump sum.

Proceedings may also be brought in the county court for periodical payments and/or a lump sum on the grounds of failure to provide reasonable maintenance for a spouse, or a child of the family, under section 27 of the Matrimonial Causes Act 1973.[9] Once a petition for divorce, nullity or judicial separation has been filed, the court may make an order for maintenance pending suit under section 22 in favour of either the petitioner or the respondent. Such an order is for periodical payments only. Periodical payments and lump sum orders may provide essential support for the applicant in the immediacy of marriage breakdown where she has no income, or only a small income, of her own. Such payments may be of particular value where one party has left the matrimonial home and there is a risk that he will default on paying the mortgage or the rent. The other party can pay the rent, mortgage or other outgoings out of the periodical payments and such payments are as good as if made by the spouse who is liable to pay; the mortgagee, landlord or other creditor cannot refuse to accept such payments.[10]

Protecting the right of occupation in the matrimonial home

In the immediacy of marriage breakdown swift attention should be given to the nature of each spouse's rights in relation to the matrimonial home. Where the matrimonial home is vested in the name of one spouse alone, there is a danger that the owning spouse may enter into some kind of transaction with a third party in relation to the property without either the knowledge or consent of the non-owner spouse. Such a transaction may give rights in the matrimonial home to the third party which are binding on the non-owning spouse. A non-owning spouse has a 'right of occupation' in the matrimonial home, and may have other rights too. Where she fails to protect her rights she may be at risk of losing them, or of

---

8   Matrimonial Causes Act 1973, s.25: see below.
9   In relation to children, the court's powers are similarly negated by s.8 of the Child Support Act 1991.
10   Matrimonial Homes Act 1983, s.1(5)

finding that they are subordinated to those of the third party; in some cases this is likely to mean that she will lose the roof over her head.

At common law each spouse had a personal right to live in the matrimonial home because he or she was married. This right was a right flowing from status and personal to the spouses only. It was not a property right and therefore it could not bind third parties. This meant that a purchaser who had notice that a spouse with merely a personal right of occupation was living in the matrimonial home could nonetheless enforce any claims he might have against the property. This doctrine left spouses, usually wives, and any dependent children living with them, vulnerable to third party claims. An extreme example arose in *National Provincial Bank Ltd v Ainsworth*,[11] when a deserting husband, and father of four children, mortgaged the family home to a bank and then defaulted on the payments due. The bank brought proceedings for possession and was successful, even though it had notice of the wife's occupation of the house. As a consequence the Matrimonial Homes Act 1967 was enacted to remedy this situation. It provided machinery to enable a spouse to protect his or her personal right of occupation against third parties. The current law is governed by the Matrimonial Homes Act 1983.[12]

Section 1(1) of the Matrimonial Homes Act 1983 provides—

'Where one spouse is entitled to occupy a dwelling house by virtue of a beneficial estate or interest or contract or by virtue of any enactment giving him or her the right to remain in occupation, and the other spouse is not so entitled, then, subject to the provisions of this Act, the spouse not so entitled shall have the following rights (in this Act referred to as "rights of occupation")—
(a) if in occupation, a right not to be evicted or excluded from the dwelling house or any part thereof by the other spouse except with the leave of the court given by an order under this section;
(b) if not in occupation, a right with the leave of the court so given to enter into and occupy the dwelling house.'

Thus it can be seen that a spouse who has no property right which entitles her to occupy the matrimonial home nonetheless has a personal right to live there. This is an important safeguard when a marriage breaks down because it prevents the owner spouse from asserting a claim to have exclusive possession of the property as sole owner. A spouse who has left the matrimonial home has a right of occupation despite the fact that he or she has not obtained the leave of the court to enter into and occupy the dwelling house. Rather the right of entry is conditional on leave being

---

11 [1965] AC 1175.
12 Which is a consolidating Act.

obtained.[13] Any other construction of the words of the statute would render the protection it affords relatively useless since, in the main, it is when relationships break down, and one spouse leaves, that recognition of the right of occupation becomes imperative.

The Act extends to those cases where the legal estate is vested in one spouse alone, but where both have a beneficial interest in the property. Section 1(11) provides that—

> '... a spouse who has an equitable interest in a dwelling house or in the proceeds of sale thereof, ...is to be treated for the purpose only of determining whether he or she has rights of occupation under this section as not being entitled to occupy the house by virtue of that interest.'

This, on its face, seems strange because a spouse with a beneficial interest in the property already has a right of occupation by virtue of that interest. Why therefore should such a spouse be given a separate right of occupation under the Act? The reason is that, because of the law relating to the registration of equitable interests, a spouse with an equitable interest could otherwise be in a more vulnerable position than a spouse with a mere right of occupation. A distinction must here be drawn between unregistered and registered land.

In the case of unregistered land, a spouse with an equitable interest could be particularly vulnerable. This is because an equitable interest is not registrable as a land charge under the Land Charges Act 1972 and therefore, if the interest is to be protected against a purchaser for value, notice of that interest must be given to such a third party by some other means. However, unless the spouse with the equitable interest is aware that a transaction involving the land is about to take place, she does not know whom to notify, or how to set about drawing her equitable interest to the purchaser's attention. She is afforded some assistance by the doctrine of 'constructive notice'. The courts have stated that, in some situations, a purchaser ought to have known about the existence of an equitable interest in the land even if in fact he did not know of it.[14] In particular, provided that a spouse remains living on the premises, it is likely that a purchaser for value will be deemed to have constructive notice of a spouse's equitable interest in the property even where the other spouse is also in occupation.[15] But of course when marriages break down one spouse usually leaves the

---

13 *Watts v Waller* [1972] 3 All ER 257.
14 And see the Law of Property Act 1925, s.199(1).
15 See *Hodgson v Marks* [1971] Ch 892, at pp 934-935; *Williams & Glyn's Bank Ltd v Boland* [1981] AC 487, at pp 505-506, 511; *Kingsnorth Finance Ltd v Tizard* [1986] 2 All ER 54; cf *Caunce v Caunce* [1969] 1 All ER 722.

home. When it is the spouse with an equitable interest only who leaves, then her equitable interest, and with it her right of occupation flowing from that interest, will probably be defeated by a purchaser for value without notice of it.[16] Section 1(11) of the Matrimonial Homes Act recognises that it is important, therefore, that a spouse with an equitable interest should be given an independent statutory right of occupation, which she can register, and thereby protect, against third parties.

In the case of registered land (which now covers most of the land in the country) a spouse with an equitable interest is in a better position because she can protect that interest through registration. Indeed, equitable interests are minor interests requiring protection on the register, and the general principle applying to registration is that a purchaser takes free of any interest which is not protected on the register. But where a spouse with an equitable interest is in actual occupation of the land, then even if she has not registered that interest it may still be protected on the basis that it is an overriding interest, which therefore binds a purchaser.[17] It is nonetheless suggested that, despite these safeguards, a spouse with an equitable interest should register her right of occupation flowing from her status as a spouse. There is always the risk in a case where a spouse claims that she has an equitable interest in the property that a court might rule that she has acquired no such interest.[18] By contrast, a spouses' right of occupation in the matrimonial home is conferred by statute. It cannot therefore be questioned, and affords her exactly the type of protection she needs in the immediacy of breakdown, namely it maintains the roof over her head.

Section 2(1) of the Matrimonial Homes Act 1983 provides that where one spouse is entitled to occupy a dwelling house by virtue of a beneficial estate or interest, then the other spouse's right of occupation is a charge on that estate or interest.[19] A spouse can protect her right of occupation by registering it in the appropriate manner. In the case of unregistered land the right is registrable as a class F land charge under the Land Charges Act 1972.[20] In the case of registered land a notice must be lodged under the Land Registration Act 1925.[1]

The only way of protecting the right of occupation against third parties who acquire an interest in the land for value is by registration, and

16 Cf *Kingsnorth Finance Ltd v Tizard*, above, where the spouse with the equitable interest returned regularly at weekends to the former matrimonial home.

17 Land Registration Act 1925, s.70(1)(g); *Williams & Glyn's Bank Ltd v Boland* [1981] AC 487.

18 Cf *Gissing v Gissing* [1971] AC 886; and see further ch 8 where the establishment of an equitable interest by an unmarried partner is discussed.

19 Provided that it has been used by the parties as a matrimonial home at some time: s.1(10).

20 S.2(7).

1 Matrimonial Homes Act 1983, s.2(8).

registration only. Failure to register a right of occupation could prove disastrous for a spouse whose only entitlement to live in the matrimonial home depends on having such a right. In the case of unregistered land the doctrine of notice does *not* apply, so that a third party who is aware that a spouse with a right of occupation is living on the premises does not take his interest in the land subject to that right of occupation *unless it has been registered*.[2] Similarly, in the case of registered land, the right of occupation is *not* an overriding interest under the Land Registration Act 1925 notwithstanding that a spouse is in actual occupation of the dwelling house.[3] So, for example, if the owner spouse were to execute a legal charge over the home in favour of a bank, that mortgage would take priority in any subsequent legal proceedings *unless* the non-owner spouse had first registered his or her occupation right. Consequently it is imperative to register the right of occupation as soon as the marriage starts to run into serious difficulties. Conversely, once registered, the statutory right of occupation takes priority and is effective against all third parties who subsequently acquire an interest in the property.[4] This gives very real protection to the non-owner spouse because no purchaser is likely to be interested in buying, or leasing, a property which is subject to a right of occupation; and no mortgagee is likely to lend money when property subject to an occupation right is offered as security for the loan.[5]

A court has no power to order any alteration of the spouses' respective rights in property whilst their marriage is subsisting. The principles which the court must apply in any proceedings which are founded on the parties' strict legal and equitable rights allow little room for manoeuvre, and the scope for the exercise by courts of discretionary powers is very small.[6] The most a court can do is to regulate the spouses' rights of occupation in the matrimonial home.[7] Furthermore, courts are most reluctant to make orders which oust one of the spouses from the home; they regard these as Draconian orders, and will only make them in compelling circumstances.[8]

2   Land Charges Act 1972, s.2(8); *Midland Bank Trust Co Ltd v Green* [1981] AC 513.

3   Matrimonial Homes Act 1983, s.2(8)(b).

4   Exceptionally, in the case of unregistered land, a purchaser who correctly searches the register, and who receives an official search certificate which does not disclose the registered class F charge, will take free: see the Land Charges Act 1972, s.10(4). The defeated spouse will be left with an action in negligence against the Chief Land Registrar or other employee of the Registry: see *Ministry of Housing and Local Government v Sharp* [1970] 2 QB 223.

5   The protection is not absolute; a spouse may lose a registered right of occupation because the court decides to terminate it under the Matrimonial Homes Act 1983, s.1(2)(a). Indeed, a court may decide to terminate the right of occupation where a purchaser has purchased property with notice of it, because it may, inter alia, take the purchaser's circumstances into account: see *Kaur v Gill* [1988] 2 All ER 288.

6   See ch 8.

7   Under the Matrimonial Homes Act 1983: see ch 5.

8   See ch 5.

A court also has power to postpone the sale of property owned by the spouses under a trust for sale where the purpose of the trust has come to an end under the Law of Property Act 1925, section 30. However, a court is likely to be reluctant to exercise its powers under the 1925 Act where divorce proceedings are anticipated. Rather, where spouses wish a court to assist them in untangling their property rights and claims, the court will expect them to take proceedings under the Matrimonial Causes Act 1973.

Financial provision and property adjustment orders—the statutory framework

The Matrimonial Causes Act 1973 establishes a specific regime for dealing with financial and property provision for spouses and children where a marriage is terminated by decree. On or after the grant of a decree of divorce, nullity or judicial separation a court has extensive powers to make financial provision and property adjustment orders. It can alter existing property rights, and generally rearrange the spouses' financial affairs in the light of their past, present and anticipated future circumstances. It is helpful at the outset to have an overview of the main features of the statutory framework. Part II of the Matrimonial Causes Act 1973 provides a comprehensive code for the provision of financial relief for the parties to a marriage and any children of the family.[9] Sections 23, 24 and 24A specify the nature of the courts' powers. Orders can be made for secured and unsecured periodical payments, for a lump sum, for the sale of property, for the creation and variation of settlements, and for rights in property to be transferred from one spouse to the other. Section 25 sets out what are sometimes referred to as the 'statutory guidelines'. These identify an extensive list of matters to which a court must have regard in deciding how to exercise its powers. Section 25A contains what are commonly known as the 'clean break' provisions. These direct a court, in all cases of divorce and nullity, to consider whether and, if so, how and when it would be just and reasonable to terminate the financial obligations of each party towards the other. Section 28 is concerned with the duration of continuing financial provision orders and the effect of remarriage. Sections 33A, 34, 35 and 36 govern a court's powers in relation to consent orders, and the validity and alteration of maintenance agreements. Section 31 empowers courts to vary or discharge certain orders for financial relief, and section 37 enables them to restrain, or set aside, dispositions of property made with the intention of defeating a claim for financial relief.[10]

9 Though in relation to the children, the courts' powers have been curtailed by the Child Support Act 1991: see above, and also ch 8.
10 References to statutory provisions in this chapter will henceforth be to the Matrimonial Causes Act 1973, unless otherwise stated.

From this brief overview it can be seen that all aspects of the spouses' financial and property affairs need to be considered within the totality of the court's powers. In practice other considerations are also likely to be influential such as how the costs of the proceedings are to be paid, whether any lump sum payment will be used to reimburse the legal aid fund, and whether such a payment will be treated as a resource for social security purposes.

Consent orders and undertakings

Identifying how the law operates in practice is complicated by the fact that practitioners are encouraged to avoid litigation when making divorce arrangements. Most financial and property arrangements are arrived at through negotiation and agreement, but such bargaining takes place in the shadow of what a court would be likely to do. When a negotiated settlement is reached, the agreement is usually embodied in what is known as a 'consent order', made under section 33A. A consent order may only contain clauses which are within the powers of the court under sections 23, 24 and 24A of the Act so, in itself, a consent order does not increase the range of possible disposals.[11] However, matters falling outside the scope of the statutory framework can be dealt with by 'undertakings'. Undertakings enable spouses to promise to do certain things which the court cannot order. For example, it is commonplace for a husband to undertake to make the mortgage repayments on the former matrimonial home, to use his best endeavours to secure the release of the wife from her own obligations to the mortgagee, and to indemnify her should she be pursued for payments owing. Or he might undertake to take out insurance on his life in order to compensate his wife for her loss of expectation of a widow's pension;[12] or to pay the children's school fees.[13] The combination of consent orders coupled with undertakings allows for a wide range of proposals to be made about how best to untangle the spouses' financial affairs, and how best to make provision for their future needs. The advantage of arrangements agreed in this manner is that they can be more flexible, and more imaginative, than the range of orders available to courts. A consent order has the same binding force as a court order made after litigation, and undertakings too are enforceable.[14] Thus, in addition to case law relating to court orders, the law relating to consent orders and undertakings forms part of the jurisprudence of financial provision and property adjustment orders. However, as the content of consent orders and undertakings are rarely

---

11 *Livesey v Jenkins* [1985] 1 All ER 106.
12 *Le Marchant v Le Marchant* [1977] 3 All ER 610.
13 *Gandolfo v Gandolfo* [1980] 1 All ER 833.
14 *Livesey v Jenkins* [1985] 1 All ER 106, per curiam.

appealed, there is little case law guidance on what terms are regarded by courts as appropriate and acceptable to them.[15]

The role of discretion

It is important to realise that the law relating to financial provision and property adjustment is not a rule-based area of law which has as its chief aim the goals of certainty and parity between one case and another. Rather agreements and orders are made within the framework of a statutory code which allows courts to exercise broad discretionary powers. It will be seen in the analysis which follows that there are no definite and settled answers to some fundamental questions of principle and policy about the nature of the spouses' rights once their marriage comes to an end. Nor can the continuing nature of their obligations to one another be stated with confidence. Thus there is no easy and straightforward answer to the question 'how will property jointly acquired and paid for during a marriage be divided and distributed between the spouses when their marriage is terminated by decree?' A reply certainly cannot be given in the absence of a substantial amount of information about each of the spouses' current and future financial and personal circumstances. Even where all relevant information has been obtained,[16] there is a wide range of possible dispositions which could either be negotiated between the spouses, or ordered by a court. Similarly, it is extraordinarily hard to respond to the question 'is there a support obligation owed by one spouse to the other after their marriage has come to an end and, if so, how will it be quantified?' The answer to this question turns on a variety of considerations, and there can often be no certainty in the response. This means that the law in this area is more than usually unpredictable. It also explains why it may take some considerable length of time to reach a negotiated settlement.

The statutory code identifies the nature of the orders which courts are empowered to make and clarifies, in the form of principles and guidelines, the matters to which a court must have regard before reaching a decision. A large body of case law emanating from the House of Lords, the Court of Appeal and the High Court provides additional guidance on how these principles and guidelines have been applied in particular factual circumstances. Why is it therefore often so difficult to identify what agreement would be the most appropriate one to make in the circumstances; and why is it nonetheless so hard to anticipate what order a court would be likely to

---

15 In practice lawyers tend to consult practitioners' texts and manuals. These contain examples and precedents around which to model a consent order. See too, Law Com Nos 103 and 112.
16 And one of the difficulties faced by practitioners is obtaining full disclosure of the opposing party's assets and income.

make? It is suggested that the answer to this question lies in the fact that the judges tend to limit their judgments to the facts before them and appear to be reluctant to articulate universal principles to be applied in all cases. Even when articulating principles, the judgments usually do not contain directions about how these principles should be translated into practical solutions. Furthermore, the courts have not always been consistent in the application of principles when faced with similar facts;[17] and it is sometimes difficult to identify which rulings point to general principles, and which are confined to the facts of the case before the court.

This is not to assert that discretionary decision-making is the same as unprincipled decision-making. However for principles to emerge, and to be followed, there needs to be some kind of shared understanding and consensus amongst the judiciary about how particular questions of law and policy might best be resolved, and sometimes this appears to be lacking. It is suggested that the judges themselves do not always feel confident about how best to determine some of the fundamental questions of principle and policy which may arise in a particular case. This may be because the guidance given in the statutory framework contains principles, and policy directives, which appear sometimes to pull in opposing directions when applied to a particular set of facts.[18] Rather, the judges have tended to emphasise that each case must be determined on its own merits and that cases have limited precedent value. The cautious approach of the judiciary to precedent in this context was clearly expressed by Ormrod LJ in *Martin v Martin*[19] when he said:

'I appreciate the point [counsel] has made, namely, that it is difficult for practitioners to advise clients in these cases because the rules are not very firm. That is inevitable when the courts are working out the exercise of the wide powers given by a statute like the Matrimonial Causes Act 1973. It is the essence of such a discretionary situation that the court should preserve, so far as it can, the utmost elasticity to deal with each case on its own facts. Therefore it is a matter of trial and error and imagination on the part of those advising clients. It equally means that the decisions of this court can never be better than guidelines. They are not precedents in the strict sense of the word.'

17 For example, contrast the approach taken to the obligation to provide periodical payments for children in *Tovey v Tovey* (1978) 8 Fam Law 80 with that in *Delaney v Delaney* [1990] 2 FLR 457.

18 For example, the clean break provisions in s.25A lean towards a spouse not receiving periodical payments, but the direction to give first consideration to the welfare of the children in s.25(1) leans towards the residential parent obtaining substantial support in her own right, since any diminution in her income will normally inevitably rebound on the children.

19 [1978] Fam 12, at p 20.

Financial provision and property adjustment orders—the court's powers

A court, when deciding what orders to make, must consider the range of its powers. These are in sections 23, 24 and 24A which provide that it may make one or more of the following orders in favour of a spouse or a child of the family:[20]

1. for unsecured periodical payments;
2. for secured periodical payments;
3. for a lump sum or sums;
4. for the transfer of property;
5. making or varying a settlement; and
6. for sale of property.

Periodical payments

There is widespread agreement that a parent should continue to have financial responsibility for his or her children where a marriage ends in divorce. The reason for this is almost self-explanatory: a child is not self-supporting, someone has to provide the income to cater for the child's daily needs, and that duty should be borne by the parents. By contrast, there is no widespread agreement that it is the duty of one spouse to provide periodical payments for the other spouse where a marriage ends in divorce. The essence of divorce is to bring all aspects of the legal relationship of husband and wife to an end. But, while one spouse continues to be financially dependent on the other, there cannot be a clean break with the past. What then are the reasons which can justify requiring one ex-spouse to make provision for the other ex-spouse's daily needs in the form of periodical payments? Why should the law make provision for this obligation to be imposed merely because, at one time, the parties were married to each other?

Before attempting to answer this question it is necessary to consider how marriage may have the effect of financially disadvantaging one of the spouses, and lead to the dependence of that spouse on the other. It is true to say that, before marriage, unmarried men and women are equal in the sense that each has an earning capacity unaffected by traditional approaches to the division of family responsibilities between men and women. After marriage this equality of opportunity is liable to alter. It is often the case that one spouse pursues his or her career while the other acts as home-maker, career-supporter and child-rearer. Usually it is the man who goes to work and climbs up the promotion ladder. Where the wife is employed, she will have time off for the birth of any children, and may spend several years out of the labour market bringing up the children

---

20 But see the restriction on making court orders for children imposed by the Child Support Act 1991, s.8.

and running the household. If either spouse has elderly parents, or other close relatives, who require care and frequent visiting, it is likely to be the wife who takes over the substantial burden of providing such attention. Where the wife remains in, or returns to, full-time employment after the birth of children, she is likely to remain at a lower level on the promotion rung than a man or a woman without a young family, and to be less well paid than her husband. Where she works part-time, she is less likely to enjoy the range of benefits associated with full-time work, such as a company car, a pension scheme, private health insurance and holiday pay.

In a situation of this kind, it may be very difficult for the wife to be financially self-sufficient where the marriage ends in divorce, and she has the day-to-day care of the children. Where the children are young, she will need to pay for child care while she is at work, and this may absorb all, or the majority, of her earnings. Where they are older, she may find it difficult to obtain well-paid employment. Where she is seeking to return to work, she is often competing with people who are already in employment, and whose skills have not become rusty through lack of use. Consequently such a wife may be able to demonstrate a need for periodical payments for herself, the alternative being that her standard of living will otherwise be drastically diminished. It can be seen that there is a tension here between the idea that courts should give recognition to the fact that marriage often leads to one spouse being economically disadvantaged in the labour market, and the idea that a spouse should be able to make a fresh start after divorce, and be able to cast aside the duties and obligations owed to a spouse once their relationship is legally over.

It could be maintained that the reasons why a divorced woman often finds it relatively hard to obtain adequately paid employment are structural within society, and that the law should not impose responsibility for this on her husband. Also, that for so long as women are expected to turn to men to make provision for their daily needs, these structures will not be broken down. However, the countervailing argument is that unless, and until, society makes provision for carers of dependent children to be paid, provides care facilities for pre-school and school-age children, expects men and women to share child care, and the care of the elderly, on an equal basis, and does not expect women to give primacy to the career ambitions of their husbands (who may, for example, have to move from one part of the country to another in order to be promoted), then husbands should continue to shoulder part of the financial cost of marriage, namely the ongoing dependency of the wife. The alternative is to let the loss lie where it falls, that is solely on her shoulders.[1]

1   See further, R Deech *The Principles of Maintenance* (1977) 7 Fam Law 229; R Deech *Financial relief: The Retreat from Precedent and Principle* (1982) 98 LQR 621; K O'Donovan *The Principles of Maintenance: An Alternative View* (1978) 8 Fam Law 180; P Symes *Indissolubility and the Clean Break* (1984) 48 MLR 44; J M Eekelaar and M Maclean *Maintenance After Divorce* (1986, Clarendon Press).

Periodical payments or clean-break?

Section 23 provides —

> '(1) On granting a decree of divorce, a decree of nullity of marriage or a decree of judicial separation or at any time thereafter ..., the court may make any one or more of the following orders, that is to say —
>
> (a) an order that either party to the marriage shall make to the other such periodical payments, for such term, as may be specified in the order;
>
> (b) an order that either party shall secure to the other to the satisfaction of the court such periodical payments, for such period, as may be so specified.'

The order directs the payer to pay the payee a sum on a periodic basis, normally weekly or monthly.

The first question to be resolved in respect of periodical payments for a spouse is whether an order ought to be made, or whether any financial dependency of one spouse on the other should immediately be brought to an end. If it is thought appropriate to make an order, the two matters then to be resolved are for how long should the order last, and how should it be quantified. It has already been indicated that periodical payments are one part of a package, one piece in the large jigsaw of principles, powers and policy considerations applying to financial provision and property adjustment orders. Particular account must be taken of the clean break provisions in section 25A, and the reference to a spouse's potential to increase her earning capacity in section 25(2)(a), when assessing whether it is appropriate for one spouse to make periodical payments to the other. The clean break provisions and the direction to consider potential earning capacity were introduced into the Matrimonial Causes Act 1973 in 1984,[2] and they have been highly influential on the development of the law during the last decade. Indeed, case law on periodical payments which precedes the clean break approach should be read with some caution, because it may reflect outdated ideas.[3]

In the past a 'blameless' wife was entitled to life-long periodical payments from her husband, and this entitlement survived divorce. The clean break provisions mark a shift in thinking away from the desirability of requiring a husband to provide continuing maintenance for his wife for the rest of

---

2   By the Matrimonial and Family Proceedings Act 1984.

3   It is suggested that Lord Denning's ruling in *Wachtel v Wachtel* [1973] 1 All ER 829, which led to the revival of the 'one third rule' for the assessment of spousal maintenance, and which for a time was highly influential, has been overtaken by fresh thinking, and an approach to periodical payments which sees them as primarily rehabilitative in the case of a relatively young spouse, or a spouse with an earning capacity.

her life, which had hitherto been a commonplace feature of court orders, towards an approach which, in appropriate cases, leads to each spouse becoming financially independent of the other. This shift had already started to permeate the reasoning of the courts before it received legislative approval. The motive for the change was to enable the spouses truly to terminate their marriage ties by settling their financial affairs in a manner which left each one free to start afresh without any continuing obligations to a former spouse. This motive was succinctly expressed by Lord Scarman in *Minton v Minton*[4] when he said: 'The law now encourages spouses to avoid bitterness after family breakdown and to settle their money and property problems. An object of the modern law is to encourage the parties to put the past behind them and to begin a new life which is not over-shadowed by the relationship which has broken down.'

The clean break provisions are contained in section 25A, which provides—

'(1) Where on or after the grant of a decree of divorce or nullity of marriage the court decides to exercise its powers ... it shall be the duty of the court to consider whether it would be approp-riate so to exercise those powers that the financial obligations of each party towards the other will be terminated as soon after the grant of the decree as the court considers just and reasonable.

(2) Where the court decides in such a case to make a periodical payments or secured periodical payments order in favour of a party to the marriage, the court shall in particular consider whether it would be appropriate to require those payments to be made or secured only for such term as would in the opinion of the court be sufficient to enable the party in whose favour the order is made to adjust without undue hardship to the termination of his or her financial dependence on the other party.

(3) Where on or after the grant of a decree of divorce or nullity of marriage an application is made by a party to a marriage for a periodical payments or secured periodical payments order in his or her favour, then, if the court considers that no continuing obligation should be imposed on either party to make or secure payments in favour of the other, the court may dismiss the application with a direction that the applicant shall not be entitled to make any further application in relation to that marriage for an order under section 23(1)(a) or (b) above.'

The following salient features should be noted about the clean break provisions: subsection (1) of section 25(A) imposes a duty on a court to

4   [1979] 1 All ER 79, at p 87.

consider whether the parties' obligations towards each other should be terminated as soon after decree as the court considers just and reasonable in all cases.[5] This is a strong directive, but it is ameliorated by the language in which the court's discretion is couched. The court must ask itself whether it is *appropriate* so to exercise its powers; and whether the outcome will be *just and reasonable*. It can be seen that neither spouse is given preferential treatment. Rather the requirement is couched in terms which allows the court to consider the circumstances of both parties.

The court's duty under subsection (2) is slightly different. It arises in a case when the court has found it appropriate to make an order for periodical payments. The court is then required to consider whether it would be appropriate to limit the term of these payments only to such term as would be sufficient to enable the recipient to adjust *without undue hardship* to the termination of his or her financial dependence on the other. Thus although the court will be considering the financial position of both parties when deciding whether it is appropriate to make an order of limited duration, the court's attention must focus on the payee when applying the undue hardship test.

An order must of course come to an end when it expires. However the initial decision to set a time-limit on the periodical payments is not necessarily final, for there is a possibility of the order being varied in the future under section 31, and this could include the extension of the term during which payments are to be made.[6] Clearly the knowledge that such an application might be made could undermine the purpose of a clean break order which is intended to bring finality to the financial dependence of the payee, albeit postponed for the duration of the order. Section 25A(2) should therefore be considered alongside section 28(1A). This provides—

> 'Where a periodical payments order or secured periodical payments order in favour of a party to a marriage is made on or after the grant of a decree of divorce or nullity of marriage, the court may direct that that party shall not be entitled to apply under section 31 for the extension of the term specified in the order.'

Thus this provision allows a court to give a direction that a party in receipt of periodical payments shall not be entitled to apply in variation proceedings for an extension of the order. In this way a postponed clean break can truly be achieved.

---

5   See *Suter v Suter and Jones* [1987] 2 All ER 336.
6   *T v T (Financial Provision)* [1988] 1 FLR 480; *Richardson v Richardson* [1993] 4 All ER 673; and see *Richardson v Richardson (No 2)* [1994] 2 FLR 1051 where the duration of limited term order was extended for a further five years to enable the wife to complete her responsibilities for bringing up the children.

Subsection (3) contains the most Draconian provision from the point of view of an applicant for a periodical payments order. It entitles a court to dismiss an application for periodical payments, and to direct that the applicant shall not be entitled to make any further application for an order under section 23(1)(a) or (b). There are no words of guidance in subsection (3) on how a court should determine whether or not a continuing obligation should be imposed on one party to make, or secure, periodical payments in favour of the other, which seems to be a weakness in the drafting of this provision. The court will, of course, follow the statutory guidelines provided in section 25 in the exercise of its powers in general, but they are not specifically focused on periodical payments orders. It seems paradoxical that a court must consider the issue of the payee's adjustment without undue hardship to an order being terminated when limiting the duration of a periodical payments order, but not when refusing to make one altogether.

Circumstances where periodical payments are likely to be ordered

Whilst in theory husband and wife are afforded equal treatment under the law, in practice it is almost always the wife who is the applicant for an order for periodical payments.[7] When are periodical payments orders in favour of a wife likely to be made? Case law suggests that she can expect to be maintained by her husband for the rest of her life where the marriage has been long-lasting, where the husband has taken on the traditional role of breadwinner, and where the wife has been a housewife.[8] She can also expect to be maintained where she has undertaken paid employment, but where her earnings are small, and her future employment opportunities are either limited, or non-existent.[9] Periodical payments may also be made in cases where the marriage has been of short duration, but where to deprive the wife of the income on which she has become reliant, at least in the short term, would be suddenly, and drastically, to reduce the standard of living to which she has become accustomed.[10] Whether this maintenance is provided in the form of periodical payments will probably depend on whether or not there are sufficient resources to capitalise them into a lump sum which, when invested, will produce an adequate income for the wife.[11]

---

7   For an example when the husband was the applicant, but where his application failed because his inability to work had largely been self-induced: see *K v K (Conduct)* [1990] 2 FLR 225.
8   *M v M (Financial Provision)* [1987] 2 FLR 1; *Boylan v Boylan* [1988] 1 FLR 282.
9   *Leadbeater v Leadbeater* [1985] FLR 789; *M v M (Financial Provision)* above.
10 *Khan v Khan* [1980] 1 All ER 497.
11 See *Attar v Attar* [1985] FLR 649, in which the court ordered capitalised periodical payments of £30,000 to enable the wife to adjust to the ending of her six-month marriage to a millionaire.

Where this is the case, a clean break arrangement of this nature is likely to be made.[12] However only those with relatively substantial incomes and assets are able to offer sufficient funds to finance a clean break order of this nature; the majority of husbands do not have these resources and they will therefore be required to continue to support their wives on a periodical basis out of income.

When the wife is looking after a dependent child of the family it is usual for an order to be made for periodical payments for her as well as the child. The reason for this is that it is impossible to anticipate how the wife's obligations to the child will affect her future earning capacity.[13] However, the Court of Appeal in *N v N (Consent Order: Variation)*[14] stated that this approach is not intended to discourage wives with children from going out to work and bringing to an end their financial dependency on their former husbands as soon as possible. A wife may also be well advised to seek periodical payments for herself in a case where the husband refuses to make a maintenance agreement for the children, and where there is likely to be a delay before her application for a maintenance assessment is processed by the Child Support Agency.

Circumstances where periodical payments are not likely to be ordered

The clean break approach has encouraged courts to make orders which bring to an end the dependence of one spouse on the other as a source of income. They have felt able to do this, even in cases when the wife is not in the position to achieve financial self-sufficiency, and even where she has children to look after, for a variety of reasons. One is because they have extensive powers to redistribute the spouses' property holdings, irrespective of who owns what as a strict matter of law. These powers enable courts to make sure that a wife obtains a fair share of the family assets, which in itself may enable her to be financially independent.[15] Often too, a wife may be awarded more in the way of capital provision than her husband because she has more pressing needs. For example, when there are several children of the family whom the wife is looking after, and where sale of the former matrimonial home is ordered, it is likely that the wife will receive substantially more than a half share in the proceeds of sale to enable her to rehouse the family nucleus.[16] In a case where resources are limited,

12 *C v C (Financial Provision)* [1989] 1 FLR 11.
13 *Waterman v Waterman* [1989] 1 FLR 380.
14 [1993] 2 FLR 868. See also *Mawson v Mawson* [1994] 2 FLR 985 where the child was aged five years. Having heard evidence as to the wife's earnings over the past 12 months, Thorpe J thought the right balance had been struck by limiting a periodical payments order for a finite term, but not including a s.28(1A) direction prohibiting an application for an extension.
15 *C v C (Financial Provision)* [1989] 1 FLR 11; and see below.
16 Cf *Chaudhuri v Chaudhuri* [1992] 2 FLR 73.

which often makes sale of the matrimonial home inappropriate, she is likely to be permitted to occupy the house at least during the period of the children's minority. Sometimes a court may give the wife a life interest in the former matrimonial home; or even transfer the husband's entire interest in the property to her. As a consequence of making one of these orders, a court may then seek to balance its comparative generosity towards the wife in capital terms, by relieving the husband of his obligation to make continuing provision for her out of income.[17]

Another reason why courts have not made orders for periodical payments for a spouse is because they have been prepared to take account of the availability of state benefits. A wife who is unemployed, and who has insufficient resources to meet her needs under criteria applied under social security legislation, will normally be entitled to claim income support. Therefore, any order she receives will normally be of no financial benefit to her because her social security payments will be reduced pound for pound. Courts have recognised that the availability of state benefits can enable it to release a husband from his obligation to support his wife.[18] A court is most likely to adopt this reasoning where the husband has acquired new dependants. The court may take the view that to require the husband to continue to pay towards the support of his wife will be to place him under too onerous a financial burden. This view was adopted in *Ashley v Blackman*[19] in proceedings to vary an existing order; but the approach has equal force to an application for an original order. The wife in *Ashley v Blackman* was in receipt of both periodical payments and state benefits.[20] The husband had remarried and had two young children. He and his second wife had a very modest income, and his obligation to make periodical payments to his first wife was putting him under considerable financial pressure. If the husband's order were to be reduced, or extinguished, the loss to the wife would be made up by an increase in her benefit payments. Therefore she would suffer no hardship from the termination of the order. The issue for the court was whether the wife should become entirely dependent on public funds, or whether the husband should be required to continue to pay for her support. This case is illustrative of the tension which frequently arises between the court's duty to preserve the public purse from unnecessary expenditure, and its duty to consider the private interests of the parties, and to authorise a clean break arrangement in appropriate cases. Waite J held that the two duties do not necessarily

---

17 *Scallon v Scallon* [1990] 1 FLR 194; *Martin v Martin* [1977] 3 All ER 762; *Hanlon v Hanlon* [1978] 2 All ER 889.

18 *Allen v Allen* [1986] 2 FLR 265; *Delaney v Delaney* [1990] 2 FLR 457; more controversially, in *Delaney* the court also said the availability of benefits could release a husband from his child support obligations. This approach has been overtaken by the Child Support Act 1991.

19 [1988] 2 FLR 278.

20 She was disabled and incapable of earning her own living.

conflict, and that a court can strike the balance which the particular circumstances of a case appear to dictate. He said that flexible orders, including phased termination, can give proper weight to both heads of policy. On the particular facts of the case before him, he found that it was a classic instance when the clean break approach should be applied, and for no order at all to be made against the husband.

It seems likely that the Child Support Act 1991 will lead to fewer orders for periodical payments for a spouse who is caring for the children of the family. Prior to the Act, a wife could expect to receive periodical payments for herself as well as periodical payments for the children. Since 1991, the first call on the absent parent's resources has been to meet his financial obligations to his children. Consequently, the wife may not herself obtain an order because the husband's spare income is entirely absorbed by child maintenance, which includes an amount for the parent with care.[1] Even where the wife was married to a man of reasonable means, it seems unlikely that she will obtain more than a nominal, or very small, order for herself in a case where there are several children to be maintained, because the quantification of the child support obligation increases for parents on higher incomes.[2]

Another reason why orders for periodical payments are not made is because a wife is sometimes reluctant to pursue her claim in a case where the husband is unwilling voluntarily to make payments. Although she would be likely to obtain an order, she may value her new-found independence from her husband, and wish to bring to an end any reliance upon him. In a case where the husband has a high income, a wife may find it demeaning to pursue an application based on her continuing needs, and prefer instead to receive a lump sum settlement. She may wish for a clean break because any other arrangement is likely to be emotionally draining. A reluctant payer is likely to be an unreliable payer, and the wife may not be prepared to become embroiled in litigation which will probably be long-lasting and acrimonious, which has the potential to lead to never-ending variation and enforcement proceedings, and where there is no certainty about its outcome.

Duration of an order for periodical payments

An order for periodical payments can last for whatever period the court thinks fit, subject to two qualifications: the term cannot begin earlier than the date of making an application for an order, and it cannot extend beyond the death of either of the parties to the marriage. Furthermore, remarriage

---

1 See *Mawson v Mawson* [1994] 2 FLR 985.
2 See ch 8.

of the payee brings the order to an end.[3] The power to back-date orders is one to which the court's attention can usefully be drawn when the paying spouse has been obdurate during the negotiations leading to court proceedings, and has refused to make periodical payments on a voluntary basis in the meanwhile. A back-dated order enables the loss suffered by the applicant eventually to be reimbursed. However, it is important to make an application for back-dating at an early stage if a back-dated order is to be of any real benefit to the applicant. Otherwise the applicant may find that the court is reluctant to back-date the order, especially when the respondent is a person of limited means, because the effect of so doing is immediately to put the respondent into arrears with respect to the payments. Therefore, it may be sensible where the respondent refuses to pay voluntarily, to bring it to his attention that an application will be made for a back-dated order, and to record this in any documentation which will eventually be placed before the court.

Section 25A(2) requires a court to consider whether it would be appropriate to require periodical payments to be made for such term as would, in the opinion of the court, be sufficient to enable the party in whose favour the order was made to adjust without undue hardship to the termination of his or her financial dependence on the other. In *Barrett v Barrett*[4] the trial judge read section 25A(2) as requiring the wife's dependency to be terminated 'unless there was a reason why it should not be'. It was held that he had misdirected himself, and that by doing so had placed too great an emphasis on termination. As Butler-Sloss LJ pointed out, 'if there is to be determination unless there is good reason not to be, then in my judgment it should have been set out in the Act. But it is not.'[5] This is a significant statement from the Court of Appeal about where the balance should lie between finding it appropriate to terminate obligations owed to a spouse, and finding it appropriate to require them to continue. In *Barrett* the difficulty experienced by women in middle age of obtaining employment was the main foundation of the court's determination that the clean break provisions should not be imposed too readily.

The key phrase in section 25A(2) is 'undue hardship'. It ties in with section 25(2)(a) which requires a court to consider each of the parties' earning capacity, including any increase in that capacity which it would be reasonable to expect each spouse to acquire. These provisions provoke three questions: first, to what extent can periodical payments be used to compensate one of the spouses for having an earning capacity which has been diminished by marriage; secondly will she be required to increase her earning capacity; and thirdly, for how long a period will she be allowed

3 Matrimonial Causes Act 1973, s.28(1).
4 [1988] 2 FLR 516.
5 Ibid, at p 519.

to adjust to making provision for herself before the periodical payments come to an end?

Rehabilitative periodical payments

One compromise solution to the tension between giving recognition to the continuance of financial obligations between spouses after divorce and the clean break principle is for a court to order what can loosely be called 'rehabilitative periodical payments'. Here the term of the order is limited in duration, its purpose being to provide temporary support for the recipient until she can adjust to the change in circumstances brought about by the divorce. Is a limited term order of this nature likely to cause hardship? It was recognised in *M v M (Financial Provision)*[6] and *Barrett v Barrett*[7] that in the case of some women who have never had paid employment, or who permanently give up work once the children are born, any order which is limited in duration is likely to cause them hardship. Such women are unlikely to obtain employment in middle age, and even less likely to do so when approaching retirement age. Also, women who have never had paid employment tend to have been married to relatively affluent men, and to move in professional circles. It may arguably be a hardship in itself to expect the ex-wife of a professional man to obtain unskilled work in her middle years, for example in a shop, or factory, or in a domestic capacity.

The relativism of hardship to the standard of living previously enjoyed by the spouses has been recognised by the courts. In *Boylan v Boylan*[8] the wife had been married to a man of substantial wealth and had enjoyed a high standard of living. After the parties had been divorced for several years the wife sought an increase in her existing order for periodical payments. The husband, who had assets in excess of £1.2 million and an income of £100,000, offered a lump sum of £40,000 in return for an order terminating the wife's periodical payments forthwith. Booth J found this offer to be quite inadequate and ordered him to pay the wife £16,000 per annum. Booth J held that it was by the wife's previous high standard of living that her reasonable requirements should be judged, and an assessment made of whether she could adjust without undue hardship to the termination of periodical payments. The court also considered whether it should limit the duration of the wife's order. It recognised that a wife's employment opportunities are bleak when she has no formal qualifications, and has never been required to apply her mind to the question of earning her living. The court therefore ruled that the only circumstances in which the wife's periodical payments could be terminated in such a way as not to

6   [1987] 2 FLR 1.
7   [1988] 2 FLR 516.
8   [1988] 1 FLR 282.

cause her undue hardship would be upon payment of a lump sum sufficient to provide her with an income comparable to that which she would receive by way of periodical payments.

Rehabilitative periodical payments orders may be particularly appropriate in relation to short-term marriages where no children have been born. It has long been the case that a young and childless wife either cannot expect to receive periodical payments at all,[9] or that any order will be of short duration.[10] However, where the parties have married in later life, or where the husband is especially wealthy, it may be thought necessary, and appropriate, to give the wife time in which to adjust to her suddenly reduced standard of living.[11] One way in which this can be achieved is by making a periodical payments order for a limited period, coupled with a direction under section 28(1A) prohibiting the wife from applying for an extension. Unless such a direction is made, the wife can make an application under section 31 to vary the order during its currency by extending its term, and the variation court has a free discretion as to whether or not to do so, though it is likely to be influenced by the fact that the original court thought a limited term order was appropriate.

It can be more difficult to assess the appropriate duration of a periodical payments order where the marriage has been short-lived, but where a child or children have been born. On the one hand a wife who is a party to a short-term marriage cannot reasonably expect to be supported by her husband indefinitely, or even for very long. On the other hand, the wife's earning capacity is likely to be impaired for a significant length of time by her child care commitments. In *Waterman v Waterman*[12] the parties were divorced after their marriage had lasted a mere 17 months. Their child, who was aged five, was living with the wife. The wife had been trained as a secretary, and had been previously employed until just before she began to live with the husband. Since the divorce she had been on training courses in order to enhance her earning capacity. The trial judge made various orders, including an order for periodical payments for the wife, which he limited in duration to five years. He also gave a direction under section 28(1A) that the wife was not entitled to apply for an extension of the term of the order. Allowing the wife's appeal in part, Sir Stephen Brown P stated that the question whether the order should be limited in duration had been one for the judge to decide in the exercise of his discretion. He expressed the view that the Court of Appeal might have come to a different conclusion, namely that it was inappropriate to set any term to the

9   *Graves v Graves* (1973) 117 Sol Jo 679; *Brady v Brady* (1973) 3 Fam Law 78.
10 See *Khan v Khan* [1980] 1 All ER 497 where periodical payments of £18 per week were ordered for a young wife for one year, thereafter reducing to £5 a week. The purpose of the initial year was to give her time to train and to find employment.
11 *Hedges v Hedges* [1991] 1 FLR 196, where 18 months was held to be the appropriate adjustment period because the marriage had been of short duration.
12 [1989] 1 FLR 380.

periodical payments order had it been considering the matter at first instance. But he reaffirmed the principle that before an appellate court can interfere with a trial judge's discretionary decision it must come to the conclusion that he was plainly wrong. He continued 'so far as the period of five years is concerned, I am bound to confess to some hesitation in accepting that assessment of the appropriate period on the facts of this case, but I am unable to say that the judge was plainly wrong in coming to that conclusion.'[13] However, the Court of Appeal did find that the judge was plainly wrong when he added the direction that the wife should not be entitled to apply for an extension of the term of the order. It described an order under section 28(1A) as a Draconian prohibition, and held that the judge had been wrong to add a prohibition preventing the wife from applying for an extension under any circumstances having regard to the fact that she was caring for a child of tender years, and the uncertainty of what her position might be in five years' time.

It is important not to approach the ratio decidendi of *Waterman v Waterman* too narrowly. It is suggested that there are two strands to the decision. The first is concerned with whether it is normally appropriate for a court to make a limited term order for a parent who is looking after a young child. It is clear that the Court of Appeal did *not* positively endorse such an approach even though the wife's appeal on that point was rejected. Rather it held that the judge had carefully reviewed the financial position and circumstances of the parties, and for this reason his decision could not be faulted. But the tenor of Sir Stephen Brown P's judgment was that he himself would not have made such an order. The second strand was whether the court should truly make a clean break order by upholding the direction under section 28(1A), or whether it should leave the door open for the wife to apply for the order to be extended should she find herself unable to support herself at the end of the five-year period. By allowing the wife's appeal against the section 28(1A) direction, the court gave significant recognition to the important truth that lack of earning capacity brought about by child care responsibilities may be a continuing problem for the wife.[14]

Limiting the duration of orders—variation traps

It is essential to ensure that an application to vary a limited term order is made before the order expires for otherwise there will be no order in existence which is capable of being varied. In *T v T (Financial Provision)*[15] a periodical payments order had been made in favour of a wife which was

---

13 Ibid, at p 386.
14 See also *Mawson v Mawson* [1994] 2 FLR 985
15 [1988] 1 FLR 480.

expressed to take effect 'until such date as the wife shall remarry or until the husband retires or further order'. After the husband retired the wife applied to vary the order. It was conceded that the court would have had jurisdiction to extend the order to beyond the husband's retirement date had the wife made her application before the husband retired, and this concession has since been confirmed in *Richardson v Richardson*.[16] But in *T v T (Financial Provision)* the court ruled that its jurisdiction had come to an end once the retirement took place. The addition of the words 'or further order' did not come to the wife's assistance because the Court of Appeal held that these words meant 'a further order in the meantime'. In the light of this ruling, care must be taken to ensure that a term is not included in an order which brings it to a premature end without due regard for whether the payee's need for periodical payments is a continuing one.

A contingency which is sometimes included in consent orders for periodical payments is that the order will cease if the wife should cohabit with another man for longer than a specified period. The risk to the wife of an order containing such a clause is that her new partner may not be in the position to maintain her himself. This is particularly likely to be the position when he has children whom he is maintaining under the Child Support Act 1991. The calculations made under the formula make no allowance for the cost of maintaining an adult partner.[17] Although courts have clearly stated that cohabitation should not be equated with remarriage when applications have been brought in variation proceedings,[18] there seems to be nothing to prevent the inclusion of a clause of this type in a periodical payments order. It seems that the wife can apply for an extension of the order before the cut-off date has been reached, provided that no direction to the contrary has been made under section 28(1A). But once the specified period of cohabitation has been fulfilled it seems that the order for periodical payments terminates automatically. Whether a fresh application can be made for a further periodical payments order, for example if the cohabitation subsequently ceases, is uncertain. But it seems extremely unlikely that this would be permitted, because there is a general rule against repeat applications being made for orders. It might be possible to persuade a court that a fresh application can be made unless a specific direction has been given under section 25A(3) that the applicant shall not be entitled to make any further application. Such an argument awaits litigation. However, the safer step would be to apply for a variation of the terms of the periodical payments order *before* the cohabitation clause (or any other term) brings the order to an end.

It is suggested that orders containing a clause that periodical payments should cease automatically if the wife should cohabit with another man

16 [1993] 4 All ER 673.
17 See ch 8.
18 See particularly *Atkinson v Atkinson* [1987] 3 All ER 849.

should be avoided. Such provisions are the modern equivalent of the old *dum casta* orders, which at one time used to stipulate that the wife must remain 'chaste' if she wished her periodical payments to continue.[19] They are objectionable in that they may lead to snooping, and may restrain the wife from forming an intimate relationship out of fear that she will lose her source of income from her ex-husband. Whereas cohabitation may provide good cause to apply for variation of an order for periodical payments, for an order to terminate automatically in the event of the wife cohabiting, irrespective of her partner's income, could cause such a wife a great deal of financial hardship.[20]

Quantification of orders for periodical payments

The quantification of periodical payments orders tends to alter in the light of social change, and to changing views on what can reasonably be expected of spouses. In all cases the assessment of how much should be paid, and for how long, will be influenced by the weight given to the various paragraphs in the statutory guidelines in section 25, by the nature of other orders or agreements which are being made, and by the clean break approach. While in any particular case one or more of the statutory guidelines may be highly pertinent, in a large number of cases the reality is how properly to allocate limited resources between spouses who each have needs, obligations, and responsibilities, when these resources are insufficient to meet each spouse's requirements.

The availability of state benefits is often an important factor in the court's calculation. Where the court knows that the first family will be equally well provided for from state funds, whether or not the husband makes periodical payments, it will often be prepared to take this into account. In this way a court is able to 'widen the purse' when considering the spouses' resources, and to refrain from making orders against the husband which will be financially onerous.[1] An extreme case is *Delaney v Delaney*[2] where Ward J, after commenting that there should be 'life after divorce' for the husband who wished to set up home with his new partner, made nominal orders only for the wife and the children. He felt able to make this decision because any order against the husband would merely reduce the wife's benefits pound for pound. However, the advent of the Child Support Act 1991 no longer allows for such an approach. Child support

---

19 Cf *Squire v Squire* [1905] P 4.
20 See further on this issue, M Hayes *Cohabitation Clauses in Financial Provision and Property Adjustment Orders: Law, Policy and Justice* (1994) 110 LQR 124.
1 See *Whiting v Whiting* [1988] 2 All ER 275 where the former wife's claim to continuing support was displaced by the needs of the man's second family, because she would be eligible for state benefits.
2 [1990] 2 FLR 457.

cannot be avoided when the state has an interest in payments being made. Where the parent with care is drawing state benefits she must authorise the child support agency to take action to recover child maintenance from the other parent.[3]

In cases where resources are limited, the requirement that a parent must first honour his obligations to his children makes it less likely that there will be money available for the support of his wife. The question then arises whether any order at all should be made in favour of the wife where there seems to be no likelihood that the husband will be able to pay a realistic amount towards her support in the foreseeable future. This is an important question for a number of reasons. Rules of court direct that a spouse's application for periodical payments should be made in the divorce petition or answer.[4] Where a court dismisses an application for periodical payments, it has power to give a direction under section 25A(3) that the applicant shall not be entitled to make any further application for periodical payments, and that direction, of course, ends the matter. It may therefore be wise for the wife to postpone making an application until such time as the husband has the means to pay. On its face, section 23(1) allows for an application to be made at any time after the grant of a decree. However, where no application is made in the petition or answer, either the parties' agreement, or the court's leave, is required before one can be pursued at a later date.[5] But at this later date the applicant might have difficulty in persuading the court to grant leave. The court might take the view that a spouse should not be rendered liable to make periodical payments long after the divorce and consequent financial arrangements have apparently been settled.

By contrast, any order for periodical payments, however small,[6] is capable of being varied upwards should either of the spouses' circumstances alter in the future. Thus a nominal order is a form of insurance against falling on hard times. Whether a court would be prepared to increase a nominal order in variation proceedings will turn on a variety of circumstances.[7] But the fact that a nominal order has been made indicates a willingness by the original court to allow the variation court to give the matter proper consideration. For example, in *Whiting v Whiting*[8] the Court of Appeal held that the trial judge had been entitled to take the view that periodical payments should be kept alive by a nominal order, in case unforeseen contingencies, such as illness or redundancy, should prevent

3   Child Support Act 1991, s.6(1); and see ch 8.
4   Family Proceedings Rules 1991, r.2.53(1).
5   Ibid, r.2.53(2).
6   Even 1p a year.
7   S.31(7).
8   [1988] 2 All ER 275; see too *Scallon v Scallon* [1990] 1 FLR 194; *Hepburn v Hepburn* [1989] 1 FLR 373.

the wife from making adequate provision for her own needs, and make it necessary for her to look again to her ex-husband for support. Hence the making of a nominal order may have profound implications for both parties.

Where there are insufficient resources to make an order in favour of the wife, because the absent parent's obligations to make payments to his children under the Child Support Act 1991 leave nothing to spare, it may nonetheless be vital to obtain a nominal order in the wife's favour. Children eventually grow up and stop being a call on the absent parent's income. The wife, as the caring parent, may then find that her own income is drastically reduced by the discontinuance of child support payments.[9] However, if the wife obtains a nominal order in her favour at the time of the original divorce settlement, she is entitled to apply at a later stage for her order to be increased.

Over the years, various rules of thumb have been applied to the quantification of periodical payments orders. These have varied according to the social circumstances of the time, and it can be misleading to seek to extrapolate principles from what was, in truth, an attempt by a higher court to provide pragmatic guidance for the lower courts on how to quantify their orders. Such rules of thumb include the so-called 'one third rule'.[10] At one stage this rule was used quite widely by courts as a starting point for assessing how much a wife should receive in the way of capital and income. When the one third rule is applied to periodical payments, the amount for the wife is calculated as follows: the income of the husband and wife is added together, and the wife is awarded an amount which will bring her income up to one third of the total sum. For example, if the husband earns £14,000 a year, and the wife earns £4,000 a year, one third of the total of their combined incomes is £6,000. Consequently, applying the one third rule, the wife will receive £2,000 a year in periodical payments from the husband.

According to Lord Denning MR in *Wachtel v Wachtel*[11] the rationale behind awarding the wife one third, rather than a different fraction, is because there are other demands on the husband's income, including the obligation to make periodical payments to the children, and because the wife will also obtain a share of the capital assets. However, although the rule gives a starting point for making calculations it has restricted value. As Sir John Arnold P subsequently stated, the one third rule has little use either where the spouses' resources are very limited, or where there is great wealth.[12] This is because the calculation simply does not work in practice in these situations. Also, the rule has largely been overtaken by

9   The formula for the quantification of child support contains an element of support for the caring parent too: see ch 8.
10 Given a new lease of life in *Wachtel v Wachtel* [1973] 1 All ER 829.
11 Above.
12 *Slater v Slater* (1982) 3 FLR 364; see too *Furniss v Furniss* (1981) 3 FLR 46.

the clean break approach to periodical payments for a wife, and by the impact of the Child Support Act 1991 on maintenance calculations for children. However, the rule may still have value in a particular case, the most likely being when there are no children of the family to be maintained.

Another calculation method is the 'net effect' approach, which in essence involves working out the husband's available resources after making various deductions, and working out the wife's resources, including the amount of a hypothetical order. The two figures can then be compared and related to their respective needs, and the hypothetical order adjusted accordingly.[13] However, while this is an acceptable method of calculating quantum, it begs the fundamental question of how to calculate the spouses' respective needs. Unless the chosen system acknowledges the importance of a base line against which to measure such needs, it is inevitable that there will be discrepancies between courts in the amount of resources which a husband is allowed to keep for his own use before making payments to the wife.

The 'subsistence level' approach does provide a base line against which to measure needs. It advises courts to ensure that the impact of any order for periodical payments should not be such as to push the remaining income of the payer below the level of income he would receive if drawing social security benefits on the income support scale rates; and not to make an order, other than a nominal order, against someone who is unemployed and living on state benefits.[14] However, the courts have not always adhered to this approach, and they have refused to elevate it to a statement of principle.[15] Rather the judges have chosen to assess for themselves how much of his income a husband needs to retain in order to support himself and any new dependants. One reason for this has been a determination by some Court of Appeal judges to impress on fathers that they have a moral obligation to support their own children, even when they clearly do not have the means to do so.[16] That moral imperative is no longer a driving force behind orders for periodical payments, because child maintenance has been transferred from the courts to the Child Support Agency. Consequently some of the pressure on courts to make orders against unemployed and poor men has been lifted. Nonetheless, applications for spousal maintenance, and for maintenance for any children of the family

13 See *Stockford v Stockford* (1981) 3 FLR 58 in which a more detailed explanation of this calculation is given; see too *Slater v Slater* above.

14 *Ashley v Ashley* [1968] P 582; *Chase v Chase* (1983) 13 Fam Law 21.

15 See *Stockford v Stockford* (1981) 3 FLR 58, in which the Court of Appeal said that the registrar and judge had both misdirected themselves when they had expressed the view that the wife's application must fail if its effect would be to reduce the husband's income below income support scale rates; see too *Freeman v Swatridge* [1984] FLR 762 where more than a nominal order was made against an unemployed man by the Court of Appeal.

16 See, for example, Ormrod LJ in *Tovey v Tovey* (1978) 8 Fam Law 80; *Freeman v Swatridge* [1984] FLR 762.

to whom the Child Support Act 1991 does not apply, must still come before the courts. Therefore whether or not the subsistence level approach is adopted as a minimum base line may still be a matter of critical importance.

It is suggested that in refusing to rule that an order should not depress the payer's income below the income support scale rate, the courts have been both seriously misguided and extraordinarily harsh. The income support scale rate is designed to meet the shortfall which exists between a man's resources and his requirements. It leaves nothing to spare over and above normal family expenditure, and indeed few would argue that income support levels provide other than a sum just adequate to cover basic needs. An order which depresses the payer's income to below this amount displays a breathtaking lack of awareness of the financial difficulties of poor people. As Finer J pointed out two decades ago: 'it is a hardship to live at [income support][17] level. It allows no extras. It is not possible to save. As time goes by, clothes, furniture, linoleum, wear out and having to replace them increases the hardship.'[18] Indeed, when a working man's income is depressed to income support level, let alone below, he will be in a worse financial position than a man who is entitled to draw benefits, because benefit claimants are automatically entitled to receive free dental treatment, free spectacles and free prescriptions. Any children are entitled to free school meals. Claimants may also be entitled to other payments, and to earn a small amount without this leading to a reduction in their benefit payments. By contrast, the working man who is required to pay maintenance enjoys no such allowances, and when he has a new family, his expenditure on his former family is not normally a deductible expense for the purpose of claiming any means-tested benefits to which he might be entitled, such as family credit.

What are the possible consequences for a man and any new family he may have if the family's income is depressed for any length of time below subsistence level because of a court order? It is likely that some of their basic living requirements may not be met. For example, an adult may go short of food, a child of clothing and shoes, and the whole family of adequate heating. It is also likely that his new relationship will be put at serious risk. Statistics reveal that one in two second marriages break down, and it is well known that financial stress is very destructive of family life. Because there is not enough money to meet all the demands on the husband's income, the order will probably fall into arrears, and enforcement proceedings may then be taken. In these proceedings the husband may then be required to pay an additional sum each week to discharge the arrears, as well as the amount originally ordered. As a result, his income decreases, his maintenance debt increases, and his ability to make proper provision for himself

17 Previously supplementary benefit.
18 *Williams v Williams* [1974] 3 All ER 377 at p 383.

and any current dependants is put in even greater jeopardy. Ultimately he risks imprisonment for non-payment.

Secured periodical payments

A secured periodical payments order is one in which payments are secured against specific property belonging to the payer. Sometimes the chosen property is income producing, and sometimes it is property against which the charge can be enforced with the sum due should the payer default on the payments. Usually the payer is required to transfer the property to trustees and to execute a deed of security. Normally the trusts of the deed provide that, so long as the payer makes the payments ordered to the payee, the income from the property on which the payments are secured should be paid to the payer. In this way the payer is allowed to retain some choice and control over how he fulfils the requirements of the order. The security will, of course, revert to the payer on the payee's death or remarriage; or to his estate when these events occur after the payer's death. A secured order has two advantages over an unsecured order: it can last for the payee's lifetime,[19] which means that when the payer dies the payee can still look to the security as a source of income; and the payee is not burdened by the enforcement problems which are often associated with unsecured orders. When an unsecured order is in existence, and the payer is determined to be obdurate in refusing to pay, one response might be to make a fresh application for a secured periodical payments order, rather than to attempt to enforce the original order.

It is suggested that full advantage should be taken of the opportunity to apply for a secured periodical payments order which lasts for the lifetime of the payee. It should be borne in mind that usually it is the wife who is the recipient of a periodical payments order; that a woman usually marries a man who is older than herself; and that the husband is statistically likely to predecease the wife. An order which survives the husband's death may make provision for a divorced woman for many years after that death occurs. Furthermore, a divorced woman is not her ex-husband's widow, which means she will lose all entitlement to a widow's pension from his pension fund. This is a major loss of income for divorced women, particularly those divorced at an age when it is too late to establish an entitlement to an adequate pension in reliance on their own pension contributions. A secured order may be one method of compensating a wife for this loss of pension income.

The other main advantage of a secured order is to be found in the improved opportunities for enforcement. Normally the payer will be able

---

19 Matrimonial Causes Act 1973, s.28(1)(b); this is by contrast with an unsecured order, which can last only for the spouses' joint lives.

to pay the sums due under the order from whatever source of income he chooses. But should he default on the payments, the trustees of the security must make payments directly to the payee from the income produced by the security. Should that income prove to be insufficient, the trustees will have power to resort to the capital. In cases where the order is secured on property which does not produce income, the amount of the arrears will be charged on the property, and the payee can realise her charge by forcing a sale. Either process could be invaluable to the payee when the payer is refusing to pay, has disappeared, has emigrated, or has defaulted for some other reason. Sometimes it might be appropriate for the order to be secured on the payer's interest in the former matrimonial home. It is relatively commonplace for sale of the former matrimonial home to be postponed to some future date when the proceeds will then be divided between the spouses in predetermined amounts, and for one spouse to be given a right to live in it in the meanwhile. In a case of this kind, the periodical payments order could be secured on the payer's postponed share and, in the event of his default, his eventual share in the proceeds of sale would be reduced by the arrears outstanding. While this arrangement would not directly assist the payee to obtain a regular income, it would ensure that the payer ultimately pays for his default, and would give the payee a growing share in the proceeds of sale of the matrimonial home, which she might need where her income has been reduced.

Lump sum orders

Section 23(1)(c) provides that the court may make an order—

> 'that either party to the marriage shall pay to the other such lump sum or sums as may be so specified.'

Although the section refers to sums in the plural, only one lump sum order can be made.[20] The plural allows for it to be paid in instalments, in which case the payments can be secured,[1] and interest can be ordered on the amount deferred.[2] An application can be made for a lump sum on the grant of a decree or at any time thereafter, but it must be remembered that the right to apply for lump sum and property adjustment orders is lost in the event of the applicant's remarriage.[3] However, provided that the application has been made before the remarriage, the court has jurisdiction even though the application is not heard until after the remarriage.

---

20 *Coleman v Coleman* [1972] 3 All ER 886.
1   S.23(3)(c).
2   S.23(6).
3   S.28(3).

One consequence of this rule, and of the rule of court which requires an applicant for an order first to obtain the leave of the court when no application has been made in the petition or answer,[4] is that it is normal practice to make an application for all types of relief at the time of the divorce. Generally speaking this practice is sensible and desirable, and it deals with the danger of a swift remarriage depriving a spouse of his or her claim to a share in the property. However, it is clearly inadvisable to apply for an order when it is obvious that the respondent is in no position to make a lump sum payment. This is because it must also be remembered that when an application for a lump sum payment is dismissed, no further application can subsequently be made. The applicant may, therefore, have everything to lose and nothing to gain from making a comprehensive application at the time of the divorce. In a case where the respondent has no capital resources, but is likely to acquire them at a later date, for example when he will probably inherit under his parent's will or intestacy, it may be wiser not to make an application at the time of the divorce, but to take the chance that leave will be granted by the court at some time in the future. Alternatively, a court may be prepared to adjourn the application for a lump sum where there is a real possibility that the respondent will shortly obtain capital out of which it can be paid.

Lump sums and clean break

A lump sum order has the advantage that it may achieve a clean break between the parties. A lump sum can be invested to produce a regular income for the applicant; consequently it may obviate the need to order periodical payments in addition. Clean break arrangements have psychological benefits for both spouses because each knows exactly what his or her financial position is, both now and in the future, and each can plan accordingly. Whilst financial dependence of one spouse on the other continues, the spouses do not usually experience their marriage as truly having been dissolved, despite the formal existence of a divorce decree. The ending of financial dependence is what truly liberates the parties from one another. It may also bring a source of acrimony to an end.[5] From the point of view of the payee, a lump sum order has the additional advantage over an order for periodical payments that it is not affected by remarriage. This principle applies whether or not the lump sum is paid all at once, or by instalments. By contrast, an order for periodical payments ends automatically if the wife remarries. Where she lives with a new partner, such cohabitation may lead to the order being reduced, or extinguished, in variation proceedings.

4   Family Proceedings Rules 1991, r.2.53.
5   *C v C (Financial Provision)* [1989] 1 FLR 11.

Lump sum orders are particularly appropriate when the marriage has been short-lived, but where the applicant needs temporary support to enable her to find employment, and otherwise adjust to the termination of the marriage. The amount of money ordered will reflect the short-term nature of the marriage. In *Leadbeater v Leadbeater*[6] the wife, who was aged 47, had been married to a very wealthy man for four years, and she had enjoyed a much enhanced lifestyle during this period. There were adequate funds to make a clean break order, but the amount the wife received when measured against her needs was reduced by 25% because of the short duration of the marriage. In *Attar v Attar*[7] the wife's marriage to her millionaire husband lasted a mere six months. Prior to the marriage she had been an air hostess earning £15,000 per annum. The court ordered that she receive a lump sum of £30,000 to enable her to adjust to the ending of the marriage. In the case of less wealthy spouses, a relatively small lump sum order (which can be paid in instalments) may be an appropriate way of assisting a financially dependent party to adjust without undue hardship to the termination of that dependence. For example, it could be used to pay for her education and training to enable her to re-enter the labour market.

Lump sums or periodical payments?

Before the advent of the Child Support Act 1991, courts would sometimes make lump sum orders against husbands which were financially onerous, but in return would relieve the husband of all, or most, of his obligation to make periodical payments for the benefit of his wife and children. Nowadays it would be most unwise for a husband to offer a large lump sum in return for an agreement by his wife not to pursue him for periodical payments, either for herself, or for the children, or to reduce the amount which would otherwise be payable. Such a husband is exposing himself to the risk that the wife may resile on the arrangement. Any term in an order, or agreement, which purports to restrict the right of a parent with care to apply to the Child Support Agency for a maintenance assessment is void.[8] Should the agency become involved at a later date, and the wife would have no choice about this if she was in receipt of state benefits,[9] the absent parent's obligation to his children would be quantified in accordance with the agency's strict arithmetical formula. This formula includes an amount which covers some of the adult carer's needs. The fact that, at an earlier agreed settlement, the caring parent has traded a lower income for higher

6   [1985] FLR 789.
7   [1985] FLR 649.
8   Child Support Act 1991, s.9(4).
9   Ibid, s.6(1).

capital provision is of no interest or concern to the agency; the absent parent will still be liable for the full amount.[10]

It is normally in the interests of a husband not to be liable to make continuing financial provision for his former wife, for he will usually wish to sever their financial as well as their legal links. But there may be occasions when he would prefer an order for periodical payments rather than to make generous capital provision for her. Lump sum and property adjustment orders once made cannot be varied.[11] In a case where the wife has, or is likely to develop, a close personal relationship with another man leading perhaps to cohabitation or remarriage, the husband may take the view that to pay his wife a substantial lump sum is like endowing her with a 'dowry' to spend on the other man. This was the belief of the husband in *Duxbury v Duxbury*.[12] He did not wish his wife to have a lump sum order because she was living with another man and was likely to spend the money on him. Also, the man was likely to inherit the residue of the money should the wife predecease him. The wife wanted to be free to live her own life in whatever manner she chose, and to spend her money on whomsoever she wished. It is when this type of conflict occurs that a question of principle arises. Does a wife have a right to a lump sum, or is it merely a claim, with the court having a free discretion to choose between a lump sum order and one for periodical payments? In *Duxbury v Duxbury* the Court of Appeal took the view that the trial court had assessed the reasonable needs of the wife, which they found in the circumstances could be provided for by a lump sum order, and that 'how she spent the money was her affair.' It therefore concluded that the husband's objection to a lump sum order, and his wish instead to make periodical payments, was ill-founded.[13] In *B v B (Financial Provision: Leave to Appeal)*[14] the husband was attempting to appeal out of time against a lump sum order because the wife had remarried a wealthy man. Of the lump sum Ward J said, 'she has her lump sum, which is the result of her contribution during the marriage, and her remarriage does not affect that in any way at all, see, for example, Mrs Duxbury.'[15]

---

10 See *Crozier v Crozier* [1994] 1 FLR 126 in which a husband had transferred his half share in the matrimonial home in exchange for a nominal order for child maintenance. This arrangement had been embodied in a consent order. Subsequently the Child Support Agency found that he was liable to pay the sum of £29 per week in child support. The husband was refused leave to appeal out of time against the consent order.

11 S.31.

12 [1990] 2 All ER 77.

13 See too *O'Donnell v O'Donnell* [1975] 2 All ER 993, in which the husband suggested a smaller lump sum and higher periodical payments. This was rejected by the court for various reasons, including that large periodical payments are a strong disincentive 'if not a prohibition' to remarriage.

14 [1994] 1 FLR 219.

15 Ibid, at p 222.

Property adjustment orders

In many families their most valuable asset is the family home, followed by such items as a car, furnishings and investments. Their assets may also include items jointly owned with a third party,[16] and property acquired since the termination of the marriage.[17] Section 24 enables a court to adjust the spouses' interests in the ownership of such property, so that it can make provision for the current circumstances of all the family members. This can be done either by ordering the out-and-out transfer of property, or that property is sold and the proceeds of sale divided between the parties, or that property is settled on one of the parties. These property adjustment orders can also be made for the benefit of any children of the family.[18]

Property transfer orders

Section 24(1)(a) provides that the court may order—

'that a party to the marriage shall transfer to the other party, to any child of the family or to such person as may be specified in the order for the benefit of such a child such property as may be so specified, being property to which the first-mentioned party is entitled, either in possession or reversion.'

Property transfer orders, like lump sum orders, may be used to bring about a clean break between the parties. When consideration is being given to making a property adjustment order it may be important to establish how each party's capital assets were acquired. In *H v H (Financial Provision: Capital Assets)*[19] Thorpe J held that the fact that the wife's capital holdings had been provided by her husband's parents was a relevant consideration, influencing him not to make any further capital provision for her. However, the estimation of the nature and extent of the spouses' interests in the family assets does not normally need to be given the same close attention as it would if the court was assessing their respective beneficial entitlements under a resulting or constructive trust. Indeed, the courts have warned practitioners against making prolonged investigations into the exact nature of each spouses' property holdings, because this often gives rise to very considerable and unnecessary expense.[20] Rather, a court will

16 See *Harwood v Harwood* [1991] 2 FLR 274 in which the husband was ordered to assign to the wife the whole of his share of the assets of a dissolved partnership.
17 See *Schuller v Schuller* [1990] 2 FLR 193.
18 See ch 8.
19 [1993] 2 FLR 335.
20 *P v P (Financial Provision)* [1989] 2 FLR 241; *B v B (Financial Provision)* [1989] 1 FLR 119.

be influenced in a loose sense by whether one spouse contributed to the acquisition of capital by the other, for example, by assisting with the building up of a business belonging in law to one of them only.[1] Where this has been the case, the court may be inclined to approach the distribution of the property between the parties in a manner which is more favourable to the applicant than it would be in a case where her contribution has been confined to domestic matters only.

The source of the acquisition of property is only one relevant factor when the court is determining whether it should be transferred. The manner in which the assets are redistributed between the parties will be affected by all the considerations in the statutory guidelines in section 25(1)(2), and the clean break approach in section 25(A). One class of assets which cannot be transferred under section 24 are rights accrued under a pension scheme, because these are not 'rights in possession or reversion' of the pensioner. However, this does not prevent a court from taking such pension rights into account as part of the pensioner spouse's assets when choosing what other orders to make. Indeed, the inability to transfer pension rights may be highly influential on orders made in respect of other property

Sale orders

Section 24A provides that—

> 'Where the court makes ... a secured periodical payments order, an order for the payment of a lump sum or a property adjustment order, then, on making that order or at any time thereafter, the court may make a further order for the sale of such property as may be specified in the order, being property in which or in the proceeds of sale of which either or both of the parties to the marriage has or have a beneficial interest, either in possession or reversion.'

This provision is an essential adjunct to those other orders, and used imaginatively it can extend and complement the court's other powers. At its simplest level it may, for example, only be possible to order a lump sum payment if property is sold to raise the necessary cash. Sometimes one spouse is obdurate about complying with an existing lump sum order. In these circumstances, provisions in section 24A may come to the assistance of the other spouse. Thus the court can order sale, but direct that the sale shall not take effect until a specified event occurs, or until after a specified

---

1   For an extreme example of going from 'rags to riches' see *Gojkovic v Gojkovic* [1990] 2 All ER 84; see too *Preston v Preston* [1982] Fam 17; *Kokosinski v Kokosinski* [1980] 1 All ER 1106.

period of time has expired.[2] This power could be used to coerce the obdurate spouse into compliance. For example, a court could order that his own home be sold if the lump sum has not been paid within a specified time. Various factors are influential in determining whether a sale order is appropriate, and sometimes such orders are clearly inappropriate. Thus if ordering the sale of the former matrimonial home will result in both spouses and their children being homeless, such an order would normally be unwise. Similarly, it may be counter-productive to liquidate assets which are income-producing when this will destroy the owning spouse's means of earning his livelihood.[3]

Where a sale order is made, it can contain a provision requiring the proceeds to be invested in a fund designed to secure an order for periodical payments for one of the parties, but such an order will cease to have effect on the death or remarriage of that party.[4] The court can require specified property to be offered for sale to a specified person.[5] In effect, this means that the court can give one spouse the first option to buy out the other spouse's share in the matrimonial home (or other specified property). This is a valuable provision where one spouse is hostile to the other acquiring a particular family asset, and where he or she plans to dispose of it to someone else. Where someone other than the spouses has a beneficial interest in the property in question, this does not prevent an order for sale being made. But that person's position must be respected by the court, which must take account of his or her representations alongside the other matters it is required to consider under section 25.[6]

Settlement orders

Section 24(1)(b), (c) and (d) provide that the court may make—

'(b) an order that the settlement of such property as may be so specified, being property to which a party to a marriage is so entitled, be made ... for the benefit of the other party to the marriage and of the children of the family or either or any of them;

(c) an order varying for the benefit of the parties to the marriage and of the children of the family or either or any of them any ante-nuptial or post nuptial-settlement ... made on the parties to the marriage;

---

2 S.24A(4).
3 *Martin v Martin* [1976] 3 All ER 625; *P v P (Financial Provision: Lump Sum)* [1978] 3 All ER 70; *P v P (Financial Provision)* [1989] 2 FLR 241.
4 S.24A(5).
5 S.24A(2)(b).
6 S.24A(6).

(d) an order extinguishing or reducing the interest of either of the parties to the marriage under any such settlement.'

A settlement arises where any property has been purchased in the spouses' joint names, or where they each have a beneficial interest in it. It includes any disposition made in favour of the spouses as spouses which makes continuing provision for them.[7] A settlement creates successive interests in land, and can be invaluable where the spouses' resources are insufficient to make adequate provision for them both, and where one spouse needs the immediate use of property more urgently than the other. It may, for example, be appropriate to direct that the matrimonial home be jointly owned, that one spouse should have exclusive use of the property for a period of time, and that the other should become entitled to his or her share in the proceeds of sale of the property when the settlement period comes to an end. In this way a settlement enables a court to make provision for one of the party's needs without entirely taking away the other party's rights in the property concerned.

Where a court wishes to extinguish the interests of one spouse under a settlement, for example, where they are joint owners of the matrimonial home, it will normally do this by making a property transfer order under section 24(1)(a). However it should be noted that an order under paragraph (a) directs one of the parties to transfer property to the other, consequently it requires the transferor's co-operation. This can create difficulties where that co-operation is not readily forthcoming, or where the transferor has disappeared. By contrast, under paragraphs (c) and (d) it is the court's order which varies, or extinguishes, a spouse's interest under an existing settlement. It may, therefore, be to the applicant's advantage to apply under either of these paragraphs rather than for a property transfer order. For example, a court could order that the settled property be held on trust for the wife absolutely. As a result, the husband's interest is extinguished immediately by operation of the court's order. The court could couple its order with a direction that the matter be referred to one of the conveyancing counsel of the court for him to execute a proper instrument to be executed by all necessary parties.[8]

Lump sum and property adjustment orders are final

Section 31 provides that lump sum and property adjustment orders cannot be varied. The policy behind section 31 is that it is desirable to achieve

---

7   *Young v Young* [1962] P 27. However, an outright transfer is not a settlement, see *Prescott v Fellowes* [1958] P 260.
8   S.30.

finality in the parties' affairs. A similar rigorous approach is taken to appeals. If such orders are to be appealed, the appeal must be lodged within five days of making the order, and not the date from when the order is to be implemented.[9] Appeals are occasionally allowed out of time, but only if the stringent conditions laid down by the House of Lords in *Barder v Caluori*[10] are satisfied. These are that new events must have occurred since the order was made; that these events invalidate the basis on which the order was made so that an appeal would be certain, or very likely, to succeed; that the new events have occurred within a relatively short time after the making of the order; that the application for leave to appeal out of time has been made reasonably promptly; and that the granting of leave does not prejudice third parties who have acted in good faith. The finality of lump sum and property adjustment orders means that, when deciding what arrangements, or orders, to make, care must be taken to anticipate future eventualities. Provision needs to be made for how such eventualities should affect the arrangements made.

The statutory guidelines

Section 25(1) and (2) specify a long list of matters to which a court must have regard when deciding whether to exercise its financial provision and property adjustment powers and, if so, in what manner. These guidelines must influence the courts in the exercise of what are essentially broad discretionary powers. No particular weight attaches to any of the matters listed in section 25(2), consequently some will assume greater importance in some cases, and lesser or no importance in others. Section 25(1) provides that—

'It shall be the duty of the court in deciding whether to exercise its powers under section 23, 24 or 24A and, if so, in what manner, to have regard to all the circumstances of the case, first consideration being given to the welfare while a minor of any child of the family who has not attained the age of eighteen.'

Section 25(2) provides that—

'As regards the exercise of the powers of the court under section 23(1)(a),(b) or (c), 24 or 24A in relation to a party to the marriage, the court shall in particular have regard to the following matters—

9   *B v B (Financial Provision: Leave to Apply)* [1994] 1 FLR 219.
10 [1987] 2 All ER 440; see too *B v B (Financial Provision: Leave to Apply)* above.

(a) the income, earning capacity, property and other financial resources which each of the parties to the marriage has or is likely to have in the foreseeable future, including in the case of earning capacity any increase in that capacity which it would in the opinion of the court be reasonable to expect a party to the marriage to take steps to acquire;

(b) the financial needs, obligations and responsibilities which each of the parties to the marriage has or is likely to have in the foreseeable future;

(c) the standard of living enjoyed by the family before the breakdown of the marriage;

(d) the age of each party to the marriage and the duration of the marriage;

(e) any physical or mental disability of either of the parties to the marriage;

(f) the contributions which each of the parties has made or is likely in the foreseeable future to make to the welfare of the family, including any contribution by looking after the home or caring for the family;

(g) the conduct of each of the parties, if that conduct is such that it would in the opinion of the court be inequitable to disregard it;

(h) in the case of proceedings for divorce or nullity of marriage, the value to each of the parties of any benefit (for example, a pension) which by reason of the dissolution or annulment of the marriage, that party will lose the chance of acquiring.'

The welfare of the children must be the court's first consideration

Sometimes legislation requires the welfare of any child affected by it to be given 'paramount' consideration by the court,[11] and sometimes that it should be the court's 'first' consideration.[12] Where the child's welfare is paramount, it overrides all other considerations and determines the course to be followed. Where the child's welfare comes first, it means that the court must give it greater weight than other considerations, but it will not necessarily prevail over the other matters which the court must bear in mind. In the case of financial provision and property adjustment orders, section 25(1) provides that 'first' consideration must be given to the welfare of any child of the family who has not attained the age of 18. In *Suter v Suter and Jones*[13] the Court of Appeal noted the distinction between 'first'

11 See the Children Act 1989, s.1(1)
12 See the Adoption Act 1976, s.6.
13 [1987] 2 All ER 336.

and 'first and paramount', and ruled that any order must be just between the parents as well as making provision for their children. However, in many cases the resources available for distribution between the parties are such that they can only cover the needs of the children, and in cases of this kind other considerations in the statutory guidelines are likely to be superfluous.

Providing for the welfare of the children means ensuring that they have adequate financial support and adequate housing. When, in the past, courts had jurisdiction to make periodical payments orders for children, judges were often determined to ensure that fathers made some contribution to the upbringing of their own children, even when they could ill afford, or arguably not afford, to pay anything at all.[14] This determination has now been taken over by the Child Support Agency, and it is undoubtedly the case that priority will continue to be given to the provision of periodical payments for children during their dependency, whether this is obtained through an application to the Agency, or through a maintenance agreement which is embodied in a consent order. The provision of periodical payments for children normally cannot be disentangled from the provision of periodical payments for the parent with care. If that person has an insufficient income in her own right, this will rebound on the children, and be prejudicial to their welfare. Accordingly there may be a conflict between the clean break provisions in section 25(A), and the welfare provision in section 25(1), because an order which limits, or terminates, periodical payments for the caring parent will reduce the family's income as a whole. It is suggested that there is a danger that the inter-relationship between the welfare of the children, and the claim of the caring parent to continue to receive periodical payments, can easily be overlooked. This is partly because the modern trend is towards the promotion of self-sufficiency for the adults, and there is no established theory that a parent with care should be entitled to receive financial support in that capacity. Indeed, the trend may be the other way, as can be seen in the comments made by the Court of Appeal in *N v N (Consent Order: Variation)*[15] where there was an unsuccessful attempt by a mother to obtain the variation of a consent order which deprived her of much needed financial support. Rather any orders have tended to be based on a mother's need for continuing financial support, and the impact of this need on the needs of the children.[16]

---

14 In *Freeman v Swatridge* [1984] FLR 762 and *Tovey v Tovey* (1978) 8 Fam Law 80 the husband's income in each case was reduced by the Court of Appeal to below subsistence level; but cf *Delaney v Delaney* [1990] 2 FLR 457 in which a far more generous, indeed arguably a far too generous, approach was taken to the husband's new liabilities when assessing what he should pay to his first family.

15 [1993] 2 FLR 868 at p 875. Compare this approach with the Child Support Act 1991 formula which includes an amount for the caring parent in the calculation of child support.

16 *Waterman v Waterman* [1989] 1 FLR 380.

In relation to housing, it is often the case that the spouse who is looking after the children is allowed to retain the use of the matrimonial home. This may be harsh on the other spouse who is forced to live in far inferior accommodation, and who cannot obtain his share in the property at least until the children grow up, and often beyond that date. But, as was said in *Browne v Pritchard*,[17] the courts must direct their attention in the first instance to the provision of homes for all concerned. Ormrod LJ pointed out that it is a complete misapprehension to think in terms of one spouse being kept out of his or her share in the fund tied up in the property, because 'investment in the home is the least liquid investment one can possibly make. It cannot be converted into cash while the children are at home and often not until one spouse dies unless it is possible to move into a much smaller and cheaper accommodation.'[18]

When making orders about the home the courts have tended to adopt one of two approaches to giving extra weight to the welfare of the children, though the thinking in each is liable to merge. Sometimes they have taken an essentially legalistic approach, looking at the words of the statute, pointing out that the obligation to give first consideration to the children ends at 18, and then giving greater weight to the rights in waiting of the spouse with an interest tied up in the property. Thus they have ordered that the property should be retained as a home for the children until they are approaching adulthood, and that the proceeds should then be shared between the spouses. The courts have done this even though they have recognised that, from the point of view of the children, the ages of 16, 17 and 18[19] are too early for the house to be sold.[20] At other times the courts have taken a broader view of family life, and have acknowledged that children do not stop needing a home merely because they reach adulthood. In some cases they have extended the period until all the children have ceased to receive full-time education.[1] In others, they have recognised that the spouse who has cared for the children during their minority will continue to wish to provide a home for the children until the children themselves marry, and to which the children can return with their own spouses, and eventually the grandchildren. When influenced by the latter approach, the courts have been inclined to transfer the entire interest in the property to the parent with care of the children as in *Hanlon v Hanlon*.[2]

17 [1975] 3 All ER 721. This was one of the first reported cases after the courts first received their financial provision and property adjustment powers in 1971.
18 Ibid, at p 725.
19 All of these ages have been chosen in reported cases.
20 See, for example, *Browne v Pritchard* [1975] 3 All ER 721.
1 See, for example, *Chamberlain v Chamberlain* [1974] 1 All ER 33.
2 [1978] 2 All ER 889. This issue is further discussed below under the heading 'The matrimonial home—what order is the most appropriate?'.

The income and earning capacity of each spouse

Paragraph (a) of the guidelines concentrates attention on the spouses' resources, that is on their real and personal property and on their income and earning capacity. It provides that the court must have regard to—

'the income, earning capacity, property and other financial resources which each of the parties to the marriage has or is likely to have in the foreseeable future, including in the case of earning capacity any increase in that capacity which it would in the opinion of the court be reasonable to expect a party to the marriage to take steps to acquire.'

Because the court's decision will influence the parties' financial affairs for many years, it is not just the present levels of income and property that must be considered; the court must also think about what these are likely to be in the foreseeable future.[3] The courts have determined that all resources are relevant. Not surprisingly, therefore, this maximisation of resources approach has brought into question some fundamental issues of principle.

The courts were initially hesitant about whether damages awarded for pain, suffering and loss of amenity could be treated as a resource, but eventually they ruled that personal injuries damages awarded under all heads of damage, including for pain and suffering and loss of amenity, could be taken into account.[4] The manner of the distribution of such damages is, of course, still a matter within the court's discretion, and likely to be influenced by paragraph (e), which looks to any mental or physical disability of either party. They have taken account of inherited wealth acquired after the parties separated, and which in no way formed part of the original matrimonial assets.[5] Expectations of inheritance give rise to difficulty because there is no knowing when the testator will die and whether his or her will may be altered. These expectations have therefore sometimes been deemed too uncertain to be included.[6] However, the courts have been prepared, in principle, to take account of all present and future resources and they have been prepared to widen the purse to the maximum extent.

---

3 Cases in the law reports, in the main, are concerned with disputed orders involving the distribution of fairly substantial assets. However the reality for many spouses is that their resources are small, especially when there are dependent children. Indeed, many have debts rather than assets: see J M Eekelaar and M Maclean *Maintenance after Divorce* (Clarendon Press, 1986).
4 *Daubney v Daubney* [1976] 2 All ER 453; *Wagstaff v Wagstaff* [1992] 1 All ER 275.
5 *Schuller v Schuller* [1990] 2 FLR 193.
6 *Michael v Michael* [1986] 2 FLR 389; *K v K (Conduct)* [1990] 2 FLR 225.

The court is not only concerned with what each spouse is actually earning, it is also engaged in estimating what each spouse could reasonably be expected to earn. If a spouse deliberately reduces his working hours, gives up a job, or is paid less than the normal rate for the work he is doing, the court can base its order on what he could earn.[7] A court may deem a man to be deliberately unemployed and make an order on the assumption that he could obtain work if he tried.[8] However, there is a risk that a court will make the assumption that a spouse could obtain work if he or she makes the effort, without there being any real evidence to substantiate this approach. The danger to the spouse who is wrongly labelled as 'work shy' by a court, and being ordered to make periodical payments on the basis of what the court believes him to be capable of earning, was graphically spelt out by Finer J in *Williams v Williams,*[9] when he reminded courts that the ultimate sanction for non-payment of periodical payments is imprisonment. He also stated that it is wrong for courts to make decisions on the footing of impressions about demeanour or generalised local knowledge, important as these factors may be, unchecked by all the hard information that may be available about a man's earning capacity and his chances of employment.

These were salutary words, which should be borne in mind particularly at times of high unemployment. There is a real risk that orders may be based on hunch and prejudice, especially if the political climate is one in which those persons who cannot obtain work are labelled as lacking the requisite initiative and drive to seek the employment which is allegedly available. Particular care also needs to be taken when an assessment is made of a non-working wife's earning capacity, and any increase in that capacity which it would be reasonable to expect her to take steps to acquire. This provision in section 25(2)(a) reinforces the clean break provisions in section 25A, and the thinking that, where appropriate, the aim should be to enable the spouses to become financially independent of one another. The Court of Appeal, in a number of judgments,[10] has recognised the difficulties experienced by middle-aged women in obtaining employment. However, courts have also been prepared to find that a non-working wife has an earning capacity, and to quantify it on what is, in reality, a speculative basis.[11] The danger of an approach which is not backed by hard evidence is that the resulting financial provision and property arrangements may prove to be insufficient to cater for the wife's needs, because account is taken of her potential earnings which never in fact

7 *Hardy v Hardy* (1981) 2 FLR 321.
8 *McEwan v McEwan* [1972] 2 All ER 708.
9 [1974] 3 All ER 377.
10 *M v M (Financial Provision)* [1987] 2 FLR 1; *Leadbeater v Leadbeater* [1985] FLR 789; *Barrett v Barrett* [1988] 2 FLR 516.
11 *M v M (Financial Provision)* above, at p 4.

materialise. It should also be borne in mind that it is much easier for a parent with young children to work when living in a two-parent household than when living as a single parent. Such matters as school holidays, and a child being ill, or off school, can more easily be coped with when parenting is shared with another.

Resources provided by a new spouse or partner

One of the most difficult issues of principle and policy which a court may have to grapple with is to what extent, if at all, it should take account of the income, earning capacity and property of a new partner when considering the spouses' resources. This difficulty is exacerbated when the new relationship is an unmarried relationship. The simple answer to the question whether property belonging to a new spouse or partner can be treated as a resource is 'yes'. There is a body of case law in which this has happened. But the extent to which a new spouse or partner's resources will influence the way the parties' own assets are distributed is not easy to assess, and the policy reasons why resources provided by such persons are taken into account are not always easy to discern.

Accommodation provided by a new spouse, or intended spouse, for one of the parties has been taken into account either as a resource under paragraph (a) or as affecting that party's financial needs under paragraph (b). When balancing the claims of each spouse to the former matrimonial home, the fact that one spouse has accommodation provided by a new spouse may lead to the postponement of the realisation of his or her interest in the property, and to the quantification of his or her share in the value of the property being reduced. For example, in *H v H (Financial Provision: Remarriage)*[12] the wife was claiming a half share in the matrimonial home on the basis of her contribution to the welfare of the family under paragraph (f). She had remarried, her second husband was wealthy, and their new home had been conveyed into their joint names. She was also being supported by her second husband's income. The court for this reason (and other reasons) rejected her claim to a half share in the property, and instead awarded her one twelfth of its value, not to be payable until the youngest child was 18. In *Martin v Martin*[13] the husband was living with a woman, whom he intended to marry, in her council house. He gave evidence that the tenancy could be transferred into their joint names. The court took account of the husband's occupation of the council house and treated it as part of his resources affecting his needs. Consequently, it gave the wife a life interest in the former matrimonial home, followed by an equal division

12 [1975] 1 All ER 367.
13 [1977] 3 All ER 762.

of the proceeds of sale.[14] Provision made for the husband by a second partner was taken into account in *Mesher v Mesher and Hall*.[15] Here the woman whom the husband intended to marry had provided a deposit for their new home. Her injection of these resources meant that the husband's housing needs were being met, whereas the wife needed to live in the former matrimonial home. The wife's greater needs led to the husband's entitlement to receive his share in the proceeds of sale of the former matrimonial home being postponed until the spouses' youngest child reached 17.

It is suggested that when a court is assessing the resources of the parties and how much the applicant wife should receive, or the respondent husband retain, what in reality it is usually doing is conducting a balancing exercise between recognising their rights under paragraph (f) and making provision for their needs under paragraph (b). Strictly speaking remarriage, or cohabitation, or their prospect, is irrelevant if the courts are solely concerned with the parties' accumulated rights at the time of marriage breakdown. Thus in *Wachtel v Wachtel*[16] there was dicta to the effect that where a wife can expect to receive a one third share in the proceeds of sale of the former matrimonial home, then whether or not she may remarry is immaterial.[17] Similarly, in *Duxbury v Duxbury*[18] the court held that the wife was entitled to a lump sum order despite the fact that she was living with another man, and was likely to spend the money on him. So, adopting a 'rights' approach to financial provision and property adjustment orders, a court might take the view that, in order to give fair recognition to a wife's claim for a share under paragraph (f),[19] she should be entitled to any amount up to a half share in the former matrimonial home, and that any resources provided by a new spouse or partner should be discounted.

However, paragraph (a) requires the court to take into account resources which the divorcing couple are likely to have in the foreseeable future, and it does not specify from where these should come; and paragraph (b) requires the court to consider the parties' respective needs. Consequently, if sale of the home, and an equal distribution of the assets, is insufficient to provide for two households, a 'needs' approach is likely to predominate. Accordingly, the position appears to be that where the resources available for distribution are being stretched, then the actual, or anticipated, contribution by a new spouse or partner will be taken fully into account by the court when it decides what orders to make. But where there is

14 This case was heavily influenced by the policy target under s.25 as originally drafted. However, the principle is clear, namely that housing provided by a new partner is a relevant consideration.
15 [1980] 1 All ER 126n.
16 [1973] 1 All ER 829.
17 See too *Trippas v Trippas* [1973] 2 All ER 1.
18 [1987] 1 FLR 7.
19 Because of her contribution to the welfare of the family.

substantial wealth to be shared between the parties, and where the applicant spouse has built up an entitlement to a share in that wealth because the marriage has been long-lasting, then resources provided by a new spouse or partner is likely to be ignored in making any strictly arithmetical calculation of the parties' respective shares, but is simply a factor to be taken into account.[20] Indeed, it will normally not be possible for a court accurately to quantify the extent of a new spouse's, or partner's, assets, because he or she cannot usually be compelled to give precise evidence of means to the court.[1] However, as the court pointed out in *Frary v Frary*,[2] where the husband cannot persuade his partner to give such evidence, he takes the risk that the court will base its order on general assertions and assumptions about the extent of the new partner's means.[3]

Periodical payments where a spouse is living with a new partner

An order for periodical payments comes to an end when a spouse remarries.[4] What is the position where the wife is living with another man? In *S v S*,[5] Waite J held that the weight given to a new partner's income will turn on such factors as the permanency of the relationship, the amount of support the wife is obtaining, and how much she needs. Where there is little money to provide for both households, money provided by a new partner may enable the court better to make provision for each spouse. For example, in *Suter v Suter and Jones*[6] Mr Jones spent every night at the wife's home (but had breakfast at his mother's house). The Court of Appeal said that he should therefore make a contribution towards the household expenses. This anticipitated contribution, which of course the court could not order Mr Jones to make, enabled the court to relieve the husband of his maintenance obligation towards the wife, and it therefore only made a nominal periodical payments order in her favour.[7]

In *Atkinson v Atkinson*[8] the argument was put that a wife who cohabits permanently with another man should not be in a better position than a

---

20   *S v S* [1987] 1 FLR 71.

1   *Wynne v Wynne and Jeffers* [1980] 3 All ER 659; *Frary v Frary* [1993] 2 FLR 696.

2   Above.

3   See too *W v W (Disclosure by Third Party)* (1981) 2 FLR 291.

4   S.28(1)(A).

5   [1987] 1 FLR 71.

6   [1987] 2 All ER 336.

7   It would be interesting to know what happened next. Did the court's order bring the relationship between the wife and Mr Jones to a premature end? Mr Jones was very much younger than the wife, and may not have wished to pay 'rent' for spending the night with her. If the relationship did end the wife could have applied for an increase in her periodical payments, as the court had refused to make a clean break order. Thus the burden of supporting the wife may not have entirely been lifted from the husband.

8   [1987] 3 All ER 849.

wife who remarries. It was pressed on the court that this argument becomes even stronger if the motive for cohabitation rather than remarriage is financial. In *Atkinson* the wife was receiving £6,000 per annum in periodical payments which she would automatically lose if she remarried. The man with whom she was living had only a very modest income, and she was therefore heavily reliant on the money she was receiving from her ex-husband. The Court of Appeal held that the fact of cohabitation is a matter to be taken into account by the court, and is conduct which it would be inequitable to disregard under paragraph (g). It referred to *Suter v Suter and Jones* and said that the financial consequences of cohabitation may be such that it would be inappropriate for maintenance to continue because the cohabitant can be expected to contribute to the running costs of the household. However, the court stated that in general there is no statutory requirement to give decisive weight to the fact of cohabitation and that it should *not* be equated with remarriage without legislative sanction.[9]

A different question arises when the respondent to an application for periodical payments, usually the husband, has remarried, or is living with another woman who has an income of her own. To what extent can the new partner's income be taken into account when assessing how much the husband ought to pay for the support of his first family? It has been held that a court cannot require a second wife directly to contribute to the periodical payments paid by a husband for the support of his former wife and children. Consequently, if the husband has no income at all of his own, and his second wife is the breadwinner in the family, no order for periodical payments can be made against the husband.[10] In *Macey v Macey*[11] it was held that a magistrates' court had erred in law when taking into account the second woman's income as part of the available funds from which an order for periodical payments could be paid. However the position is a subtle one. In *Macey v Macey* the court held that where the husband derives benefits from his new partner's income, which means that a greater part of his own income is available to pay maintenance to his first wife and children, an order can be made on the basis that the husband does not need his money to support his new family.[12] This has the practical consequence that a husband can be ordered to pay more by way of periodical payments to his first family when his new partner has her own income, than he would be required to do where she has not.

9 The wife's payments were reduced to £4,500.
10 *Brown v Brown* (1981) 3 FLR 161; *Berry v Berry* [1986] 1 FLR 618.
11 (1981) 3 FLR 7.
12 See too *Wilkinson v Wilkinson* (1980) 10 Fam Law 48.

Policy and a second partner's income

Whether the income of a second wife, or partner, should be taken into account when assessing a husband's ability to pay for the support of his first wife and children is a contentious issue, which tends to give rise to considerable animosity and strongly held views. On the one hand, the husband and his new partner may enjoy quite a good income when their resources are pooled, but on the other hand, if a court orders the husband to pay a large amount by way of periodical payments to his ex-wife, as well as to his children, the second wife or partner is likely to be extremely resentful that her earnings are treated as a relevant consideration. The Law Commission, when conducting a review of the working of the Matrimonial Causes Act 1973 at the beginning of 1980, wrote in their discussion paper that they had been told of cases in which second wives alleged that they had postponed having children, and in which husbands claimed to have been sterilised, because they could not afford to start a new family.[13] In their final report, the Commission observed that responses to the discussion paper revealed that such feeling was indeed widespread.[14]

Many first wives complained equally strongly to the Law Commission that they, and their children, were living in poverty, because the amount they were receiving in periodical payments was totally inadequate to provide for their needs, whereas, by contrast, the husband and his new partner were enjoying a far higher standard of living.[15] Many first wives deeply resented being forced to rely on inadequate state benefits, and the severe drop in their living standards, caused by the breakdown of the marriage. They felt this particularly strongly where the husband had remarried, and was able to enjoy a comparatively high standard of living with his new partner.[16] Many first wives were angered by the fact that their children had a very low standard of living compared to other children. They found that, as divorced mothers, they did not have the earning capacity to lift their children out of poverty. Consequently they saw no reason why the children's father should not take proper financial responsibility for his children, and for his ex-wife as the parent with care.

Although some of the concerns of husbands and second partners were addressed when the clean break provisions were introduced,[17] in essence the conflict between these two opposing points of view remains. Is the law unfair, as many second wives or partners, and many first wives, would continue to claim? It could be argued that a second wife must take her

---

13 Law Com No 103, para 26.
14 Law Com No 112, para 41.
15 Law Com No 103, paras 27 and 28.
16 Note the wide discrepancy in the spouses' incomes in *Macey v Macey* (1981) 3 FLR 7.
17 By the Matrimonial and Family Proceedings Act 1984.

husband 'subject to all existing encumbrances'.[18] Only a lawyer would choose to express personal relationships in these terms, but the terminology is apt. It is suggested that a second marriage cannot be a fresh start because prior obligations have been incurred which are continuing. It is wrong that a husband should be allowed to escape his liability to his first wife and children by pleading he needs his income to support himself and his second family, when his second wife has her own means of support. But equally it is wrong for a first wife to continue with her dependency unnecessarily. Surely the questions for the court should be: what are the husband's needs in the light of the resources provided by his new partner; how do the second family's resources compare with those of the first family; and how can the claims of each family fairly be balanced one against the other?

It is suggested that the basis of the conflict between the two households arises from the fact that, generally speaking, motherhood forces women into financial dependency. During marriage a wife is therefore forced to look to her husband both for the support of their children, and for her own support, and this situation does not alter simply because the couple divorce. Where a man remarries, or lives, with another woman, and children are born, an almost identical relationship of dependency often comes into being. Hence each woman may properly complain that the husband has insufficient resources to provide herself, and her children, with adequate support. The first wife will complain that the husband's income is being absorbed by his new responsibilities. The second wife will complain that her earnings are being used to keep the husband's first family in addition to her own. It is suggested that both points of view are equally valid. They reveal the sad, but inescapable, fact that the vast majority of men and women neither earn enough, nor own enough, to be able to afford to move from one relationship to another, and to have more children by second partners, without the income of both households being drastically reduced.

Financial needs, obligations and responsibilities

Paragraph (b) of the guidelines requires the court to take account of—

> 'the financial needs, obligations and responsibilities which each of the parties to the marriage has or is likely to have in the foreseeable future'.

It is a paragraph to which the courts tend to give great weight. Thus in *S v S*[19] Ormrod LJ said that if the court's attention is concentrated primarily

18 *Roberts v Roberts* [1968] 3 All ER 479, per Rees J.
19 [1977] 1 All ER 56.

on needs, the calculation of financial provision and property adjustment orders then becomes easier, more logical and more constructive. Certainly where resources are limited, paragraph (b) tends to take priority.[20] And giving primacy to needs is particularly pertinent when there are dependent children, as their welfare must be the court's first consideration.[1] The words 'obligations and responsibilities' embrace obligations not only to the ex-spouse and children, but also other family obligations, such as to elderly parents or other relatives. And of course it is these words which allow the claims of any new dependants to be brought into the weighing-up process. Thus if by the time the court makes its order one of the parties has remarried and undertaken financial responsibility for a new spouse and her children, or if he is cohabiting and has taken on similar obligations, this must be taken into account.

The court is looking not only at the parties' current needs when their children are dependent, but also at their likely future needs when the children have grown up. The relevance of future needs to financial provision and property adjustment arrangements is one reason why an agreed solution may be difficult to reach. How far, for example, should the parties try to anticipate future events such as ill-health, remarriage, cohabitation and employment prospects? Here there is uncertainty. The Act is undoubt-edly concerned with likelihoods rather than mere possibilities. However, the pressure to look to the future is only acute in respect of lump sum and property adjustment orders because these cannot be varied at a later date should the parties' circumstances alter significantly.[2] By contrast, period-ical payments orders can be varied if either of the spouses' circumstances change. Consequently, courts are inclined to look to the immediacy of the parties' needs when quantifying the amount of a periodical payments order, and tend to leave the door open to make provision for change should their needs alter.[3]

The prospect of a wife's remarriage or cohabitation causes particular difficulties. Arguably it is irrelevant. If the wife can properly expect to receive a share in the proceeds of sale of the former matrimonial home then whether or not she may remarry is immaterial, and has been held to be so.[4] However, property adjustment orders are often made not only in recognition of a wife's legitimate expectation to receive a fair share of the family assets, but also in response to her needs, and the needs of the parties' children. Where the wife remarries, the main reason for making a

---

20 See, for example, *Smith v Smith* [1975] 2 All ER 19n; *Suter v Suter and Jones* [1987] 2 All ER 336; *Wells v Wells* [1992] 2 FLR 66.
1   S.25(1).
2   S.31(2). Furthermore, a lump sum or property adjustment order cannot be made on an application to vary a periodical payments order: s.31(5).
3   See above.
4   See the dicta in *Wachtel v Wachtel* [1973] 1 All ER 829; *Trippas v Trippas* [1973] 2 All ER 1.

substantial order in her favour may be brought to an end, because her new husband has his own resources. It may then seem manifestly unfair that a lump sum order, or a property adjustment order, which was made to reflect the spouses' respective needs at the time of breakdown, has the effect not only of depriving the husband for all time of his share in the spouses' capital assets, but also, in some cases, of endowing the wife's second husband, or partner, with a house paid for by the first husband.[5]

This point is well illustrated by *Chaudhuri v Chaudhuri*[6] which provides a salutary example. Here the home had been transferred to the wife subject to a charge for one quarter of the proceeds of sale in favour of the husband. The wife, who was caring for the children, had remarried a year after this order had been made, and their elder child had gone to live with the husband. Leave to appeal out of time was refused, because the original order had contemplated the possibility of the wife remarrying, and because too much time had elapsed since the original order was made. In *Clutton v Clutton*[7] the Court of Appeal referred to the resentment a husband may feel when his house is occupied by the wife and her new husband or partner. The court approved the custom of making provision for this contingency occurring by making property adjustment orders under which the husband's interest in the house is postponed and becomes realisable in the event of the wife's remarriage or cohabitation.[8]

The standard of living before the breakdown of the marriage

Paragraph (c) of section 25(2) requires the court to take account of—

> 'the standard of living enjoyed by the family before the breakdown of the marriage.'

In the case of families of limited, or average, means it is inevitable that the standard of living of each spouse will fall because resources, which are adequate to keep one family at a standard of living which allows for small luxuries, when divided between two households will often barely keep each household in necessities. However, the issue to be resolved in the case of a divorced wife of a rich man is whether she can expect to maintain the standard of living which she enjoyed when married to him. Cases which occurred before 1984 must be treated with caution, because the policy of the legislation was to sustain the wife's standard of living so far as this was possible in the circumstances. However, it seems likely that a wife in

---

5   Cf *Wells v Wells* [1992] 2 FLR 66 (but decided in June 1980) where the husband was fortunate in being granted leave to appeal out of time against such an order.

6   [1992] 2 FLR 73.

7   [1991] 1 All ER 340.

8   See below.

circumstances like the wife in *Preston v Preston*[9] would still receive a similar settlement. In that case Ormrod LJ said 'the wife of a millionaire and 23 years married is entitled to expect a very high standard of living which would include a home in a house or flat at the top end of the market, and probably a second home in the country or abroad, together with a very high spending power'. In *Boylan v Boylan*[10] the wife's standard of living was considered in the context of the clean break provisions. Here it was held that it would be wrong to construe the words 'undue hardship' as referring solely to the needs of a former wife when assessing her ability to adjust to the termination of periodical payments. Rather her reasonable requirements should be judged by the standard that she was the former wife of a man of substantial wealth.[11]

The age of each party and the duration of the marriage

Paragraph (d) directs the court's attention to —

'the age of each party to the marriage and the duration of the marriage.'

In the light of this provision, a court is likely to want to be given information about the following matters: the impact of an unemployed wife's age on whether she can be expected to obtain work; how old she will be when the children cease to be dependent; where the husband is unemployed, whether, at his age, he can expect to gain further employment; where both parties are in middle age, what their financial positions will be on retirement. A wife in middle age with no, or only a limited, earning capacity, is likely to be awarded a more substantial share in the capital assets than a younger wife, as in *Martin v Martin*,[12] where the wife was given a life interest in the former matrimonial home. In *Jones v Jones*[13] the entire interest in the matrimonial home was transferred to the wife because she might be rendered homeless in middle age if the husband retained an interest in the property.[14] A property transfer order was made in *Hanlon v Hanlon*[15]

---

9   [1982] 1 All ER 41 at p 48.
10 [1988] 1 FLR 282.
11 It was therefore held that the only way in which the wife's right to periodical payments could be terminated, in such a way as not to cause her undue hardship, would be by the payment to her of a lump sum sufficient to provide her with an income comparable to the amount she was receiving in periodical payments; see too *B v B (Financial Provision)* [1990] 1 FLR 20; *R v R (Financial Provision: Reasonable Needs)* [1994] 2 FLR 1044.
12 [1977] 3 All ER 762.
13 [1975] 2 All ER 12.
14 Though this decision was also strongly influenced by the fact that the husband's violence had deprived the wife of her earning capacity.
15 [1978] 2 All ER 889.

mainly because a middle-aged wife needed the home for the four children of the marriage.

The age of the husband was an important consideration in *Greenham v Greenham*.[16] The trial judge had ordered that the former matrimonial home, in which the husband was living, should be sold when the husband attained the age of 70. He was held to have been wrong to include this provision. Even though the husband would probably be in a secure financial position at that age, and would be able to afford to pay the wife her share in the property, it was unreasonable to force him to move house at the age of 70. In *S v S*[17] the parties had married when both were aged over 50, and because of her age and circumstances the wife had pressing housing needs. However the marriage had lasted a mere two years, which made it unreasonable to expect the husband to make very substantial financial provision for her. The court arrived at an imaginative solution. It ordered the husband to settle on the wife a sufficient sum to buy a house, the object being that the capital invested in the house would revert to the husband, or to his estate, on the wife's death. This would mean that, in the long run, the husband's family would not be deprived of the capital represented by the house, whereas the wife would have a reasonable home to live in during her lifetime.

The weight given to the duration of the marriage is liable to vary in accordance with whether the fact of marriage has brought about adverse financial circumstances for one of the spouses. On the one hand, if the wife is young and the marriage has been short-lived she cannot expect much, if anything at all, in the way of periodical payments or property adjustment provision.[18] But if she has given birth to children, then she will need periodical payments for herself as well as the children, and she will have a greater need than the husband to occupy the former matrimonial home.[19] In a case where a wife has been married for a short period to a wealthy husband, the court is likely to apply the clean break provisions. Thus in *Attar v Attar*[20] and *Hedges v Hedges*[1] the court made orders designed to give the wives time in which to adjust to their suddenly reduced standard of living, and then terminated the husbands' obligations entirely. In *Leadbeater v Leadbeater*[2] the court ordered the payment of a lump sum, which was less than the wife could have expected if the marriage had lasted for longer.

Giving weight to the duration of the marriage can enable courts to do justice between the spouses in relation to their respective property holdings.

16   [1989] 1 FLR 105.
17   [1977] 1 All ER 56.
18   *Graves v Graves* (1973) 117 Sol Jo 679; *Brady v Brady* (1973) 3 Fam Law 78.
19   *Cumbers v Cumbers* [1975] 1 All ER 1.
20   [1985] FLR 649.
1   [1991] 1 FLR 196.
2   [1985] FLR 789.

Under the general law, where property is conveyed into the parties' joint names both legally and beneficially, and where there is an express declaration of trust as to the distribution of the proceeds of the trust for sale, this is conclusive in respect of their entitlement.[3] But this may be quite unjust having regard to their financial contribution to its acquisition, and when the purpose for its joint acquisition has failed to materialise, namely a happy marriage. Thus if, for example, the husband buys a house using all his resources, and perhaps inherited wealth, which is conveyed to him and his wife jointly, then the starting position is that they are joint owners of the property. But if their marriage is short and childless, why should the wife receive a half share in the proceeds of sale? In *Taylor v Taylor*[4] the husband alone had paid for the spouses' jointly-owned property. The marriage lasted for four months and the parties actually lived together for a mere 20 days. Reeve J ordered the whole of the wife's interest to be transferred to the husband.[5]

It is becoming increasingly commonplace for couples to live together as husband and wife before they marry. Consequently the issue has arisen in various cases whether pre-marital cohabitation can be taken into account. This is a particularly important issue in a case where the wife has given birth to the husband's children during the period of cohabitation, so that she has pressing needs for financial assistance. In *Kokosinski v Kokosinski*[6] the parties lived together for 25 years and had a son. Then they were married, but the marriage lasted for only 12 months. The court held that the period between the ceremony and the breakdown was likely to be the most material consideration. It also held that the 'welfare of the family' in paragraph (f) referred only to events which had occurred after the marriage took place. However, the judge pointed out that the court also must have regard to conduct,[7] and to all the circumstances of the case, and under both of these it could take account of behaviour which had occurred outside the span of marriage, at least in a case where the conduct had affected the finances of the other spouse.[8] In *Foley v Foley*[9] the parties had lived together for seven years and had three children, and then were married for eight years. The court treated the period when they were living together as 'one of the circumstances' to which the court was required to have regard, the weight to be attached to it being a matter for the court's discretion. It held

---

3 See for example *Goodman v Gallant* [1986] Fam 106; and see ch 8.
4 (1974) 119 Sol Jo 30.
5 It is interesting to note that, in the case of cohabitants, the courts have no power to redress this type of injustice.
6 [1980] 1 All ER 1106.
7 Now under para (g), then under the final target in s.25(1).
8 But it should be noted that the wife did not obtain the type of order she would have obtained had the marriage lasted for 25 years. She obtained a lump sum which was less than the amount she was seeking, and might have expected to obtain, and no periodical payments.
9 [1981] 2 All ER 857.

it was entitled to give less weight to the period of cohabitation than to events occurring during the marriage, although the court also said that, where the parties cannot marry, the court could regard their cohabitation as a very weighty factor.[10] In *S v S (Financial Provision) (Post-Divorce Cohabitation)*[11] the court took into account not just the parties' six years' pre-marital cohabitation, but also their 15 years' post-marital cohabitation.

Any physical or mental disability of either of the parties to the marriage

Paragraph (e) requires the court to take account of—

> 'any physical or mental disability of either of the parties to the marriage'.

There does not appear to be any case in which this factor has been directly referred to.[12] It sometimes happens that a disabled spouse has resources in the form of damages for personal injuries. In principle damages are treated as any other property available for reallocation after divorce, though the courts are likely to take account of their compensatory nature when determining the order to be made.[13] The courts have yet to determine to what extent the needs of a disabled party should impose an obligation on the other spouse to provide financial support which exceeds the norm.[14] For example, should there be a life-long obligation to provide periodical payments for a disabled spouse where the marriage has been relatively short-lived, and where an immediate or deferred clean break order would normally be considered appropriate? This raises the broader question of when the private obligations of ex-spouses to one another should end, and when those of the welfare state should take over. This is an issue of principle which has not been directly addressed by either the Law Commission or the courts.

Contributions made to the welfare of the family

Paragraph (f) focuses attention on—

10 In *Foley v Foley* the wife was awarded a lump sum payment of £10,000, rather than £14,000 which she claimed to be her one third share of the spouses' combined assets.
11 [1994] 2 FLR 228
12 The needs of the *child* of the marriage who had a serious kidney complaint were an important consideration in *Smith v Smith* [1975] 2 All ER 19n.
13 *Daubney v Daubney* [1976] 2 All ER 453; *Wagstaff v Wagstaff* [1992] 1 All ER 275.
14 In *Chadwick v Chadwick* [1985] FLR 606 the Court of Appeal declined to take account of the wife's disability when determining what order to make in respect of the matrimonial home: see below.

'the contributions which each of the parties has made or is likely in the foreseeable future to make to the welfare of the family, including any contribution by looking after the home or caring for the family.'

It is designed to correct the imbalance that often exists in the parties' strict property rights under the general law. In many marriages the spouses arrange their finances on the basis that the husband is the sole or main breadwinner, and the wife makes no direct contribution to the purchase of the matrimonial home and other substantial items such as the furniture and the car. Where property is owned solely by the husband, the fact that the wife has contributed towards the general well-being of the family by looking after the children, running the household, and paying for various small items does not give her any beneficial entitlement to a share in the property under the general law.[15] This was expressed with compelling imagery by Lord Simon of Glaisdale when he wrote: 'The cock bird can feather his nest precisely because he is not required to spend most of his time sitting on it.'[16]

The principle that each spouse should normally be entitled to receive a share in the family assets on marriage breakdown is sharply illustrated by the facts of *Smith v Smith*.[17] A lump sum order of £54,000 had been made in favour of the wife under which she received a little less than half of the combined value of the matrimonial home (which was in the husband's sole name), and investments made up partly from savings and partly from the husband's pension lump sum. The purpose of the order had been to give the wife sufficient resources from which to buy a house in order to meet her needs. She had no capital assets of her own. Six months after the order was made the wife committed suicide, leaving her estate to her daughter. The husband appealed against the order and the judge set it aside on the ground that the wife no longer had any needs. On a further appeal by the daughter, the Court of Appeal ruled that the basis of the wife's award had not only been to make provision for her needs, it had also been to reflect her significant contribution to the spouses' long marriage, and that a wife who had few, or no, needs had a right to have that contribution recognised in money terms. However, since a significant proportion of the lump sum had been to make provision for the wife, and since the husband was the only one now with future needs, it would be just to the husband to make a substantial downward adjustment of the wife's award. It was reduced to £25,000.

---

15 *Gissing v Gissing* [1970] 2 All ER 780; *Lloyds Bank plc v Rosset* [1990] 1 All ER 1111; and see ch 8.
16 *With All My Worldly Goods* (1964, Holdsworth Club).
17 [1991] 2 All ER 306.

However, it can be misleading to describe the non-owner spouse's claim to a share in the matrimonial assets as a 'right' or an 'entitlement'.[18] Rather what she has is a claim which will almost certainly be recognised in some manner if presented to a court. But until she presents her claim she has no rights in relation to property owned solely by her husband. Thus if the wife remarries before making an application for a property adjustment order, any 'rights' she has will be lost, because the court no longer has jurisdiction to make an order. If she dies before her application is heard her 'rights' die with her; her claim for a property adjustment order does not accrue for the benefit of her estate.[19] Because the claiming spouse is dependent on a court exercising its discretion to award her a share in the family assets, she is also vulnerable to her claim being denied for moralistic reasons. In *H v H (Financial Provision: Remarriage)*[20] the court applied the concept of earning to the wife's claim to receive a share in the proceeds of sale of the matrimonial home. The wife had deserted the husband and gone to live with another man. Sir George Baker P awarded her merely one twelfth of the value of the matrimonial home because 'if the job is left unfinished you do not earn as much.' It is suggested that it is very unlikely that the court could properly have used that reason for reducing the wife's interest in the property from one half to one twelfth had the spouses been beneficial joint owners of the matrimonial home.[1]

Conduct

The extent to which the conduct of the parties should be taken into account when making financial provision and property adjustment orders is a controversial issue. When, in 1980, the Law Commission issued a discussion paper which included the question of what policy ought to be adopted on the impact of conduct,[2] they received a considerable body of conflicting comment in reply. Many individuals felt a considerable sense of injustice because the court had not been prepared to take account of the other spouse's behaviour.[3] Despite this the Law Commission expressed the view that courts cannot reasonably be expected to apportion responsibility for

18 See Bagnall J in *Harnett v Harnett* [1973] 2 All ER 593 at p 601.
19 On this, see the note by R Spon Smith (1992) 22 Fam Law 421.
20 [1975] 1 All ER 367; the court's decision was also strongly influenced by the fact that the wife had remarried by the time of the hearing and her new husband was making provision for her needs.
1   See too, *Schuller v Schuller* [1990] 2 FLR 193 where the wife, who had been married for 21 years, was awarded only six per cent of the value of the house, because she had inherited property after the parties parted.
2   Law Com No 103.
3   Law Com No 112, para 36.

breakdown in any save exceptional circumstances. They relied in particular on the words of Ormrod J in *Wachtel v Wachtel*[4] when he said:

'The forensic process is reasonably well adapted to determining in broad terms the share of responsibility of each party for an accident on the road or at work because the issues are relatively confined in scope, but it is much too clumsy a tool for dissecting the complex inter-actions which go on all the time in a family. Shares in responsibility for breakdown cannot be properly assessed without a meticulous examination and understanding of the characters and personalities of the spouses concerned, and the more thorough the investigation the more the shares will, in most cases, approach equality.'

The Law Commission also gave more pragmatic reasons for rejecting an inquiry into the parties' mutual recriminations in other than exceptional cases. These included that it would be expensive of court time and legal aid; that resurrecting past matters, sometimes stretching back over many years, for forensic investigation would not assist the parties to come to terms with their deep feelings about the breakdown of their marriage; and that such feelings are better dealt with during conciliation.[5] Paragraph (g) requires courts to take account of

'the conduct of each of the parties, if that conduct is such that it would in the opinion of the court be inequitable to disregard it.'

This wording does, of course, leave wide open the question of when it will be so inequitable. The courts have generally been reluctant to give weight to immoral conduct except when it has been 'obvious and gross';[6] or conduct which has been 'of the kind that would cause the ordinary mortal to throw up his hands and say, "surely that woman is not going to be given any money" or "is not going to get a full award" '.[7] Consequently they have refused to penalise a spouse who has committed adultery, or otherwise behaved in a manner which has caused offence or distress to the other party, taking the view that this would be to 'impose a fine for supposed misbehaviour in the course of an unhappy married life'.[8] However, reasonable people apply different moral standards to certain forms of behaviour, and some may be more prepared than others to find that the conduct is

4   [1973] 1 All ER 113, at p 119.
5   Law Com No 112, para 37.
6   Per Lord Denning in *Wachtel v Wachtel* [1973] 1 All ER 829.
7   *W v W (Financial Provision: Lump Sum)* [1976] Fam 107, per Sir George Baker P at p 114.
8   *Wachtel v Wachtel* [1973] 1 All ER 829.

susceptible of forgiveness.[9] The assessment of when conduct will be regarded as relevant is made more difficult by the fact that the courts have held that conduct does not necessarily carry any imputation of moral blame, rather it means behaviour of the greatest importance in the marriage.[10] Thus determining when a court is likely to take the view that it would be inequitable to disregard conduct is not easy.

As an illustration of how difficult it is to predict when a court will give weight to one spouse's apparent misconduct it is instructive to look at *Kyte v Kyte*[11] as it passed through the hierarchy of the court system. The registrar found that it would be inequitable to disregard the wife's conduct, yet the judge held that conduct was not relevant and did not apply. Finally the Court of Appeal held that there had been such an imbalance of conduct as between the husband and wife that it would be inequitable to ignore it. This divergence of opinion reflects research findings made in the 1970s which revealed that registrars tended to differ considerably in the account they took of conduct when choosing the level of their orders.[12] This may be even more marked nowadays. In *Kyte v Kyte* Purchas LJ said that the wording of paragraph (g) may give courts a broader discretion than they had hitherto enjoyed when applying the test of 'gross and obvious conduct'.[13]

The moral imperative to have regard to conduct probably commands very wide acceptance when the facts of a case are very heavily weighted in favour of one spouse and against the other. An example is *Evans v Evans*,[14] in which the facts were particularly sympathetic towards the husband. He had conscientiously paid maintenance for his ex-wife for many years, and it was only when she was convicted of inciting others to kill him that he applied to have the order terminated. Not surprisingly the court granted his application. More controversial is the situation when one of the parties has allegedly behaved badly and the other has been blameless, but when that behaviour cannot be characterised as totally immoral. An example arose in *Robinson v Robinson*[15] when the wife had deserted her husband because she was unhappy with army life overseas. The Court of Appeal upheld a ruling by magistrates that the amount of maintenance awarded to the wife should be reduced and limited in time to reflect the blameless-

9 Compare the approach of Bagnall J in *Harnett v Harnett* [1973] 2 All ER 593 with that of Lawton LJ in *Blezard v Blezard* (1979) 9 Fam Law 249.
10 *West v West* [1977] 2 All ER 705.
11 [1987] 3 All ER 1041.
12 W Barrington Baker, J Eekelaar, C Gibson and S Raikes *The Matrimonial Jurisdiction of Registrars* (1977) Wolfson College, Oxford, Centre for Socio-Legal Studies, SSRC, pp 20-27.
13 He said it was not necessary to decide whether this was the case because the behaviour of the wife satisfied the test under either approach.
14 [1989] 1 FLR 351. See also *Whiston v Whiston* [1994] 2 FLR 906, where payments were reduced to a bigamous wife.
15 [1983] 1 All ER 391.

ness of the husband, and the blameworthy behaviour of the wife. This ruling appeared to cut across the thinking in *Wachtel v Wachtel,* namely that the legal process is not suited to the allocation of blame for marriage breakdown because of the complexity of the married relationship. *Robinson v Robinson* was arguably nothing more than a case of simple desertion, and it is suggested that to characterise the wife and husband as 'blameworthy' and 'blameless' may have been to fall into the trap which the Court of Appeal had hitherto been anxious to avoid.[16] The relationship between husband and wife is usually too subtle to be analysed in the black and white terms of being 'at fault' and 'faultless'.[17]

Probably the least questionable circumstance in which this provision has been satisfied is when the conduct of one spouse has had a direct bearing on the spouses' financial and property position. In *Jones v Jones*[18] the husband had attacked his wife, injuring her so severely that he impaired her earning capacity. The Court of Appeal found that it would be repugnant to justice not to take the husband's conduct into account when securing the position of the wife in the future. In *H v H (Financial Provision: Conduct)*[19] the husband violently assaulted his wife as a result of which he was sent to prison for wounding and attempted rape. This meant that the husband was no longer able to support his wife and children to the standard which had preceded the attack. She had been left in a psychologically vulnerable position. The husband's conduct was one of the factors which influenced Thorpe J to transfer the husband's half share in the matrimonial home to the wife. In *Martin v Martin*[20] the husband had not behaved in an immoral manner, but he had lost money in successive unsuccessful business ventures. The court held that he could not claim the same share in the family assets as he would have been entitled to had he behaved reasonably.[1] Thus in each of these cases there was a causative link between the conduct of one of the spouses and the parties' current financial circumstances which it was inequitable to disregard.

Paragraph (g) is but one of the several matters to be taken into account, and the courts have, in the main, made efforts to minimise litigation which focuses on conduct. But, while it is a factor, it provides spouses with a financial motive to litigate. The disadvantage of treating conduct as a discrete consideration is that to do so may foster further animosity between

16 The ruling also indirectly penalised the child of the family. The mother's maintenance was reduced and limited in time, and she therefore was left with insufficient resources to provide for them both.
17 For example adultery, even though it appears to be the cause of the breakdown, may in reality be an indication of pre-existing disharmony.
18 [1975] 2 All ER 12.
19 [1994] 2 FLR 801.
20 [1976] Fam 335.
1 See too *Bryant v Bryant* (1976) 120 Sol Jo 165; *Weisz v Weisz* (1975) Times, 16 December; *Hillard v Hillard* (1982) 12 Fam Law 176.

the parties. It has been recognised that it is unhelpful for divorce petitions to contain allegations and counter-allegations about behaviour, and proposals to reform the divorce law would eliminate this.[2] However, lawyers and mediators are likely to be pressed into hearing details about the parties' conduct while ever it is a relevant matter. The present law is also in danger of being perceived as unfair because it is unclear which kind of conduct should be ignored, and which it is inequitable to disregard.[3]

This raises the question whether, as a matter of policy, it would be more beneficial for issues of conduct to be subsumed within the other paragraphs in section 25(2). It is suggested that this might help to avoid allegations being made which can be both inflammatory, and distressing, to the spouses personally, and may be damaging to their children. For example where, as in *Robinson v Robinson*[4] and *West v West*,[5] one spouse deserted the other at an early stage in the marriage, this could have been considered under paragraphs (d) or (f), which focuses on the duration of the marriage, and contributions to the welfare of the family. Even extreme cases like *Jones v Jones*,[6] in which the husband attacked the wife with a knife, or *H v H (Financial Provision: Conduct)*,[7] where the husband's attack on his wife had led to his imprisonment, and to her being psychologically harmed, could probably have adequately been considered under paragraphs (a),(b) and (e). These focus on each spouse's earning capacity, resources, needs and any physical or mental disabilities. The fact that the husband's conduct had caused the wife's loss of earning capacity, and increased her needs, would clearly have been relevant, yet the resultant order, if perceived as a matter of causation rather than reflecting guilt and innocence, could not have been characterised as punishing him twice, which was arguably unfair.[8] Where a spouse has squandered resources, as in *Martin v Martin*,[9] this could be considered as a matter relating to the spouses' resources. While some situations would not easily fall within the other paragraphs in the section,[10] abolishing conduct as a separate category would be more in keeping with the moral neutrality which proposals emanating from the Lord Chancellor's Department suggest should be adopted in relation to the ground for divorce.[11] The counter-argument to this is that it is highly

2 See ch 6.
3 See too the research findings of W Barrington Baker, J Eekelaar, C Gibson and S Raikes *The Matrimonial Jurisdiction of Registrars* (Wolfson College, Oxford, 1977).
4 [1983] 1 All ER 391.
5 [1977] 2 All ER 705.
6 [1975] 2 All ER 12.
7 [1994] 2 FLR 801.
8 See the note on *Jones v Jones* by E Ellis (1976) 39 MLR 97.
9 [1976] Fam 335.
10 It is hard to see where *Evans v Evans* [1989] 1 FLR 351 would fall, but it might have been considered under the clean break provisions in s.25(A).
11 *Looking to the Future* (HMSO, 1984); and see ch 6.

offensive if persons who have behaved in a violent manner, such as the husbands in *Jones v Jones* and *H v H (Financial Provision: Conduct)*, do not have their conduct positively condemned in proceedings ancillary to the divorce itself.

Loss of pension

Paragraph (h) directs the court to have regard to

'in the case of proceedings for divorce or nullity of marriage, the value to each of the parties of any benefit (for example, a pension) which by reason of the dissolution or annulment of the marriage, that party will lose the chance of acquiring.'

The loss of an occupational pension scheme entitlement usually represents a real deprivation to a spouse, particularly one divorced in middle age.[12] This is because a divorced wife is no longer her husband's widow for the purposes of his pension scheme and therefore, if he should predecease her, she will not obtain a widow's pension. Similarly, if the wife has a pension scheme which pays benefits to a widower, the husband will not be able to benefit from it if the parties divorce. Where spouses divorce fairly late in life their opportunity to make adequate substitute pension arrangements is likely to be limited. Indeed it may be sensible to discuss the alternative decree of judicial separation with middle aged, or elderly, persons contemplating ending their marriage.[13] Where remarriage is not contemplated it may be wiser for each spouse to stay married, but legally separated. With a decree of judicial separation they can obtain orders for financial provision and property adjustment in the same way as divorcing spouses can, but also retain their pension entitlements.

When resources are available it may be possible to compensate a spouse for loss of future pension rights; for example, the husband might be ordered to transfer capital to the wife which she could invest; or he might be required to transfer his entire interest in the matrimonial home to her; or he might be ordered to pay his wife a lump sum, the date of payment to be postponed until he receives his own lump sum payable on retirement. Other methods could include requiring the husband either to purchase an annuity for his wife, or take out insurance on his own life. It lies outside the scope of the court's powers to order a husband to make this type of insurance arrangement, but he might be persuaded to agree to such a settlement if faced

---

12 See J Masson *Pensions, Dependency and Divorce* [1986] JSWL 343; J Masson *Pensions: A Scheme for Divorcing Couples* (1993) 23 Fam Law 479.
13 S.17.

with the alternative of an inflated property transfer order. Pension entitlements vary from one pension scheme to another, and it is essential to look at the details of the scheme and how they affect the spouses' positions. On rare occasions it may be possible to treat a pension scheme as a post-nuptial settlement which can be varied under section 24(1)(c).[14] The state pension arrangements are also affected by divorce and must similarly be examined.

Special protection for respondents to divorces based on two or five years of living apart

When, in 1969, divorce law was extended to enable a spouse to petition for divorce even though he or she had been the 'guilty' party, and even though the respondent had not committed a 'matrimonial offence', there was some considerable concern that the financial consequences of a decree could cause very substantial hardship to some women divorced in middle age. There was also a fear that a spouse might be persuaded to agree to a divorce without having fully appreciated the financial implications of doing so. Consequently special financial protection for respondents to a decree based on the two- and five-year separation facts is provided.[15]

Grave financial hardship as a defence

Where the only fact being relied on for divorce is under section 1(2)(e), namely that the parties have lived apart for a continuous period of five years, the respondent can oppose the grant of a decree under section 5 on the ground that the dissolution of the marriage will result in grave financial or other hardship, and that it would be wrong in all the circumstances to dissolve the marriage. Grave financial hardship is not defined, but section 5(3) provides that hardship includes the loss of the chance of acquiring any benefit which the respondent might acquire if the marriage were not dissolved. The courts have ruled that the correct approach is for the court first to determine whether the divorce will cause the respondent grave financial hardship. Only if this is established should it then go on to consider whether in all the circumstances the marriage should be dissolved.[16] The reported case law on section 5 has focused on the wife's loss of pension rights. It is important here to distinguish between the wife's claim to a share in the husband's personal pension, and her loss of a chance of

14 *Brooks v Brooks* [1993] 4 All ER 917.
15 See ch 6 on divorce generally, and for discussion of the five facts which must be established to prove irretrievable breakdown of marriage.
16 *Parker v Parker* [1972] 1 All ER 410; *Le Marchant v Le Marchant* [1977] 3 All ER 610; *Jackson v Jackson* [1993] 2 FLR 848.

acquiring a widow's pension because she is divorced. Although a wife has no entitlement to income from her husband's pension scheme, she can nonetheless gain from it indirectly through the award of periodical payments or a lump sum from the income produced. It is therefore improbable that such a loss will fall within section 5. It is when it is thought likely that the husband will predecease the wife that the loss to her of a widow's pension can amount to a serious form of financial hardship, since it may not be possible to compensate her by other orders made under sections 23 and 24.

The question to ask is: 'How will the wife's pension position be affected by divorce?' Importantly, however, there is no point in claiming that she will lose her pension entitlement if the loss that entails will be made up by income support. The source of her future income does not matter provided that the loss will be made up pound for pound.[17] As Finer J emphasised in *Reiterbund v Reiterbund*,[18] there is no shame to be attached to the receipt of state benefits, and the law has a duty to foster this attitude. There is also little point in a relatively young wife seeking to rely on this provision, because its main purpose is to protect respondent wives who have reached middle age from losing financial security. Therefore the chances of a young wife being able to establish the defence are remote.[19] In *Julian v Julian*[20] the loss of pension could not be compensated from the husband's other resources, and there was a substantial monetary gap between the financial provision the husband could provide and the financial benefits the wife would receive if she remained married. As this loss would cause the wife grave financial hardship the decree was consequently refused. However, a wife is not entitled to be compensated pound for pound for what she will lose; rather it is the grave nature of the hardship which she must establish, not that divorce will cause her financial loss.[1]

The respondent must also overcome the additional hurdle of persuading the court that it would be 'wrong' to dissolve the marriage. In *Reiterbund* the court ruled that wrong must be construed as meaning unjust, and that the court must exclude from its consideration the fact that the petition had been brought by a 'guilty' husband against a non-consenting wife as this would be tantamount to striking out the five year living apart ground for divorce. However, where the respondent has behaved in a wrongful manner towards the petitioner this may lead to the grant of a decree despite a finding that the respondent will suffer grave financial hardship.[2]

17 *Reiterbund v Reiterbund* [1974] 2 All ER 455; *Jackson v Jackson* above.
18 Above.
19 *Mathias v Mathias* [1972] 3 All ER 1.
20 (1972) 116 Sol Jo 763; see too *Brickell v Brickell* [1973] 3 All ER 508; *Johnson v Johnson* (1982) 12 Fam Law 116.
1 *Le Marchant v Le Marchant* [1977] 3 All ER 610.
2 *Brickell v Brickell* [1973] 3 All ER 508; disapproving dictum to the contrary in *Dorrell v Dorrell* [1972] 3 All ER 343.

Courts have been extremely reluctant to allow the grave financial hardship defence to succeed, because to do so will keep a marriage in existence which has undoubtedly irretrievably broken down. Rather the courts have found their own means of alleviating a spouse's hardship. For example in *Parker v Parker*[3] the wife's loss of pension rights was found to amount to grave financial hardship, but the court found that this could be alleviated by the husband purchasing a deferred annuity for the wife. One matter which exercised the mind of the court, and which was fundamental to its decision to grant the decree, was what steps could be taken to ensure that the husband would continue to pay the annual insurance premium. It found that the husband could secure this obligation by taking out a second mortgage on the house. Similarly in *Le Marchant v Le Marchant*[4] the Court of Appeal compelled a husband to 'volunteer' a solution, by withholding the decree until he made an acceptable proposal to alleviate the wife's hardship.[5]

Special protection for certain respondents after decree nisi

The disadvantage of defending a divorce under section 5 is that the only relief available is the refusal of a decree. But the respondent, as well as the petitioner, may not wish to remain bound up in a marriage which has irretrievably broken down. A respondent wife's fear of divorce may relate to its financial consequences rather than to her change in status. In this situation section 10 may come to her aid. Section 10 gives special protection to the respondent in divorce cases where a decree nisi has been obtained in reliance on either the two- or five-year separation fact. This protection is *not* given to spouses who divorce their partner because he or she has committed adultery, or behaved in such a way that the petitioner cannot reasonably be expected to live with the respondent, or deserted the petitioner for more than two years. It is also only given to the *respondent* to the petition, although in practice the choice of who is the petitioner and who is respondent to a petition based on the two-year separation fact may be entirely fortuitous. It may therefore be important to have all this in mind at the outset of divorce proceedings when determining which fact should be relied on to evidence the irretrievable breakdown of the marriage, and who should be the petitioner.

3   [1972] 1 All ER 410.
4   [1977] 3 All ER 610.
5   It should be recalled that the court only has power to make orders which fall within ss.23 and 24; insurance arrangements will often fall outside the scope of these powers, but they may nonetheless be a very important method of dealing with lost pension rights, either under s.25(2)(h), or under ss.5 and 10.

Section 10(1) empowers the court to rescind the decree nisi in a case where the petitioner has misled the respondent (whether intentionally or unintentionally) about any matter which the respondent took into account in deciding to give consent to the decree being granted. Whilst the risk of this happening appears to be remote, a petitioner could in some circumstances be well advised to take advantage of section 7 in order to ensure that section 10 cannot be raised. Section 7 enables either party to a divorce to bring before the court any agreement or proposed agreement and the court can express its opinion on its reasonableness. Such a step might also prevent the petitioner falling foul of section 10(2) and (3).

Under section 10(2) a respondent may apply to a court for consideration of her financial position after divorce, in which case, by virtue of the provisions contained in section 10(3), the court hearing the application—

'shall consider all the circumstances including the age, health, conduct, earning capacity, financial resources and financial obligations of each of the parties, and the financial position of the respondent as, having regard to the divorce, it is likely to be after the death of the petitioner should the petitioner die first; and, subject to subsection (4) ... the court shall not make the decree absolute unless it is satisfied:
(a) that the petitioner should not be required to make any financial provision for the respondent, or
(b) that the financial provision made by the petitioner for the respondent is reasonable and fair or the best that can be made in the circumstances.'

This provision affords the respondent valuable protection where the petitioner is being unreasonable, or obdurate, over financial arrangements, or where he is in arrears with payments due under an existing order. In *Griffiths v Dawson & Co*,[6] Ewbank J said that the first step any competent solicitor should take to protect the wife's position when consulted by a wife in her late middle age, who has been married for many years to a man in pensionable employment, and who is being divorced against her will, is to make an application under section 10. He said that the purpose of making such an application is not to obtain a hearing in court; rather it is to hold up the decree absolute, whilst financial matters are being looked into. This step prevents a wife from ceasing to be a wife, and thereby losing her right to a widow's pension, until the investigation has been made. In *Garcia v Garcia*[7] the wife was able to use this section to delay the grant of decree nisi because her Spanish husband owed her £4,000 in unpaid

6   [1993] 2 FLR 315.
7   [1992] 1 FLR 256.

maintenance for their child. In *Wilson v Wilson*[8] the Court of Appeal ruled that a petitioner cannot circumvent the protection afforded by subsection (3) by making mere proposals. The court pointed out that the subsection requires the provision to have been made, and that to allow it to be satisfied by proposals only might enable the husband subsequently to resile from them, leaving the wife without protection.

However, the court has some discretion over whether or not to make the decree absolute once the inquiry under subsection (3) has been conducted. Subsection (4) states that—

'The court may if it thinks fit make the decree absolute not-withstanding the requirements in subsection (3) if—

(a) it appears that there are circumstances making it desirable that the decree should be made absolute without delay, and

(b) the court has obtained a satisfactory undertaking from the petitioner that he will make such financial provision for the respondent as the court may approve.'

But again the courts have been careful to ensure that this provision does not undermine the overall protective purpose of the section. In *Grigson v Grigson*[9] the husband had failed, even in outline, to give an indication of the kind or amount of financial provision he would make. He merely said he would do so. It was held that, on a true construction of the subsection, the court must approve proposals submitted by the petitioner at least in outline, and then obtain an undertaking from him that they will be given effect, before proceeding to decree absolute. It was not sufficient for the petitioner merely to give an undertaking that he would 'make such financial provision as the court may approve' at some specified date in the future. Essentially, the provisions in section 10 provide the respondent to a divorce based on the two- or five-year separation facts with a 'bargaining chip', and where the petitioner is being unreasonable when negotiating financial and property arrangements, it is a bargaining chip which may sometimes usefully be exploited.

The matrimonial home—what order is the most appropriate?

The fact that parties are divorcing does not mean that they must adopt a confrontational stance. It is often the case that one, or both, parties wants to secure an arrangement which is fair to each of them, but they need

8   [1973] 2 All ER 17.
9   [1974] 1 All ER 478.

guidance on how this can best be achieved. Prolonged negotiation, and extensive litigation, over financial provision and property adjustment arrangements after divorce is very expensive for the parties.[10] Cases abound in which the spouses' resources have been relatively limited, and in which the costs of the proceedings have absorbed a sizeable percentage of their assets. For example, in *P v P (Financial Provision)*[11] Anthony Lincoln J said: 'Once again I am confronted with the fact that the total realisable funds of the family have been severely reduced by the incurring of vast costs by both sides in order to resolve an issue as to the value of their respective shareholding'. In *C v C (Financial Provision)*[12] Ewbank J commented, almost in passing, that the costs of the financial part of the case amounted to £160,000, with more costs owing for the divorce. Clearly, neither party gains if money and resources which could be used to benefit the spouses and their children are unnecessarily spent on paying lawyers' fees.

At various time the judges have issued guidance to lawyers on how they should seek to minimise the costs of matrimonial proceedings, about which the judges have frequently expressed concern.[13] The magnitude of the problem was demonstrated by the need to issue a Practice Direction that the court will require an estimate of the approximate amount of costs on each side before it can make a lump sum award.[14] Very specific guidance was provided for practitioners by Booth J, in concurrence with the President of the Family Division, in *Evans v Evans*.[15] This was designed to promote the efficient handling of cases, to identify and define the issues to be resolved, and to encourage the reaching of a settlement. Lawyers were instructed to keep their clients informed of the costs at all stages of the proceedings. One process which can assist is to issue what is known as a '*Calderbank* letter'[16] in which the right is reserved to draw the court's attention to an offer to settle the arrangements on specified terms, after the court has made its judgment. If the amount ordered by the court is equal to, or less than, the amount offered, the court can order the successful party to pay the other side's costs as from the date of the letter.

Often the parties' only major asset is the matrimonial home and it may require some ingenuity to make provision for each spouse. But there is a danger that, by the time the lawyers have finished negotiating over what

---

10 See, for example, *B v B (Financial Provision)* [1989] 1 FLR 119, in which some £50,000 was spent by the spouses in support of their conflicting views of the extent and value of the husband's assets.

11 [1989] 2 FLR 241 at p 242.

12 [1989] 1 FLR 11.

13 See particularly *P v P (Financial Provision)* [1989] 2 FLR 241.

14 *Practice Direction* [1982] 2 All ER 800.

15 [1990] 2 All ER 147.

16 Stemming from *Calderbank v Calderbank* [1975] 3 All ER 333.

should happen to the house, and to its contents, the property is likely to be worth much less than it was originally. Indeed, how the costs will be paid is often a factor which influences the final order. Where a spouse who remains in the property is legally aided, the costs of the proceedings will be a charge on the property, with interest accumulating the longer the charge remains unredeemed. The main methods of disposition of the matrimonial home are described below, and the discussion which follows is aimed at assisting the negotiation process, so that unnecessary costs are avoided. The discussion therefore focuses on what arrangements might reasonably be agreed as much as it does on what orders the courts have made. When considering the appropriateness of particular orders, and choosing between them, the advantages and disadvantages inherent in the different types of order need to be identified and weighed in the light of the range of the court's other powers, the parties' particular circumstances, and the application to them of the statutory guidelines.[16a]

The property to be sold and the proceeds of sale divided

The attractive feature of an agreement, or order, in which the matrimonial home is sold, and the proceeds of sale divided between the parties, is that each spouse is enabled to realise his or her investment in the property. It is particularly appropriate where there are no children, and where each spouse can be adequately housed in alternative accommodation from his or her share of the proceeds. It is also appropriate where the spouses are young. They can go their separate ways, using their shares in the money realised as a down payment on fresh property should they so wish. In *Scallon v Scallon*[17] the court took the view that it was more fair to divide the property between the spouses than to transfer it to one spouse only and make a clean break order. The spouses were beneficial co-owners. The original order of the registrar was that the husband's interest in the matrimonial home be transferred to the wife, and that all the wife's other financial claims be dismissed. The husband appealed, stating that he had debts and contending that the order had left him with no capital assets. It was ordered that the house be sold, and that the net proceeds be divided three fifths to the wife and two fifths to the husband. The court took the view that this would give the wife sufficient with which to house herself, but ruled that she should have the additional protection of a nominal periodical payments order in case she should need maintenance in the future.[18]

16a See too, M Hayes and G Battersby 'Property Adjustment: Order or Disorder in the Former Matrimonial Home' (1985) 15 Fam Law 213; M Hayes and G Battersby 'Property Adjustment: Further Thoughts on Charge Orders' (1986) 16 Fam Law 142.

17 [1990] 1 FLR 194.

18 The importance of a nominal periodical payments order is explained above.

Scallon v Scallon was also concerned with the vexed issue of legal aid, and whether the loan from the Legal Aid Fund must be repaid when the property is sold. If any property is 'recovered or preserved' for a person who has been assisted by legal aid, the Legal Aid Fund has first charge on any such property in order to recoup its expenditure on legal fees. Only the first £2,500 of a lump sum, or the value of any property, is exempt.[19] However, since 1989 the Legal Aid Board has had the power to postpone the enforcement of its charge where the money, or property, is to be used for the purchase of a home for the assisted person. In *Scallon v Scallon* the wife asserted that the court had failed to take account of the impact of the charge on her means, and that once she had paid her legal aid contribution she would have insufficient money with which to buy a new home. However the Court of Appeal, while recognising that postponement of the realisation of the charge is a discretionary power, said that it was right to assume that the Board would not seek to frustrate the order of the court by refusing to exercise its discretion, and by realising its charge immediately.

There are advantages and disadvantages in selling the matrimonial home. Sale promotes a clean break and finality. It also allows for flexibility because the division of the proceeds of sale can reflect the criteria in the statutory guidelines. For example, the parent with care of the children could receive a larger percentage of the proceeds than the other spouse, reflecting the requirement that the children's interests must be put first.[20] The disadvantage of immediate sale is that the proceeds may be insufficient for the purchase of two new properties, particularly at times of rapidly inflating house prices. Sale, where there are children, also means that the children lose their home at a time when they are likely to be suffering distress at the termination of their parents' marriage, and experiencing the loss of the day-to-day presence of one parent. When moving to a new house will involve losing the companionship and support of friends in the neighbourhood, or going to a new school, this may be to deprive the children of much needed emotional security. It may also make the position of the caring parent who is in, or who is seeking, employment more difficult, because she may have built up a network of persons on whom she can rely to assist her with care of the children while she is out at work.[1] In *R v R (Financial Provision: Reasonable Needs)*[1a] Sir Stephen Brown P held that

---

19 Cf *Mortimer v Mortimer-Griffin* [1986] 2 FLR 315, in which the husband's lump sum was limited to this amount as any larger sum would have been recouped by the Legal Aid Fund. By taking account of this factor, the courts have widened the purse of available resources in a manner similar to that in which they have taken account of state benefits when making periodical payments orders: see above.

20 S.25(1).

1 Cf *Chaudhuri v Chaudhuri* [1992] 2 FLR 73, in which it had been a central part of the wife's case that she needed to stay in the matrimonial home in order to provide a secure home for the children in a neighbourhood where she would have the support of friends.

1a [1994] 2 FLR 1044.

it was wholly unreasonable to order the sale of the former matrimonial home in which the wife had lived for 17 years simply because it provided her with accommodation in excess of her needs. The husband, who was extremely wealthy, had rehoused himself in luxurious accommodation. Sir Stephen Brown P ruled that as it was not necessary for the wife to leave because of a lack of resources, it would therefore be unreasonable to require her to do so.

The property to be vested in the sole name of one of the spouses

A court has been willing to order that the matrimonial home should belong solely to one of the parties where it forms only one part of the spouses' capital assets. Thus where in *Hanlon v Hanlon*[2] one spouse enjoyed secure accommodation as part of his employment; or, as in *H v H (Financial Provision: Remarriage)*,[3] had acquired an interest in property through marriage to another; or had additional wealth as a result of inheritance, as in *Schuller v Schuller*,[4] the property was vested in the name of one spouse alone. Essentially, what the court was doing in those cases was taking account of all available resources under section 25(2)(a), and using the matrimonial home to house one of the parties secure in the knowledge that the other was provided for. Although one spouse was obtaining a disproportionate share in the matrimonial home, this could be justified by reference to each spouses' needs under section 25(2)(b) and, where there were children, by the requirement under section 25(1) to give first consideration to their interests.

Sometimes the owner spouse is required to pay a lump sum to compensate the other for the loss of his or her share in the matrimonial home. Such an order is similar in effect to one in which sale of the home is ordered, because in each case both acquire a share in the value of the property. However, in many instances the owner spouse will not have sufficient resources to make such a payment. Another way of compensating a spouse for giving up his or her claim to a share in the matrimonial property is to make no order for periodical payments. In *Hanlon v Hanlon*[5] the husband, who was living rent free in a police flat, was ordered to transfer his entire interest in the matrimonial home to his wife who was looking after their four children, and in return he was no longer required to make periodical payments for the two children who were still dependent. Similarly, in *Smith v Smith*[6] the husband was ordered to transfer his half interest in the

2   [1978] 2 All ER 889, in which the husband lived rent-free in a police flat.
3   [1975] 1 All ER 367.
4   [1990] 2 FLR 193.
5   [1978] 2 All ER 889.
6   [1975] 2 All ER 19n.

matrimonial home to his wife despite the fact that, unlike the husband in *Hanlon v Hanlon*, he had no other secure accommodation. His wife had a pressing need for the home because their child had a serious kidney complaint. In return no periodical payments were ordered for the wife, and only a modest sum for the child. However, a husband would be very unwise to accept such an arrangement in relation to his child, because he is vulnerable to an application being made at any time to the Child Support Agency by the parent with care. The fact that a property transfer order has been made on the basis that child support will not be ordered is of no relevance to how the Agency applies the maintenance formula.[7] But where there are no children, a transfer of property may usefully be made in return for an agreement from the wife that she will not seek periodical payments. This also has the advantage that it achieves a clean break.

It is possible that the conduct of one of the parties may lead the court to make an order which secures the matrimonial home for the other. In *Jones v Jones*[8] the husband had attacked the wife with a knife severing the tendons of a hand. The trial judge had ordered that the house be transferred to the wife, but that she should pay the husband a sum equal to one fifth of the equity when the youngest of their five children ceased to be a dependant. The wife appealed on the ground that at that time she would be aged 50, and incapable of earning a living by reason of the injuries inflicted on her by her husband. Clearly the husband had behaved in a manner which it would be repugnant to justice to disregard,[9] and the Court of Appeal found that it would be unjust to the wife that she should be required to sell the house and to find somewhere else to live in order to pay the husband his share. Accordingly, the court ordered that the whole beneficial interest be vested in her. In *Jones v Jones* the conduct of the husband had a direct bearing on the wife's financial circumstances. Similarly, where the husband has dissipated the family assets or failed to make periodical payments in the past, a court may choose to make an order transferring the home to the wife.[10] Here the court is influenced by conduct not so much because it is immoral, but because it has the effect of reducing the spouses' assets on divorce, and therefore the choice of orders available.

The advantage of an order under which the matrimonial home is vested in the name of one of the spouses is that it brings about finality, certainty and facilitates a clean break. It means that the occupying spouse is not in the position of being fearful that she will have to sell the property at some date in the future in order that the other spouse can have his share.[11] Where the other spouse can be compensated for his or her loss by a lump sum payment, raised perhaps through the property being mortgaged, or

---

7   *Crozier v Crozier* [1994] 1 FLR 126. See also *Smith v McInerney* [1994] 2 FLR 1077.
8   [1975] 2 All ER 12.
9   Under what would now be s.25(2)(g).
10 *Bryant v Bryant* (1976) 120 Sol Jo 165.
11 See *Hanlon v Hanlon* [1978] 2 All ER 889; *Mortimer v Mortimer-Griffin* [1986] 2 FLR 315.

remortgaged, that solution may be accepted as fair by both parties, and can bring about a parity between them. However, often there are no resources from which a lump sum payment can be made, and the owning spouse will not have a large enough income to finance a second mortgage. It has been seen that transferring the home in exchange for no continuing liability to make periodical payments is often not a realistic option when there are children to be maintained, bearing in mind that the formula for assessing child support includes a sum for the caring parent. Yet unless a sole ownership order is made with compensating provisions, it may give unfair weight to one spouse's needs at the expense of the other spouse's rights. This position is exacerbated when the order has been based on the parties' respective needs, and if the needy spouse's circumstances change for the better after the order in her favour has been finalised; for example if she remarries,[12] comes into an inheritance, or obtains gainful employment. At this stage there is no way of correcting the imbalance of the original distribution of the property.[13]

Satisfying the immediate needs of one spouse at the time of divorce should not necessarily outweigh the legitimate expectation of the non-residential spouse to have some share in the property, the purchase of which he has paid towards, at a future date. Certainly if both spouses have contributed towards the purchase of the house, either financially or in kind by looking after the home and caring for the family, then, applying paragraphs (c) and (f), looking to the parties' standard of living and contribution to the welfare of the family, it may seem inequitable to deprive one spouse of any share in the parties' only substantial asset.

It is suggested that an example arose in *Schuller v Schuller*.[14] After the parties separated the wife went to work for an elderly friend who died shortly afterwards. By his will he left the wife a flat worth £130,000, and his residuary estate worth £4,000. The husband was living in the former matrimonial home of which he was the sole owner, and which was worth £143,000. The parties had been married for 21 years. The wife had worked throughout the marriage, except when the children were young, and both had pooled their resources towards the family's living expenses. On the wife's application for financial provision and property adjustment, the trial judge made an order that a lump sum of £8,500 should be paid to the wife and dismissed all her other claims. The wife appealed, contending the decision was unjust because, she said, after-acquired assets should not be treated in the same way as money acquired during the marriage. She also claimed that she had a right to share in the family assets which amounted to more than a six per cent share. The judge's order was upheld on appeal,

12 Cf *Wells v Wells* [1992] 2 FLR 66.
13 *Chaudhuri v Chaudhuri* [1992] 2 FLR 73.
14 [1990] 2 FLR 193.

the Court of Appeal ruling that the word 'resources' in section 25(2)(a) was entirely unqualified, and that a court should approach the distribution of assets realistically and take account of all available resources. Adding the assets together and attempting to achieve parity between the parties was, the court said, an acceptable approach.

The outcome in *Schuller v Schuller* was arguably unfair to the wife because, had an order been made at the time of their separation, she could probably have expected to receive about a half share in the property.[15] It is suggested that there were other options which might have been explored which could have given greater recognition to the wife's claim to an entitlement to share in the family assets under paragraphs (d) and (f) of the statutory guidelines (which are concerned with the duration of the marriage, and the contribution made to the welfare of the family). For example, an order in which the husband would be allowed to live in the property for the remainder of his life, with the wife receiving a far greater proportion than six per cent of the proceeds of sale on his death, could have ensured that his needs were met during his lifetime, and at the same time could have given proper recognition to the wife's right to a fair share in the family assets accumulated during the marriage.

Retaining an interest for each spouse in the matrimonial home

The dilemma a court faces in making an order is how can arrangements be made in relation to the matrimonial home which give proper recognition to the rights of both spouses; protect the financially dependent spouse and any children of the family; create a clean break where appropriate; and allow for an adjustment of the position if the circumstances of the parties alter? Clearly these very different objectives nearly always conflict. The usual response to this dilemma is to make an order under which each spouse retains some type of interest in the former matrimonial home. One method is to make a co-ownership order. Another is to transfer the property into the sole name of one spouse but to require the owner spouse to execute a charge over it in favour of the non-owner. In either case one spouse will have a right to live in the property, and the trust for sale, or the realisation of the charge, will be postponed until one or more of various specified contingencies occurs. These two methods will therefore be considered together, and the differing ways of achieving certain objectives under the two orders will be explained.

One of the most difficult questions to be determined in co-ownership and charge cases is when should the trust for sale become operative, or

---

15 Her inheritance could not have been anticipated, and was a windfall after the marriage had come to an end.

when should the person with the charge be entitled to demand that the charge should now be enforceable? In either case this will often mean that the house must be sold, so that the chosen time has very serious implications for the occupying spouse. Equally, the non-occupying spouse has a very real interest in the choice of eventualities in the order which will lead to him being able to realise his interest in the property.

Various eventualities present themselves, these include:
1. the youngest child of the family reaching a specified age, or completing full-time education;
2. the death of the wife;
3. the remarriage of the wife;
4. the wife's cohabitation with another man;
5. the sale of the property.

Usually several of these events are included in the order, which is often made in terms that the property should be sold, or the charge should be enforceable, where one of them occurs, whichever is the earliest.

A *Mesher* order

An order that the trust for sale should be postponed, or the charge should not be redeemable until the youngest child reaches a specified age, is often referred to as a *Mesher* order.[16] The original *Mesher* order involved a settlement of the property on the spouses on trust for sale in equal shares, sale postponed until the youngest child reached 17. But the term a '*Mesher* order' is now used by lawyers to describe any order under which one of the spouses is kept out of his or her share in the former matrimonial home until a specified event relating to the children occurs.[17] Typically the chosen age is 18. Sometimes it has been defined more generously as the date when the youngest child completes full-time education, but sometimes it has been fixed less generously at 17 or even 16.[18]

There are obiter dicta in *Clutton v Clutton*[19] which suggest that a *Mesher* order may be appropriate where the spouses' assets are amply sufficient to house both parties if the home is sold immediately, but when the interests of the children require that they remain in the home for the time being. In such a case, said Lloyd LJ, it may be sensible and just to postpone sale until the children have left home, since the proceeds will be sufficient to enable the wife to rehouse herself. However, he continued, 'but where there

16 *Mesher v Mesher and Hall* [1980] 1 All ER 126n.
17 See, for example, *Carson v Carson* [1983] 1 All ER 478, in which the property was ordered to be held on trust for sale for the spouses jointly until the youngest child attained 18, or completed full-time education.
18 *Hector v Hector* [1973] 3 All ER 1070, which seems an incredibly young age to choose.
19 [1991] 1 All ER 340.

is doubt as to the wife's ability to rehouse herself, on the charge taking effect, then a *Mesher* order should not be made'.[20] This statement highlights the reservations which the courts have expressed about *Mesher* orders in recent years. They have dropped out of favour because they are said to store up problems for the future.[1] When the children reach the specified age it may turn out to be the case that the parent who has been looking after them in the former matrimonial home, usually the wife, does not have enough remaining money after sale of the property, or redemption of the charge, to buy a new property.[2]

Another disadvantage of a *Mesher* order is that children do not stop needing a family home merely because they leave school, complete further education or start work. It is noticeable that in those cases where the children were not expected to go into higher, or further, education the courts have sometimes alighted on 17 as the date for sale.[3] Yet surely such orders are based on inappropriate expectations of independence at such a young age, and they fail to recognise that the crucial date may arise at a time when a child is taking important examinations.[4] If it is thought necessary to specify an age then 21 seems more suitable.[5] This is a higher age than the ages of 17 or 18 which bring to an end the obligation of parents to make periodical payments for their children (unless the child is receiving further education or training).[6] Also, once they reach majority, the children of the family are no longer the court's first consideration under section 25(1). However they can still be characterised as an obligation and responsibility under section 25(2)(b), and it is suggested that the higher age is justifiable because there is arguably a difference between an obligation to maintain a child, and an obligation to continue to provide him with a home. Whilst it may be realistic to expect a child to be able to earn a living once he attains his majority, it is usually not realistic to expect him to earn sufficient income to rent, or buy, adequate accommodation. Furthermore, there are sound social policy reasons for enabling young adults to remain in the family home for some period of time after reaching 18. These include that they will continue to benefit from the influence and guidance of their parents; that they are less likely to become involved in crime or drug abuse when living in a steady environment; that they are more likely to delay marrying, or cohabiting, and having children of their own before they have sufficient resources to make proper provision for

---

20 Ibid, at p 343.
1 *Carson v Carson* [1983] 1 All ER 478.
2 *Hanlon v Hanlon* [1978] 2 All ER 889.
3 As in *Mesher v Mesher and Hall* [1980] 1 All ER 126n itself.
4 Relying, probably, on the fact that a parent will normally not try to force a sale at an inappropriate stage in his child's life. But should the date of sale, which relates so directly to the welfare of the child, be left to the goodwill of the non-residential parent?
5 As in *Alonso v Alonso* (1974) 4 Fam Law 164.
6 S.29(1)(2)(3).

their own family; and that students in higher education need a home to return to in vacations.[7]

Another disadvantage of a *Mesher* order[8] is that it makes the assumption that the children will continue to make their permanent home with the parent to whom the house has been transferred throughout their minority. But this may sometimes come into conflict with reality, and with the philosophy of the Children Act 1989. This philosophy is founded on the premise that after divorce each parent continues to have equal parental responsibility for their children. It also builds on the notion that parents should be encouraged to make their own arrangements about their children, and that court orders should not be made which settle the arrangements as to where the children are to live unless such an order is better for the children.[9] In the case of a charge order, there is no power to retransfer the former matrimonial home should either the children wish, or a court order, that they move from one parent to the other. A co-ownership order containing a provision that one spouse is entitled to remain in the matrimonial home until the children reach a specified age similarly does not provide for this eventuality. Rather, in either case, the spouses are locked into a fixed property arrangement which cannot be departed from unless both agree. Thus the situation could arise in which the wife is entitled to remain in the former matrimonial home, sale of the property, or enforcement of the charge, to be postponed until the children reach a specified age, but in which one, or all, of the children have gone to live with the husband. Thus in *Chaudhuri v Chaudhuri* [10] the husband found himself locked into an arrangement whereby he received only one third of the proceeds of sale of the property even though his wife had remarried, and a child of the family had come to live with him.

How might the problem of the children moving house be anticipated and provision be made for it in advance of it occurring? It is suggested that in the case of co-ownership, because this is a settlement, this allows for considerable flexibility. Thus, for example, it would be possible (although apparently unprecedented) to settle the property so that the right of occupation is vested in whichever parent is providing a home for the children, with liberty to apply for the transfer of the occupation right if that situation alters. It would also be possible to order that the trust for sale should come to an end if one or more of the children moves to live with the non-occupying spouse. In the case of a charge order, it could be made a term of the order that an application can be made to enforce the charge if

7 Contrast the approaches to the continuing need of the children for the family home taken in *Hanlon v Hanlon* [1978] 2 All ER 889 and *Chamberlain v Chamberlain* [1974] 1 All ER 33.
8 Which does not yet appear to have troubled the courts.
9 Children Act 1989, s.1(5); and see further ch 2.
10 [1992] 2 FLR 73.

one or more of the children moves to live with the parent who is not the owner of the former matrimonial home.

In a case where the problem has actually arisen, and the children have already moved to live with the parent who is out of the former matrimonial home, it might be possible to obtain a sale order under section 24A, but this seems very doubtful. In *Thompson v Thompson*[11] spouses remained co-owners of the matrimonial home, and sale of the property had been postponed until the children reached 17 or further order. However, the wife wanted to move. The husband refused to agree to sale because he feared losing contact with his children. The wife therefore applied to the court for a further order compelling the husband to consent to the sale of the property. It was held by the Court of Appeal that provided the order included a 'liberty to apply' provision, the court had jurisdiction to order a sale under section 24A. But it also held that a sale order must be seen as a *working out* of the original order and not a *variation* of it.[12] It held that an early sale at the instance of the party for whose protection the order had been made would give effect to the original order rather than vary it.

However, *Thompson v Thompson* should be contrasted with *Taylor v Taylor*,[13] in which it was held that there is jurisdiction to hear an application for an earlier sale under section 24A, whether or not the original order gives liberty to apply. But, it was held that the court had been wrong to order an earlier sale under section 24A without hearing evidence, or exercising its discretion, on the merits of the case. More significantly, it was further held that the discretion to order an earlier sale will not be exercised if the consequence will be to displace rights which have already vested under the earlier order. It is therefore suggested that for a court to order an earlier sale against the wishes of a wife who has the benefit of a *Mesher* order would amount to a variation of the order, and the displacement of her rights, even though the children had moved to live with the husband. It is therefore suggested that a sale order could not be made where the children move house.

It is probably the case that one of the reasons why *Mesher* orders have fallen into so much disfavour is because the original orders were settlement orders. The courts seemed to proceed on the assumption that in cases of co-ownership, where the original conveyance directed an equal division of the proceeds of sale,[14] that this division should be preserved, so that the only effect of the *Mesher* order was to postpone the sale. Clearly, if the proceeds of sale must be evenly divided between the parties when the property is sold then such an order can quite properly be described as one

11 [1985] 2 All ER 243.
12 S.31 provides that property adjustment orders are final. They cannot therefore be varied at a later date.
13 [1987] 1 FLR 142.
14 Whether as joint tenants or tenants in common.

in which the 'chickens come home to roost',[15] because it does not make adequate provision for the occupying spouse to purchase an alternative home. But the court, when making a *Mesher* order, has the power to redistribute the proceeds of sale in whatever proportions it thinks fit, so as to make adequate provision for the occupying spouse when the time for sale arrives. Where there is an outright transfer to one spouse, with the interest of the other spouse preserved by means of a charge over the property, the charge can be for any amount. It is normal for the charge to be for a proportion of the proceeds of sale of the property, rather than for a fixed sum, because this arrangement has the advantage that it anticipates the effects of both inflation, and reduction, in house values.

Where the non-residential spouse's share is for a relatively small proportion of the total value of the property, its realisation when the children grow up may not cause the owner too much hardship. Even where a wife is forced to sell the property in order to pay the husband his share, she may be able to buy adequate alternative accommodation for herself, and any remaining children living with her, with her own share of the sale proceeds, bearing in mind that she will probably no longer need a property with so many rooms when one or more of the children have left home. It is suggested that the impact of the Child Support Act 1991 on the courts' property adjustment powers, namely that property transfer orders cannot be 'traded' for no, or low, periodical payments orders for children, makes it likely that there will be a revival in the use of *Mesher* orders. It is suggested that it may be that it is the quantification of each spouses' share which should be approached with more caution, rather than whether the independence of the children should be the factor which precipitates sale.

The effect of remarriage or cohabitation

One spouse, usually the wife, may have a particularly pressing need to be accommodated in the former matrimonial home. Sometimes this need is likely to continue for the rest of her life. Because one of the main concerns of the court is to make sure that, wherever possible, each spouse is securely housed, it has sometimes been thought appropriate to order that the wife should be allowed to live in the property for the rest of her life. This means that the husband will never himself obtain his share in the property if he predeceases her. He must draw what comfort he can from the knowledge that his share will at some time enure to the benefit of his estate. However, usually such an order contains the contingencies that the property should be sold, or the charge be realisable, 'if the wife should remarry or cohabit with another man'. This is often described as a *Martin*[16] order.

15 See *Carson v Carson* [1983] 1 All ER 478 at p 482.
16 After *Martin v Martin* [1977] 3 All ER 762.

In *Clutton v Clutton*[17] the Court of Appeal ruled that the trial judge had been wrong to order the transfer of the matrimonial home to the wife free of any charge in favour of the husband. It emphasised that the clean break approach did not mean that the court should disregard other considerations, and deprive one spouse for all time of any share in the matrimonial home. In *Clutton v Clutton* both spouses were aged 48 and were divorcing after a 20-year marriage. Their only asset of substance was the matrimonial home, the equity in which was worth about £50,000. The husband was earning about £20,000 per annum but had substantial debts. The wife had an income of £66 per week working part-time as a typist. She was having a stable sexual relationship with a man, but she said that she did not intend either to marry him, or to cohabit with him. The Court of Appeal considered whether remarriage, or cohabitation, should affect the wife's future position, and found that it should. The essence of the court's judgment was that it would be unfair to the husband if he lost his entire interest in the property through the wife obtaining an outright transfer order, if she was later joined in the house by a new husband, the latter having contributed nothing towards its acquisition. In relation to cohabitation, Lloyd LJ said that, if the reason underlying the clean break principle is the avoidance of bitterness, 'then the bitterness felt by the husband when he sees the former matrimonial home occupied by the wife's cohabitee must surely be greater than the bitterness felt by the wife being subject, as she fears, to perpetual supervision'.[18] The court therefore ordered that the sale of the house should be postponed until the wife died, remarried or cohabited with another man, and that the proceeds should then be divided on the basis of two thirds to the wife and one third to the husband.

Consider the effect of such an order, namely that the charge should be enforceable by the husband, or that the property should be sold, in the event of the wife's remarriage, and measure it against the principle that it is normally fair that each spouse is entitled to a share in the value of the former matrimonial home. Look at it first from the point of view of the husband. His position was succinctly expressed by Ormrod LJ in *Leate v Leate*[19] when he recognised that it is 'very galling' for a husband if the family assets are handed over to the wife who then remarries. It could strongly be asserted on behalf of the husband that remarriage is a new relationship which should not be subsidised in any way by an ex-husband. He could argue that a wife who has remarried has all the protection of the legal code which surrounds that new marriage, and that her ex-husband's obligation to provide her with housing should now be brought to an end. Indeed, on behalf of the husband it could be asserted that, if remarriage is not a contingency which should precipitate him acquiring his share in the

17 [1991] 1 All ER 340.
18 Ibid, at p 345.
19 (1982) 12 Fam Law 121.

property, it is hard to think of what other change of circumstance should bring this about.

But now consider such a clause from the point of view of the wife. It could be asserted that it may act as a serious restraint on her remarrying, or on her being able to do so only at the cost of losing her home and, where there are children, the children's home too. Such a clause is based on the assumption that her new husband will either be able to provide her with accommodation, or that he will be able to buy out the husband's share in the former matrimonial home. But this may prove to be incorrect. It could also be pointed out that, where the wife is in receipt of periodical payments, her entitlement to these comes to an end on remarriage.[20] Thus remarriage, for her, will mean that not only will she lose her source of income, she may also lose the roof over her head and, when there are children, over their heads too. Yet, the wife is not at risk of losing her home (and may continue to receive periodical payments) provided that she does not remarry. It could be maintained on behalf of the wife that the insertion of the contingency of remarriage is liable to perpetuate the wife's tie to her ex-husband; it is liable to dissuade her from making a fresh start; and that it is a restraint on marriage which is arguably contrary to public policy.[1]

In *Clutton v Clutton* the Court of Appeal not only made remarriage a reason for the property being sold, it also said that the wife's 'cohabitation with another man' should have the same effect. In *Chadwick v Chadwick*[2] the Court of Appeal specifically endorsed the inclusion of such a cohabitation clause. Here, after divorce, the trial court had ordered that the former matrimonial home be held in joint names on trust for sale, with the wife to have sole occupation of the property unless she decided to move, or to remarry, or to cohabit with another man. On the occurrence of any of these events the house was to be sold and the proceeds divided equally between her and her former husband. The wife, who was severely disabled, appealed on two grounds: (i) that she might wish to move in order to live nearer the hospital where she had regular medical appointments; and (ii) that any new spouse or partner might not have enough resources to be able to assist her with the purchase of the specially adapted accommodation which she needed. She argued that, in either situation, her share in the proceeds of sale might not be sufficient to enable her to buy a new home, and therefore that the order put her at risk of being rendered homeless. The husband's position was that he had no other major resources, and he was purchasing a new property with the assistance of a one hundred per cent mortgage.

20 S.28(1)(a).
1   Is there even a faint chance that it could be found to be contrary to Art.8 of the European Convention of Human Rights, namely that 'everyone has a right to respect for his private and family life'?
2   [1985] FLR 606; see too *Simpson v Simpson* [1984] CA Transcript 119; *Hendrix v Hendrix* [1981] CA Transcript 57.

Approving and upholding the trial judge's order, Cumming Bruce LJ stated that in order to do justice to the husband it was necessary to impose some 'real inconvenience' on the former wife, which here meant that if she remarried or cohabited the house must be sold. He continued:

'That imposes on her the necessity, if she decides either to marry another gentleman or to cohabit with another gentleman, to select as her consort a gentleman who is in a position to provide her with accommodation suitable to her needs. [If] she does decide to marry or to cohabit with a gentleman who cannot provide her with such accommodation, that must be regarded as a grave misfortune which she will bring upon herself. Although material considerations are sometimes not the main considerations that lead spouses to the altar, they are not irrelevant.'[3]

It is suggested that the practice of equating cohabitation with remarriage may give rise to problems. Firstly, it will not always be clear whether or not the wife is cohabiting. For example, is she cohabiting when a long-distance lorry driver spends part of the week with his parents and the other part with her? Was Mr Jones, the co-respondent in *Suter v Suter and Jones*,[4] who slept each night with the wife but had his breakfast at his mother's house, cohabiting? It may also not be clear for how long the cohabiting relationship must last before it can precipitate sale of the property. Sometimes a time provision is included in the order such as 'the property to be sold if the wife should cohabit with another man for a period exceeding six months'. But even this may be uncertain in its application. For example, what would be the position if the cohabitation continued for more than six months, but then came to an end. Would the husband nonetheless be entitled to demand that the property now be sold in accordance with the court's order? This could place the wife, and any children living with her, in a very vulnerable position, for now she could turn to neither man for a roof over her head.

It appears both anomalous, and contradictory, that the courts have equated cohabitation with remarriage for the purposes of precipitating sale of the matrimonial home, but not for the purposes of terminating periodical payments in an application brought in variation proceedings. In *Atkinson v Atkinson*[5] the Court of Appeal was emphatic that it is for Parliament, not the courts, to determine whether the fact of cohabitation should automatically bring to an end the right of a wife to receive periodical payments, and it refused either to extinguish, or even substantially to

3   Ibid, at p 608.
4   [1987] 2 All ER 336.
5   [1987] 3 All ER 849.

reduce, the cohabiting wife's order, despite evidence that the wife had deliberately refrained from marrying because remarriage would lead to the termination of her periodical payments. Courts also appear to have lost sight of the principle expounded in *Duxbury v Duxbury*[6] that, after divorce, a wife should be free to live as she chooses and to spend money on, or provide a home for, whomsoever she wishes. In *Clutton v Clutton*[7] the wife argued that a cohabitation clause would encourage constant surveillance of her private life by her husband. This fear was dismissed by the court, but it seems likely that steps to obtain evidence to confirm his suspicions will sometimes be taken by a husband who suspects that his wife is cohabiting when this is denied. This type of 'snooping' is at best distasteful and, at worst, may amount to an invasion of her privacy.

It is suggested that it is most unfortunate that courts have advocated the making of orders in which cohabitation is a factor which automatically precipitates sale of the home, or the right to realise the charge. Cohabitation does not give a wife the same security as remarriage. She has no right to live in any new property purchased solely by her cohabitant. If her cohabiting relationship comes to an end, she has no claims against her new partner for financial provision and property adjustment orders. Should her cohabitant die, she has no automatic succession rights and no pension rights. Thus there are no safeguards, let alone guarantees, that a cohabiting relationship will make provision for a wife's future needs, which was the fear of the wife in *Chadwick v Chadwick*.[8] It is suggested that it would be more acceptable, and less gender-biased,[9] if orders were made in such a manner as to allow the courts to respond in the most appropriate manner to the eventualities of the wife's remarriage, or cohabitation, if and when they occur. This could be achieved by giving the husband 'liberty to apply' to the court for an order that jointly-owned property should now be sold, or that he should be entitled to realise his charge, if the wife should remarry, or cohabit with another man. This allows the court to deal with the issue, on its merits, at the time when it happens. In some cases it will be appropriate to order immediate sale. In others the needs of the wife compared to those of the husband may be such as to persuade the court that to order sale, or the realisation of the charge, would cause her too much hardship. It should be recalled that unless the wife remarries, or cohabits, the husband will, in any event, be deprived of his share of the property. So that to make these eventualities automatic factors precipitat-

6   [1987] 1 FLR 7.

7   [1991] 1 All ER 340.

8   [1985] FLR 606. See further M Hayes *Cohabitation Clauses in Financial Provision and Property Adjustment Orders: Law, Policy and Justice* (1994) 110 LQR 124.

9   It is suggested that it is most unlikely that a court would order that a husband who remains in occupation of the matrimonial home under a *Martin* or *Mesher* order should be forced to sell the home if he should remarry, or cohabit, with another woman. The assumption is more likely to be made that such a union will add to the husband's responsibilities, rather than provide him with additional resources.

ing sale is arguably to put a strong, and unacceptable, restraint on the wife forming an intimate relationship with a new partner.

Overcoming the 'moving house' problem

In cases of co-ownership, the courts seem invariably to have ordered that the parties' respective interests in the fund must be distributed on sale of the matrimonial home; and where making charge orders almost invariably to have provided that the charge is realisable when the property is sold. However, this contingency may cause particular hardship to the wife who wishes to move house. Whether there has been a limited term order, as in the case of a *Mesher* order, or a *Martin* order giving the wife a right to live in the house for life, the security afforded by that order disappears if the property is sold at an earlier date, and the proceeds of sale are divided. The wife may wish to move for various reasons such as to take up an offer of employment, to be closer to the children's schools, to care for elderly parents, or to be near to a hospital.[10] Yet the effect of the order may prevent her from moving.

How might the moving-house problem be overcome? In co-ownership cases the property is already vested in trustees (usually the husband and wife) on trust for sale. It is suggested that any order or agreement should impose a specific duty on the husband and wife to reinvest the proceeds of sale in a new property, where the wife makes such a request. But in order to be fair to the husband, the order or agreement could include a provision allowing him liberty to apply for the proceeds to be divided when the sale occurs. This would enable the court to consider the respective merits of the spouses' positions at that time. In cases where there is a charge, provision could be made that the charge should not be realisable on sale of the property, provided that the proceeds of sale are reinvested in new property which is similarly intended to provide a home for the wife, and any dependent children who are living with her, the charge to be attached to the new property. Again, in order to be fair to the husband, liberty to apply for realisation of the charge when the property is sold could be given.

Does it seem likely that courts would be willing to accept such a flexible approach? There is no reason in principle why they should not. The answer probably would depend on how they perceive the way in which it would affect the balance of interests between the husband and wife.[11] On the one

10 Cf *Chadwick v Chadwick* [1985] FLR 606.
11 For an unusual example see *Greenham v Greenham* [1989] 1 FLR 105, in which the Court of Appeal deleted a provision requiring a husband who was occupying the former matrimonial home to pay his wife 20 per cent of its value when he reached his 70th birthday. The court said that although he would have sufficient capital and income to do so, it would still involve him in having to move house at an age when he might not wish to do so.

hand, if the main focus of the original order was to make provision for the wife's needs, then an order which would ensure that those needs will continue to be provided for, should she wish to move house, might well be considered desirable. It could usefully be pointed out that one reason for the wife's desire to move might be because she has employment opportunities elsewhere and that, were she to obtain employment, this could bring about a clean break from any periodical payments requirements imposed on the husband. Thus both parties would gain from such an arrangement. On the other hand, if the court's focus has been on the preservation of the absent spouse's share in that particular piece of property, then it would be likely to be reluctant to allow for such a scheme. In *Chadwick v Chadwick*,[12] which appears to be the only reported case which directly deals with this matter, the Court of Appeal was entirely unsympathetic to the wife's position.

Are more open-ended orders preferable?

It has been suggested above that the insertion in orders of specific contingencies which will give rise to the enforcement of the trust for sale, or the entitlement to demand that the property subject to the charge should now be sold, have the potential to cause hardship for the occupying spouse. This potential may dissuade a court from making an order containing a specific contingency, as in the case of *Mesher* orders, which have fallen out of favour for this reason. Yet a refusal to contemplate a *Mesher* order may cause equal hardship for the non-occupying spouse if the other option is a *Martin* order. Such an order often means that the husband never realises his share in the property during his lifetime. An alternative approach is for courts to make more open-ended orders. Sometimes they have done this by inserting a contingency in an order, but also including a clause which gives either spouse 'liberty to apply to the court for an earlier sale of the property, or earlier realisation of the charge'. An even more open-ended order is one in which sale is postponed until 'the parties consent to the sale or until further order of the court, with liberty to apply'.

The disadvantage of a more open-ended type of order is that it is vague and leaves the parties in a state of uncertainty. It is difficult for either of them to make plans if they do not know what events might precipitate sale. Also, when they cannot agree that the appropriate time for sale has now been reached, they may then become embroiled in further litigation, which is costly. However, an open-ended order has the advantage that the merits of ordering a sale can be reviewed at the time of the application. Thus where, for example, the youngest child has not yet reached 18, but

12 [1985] FLR 606.

where the husband has a particularly pressing need to realise his share in the property, this would allow the husband to take the matter back to court. Where the wife is in fact in the position to be able to accommodate herself from her share in the property, or able to buy the husband out, the court could take account of this when reaching its decision. Equally, if the youngest child has reached 18, but where both the wife and the 'child' have pressing needs to remain in the property, and where the husband is adequately accommodated elsewhere, this too could be borne in mind by the court when determining whether sale should be ordered. It has been argued that an order which states that the property must be sold where the wife cohabits with another man may be unduly restrictive. But a more open-ended order, which would give the husband liberty to apply in the event of his wife's cohabitation would be fair to him, but would also allow the wife to form a relationship with a man of limited means, without the fear of automatically losing the roof over her head.

Normally, the proportion each spouse will receive in the proceeds of sale of the property is fixed at the time when the order is made. However this is not imperative, and in *Sakkas v Sakkas*[13] Wood J ordered that the property be held on trust for sale, sale to be postponed until the younger child attained the age of 20. He further ordered that before the house was sold the matter should be brought back before the court for directions to be given as to the proportions in which the proceeds were to be divided. Again there is uncertainty, and the potential for further litigation is actually built into the court's order; however such an order has the advantage of flexibility and gives the opportunity to achieve fairness when the date for sale arrives.

Choosing between co-ownership or a charge

It has been seen that there is a choice to be made where each spouse retains an interest in the former matrimonial home. Should they be co-owners, or should the property be transferred into the sole name of one party and the interest of the other be protected by giving him a charge over the property?

Co-ownership

There are various considerations which might usefully be borne in mind when making this choice. In many cases co-ownership will be the starting position because it has become increasingly common for the matrimonial home to be conveyed into the spouses' joint names, usually as joint tenants.

13 (1987) 17 Fam Law 414.

When determining what should happen to the matrimonial home it may be the easiest solution simply to maintain the joint tenancy. This has two significant consequences: first, on the death of one joint tenant the whole beneficial interest enures to the benefit of the survivor; and secondly, the property is held on trust for sale and each spouse's share in the proceeds of sale is fixed at 50 per cent. Therefore, when a marriage breaks down, one of the first matters to consider when the property is held on a joint tenancy is whether it should be severed. Succession rights through operation of the doctrine of survivorship may represent what the parties wish, especially where the home is being used for the children, or where each spouse agrees that, in the event of death, the surviving parent should own the house. However, where there is no such joint intention, a spouse who fails to sever the joint tenancy and then dies is likely to have his or her testamentary wishes defeated by operation of the right of survivorship.

It is suggested that a conscious decision should always be made about whether to sever the joint tenancy at an early stage in divorce proceedings. If the divorce proceedings are concluded before the death, presumably questions of severance will be dealt with by the court under section 24. The danger lies if either party dies before the conclusion of the divorce proceedings. Here, in the absence of severance, the survivor takes all. For example, in *McDowell v Hirschfield Lipson & Rumney and Smith*[14] the husband and wife were joint tenants of the matrimonial home. The husband had petitioned for divorce after living apart from his wife for more than five years. He had been living with another woman, the plaintiff, and she had borne him two children. The husband had died while the divorce proceedings were pending, and there had been no express severance of the joint tenancy. The court held that, for severance to be implied, there must be shown a course of dealing in which both parties clearly evince an intention that the property should henceforth be held in common and not jointly, and this the plaintiff had failed to establish. The husband's interest therefore passed to the wife. The other danger in simply allowing a joint tenancy to continue is that such an arrangement is dependent on trust and co-operation between ex-spouses in circumstances which cannot be foreseen. There is always the risk that one of the spouses might sever the joint tenancy at some future date, and devise his or her share to a third party, without the other spouse being aware of the implications of severance for succession purposes.

Another problem associated with preserving the joint tenancy is that if the property is sold during the lifetime of the spouses the proceeds of sale must be equally distributed between them. This may mean that one of the parties has insufficient resources with which to purchase a new property. It may therefore be more appropriate to retain co-ownership, but for the

14 [1992] 2 FLR 126; see too *Harris v Goddard* [1983] 3 All ER 242.

parties, or the court, to convert the joint tenancy into a tenancy in common and to alter the proportionate share of each spouse's beneficial interest in the property, after taking account of the different factors in section 25.

Where it is agreed that the spouses are already co-owners in equity, but where the legal title is in the name of one spouse alone, say the husband, it is important to ensure that the name of the wife is added to the legal title so that she is equally in control of the property for the future. Otherwise the wife's position as against a purchaser could be put at risk. There is some danger that her beneficial interest could be defeated by sale of the property without her knowledge, or she might find that the property has been used as security for a loan without her consent.[15] Of course, where each spouse's name is on the legal title, then each must be involved in any future transactions concerning the property. The advantages and disadvantages of such an arrangement need to be considered when deciding whether co-ownership or a charge is the better way of maintaining an interest in the property for both spouses. Where the spouses are hostile to one another, or where there is likely to be disagreement over sale, or other transactions, concerning the property, then any arrangement which depends on the parties' future co-operation is to be avoided. However, such lack of co-operation may be able to be overcome where the obduracy of one co-owner threatens to defeat the court's original order. In *Harvey v Harvey*[16] the husband flatly refused to join with the wife in applying for a second mortgage and improvement grant to effect repairs to the property. The court ordered the appointment of a receiver of the husband's interest in the property, who would be invited to act on the husband's behalf on the applications which the wife wished to make.

The advantage of co-ownership over a charge order is that it allows for more flexibility, because it is possible to create the settlement in such a way that it can be responsive to changes in circumstances. This could be particularly valuable where there are dependent children of the family, and when any order must reflect the needs of the parent caring for the children to provide them with a home. The Children Act 1989 places considerable emphasis on the continuing parental responsibility of each parent after divorce, and where both parents maintain involvement with their children there may be a real possibility that the children may wish to move from one parent to the other during the course of their upbringing. It would be unfortunate, and not in the interests of the children which section 25(1) requires should be given first consideration, if such a move was impossible because of inflexible arrangements about the use of the matrimonial home during their minority. Where it seems likely that the

---

15 The wife's position depends on points discussed earlier in relation to the doctrine of notice.
16 [1987] 1 FLR 67.

parties will agree, or a court may wish to order, a change of residence for a child, then continuing co-ownership of the property may best provide for this eventuality. It would be possible to settle the property so that the right of occupation is vested in whichever parent is providing a home for the children, with liberty to apply for the transfer of the occupation right if that situation alters. This would allow for the situation where the children move from one parent to the other after the financial and property arrangements have been completed.

A charge

It seems that the most liked method of preserving the absent spouse's interest is by means of a charge. The legal estate and entire beneficial interest in the matrimonial home is vested in the sole name of one spouse, but the owner spouse is required to execute a charge over it in favour of the other spouse to secure to him the payment of a sum of money. It is particularly popular where the property is mortgaged. Many mortgagees, that is the banks and building societies, will release a husband from his personal covenants under the mortgage on the wife giving an undertaking to take full responsibility for these, and vice versa. If the husband should then wish to obtain a fresh mortgage to purchase a new home, he will be in a better position to do so because he has no liabilities. Indeed, he may even be able to claim that he is particularly creditworthy because he has a charge on property, which he will be able to enforce at some time in the future. Thus a charge order is usually advantageous for the husband.

The advantage of a charge order from the wife's point of view is that she now has full control over the property, and can deal with it without consulting the husband. This is in contrast to her position where there is co-ownership. She is also entitled to redeem the charge at any time, thereby ending the husband's claim over the property.[17] However, the wife could well find herself in the position of owning property subject to two, and possibly three, charges, namely the original mortgage, the husband's charge and, in cases when she has been legally aided, the charge in favour of the Legal Aid Fund. Consequently she would be unlikely to be able to raise any further loan for such things as improvements and repairs using the home as security. By contrast, where there is co-ownership and just one charge by way of a mortgage, or two where she has been legally aided, the wife may more easily be able to use the home as security for a loan. However she will need the husband's agreement where he is the co-trustee, which is likely to be the case, and this can cause problems.[18]

17 *Popat v Popat* [1991] 2 FLR 163.
18 See the particular difficulties which arose in *Harvey v Harvey* [1987] 1 FLR 67.

Negotiating and mediating a fair settlement

It is suggested that negotiation over financial and property provision should concentrate on what would be the most fair and reasonable arrangement for both parties, bearing in mind that the Act provides that the welfare of the children must come first, and that the appropriateness of a clean break arrangement should always be considered. It does neither of the parties a service to raise false expectations about how much property and income he or she can expect to retain or receive. Where unrealistic expectations have been raised, these can prove to be a real impediment to obtaining a reasonable negotiated settlement. Yet if the parties are forced to litigate, the legal costs will often outweigh any advantage accruing to a spouse who obtains a more beneficial order than the one which could be agreed upon. It can be seen from the above analysis of the courts' powers, and the various ways in which the courts have chosen to exercise them, that there are no easy and obvious answers as to how agreements and orders for financial provision and property adjustment should be determined. In recent years, a process known as 'mediation' has been used by some parties, whereby a mediator, who may be a lawyer, helps to mediate a settlement between them. Each party is then advised to check the arrangements agreed with his or her own independent lawyer. This process can work very well when spouses are willing to try to sort out their affairs in a non-adversarial manner. Mediation also has the advantage which attaches to any genuinely agreed settlement, namely that each of the parties takes responsibility for the decision which is finally reached, and resentment and bitterness may consequently be minimised. Mediation, of course, will not work for all people, but in appropriate cases it can be another useful tool in assisting couples to reach agreement over their property and finances.[19]

---

19 Mediation is a major element in Government's proposals for reforming the law of divorce. See further ch 6.

Chapter 8

Child support, and homes for unmarried partners and children

Chapter 8

Child support, and homes for unmarried partners and children

Child support—equal treatment for children

When a marriage breaks down, and where there are dependent children of the family, the parent who is looking after the children will normally expect his or her ex-spouse to contribute towards the children's maintenance until they complete their education. Such a parent may also wish to obtain lump sum and property adjustment orders for the benefit of the children. Similarly, when an unmarried couple with children separate, the children need to be provided with a home and to be maintained, and the parent with care may wish to look to his or her ex-partner to make some financial and property provision for them. Sometimes a child is the product of a more casual intimate relationship between his or her mother and father; indeed, in some cases the mother may be uncertain who the father is, or the father may not know that he is a father. But of course a child of a casual union has just as much need of financial support and shelter as does a child born into a more conventional family unit containing two parents. It will be seen that all such children are treated in an equal manner under the Child Support Act 1991. Provided that appropriate steps are taken by a parent, or other person with care of the child, to obtain child support maintenance, the law will oblige the child's 'absent parent'[1] to make regular payments for the benefit of his or her own child. These payments will be quantified applying the same principles and the same criteria irrespective of the circumstances surrounding the child's birth.

In relation to requiring parents to make more substantial provision for the benefit of children, it will be seen later in this chapter that a court may make orders which require a parent to settle property for the benefit of a child, to make a lump sum payment for the benefit of the child, and to transfer property for the benefit of the child under the Children Act 1989,

---

1   See below for discussion of the meaning of this term.

irrespective of whether the parents are married or unmarried.[2] However, children of married parents, and children who have been treated as children of the family by a parent and step-parent, have the additional advantage that they are likely to benefit from orders made in favour of spouses.

The Child Support Agency

Although, on their face, various statutes appear to give powers to courts to order parents to make periodical payments for the benefit of their children, these statutes are misleading.[3] They must be read in conjunction with the Child Support Act 1991 which has drastically curtailed the scope of the courts' powers. Since 1993 new claims for child maintenance have been handled outside the court system by an administrative agency called the Child Support Agency, which was established by the Child Support Act 1991. The Child Support Agency is a part of the Department of Social Security. Its responsibility for all child support maintenance cases is being phased in gradually, and it will not become fully operational until April 1997. Its role is to make a maintenance assessment and to collect and enforce maintenance payments for children. It is staffed by child support officers who must apply rules rather than exercise discretion when making decisions, and a formula is used to calculate how much child maintenance is payable. Court orders for periodical payments for children can no longer be made except in a residue of cases.[4]

Terms used in the Child Support Act 1991

A child for whom child maintenance is payable under the Child Support Act 1991 is called a 'qualifying child' and the Act uses specific language to describe the relationship between a 'qualifying child' and his parents, or between the child and the person who is looking after him.

Section 3 provides —

'(1) A child is a "qualifying child" if—
(a) one of his parents is, in relation to him, an absent parent; or

2   S.15 and Sch.1. Orders can also be made that property is transferred, and a lump sum payment made, directly to the child.
3   Matrimonial Causes Act 1973, s.23; Domestic Proceedings and Magistrates' Courts Act 1978, s.2; Children Act 1989, s.15 and Sch.1.
4   S.8(3) of the Child Support Act 1991 provides that a court shall not exercise any power which it would otherwise have to make, vary or revive orders for child maintenance in any case where a child support officer would have jurisdiction to make a maintenance assessment.

(b) both of his parents are, in relation to him, absent parents.

(2) The parent of any child is an "absent parent", in relation to him, if—

(a) that parent is not living in the same household with the child; and

(b) the child has his home with a person who is, in relation to him, a person with care.

(3) A person is a "person with care", in relation to any child, if he is a person—

(a) with whom the child has his home;

(b) who usually provides day to day care for the child (whether exclusively or in conjunction with any other person); and

(c) who does not fall within a prescribed category of person.'

Language used in legislation designed to deal with family situations may have symbolic and emotional significance for the persons concerned and therefore the selection of words in such legislation is important. It is suggested that the choice of language in the Child Support Act 1991 is unfortunate because it is insensitive to the feelings of so-called 'absent parents'. Many parents who are so described find the term offensive. They claim that the term could be understood to carry with it the connotation that the 'absent parent' has in some sense abandoned his child, is feckless in his dealings with the child, or is otherwise failing to show the child any love, care, affection or interest. It is suggested that it would have been preferable if the Child Support Act 1991 had been drafted in a manner which emphasised the continuing responsibility of both parents for the financial support of their child without using language which is arguably pejorative of one of them.

Assessment of maintenance by the Child Support Agency

Applications for child maintenance are made on a maintenance application form by the parent or other person with care. The applicant must provide a substantial amount of information including detailed information about her personal circumstances and those of her partner; the circumstances of any children under 19 who are living with her; the circumstances of the absent parent; her income from all sources; and her housing arrangements. Once a properly completed maintenance application form has been received by the Child Support Agency the absent parent will be sent a maintenance enquiry form. The absent parent too must provide the Agency with a substantial amount of information, including detailed information about his personal circumstances and whether he accepts that he is the parent of the child or children named;[5] the circumstances of any children under 19 who are living with him; his own income and that of his partner from all sources; and his housing arrangements. He must complete and return the maintenance enquiry form to the Child Support Agency within 14 days. Should he fail to do so the Agency is entitled to make an interim maintenance assessment. Since such an assessment is usually higher than the amount of child maintenance the absent parent would be required to pay if it was calculated under the formula, he has a strong incentive to reply swiftly.

All of this data is used to calculate, with the use of the formula, how much child support maintenance should be paid.

Calculations made under the formula progress through five stages:

1. the maintenance requirement;
2. the exempt income calculation;
3. the assessable income calculation;
4. the maintenance assessment calculation; and
5. the protected income calculation.

There are various rules which relate to the calculation of the formula at each of these five stages, and identifying the relevant information which is needed at any stage can be extremely complicated. Detailed provisions, which influence the calculation of the formula, are contained in several sets of Regulations. Only a rough calculation can be made of how much each parent will be required to contribute to the support of his or her child unless full account is taken of these provisions, which are very complex. Basic guidance only is given below on how each stage of the formula is calculated.[6]

The maintenance requirement

The maintenance requirement is the minimum amount considered necessary for the maintenance of a child or, where there is more than one qualifying child, all of them. The calculation is based on income support rates, and the following must be added together:

*   the personal allowance for each child;[7]

---

5   A parent cannot delay the payment of child maintenance by falsely denying parentage. His liability to pay will be back-dated to the effective date of the maintenance assessment, and arrears will simply accrue.

6   For a detailed consideration of the operation of the Act, and worked examples, see R Bird *Child Maintenance, The Child Support Act 1991* (Family Law, 1993); A Garnham and E Knights *Child Support Handbook* (Child Poverty Action Group, 1993-4). However, it should be noted that there have been amendments to the level of allowances under the formula since these books were published. A computer program has the advantage that it can be updated when benefit rates alter, or if other changes to the formula are made, see *Child's Pay*, Family Law Bar Association (1994).

7   This varies according to the child's age.

- the personal allowance for an adult aged 25 or over;[8]
- the family premium;
- the lone parent premium where the parent with care has no partner.

From this must be deducted:

- child benefit for all children.

The total is the basic maintenance requirement for the child or children. Once that basic requirement has been met a parent will be required to pay an additional amount towards the support of his child where he has sufficient income to do so.

The following four steps are about how each parent's contribution to the maintenance requirement is calculated.

The exempt income calculation

'Exempt income' means the amount of income a parent is entitled to keep before being required to pay child maintenance. The Child Support Act 1991 recognises that the first call on a parent's income is to make provision for his own needs and for the needs of any of his own children who are living with him, and allowance is made for this. However, the formula is strictly rule-based and allows no scope for the exercise of discretion except in a few clearly defined circumstances. It makes no allowance for individual financial pressures on an absent parent, unless these financial pressures fall within the scope of the data used to calculate the application of the formula. An absent parent may be deeply in debt, give financial assistance to elderly parents, be supporting a wife or partner, be supporting step-children, incur substantial travel costs when visiting his child, or otherwise have financial liabilities which are an especially heavy drain on his resources. None of these matters are relevant to the calculation of his exempt income because they fall outside the scope of the allowances made in the relevant part of the formula.

A parent's exempt income is calculated by adding together:

- the personal allowance for an adult aged 25 or over;
- the personal allowance for any of his own children who are living with him;
- the family premium where there are such children living with him;
- the lone parent premium where there are such children and the parent has no partner; and
- the housing costs of the parent and any of his own children living with him.

Additional allowances are given where the parent, or any of his own children, are disabled, or where the parent would qualify for the income support carer premium.

---

8   This is irrespective of the age of the parent with care.

Although an absent parent's exempt income includes an allowance for any child of his own whom he is supporting, this provision may not be as generous as it seems. Where the absent parent has a child by a new partner, that person's liability to support their child is taken into account when the absent parent's exempt income is calculated. Where the new partner can be expected to contribute to the support of their child the allowances made in relation to the child are divided between them, and the absent parent's exempt income is reduced proportionately.

Assessable income

A parent's assessable income is the income available for child maintenance. It is calculated by taking the parent's net income and subtracting his exempt income; the remainder is his assessable income. A parent's net income is almost invariably less than his gross income because certain sums can first be deducted.[9] Each parent is liable to maintain his or her children who are living with the parent with care and therefore the assessable income of each parent must be calculated; but of course only the absent parent actually makes a payment of child maintenance.

The maintenance assessment

The maintenance assessment is calculated by adding together the assessable income of each parent and dividing the total by two; the final figure is the sum available for the support of the child. (Where the parent with care has no assessable income, such as when she is living on income support, only the assessable income of the absent parent is divided by two.) The maintenance assessment is then compared with the maintenance requirement. Where it is less than, or equal to, the maintenance requirement, the absent parent is required to pay 50 per cent of his assessable income.[10] Where the maintenance assessment is more than the maintenance requirement, the formula allows for an additional amount of maintenance to be payable. The parent then has two assessable incomes, in effect, out of which he must make a contribution. Basic assessable income, which will be paid on a 50 per cent basis and which will be put towards the maintenance requirement, and additional assessable income. The additional assessable income is the balance left over after the parent has met his share of the maintenance requirement. He is then required to contribute

9   The calculation of a parent's net income is governed by regulations which specify which income must be included and which can be excluded.
10 Subject to his protected income.

on a 25 per cent basis out of this extra income until a maximum figure is reached; this ceiling is calculated with reference to income support rates.[11] Thus where one or both parents have high incomes the child benefits accordingly because his maintenance is assessed with regard to that income.

Protected income

It has been seen already that no allowance is made for the cost of maintaining a new spouse or partner and any step-children living in the absent parent's household when the absent parent's assessable income is calculated. In some cases this could mean that a 50 per cent deduction from the absent parent's assessable income could push his remaining income for the support of his present household to below subsistence level. Therefore, before finalising how much an absent parent must pay, it is necessary to establish his protected income level.

The protected income calculation is made with reference to income support rates; the following amounts are added together:

- the personal allowance for an adult aged 25 or over; or
- the personal allowance for a couple;
- the allowance for each child;
- any premiums which would be paid if income support was claimed;
- reasonable housing costs for the family;
- council tax liability;
- a fixed margin above income support rates;[12]
- a further margin of a percentage of the family's income above the income support level.[13]

An absent parent's protected income is calculated by adding together all income coming into his current family, including the income of a partner and any children living in the household. If the maintenance contribution which the absent parent is required to make reduces his remaining disposable income to below the level of his protected income, his contribution will be reduced by the difference between the two amounts.

Who *must* use the Child Support Agency?

When marriages and unmarried relationships break down and the parent with care of the children has no source of income, or where her income is

---

11 Currently the income support personal allowance for each child plus the amount equal to the family premium multiplied by three.

12 Raised in 1994 from £8 to £30.

13 Raised in 1994 from 10 per cent to 15 per cent.

insufficient for the family's requirements, she will usually turn to the state for assistance, and she will normally be eligible for some form of welfare benefits. Clearly the cost of maintaining single parents and their children imposes a heavy burden on state funds, and one of the main factors which motivated the establishment of the Child Support Agency was to save public expenditure on welfare benefits. It was asserted by the government that if parents have the means to maintain their own children, the cost of such maintenance should not fall on the taxpayer.[14] Normally only the state will benefit financially from the pursuit of an absent parent for maintenance when the parent with care and her children are supported by benefits. The children will gain financially only if the amount which the absent parent is required to pay in child support maintenance exceeds the amount in benefits which is being paid to the parent with care. The Act therefore imposes a degree of compulsion on the parent with care to co-operate with the Agency because otherwise she has little motivation to do so; indeed she may have strong reasons for wishing to have no further involvement with the absent parent. Section 6(1) states that a parent with care of a child who is in receipt of income support, family credit or disability working allowance *shall* authorise the Child Support Agency to take action to recover child support from the absent parent if required to do so by the Agency. Where she refuses to do so, and where she refuses to provide information required by the Agency under section 6(9) to enable the absent parent to be traced and a maintenance assessment to be made, she is at risk of a direction being made under section 46 that her benefits be reduced.

These are Draconian provisions. They present the parent with care with a stark choice: either co-operate with the Agency or suffer a reduction in benefits as a penalty for non-compliance. As any reduction in an already very low income is likely to cause the parent with care and her children very real financial hardship, the threat of such a reduction is likely to persuade her to comply with the Agency's demands. However, the Act recognises that there are some situations in which the parent with care will have good cause to refuse to authorise the Agency to take action to recover child support maintenance from the absent parent, and good cause to refuse to identify the father. Section 6(2) provides that the parent with care who is supported by state benefits shall not be required to authorise the Agency to recover child support maintenance where she can persuade a child support officer that there are reasonable grounds for believing that—

'(a) if the parent were to be required to give that authorisation; or
(b) if she were to give it,
there would be a risk of her, or of any child living with her, suffering harm or undue distress as a result.'

14 See the White Paper which preceded the Act, *Children Come First* Cm 1264, vol 1, para 2.1.

Similarly, where a child support officer is considering whether to impose a benefit reduction for failure to comply with section 6(1) or (9), section 46(3) provides that these same matters must be considered.

No guidance is given in the Act on the meaning of 'harm or undue distress' and sections 6(2) and 43(6) are rare examples of provisions in the Act which allow scope for the exercise of discretion. However, statements of policy have been issued to child support officers on how that discretion should be exercised; in particular, guidance has been given on those matters which are not considered distressing enough to count as a reason for non co-operation.[15] During the passage of the Bill through the House of Lords, Lord Henley expressed the view that '... if on the evidence before us we are satisfied that there has been a history of violence in a case or a parent has a well-founded fear that seeking maintenance will put her or the child at risk of violence that will amount to good cause.'[16] There is evidence to suggest that it is such an approach which has been adopted. It seems that it is only the risk of real physical harm which can exempt a parent with care from her obligation to authorise the Agency to take action.[17] However, there is also evidence to suggest that there is a lack of consistency in practice on how cases of this kind are approached, with some child support officers requiring very strong reasons, accompanied by proof, before they are satisfied that harm or distress is likely to be suffered, and others being willing simply to accept the word of the parent with care.[18]

The following are examples of situations which would almost certainly not amount to sufficient cause for the purposes of establishing harm or undue distress: a fear that if the absent parent were to be required to support the child he might also demand to have contact with the child although he has not had contact for many years; a fear that a positive relationship between the child and the absent parent would be jeopardised if the Agency were to require the absent parent to maintain the child, or to increase the amount that he has been paying voluntarily; a wish not to reveal the name of the father because he is a married man and such a revelation would be likely to cause the breakdown of his marriage; a fear that the parent with care's current family relationships would be disrupted. These are very real fears and concerns, and a substantial body of evidence is emerging that parents with care are being pressurised into making a maintenance application for their children against their own wishes and better judgment. Many parents have alleged that rather than improving the lot of their child, the Agency's involvement in their lives has led to their children suffering harm and distress.[19] It is suggested that insufficient

15 See A Garnham and E Knights *Putting the Treasury First* (Child Poverty Action Group, 1994) p 86.
16 *Official Report*, 14 March 1991, col 386.
17 *A Garnham and E Knights*, pp 84-92.
18 Ibid.
19 Ibid.

thought was given to the impact of the Child Support Act 1991 on the stability of family life, and that one of the sad outcomes of the Act is likely to be the breakdown of those family units which are particularly vulnerable to strain brought about by the inflexibility of the Act's requirements.

The formula and the very poor

The Act is based on the principle that all absent parents are expected to make some contribution towards the maintenance of their own children. Even when an absent parent's only source of income is income support he will be required by the Agency to pay a minimum amount in child support. This is currently set at five per cent of the amount of the income support personal allowance for an adult. Only the very poorest absent parents are exempt.[20] Thus even when under the normal rules of the formula an absent parent's contribution would be nil, or less than the minimum amount, he is nonetheless required to make this minimum payment. Where such an absent parent is in receipt of income support, which will normally be the case, the minimum payment will be deducted directly from the amount which he receives. The deduction can be made from a partner's income support where the partner is claiming for a couple.

The minimum payment provision resiles from the principle that an absent parent should pay child support only in those cases where he can afford to pay. Pushing an absent parent's income to below the minimum amount deemed sufficient for income support purposes is to push him below the poverty line, and the effects of this will be cumulative. Losing 5 per cent of the income support personal allowance simply for a week may not create undue difficulty for an absent parent; but losing that income for an indefinite period is likely to cause him extreme financial hardship. It is suggested that it is of no benefit to a child to impoverish his absent parent through the token gesture of requiring the absent parent to pay maintenance. Indeed, a parent who has no spare money at all, and who lives some distance away from his child, is unlikely to be able to afford to maintain contact with his child. It is suggested that, from the child's point of view, it is far more important that his absent parent fulfils his duty to show the child affection, care and interest by visiting the child and otherwise being involved in the child's upbringing than that he pays small sums of money towards the child's maintenance. It is suggested that the minimum payment requirement is completely unacceptable and that the law here is engaging in the symbolic assertion of parental responsibility

20 Namely those in receipt of certain sickness and disability benefits, supporting other children, prisoners, under 18 and in receipt of income support, and defined by the Act as children.

at the expense of those who can least afford it, and at the expense of the emotional well-being of the children concerned.

The formula and step-children

Normally the provisions of the formula disregard any financial obligations which an absent parent has taken on in relation to step-children when calculating how much he must pay towards the support of his own children. The formula takes account of the fact that the absent parent is supporting step-children, or that his new partner is supporting her own children from a previous relationship, only when the protected income level is assessed.[1] All other aspects of the formula are premised on the assumption that step-children are being supported by their own absent parent, whether or not they are in fact being so supported. This is the case even where the step-child's absent parent is dead.

It is suggested that the approach of the Act to the financial support of step-children is unrealistic in financial terms and damaging in family policy terms. Bringing up a child is expensive, and providing a child with opportunities to develop his full potential by extending his knowledge, experience and skills usually costs a considerable amount of money. Where a step-child forms part of a household in which there are other children it is particularly important, in the interests of the welfare of such a child, that he is treated in the same manner as a child who is the child of both parents. Yet no allowance is made in the formula for the costs incurred by a step-parent in making provision for a step-child; even in those cases where the child's own absent parent is not maintaining him, or where the amount of support which the absent parent is providing is below the child's maintenance requirement, no corresponding adjustment is made. It is therefore suggested that the Act does not treat all children equally, but that, on the contrary, it discriminates financially against step-children.

Furthermore, although the Act is consistent in its approach to the step-parent relationship, the reality of the effect of the formula on different family units containing step-children may be significantly different. As has been seen, the fact that an absent parent is providing support for step-children is disregarded when his exempt income is calculated. Thus an absent parent may be supporting several children out of his income, but the law will treat him as if the only financial liability he has is towards his own children.[2] By contrast, the parent with care may have no income

1   See above.
2   Unless his income is very low so that such obligations are taken into account when calculating his exempt income. In such a case the income of any partner is taken into account which correspondingly reduces the amount of the absent parent's exempt income.

of her own but she may be receiving support for her child from a new partner (who may be very wealthy). However, the new partner's contribution to the support of the child is treated as irrelevant when the formula is calculated. The law treats the parent with care and the absent parent as the only persons who are maintaining their child. It is suggested that for the formula totally to disregard the benefits of income provided by a step-parent for the support of a step-child is just as unwise as it is to disregard a step-parent's obligations to step-children living in his household. Where disregarding a new partner's income leads to considerable disparity between the total income of the family unit in which the parent with care is living, and the total income of the family unit in which the absent parent is a member, this is likely to be perceived as unfair, and therefore as unjust.

In family policy terms, it is suggested that one of the more depressing features of the Act is that it has entirely discarded the concept of a 'child of the family'. This concept has been a feature of child maintenance legislation for decades. It is particularly apposite to families in which there are step-children. It is based on the notion that a spouse who has treated a child who is not his own child as a child of the family has responsibilities to that child. In the past, when courts made maintenance orders for children, it meant that courts could make orders against a spouse for the maintenance of a child who was not his own child, and indeed this power survives the Act.[3] But it also meant that financial obligations and responsibilities taken on in relation to step-children could be taken into account when a court was assessing how much a parent should pay for the support of his own children by a prior marriage or relationship. The competing claims of the children in both families could be balanced one against the other, and the law turned its face away from making fine distinctions between 'legal' and 'moral' responsibilities.[4]

It is suggested that the Act is refusing to recognise the reality of family life in modern Britain, in which large numbers of first family units break down and in which large numbers of persons form second family relationships. It is suggested that there is a real danger that the Act will cause the breakdown of some of these second family units: lack of money is often a cause of family strife, and the simplistic reasoning in the Act that step-children should be provided for by their own absent parent ignores the reality that sometimes they are and sometimes they are not. It is suggested that there is a strong link between the source of financial support for children and the quality of the inter-personal relationships within families, particularly where natural children and step-children are members of the same household. It is therefore suggested that it is highly desirable for law to encourage step-parents to take on some financial

---

3   See below.
4   See particularly *Roberts v Roberts* [1968] 3 All ER 479 for an historical analysis of case law on this issue.

responsibility for step-children. Such a policy assists in promoting commitment to a step-child by a step-parent and the cohesion of second family units.

Options available to parents with care who are not living on benefits

A parent with care of a child who is not in receipt of benefits cannot be compelled to authorise the Child Support Agency to pursue the absent parent for maintenance. If the parent with care chooses to support her child entirely from her own resources she is entitled to do so, even though the child would receive considerably more in child support if his absent parent were required by the Agency to make provision for him. In some cases pursuing child support maintenance carries with it the attendant risk that the absent parent may, as a consequence, wish to have other types of involvement in his child's upbringing, and the parent with care may not wish to take this risk. An example might be where the child was born at a time when the mother was unmarried, where she has subsequently married another man, and where the child's natural father does not know of the child's existence. Where the mother does not want the child's natural father to play any part in the life of the child for fear that this will disrupt the new family unit she has a choice: she can decide whether she is willing to take on the entire financial burden of raising the child, perhaps with the assistance of her husband or partner, or whether to involve the natural father by authorising the Agency to make a maintenance assessment against him. However, it has been seen that this choice is taken from the parent with care if, for any reason, she, or any new partner with whom she is living, should be forced to claim state benefits at some time in the future.

Child maintenance agreements

In most cases the parent with care is likely to wish to obtain financial provision for the child from the other parent. However, where parents are able to agree over child maintenance they may not wish to involve the Agency in the regulation of their financial affairs. Some parents may find submitting their personal lives and financial circumstances to the scrutiny of government officials distasteful and intrusive. The Agency has extensive powers to obtain information from a variety of sources, including employers, local authorities and the Inland Revenue, and a parent may prefer not to risk such enquiries being made.[5] Instead parents may prefer to make their own agreement about financial provision for their children. The private

5   Child Support Act 1991, s.14 and Sch.2.

ordering of the parents' financial arrangements for their children may be in the interests of both parents. Fees are payable where the services of the Agency are used, and each parent can therefore save money by not using the Agency.[6]

However, there are pitfalls in making a maintenance agreement. Whilst section 9(2) of the Child Support Act 1991 provides that nothing in the Act shall be taken to prevent any person from entering into a maintenance agreement, subsections (3), (4) and (5) of section 9 provide that—

'(3) The existence of a maintenance agreement shall not prevent any party to the agreement, or any other person, from applying for a maintenance assessment with respect to any child to or for whose benefit periodical payments are to be made or secured under the agreement.

(4) Where any agreement contains a provision which purports to restrict the right of any person to apply for a maintenance assessment, that provision shall be void.

(5) ... no court shall exercise any power that it has to vary any agreement so as—
(a) to insert a provision requiring the absent parent to make or secure the making of periodical payments by way of maint-enance ... to or for the benefit of that child; or
(b) to increase the amount payable under such a provision.'

Thus the Act makes it clear that the jurisdiction of the Child Support Agency cannot be ousted by a maintenance agreement.

The effect of section 9 is to put the parent with care in a powerful position in a case where the absent parent fails to pay the amount agreed under the terms of the agreement. Where that amount exceeds the amount which the parent with care would receive were she to apply to the Agency, she can rely on the contractual force of the agreement and take steps to enforce it just like any other contract. Where the amount she receives is less than that which she would receive under a maintenance assessment the combined effect of section 9(3) and (4) is to enable her to go behind the terms of the agreement and to apply to the Agency for child support maintenance at any time. Indeed, in a case where the parent with care later applies for state benefits she will have no choice but to resile on the agreement and to authorise the Agency to pursue her claim.[7] It is suggested that it is therefore essential that the amount of child support maintenance

6 Only the poorest parents are exempt from paying fees. These are based on the full economic cost of running the Agency; at the time of writing the assessment fee was £44 per year and the collection fee was £34 per year.
7 S.6(1), see above.

which the parent with care would receive under a maintenance assessment is calculated before a child maintenance agreement is finalised. Otherwise any maintenance agreement in favour of a child has the potential to be unfair to one of the parties, particularly the absent parent.

Periodical payments for children who fall outside the Child Support Act 1991

For the purposes of the Child Support Act 1991, a qualifying child is a child who is the natural child of both parents, or who has been adopted by both parents;[8] a child is defined as being under 16, or under 19 but in receipt of full-time education;[9] and the jurisdiction of a child support officer extends to those cases where the child, the absent parent and the parent with care are all habitually resident in the United Kingdom.[10] Courts are prevented from making orders for periodical payments for all such children,[11] but they still have jurisdiction to make periodical payments orders in relation to children who fall outside the scope of the Act.[12] Moreover, they can make orders which are designed to pay school and other education and training fees.[13] Where the absent parent is wealthy, and where a court is therefore satisfied that the amount of child support maintenance payable under the alternative formula mentioned in paragraph 4(3) of Schedule 1 makes it appropriate for the absent parent to make periodical payments under a maintenance order *in addition* to child support maintenance, it may so order.[14]

A 'child of the family'

Because a qualifying child must be biologically related to both parents for the purposes of the Child Support Act 1991, children who have been treated as 'children of the family' are excluded from its scope. A child of the family is a concept which applies only to parties to a marriage; it does not apply to unmarried unions.[15] It means in relation to the parties to a marriage—

---

8 S.3.
9 S.55.
10 S.44.
11 S.8.
12 That is such children who are not 'qualifying children' within the meaning of s.3; who are not children within the meaning of s.55; and those children for whom a child support officer has no jurisdiction to make a maintenance assessment under s.44.
13 S.8(7).
14 Child Support Act 1991, s.8(6); see too sub-ss.(8) and (9) which allow special orders to be made for disabled children.
15 *J v J (A Minor: Property Transfer)* [1993] 2 FLR 56.

'(a) a child of both of those parties; and
(b) any other child, not being a child who is placed with those parties as foster parents by a local authority or voluntary organisation, who has been treated by both of those parties as a child of their family.'[16]

A step-child is the most obvious child to fall within this definition. Indeed, there appear to be no reported cases where it has been found that any child other than a step-child falls within its scope.[17]

Orders for financial provision for children of the family may be made in divorce proceedings and in proceedings between spouses brought before magistrates. However, the widest scope for orders is under the Children Act 1989, Schedule 1, because not only may parties to a marriage apply for an order, but also any parent, guardian or person with a residence order with respect to the child may apply.[18] Furthermore, the definition of a parent extends to any party to a marriage (whether or not subsisting) in relation to whom the child concerned is a child of the family.[19] Thus a step-parent who has care of the child can apply for an order for periodical payments.

In deciding whether to exercise its powers and to make an order,[20] and if so in what manner, the court must have regard to the financial and other circumstances of all parties including the child.[1] Paragraph 4(2) of Schedule 1 is of particular relevance to orders for children of the family; it provides—

'In deciding whether to exercise its powers under paragraph 1 against a person who is not the mother or father of the child, and if so in what manner, the court shall in addition have regard to—
(a) whether that person assumed responsibility for the child and, if so, the extent to which and the basis on which he assumed that responsibility and the length of the period during which he met that responsibility;

---

16 Children Act 1989, s.105(1); the same definition appears in the Matrimonial Causes Act 1973, s.52(1) and the Domestic Proceedings and Magistrates' Courts Act 1978, s.88(1).
17 However, there is no reason why other children should not be able to look to the parties to a marriage for periodical payments if the marriage breaks down. Examples might be an orphaned relative who has lived with the parties and has been treated as a child of their family; or a foster child who was placed privately, who has been treated as a child of the family for some considerable time, and whose parents cannot support him financially.
18 Sch.1, para 1.
19 Sch.1, para 16(2).
20 The orders can include lump sum, settlement and property adjustment orders for children of a marriage, children of the family and children of an unmarried relationship, these orders are discussed below.
1 Sch.1, para 4(1).

(b) whether he did so knowing that the child was not his child;

(c) the liability of any other person to maintain the child.'

In this respect the legislation acknowledges that the obligation owed to a child of the family may be different from that which is owed by a parent to his or her own child. Nonetheless, the concept of the child of the family recognises that a person who chooses to marry someone who already has children takes on responsibility for the children as well as for his spouse. If the marriage ends, this responsibility may involve making financial and property provision for these children, which is tempered only by the liability of anyone else to maintain the child.

Before any obligation can be imposed, it must first be established that the non-parent has treated the child as a child of the family. This is a question of fact turning on evidence of how he behaved towards the child.[2] Where a child lives in the same household with a step-parent for some considerable period of time it is almost inevitable that he or she will be treated as a child of the family.[3] On the other hand, if the child has her home with other family members, but visits her parent and step-parent, this does not make her a child of the family and the step-parent potentially financially responsible for her if the marriage breaks down.[4] A child can be treated as a child of the family where a husband has treated him as such in the mistaken belief that the child is his own child. In *W(RJ) v W(SJ)*[5] a husband was deceived by his wife about the paternity of their two children, and after the marriage broke down blood tests revealed that he was not the father. Prior to that the husband had treated the children as his own children. The question for the court was could the children be treated as children of the family despite the husband's lack of knowledge about their true paternity? Park J held that both children had been treated as children of the family and that the husband's lack of knowledge of the facts relating to the children's paternity was immaterial to their status.

However, lack of knowledge on the part of a deceived husband is highly material to whether he should be ordered to make provision for a child who is a child of the family but not his own. The court is required to consider the basis on which such a husband had assumed and discharged his financial responsibility for the child and whether he did so knowing that the child was not his own. It was implicit in the judgment in *W(RJ) v W(SJ)* that no order for financial provision would be made against the husband. Where a husband is deceived before the child's birth into believing that he is the father of his wife's expected child, but where when the child is born it is clear to him that the child is not his child, and where he has

2   *Teeling v Teeling* [1984] FLR 808.
3   *Carron v Carron* [1984] FLR 805.
4   *D v D* (1981) 2 FLR 93.
5   [1971] 3 All ER 303.

nothing further to do with the child, then the child is not a child of the family. As the court held in *A v A (Family: Unborn Child)*,[6] it is only possible to behave towards a child, and therefore to treat it as a child of the family, after it is born.

In relation to a step-child who has been treated as a child of the family, the obligation of the step-parent to make provision for the child is tempered by the liability of any other person to maintain the child. Whilst this liability has always been of relevance, it seems likely that it will take on greater significance in the light of the changes brought about by the Child Support Act 1991.[7] This Act emphasises that primary responsibility for child support remains with the natural parent regardless of events, and regardless of the length of time for which a step-parent has been providing for the child. A step-parent who is pursued for child maintenance in the courts will therefore normally be well advised to insist that the applicant first seeks to obtain support for the child from his natural parent through the intervention of the Child Support Agency.

It is suggested that there is a real risk that the concept of the child of the family, and with it the concomitant financial responsibility, will wither and die in response to the radical change of approach to child maintenance brought about by the Child Support Act 1991. Now that a structure has been established under which all natural parents are obliged to make provision for their own children according to a universal formula, it may be perceived as unfair to burden step-parents and deceived husbands with financial responsibility for children who are not their own through the mechanism of court orders. The notion that this is unfair and unduly burdensome is particularly likely to be expressed in those cases where such men are already supporting their natural children in accordance with the provisions of the formula, and where no allowance has been made in the formula for the costs of maintaining a step-child. However, if this approach were to take root, many step-children could find that they are deprived of adequate financial support when the marriage between their parent and step-parent breaks down. Such children are often financially dependent on their step-parents, and unless step-parents are required to provide step-children with support, the household in which the children live after the breakdown may be reduced to relying on income support payments as their only source of income. Where this would lead to a drastic reduction in the step-child's standard of living the welfare of such a child would be liable to suffer disproportionately to other children. Whilst the majority of children experience some material deprivation after divorce, it is suggested that step-children may be particularly vulnerable to this unless full use is made of the courts' powers under the child of the family provisions.

6   [1974] 1 All ER 755.
7   As explained above.

Beneficial entitlement to the family home when unmarried partners separate

Where an unmarried partnership comes to an end the man and woman face identical problems to those which usually confront a married couple whose marriage breaks down, namely, how is one home to be shared between two persons who each have rights and needs, and how is provision to be made for housing the children? But at this point the similarity between married and unmarried couples ends. Although their problems are the same, the solutions are different. Beneficial entitlement to ownership of the family home is governed by principles of law and equity which apply to spouses just as they do to unmarried couples.[8] Many of the cases discussed below concerned a husband and wife, but it is now rare for disputes between spouses relating to their rights in the home to be determined by these principles.[9] Spouses now have the benefit of a statutory regime which takes regard of their married status and which allows courts to respond flexibly to their specific circumstances. Thus a spouse has a statutory right of occupation of the matrimonial home pending the grant of a decree irrespective of any rights of ownership he or she may have;[10] and where the marriage is ended by decree, the court has power to alter the parties' existing property rights.[11] But there is no such statutory right of occupation or property adjustment regime available to unmarried couples; in particular, the courts have no power to make an order about the house, or any other property, on the basis that it would be fair and reasonable between the parties, and would make proper provision for their children. Instead the entitlement of unmarried partners to ownership and occupation of the family home is governed by principles of law and equity, and these do not allow for the exercise of discretion to alter the parties' existing rights in order to achieve a just result.[12]

A declaration of trust respecting land must be in writing

The starting point for determining the parties' respective rights in the land is to look at the conveyance or other document of title; this establishes who has legal title to the property. It may be alleged that the person with

---

8 In the case of spouses, the outcome may be influenced by the presumption of advancement: see *Pettitt v Pettitt* [1969] 2 All ER 385.
9 Where a third party has a claim on the property then the spouses' respective rights in the property take on a different significance, as in *Lloyds Bank plc v Rosset* [1990] 1 All ER 1111 which is discussed below.
10 Under the Matrimonial Homes Act 1983: see ch 7.
11 Under the Matrimonial Causes Act 1973: see ch 7.
12 *Burns v Burns* [1984] 1 All ER 244.

the legal title (assumed here to be the man) has made a gift of the land to the woman. However, a basic rule of property law is that 'all conveyances of land or of any interest therein are void for the purpose of conveying or creating a legal estate unless made by deed.'[13] Thus with regard to the legal estate there is certainty, and any informal written transaction designed to dispose of the legal estate is void.[14]

It is where one of the parties (assumed here to be the woman) alleges that the man holds the property on trust for her beneficially that the law becomes more complex. Section 53(1)(b) of the Law of Property Act 1925 states that—

> 'a declaration of trust respecting land or any interest therein must be manifested and proved by some writing signed by some person who is able to declare such a trust or by his will.'[15]

Without such writing, any declaration is void. Thus in *Lloyds Bank plc v Rosset*[16] the wife claimed a beneficial entitlement to a share in the matrimonial home which had been conveyed into the sole name of her husband on the basis that this had been agreed between the parties. Responding to her claim, Lord Bridge said:

> 'Even if there had been the clearest oral agreement between Mr and Mrs Rosset that Mr Rosset was to hold the property in trust for them both as tenants in common, this would of course have been ineffective since a valid declaration of trust by way of gift of a beneficial interest in land is required by section 53(1) of the Law of Property Act 1925 to be in writing.'[17]

Sometimes there is an express declaration of beneficial entitlement in the conveyance; where there is, that concludes the question of title as between the parties for all time, and in the absence of fraud or mistake at the time of the transaction the parties cannot go behind it at any time thereafter.[18] For example, in *Leake v Bruzzi*[19] the wife successfully appealed against an order that she was entitled to a one third share, and her husband to a two thirds share, in the beneficial interest in the matrimonial home.

13 Law of Property Act 1925, s.52(1).
14 See *Crago v Julian* [1992] 1 WLR 372 in which it was held that a deed is necessary even to assign an informal weekly tenancy.
15 S.53(1)(c) imposes a similar requirement for writing in relation to the disposition of an equitable interest or trust subsisting at the time of the disposition.
16 [1990] 1 All ER 1111.
17 At p 1116.
18 Per Lord Upjohn in *Pettitt v Pettitt* [1969] 2 All ER 385 at p 407; *Re John's Assignment Trusts* [1972] 2 All ER 210n.
19 [1974] 2 All ER 1196.

The house had been conveyed into the sole name of the husband, but on the same day a trust deed had been executed by the parties which declared that the husband held the property on trust for both parties as joint tenants beneficially. The trial judge had made his order for unequal apportionment on the basis of the parties' respective contributions to the purchase of the property. Allowing the wife's appeal, the Court of Appeal held that the court was not entitled to go behind the terms of the trust deed, that it was conclusive of the parties' respective beneficial interests in the home and that therefore the wife was entitled to a half share. Thus in an extreme case, where the man alone has paid for the property but where it was conveyed into the parties' joint names with an express declaration that it is held by them as beneficial joint tenants, each is entitled to a half share in the proceeds of sale of the property despite the fact that the woman has made no financial contribution towards its acquisition.

Resulting, implied or constructive trusts

The more difficult cases are those where one party is claiming that it would be unconscionable to allow the other to retain the entire beneficial interest in the property, but where there is no written declaration of trust falling within section 53(1)(b). Section 53(2) makes provision for this. It states that—

'This section does not affect the creation or operation of resulting, implied or constructive trusts'.

The concept of the resulting, implied or constructive trust enables equity to require the legal owner of land to hold the property on trust for another where it would be inequitable to allow him to deny the other a beneficial interest in the land. The broad determining principle is that equity will step in and impose a trust where not to do so would allow the legal owner unjustly to enrich himself at the expense of the other. However, the subsection is silent on how courts should decide whether one of these trusts has arisen. It is the courts themselves which have created the principles, and it will be seen that they have adopted an approach which makes little allowance for the vague and haphazard way in which couples often deal with their financial and property affairs when they are living together in harmony.[20] In *Pettitt v Pettitt*[1] the House of Lords made it clear that beneficial ownership of land is determined by principles which have

---

20 Yet surely such a trusting approach is to be encouraged; there is something rather clinical and pessimistic about the modern trend to draw up contracts at the start of a relationship to determine how the parties assets will be distributed if the relationship breaks down.

1 [1969] 2 All ER 385.

universal application and that where spouses are involved they are not entitled to receive special treatment. The courts have ruled on several occasions that the fact that the parties are married, or that they have lived together as husband and wife, or that the woman has brought up the parties' children and generally run the household, is of no relevance when applying general principles of law and equity to determine their respective rights in the family home.[2]

Direct financial contribution to the purchase price

Consider first the situation where the legal title is in the joint names of an unmarried couple, but where there is no express declaration of the parties' beneficial entitlement. In *Bernard v Josephs*[3] the Court of Appeal held that there is no presumption that they are beneficial joint tenants or that they are beneficial tenants in common. Rather the court will consider all the circumstances to ascertain their intentions including their respective contributions to the purchase price and other subsequent contributions. It may conclude that a different apportionment than half and half reflects the parties' intentions. But where the house has been purchased in joint names in order to provide the parties with a home, where each has contributed to the purchase price and where they have subsequently pooled their resources, the proper inference to draw is that they intended to have equal shares in the house.

Consider now the situation where the property is conveyed into the sole name of one party, and where there is no declaration of beneficial entitlement. Here equity presumes that the owner of the legal estate has the sole beneficial entitlement. In order to rebut this presumption and to be beneficially entitled, the party without the legal estate must establish that the legal owner holds the property, or a share in the property, as trustee for him or her. How can this be done? The most straightforward case is where the property is purchased outright and where the person whose name is not on the legal title makes a direct financial contribution to the purchase price. This could be intended to be a gift, or a loan, or as consideration for a share in the beneficial interest in the land. If the evidence is neutral equity will assume the latter and find that there is a resulting trust. As Lord Diplock said in *Gissing v Gissing*, 'the prima facie inference is that their common intention was that the contributing spouse

---

2   The leading cases are *Pettitt v Pettitt* [1969] 2 All ER 385; *Gissing v Gissing* [1970] 2 All ER 780; *Burns v Burns* [1984] 1 All ER 244; and *Lloyds Bank plc v Rosset* [1990] 1 All ER 1111.

3   [1982] 3 All ER 162.

should acquire a share in the beneficial interest in the land in the same proportion as the sum contributed bears to the total purchase price'.[4]

Where, as is more common, the financing of the transaction is out of moneys advanced on mortgage repayable by instalments, if the person whose name is not on the legal title contributes to the mortgage instalments, even if she did not contribute to the original deposit, it may be reasonable to infer a common intention from the outset that she should share in the beneficial interest, or to infer a fresh agreement reached after the original conveyance that she should acquire a share.[5] Furthermore, the contribution need not be directly to the mortgage instalments; where a person contributes to the initial deposit and then uses her money to meet joint household expenses so as to enable her partner to pay the mortgage, this would be consistent with a common intention that the parties will share the beneficial interest in the property.[6] It is, however, essential that such a contribution releases the partner's income to pay the mortgage instalments, and that without it he would not be able to afford to keep up payments and fulfil his other financial commitments.[7]

Common intention and detrimental reliance

More difficult is the situation where one of the parties makes an indirect contribution to the acquisition of the property and claims that this gives rise to a constructive trust. In three leading cases,[8] the House of Lords have emphasised that the key issue to be resolved is whether the parties had a common intention at the time that the property was acquired that its ownership should be shared between them, and whether the non-owner acted to her detriment, or significantly altered her position, in reliance on that common intention. It is only where both common intention and detrimental reliance are established that a constructive trust arises.

---

4   [1970] 2 All ER 780 at p 791. For an example of where various properties had been conveyed into the sole name of the husband, but where the wife had provided all the money, see *Heseltine v Heseltine* [1971] 1 All ER 952. It was held that the husband held the entire beneficial interest in the properties on resulting trust in favour of the wife.
5   Ibid per Lord Diplock at p 792. See too *Burns v Burns* [1984] 1 All ER 244 per Fox LJ at p.251:'[There is] a possibility that while, initially, there was no intention that the claimant should have any interest in the property, circumstances may subsequently arise from which the intention to confer an equitable interest on the claimant may arise (eg the discharge of a mortgage or the effecting of capital improvements to the house at his or her expense). Further subsequent events may throw light on the initial intention.'
6   See too *Grant v Edwards* [1986] 2 All ER 426.
7   *Gissing v Gissing* [1970] 2 All ER 780; *Burns v Burns* [1984] 1 All ER 244.
8   *Pettitt v Pettitt* [1969] 2 All ER 385; *Gissing v Gissing* [1970] 2 All ER 780; and *Lloyds Bank plc v Rosset* [1990] 1 All ER 1111.

The courts are not permitted to ascribe a common intention to the parties which they never had, but which the court is satisfied they would have had if they had thought about the matter.[9] Thus the issue to be resolved is 'what did the parties actually intend?' rather than what can it be assumed that they intended. But how can a person prove that the parties intended that the property should be jointly owned where there is no written evidence to this effect and where she has made no direct financial contribution to its acquisition? As Lord Hodson said in *Pettitt v Pettitt*,[10] 'the conception of a normal married couple spending the long winter evenings hammering out agreements about their possessions appears grotesque...'. Even if unmarried partners are more cautious than spouses, and more aware that they need to have some kind of understanding about their respective ownership of property, it is suggested that normally they will not formalise any arrangement, and that they too will tend to act on tacit understandings. But once an unmarried couple part, particularly where their parting is accompanied by feelings of hostility, their respective memories are likely to become selective and self-serving about what they agreed about the family home. Moreover, in *Bernard v Josephs*[11] it was said that the nature of the relationship is an important factor when considering the inference to be drawn from the way in which the parties had conducted their affairs, and it was essential for the court to be satisfied that the relationship between the parties was intended to involve the same degree of commitment as a marriage before applying the principles applicable to a married couple. The fact that the relationship is one of cohabitation rather than marriage may therefore have an important bearing on the ascertainment of their common intention, and on the determination of the appropriate apportionment of their respective rights in the property. As Griffiths LJ said, 'each case will depend on its own facts, and I only warn against a blithe assumption that all couples living together are to be regarded as no different from a married couple.'[12]

It is clear from Lord Bridge's speech in *Lloyds Bank plc v Rosset*[13] that the evidence to establish a constructive trust can relate either to oral statements or to conduct. He said that the first question to be resolved is whether:

> 'there has at any time prior to acquisition, or exceptionally at some later date, been any agreement, arrangement or understanding reached between [the parties] that the property is to be shared beneficially. The finding of an agreement or arrangement to share in this sense can only, I think, be based on evidence of express

9   *Pettitt v Pettitt* above.
10 [1969] 2 All ER 385 at p 403.
11 [1982] 3 All ER 162.
12 Ibid, at p 170.
13 [1990] 1 All ER 1111 at p 1118.

discussions between the partners, however imperfectly remembered and however imprecise their terms may have been.'

This emphasis on express discussions between the parties means that:

'The tenderest exchanges of a common law courtship may assume unforeseen significance many years later when they are brought under equity's microscope and subjected to an analysis under which many thousands of pounds of value may be liable to turn on fine questions as to whether the relevant words were spoken in earnest or in dalliance and with or without representational intent.'[14]

An example of such an informal oral arrangement arose in *Eves v Eves*.[15] An unmarried couple, who had a child, decided to buy a house. The man provided the deposit and paid the mortgage. At the time of the purchase the man told the woman that 'it was to be their house and a home for themselves and their children'. He said that as she was under 21 it could not be in joint names but had to be in his name alone. He said that, but for her age, it would have been purchased in joint names. In fact he was being dishonest, and all along he intended that the property should be his alone. However, the woman accepted his explanation. The house itself was in a very dirty and dilapidated condition, and the woman did a great deal of work in both the house and garden to make it habitable.[16] Subsequently the man left her and married someone else.[17] The Court of Appeal held that the man clearly led the woman to believe that she would have some undefined interest in the property. This in itself was not enough to create a beneficial interest in her favour. But where it was part of the express or implied agreement between the parties that the woman would contribute some of her labour towards the renovation of the house in which she was to have some beneficial interest, then the law would impose a trust.[18]

In *Grant v Edwards*[19] the house was conveyed into the sole name of the man because the woman was married. Here too the man falsely led the woman to believe that her name was being excluded from the title deeds for good reason; he told the woman that were she to be a joint legal owner this might prejudice her position in the matrimonial proceedings which were pending between her and her husband. Subsequently the woman made substantial indirect contributions towards the mortgage repayments by applying her earnings towards the joint household expenses, without

14 *Hammond v Mitchell* [1992] 2 All ER 109 at p 121, per Waite J.
15 [1975] 3 All ER 768.
16 She did a considerable amount of painting and decorating, broke up concrete in the garden, demolished and rebuilt a shed and prepared the garden for turfing.
17 The woman by now had given birth to their second child.
18 Quantified here as one quarter of the equity.
19 [1986] 2 All ER 426.

which the mortgage instalments could not have been paid by the man. The Court of Appeal held that the man's statement that the woman's name would be on the title deeds but for the matrimonial proceedings was sufficient to show the necessary common intention that the ownership should be shared.[20]

Conduct which is insufficient to give rise to a trust

Failure to establish an agreement or arrangement is not necessarily fatal to the claimant's case. Evidence relating to the parties' conduct may be sufficient to establish a constructive trust where the conduct is such that the court can infer that the parties commonly intended that the beneficial ownership of the property should be shared. However, in *Lloyds Bank plc v Rosset*[1] Lord Bridge stated that:

'In this situation direct contributions to the purchase price by the partner who is not the legal owner, whether initially or by payment of mortgage instalments, will readily justify the inference necessary to the creation of a constructive trust. But, as I read the authorities, it is at least extremely doubtful whether anything less will do.'

In *Lloyds Bank plc v Rosset* the issue to be resolved was whether Mrs Rosset had acquired a beneficial interest in the matrimonial home, a derelict farmhouse, which had been purchased in her husband's sole name, and which she had helped to renovate. Mr Rosset had used the property as security for a bank loan without Mrs Rosset's knowledge and when he was unable to repay the loan the bank started proceedings for possession and sale of the property. Mrs Rosset resisted the bank's claim. She alleged that she had made a significant contribution to the acquisition of the property by the work she had personally undertaken in the course of its renovation. This included doing some painting and decorating (for which she had a particular expertise), designing two rooms, co-ordinating work with the builders and engaging in various other tasks connected with the house. She claimed that the parties had a common intention that she should share in the ownership of the property and that therefore she had a beneficial interest under a constructive trust.[2] The trial judge and the Court of Appeal

---

20 At one stage the man paid insurance moneys relating to the house into a savings account in the parties' joint names, which reinforced the evidence of how the parties intended the property to be shared, namely that it should be owned jointly.

1 [1990] 1 All ER 1111, at p 1119.

2 She therefore claimed that she had an overriding interest under s.70(1)(g) of the Land Registration Act 1925 which would prevail against the bank because she had been in actual occupation of the land on the date when the bank's charge was registered. The third party aspects of this and other cases are beyond the scope of this book.

were each satisfied that Mr and Mrs Rosset had had the necessary common intention that she should have an interest in the property, that she had acted on the basis of that common intention to her detriment, and that therefore she had acquired an equitable interest under a constructive trust. However, Lord Bridge, stating the unanimous opinion of the Law Lords, ruled that the two inferior courts had been wrong. Why?

Mrs Rosset failed in her claim because she could not establish that the spouses had a common intention that ownership of the property be shared either by proving that the parties had informally agreed to this, or by establishing conduct on her own part such that the court should infer an agreement. Lord Bridge reasoned in the following manner: he stressed that there must be a common intention between the parties to share the ownership of the property where it is alleged that there is a common intention that the property should be shared beneficially. He said that 'the expectation of parties to every happy marriage is that they will share the practical benefits of *occupying*[3] the matrimonial home whoever owns it. But this is something quite distinct from sharing the *beneficial interest*[4] in the property asset which the matrimonial home represents.'[5] He emphasised this further when he said 'neither a common intention by spouses that a house is to be renovated as a "joint venture" nor a common intention that the house is to be shared by the parents and children as the family home throws any light on their intentions with respect to the beneficial ownership of the property.'[6]

In relation to Mrs Rosset's efforts in respect of the renovation of the property, from which the trial judge had drawn the inference of a common intention that she should have a beneficial interest, Lord Bridge said:

> 'By itself this activity, it seems to me, could not possibly justify such an inference. It was common ground that Mrs Rosset was extremely anxious that the new matrimonial home should be ready for occupation before Christmas if possible. In these circumstances it would seem the most natural thing in the world for any wife, in the absence of her husband abroad, to spend all the time she could spare and to employ any skills she might have, such as the ability to decorate a room, in doing all she could to accelerate progress of the work quite irrespective of any expectation she might have of enjoying a beneficial interest in the property'[7]...' On any view the monetary value of Mrs Rosset's work expressed as a contribution

3 Emphasis added.
4 Emphasis added.
5 Ibid, at p 1115.
6 Ibid, at p 1117.
7 Ibid, at p 1115.

to a property acquired at a cost exceeding £70,000 must have been so trifling as to be almost de minimis.'[8]

Thus Lord Bridge not only took the view that this conduct could not justify the inference that there had been a common intention that Mrs Rosset should have a beneficial interest in the matrimonial home, he also characterised her contribution as so trifling that it was doubtful whether it amounted to sufficient detriment.

The courts have not been prepared to recognise that when a woman runs the household and looks after the children, this releases the man to be able to devote his energies to earning.[9] It is suggested that they have reached decisions within a framework which fails to recognise the realities of domestic life where there are children living in the household. It is extremely difficult to combine full-time employment with child care responsibilities, and it is suggested that many men would not be able to remain in employment and pay the mortgage if they had to combine their employment responsibilities with looking after the children and doing domestic tasks. The clearest example of courts giving no monetary value to the contribution which women make to the successful running of a household arose in *Burns v Burns*.[10] The couple were unmarried but had lived together as husband and wife for 19 years; they were known as Mr and Mrs Burns and Mrs Burns had had two children. There was no express declaration that Mrs Burns should have a share in the beneficial ownership of the matrimonial home, nor had she made any direct financial contribution to its acquisition such as to give rise to a resulting trust. At no time did Mr Burns ask her to contribute to the household expenses in order to relieve the financial burden on him, and her purchases did not release his earnings to enable him to pay the mortgage. Mrs Burns nonetheless sought to establish a common intention that she should have a beneficial interest on the grounds that she had brought up the children, done domestic tasks, had redecorated the interior of the house, had used her earnings to contribute towards the housekeeping expenses and had bought fixtures and fittings and various consumer durables. The Court of Appeal held that none of this expenditure was referable to the acquisition of the house. It held that paying for chattels[11] and decorating the property did not amount to evidence of a common intention that she should have an interest in the house.[12] It had no hesitation in dismissing her claim based on her domestic contributions and role as mother of the children.

8 Ibid, at p 1118.
9 During the 1970s Lord Denning made efforts in this direction, but these have been overtaken by the return to narrow orthodoxy.
10 [1984] 1 All ER 244.
11 See too Viscount Dilhorne in *Gissing v Gissing* [1970] 2 All ER 780 at p 786.
12 See too *Pettitt v Pettitt* [1969] 2 All ER 385 at p 416, where Lord Diplock was dismissive of the notion that handiwork around the house by a husband should give rise to him acquiring a beneficial interest in the property owned by the wife.

Thus Mrs Burns, who properly fulfilled her parental responsibilities to her children by spending their formative years in caring for them, was nonetheless denied any share in the property which had been the family home for 19 years. Mr Burns, on the other hand, was entitled to retain the entire beneficial interest in a property which Mrs Burns had cleaned, decorated and otherwise looked after and in which she had laboured for his benefit as well as for the benefit of herself and their children. The Court of Appeal felt some limited sympathy for Mrs Burns' position, but held that it was not for the courts to attempt to remedy any inequity; this was a matter for Parliament. But of course, it could be said that it was the courts which created the inequity in the first place by adopting a narrow and money-based approach to contributions towards the acquisition of the matrimonial home. Parliament imposed no restrictions on their powers when it enacted section 53(2) of the Law of Property Act 1925. If courts take the view that they are reaching inequitable decisions surely it is up to them to think again about when a resulting, implied or constructive trust should be imposed. It is courts which have created the unfairness to women like Mrs Burns by requiring that evidence to establish a trust must be directly referable to the purchase of the property, and that detrimental reliance must consist of making substantial contributions to the purchase or improvement of the property. As a consequence they have denied many non-earning women who live with men to whom they are not married any security in the form of continuing shelter for themselves and their children if the relationship breaks down.

Proprietary estoppel

The law relating to proprietary estoppel is complex and 'the doctrine has rarely been defined in one clear analytical formula, but has instead been expounded at different times by different judges in slightly divergent terms.'[13] Proprietary estoppel prevents the owner of land from insisting on his strict legal rights. It arises where a person is deliberately misled into believing, or mistakenly believes, that she has a present interest in property owned by another, or that she will be given such an interest in the future. The owner of the property must have assured, encouraged or acquiesced in her wrongful or mistaken belief. The non-owner must further establish that she relied on this belief and that, as a consequence, she has suffered detriment. Hence the notions of justice and fairness which have informed decisions on proprietary estoppel are similar to those which have persuaded courts to find an implied, resulting or constructive trust, namely that it would be unconscionable if equity did not intervene.[14]

13 K Gray *Elements of Land Law* (Butterworths, 2nd edn) pp 313-4. Ch 11 provides a detailed exposition.
14 *Re Basham (Deceased)* [1987] 1 All ER 405.

Detrimental reliance will usually, but not necessarily, involve the expenditure of money. Thus in *Greasley v Cooke*,[15] Doris Cooke had lived all her adult life with the same family, living as man and wife with one brother, working in the house without payment, looking after a mentally ill member of the household, and remaining there after several members of the family had left or died. She had been encouraged by the family to believe that she could regard the property as her home for the rest of her life and she therefore did not ask for payment for what she did. At the age of 62 she was told to leave the house by the one surviving brother. The trial judge held that her belief that she could remain in the house for as long as she lived had been induced by assurances given to her by family members, but that she had failed to prove that she had acted to her detriment in reliance on these assurances. The Court of Appeal held that it was to be presumed that she had acted on the faith of these assurances and that it was up to those who wished to evict her to prove that she had not acted to her detriment by remaining in the house, and they had failed to do so. It therefore granted her a declaration that she was entitled to remain rent free in the house for the rest of her life.[16]

Where a woman has been assured that she will be able to remain in property owned by her partner, and where she spends money on the property in reliance on that assurance, equity may grant her a remedy. In *Pascoe v Turner*,[17] after the breakdown of their relationship, Mr Pascoe told Mrs Turner, with whom he had been living for 10 years, that the house and its contents were hers. However, no conveyance of the property was ever drawn up. Therefore, although there was evidence of intention by Mr Pascoe to make a gift of the house to Mrs Turner, it was an imperfect gift.[18] However, Mrs Turner, having been told that the house was hers, set about improving it and spent a substantial sum on the property. Mr Pascoe allowed this to happen and at no time suggested that she was putting her money and her labour into his house. Subsequently he brought proceedings for possession. The court found that Mrs Turner had not acquired a beneficial interest under a constructive trust because there had been no common intention that the ownership be shared at the time when the property was acquired. However, it ruled that Mr Pascoe had encouraged or acquiesced in the manner in which Mrs Turner had changed her position for the worse and therefore that equity should grant her a remedy. The nature of the remedy was at large. It was clear that the beneficial ownership of the property still remained with Mr Pascoe. The Court of Appeal therefore took the view that the choice lay between two alternatives: either the equity could be satisfied by granting a licence to Mrs Turner to occupy the house

15 [1980] 3 All ER 710.
16 In *Re Basham (Deceased)*[1987] 1 All ER 405, the plaintiff also worked without receiving payment.
17 [1979] 2 All ER 945.
18 Law of Property Act 1925, s.52(1): see above.

for her lifetime, or there should be a transfer to her of the fee simple. The court chose the latter and required Mr Pascoe to perfect his gift by conveying the fee simple.

It is suggested that the outcome in *Pascoe v Turner* was generous and clearly influenced by the fact that the court regarded Mr Pascoe as a man who would pursue his purpose of evicting Mrs Turner from the house by any legal means at his disposal, and that therefore Mrs Turner needed a remedy which would be effective to protect her against 'future manifestations of Mr Pascoe's ruthlessness.' It rejected the remedy of granting her a licence to live in the house for the rest of her life because she could not protect this right against a purchaser for value without notice.[19] Also, a licensee cannot charge property as security for a loan, which the court thought she might need in order to effect repairs. A licence has the further disadvantage that the legal owner is entitled to enter the property in order to carry out necessary maintenance and repairs, and this right could have been used by Mr Pascoe as an excuse to act in ways which would have derogated from Mrs Turner's enjoyment of the use of the property.

It is clear, once the equity has been established, that it is for the court to decide how it should be satisfied in the light of the assurances and the nature of the detrimental reliance.[20] Despite the Court of Appeal's strictures in *Pascoe v Turner,* an irrevocable licence may appear, on its face, to be the most appropriate remedy in a case of proprietary estoppel arising between unmarried partners. In many cases it may be thought most closely to mirror the assurance given to the aggrieved party that she will always have a home in the property.[1] It also seems likely that a claim that the owner intended to make an out-and-out gift of the property will normally be difficult to substantiate. Moreover, a court will probably be reluctant to make an order which requires the legal owner to transfer the legal estate and entire beneficial interest to the other, for such an order is Draconian, and one which courts are hesitant to make even in cases where they have property adjustment powers, unless the circumstances are compelling.[2] However, it is suggested that the remedy of a licence should nonetheless be avoided at all costs. As the Court of Appeal recognised in *Pascoe v Turner,* a licence does not afford the licensee adequate protection against a

---

19 At the time the court's concern was with her inability to register the licence, but since then it has been made clear that a licence is not a proprietary interest: see below.

20 Thus in *Re Basham (Deceased)* [1987] 1 All ER 405 the plaintiff had been encouraged to believe that she would inherit a cottage in return for caring for the deceased. Since the plaintiff had subordinated her own interests and wish to move away in reliance on this belief it was held that she was entitled to inherit the cottage.

1 Cf *Greasley v Cooke* [1980] 3 All ER 710; see too *Inwards v Baker* [1965] 1 All ER 446. In *Matharu v Matharu* [1994] 2 FLR 597, in an action brought by a daughter-in-law against her father-in-law, the Court of Appeal held that a licence for life, rather than an unquantifiable beneficial interest, was the most appropriate remedy.

2 See ch 7.

determined owner who is prepared to act with 'ruthless disregard of the obligations binding on conscience'; and it has subsequently been made clear in *Ashburn Anstalt v Arnold*[3] that a licence does not bind third parties at all. Irrespective of notice, a purchaser is not bound by a licence because the Court of Appeal ruled that a licence does not create a proprietary interest in land.[4]

It is suggested instead that the non-owner should seek an order which grants her one of the traditional estates in land, because such an estate would protect her against the claims of third parties. It would also provide her with better protection against harassment by the other party than would a licence. The court has a range of options at its disposal when determining the nature of the equity to which the estoppel gives rise, and it is suggested that it should look to the ways in which the courts have handled orders relating to the former matrimonial home under the Matrimonial Causes Act 1973 when considering models for orders.[5] For example, where there is evidence of substantial detrimental reliance, the court could settle the property for life on the claiming woman. Although this would have the disadvantage that it creates a settlement under the Settled Land Act 1925, it would have the advantage that the woman could dispose of the property and use the proceeds to buy fresh accommodation should she wish to move house. Another possibility would be to order that the property be transferred to trustees for sale, the woman to be allowed to live there for life (or until some fixed date), and no sale to take place without her consent during her lifetime (or until the fixed date).[6] Or it could order the owner to transfer the property to the woman, but preserve an interest in it for him by requiring the woman to execute a charge over the property in his favour, not to be realisable until some future date. Perhaps the nearest equivalent to the grant of a licence would be to order the owner to grant the non-owner party a lease at a nominal rent.[7] Where the owner has succeeded in driving the woman from the home the court could require him to pay compensation.[8]

However, as with the constructive trust, the courts have maintained a tight control over when equity will intervene to assist an unmarried partner who is relying on proprietary estoppel to remain in occupation of the former family home. The courts have not easily been satisfied that the case is one in which the courts should prevent the owner from exercising his strict

---

3   [1989] Ch 1.
4   *Ashburn Anstalt v Arnold* was concerned with contractual licences, but it is suggested that it is inconceivable that the courts would take a different approach and give proprietary status to a licence granted by a court in a case of proprietary estoppel.
5   See ch 7.
6   Cf *Allen v Allen* [1974] 3 All ER 385.
7   *Griffiths v Williams* (1977) 248 Estates Gazette 947.
8   Cf *Tanner v Tanner* [1975] 3 All ER 776.

legal rights. Thus in *Coombes v Smith*[9] Mrs Coombes, a married woman, formed a relationship with Mr Smith, a married man, and had his child. Mr Smith bought a house intended for them both, but although Mrs Coombes moved in, he never did. He refused her requests to put the property in joint names, but reassured her that he would always look after her. He paid the bills and the mortgage and frequently visited her and their child. Mrs Coombes decorated the house on a number of occasions and tidied the garden. When their relationship eventually broke down Mrs Coombes sought an order that Mr Smith transfer the property and its contents to her absolutely, or alternatively a declaration that he was bound to allow her to occupy the property and to use its contents for the rest of her life.

Mr Smith conceded that Mrs Coombes had an equity to remain in the property until their daughter reached 17. (No explanation is given as to why this concession was made, but it seems likely that it was made because Mrs Coombes was relying on *Tanner v Tanner*,[10] where the Court of Appeal had found that a woman with twins had a contractual licence to remain in the property so long as the children were of school age.) However, Mr Smith asserted that Mrs Coombes had no entitlement to remain in the property after that time. The court upheld his claim. It held that Mrs Coombes' belief that Mr Smith would always provide her with a roof over her head was quite different from a belief that she had the legal right to remain there against his wishes, and therefore she was unable to establish that she had acted under a mistaken belief that she had security of tenure. It distinguished *Pascoe v Turner* on the grounds that there were no words of gift, and there were no improvements made to the property made on the mistaken belief that the property was hers.

But the most significant feature of the judgment from the point of view of a woman who is claiming that she has a licence to remain in her ex-partner's house is the manner in which the court approached the assurance given by Mr Smith to Mrs Turner 'that he would never see her without a roof over her head'. It held that all that amounted to was an assurance that Mrs Turner was a licensee at the will of Mr Smith. It did not provide evidence of what would happen in the event of the relationship breaking down. The court further held that even if Mrs Coombes had been led to believe that she had a right to remain in the property for the rest of her life, she had not behaved in a way which was detrimental to her. It held that it would be wholly unreal to find that she had allowed herself to become pregnant in reliance on some mistaken belief as to her legal rights, and in any event allowing oneself to become pregnant could not amount to detriment in the context of proprietary estoppel. Similarly, her act of leaving

9   [1986] 1 WLR 808.
10 [1975] 3 All ER 776.

her husband and moving into the property could not amount to detrimental reliance. Nor did any detriment arise from her having decorated the property, as this was done in the context of her continuing relationship with Mr Smith. Thus proprietary estoppel will not come to the assistance of a woman who has lived with a man who has assured her that he will always provide her with a home.

There is certainly a realism in the courts' view that assurances made by the owning party about property rights when an unmarried cohabiting relationship is happy are almost certainly not intended to have binding force when the relationship breaks down. Proprietary estoppel, like the constructive trust, cannot handle the disadvantageous situation in which an unmarried partner, usually the woman, finds herself when her relationship with her partner breaks down and where she has not paid for, or contributed towards, the cost of the roof over her head. The law relating to the acquisition of a beneficial interest in the family home, and the law of proprietary estoppel, are not truly a part of family law; they are about property law and its amelioration by equity. It is persons who have been living in a family relationship who usually need to rely on equity at its most generous, but it has been seen that this generosity is limited by doctrines which have universal application. Equity has a part to play in assisting the unmarried where there is unfairness, but this part is limited. Only the introduction of a property adjustment scheme, similar to that available to spouses, would be able to rearrange the rights of unmarried partners. Whether such a scheme would be more just is itself an interesting matter for debate.[11]

Lump sum, settlement and property transfer orders in favour of children

When spouses divorce, the court's first consideration must be for the welfare of their children, including step-children, when determining what orders should be made for financial and property provision.[12] Capital orders in the form of orders for the payment of lump sums, the creation or variation of settlements and the transfer of property can be made in favour of a party to the marriage, in favour of the children themselves, or in favour of both. In practice, property adjustment orders on divorce are almost invariably made in favour of the spouses, but the nature of the order is strongly influenced by the needs of the children. In particular, a court will be anxious to ensure that the parent with the care of dependent children has adequate housing for the children during their minority, and where

11 R Deech *The Case Against the Legal Recognition of Cohabitation* and E Clive *Marriage: An Unnecessary Legal Concept* in J M Eekelaar and S M Katz (eds) *Marriage and Cohabitation in Contemporary Societies* (1980, Butterworths, Toronto).

12 Matrimonial Causes Act 1973, s.25(1).

resources are limited the court will normally postpone the claim of the non-residential parent to realise his or her share in the capital invested in the matrimonial home until the children reach adulthood.[13] In this way, although lump sum, settlement and property transfer orders are not made directly in favour of, or for the benefit of, the children of the family, they are nonetheless designed to inure to their benefit.

The courts have, however, turned their face away from making capital orders for children which will benefit them beyond the stage where they complete their full-time education. Section 29 of the Matrimonial Causes Act 1973 provides that no financial provision order and no order for the transfer of property shall be made in favour of a child who has reached 18 save where the child is continuing to receive education or training, or unless there are special circumstances. In *Lord Lilford v Glynn*[14] the Court of Appeal made it clear that the wealth of a parent does not amount to special circumstances. It held that it had been wrong to order a millionaire father to settle a lump sum on trust for each of his children to make provision for the payment of an income to them for their lifetime. As Orr LJ said, 'even the richest father ought not to be regarded as under "financial obligations and responsibilities" to provide funds for the purposes of such settlement as are envisaged in this case on children who are under no disability and whose maintenance and education are secure.'[15] In *Kiely v Kiely*[16] a father living in more modest circumstances had been ordered to pay a lump sum to each of his children when the younger child reached 18. When allowing the father's appeal, the Court of Appeal reiterated the approach that a parent's obligations end when his child reaches 18. It held that there was nothing special about the circumstances which entitled these children to different treatment.[17] It is also clear that the courts will not allow a capital order to be made in favour of the children of the parties rather than to one of the parties themselves if the purpose of this arrangement is to defeat the statutory charge imposed by the Legal Aid Board.[18]

Financial provision and property adjustment orders for children of unmarried parents

Whilst the children of divorcing parents can be provided with a roof over their heads by orders made between the spouses, children of unmarried

13 See ch 7.
14 [1979] 1 All ER 441.
15 Ibid, at p 447. See too Scarman LJ in *Chamberlain v Chamberlain* [1974] 1 All ER 33 at p 38.
16 [1988] 1 FLR 248.
17 The father had originally been ordered to make periodical payments for his wife and children. Shortly afterwards he ceased to make such payments, and they were subsequently reduced to a nominal sum.
18 *Draskovic v Draskovic* (1981) 11 Fam Law 87.

parents enjoy no such advantage because there is no property adjustment regime applying to unmarried parents. Also, where a child is living with a person other than a parent, and where that person has a residence order, and consequently has parental responsibility for the child, there is no system under which she can obtain an order for financial provision and property adjustment for herself in order to house the child or otherwise provide for him financially. However, since the implementation of the Family Law Reform Act 1987, courts have had wide powers to make orders in favour of children on an application made on their behalf by adults.[19] These powers were extended by the Children Act 1989, which added to the persons who are entitled to apply for an order on behalf of a child. It is now the case that any parent (including a step-parent), guardian or person in whose favour a residence order is in force can apply to the court to make one or more orders for the benefit of the child, or to the child himself.[20] These orders are—

'(c) an order requiring either or both parents of a child—
    (i) to pay to the applicant for the benefit of the child; or
    (ii) to pay to the child himself,
such lump sum as may be so specified;
(d) an order requiring a settlement to be made for the benefit of the child, and to the satisfaction of the court, of property—
    (i) to which either parent is entitled (either in possession or in reversion); and
    (ii) which is specified in the order;
(e) an order requiring either or both parents of a child—
    (i) to transfer to the applicant for the benefit of the child; or
    (ii) to transfer to the child himself,
such property to which the parent is, or the parents are, entitled (either in possession or in reversion) as may be specified in the order.'[1]

Once a child reaches 18, and where he is receiving education or training, he can apply for an order in his own right against his mother or father, but not against a step-parent. However, the court's powers are limited to making an order for periodical payments and a lump sum only.[2]

---

19 The Family Law Reform Act 1987 inserted ss.11B and C into the Guardianship of Minors Act 1971.
20 S.15(1) and Sch.1, para 1(1).
1 Sch.1, para 1(2) (c),(d) and (e).
2 Ibid, paras 2 and 4(4)(b).

The criteria for making financial and property orders in favour of children

The principle that the child's welfare must be the court's paramount consideration when a court determines a question with respect to his upbringing does not apply to orders made under Schedule 1. Section 105 states that 'upbringing' does not include a child's maintenance.[3] Instead, paragraph 4 states the matters to which the court shall have regard in making orders for financial and property provision for children are all the circumstances, including—

'(a) the income, earning capacity, property and other financial resources which each person mentioned in sub-paragraph (4) has or is likely to have in the foreseeable future;

(b) the financial needs, obligations and responsibilities which each person mentioned in sub-paragraph (4) has or is likely to have in the foreseeable future;

(c) the financial needs of the child;

(d) the income, earning capacity (if any), property and other financial resources of the child;

(e) any physical or mental disability of the child;

(f) the manner in which the child was being, or was expected to be, educated or trained.'

The persons mentioned in sub-paragraph (4) are any parent, the applicant and any other person in whose favour the court proposes to make the order.

In *K v K (Minors: Property Transfer)*[4] the Court of Appeal emphasised that the balancing exercise contemplated by these provisions must always be carried out, and that the needs of the parents cannot simply be subordinated to those of the children. In *K v K*, a father of four children had been ordered to transfer to their mother 'for the benefit of the children of the family' his interest in a joint tenancy of the council house in which the family were living.[5] However, when arriving at his decision, the judge had omitted to refer to the criteria governing orders for children. In particular he had not taken account of the father's nine years of accrued rights under the right to buy provisions of the Housing Act 1980, his ability to find and pay for other accommodation, and his very low income. Ordering a retrial, the Court of Appeal held that the judge had erred in principle in failing to conduct this balancing exercise, and therefore that his decision was one with which the court could and must interfere. However, the court

---

3   Indeed, as Ward J said in *A v A (A Minor: Financial Provision)* [1994] 1 FLR 657 at p 667: 'Somewhat to my surprise and for reasons I cannot understand, welfare plays no express part in the considerations to which I have to have regard.'

4   [1992] 2 All ER 727.

5   Under s.11B(2)(d) of the Guardianship of Minors Act 1971.

gave no indication of how much weight should be given to the needs of the children when balancing these against the needs and accrued rights of the father. It was further argued on behalf of the father that the judge had exceeded his powers and that any order for the benefit of a child had to be for the child's direct financial benefit. The Court of Appeal rejected this argument; it found that the order was for the purpose of enabling the mother to provide a home for the children and that therefore it was for the children's benefit.[6]

It must be remembered that a court is not empowered to order one unmarried parent to transfer property for the benefit of the other parent. Nonetheless, in *K v K (Minors: Property Transfer)* the judge ordered the father to transfer his tenancy in property to the mother, and the Court of Appeal held that it lay within his power to do so. This was a crucial ruling in an area of law which, until then, had generated surprisingly little case law. Its importance lies in the fact that although the order was for the benefit of the children, it would in fact benefit their mother long after they had ceased to be dependent on her. Indeed, it would provide her with housing for the rest of her life. Thus the approach in *K v K* allows courts not only to protect the children and their residential parent from being rendered homeless during the children's minority, but also extends that protection to beyond the stage where the parenting role comes to an end.[7]

However, the approach taken in *K v K (Minors: Property Transfer)* seems to have been unique, and is probably limited to cases involving the transfer of a council tenancy. The courts have been emphatic in cases involving children of divorcing parents that orders for the benefit of children should make provision for them during their minority, but should not be designed to extend beyond that stage in their lives.[8] This principle has been applied with equal force to children of unmarried parents. The courts have adopted this approach even where the parent against whom the order is made is extremely wealthy and could well afford to make life-long provision for the child. In *A v A (A Minor: Financial Provision)*,[9] the father of one child of a family of three children was a multi-millionaire. The mother applied, inter alia, for an outright transfer of property either to herself for the benefit of the child, or to the child herself. Ward J rejected her application, and ordered that the house owned by the father, in which the mother and the three children were living, should be settled on the child during her

6   See too *Pearson v Franklin* [1994] 2 All ER 137, where the Court of Appeal advised a mother who had failed to obtain an injunction to oust the children's father from the home to apply for the transfer of the tenancy under s.15 and Sch.1.

7   Other examples arise in the area of implied, resulting and constructive trusts and proprietary estoppel, which are discussed above.

8   *Chamberlain v Chamberlain* [1974] 1 All ER 33; *Lord Lilford v Glynn* [1979] 1 All ER 441; *Kiely v Kiely* [1988] 1 FLR 248; *H v P (Illegitimate Child: Capital Provision)* [1993] Fam Law 515.

9   [1994] 1 FLR 657.

minority or until she completed full-time education. In relation to the child's mother, he said:

> 'The mother's obligation is to look after [the child], and [the child's] financial need is to provide a roof over the head of her caretaker. It is, indeed, a father's obligation to provide the accommodation for the living-in help which [the child] needs. Consequently, it must be a term of the settlement that while [the child] is under the control of her mother and thereafter for so long as [the child] does not object, the mother shall have the right to occupy the property to the exclusion of the father and without paying rent therefor for the purpose of providing a home and care and support for [the child].'[10]

It is suggested that this was an extraordinarily legalistic approach to the mother's role in caring for a child. Moreover, the notion that the child should be entitled to object to her mother continuing to occupy the family home once she reached the age when she was no longer under the control of her mother is truly horrifying. It cannot be in the interests of a child that she should have this kind of power over her parent, and it was an order which had the potential to be extraordinarily damaging to the relationship between the child, her mother and her siblings. Yet giving children the authority to treat their mother in an immoral fashion mirrors the present powers of the unmarried parent, usually the father, who is sole owner of the family home, in relation to the mother. The father has no obligation to make provision for the mother of his children in her own right, and he can literally cast her into the street once his children have reached their majority.

This is illustrated by *T v S (Financial Provision for Children)*.[11] A district judge ordered the father of five children to buy a small property for the mother and the children, the property to be held by trustees with a power of sale postponed until the youngest surviving of the children reached 21, or ceased full-time education whichever was the sooner. In that event, the property was to pass to the five children, or to such of them as survived, in equal shares. The father took the view that the property was his property and that it should eventually be restored to him. He also asserted that the judge's order would almost certainly result in the children together allowing their mother to continue to live in the house. Allowing the father's appeal, Johnson J held that the children had no continuing claim on their father after they had ceased full-time education. He therefore extended the duration of the settlement by postponing the father's interest until the

---

10 Ibid, at p 663.
11 [1994] 2 FLR 883.

youngest child had completed full-time education, including tertiary education, but ordered that upon the trust for sale coming into effect, the property should revert to the father and should not be the property of the children equally. He rejected the option that the father should pay a lump sum to the mother for the benefit of the children because it would provide a windfall to the mother. In relation to the settlement, he recognised that it was extremely unlikely that the children would insist on their share of the settlement being released if this had the consequence that their mother would be put out of their home, but he took it out of the power of the children to make continuing provision for her. As he said: 'The sadness here is that, after a long and seemingly happy relationship, this mother of five children, never having been married to their father, has no rights against him of her own. She has no right to be supported by him in the short, still less the long term; no right in herself to have even a roof over her head.'[12]

Thus an unmarried parent who brings up the children has no continuing claim for support and shelter in her declining years. This is surely indefensible. It is an area of law which is ripe for reform, and the Law Commission are presently seised of the matter. It is to be hoped that some radical proposals for change will have been made before this book appears in a second edition.

12 Ibid, at p 889-90.

Index